Interpersonal Communication

Everyday Encounters 5e

Julia T. Wood

FROM THE WADSWORTH SERIES IN COMMUNICATION STUDIES

Adler/Proctor/Towne	*Looking Out/Looking In,* Eleventh Edition
Backlund/Williams	*Readings in Gender Communication*
Baxter/Babbie	*The Basics of Communication Research*
Benjamin	*Principles, Elements, and Types of Persuasion*
Bettinghaus/Cody	*Persuasive Communication,* Fifth Edition
Borchers	*Rhetorical Theory: An Introduction*
Braithwaite/Wood	*Case Studies in Interpersonal Communication: Processes and Problems*
Brummett	*Reading Rhetorical Theory*
Campbell/Huxman	*The Rhetorical Act,* Third Edition
Conrad/Poole	*Strategic Organizational Communication,* Sixth Edition
Cragan/Wright/Kasch	*Communication in Small Groups: Theory, Process, Skills,* Sixth Edition
Crannell	*Voice and Articulation,* Third Edition
Dwyer	*Conquer Your Speech Anxiety,* Second Edition
Freeley/Steinberg	*Argumentation and Debate: Critical Thinking for Reasoned Decision Making,* Eleventh Edition
Geist-Martin/Ray/Sharf	*Communicating Health: Personal, Cultural and Political Complexities*
Goodall/Goodall	*Communicating in Professional Contexts: Skills, Ethics, and Technologies,* Second Edition
Griffin	*Invitation to Public Speaking,* Second Edition
Hall	*Among Cultures: The Challenge of Communication,* Second Edition
Hamilton	*Essentials of Public Speaking,* Third Edition
Hamilton	*Communicating for Results: A Guide for Business and the Professions,* Seventh Edition
Hoover	*Effective Small Group and Team Communication,* Second Edition
Huglen/Clark	*Argument Strategies from Aristotle's Rhetoric*
Isaacson/Saperstein	*The Art and Strategy of Service-Learning Presentations,* Second Edition
Jaffe	*Performing Literary Texts: Concepts and Skills*
Jaffe	*Public Speaking: Concepts and Skills for a Diverse Society,* Fifth Edition
Knapp/Hall	*Nonverbal Communication in Human Interaction,* Sixth Edition
Larson	*Persuasion: Reception and Responsibility,* Eleventh Edition
Littlejohn/Foss	*Theories of Human Communication,* Eighth Edition
Lumsden/Lumsden	*Communicating in Groups and Teams: Sharing Leadership,* Fourth Edition
Lumsden/Lumsden	*Communicating with Credibility and Confidence: Diverse People, Diverse Settings,* Third Edition
Metcalfe	*Building a Speech,* Sixth Edition
Miller	*Organizational Communication: Approaches and Processes,* Fourth Edition
Morreale/Spitzberg/Barge	*Human Communication: Motivation, Knowledge, and Skills,* Second Edition
Natalle/Bodenheimer	*The Woman's Public Speaking Handbook*
Rothwell	*In Mixed Company: Communicating in Small Groups and Teams,* Sixth Edition
Rubin/Rubin/Piele	*Communication Research: Strategies and Sources,* Sixth Edition
Samovar/Porter	*Communication Between Cultures,* Sixth Edition
Samovar/Porter	*Intercultural Communication: A Reader,* Eleventh Edition
Sellnow	*Confident Public Speaking,* Second Edition
Sprague/Stuart	*The Speaker's Compact Handbook*
Sprague/Stuart	*The Speaker's Handbook,* Seventh Edition
Verderber/Verderber	*The Challenge of Effective Speaking,* Thirteenth Edition
Verderber/Verderber	*Communicate!,* Eleventh Edition
VerLinden	*Critical Thinking and Everyday Argument*
West/Turner	*Understanding Interpersonal Communication: Making Choices in Changing Times*
Williams/Monge	*Reasoning with Statistics: How to Read Quantitative Research*
Wood	*Communication in Our Lives,* Fourth Edition
Wood	*Communication Mosaics: An Introduction to the Field of Communication,* Fourth Edition
Wood	*Communication Theories in Action: An Introduction,* Third Edition
Wood	*Gendered Lives: Communication, Gender, and Culture,* Seventh Edition
Wood	*Interpersonal Communication: Everyday Encounters,* Fifth Edition
Wood	*Relational Communication: Continuity and Change in Personal Relationships,* Second Edition
Wood/Duck	*Composing Relationships: Communication in Everyday Life*

Interpersonal Communication

EVERYDAY ENCOUNTERS

Edition 5

Julia T. Wood

*Lineberger Distinguished Professor
of Humanities*
THE UNIVERSITY OF NORTH
CAROLINA AT CHAPEL HILL

WADSWORTH
CENGAGE Learning™

Australia • Brazil • Japan • Korea • Mexico • Singapore • Spain • United Kingdom • United States

WADSWORTH
CENGAGE Learning

Interpersonal Communication:
Everyday Encounters, 5e
Julia T. Wood

Publisher: Holly J. Allen

Acquisitions Editor: Jaime Perkins

Senior Development Editor: Greer Lleuad

Assistant Editor: Lucinda Bingham

Editorial Assistant: Laura Localio

Senior Technology Project Manager: Jeanette Wiseman

Managing Marketing Manager: Kimberly Russell

Marketing Assistant: Alexandra Tran

Senior Marketing Communications Manager: Shemika Britt

Project Manager, Editorial Production: Megan E. Hansen

Creative Director: Rob Hugel

Executive Art Director: Maria Epes

Print Buyer: Barbara Britton

Permissions Editor: Bob Kauser

Production Service: Mandy Hetrick, Lachina Publishing Services

Photo Researchers: Myrna Engler/Jane Sanders-Miller

Copy Editor: April Wells-Hayes

Cover Designer: Laurie Anderson

Cover Images: Clockwise from top:
© John Feingersh/
CORBIS; © Franco Vogt/CORBIS;
© Royalty-Free CORBIS

Compositor: Lachina Publishing Services

For product information and technology assistance, contact us at
Cengage Learning Customer & Sales Support, 1-800-354-9706

For permission to use material from this text or product,
submit all requests online at **cengage.com/permissions**
Further permissions questions can be emailed to
permissionrequest@cengage.com

Library of Congress Control Number: 2005938049

ISBN-10: 0-495-00653-X

ISBN-13: 978-0-495-00653-4

Wadsworth
10 Davis Drive
Belmont, CA 94002-3098
USA

Cengage Learning is a leading provider of customized learning solutions with office locations around the globe, including Singapore, the United Kingdom, Australia, Mexico, Brazil, and Japan. Locate your local office at:
international.cengage.com/region

Cengage Learning products are represented in Canada by Nelson Education, Ltd.

For your course and learning solutions, visit **academic.cengage.com**

Purchase any of our products at your local college store or at our preferred online store **www.ichapters.com**

Printed in China
4 5 6 7 11 10 09 08

For Michelle who helps me stay young as I help her grow up.

BriefContents

Part One *The Fabric of Interpersonal Communication*

Chapter **1**

Part Two *Weaving Communication into Relationships*

Chapter **7**

DetailedContents

Chapter 3

Chapter 4

Chapter 5

Chapter 6

Part Two *Weaving Communication into Relationships*

Chapter 7

Emotions and Communication 185

Chapter 8

Communication Climate: The Foundation of Personal Relationships 213

Chapter 9

Chapter 10

Chapter 11

Chapter 12

Preface

Interpersonal Communication: Everyday Encounters offers a distinct approach to the introductory course in interpersonal communication. First, this book integrates theories, research, and practical skills from the field of communication and supplements them with scholarship from other fields. A second distinguishing feature is an attention to significant trends that affect interpersonal communication in the 21st century: social diversity, the increasing number of long-distance relationships, and the influence of technology on interpersonal interaction. Third, this book offers unique pedagogical features that encourage students to engage theories and concepts and apply them to their lives.

Focus on Communication

In writing this book, I've centered communication research and theory and complemented it with work from other fields. Interpersonal communication is a well-established intellectual area, complete with a base of knowledge, theories, and research developed by communication scholars. The maturation of interpersonal communication as an intellectual area is evident in the substantial original research published in academic journals and scholarly books. Consistent with the scholarly growth of the communication discipline, *Interpersonal Communication: Everyday Encounters* features current research by communication scholars. For example, Chapter 7, which focuses on emotions, highlights research on comforting communication that has been conducted by Brant Burleson and his colleagues; Chapters 10 and 11 call attention to the importance of everyday, routine communication in friendships and romantic relationships, which is a rising focus of scholarship (Wood & Duck, 2006); and all chapters draw on communication scholars' research on the ways that cultures and social communities shape communication styles.

Scholarship in other fields can also enhance understanding of communication. For this reason, *Interpersonal Communication: Everyday Encounters* incorporates research from other fields. For example, research in psychology deepens our understanding of the role of attributions in interpersonal perception. Ongoing work in anthropology, sociology, and psychology enriches insight into differences in communication that are influenced by gender, economic class, sexual orientation, ethnicity, and race.

Because interpersonal communication inevitably involves ethical challenges and choices, I've woven discussions of ethics into this book. I identify ethical issues and choices related to interpersonal communication. For example, what do we do when the value of supporting a friend seems to conflict with the value of being honest? How do we communicate when our needs are in tension with those of close friends or intimate partners? These and other ethical issues are integrated into this book. As a result, students who read it will gain an appreciation of the ethical as well as the practical nature of interpersonal communication.

Attention to Significant Social Trends

Interpersonal Communication: Everyday Encounters speaks to the context of students' lives today. To do this, I have given attention to social trends, issues, and concerns that characterize the 21st century in Western culture.

SOCIAL DIVERSITY One clear issue of importance in today's society is social diversity. The United States, like many other countries, is enriched by a cornucopia of people, heritages, customs, and ways of interacting. *Interpersonal Communication: Everyday Encounters* reflects and addresses social diversity by weaving it into the basic fabric of interpersonal communication.

Addressing diversity adequately entails more than tacking paragraphs on gender or race onto conventional coverage of topics. Rather than having a separate chapter on social diversity, I have integrated attention to race, economic class, gender, age, and sexual orientation into the book as a whole. I think this approach allows students to understand the importance of diversity in all forms of communication and contexts of interaction. For example, in exploring self-concept, I examine race, gender, and sexual orientation as core facets of identity that shape how people communicate and interpret the communication of others. You'll also find numerous examples of ways in which diversity affects communication in the workplace, which is increasingly populated by people from different cultures and communities. Chapter 11, on romantic relationships, discusses research on interracial, gay, and lesbian romances, and Chapter 12, on family communication, includes research on a range of families, including ones that are not white, middle class, and heterosexual.

To discourage stereotyped thinking about groups of people, I rely on qualifying adjectives. For instance, when citing research about differences between Hispanic and European American communication patterns, I refer to "most Hispanics" and what is "typical of European Americans." My intent is to remind students that generalizations are limited and may not apply to all members of a group.

To further weave diversity into *Interpersonal Communication: Everyday Encounters,* I have highlighted "Communication in Everyday Life" features that emphasize connections between communication and diversity.

TECHNOLOGIES OF COMMUNICATION A second defining feature of our era is technology, which is increasingly part of our interpersonal, social, and professional lives. Throughout the book, I've included examples of many ways in which technologies intersect with interpersonal communication. One way technology has affected interpersonal communication is by making it possible for people to meet others and form and sustain relationships online. The extent to which people today rely on technologies to build and develop relationships is evident in findings from recent surveys:

- More than 900 million people use the Internet; 200 million of those are North Americans (ClickZ Stats staff, 2004; Pew Internet and American Life Project, 2004).
- Each day, about 84 million Americans send e-mail messages to friends and family members (Baym, 2002).
- An increasing number of people belong to online support groups and online religious congregations (Howard & Jones, 2004).

- 69% of teens and college students who are online use instant messaging (Carl, 2006; Pew Internet and American Life Project, 2004).
- Online dating has grown in popularity; some people prefer to develop new relationships online rather than face-to-face (Silverstein & Lasky, 2004).
- 44 million people work in virtual offices (Telework Advisory Group, 2005).

Because many students today form and conduct relationships at least partially online, this edition of *Interpersonal Communication: Everyday Encounters* integrates research on online communication into discussions of language, nonverbal communication, climate, expression of emotions, and friendships and romantic relationships. In addition, I have highlighted "Communication in Everyday Life" features that emphasize communication and technology.

Another impact of technology on interpersonal interaction is the ease with which we can now learn about and interact with others who live in different parts of the world and in vastly different social, material, and personal circumstances. The Internet, the web, and interactive technologies have truly shrunk the distance between people and cultures. Whether or not your campus is culturally diverse, all of us today have the ability to interact with people from diverse backgrounds.

To be effective in today's world, students need not only to learn about diversity but also to gain competence in the technologies that are making interaction among members of different cultures and social groups more common. This edition of *Interpersonal Communication: Everyday Encounters* meets that need by connecting the content in the textbook with technologies that enhance students' learning.

Along with the textbook, students are able to use dynamic technological resources, including website InfoTrac® College Edition and an interactive book companion website. They're part of the overall learning package that makes up this edition.

In addition to the technological resources just mentioned, I've integrated technology into the text itself. I suggest a number of websites and online sources for students who want to learn more about particular topics and online resources they may consult to answer end-of-chapter questions and to respond to the case studies that conclude each chapter.

ENHANCED COVERAGE OF TIMELY TOPICS This edition also features expanded coverage of topics and issues that have increased importance in this era. There is a full chapter on friendships because so many of my students tell me that friendships are increasingly important to them in the face of the growing number of broken marriages and geographically dispersed families. The chapter notes the use of technology in keeping friends in touch across the distances that separate them. The chapter on romantic relationships addresses abuse and violence between intimates, and it discusses using communication to negotiate safer sex in an era shadowed by sexually transmitted diseases, including HIV-AIDS. I also include a discussion of communication in long-distance relationships, which are part of the lives of many of us.

Pedagogical Features

In addition to this book's distinct conceptual emphases, there are pedagogical features specifically designed to make the book engaging and useful to contemporary students.

First, I've adopted a **conversational tone** to invite students to engage ideas in this book. I use contractions, as people do in everyday conversations. Also, I include examples of everyday interactions so that abstract ideas are clarified in practical ways. In my writing, I share with students some of the communication challenges and encounters that have surfaced in my life. The conversational writing style is intended to invite students to interact personally with the concepts, principles, and skills presented in this book.

My voice is not the only one students will encounter in this book. All chapters are enhanced by **student commentaries** that were written by students in interpersonal communication classes at my university and other colleges and universities around the nation. The experiences, insights, and concerns expressed by these students broaden the conversation to include a wide range of perspectives.

This edition of *Interpersonal Communication: Everyday Encounters* features an **interactive pedagogical toolkit** that is designed to maximize the instructional potential of technologies and to connect book content and students to our larger, wired world. Pedagogical features—in text and online— promote development of interpersonal communication skills. If you order **1pass** packaged with the text, your students will have access to this interactive toolkit; 1pass provides your students with one-stop access to the *Everyday Encounters* premium book companion website and InfoTrac College Edition.

The **password-protected Everyday Connections premium website** consists of a number of integrated components. The first is a link to **InfoTrac College Edition,** a world-class online library students can use to learn more about subjects covered in chapters and to conduct research. The second component is **chapter-by-chapter online resources,** including hotlinks, quizzes, glossary terms, and interactive activities. Students can complete activities and quizzes online and, if requested, submit them to their instructors electronically. Finally, cases from the text are presented as **visual and audio scenarios.** This feature allows students to read, watch, listen to, critique, and analyze actual communication encounters.

Please note: If you want your students to have access to the premium online resources, please be sure to order this option for your course. If you do not order this option, your students will not have access to this online content. Use **ISBN: 0-495-16240-X** to bundle this content, at no additional charge to your students, with every new copy of the text. Access to 1pass can also be purchased separately by visiting **academic.cengage.com/communication/wood interpersonal5** and clicking on "Purchase 1pass Now!" on the left-hand navigation bar. *Contact your local Cengage sales representative for more details.*

Pedagogical features are also woven into the text itself. Each chapter includes **"Everyday Applications," exercises** that encourage students to apply concepts and principles discussed in the text to their own lives. As mentioned earlier, many of these are also available online at the Everyday Connections premium website. Each chapter also includes a number of **"Communication in Everyday Life" features,** which highlight interesting research and examples of interpersonal communication. To call students' attention to interpersonal communication in relation to the workplace, technology, and social diversity, I highlight relevant features with the designations *"Work," "Technology,"* and *"Diversity."*

A third pedagogical feature is **"Continuing the Conversation."** Before each chapter summary, you will find a short case study that continues the conversation of the chapter by allowing students to see how theories and principles they have read about show up in everyday life. The "Continuing the Conversation" cases can be elaborated through interactive videos available on the Everyday Connections website. Finally, I've written **questions that invite students to engage in further reflection and discussion** of ideas covered in each chapter. Some questions focus specifically on ethical issues in interpersonal communication, and some call for research using InfoTrac College Edition.

Changes in the Fifth Edition

Interpersonal Communication: Everyday Encounters has evolved in response to feedback from instructors and students as well as new research in communication and kindred disciplines. Eight significant changes mark this edition.

··· First, in response to instructors' suggestions, I have added a full chapter on communication in families. I believe this addition allows the book to cover more fully the range of contexts in which interpersonal communication takes place.

··· Second, I have strengthened attention to the workplace. Many students and instructors who used previous editions encouraged me to give stronger coverage to the role of interpersonal communication in professional contexts. In response, I've integrated discussion of communication on the job into discussions of concepts and principles presented throughout the book.

··· Third, I have included findings from more than 150 new research references that reflect the latest scholarship related to interpersonal communication.

··· Fourth, this edition gives more attention to online communication because that is so much a part of many students' lives and their interpersonal relationships.

··· Fifth, in response to reviewers' suggestions, I have reorganized Chapter 2 to more clearly explain how we develop selves through communicating with particular others and the generalized other. I have also enlarged coverage of ways we can use communication to promote self growth.

··· Sixth, in Chapter 11 I have expanded discussion of safer sex to include STDs other than HIV-AIDS and to address common and dangerous misconceptions many students hold.

··· Seventh, throughout the book I have increased in-text and student voice examples of parent–child, teacher–student, and boss–employee interactions and communication by older people.

··· Finally, in revising this edition, I have worked to avoid the tendency for books to grow longer with each new edition. I've tightened discussions and removed outdated material. As a result, this edition includes new information in all chapters, as well as a new chapter, without having become substantially longer than previous editions.

Additional Resources for Instructors

Accompanying *Interpersonal Communication: Everyday Encounters* are many instructional resources. An extensive *Instructor's Resource Manual*, coauthored by Narissra Carter of Texas Tech University and me, supplements the textbook. The manual discusses philosophical and pragmatic considerations involved in teaching the introductory course in interpersonal communication. It also includes suggestions for course emphases, sample syllabi, exercises and films appropriate for each chapter, journal items, panel ideas, and a bank of test items.

The *Student Companion,* coauthored by Debi Iba of Texas Christian University and me, includes interactive content outlines, vocabulary terms for key concepts, activities, Internet addresses, and self-test questions for each chapter.

A third resource for instructors is the *Multimedia Manager/Instructor's Resource CD-ROM,* which includes an electronic version of the Instructor's Resource Manual, *ExamView*® Computerized Testing, and the *Multimedia Manager* predesigned Microsoft® PowerPoint® presentations. This resource is available to qualified adopters. Please consult your local sales representative for details.

Acknowledgments

Although my name is the only one that appears as the author of this book, many people have contributed to it. I am especially indebted to my former acquisitions editor at Wadsworth, Annie Mitchell. From the start, she was a full partner in this project. Her interest and insights greatly enhanced the content of this book, and her amazing sense of humor and fun made working with her a joy.

Also essential to the birth of this book were members of the publishing team who transformed an unembroidered manuscript into the final book you are holding. Specifically, I thank Holly Allen, publisher; Jaime Perkins, my new acquisitions editor; Greer Lleuad, senior development editor; Kim Russell, managing marketing manager; Megan Hansen, production project manager; Jeanette Wiseman, senior technology project manager; John Gahbauer, assistant editor; Laura Localio, editorial assistant; Alexandra Tran, marketing assistant; Shemika Britt, senior advertising project manager; April Wells-

Hayes, copyeditor; and Mandy Hetrick, project manager of Lachina Publishing Services, Inc.

In addition to the editorial and production teams at Wadsworth and Lachina, I am grateful to the many students and teachers who reviewed versions of the manuscript and whose comments and suggestions improved the final content of the book. For the first edition, I thank Patricia Amason, University of Arkansas; Lucinda Bauer, University of North Carolina at Chapel Hill; Betsy W. Bach, University of Montana; Cherie L. Bayer, Indiana University; Kathryn Carter, University of Nebraska, Lincoln; Joseph S. Coppolino, Nassau Community College; Laverne Curtis-Wilcox, Cuyahoga Community College; Michelle Miller, University of Memphis; John Olson, Everett Community College; William Foster Owen, California State University, Sacramento; Nan Peck, Northern Virginia Community College, Annandale Campus; Mary Jo Popovici, Monroe Community College; Sharon A. Ratliffe, Golden West College; Susan Richardson, Prince George's Community College; Cathey S. Ross, University of North Carolina, Greensboro; Kristi A. Schaller, Georgia State University; Michael Wallace, Indiana University/Purdue University at Indianapolis; and the students at North Virginia Community College, Annandale Campus, and University of Arkansas who class-tested the book.

For the second edition, thank you to reviewers Lynn Badertscher, Fresno City College; Diane Boynton, Monterey Peninsula College; Larry Nadler, Miami University of Ohio; John Olson, Everett Community College; Sally Planalp, University of Montana; Valerie Randhawa, Harrisburg Area Community College; and Susan Richardson, Prince George's Community College.

For the third edition, thanks go to reviewers Dale Ash, Prince George's Community College; Betsy Bach, University of Montana; Marion Boyer, Kalamazoo Valley Community College; Steve Coffman, Montana State University, Billings; Layne Dearden, Ricks College; Michelle Gorthy, Cuyamaca College; Karin M. Hilgersom, Spokane Community College; Frances Johnson, University of Central Florida; Scott D. Johnson, University of Richmond; Richard Katula, Northeastern University; Shelley D. Lane, Collin County Community College; Barbara Malinauskas, Murray State University; Kelly McCornack, Michigan State University; Steve McCornack, Michigan State University; Michael Monsour, University of Colorado at Denver; Deborah McGee, Texas Tech University; Lisa Orick, Albuquerque Technical Vocational Institute; Joel C. Passey, Weber State University; Susan L. Richardson, Prince George's Community College; Bob Schuessler, North Seattle Community College; Deborah Shelley, University of Houston; Deborah Stieneker, Arapahoe Community College; Karen Strother-Jordan, Oakland University; Joyce Taylor, City College of San Francisco; Terry Turner, Shasta College; Jill Tyler, University of South Dakota; Jerry L. Winsor, Central Missouri State University; Janet Yeddes, Kean University; and Miriam Zimmerman, College of Notre Dame.

For the fourth edition, thank you to reviewers Stephanie Ahlfeldt, North Dakota University, Fargo; Walter Bernstein, Western Connecticut State University; Stephanie Coopman, San Jose State University; Mary Gill, Buena Vista University; Lori Halverson-Wente, Rochester Community and Technical College; Bud Hazel, Gonzaga University; Willie Johnson, Normandale Community College; Suzanne Kurth, University of Tennessee, Knoxville; Shelley Larson, Washtenaw Community College; Amy London, College of the Canyons; Nan Peck, Northern Virginia Community College, Annandale; Linda Rea, Hiram College; Vicki Shook, Cabrillo College; Vicki Welch, Dakota Wesleyan University; Shawnalee Whitney, University of Alaska, Anchorage; Alaina Winters, Heartland Community College; and Deborah Woolridge, Coe College.

And finally, my thanks to the reviewers and survey respondents for this edition: Michael D. Crum, Coastal Carolina Community College; H. L. Lee Gillis, Georgia College & State University; Victoria Leonard, College of the Canyons; Polly McMahon, Spokane Falls Community College; Loretta L. Pecchioni, Louisiana State University; Narissra Punyanunt-Carter, Texas Tech University; Stuart Schrader, Indiana University–Purdue University, Indianapolis; and Mike Searcy, University of Illinois, Springfield.

Finally, I am indebted to family and friends who enrich my life. At the top of that list is Robbie (Robert) Cox, my partner in love, life, adventure, and mischief for more than 30 years. He cheers with me when writing is going well and bolsters my confidence when it isn't. He provides a critical ear when I want a sounding board and privacy when I am immersed in a project. Along with Robbie, I am fortunate to have the love and support of my sister Carolyn and my close friends, Nancy, Todd, and Linda Becker. And, of course, always, I appreciate the love and patience of the four-footed members of my family: Cassidy, Sadie Ladie, and Wicca. Unlike my two-footed friends, these three keep me company when I am writing at 2 or 3 in the morning.

Julia T Wood

January 2006

Introduction

Starting the Conversation

When I was 20 years old, something happened that profoundly changed the rest of my life: I took my first interpersonal communication class. A new world of meaning opened up for me as I learned about the power of communication to enhance or harm personal, social, and professional relationships. The more courses I took, the more fascinated I became, so I decided to make a career of studying and teaching interpersonal communication. I wrote *Interpersonal Communication: Everyday Encounters* because I wanted to awaken you to the wonder of interpersonal communication as my first course awakened me.

In the opening pages of this book, I'll introduce you to the field of interpersonal communication, to myself, and to some of the special concerns and issues that surround interpersonal communication in this era.

The Field of Communication

The field of communication has a long and distinguished intellectual history. It dates back to ancient Greece, where great philosophers such as Aristotle and Plato taught rhetoric, or public speaking, as a necessary skill for participation in civic life. In the 2,000 years since the communication field originated, it has expanded to encompass many kinds of interaction, including group discussion, family communication, oral traditions, organizational communication, and interpersonal communication.

In recent years, interest in interpersonal communication has mushroomed, making it one of the largest and most vibrant areas in the discipline. Student demand for courses in interpersonal communication is rising. Scholars have responded by conducting more research and offering more classes that help students learn to interact effectively in their everyday interpersonal encounters.

Reflecting the intellectual maturity of the field, communication theory and research offer rich insight into the impact of interpersonal communication on individual identity and personal, social, and professional relationships. In the chapters that follow, we'll learn what scholars have discovered about the effects of communication on our self-concepts and our relationships with others. We'll also discover how communication creates defensive or supportive climates and how it shapes constructive or unproductive ways of expressing feelings, listening, managing conflict, and building relationships.

Because interpersonal communication in its many forms is central to personal, social, and professional life, its concerns intersect with other disciplines that study human behavior. Thus, research in communication contributes to and draws from work in such fields as psychology, business, sociology, anthropology, and counseling. The interdisciplinary mingling of ideas enriches the overall perspective on human interaction that you will find in *Interpersonal Communication: Everyday Encounters.*

© Michael Krasowitz/Taxi/Getty Images

A Personal Introduction

When I was an undergraduate, most of the books I read seemed distant and impersonal. I never had the feeling a real human being had written them, and authors never introduced themselves except by stating their titles. Certainly, that's no way to begin a book about interpersonal communication! I'd like to personally introduce myself and explain my reasons for writing this book.

I'm in my mid-fifties, and I'm more excited than I've ever been about life and its possibilities. My teaching and research, as well as ongoing conversations with students, colleagues, friends, and intimates, enrich my life and fuel my energies. Because my students teach me so much, I've included many of their comments, taken from journals they've kept in interpersonal communication classes taught by me and by instructors at other schools. It's likely that you'll agree with some of the students' comments, disagree with others, and want to think further about still others. However you respond to their ideas, I suspect that, like me, you will find them interesting, insightful, and often challenging.

Teaching is one of my passions. I love collaborating with students as we work to enhance their perspectives and develop skills that increase their effectiveness in everyday encounters. I am also passionate about research. I find it exciting to design and conduct studies, often in an effort to find answers to questions that students raise in my classes. My research, as well as that of many other scholars, is included in this book.

Although teaching, research, and writing occupy a great deal of my time, I have other interests as well. I cherish close relationships and spend much time with Robbie (Robert) Cox, who has been my partner for more than 30 years, and with special friends who grace my life: Carolyn, Nancy, Linda Becker, and Todd. My friendships with these people continuously enlarge my appreciation of the vital role of interpersonal communication in our lives.

I can also tell you that I am a European American, Southern, middle-class, heterosexual, married

Communication in Everyday Life
About Vocabulary in This Book

Because the subject of social diversity is woven into this book, it's important to think carefully about the language used to refer to social groups. Drawing on research, I present generalizations about how members of various groups think about and engage in communication. Whenever possible, I cite research done by members of the groups we are discussing so we understand groups from the perspectives of insiders. But the generalizations researchers identify are only that: generalizations. They are not universal truths that apply to all members of a group. There are always exceptions to generalizations. As you read, you may discover that you are a living exception to some of the generalizations about groups to which you belong. If so, you may want to reflect on the reasons you depart from group tendencies.

Generalizations should not be used to stereotype members of particular groups. For instance, in Chapter 4 you will read about gendered speech communities. You will learn how women and men typically—but not always, not in every case—differ in some of their communication. You will also learn about communication patterns in some traditional African American communities. The general patterns you read about don't describe every woman or man or every African American. Any of us may not follow the usual patterns of our groups, because of individual differences or because we belong to multiple groups.

The key point to keep in mind as you read is this: Generalizations are both important and limited. They are important because they inform us of general patterns that can be useful starting points in our efforts to understand and interact with others. We can't learn about social diversity if we cannot discuss particular social groups. At the same time, generalizations are limited because they do not necessarily tell us about any single individual who belongs to a group, such as men or Asian Americans. Thus, it's important to qualify generalizations. You'll notice that I use words such as *usually, typically,* and *in general.* These are to remind us that there are exceptions to generalizations, so we can never assume that a generalization applies to a specific person.

woman who strives to live in ways that are consistent with my spiritual values. Each facet of my identity shapes how I communicate, just as your race, class, gender, spirituality, and sexual orientation shape your communication. For instance, I don't know what it is like to be a man, to be in a same-sex romantic relationship, or to live in poverty. However, my identity doesn't mean that I, or you, can't learn to understand and respect the experiences of people who differ—sometimes radically—from us.

We can expand our personal horizons by interacting with others, particularly people who are different from us. As I talk with students, colleagues, friends, and acquaintances of other races, sexual orientations, ages, religions, and so forth, I learn about their views and values, and I see how their experiences have shaped their interpersonal communication. In addition to face-to-face interaction, I gain appreciation of human diversity through communication technologies that allow us to interact with others around the globe and to learn about worlds and experiences that differ from our own.

Because I am middle-class, I have been fortunate not to suffer economic deprivation. Yet, I interact with many people who are struggling economically, and I've gained some insight into the views, values, hardships, and pleasures that make up the fabric of their lives. Although my heterosexuality means that I don't have personal experience in gay, lesbian, bisexual, or transsexual relationships, I have learned a good deal about these relationships from reading and talking with friends, colleagues, and students.

All of us are limited by our own identities and the experiences and understandings they have—and have not—given us. Yet, this doesn't mean we have to be completely ignorant of those who are different from us. In fact, the more we interact with a range of people, the more we discover we have important similarities as well as interesting differences. Learning about both is essential for ethical, effective participation in our pluralistic world.

Years ago, Marshall McLuhan (McLuhan & Fiori, 1967) predicted that technology would create a global village. Mass media took the first steps toward creating a global village. Since then, technologies of communication have enhanced our ability to connect with others and visit faraway places. On the web, we can get news clips and virtual tours of everything from real estate to political and social events around the world.

Communication in Everyday Life
A Kaleidoscopic Culture

Between 1980 and 1990, the Hispanic population in the United States grew by more than 50%; by 2003, Hispanics constituted 12% of the population (Jandt, 2004). The U.S. Census Bureau (2004) projects that, by the year 2030, non-Hispanic whites may represent fewer than 50% of the U.S. population under age 18 (Cose, 2000).

The number of Asian and Pacific Islanders in the United States has more than doubled in the past 10 years. If current immigration trends continue as predicted, by 2050 there will be no single majority group in the country (Bates, 1994).

To learn more about changing demographics in the United States, go to http://www.census.gov. Read information in the "People" category under "Estimates and Projections."

In September 2001, most of us relied on television and the Internet for coverage of the terrorist attacks on the Pentagon and the World Trade Center's twin towers in New York City. Although most of us were not at the terrorists' targets, we could be there virtually, and we could connect with others who were also shocked by the events. On that dark day and those that followed, most of us reached out to others both nearby and far away. We felt a need to connect. We also felt a need to come to some understanding of what had happened. So we talked and listened, we watched television and listened to the radio, we e-mailed friends and visited chat rooms, all the while gathering perspectives to help us make sense of the attacks.

Yet, we don't need dramatic events such as the terrorist attacks to remind us of the need to connect with others and learn from them. In our era, it is essential to learn about and respect perspectives that are different from our own and from those of the communities in which we were raised. It's very likely that you will have neighbors of different ethnic backgrounds from your own. It's even more likely— almost guaranteed—that you will work with people of diverse races, sexual orientations, and spiritual commitments. If you have children, they may date people of many races and religious backgrounds. These are but a few examples of the ways in which social diversity is increasingly part of our lives. Our ability to be comfortable and effective in the years ahead depends vitally on our skill in communicating well with a range of people.

Diversity in Interpersonal Life

The social diversity of modern life fosters two types of insight. The more obvious one is increased understanding of and respect for perspectives and ways of communicating that differ from our own. Less obvious but equally important is the insight into ourselves that comes from learning about those who differ from us in certain ways. For instance, Western cultures define "normal" as European American, heterosexual, middle-class, and able bodied. Gay and lesbian orientations often are seen as deviations from the culturally created norm of heterosexuality. This means that gays, bisexuals, lesbians, and transgendered people understand their sexual orientations in relation to the heterosexual standard the culture represents as natural. However, heterosexuals often do not understand their sexual orientation in relation to other sexual orientations, because heterosexuality is regarded as the norm in the United States.

Similarly, African Americans, Asian Americans, Hispanics, and people of other ethnic and racial groups realize how they differ from European Americans more than European Americans perceive how they differ from people of color. We can also see our competitive attitude toward athletics in a new light when we consider the Japanese preference for tied scores in sporting events so that neither side loses face. It is difficult to be aware of whiteness, heterosexuality, middle-class status, or competitiveness, because cultural practices make these qualities appear natural and right. Thus, learning about people in other cultures and people who are outside of what the culture defines as mainstream inevitably teaches us about the mainstream as well.

The diversity of our society offers both opportunities and challenges. Differences in gender, race, class, cultural heritage, sexual orientation, age, physical and mental abilities, and spiritual belief present us with a rich array of perspectives on identity and interaction. Exploring variations among us enhances our appreciation of the range of human behavior and

the options open to us as people and as communicators. At the same time, diversity can complicate interaction because people may communicate in dissimilar ways and misunderstand one another, as Yih-Tang Lin notes in her commentary.

> **YIH-TANG LIN** When I first came here to school, I was amazed at how big the rooms in dormitories are, so I remarked on this. All of the Americans had a laugh at that and thought I was joking. In my country, individuals have very little space, and houses are tight together. The first time an American disagreed with me, I felt angry that he would make me lose face. We don't ever contradict another person directly. I have had many miscommunications in this country.

The process of socialization teaches us how to communicate and interpret what others say and do. This means that communication goals and styles vary according to the experiences, values, and norms of particular social groups. Asian Indians and Eastern Europeans may have learned different ways of disclosing personal information and interacting in the workplace, just as women and men may have been socialized to listen with different styles. For this reason, we must understand diversity as part of the overall fabric of interpersonal communication in our everyday lives.

In this book, we will consider many ways in which diversity intersects with communication. For instance, we'll discover that women and men, in general, rely on both similar and distinct types of communication to create closeness. We'll also learn that race and ethnicity influence how people interact.

Weaving diversity into how we think about interpersonal communication enlarges understandings of communication and the range of people and perspectives it involves. Cherrie, a student in one of my courses, makes this point effectively in her commentary.

> **CHERRIE** I am Hispanic, and I am tired of classes and books that ignore my people. Last year, I took a course in family life, and all we talked about was Western, middle-class families. Their ways are not my ways. A course on family should be about many kinds of families. I took a course in great literature, and there was only one author who was not Western and only three who were women. It's not true that only white men write great literature.

Communication in Everyday Life
Global Students

DIVERSITY

Isabelle de Courtivron is the director of the Center for Bilingual/Bicultural Studies at the Massachusetts Institute of Technology. Her experience working with bilingual and bicultural students leads her to observe that many of today's college and university students are "citizens of a time rather than a place" (Courtivron, 2000, p. B4). By this, she means that many students today form their identities not only from the history of their own families but also from knowledge of and interaction with people and events from all over the world. Most campuses include many international students and students who are first-generation Americans who balance the identities urged by their parents' culture with those encouraged in the United States.

Students who straddle cultural boundaries often feel pulled in different directions: to respect the traditions of their parents and to participate in the traditions of the society in which they currently live. Many bilingual students have families in which English is spoken rarely if ever. In addition, many students whose parents speak English and were born in the United States feel that they have one foot in each of two cultures: Hispanic culture and American culture, black culture and white culture, Native American culture and mainstream American culture. Living in two cultures involves living with contradictions.

Yet it also leads to a profound appreciation of the fact that all cultures—and all their norms and practices—are socially constructed. To understand two cultures intimately is to understand that social, political, professional, and personal codes of behavior can be organized in many ways and that no one way is absolute. In turn, this enables more thoughtful consideration of the practices in any specific culture and more openness to the world's multiplicity (Anzaldúa, 1987; Rodriguez, 1982).

Most Americans expect higher education to play a major role in preparing students to function effectively in a diverse society. More than 60% of today's college students expect to socialize with people outside their own racial and ethnic groups (Farrell, 2005).

Cherrie and others who were not born and raised in the United States also have much to teach students who are native citizens of the United States, as Carl's commentary reveals.

© Betty Press/Woodfin Camp & Associates

CARL At first, I was really put off by the two students in our class who were from China. Like when we talked about conflict and they just didn't get it—I mean, that's the way it seemed to me when they said they tried to avoid it. But the more I listened to them, the more I saw that they were really saying there are ways for people to work around differences without having to attack each other or make the other person look bad. It's really different than how I was brought up—you know, stand your ground, muster your arguments, win! I'm still not sure I really get their perspective, but it does make me think about whether I always need to be so fast to try to beat the next guy.

Like many of us, Carl's first inclination is to view ways other than his own as inferior. Yet, Carl moved beyond that starting point. He worked to consider his Chinese classmates' perspectives on conflict on their terms, in the context of their culture. In turn, they enlarged Carl's perspective on ways to deal with conflict. Like Carl, most of us will not always find it easy to appreciate or respect ways that are different from our own. Yet the struggle is worthwhile because it can enrich us personally and enable us to participate more effectively in our global village, where there are many, many perspectives on life and communication.

· · · · · · · · · ·

Weaving the Book

I've written this book in a conversational tone so that you can connect with the ideas in the pages that follow. Another reason I chose to use a personal tone is that I want you to understand that there is a real person behind the words you read. Like you, I am interested in interpersonal communication, and I am continually trying to figure out how to be more effective in my everyday encounters with others. In this book, I share some of the ideas and skills that enhance my interactions, and I hope you will find them valuable in your life.

In addition to my voice, you'll encounter the voices of students like Cherrie, Carl, and Yih-Tang Lin. In reading their commentaries, you'll discover that some of them are much like you and that others are quite different. I believe we can learn both from those who are similar to us and from those who differ from us. I think you will find, as I do, that it is enlarging to encounter a range of perspectives and issues relevant to interpersonal interaction.

Learning about interpersonal communication involves encounters with others, with ourselves, and with the world of ideas. I've woven these kinds of encounters into the text as "Student Voices" and features titled "Everyday Application" and "Communication in Everyday Life." As noted earlier, the "Student Voices" invite you to encounter others and to consider their perspectives on interpersonal communication. "Everyday Applications" invite you to apply material discussed in the text to your own life. Some of the "Everyday Applications" show you how to develop a

Communication in Everyday Life
A Global Village

What would the world be like if it really were a village? To give us an idea, the U.S. Census Bureau (1999) figured out who we would be if the entire world were a village of 1,000 people.

5 Oceanians/Pacific Islanders	123 Latin Americans
49 North Americans	579 Asians
122 Africans	122 Others

Of these people, there would be

169 Catholics	93 People of other religions
69 Protestants	184 People who are atheists,
99 Christians of other types	agnostics, or otherwise
192 Muslims	uncommitted to
137 Hindus	a particular religion
57 Buddhists	

particular communication skill; others ask you to reflect on ideas we've discussed to discover how those ideas surface in your everyday encounters. The "Communication in Everyday Life" features extend chapter coverage by spotlighting interesting research and news items about interpersonal communication. When this information is particularly relevant to cultural diversity, the workplace, or technology, I call that to your attention. Finally, each chapter concludes with a feature titled "Continuing the Conversation." These are short case studies that allow you to see how concepts, theories, and principles discussed in the chapter affect real-life interactions. Each of these features is woven into the text, just as encounters with ourselves, others, and ideas are woven into the fabric of our everyday lives.

Interpersonal Communication: Everyday Encounters is my effort to give back to all the students who have taught me so much. It's also a way to contribute to the field that continues to enrich my life and to make teaching communication a continuous joy for me. I hope this book will enhance your appreciation of the power of interpersonal communication in our relationships. I also hope it will motivate you to apply the principles and skills presented here in your everyday life.

Julia T Wood

The University of North Carolina at Chapel Hill

A First Look at Interpersonal Communication

Ryan McVay/Photodisc/Getty Images

"Exploration is really the essence of the human spirit."

Frank Borman

You've been interviewing for 2 months, and so far you haven't gotten a single job offer. After another interview that didn't go well, you run into a close friend, who asks what's wrong. Instead of just offering quick sympathy, your friend suggests the two of you go to lunch and talk. Over pizza, you disclose that you're starting to worry that you won't find a job, and you wonder what's wrong with you. Your friend listens closely and lets you know he cares about your concerns. Then, he tells you about other people he knows who also haven't yet gotten job offers. All of a sudden, you don't feel so alone. Your friend reminds you how worried you felt last term when you were struggling with your physics course and then made a B on the final. As you listen to him, your sagging confidence begins to recover. Before leaving, he tells you about a website called Virtual Interview that allows you to practice interviewing skills and works with you to come up with some new strategies for interviewing. By the time you leave, you feel hopeful again.

Interpersonal communication is central to our everyday lives. We count on others to care about what is happening in our lives and to help us sort through problems and concerns. We want them to share our worries and our joys. In addition, we need others to encourage our personal and professional growth. Friends and romantic partners who believe in us often enable us to overcome self-defeating patterns and help us become the people we want to be. Co-workers who give us advice and feedback help us increase our effectiveness on the job. And sometimes we just want to hang out with people we like, trust, and have fun with.

We communicate to develop identities, establish connections, coordinate efforts with others, deepen ties over time, and work out problems and possibilities. In the workplace, interpersonal communication is equally important. Jerry Winsor, Dan Curtis, and Ronald Stephens (1997) asked 400 managers in a wide range of organizations which applicant skills are most important in their hiring decisions. Topping the list was oral communication. The managers said that, to get hired and to advance in careers, people needed to work effectively with others, listen well, and give feedback effectively. The importance of interpersonal communication to professional success is confirmed by other studies (Cooper, Seibold, & Suchner, 1997; Wagner, 2001; Waner, 1995). In short, interpersonal communication is central to our effectiveness and our everyday lives. It is the lifeblood of meaningful relationships in personal, social, and professional contexts.

In this chapter, we take a first look at interpersonal communication. We start by considering how communication meets important human needs. We then distinguish interpersonal communication from communication in general. Next, we examine models of communication, define interpersonal communication, and identify principles and skills of effective interpersonal communication. After reading this chapter, you should understand what interpersonal communication is (and is not), why it matters in our lives, and what skills and principles make up competent interpersonal communication.

The Interpersonal Imperative

Have you ever thought about why we communicate with others? Psychologist William Schutz (1966) developed interpersonal needs theory, which asserts that our tendency to create and sustain relationships depends on how well they meet three basic needs. The first need is for affection, the desire to give and receive love and liking. The second need is for inclusion, the desire to be social and to be included in groups. The third need is for control, which is a desire to influence the people and events in our lives.

Expanding Schutz's ideas, Abraham Maslow (1968) proposed that we communicate to meet a range of human needs. According to Maslow, basic needs must be satisfied before we can focus on those that are more abstract (Figure 1.1). *Student Companion:* Activity 1.1.

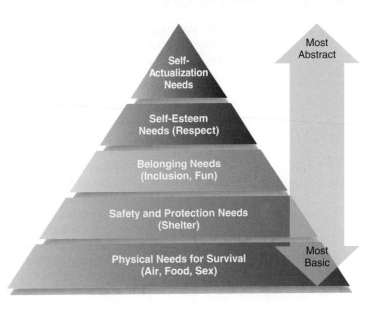

FIGURE 1.1

Maslow's Hierarchy of Needs

PHYSICAL NEEDS

At the most basic level, humans need to survive, and communication helps us meet this need. To survive, babies must alert others when they are hungry or in pain. And others must respond to these needs, or the babies will die. Beyond survival, children need interaction if they are to thrive. Linda Mayes, a physician at the Child Study Center at Yale University, reports that children can suffer lasting damage if they are traumatized early in their lives. Trauma increases the stress hormones that circulate through infants' fragile brains. One result is inhibited growth of the limbic system, which controls emotions. Adults who have suffered abuse as children often have reduced memory ability, anxiety, hyperactivity, and impulsiveness (Begley, 1997). Further, good communication between doctors and patients is related to effective treatment and to patients' mental well-being (Fleishman, Sherbourne, & Crystal, 2000).

As we grow older, we continue to rely on communication to survive and to thrive. We discuss medical problems with doctors to stay healthy, and our effectiveness in communicating affects what jobs we get and how much we earn to pay for medical care, food, leisure activities, and housing. Furthermore, researchers have amassed impressive evidence to document the close link between physical health and relationships with others (Kupfer, First, & Regier, 2002; Lane, 2000; Segrin, 1998). Heart disease is more common among people who lack strong interpersonal relationships (Ornish, 1998), and arthritis patients who have strong social support experience less severe symptoms and live longer than patients without such support (Whan, 1997).

SAFETY NEEDS

We also meet safety needs through communication. If your roof is leaking or if termites have invaded your apartment, you must talk with the property manager or owner to get the problem solved so that you have safe shelter. If someone is threatening you, you need to talk with law enforcement officers to gain protection. If your friend has been drinking, and you take the car keys and say, "I'll drive you home," you may save a life. We may go online to research symptoms we have or to learn about medical conditions that our friends or family members have developed. In an era when AIDS and other sexually transmitted diseases are widespread, couples must talk with each other about safer sex. The ability to discuss private and difficult issues having to do with sex is essential to our safety, although it may be embarrassing, as Navita comments.

> **NAVITA** It's funny, but it's harder to talk about sex than to have it. I'm having to learn how to bring up the topic of safety and how to be assertive about protection. I used not to do that because it's embarrassing, but I'd rather be embarrassed than dead.

Communication also helps protect us from dangers and harms. When foods are determined to be unsafe, news media inform the public. Car manufacturers send owners recall messages when defects in a model are found. Workers persuade managers to do something about unsafe working conditions, and professionals communicate with each other to do their jobs. Communication is needed, too, to protect us from environmental toxins. Residents in communities with toxic waste dumps must communicate with officials and media to call attention to environmental toxins that endanger their physical survival and safety.

BELONGING NEEDS

The third level in Maslow's hierarchy is belonging, or social, needs. All of us need others in order to be happy, to enjoy life, to feel comfortable on the job, and to fit into social groups. We want others' company, acceptance, and affirmation, and we want to give acceptance and affirmation to others.

We communicate to meet belonging needs by talking with others, sharing thoughts and feelings online, watching films together, and working on project teams. Also, interpersonal communication introduces us to ideas that broaden our perspectives. Perhaps, after talking with someone, you've thought, "I never saw it that way before" or "Gee, that really changes my attitude." In his commentary, James notes the importance of this type of communication.

> **JAMES** I'm not usually a really social person, but after the 9/11 attack, I needed to be around other people. I think a lot of people did. We needed to connect with others. It was almost like we felt our community had been destroyed and we were trying to rebuild it by talking with others.

The connection between belonging needs and well-being is well established. One study found that people who lack strong social ties are 200% to 300% more likely to die prematurely than those whose social ties are strong (Narem, 1980). Other reports conclude that heart disease is far more prevalent in people lacking strong interpersonal relationships than in those who have healthy connections with others (Cowley, 1998; Kupfer et al., 2002; Ornish, 1999; Ruberman, 1992). Belonging is also important in our careers. We want to feel that we're a part of work groups, and we want to be part of the formal and informal communication networks in organizations.

A particularly dramatic finding is that people who are deprived of human interaction over a long time may fail to develop a concept of themselves as humans. The "Communication in Everyday Life" feature on page 13 summarizes two extreme examples of the effects of social isolation. The first case is that of Victor, a wild boy found in France in 1800; the second case is that of Ramu, or *Ghadya Ka Bacha,*" the "wolf boy" (Gerstein, 1998; Shattuck, 1994). Doctors who examined Ramu concluded that he was a feral child, which means he was raised in the wild with little or no human contact. As a result, he did not have a sense of himself as a person or a human being. His self-concept and self-esteem were shaped by those with whom he interacted, presumably wolves.

Two other cases are documented by sociologist Kingsley Davis (1940, 1947). Anna and Isabelle, two girls who were not related to one another, received minimal human contact and care during the first 6 years of their lives. Authorities who discovered the children reported that both girls lived in dark, dank attics. Anna and Isabelle were so undeveloped intellectually that they behaved like 6-month-olds. Anna was startlingly apathetic and unresponsive to others. She did not progress well despite care, contact, and nutrition. She died 4 years after she was discovered. Isabelle fared better. When she was found, she communicated by grunts and gestures and was responsive to human interaction. After 2 years in systematic therapy, Isabelle's intelligence approached normal levels for her age.

How do we explain the difference between these two isolated children and what happened to them? There was one major difference. Anna was left alone all the time and had no human contact. Food was periodically put in her room, but nobody talked to her or played with her. Isabelle, on the other hand, shared her space with her mother, who was deaf and mute. The family had renounced both of them and sequestered them with each other.

Although Isabelle didn't have the advantage of normal family interaction, she did have contact with a mother who loved her. Because the mother was deaf and mute, she couldn't teach Isabelle to speak, but she did teach Isabelle to interact with gestures and sounds that both of them understood. Thus, Isabelle suffered less extreme deprivation than Anna.

The need for social contact continues throughout our lives. Even people who have been raised with normal social interaction can be affected if such interaction is lacking later in life. People who have few friends are more likely to experience depression, anxiety, and fatigue (Jones & Moore, 1989; Segrin, 1998).

Communication in Everyday Life
Missing Socialization

Most of us take socialization for granted. We are born into families, and they socialize us as members of the human world of meaning and action. But what if there were no humans around to socialize you? Would you still be human? The question of what it means to be human is at the heart of two extraordinary stories of "wild children" who appear to have grown up without human contact (Douthwaite, 2002; Gerstein, 1998; Shattuck, 1994).

The first case took place in 1800. One day, French hunters found a strange creature in the woods. They were unsure what the creature was—perhaps a wild pig or monkey, they thought. The hunters tied the creature to a pole and brought it out of the woods for villagers to see. Quickly, it was determined that the creature was a human boy—filthy, naked, mute, and wild, but human nonetheless. When scientists were consulted, they said the boy was severely mentally disabled and unteachable. However, Jean-Marc Gaspard Itard disagreed. He was a young doctor who devoted many years to trying to socialize the wild boy, whom he named Victor. Itard was not successful, perhaps because Victor had missed human socialization during a critical developmental period early in life. The story of Victor is portrayed in François Truffaut's film *The Wild Child*.

A second case occurred in India in the mid-20th century. A young, naked, starving boy found his way to the hospital at Balrampur, India. He showed no ability to interact with people and had heavy calluses as though he moved on all fours. In addition, there were scars on the boy's neck as though he had been dragged by animals. The boy, named Ramu by the hospital staff, spent most of his time playing with a stuffed animal, as a wild animal might in its lair. He showed no interest in communicating; indeed, he seemed to feel no connection with other people. Ramu howled when he smelled raw meat in the hospital kitchen more than 100 yards from his room—far too great a distance for the human sense of smell to detect a scent. Ramu also didn't eat like a human; he tore meat apart and lapped milk from a container. Most of the doctors and scientists who examined Ramu concluded that he was a "wolf boy"—"*Ghadya Ka Bacha*" in the Indian language—who had grown up in the wild and had been socialized by wolves.

SELF-ESTEEM NEEDS

Moving up Maslow's hierarchy, we find self-esteem needs, which involve valuing and respecting ourselves and being valued and respected by others. As we will see

Communication in Everyday Life
Interpersonal Communication on the Job

When the National Association of Colleges and Employers asked 480 companies what applicant qualities and abilities were most important to them in making hiring decisions, communication skills were at the top of the list (Schneider, 1999). According to the employers, effective job performance depends critically on skills such as expressing oneself clearly, listening well to others, creating productive working climates, and being sensitive to differences in how people perceive communication.

The employers noted that they see far too many applicants who don't know how to articulate their ideas clearly or how to interact effectively with others. Interpersonal communication skills are a key asset in applying for a job and for advancement in a career.

To find out more about the relationship between effective interpersonal communication and career success, go to http://www .natcom.org/research/Roper/how_Americans_communicate.htm.

in Chapter 2, communication is the primary way we figure out who we are and who we can be. We gain our first sense of self from others who communicate how they see us. Parents and other family members tell children they are pretty or plain, smart or slow, good or bad, helpful or difficult. As family members communicate their perceptions, children begin to form images of themselves.

This process continues throughout life as we see ourselves reflected in others' eyes. In elementary school, our teachers and peers influence our perceptions of how smart we are, how good we are at soccer, and how attractive we are. As we date and form romantic relationships, our partners reflect their views of us as loving or unloving, generous or selfish, open or closed, and trustworthy or untrustworthy. In professional life, our co-workers and supervisors communicate in ways that suggest how much they respect us and our abilities. Through all the stages of our lives, our self-esteem is shaped by how others communicate with us. People who lack strong interpersonal communication skills are unlikely to rise to the top of their fields, and many of them suffer lowered self-esteem as a result (Morreale, 2001).

SELF-ACTUALIZATION NEEDS

According to Maslow, the most abstract human need is self-actualization. Maslow (1954/1970) defined *self-actualization* as fully developing and using our unique "talents, capacities, potentialities" (p. 150). To achieve this, we need to refine talents that we have already developed to some degree, while we also cultivate new potentials in ourselves. As humans, we seek more than survival, safety, belonging, and esteem. We also thrive on growth. Each of us wants to cultivate new dimensions of mind, heart, and spirit. We seek to enlarge our perspectives, engage in challenging and different experiences, learn new skills, and test ourselves in unfamiliar territories. To become our fullest selves—to self-actualize—we must embrace the idea that we are always evolving, growing, changing.

Communication fosters our personal growth. Therapists can be powerful resources in helping us identify our potentials. Often, therapy assists us in our quest to know, understand, and improve ourselves (Maslow, 1959/1970). In addition, friends, family, co-workers, and teachers can help us recognize promise in ourselves that we otherwise might not see. For me, one such person was my father, who told me I had some ability as a writer. He encouraged me to write, and he taught me how to edit and

rewrite so that I developed my skill as a writer. Had he not nurtured this dimension in me, I doubt that writing would be a major part of my life today. Adam recalls how such a person affected him in his first job.

> **ADAM**   Mr. Bentley really helped me when I had my first job. It wasn't much—just serving at a sandwich shop—but he mentored me. He noticed I was awkward interacting with people, and he said I could learn social skills. He showed me how to be more effective—how to make customers feel comfortable, how to notice subtle cues that they needed something. Before that job, I'd thought of myself as kind of an introvert, somebody not very good with people. But Mr. Bentley saw a possibility in me that I hadn't seen in myself, and, as a result, I developed social skills and confidence that I never had before.

Another way in which we seek personal growth is by experimenting with new versions of ourselves. For this, too, we rely on communication. Sometimes we talk with others about ways we want to grow. At other times, we try out new styles of identity without telling anyone what we're doing. Some people experiment with their identities in chat rooms, where visual cues won't expose their color, sex, age, or other characteristics. For instance, some people engage in gender swapping in online communication—males present themselves as females, and females present themselves as males (Baym, 2002). Gender swapping allows us to imagine ourselves as the other sex and to try on an identity that is divorced from our physical one. In both online and face-to-face communication, we see how others respond, and we decide whether we like the effects of the new identity or whether we need to go back to the drawing board. We could not assess changes in ourselves without feedback from others. Lashelle's commentary stresses this point.

> **LASHELLE**   A person who changed my life was Mrs. Dickenson, my high school history teacher. She thought I was really smart, and she helped me see myself that way. I'd never considered myself all that intelligent, and I sure hadn't thought I would go to college, but Mrs. Dickenson helped me to see a whole new image of who I could be. She stayed after school a lot of days to talk to me about my future and to help me get ready for the SAT. If it weren't for her, I wouldn't be in college now.

Others also help us self-actualize through inspiration and teaching. Mother Teresa was well known for inspiring others to be generous, compassionate, and giving. She had the ability to see the best in others and to help them see it in themselves. Mohandas Gandhi embodied the principle of nonviolent resistance so gracefully and effectively that he inspired thousands of Indians to define themselves as nonviolent resisters. Years later, in the United States, the Reverend Martin Luther King Jr. followed Gandhi's example with his nonviolent resistance of racism. Spiritual leaders such as Lao-tzu, Confucius, Jesus, Muhammad, and Buddha also inspire people to grow personally. As we interact with teachers and leaders who inspire us, we may come to understand their visions of the world and of themselves and may weave them into our own self-concepts.

© Nita Winter

The likelihood of meeting the needs Maslow discussed depends on our ability to participate effectively in a very diverse social world. Western culture includes people of different ethnicities, genders, social classes, sexual orientations, ages, spiritual commitments, and abilities. Consider a few signs of the increasing diversity in the United States:

··· At the headquarters of technology giant Cisco Systems, the workforce is 45% Asian.
··· By 2020, the number of people of Asian descent living in the United States will have doubled, increasing from 10 million to 20 million (Meacham, 2000).
··· In 1998, the U.S. Census recorded more than 1.3 million racially mixed marriages (Clemetson, 2000).
··· Between 1970 and 2000, the white population in Santa Clara County, California, dropped from 82% to 49% (Breslau, 2000).
··· In the past two decades, more than 20 million people from other countries have moved legally to the United States (Zachary, 2002).
··· In 1860, the U.S. Census had only three categories for race: white, black, and quadroon. Now there are thirty (Meacham, 2000).

Most of us realize the need to understand and learn from others who differ from us. In a recent national survey of people between the ages of 25 and 65, 79% of respondents said it was either "very important" (55%) or "important" (24%) to teach students to get along with people from different backgrounds (*Survey*, 2004, p. 35).

Through interaction with others, we learn about experiences, values, customs, and lifestyles that differ from our own. In addition, we share our experiences and values with people who seem unlike us in certain ways. Through interaction, people come to understand their differences and similarities, and this fosters personal growth. Friendships between people with different cultural backgrounds enlarge perspective and appreciation of the range of human values and viewpoints (Bernard, 2004). Interacting with a range of people allows us to notice not only differences between others and ourselves but also our similarities. This idea is expressed by poet laureate Maya Angelou (1990) in the poem "Human Family," in which she writes, "We are more alike, my friends, than we are unalike."

Participating effectively in a diverse social world is critical to success in professional life. Today's and tomorrow's employers think it is very important for employees to be able to interact effectively with different kinds of people, but the

Communication in Everyday Life
Communicating in a Multicultural World

Communicating effectively with diverse people begins with learning how people in different cultures view communication and actually practice it. One excellent resource for learning more is the website of the Society for Cross-Cultural Research. In addition to presenting a wealth of good information, this site provides links to many other intercultural communication sites. Go to http://www .sccr.org/. Communicating comfortably and effectively with diverse people is also essential to career success as organizations become increasingly global and diverse. This site, focused on workplace diversity, offers good information and links to other sites: http:// www.ilr.cornell.edu/library/subjectGuides/workplaceDiversity .html.

Everyday Application
Communication and Your Needs

Keep a diary of your communication for the next 3 days. Note the people you talk to, what is said, and how you feel about each interaction.

After you've completed a 3-day diary, go back and classify each interaction according to one of the six needs we discussed. How much of your communication focuses on each need?

Physical survival   Self-esteem

Safety   Self-actualization

Belonging

To what extent does the effectiveness of your interactions depend on your ability to understand social diversity? For a similar activity, complete *Student Companion: Activity 1.2.*

majority of job applicants cannot do this. For example, U.S. citizens who are sent overseas to work in multinational corporations often do not adapt as well as citizens of other countries adapt to working in the United States. Between 20% and 50% of U.S. employees cannot adjust to overseas job assignments and must return home (Mendenhall, Dunbar, & Oddou, 1987).

Doctors, too, need to adapt to cultural differences (Mangan, 2002). For example, some Hispanic patients are reassured by eye contact, whereas some patients from traditional Asian backgrounds are uneasy when looked at directly. Social workers need to understand that many people of Spanish and Asian heritage have extended families that are much larger than most Caucasian families. German-born people are more likely to leave work at the formal quitting time. Others would be mistaken if they interpreted this as a sign that workers of German origin are less committed professionals than those who work late. In the 21st century, one of the most vital functions of communication is to enlarge our understanding of others so that we can participate in a diverse world.

So far, we've seen that interpersonal communication is a primary way to meet a range of human needs. Now, we need to define interpersonal communication precisely. We'll first consider three efforts to model the communication process. Following that, we'll define interpersonal communication and discuss key aspects of our definition.

Models of Interpersonal Communication

A **model*** is a representation of what something is and how it works. Early models of interpersonal communication were simplistic, so we will discuss them very briefly. We'll look more closely at a current model that offers sophisticated insight into the process of interpersonal communication.

---

*Boldfaced terms are defined in the glossary at the end of the book.

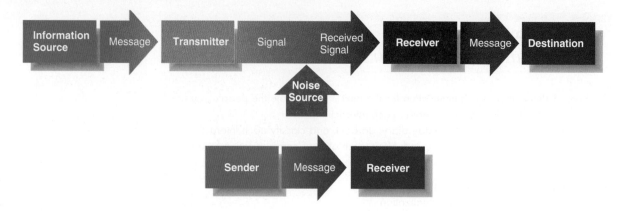

FIGURE 1.2

The Linear Model
of Communication
Adapted from Shannon & Weaver, 1949.

LINEAR MODELS

The first model of interpersonal communication (Laswell, 1948) depicted communication as a linear, or one-way, process in which one person acts on another person. This was a verbal model that consisted of five questions describing a sequence of acts that make up communication:

Who?
Says what?
In what channel?
To whom?
With what effect?

A year later, Claude Shannon and Warren Weaver (1949) offered a revised model that added the feature of noise. **Noise** is anything that causes a loss of information as the information flows from source to destination. Noise might be static in a phone line or activities going on that distract the sender or receiver of information. (Figure 1.2 shows Shannon and Weaver's model.)

These early **linear models** had serious shortcomings. They portrayed communication as flowing in only one direction, from a sender to a passive receiver. This implies that listeners never send messages and that they absorb only passively what speakers say. But this isn't how communication really occurs. Listeners nod, frown, smile, look bored or interested, and so forth, and they actively work to make sense of others' messages. Linear models also erred in representing communication as a sequence of actions in which one step (listening) follows an earlier step (talking). In actual interaction, however, speaking and listening often occur simultaneously or overlap. As you talk to friends, you notice whether they seem engaged or bored. If they nod, you're likely to continue talking; if they yawn or turn away from you, you might stop. On the job, co-workers exchange ideas, and each listens and responds while the others speak; those who are speaking are also listening for cues from others. Online, as we compose our messages, comments from others pop up on our screens. At any moment in the process of interpersonal communication, all participants are sending and receiving messages and adapting to one another.

INTERACTIVE MODELS

Interactive models portrayed communication as a process in which listeners give **feedback,** which is response to a message (Weiner, 1967). In addition, interactive models recognize that communicators create and interpret messages within personal fields of experience (see Figure 1.3). The more communicators' fields of experience overlap, the better they can understand each other. When fields of experience don't overlap enough, misunderstandings may occur. Lori Ann's commentary gives an example of this type of misunderstanding.

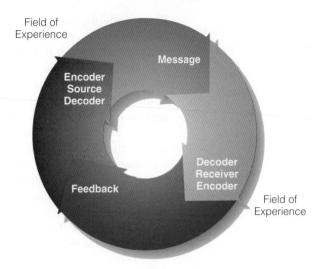

> **LORI ANN** I was born in Alabama, and all my life I've spoken to people whether I know them or not. I say "hello" or something to a person I pass on the street, just to be friendly. When I went to a junior college in Pennsylvania, I got in trouble for being so friendly. When I spoke to guys I didn't know, they thought I was coming on to them or something. And other girls would just look at me like I was odd. I'd never realized that friendliness could be misinterpreted.

FIGURE 1.3

The Interactive Model of Communication
Adapted from Schramm, 1955.

Although the interactive model is an improvement over the linear model, it still portrays communication as a sequential process in which one person is a sender and another is a receiver. In reality, everyone who is involved in communication both sends and receives messages. Interactive models also fail to capture the dynamic nature of interpersonal communication and the ways it changes over time. For example, two people communicate more openly and casually after months of exchanging e-mail messages than they did the first time they met in a chat room. Two co-workers communicate more easily and effectively after months of working together on a project team.

TRANSACTIONAL MODELS

The **transactional model** of interpersonal communication emphasizes the dynamism of interpersonal communication and the multiple roles people assume during the process. In addition, this model includes the feature of time to call our attention to the fact that messages, noise, and fields of experience vary over time (See Figure 1.4).

The transactional model recognizes that noise is present throughout interpersonal communication. In addition, this model includes the feature of time to remind us that people's communication varies over time. Each communicator's field of experience and the shared field of experience between communicators changes over time. As we encounter new people and have new experiences that broaden us, we change how we interact with others. As we get to know others over time, relationships may become more informal and intimate. For example, people who meet online sometimes decide to get together face to face, and a serious friendship or romance may blossom.

The transactional model also makes it clear that communication occurs within systems that affect what and how people communicate and what meanings are created.

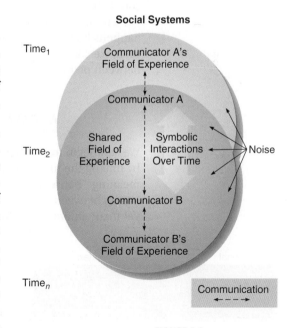

FIGURE 1.4

The Transactional Model of Communication

Those systems, or contexts, include the shared systems of both communicators (shared campus, town, workplace, social groups, and culture) and the personal systems of each person (family, religious association, friends).

Finally, we should emphasize that the transactional model doesn't label one person a sender and the other a receiver. Instead, both people are defined as communicators who participate equally and often simultaneously in the communication process. This means that, at a given moment in communication, you may be sending a message (speaking or nodding your head), receiving a message, or doing both at the same time (interpreting what someone says while nodding to show you are interested). Because communicators affect each other (Rothwell, 2004), interpersonal communication involves ethical responsibilities. Our verbal and nonverbal behaviors can enhance or diminish others, just as their communication can enhance or diminish us.

Now that we have examined models of interpersonal communication and learned what is involved in the process, we're ready to develop a precise definition.

. . . .

Defining Interpersonal Communication

When asked to distinguish interpersonal communication from communication in general, many people say that interpersonal communication involves fewer people, often just two. According to this definition, an exchange between a homeowner and a plumber would be interpersonal, but a conversation involving parents and three children would not. Although interpersonal communication often involves only two or three people, this isn't a useful definition.

Perhaps you are thinking that intimate contexts define interpersonal communication. Using this standard, we would say that a couple on a first date in a romantic restaurant engages in more interpersonal communication than an established couple in a shopping mall.

The best way to define interpersonal communication is by focusing on what happens between people, not where they are or how many are present. For starters, then, we can say that interpersonal communication is a distinct type of interaction between people.

A COMMUNICATION CONTINUUM

We can begin to understand the unique character of interpersonal communication by tracing the meaning of the word *interpersonal*. It is derived from the prefix *inter*, meaning "between," and the word *person*; interpersonal communication literally occurs between people. In one sense, all communication happens between people, yet many interactions don't involve us personally. Communication exists on a continuum from impersonal to interpersonal (see Figure 1.5).

Much of our communication involves no personal interaction. Sometimes we don't acknowledge others as people at all but treat them as objects; they bag our groceries, direct us around highway construction, and so forth. In other instances, we do acknowledge people, yet we interact with them in terms of their social roles rather than as unique individuals. For instance, I often run into neighbors when I'm walking my dog, Cassidy. We engage in small talk and

FIGURE 1.5

The Communication Continuum

perhaps comment on home projects. Through this kind of interaction, we acknowledge each other as people, but we don't engage in intimate talk. With a select few people, we communicate in deeply personal ways. These distinctions are captured in poetic terms by the philosopher Martin Buber (1970), who distinguished among three levels of communication: I–It, I–You, and I–Thou.

I–It Communication In an I–It relationship, we treat others very impersonally, almost as objects. In **I–It communication,** we do not acknowledge the humanity of other people; we may not even affirm their existence. Salespeople, servers in restaurants, and clerical staff often are treated not as people but as instruments to take our orders and deliver what we want. In the extreme form of I–It relationships, others are not even acknowledged. When a homeless person asks for money for food, some people do not even respond but look away as if the person weren't there. In dysfunctional families, parents may ignore children, thereby treating the children as things—as "its"—not as unique individuals. Students on large campuses may also feel they are treated as "its," not as people. Jason, a sophomore in one of my classes, makes this point.

> **JASON** At this school, I get treated like a number a lot of the time. When I go to see my adviser, he asks what my identification number is—not what my name is. Most of my professors don't know my name. In high school, all the teachers called on us by name. It felt more human there. Sometimes I feel like an "it" on this campus.

I–You Communication The second level Buber identified is **I–You communication,** which accounts for the majority of our interactions. People acknowledge one another as more than objects, but they don't fully engage each other as unique individuals. For example, suppose you go shopping, and a salesclerk asks, "May I help you?" Chances are you won't have a deep conversation with the clerk, but you might treat him or her as more than an object (Wood, 2006). Perhaps you say, "I'm just browsing today. You know how it is at the end of the month—no money." The clerk might laugh and commiserate about how money gets tight by the end of each month. In this interaction, the clerk doesn't treat you as a faceless shopper, and you don't treat the clerk as just an agent of the store.

I–You relationships may also be more personal than interactions with salesclerks. For instance, we talk with others in classes, on the job, and on sports teams in ways that are somewhat personal. The same is true of interaction in chat rooms, where people meet to share ideas and common interests. Interaction is still guided by our roles as peers, as members of a class or team, and as people who have common interests. Yet we do affirm the existence of others and recognize them as individuals within those roles. Teachers and students often have I–You relationships. In the workplace, the majority of our relationships are of the I–You sort. We communicate less deeply with most people in our social circles than with those we love most. Casual friends, work associates, and distant family members typically engage in I–You communication.

I–Thou Communication The rarest kind of relationship involves **I–Thou communication.** Buber regarded this as the highest form of human dialogue because each person affirms the other as cherished and unique. When we interact on an I–Thou level, we meet others in their wholeness and individuality. Instead of dealing with them as occupants of social roles, we see them as unique human beings whom we know and accept in their totality. In I–Thou communication, we open ourselves fully, trusting others to accept us as we are, with our virtues and vices, hopes and fears, strengths and weaknesses.

Buber believed that only in I–Thou relationships do we become fully human, which for him meant that we discard the guises we use most of the time and allow ourselves to be completely genuine (Stewart, 1986). Much of our communication involves what Buber called "seeming," in which we're preoccupied with our image and careful to manage how we present ourselves. In I–Thou relationships, however, we engage in "being," through which we reveal who we really are and how we really feel. I–Thou relationships are not common, because we can't afford to reveal ourselves totally to everyone all the time. Thus, I–Thou relationships and the communication in them are rare and special.

FEATURES OF INTERPERSONAL COMMUNICATION

Building on Buber's poetic description, we can define **interpersonal communication** as selective, systemic, unique, processual transactions that allow people to

© Mugshots/Gabe Palmer/CORBIS Stock Market

reflect and build personal knowledge of one another and create shared meanings. We'll discuss the key terms in this definition so that we have a common understanding of interpersonal communication.

Selective First, as we noted earlier, we don't want to communicate intimately with the majority of people we encounter. In some cases, we neither want nor need to communicate with others even at the I–You level. For instance, if we get a phone call from a pollster, we may only respond to the questions and not engage the caller in any personal way. We invest the effort and take the risks of opening ourselves fully with only a few people. As Buber realized, most of our communication occurs on I–It or I–You levels. This is fine because I–Thou relationships take more time, energy, and courage than we are willing to offer to everyone.

Communication in Everyday Life
Poor Interpersonal Communication as the Number One Cause of Divorce

Poll results reported in 1999 show that a majority of people perceive communication problems as the number one reason marriages fail (Roper poll, 1999). The research organization Roper Starch asked 1,001 Americans a variety of questions about the role of communication in their lives. One finding overshadowed all others: Regardless of age, race, sex, or income level, Americans reported that communication problems are the most common cause of divorce; 53% of those who were polled said that ineffective communication was the principal reason for divorce. Compare this with the frequency with which people named other causes of divorce: money problems, 29%; interference from family members, 7%; sexual problems, 5%; previous relationships, 3%; and children, 3%. To read the full results of this poll, go to http://www.natcom.org/research/Roper/how_Americans_communicate.htm.

Use your InfoTrac College Edition to find out more about the relationship between successful relationships and effective interpersonal communication. Conduct key word searches for these terms: *marriage and communication, intimacy and communication,* and *relationships.*

Systemic Interpersonal communication is also **systemic,** which means that it takes place within various systems. As the transactional model notes, communication occurs in contexts that influence events and the meanings we attribute. The communication between you and me right now is embedded in multiple systems, including the interpersonal communication course, academic institutions, and American society. Each of these systems influences what we expect of each other, what I write, and how you interpret what you read. The ways people communicate also vary across cultures. Whereas North Americans tend to communicate assertively and look at one another, in some traditional Asian societies assertion and eye contact are considered rude. Traditional Native Americans tend to be less verbal than most Americans of European heritage (Braithwaite, 1990).

Consider an example of the systemic character of communication. Suppose Ian gives Cheryl a solid gold pendant and says, "I wanted to show how much I care about you." What do his words mean? That depends in large part on the systems within which he and Cheryl interact. If Ian and Cheryl have just started dating, an expensive gift means one thing; if they have been married for 20 years, it means something different. On the other hand, if they don't have an established relationship, and Cheryl is engaged to Manuel, Ian's gift may have yet another meaning. What if Ian argued with Cheryl the previous day? Then, perhaps, the gift is to apologize more than to show love. If Ian is rich, a solid gold pendant may be less impressive than if he is short on cash. Systems that affect what this communication means include Cheryl's and Ian's relationship, their socioeconomic classes, cultural norms for gift giving, and Cheryl's and Ian's personal histories. All these contexts affect their interaction and its meaning.

Because interpersonal communication is systemic, situation, time, people, culture, personal histories, and so forth interact to affect meanings. We can't just add up the various parts of a system to understand their impact on communication. Instead, we have to recognize that all parts of a system interact; each part affects all others. In other words, elements of communication systems are interdependent; each element is tied to all the other elements.

Recall also that all systems include noise, which is anything that distorts communication or interferes with people's understandings of one another. Noise in communication systems is inevitable, but we can be aware that it exists and try to compensate for the difficulties it causes.

There are four kinds of noise. *Physiological noise* is distraction caused by hunger, fatigue, headaches, medications, and other factors that affect how we feel and think. *Physical noise* is interference in our environments, such as noises made by others, overly dim or bright lights, extreme temperatures, and crowded conditions. *Psychological noise* is qualities in us that affect how we communicate and how we interpret others. For instance, if you are preoccupied with a problem, you may be inattentive. Likewise, prejudice and defensive feelings can interfere with communication. Our needs may also affect how we interpret others. For example, if we really need affirmation of our professional competence, we may be predisposed to perceive others as communicating more praise for our work than they really do. Finally, *semantic noise* exists when words themselves are not mutually understood. Authors sometimes create semantic noise by using jargon or unnecessarily technical language. For instance, to discuss noise, I could write, "Communication can be egregiously obstructed by phenomena extrinsic to an exchange that actuate misrepresentations and symbolic incongruities." Although that sentence may be accurate, it's filled with semantic noise.

CARMELLA   I wish professors would learn about semantic noise. I really try to pay attention in class and to learn, but the way some faculty talk makes it impossible to understand what they mean, especially if English is a second language. I wish they would remember that we're not specialists like they are, so we don't know all the technical words.

In summary, when we say that communication is systemic, we mean three things. First, all communication occurs within multiple systems that affect meanings. Second, all parts and all systems of communication are interdependent, so they affect one another. Finally, all communication systems have noise, which can be physiological, physical, psychological, or semantic.

Unique   At the deepest level, interpersonal communication is also unique. In relationships that go beyond social roles, every person is unique and therefore irreplaceable. We can substitute people in I–It relationships and even in I–You relationships (one clerk can ring up purchases as well as another; we can get another racquetball buddy), but we can't replace intimates. When we lose intimates, we find new friends and romantic partners, but they aren't interchangeable with the ones we lost.

Just as every person is unique, so is each friendship and romantic relationship. Each develops its own distinctive patterns and rhythms and even special vocabulary that are not part of other interpersonal relationships. In the process of becoming close, people work out personal roles and rules for interaction, and these may deviate from general social rules and roles (Duck, 2006; Dainton, 2006; Wood, 2006). With one friend, you might go skating and get together for athletic events. With a different, equally close friend, you might talk openly about feelings. My sister Carolyn and I constantly play jokes on each other and engage in verbal duels in which we try to one-up each other. Another close friend of mine doesn't enjoy verbal jousting, so it's not part of our interaction. As these examples show, interpersonal communication involves unique people who interact in relation to each other.

Processual Interpersonal communication is an ongoing, continuous **process.** This means, first, that communication evolves over time, becoming more personal as people interact. Friendships and romantic relationships gain depth and significance over the course of time, and they may also decline in quality over time. Relationships on the job also evolve over time. Ellen may mentor Craig when he starts working at her firm, but over time they may become equal colleagues. Because relationships are dynamic, they don't stay the same but continually change just as we do.

> **JANA** My daughter is my best friend, but it wasn't always that way. As a child, she was very shy and dependent. She was a sullen teenager who resented everything I said and did. Now that she's 22, we've become really good friends. But even now, our relationship has all of the echoes of who we were with each other at different times in our lives.

An ongoing process also has no discrete beginnings and endings. Figure 1.4 on page 19 highlights the processual character of interpersonal communication by including time as a dynamic, changing feature. Suppose a friend stops by and confides in you about a troubling personal problem. When did that communication begin? Although it may seem to have started when the friend came by, earlier interactions may have led the friend to feel that it was safe to talk to you and that you would care about the problem. We can't be sure, then, when this communication began. Similarly, we don't know where it will end. Perhaps it ends when the friend leaves, but perhaps it doesn't. Maybe your response to the problem helps your friend see new options. Maybe what you learn changes how you feel toward your friend. Because communication is ongoing, we can never be sure when it begins or ends.

Because interpersonal interaction is a process, what happens between people is linked to both past and future. In our earlier example, the meaning of Ian's gift reflects prior interactions between him and Cheryl, and their interaction about the gift will affect future interactions. All our communication occurs in three temporal dimensions: past, which affects what happens now; present; and future, which is molded by what occurs in this moment (Dixson & Duck, 1993; Wood, 2006). How couples handle early arguments affects how they deal with later ones. Yesterday's e-mail response from a friend influences what we write today and, in turn, what our friend may write back tomorrow. In communication, past, present, and future are always interwoven.

The ongoing quality of interpersonal communication also suggests that we can't stop the process, nor can we edit or unsay what has been said. In this sense, communication is irreversible: We can't take it back. This implies that we have an ethical responsibility to recognize the irreversibility of communication and to communicate carefully.

© Ariel Skelley/CORBIS

Transactional   Interpersonal communication is a process of transaction between people. As you speak to a friend, your friend smiles; as your supervisor explains an idea, you nod to show you understand; as your parent scolds you, you wrinkle your brow resentfully. In interpersonal encounters, all parties communicate continually and simultaneously.

The transactional nature of interpersonal communication implies that communicators share responsibility for effectiveness. We often say, "You didn't express yourself clearly" or "You misunderstood me," as if understanding rested with a single person. In reality, responsibility for good communication is shared. One person cannot make communication successful, nor is one person totally responsible for problems. Misunderstandings often arise in e-mail and online communication because feedback tends to be delayed, a problem that instant messaging can decrease. Another limitation of online communication is the inability to convey inflection and nonverbal behaviors, such as winks, that tell another we are joking. Sometimes we add emoticons, such as :) or :(, to signal emotions online. Because interpersonal communication is an ongoing, transactional process, all participants share responsibility for its effectiveness.

Individual   From Buber, we learned that the deepest level of interpersonal communication involves engaging others as individuals who are unlike anyone else. When we communicate this way, we don't speak from social roles (teacher–student, boss–employee, customer–salesclerk). Instead, in I–Thou communication, we treat others, and are treated by them, as individuals. This is possible only if we learn who they are and if they, in turn, come to understand us as distinct individuals unlike anyone else. We come to understand the unique fears and hopes, problems and joys, needs and abilities of people as we interact with them meaningfully over a period of time. As trust builds, people disclose personal information that allows insight into their unique selves.

Personal   Interpersonal communication fosters personal knowledge and insights. To connect as unique individuals, we have to get to know others personally and understand their thoughts and feelings. With colleagues whom I have known for more than 25 years, I understand some of their worries, concerns, and personal issues in ways I didn't when we first became colleagues. Longtime friends have a history of shared experiences and knowledge that allow them to interact more fully than casual friends can.

Interpersonal communication also creates personal knowledge. As our relationships with others deepen, we build trust and learn how to communicate in ways that make each other feel comfortable and safe. The personal knowledge we gain over time in relationships encourages us to know and be known: We share secrets, fears, and experiences that we don't tell to just anyone. This is part of what Buber meant by "being" with others. Personal knowledge is a process, one that grows and builds on itself over time as people communicate interpersonally. Sometimes, we may even feel that our closest friends know us better than we know ourselves, as Lizelle explains.

> **LIZELLE**   What I like best about long-term relationships is all the layers that develop. I know the friends I've had since high school in so many ways. I know what they did and felt and dreamed in high school, and I know them as they are now. They have the same kind of in-depth knowledge of me. We tell each other everything, so it sometimes seems that my deepest friends know me better than I know myself.

Sharing personal information and experiences highlights the ethical dimension of interpersonal communication. We can use our knowledge to protect people we care about. We can also use it to hurt those people; for example, personal knowledge allows us to attack vulnerabilities others have revealed to us. Ethical communicators choose not to exploit or treat casually personal information about others.

Meaning Creating   The heart of interpersonal communication is shared meanings between people (Duck, 1994a, 1994b). We don't merely exchange words when we communicate. Instead, we create meanings as we figure out what each other's words and behaviors stand for, represent, or imply. Meanings grow out of histories of interaction between unique persons. For example, my partner, Robbie, and I are both continually overcommitted professionally, and we each worry about the pace of the other's life. Often, one of us says to the other, "*Bistari, bistari.*" This phrase will mean nothing to you unless you know enough Nepalese to translate it as meaning "Go slowly, go gradually." When one of us says, "*Bistari, bistari,*" we not only suggest slowing down but also remind each other of our special time living and trekking in Nepal.

Most close friends and romantic partners develop vocabularies that have meaning only to them. People who work together also develop meanings that grow out of their interactions over time. Once, in my department, faculty members argued for 30 minutes over whether we wanted a semicolon or a dash in a sentence that was part of our mission statement. Now, whenever we start debating small issues, one of us is bound to say, "Semicolon or dash?" Usually this evokes laughter and persuades us to abandon a trivial argument.

You may have noticed that I refer to *meanings,* not just one meaning. This is because interpersonal communication involves two levels of meaning (Watzlawick, Beavin, & Jackson, 1967). The first level, called the **content meaning,** deals with literal, or denotative, meaning. If a parent says to a 5-year-old child, "Clean your room now," the content meaning is that the room is to be cleaned immediately.

The second level is the **relationship meaning.** This refers to what communication expresses about relationships between communicators. The relationship meaning of "Clean your room now" is that the parent has the right to order the child; they have an unequal power relationship. If the parent had said, "Would you mind cleaning your room?" the relationship meaning would have reflected a more equal relationship. Suppose a friend says, "You're the only person I can talk to about this," and then discloses something that is worrying him. The content level includes the actual issue itself and the information that you're the only one with whom he will discuss this issue. But what has he told you on the relationship level? He has communicated that he trusts you, he considers you special, and he probably expects you to care about his troubles.

> **ANI**   My father needs to learn about relationship meanings. Whenever I call home, he asks me if anything's wrong. Then he asks what the news is. If I don't have news to report, he can't understand why I'm calling. Then Mom gets on the phone, and we talk for a while about stuff—nothing important, just stuff. I don't call to tell them big news. I just want to touch base and feel connected.

Cultures vary in how much they emphasize content- and relationship-level meanings. In high-context cultures, great emphasis is put on holistic understanding of meanings. Words themselves have little meaning until placed in the context of particular people, relationships, and histories. In low-context cultures, the content level of meaning is given greater priority. Words and literal meaning are

Communication in Everyday Life
Pillow Talk

Most people in close relationships develop private vocabularies to express themselves to each other in unique ways. Siblings create nicknames that often follow them into adult life (Nicholson, 2006). Couples report having private nicknames for one another ("the red-head," "noodle brain"), special codes for indicating that they want to make love ("Want to read in bed tonight?"), and teasing routines and mock insults used to show affection. Researchers also discovered that closeness between partners seems linked to how extensive a private language they have developed. Thus, it may be that communication is not only the messenger of loving feelings but also the creator ("Public Pillow Talk," 1987).

emphasized. The United States is a low-context culture, whereas many Asian cultures are high-context ones (Lim, 2002).

Scholars have identified three general dimensions of relationship-level meanings. The first dimension is responsiveness, and it refers to how aware of others and involved with them we are. Perhaps you can remember a conversation you had with someone who shuffled papers and glanced at a clock or kept looking at a computer screen while you were talking. If so, you probably felt she wasn't interested in you or what you were saying. Low responsiveness is communicated on the relationship level of meaning when people don't look at us or when they are preoccupied with something other than talking with us. Higher responsiveness is communicated by eye contact, nodding, and feedback that indicates involvement (Richmond & McCroskey, 2000).

A second dimension of relationship meaning is liking, or affection. This concerns the degree of positive or negative feeling that is communicated. Although liking may seem synonymous with responsiveness, the two are actually distinct. We may be responsive to people we don't like but to whom we must pay attention, and we are sometimes preoccupied and unresponsive to people about whom we care. We communicate that we like or dislike others by what we actually say as well as by tone of voice, facial expressions, how close we sit to them, and so forth.

Power, or control, is the third dimension of relationship meaning. This refers to the power balance between communicators. A parent may say to a 5-year-old, "Clean your room because I say so, that's why." This communicates that the parent has the

Everyday Application
Levels of Meaning

For the next 48 hours, focus on relationship meanings in your communication. Record examples of the following:

··· Communicating responsiveness
··· Communicating lack of responsiveness
··· Expressing liking
··· Expressing dislike
··· Expressing superiority
··· Expressing subordination
··· Expressing equality

What does this tell you about the relationship issues being negotiated and expressed in your relationships? *Student Companion:* Activity 1.4 and Activity 1.5 provide additional opportunities to identify levels of meaning in your communication with others.

power to tell the child what to do. Friends and romantic partners sometimes engage in covert power struggles on the relationship level. One person suggests going to a particular movie and then to dinner at the pizza parlor. The other responds by saying she doesn't want to see that movie and isn't in the mood for pizza. They could be arguing on the content level about their different preferences for the evening. If arguments over what to do or eat are recurrent and heated, however, chances are the couple is negotiating power. In interpersonal relationships, the relationship level of meaning often is the most important, for it sets the tone for interaction and for how people feel about each other. *Student Companion:* Activity 1.8.

Thus far, we have seen that communication exists on a continuum, ranging from impersonal to interpersonal. We've also learned that it is best understood as a transactional process, not a linear exchange or an interaction. Based on the transactional model, we defined interpersonal communication as a selective, systemic, unique, and ongoing process of transaction between people who reflect and build personal knowledge of one another as they create meanings. Meanings, we have seen, reflect histories of interaction and involve both content and relationship levels. Building on this definition, we're now ready to identify basic principles of interpersonal communication.

Principles of Interpersonal Communication

Our first look at interpersonal communication suggests eight basic principles for effectiveness.

PRINCIPLE 1: WE CANNOT NOT COMMUNICATE

Whenever people are together, they communicate. We cannot avoid communicating when we are with others, because they interpret what we do and say as well as what we don't do and don't say. Even if we choose to be silent, we're communicating. What we mean by silence and how others interpret it depend on cultural backgrounds.

Because Westerners typically are more verbal than many cultural groups, they are likely to regard silence as a signal of lack of knowledge, anger, or disinterest. Some Native Americans and members of many Eastern cultures might interpret silence as thoughtfulness or respect. Either way, silence communicates.

Even when we don't intend to communicate, we do so. We may be unaware of a grimace that gives away our disapproval or an eye roll that shows we dislike someone, but we are communicating nonetheless. Unconscious communication often occurs on the relationship level of meaning as we express feelings about others through subtle, often nonverbal communication. Regardless of whether we aim to communicate and whether others understand our intentions, we continuously, unavoidably communicate.

PRINCIPLE 2: INTERPERSONAL COMMUNICATION IS IRREVERSIBLE

Perhaps you have been in heated arguments in which you lost your temper and said something you later regretted. It could be that you hurt someone or revealed something about yourself that you meant to keep private. Later, you might have tried to repair the damage by apologizing, explaining what you said, or denying what you revealed. But you couldn't erase your communication; you couldn't unsay what you said. You may have had similar experiences when communicating by e-mail. Perhaps you read a message that made you mad, and you dashed off a pointed reply, sent it, and then wished you could unsend it. The fact that communication is irreversible reminds us that what we say and do matters. It has impact. Once we say something to another person, our words become part of the relationship. Remembering this principle keeps us aware of the importance of choosing when to speak and what to say—or not to say!

PRINCIPLE 3: INTERPERSONAL COMMUNICATION INVOLVES ETHICAL CHOICES

Ethics is the branch of philosophy that focuses on moral principles and codes of conduct. Ethical issues concern right and wrong. Because interpersonal communication is irreversible and affects others, it always has ethical implications. What we say and do affects others: how they feel, how they perceive themselves, how they think about themselves, and how they think about others. Thus, responsible people think carefully about ethical guidelines for communication. For instance, should you not tell someone something that might make him less willing to do what you want? If you read a message in a chat room that makes you angry, do you fire off a nasty reply, assuming that you will never meet the person and so won't face any consequences? Do you judge another person's communication from your own individual perspective and experience? Or do you try to understand her communication on her terms and from her perspective? In work settings, should you avoid giving negative feedback because it could hurt others' feelings? In these and many other instances, we face ethical choices.

Richard Johannesen (1996) has devoted most of his career to studying the ethical aspects of human communication. He says that ethical communication occurs when people create relationships of equality, when they attend mindfully to each other, and when their communication demonstrates that they are authentic, empathic, supportive, and confirming of each other. Because interpersonal communication affects us and others, ethical considerations are always part of our interactions. Throughout this book, we note ethical issues that arise when we interact with others. As you read, consider what kinds of choices you make and what moral principles guide your choices.

PRINCIPLE 4: PEOPLE CONSTRUCT MEANINGS IN INTERPERSONAL COMMUNICATION

Human beings construct the meanings of their communication. The significance of communication doesn't lie in words and nonverbal behaviors. Instead, meaning arises out of how we interpret communication. This calls our attention to the fact that humans use symbols, which sets us apart from other creatures.

As we will see in Chapter 4, **symbols,** such as words, have no inherent or true meanings. Instead, we must interpret them. What does it mean if someone says, "You're sick"? To interpret the comment, you must consider the context (a counseling session, a professional meeting, after a daredevil stunt), who said it (a psychiatrist, a supervisor, a subordinate, a friend, an enemy), and the words themselves, which may mean various things (a medical diagnosis, a challenge to your professional competence, a compliment on your zaniness, disapproval).

In interpersonal communication, people continuously interpret each other. Although typically we're not aware that we assign meanings, inevitably we do so. Someone you have been dating suggests some time away from each other, a friend turns down invitations to get together, or your supervisor at work seems less open to conversations with you than in the past. The meanings of such communications are neither self-evident nor inherent in the words. Instead, we construct their significance. In close relationships, partners gradually coordinate meanings so that they share understandings of issues and feelings important to their connection. When a relationship begins, one person may regard confrontation as healthy, and the other may avoid arguments. Over time, partners come to share meanings for conflict—what it is, how to handle it, and whether it threatens the relationship or is a path to growth.

The meanings we attribute to conflict and other aspects of communication are shaped by cultural backgrounds. Because standing up for your own ideas is emphasized in the United States, many people who were born and raised in this country value confrontation more than do many Asians who were raised in traditional Asian families. Conflict means different things to each group.

BYRON Sometimes my buddies and I will call each other "boy" or even "black boy," and we know we're just kidding around. But if a white calls me "boy," I get real mad. It doesn't mean the same thing when they call us "boy" that it does when we call ourselves "boy."

Even one person's meanings vary over time and in response to experiences and moods. If you're in a good mood, a playful gibe might strike you as funny or as an invitation to banter. The same remark might hurt or anger you if you're feeling down. The meaning of the gibe, like all communication, is not preset or absolute. Meanings are created by people as they communicate in specific contexts.

PRINCIPLE 5: METACOMMUNICATION AFFECTS MEANINGS

The word *metacommunication* comes from the prefix *meta*, meaning "about," and the root word *communication*. Thus, **metacommunication** is communication about communication. For example, during a conversation with your friend Pat, you notice that Pat's body seems tense and her voice is sharp. You might say, "You seem really stressed." Your statement metacommunicates about Pat's nonverbal communication.

Metacommunication may be verbal or nonverbal. We can use words to talk about other words or nonverbal behaviors. If an argument between Joe and Marc gets out of hand, and Joe makes a nasty personal attack, Joe might say, "I didn't really mean what I just said. I was just so angry it came out." This metacommunication may soften the hurt caused by the attack. If Joe and Marc then have a productive conversation

© Boiffin Vivier/Photo Researchers, Inc.

about their differences, Marc might conclude by saying, "This has really been a good talk. I think we understand each other a lot better now." This comment verbally metacommunicates about the conversation that preceded it.

We also metacommunicate nonverbally. Nonverbal metacommunication often reinforces verbal communication. For example, you might nod your head while saying, "I really know what you mean." Or you might move away from a person after you say, "I don't want to see you anymore." Yet, not all nonverbal metacommunication reinforces verbal messages. Sometimes, our nonverbal expressions contradict our verbal messages. When teasing a friend, you might wink to signal you don't mean the teasing to be taken seriously. Or you might smile when you say to a friend who drops by, "Oh, rats—you again!" The smile tells the friend you welcome the visit despite your comment to the contrary.

Metacommunication can increase understanding. For instance, teachers sometimes say, "The next point is really important." This comment signals students to pay special attention to what follows. A parent might tell a child, "What I said may sound harsh, but I'm only telling you because I care about you." The comment tells the child how to interpret a critical message. A manager tells a subordinate to take a comment seriously by saying, "I really mean what I said. I'm not kidding." On the other hand, if we're not really sure what we think about an issue, and we want to try out a stance, we might say, "I'm thinking this through as I go, and I'm not really wedded to this position, but what I tend to believe right now is . . . ." This preface to your statement tells listeners not to assume that what you say is set in stone.

We can also metacommunicate to check on understanding: "Was I clear?" "Do you see why I feel like I do?" "Can you see why I'm confused about the problem?" Questions such as these allow you to find out whether another person understands what you intend to communicate. You may also metacommunicate to find out whether you understand what another person expresses to you. "What I think you meant is that you are worried. Is that right?" "If I follow what you said, you feel trapped between what you want to do and what your parents want you to do. Is that what you were telling me?" You may even say, "I don't understand what you just told me. Can you say it another way?" This question metacommunicates by letting the other person know you did not grasp her message and that you want to understand.

Effective metacommunication also helps friends and romantic partners express how they feel about their interactions. Linda Acitelli (1988, 1993) has studied what happens when partners in a relationship talk to each other about how they perceive and feel about their interaction. She reports that women and men alike find metacommunication helpful if there is a conflict or problem that must be addressed. Both sexes seem to appreciate knowing how the other feels about their differences; they are also eager to learn how to communicate to resolve those differences. During a conflict, one person might say, "I feel like we're both being really stubborn. Do you think we could each back off a little from our positions?" This expresses discontent with how communication is proceeding and offers an alternative. After conflict, one partner might say, "This really cleared the air between us. I feel a lot better now."

> **TARA**   I never feel like an argument is really over and settled until Andy and I have said that we feel better for having thrashed out whatever was the problem. It's like I want closure, and the fight isn't really behind us until we both say, "I'm glad we talked," or something to say what we went through led us to a better place.

Acitelli also found that women are more likely than men to appreciate metacommunication when there is no conflict or immediate problem to be resolved. While curled up on a sofa and watching TV, a woman might say to her male partner,

Everyday Application
Improving Your Metacommunication

For each of the scenarios described here, write out one verbal or nonverbal metacommunication that would be appropriate to express your feelings about what has been said or to clarify understanding.

1. A friend tells you about a problem with his parents, and you aren't sure whether your friend wants advice or just a safe person with whom to vent feelings.

Metacommunication

_____
_____
_____

2. You are arguing with a person who seems more interested in winning the argument than in working things through so that both of you are satisfied. You want to change how the argument is proceeding.

Metacommunication

_____
_____
_____

3. Your manager at work routinely gives you orders instead of making requests. You resent it when she says to you, "Take over the front room," "Clean up the storeroom now," and "I want you in early tomorrow." You want to change how your manager expresses expectations for your performance.

Metacommunication

_____
_____
_____

4. Lately, someone who used to be a close friend seems to be avoiding you. When you do see the friend, he seems eager to cut the conversation short. He doesn't meet your eyes and doesn't tell you anything about his life anymore. You want to know what is going on and how to interpret his communication.

Metacommunication

_____
_____
_____

5. You have just spent 10 minutes telling your father why you want to study abroad next year. Earlier, your father said that studying abroad was just an extravagance, but you've tried to explain why it will broaden your education and your marketability when you look for a job next year. You aren't sure your father has understood your points.

Metacommunication

_____
_____
_____

You can complete this activity online and, if requested, submit it to your instructor under "Chapter Resources for Chapter 1" at the Everyday Connections website. See the end of this chapter for information about accessing this website.

"I really feel comfortable snuggling with you." This comments on the relationship and on the nonverbal communication between the couple. According to research by Acitelli and others (Wood, 1997, 1998), men generally find talk about relationships unnecessary unless there is an immediate problem to be addressed. Understanding this gender difference in preferences for metacommunication may help you interpret members of the other sex more accurately.

PRINCIPLE 6: INTERPERSONAL COMMUNICATION DEVELOPS AND SUSTAINS RELATIONSHIPS

Interpersonal communication is the primary way we build, refine, and transform relationships. Partners talk to work out expectations and understandings of their interaction, appropriate and inappropriate topics and styles of communicating, and the nature of the relationship itself. Is it a friendship or a romantic relationship? How much and in what ways can we count on each other? How do we handle disagreements—by confronting them, ignoring them, or using indirect strategies to restore harmony? What are the bottom lines, the "shalt not" rules for what counts as unforgivable betrayal? What counts as caring—words, deeds, both? Because communication has no intrinsic meanings, we must generate our own in the course of interaction.

Communication also allows us to construct or reconstruct individual and joint histories. For instance, when people fall in love, they often redefine former loves as "mere infatuations" or "puppy love" but definitely not the real thing. When something goes wrong in a relationship, partners may work together to define what happened in a way that allows them to continue. Marriage counselors report that couples routinely work out face-saving explanations for affairs so that they can stay together in the aftermath of infidelity (Scarf, 1987). Partners often talk about past events and experiences that challenged them and ones that were joyous. The process of reliving the past reminds partners how long they have been together and how much they have shared. As partners communicate thoughts and feelings, they generate shared meanings for themselves, their interaction, and their relationship.

Communication is also the primary means by which intimates construct a future for themselves, and a vision of shared future is one of the most powerful ties that link people (Dixson & Duck, 1993; Wood, 2006). Romantic couples often dream together by talking about the family they plan and how they'll be in 20 years. Likewise, friends discuss plans for the future and promise reunions if they must move apart. Communication allows us to express and share dreams, imaginings, and memories and to weave all of these into the joint world of relational partners.

KAREN I love talking about the future with my fiancé. Sometimes, we talk for hours about the kind of house we'll have and what our children will be like and how we'll juggle two careers and a family. I know everything won't work out exactly like we think now, but talking about it makes me feel so close to Dave and like our future is real.

PRINCIPLE 7: INTERPERSONAL COMMUNICATION IS NOT A PANACEA

As we have seen, we communicate to satisfy many of our needs and to create relationships with others. Yet it would be a mistake to think communication is a cure-all. Many problems can't be solved by talk alone. Communication by itself won't end hunger, abuses of human rights around the globe, racism, intimate partner violence, or physical diseases. Nor can words alone bridge irreconcilable differences between people or erase the hurt of betrayal. Although good communication may increase understanding and help us solve problems, it will not fix everything. We should also realize that the idea of talking things through is distinctly Western. Not all societies think it's wise or useful to communicate about relationships or to talk extensively about feelings. Just as interpersonal communication has many strengths and values, it also has limits, and its effectiveness is shaped by cultural contexts.

PRINCIPLE 8: INTERPERSONAL COMMUNICATION EFFECTIVENESS CAN BE LEARNED

It is a mistake to think that effective communicators are born, that some people have a natural talent and others don't. Although some people have extraordinary talent in athletics or writing, all of us can become competent athletes and writers. Likewise, some people have an aptitude for communicating, but all of us can become competent communicators. This book and the course you are taking should sharpen your understandings of how interpersonal communication works and should help you learn skills that will enhance your effectiveness in relating to others.

Guidelines for Interpersonal Communication Competence

Sometimes we handle interactions well, and in other cases we are ineffective. What are the differences between effective and ineffective communication? Scholars define **interpersonal communication competence** as the ability to communicate effectively and appropriately. Effectiveness involves achieving the goals we have for specific interactions. In different situations, your goals might be to explain an idea, to comfort a friend, to stand up for your position, to negotiate a raise, or to persuade someone to change behaviors. The more effectively you communicate, the more likely you are to be competent in achieving your goals.

Competence also emphasizes appropriateness. This means that competent communication is adapted to particular situations and people. Language that is appropriate at a party with friends may not be appropriate in a job interview. Appropriateness also involves contexts. It may be appropriate to kiss an intimate in a private setting but not in a classroom. Similarly, many people choose not to argue in front of others but prefer to engage in conflict when they are alone.

Five skills are closely tied to competence in interpersonal communication: (1) developing a range of communication skills, (2) adapting communication appropriately, (3) engaging in dual perspective, (4) monitoring communication, and (5) committing to effective and ethical interpersonal communication. We'll discuss each of these skills now.

DEVELOP A RANGE OF SKILLS

No one style of communication is best in all circumstances, with all people, or for pursuing all goals. Because what is effective varies, we need to have a broad repertoire of communication behaviors. Consider the different skills needed for interpersonal communication competence in several situations.

To comfort someone, we need to be soothing and compassionate. To negotiate a good deal on a car, we need to be assertive and firm. To engage constructively in conflict, we need to listen and build supportive climates. To support a friend who is depressed, we need to affirm that person, demonstrate that we care, and encourage the friend to talk about problems. To build good work relationships, we need to know how to communicate supportively, how to express our ideas clearly, and how to listen well. Because no single set of skills composes interpersonal communication competence, we need to learn a range of communicative abilities. To learn about how interpersonal communication skills training is promoted on business web pages, complete *Student Companion:* Activity 1.9.

ADAPT COMMUNICATION APPROPRIATELY

The ability to communicate in a range of ways doesn't make us competent unless we also know which kinds of communication to use in specific interactions. For instance, knowing how to be both assertive and deferential isn't useful unless we can figure out when each style of communication is appropriate. Although there is no neat formula for adapting communication appropriately, it's generally important to consider personal goals, context, and the people with whom we communicate.

Your goals for communication are a primary guideline for selecting appropriate behaviors. If your purpose in a conversation is to give emotional support to someone, then it isn't effective to talk at length about your own experiences. On the other hand, if you want someone to understand you better, talking in depth about your life may be highly effective. If your goal is to win an argument and get your way, it may be competent to assert your point of view, point out flaws in your partner's ideas, and refuse to compromise. If you want to work through conflict in a way that doesn't harm a relationship, however, other communication choices might be more constructive.

> **MARY MARGARET**   For most of my life, I wasn't at all assertive, even when I should have been. Last spring, though, I was so tired of having people walk all over me that I signed up for a workshop on assertiveness training. I learned how to assert myself, and I was really proud of how much more I would stand up for myself. The problem was that I did it all the time, regardless of whether something really mattered enough to be assertive. Just like I was always passive before, now I'm always assertive. I need to figure out a better way to balance my behaviors.

Context is another influence on decisions of when, how, and about what to communicate. It is appropriate to ask your doctor about symptoms during an office exam, but it isn't appropriate to do so when you see the doctor in a social situation. When a friend is feeling low, that's not a good time to criticize, although at another time criticism might be constructive. When communicating online, skilled communicators compensate for the lack of nonverbal cues by adding emoticons and expressing warmth explicitly (Baym, 2002; Parks & Roberts, 1998).

Remembering Buber's discussion of the I–Thou relationship, we know it is important to adapt what we say and how we say it to particular people. As we have seen, interpersonal communication increases our knowledge of others. Thus, the more interpersonal the relationship, the more we can adapt our communication to unique partners. Abstract communicative goals, such as supporting others, call for distinct behaviors in regard to specific people. What feels supportive to one friend may not to another. One of my closest friends withdraws if I challenge her ideas, yet another friend relishes challenges and the discussions they prompt. What is effective in talking with them varies. We have to learn what our intimates need, what upsets and pleases them, and how they interpret various kinds of communication. Scholars use the term **person-centeredness** to refer to the ability to adapt messages effectively to particular people (Bernstein, 1974; Burleson, 1987; Zorn, 1995). Appropriately adapted communication, then, is sensitive to goals, contexts, and other people.

ENGAGE IN DUAL PERSPECTIVE

Central to competent interpersonal communication is the ability to engage in **dual perspective,** which is understanding both our own and another person's perspective, beliefs, thoughts, or feelings (Phillips & Wood, 1983). When we adopt dual perspective, we understand how someone else thinks and feels about issues. To meet another person in genuine dialogue, we must be able to realize how that person views himself or herself, the situation, and his or her own thoughts and feelings. We may personally see things much differently, and we may want to express our perceptions. Yet, we also need to understand and respect the other person's perspective.

People who cannot take the perspectives of others are egocentric. They impose their perceptions on others and interpret others' experiences through their own eyes. Consider an example. Roberto complains that he is having trouble writing a report for his supervisor. His co-worker Raymond responds, "All you have to do is outline the plan and provide the rationale. That's a snap." "But," says Roberto, "I've always had trouble writing. I just block when I sit down to write." Raymond says, "That's silly. Anyone can do this. It just took me an hour or so to do my report." Raymond has failed to understand how Roberto sees writing. If you have trouble writing, then composing a report isn't a snap, but Raymond can't get beyond his own comfort with writing to understand Roberto's different perspective.

ASHA   Sometimes it's very difficult for me to understand my daughter. She likes music that sounds terrible to me, and I don't like the way she dresses sometimes. For a long time, I judged her by my own values about music and dress, but that really pushed us apart. She kept saying, "I'm not you. Why can't you look at it from my point of view?" Finally, I heard her, and now we both try to understand each other's point of view. It isn't always easy, but you can't have a relationship on just one person's terms.

As Asha says, engaging in dual perspective isn't necessarily easy, because all of us naturally see things from our own points of view and in terms of our own experiences. Parents often have trouble understanding the perspectives of children, particularly teenagers (Fox & Frankel, 2005). Yet, we can improve our ability to engage in dual perspective (Greene & Burleson, 2003). Three guidelines can help you increase your ability to take the perspective of others.

© David Joel/Getty Images/Stone

··· First, be aware of the tendency to see things from your own perspective, and resist that inclination.
··· Second, listen closely to how others express their thoughts and feelings, so you gain clues of what things mean to them and how they feel.

··· Third, ask others to explain how they feel, what something means to them, or how they view a situation. Asking questions and probing for details communicates on the relationship level that you are interested and that you want to understand. Making a commitment to engage in dual perspective and practicing the three guidelines just discussed will enhance your ability to recognize and respond to others' perspectives.

MONITOR YOUR COMMUNICATION

The fourth ability that affects interpersonal communication competence is **monitoring,** which is the capacity to observe and regulate your own communication. Most of us do this much of the time. Before bringing up a touchy topic, you remind yourself not to get defensive and not to get pulled into counterproductive arguing. During the discussion, Chris says something that upsets you. You think of a really good zinger but stop yourself from saying it, because you don't want to hurt Chris. In each instance, you monitored your communication.

Monitoring occurs both before and during interaction. Often, before conversations we indicate to ourselves what we do and don't want to say. During communication, we stay alert and edit our thoughts before expressing them. Online communication offers us especially effective ways to monitor our communication. We can save messages, reread them to see if they express what we really intend, and edit them before sending (Baym, 2002). Our ability to monitor allows us to adapt communication in advance and gauge our effectiveness as we interact.

Of course, we don't monitor all the time. When we are with people who understand us or when we are talking about unimportant topics, we don't necessarily need to monitor communication with great care. Sometimes, however, not monitoring can result in communication that hurts others or that leads us to regard ourselves negatively. In some cases, failure to monitor results from getting caught up in the dynamics of interaction. We simply forget to keep a watchful eye on ourselves, and so we say or do things we later regret. In addition, some people have poorly developed monitoring skills. They have limited awareness of how they come across to others. Communication competence involves learning to attend to feedback from others and to monitor the impact of our communication as we interact with them.

COMMIT TO EFFECTIVE AND ETHICAL COMMUNICATION

The final requirement for interpersonal competence is commitment to effective and ethical communication. This commitment requires that you invest energy in communicating ethically with others as unique human beings. This implies that you can't treat another person as merely a member of some group, such as men, co-workers, or customers. Responding to another as a unique and valuable person also means you can't dismiss the other person's feelings as wrong, inappropriate, or silly. Instead, you must honor the person and the feelings he or she expresses, even if you feel differently.

A commitment to effective and ethical communication also includes caring about yourself and your ideas and feelings. Just as you must honor those of others, you must respect yourself and your own perspective. Finally, competent communicators are committed to the communication process itself. They realize that it is interactive and always evolving, and they are willing to deal with that complexity. In addition, they are sensitive to multiple levels of meaning and to the irreversibility of communication. Commitment, then, is vital to relationships, other people, ourselves, and communication.

In sum, interpersonal communication competence is the ability to communicate in ways that are interpersonally effective and appropriate. The five requirements for competence are (1) developing a range of communication skills; (2) adapting them appropriately to goals, others, and situations; (3) engaging in dual perspective; (4) monitoring communication and its impact; and (5) committing to effective and ethical interpersonal communication. Consider which aspects of communication competence you would most like to improve, and make a contract with yourself to work on them during this course.

Everyday Application
Improving Communication Competence

··· How competent are you in various communication skills?
··· Describe communication situations in which you don't feel you are as competent as you'd like to be.
··· How well do you adapt your communication to different goals, situations, and people?
··· How consistently and effectively do you engage in dual perspective when interacting with others? How can you tell when you really understand another's point of view?
··· How well do you monitor your communication so that you gauge how you come across to others?
··· Describe your commitments to others, to relationships, to yourself, and to the interpersonal communication process.

You can assess your satisfaction with your ability to communicate in different situations online under "Chapter Resources for Chapter 1" at the Everyday Connections website or by completing *Student Companion: Activity 1.6.*

Case Study: Continuing the Conversation

The following conversation is featured at the Everyday Connections website under "Chapter Resources for Chapter 1." Click on the link "The New Employee" in the left-hand menu to launch the video and audio scenario scripted below.

Your supervisor asks you to mentor a new employee, Toya, and help her learn the ropes of the job. After 2 weeks, you perceive that the new person has many strengths. She is responsible and punctual, and she takes initiative on her own. At the same time, you realize that Toya is careless about details: She doesn't proofread reports, so they contain errors in spelling and grammar, and she doesn't check back to make sure something she did worked. You've also noticed that Toya seems very insecure and wants a lot of affirmation and praise. You want to give her honest feedback so she can improve her job performance, yet you are afraid she will react defensively if you bring up her carelessness. You ask Toya to meet with you to discuss her first 2 weeks on the job. The meeting begins:

You: Well, you've been here for 2 weeks. How are you liking the job?

Toya: I like it a lot, and I'm trying to do my best every day. Nobody has said anything, so I guess I'm doing okay.

You: Well, I've noticed how responsible you are and how great you are about being a self-starter. Those are real strengths in this job.

Toya: Thanks. So I guess I'm doing okay, right?

You: What would you say if someone suggested that there are ways you can improve your work?

Toya: What do you mean? Have I done something wrong? Nobody's said anything to me. Is someone saying something behind my back?

1. What would you say next to Toya? How would you meet your ethical responsibilities as her mentor and also adapt to her interpersonal needs for reassurance?

2. What degree of responsibility do you have to Toya, your supervisor, and the company? How can you reflect thoughtfully about potential tensions between these responsibilities?

3. How would your communication differ if you acted according to a linear or transactive model of communication?

You can critique and analyze this encounter based on the principles you learned in this chapter by responding to the questions included under "Conversation Analysis" at the website. By clicking the "Submit" button at the end of the form, you can compare your work to my suggested responses. Let's continue the discussion online!

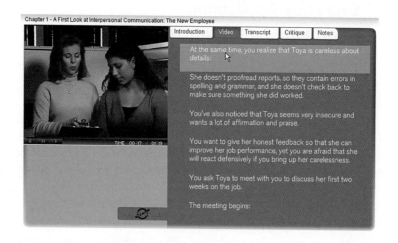

Chapter Summary

In this chapter, we launched our study of interpersonal communication. We began by noting that communication is essential to our survival and happiness. Communicating with others allows us to meet basic needs for survival and safety as well as more abstract human needs for inclusion, esteem, self-actualization, and effective participation in a socially diverse world.

We looked at three different models of the process. The best model is the transactional one because it emphasizes the dynamic nature and the systemic quality of interpersonal communication and because it recognizes that people simultaneously send and receive messages. This model is the foundation of our definition of interpersonal communication as a selective, systemic, unique, and ongoing process of interaction between people who reflect and build personal knowledge and create meanings. We also learned that communication exists on a continuum that ranges from impersonal (I–It) to interpersonal (I–Thou). Fully interpersonal communication occurs when people engage each other as full, unique human beings who create meanings on both content and relationship levels.

We discussed eight principles of interpersonal communication. First, it is impossible not to communicate. Whether or not we intend to send certain messages and whether or not others understand our meanings, communication always occurs when people are together. Second, communication is irreversible because we cannot unsay or undo what passes between us and others. Third, interpersonal communication always has ethical implications. The fourth principle maintains that meanings reside not in words but rather in how we interpret them. Fifth, metacommunication affects meanings in interpersonal interaction. Sixth, we use communication to develop and sustain relationships. In fact, communication is essential to relationships because it is in the process of interacting with others that we develop expectations, understandings, and rules to guide relationships. Seventh, although communication is powerful and important, it is not a cure-all. The eighth and final principle is that effectiveness in interpersonal communication can be learned through committed study and practice of principles and skills.

Competent interpersonal communicators interact in ways that are effective and appropriate. This means that we should adapt our ways of communicating to specific goals, situations, and others. Effectiveness and appropriateness require us to recognize and respect differences that reflect personal and cultural backgrounds. Guidelines for doing this include developing a range of communication skills, adapting communication sensitively, engaging in dual perspective, monitoring our own communication, and committing to effective and ethical interpersonal communication. In later chapters, we focus on developing the skills that enhance interpersonal communication competence.

Everyday Connections Online

Now that you've read Chapter 1, go to the *Everyday Connections* premium website at academic.cengage.com/communication/woodinterpersonal5plus for quick access to the electronic study resources that accompany this text. The

website gives you access to the "Continuing the Conversation" video scenario and questions featured in this chapter, to InfoTrac College Edition, to maintained and updated web links, and to the study aids for this chapter, including a digital glossary, review quizzes, and the chapter activities. For more information about this text's electronic learning resources, consult the **1pass card** that came with each

new copy of this book, or visit academic.cengage.com/communication/woodinterpersonal5.

Key Concepts

Audio flash cards of the following key terms are available on the Everyday Connections website. Use the flash cards to improve your pronunciation of text vocabulary.

content meaning	interpersonal communication	linear model	process
dual perspective		metacommunication	relationship meaning
ethics	interpersonal communication competence	model	symbols
feedback		monitoring	systemic
I–It communication	I–Thou communication	noise	transactional model
interactive model	I–You communication	person-centeredness	

For Further Thought and Discussion

1. Use each of the three models presented in this chapter to describe an interpersonal communication encounter. What does each model highlight? What does each model neglect or ignore? Which model best explains the process of interpersonal communication?

2. Interview a professional in the field you plan to enter. Ask him or her to explain the communication skills needed for success and advancement in the field. Which skills do you already have? Which ones do you need to develop or improve? Write out a personal action plan for using this book and the course it accompanies to enhance your effectiveness in interpersonal communication.

3. Go to the placement office on your campus, and read descriptions of job openings. Record the number of job descriptions that call for communication skills. Share your findings with others in your class.

4. Identify a relationship of yours that has become closer over time. Describe the earliest stage of the relationship. Was it an I–It or an I–You relationship at that time? Dur-

ing that early stage of the relationship, what did you talk about? Were there topics or kinds of talk you avoided? Now, describe the current relationship. What do you now talk about? Can you identify differences over time in your own and the other person's shared fields of experience?

5. Use your InfoTrac College Edition to read "Psychological Health and Change in Closeness in Platonic and Romantic Relationships" by Duncan Cramer and Marie Donachie. Which aspects of interpersonal communication does this article suggest are related to psychological health and closeness in relationships?

6. The National Communication Association's Credo on Communication Ethics provides guidelines for ethical communication. Learn about these by visiting http://www.natcom.org/conferences/ethics/ethicsconfcredo99.htm.

Communication and the Creation of Self

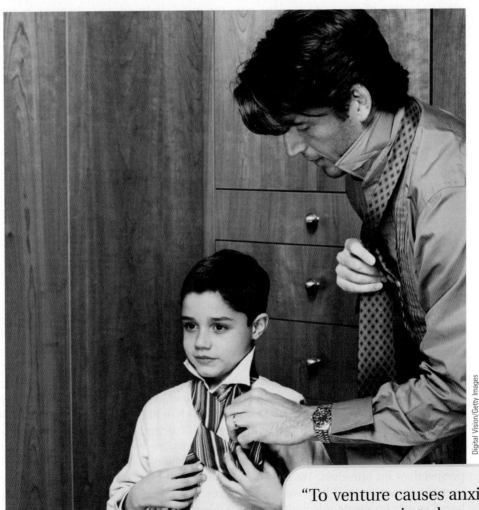

Digital Vision/Getty Images

"To venture causes anxiety, but not to venture is to lose one's self."

Søren Kierkegaard

I am a singer. I am short. I am shy. I am a sister. I am a brother. I am a parent. I am a goalie. I am a student. I am a woman. I am a man. I am gay. I am straight. I am a Christian. I am Hispanic. I am white. I am black. I am Asian American.

Who are you? How has your view of yourself changed over the years? At age 5, perhaps you defined yourself as your parents' daughter or son. In high school, you may have described yourself in terms of academic strengths ("I'm good at math and science"), athletic endeavors ("I'm a forward on the team"), leadership positions ("I'm president of the La Rosa Club"), friends and romantic partners ("I'm going steady with Cam"), or future plans ("I'm starting college next year" or "I'm going to start a dot.com business"). Now that you're in college, you're likely to see yourself in terms of a major, a career path, and perhaps relationships that you hope will span the years ahead. You've probably also made some decisions about your sexual orientation, spiritual commitments, and political beliefs.

As you think about the different ways you've defined yourself over the years, you'll realize that the self is not something that we fix at one point in life, after which it remains stable. Instead, the self is an ongoing process that evolves throughout our lives. One of the most important influences on the self is communication. In this chapter, we explore how the self is formed and changed in the process of communicating with others. We also discuss ways in which you can challenge and change aspects of your self that hold you back from becoming who you want to be.

······

What Is the Self?

The **self** arises in communication and is a multidimensional process of internalizing and acting from social perspectives. Although this is a complicated way to describe the self, it directs our attention to some important propositions about this very complicated concept.

THE SELF ARISES IN COMMUNICATION WITH OTHERS

Babies aren't born with clear understandings of who they are. Instead, we develop a self in the process of communicating with others. As we interact with others, we import, or internalize, their perspectives so that we come to share many of their perspectives as well as many of their perceptions of who we are.

From the moment we enter the world, we interact with others. As we do, we learn how they see us, and we take their perspectives inside ourselves. This process usually begins in the family as we learn how our parents, siblings, and other relatives view us. Later, as we interact with peers and teachers, we gain additional perspectives on ourselves. Still later, when we take jobs, we learn how co-workers and supervisors see us as employees. We also tune into media, which give us additional perspectives on ourselves. We internalize many of these views, and they become part of who we are and how we see ourselves. Thus, how we perceive ourselves is based largely on the people with whom we interact.

George Herbert Mead (1934) devoted his career to understanding how the self develops through communication. According to Mead, we develop selves by internalizing two kinds of perspectives that are communicated to us: the perspectives of particular others and the perspective of the generalized other. Let's now look more closely at these two types of social perspectives, on which we rely to define ourselves and to guide how we think, act, and feel.

PARTICULAR OTHERS

The first perspectives that affect us are those of particular others. **Particular others** are specific people who are significant to us. They include family members, peers, teachers, and other individuals who are especially important in our lives. As babies interact with particular others in their world, they learn how others see them. This is the beginning of a self-concept. Notice that the self starts from outside—from how particular others view us.

For most of us, family members are the first major influence on how we see ourselves. Mothers, fathers, siblings, and often day-care providers are particular others who are significant to most infants. In addition, some families include aunts, uncles, grandparents, and others who live together. Hispanics and African Americans, in general, have larger extended families than do most European Americans; children in such families often have more family members who affect how they see themselves (Gaines, 1995). In India, too, the extended family is very important. Traditional Indian families often include grandparents, aunts, uncles, and even second and third cousins who live together in the same household (Lustig & Koester, 1999). Among some Native Americans, everyone in a clan is considered family (Locke, 1992).

Parents and other individuals who matter to us communicate who we are and what we are worth through direct definitions, reflected appraisals, scripts, and attachment styles (see Figure 2.1). If parents communicate to children that they are special and cherished, the children are likely to see themselves as worthy of love. On the other hand, children whose parents communicate that they are not wanted or loved may come to think of themselves as unlovable.

Direct Definition As the term implies, **direct definition** is communication that tells us who we are by explicitly labeling us and our behaviors. Family members, as well as peers, teachers, and other individuals, define us by how they describe us. For instance, parents often communicate gender roles directly by telling us what boys and girls do and don't do. "Nice girls don't play rough," "You should help Mom around the house," and "Don't get your clothes dirty." Sons, on the other hand, are more likely to be told, "Go out and get 'em," "Stick up for yourself," and "Don't cry." As we hear these messages, we pick up our parents' and our society's gender expectations.

Communication in Everyday Life
What Is the Self?

Cultures vary in how they view the self and even in when they believe social identity begins. In the United States, a person is thought to exist at least when biological birth occurs, and many Americans believe that a fetus is a human self. Yet, in some societies, birth—and certainly not the stages prior to birth—isn't regarded as the start of selfhood (Morgan, 1996).

The Arunta of Central Australia consider a child born prematurely to be a nonperson, an animal that mistakenly has entered the body of the pregnant woman. In Ghana, a newborn is a nonperson until it has lived for 7 days. If the child doesn't live that long, members of the society believe that it was a spirit child, not a human being. Parents in Ghana do not mourn a baby that dies before the seventh day, because their society has taught them that such a being was a mistake and that they should be glad it is gone. The Tallensi people of Africa traditionally have not regarded twins as human until they have lived for a full month.

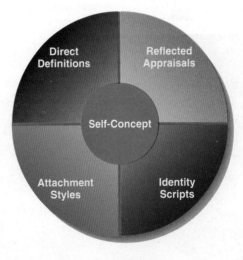

FIGURE 2.1

Family Influences on Self-Concept

© Spencer Grant/Stock Boston, LLC.

Positive direct definitions enhance our self-esteem: "You're smart," "You're strong," "You're great at soccer." Negative direct definitions can damage children's self-esteem (Brooks & Goldstein, 2001): "You're a troublemaker," "You're stupid," "You're impossible." Negative messages can demolish a child's sense of self-worth. Andrew Vachss (1994), who fights for children's rights, believes that emotional abuse is just as damaging as other forms of abuse.

Particular others often provide us with direct definitions of our racial and ethnic identities. In cultures with a majority race, members of minority races often make special efforts to impart racial identity to children. According to Susan Mosley-Howard and Cheryl Burgan Evans (1997), many African American parents and grandparents teach children to take pride in the strength and struggle that are part of African Americans' history. Many African American families also feel they must teach children that racism still exists in the United States (Mosley-Howard & Evans, 1997). Thus, the ethnic training in many African American families stresses both positive identification with black heritage and awareness of prejudice on the part of people who are not black.

Direct definition also takes place as particular others respond to children's behaviors. If a child clowns around, and parents respond by saying, "What a cut-up; you really are funny," the child learns to see herself or himself as funny. If a child dusts furniture and receives praise ("You're great to help clean the house"), helpfulness is reinforced as part of the child's self-concept. From direct definition, children learn what others value in them, and this shapes what they come to value in themselves. I still have vivid memories of being shamed for a B in reading on my first-grade report card. Just as intensely, I recall the excessive praise heaped on me when I won a reading contest in fourth grade. By then, I had learned what I had to do to get approval from my family. Through explicit labels and responses to our behaviors, family members and others who matter to us provide direct definitions of who we are and—just as important—who we are supposed to be.

© Misser/Explorer/Photo Researchers, Inc.

Berry Brazelton is a renowned pediatrician and a professor emeritus of pediatrics at Harvard Medical School. According to Brazelton (1997), parents and other family members boost or impair children's self-esteem by their responses to children's behavior. Especially important is responding with enthusiasm to a child's accomplishments. When a baby masters walking, she or he will show a look of delight at this new achievement. For that feeling to be complete, however, the child needs positive responses from others. Family members need to smile and say, "Wow, you did it!" Brazelton says that how a child is treated in the first 8 months of life sets the child's expectation of success or failure in life. If the child's accomplishments are noticed and praised, the

Leigh M. Wilco

child progressively gains self-confidence and undertakes increasingly difficult challenges. On the other hand, if the child's achievements are not noted and affirmed, the child is a candidate for low self-expectations and defeating self-fulfilling prophecies.

Reflected Appraisal   If we do not perceive or accept particular others' direct definitions of us, these definitions might not become part of how we see ourselves. **Reflected appraisal** is another's view of us. Another person's appraisal of us affects how we see ourselves. This concept is similar to the *looking glass self*, based on Charles Cooley's poetic comment, "Each to each a looking glass / Reflects the other that doth pass" (1961, p. 5). Others are mirrors for us—the views of ourselves that we see in them (our mirrors) shape how we perceive ourselves. If others communicate that they think we are smart, we are likely to reflect that appraisal in how we act and think about ourselves. If family members communicate that they see us as dumb or unlikable, we may reflect their appraisals by seeing ourselves in those ways.

The appraisals of us that parents express let us know when our behaviors are not acceptable. Did your parents ever tell you that something you said or did was inappropriate? Did they ever punish you for misbehaving? If so, you know how effectively others' appraisals can communicate that they regard our behaviors as unacceptable.

Peers also communicate their perceptions of us. When we accept them, peers' reflected appraisals affect how we see ourselves. The importance of peers' reflected appraisals is illustrated by this amusing example from Don Monkerud's (1990) research. Jeremy Bem was raised by parents who were committed to nonsexist child rearing. When Jeremy put barrettes in his hair, his parents expressed neither surprise nor disapproval. But a different response greeted Jeremy when he wore his barrettes to nursery school. His male peers repeatedly told him that "only girls wear barrettes." Jeremy tried to tell them that wearing barrettes had nothing to do with being a boy or a girl, but his peers were adamant that he couldn't be a boy if he wore barrettes.

Communication in Everyday Life
The Role of Fathers in Socializing Children

For years, mothers have been regarded as essential to children's development. We've all heard about "maternal instinct" and "mothers' intuition." Yet, mothers are only half the picture. Fathers play important roles in children's development, and the roles they play tend to be distinct from those of mothers.

Fathers seem more likely than mothers to challenge and stretch children to achieve more. Fathers urge children to take initiative, to tolerate risks, and to experiment with unfamiliar activities and situations. Fathers also tend to focus on playing with their children, and fathers' play generally is physically stimulating. Roughhousing with fathers seems to develop children's courage and willingness to take risks.

Mothers, in contrast, seem to specialize in protecting children and emotionally reassuring them. Mothers, more than fathers, accept children at their current levels and don't push them to go further. Mothers also spend more of their time with children in caretaking activities than in play.

Researchers who have studied parents' interactions with children conclude that fathers and mothers typically contribute in unique and valuable ways to their children's development and self-esteem (Popenoe, 1996; Stacey, 1996). Fathers especially seem prepared to help their sons and daughters develop confidence, autonomy, and high expectations of themselves. Mothers are more likely to provide children with a sense of self-acceptance and to teach them to be sensitive to others. Researchers conclude that both mothers and fathers make substantial and unique contributions to the full development of children.

A number of groups support active fathering and provide information about the impact fathers can have on children. Two websites you might want to visit are the American Fathers Coalition at http://www.acfc.org and the National Fatherhood Project at http://www.hsrc.ac.za/fatherhood.

Finally, in frustration, Jeremy pulled down his pants and declared that, because he had a penis, he was a boy. The other boys laughed at this and informed Jeremy, "Everybody has a penis; only girls wear barrettes" (1990, p. 83).

We don't have a record of how Jeremy and his barrettes fared after this incident, but we do know that Jeremy, like all of us, was affected by his peers' appraisals of him. The reflected appraisals of peers join with those of family members and shape the images we have of ourselves.

TALMIDGE During high school, a lot of my friends thought I was too religious. They would kid me about being "Goody Two-Shoes" because I didn't drink or do other things that most of them did. In college, I've found more Christian friends who respect what I stand for. They make me feel better about myself.

One way to think about reflected appraisals is to realize that others can behave as uppers, downers, and vultures. People act as **uppers** when they communicate positively about us and reflect positive appraisals of our self-worth. They notice our strengths, see our progress, and accept our weaknesses and problems without discounting us. When we're around uppers, we feel more upbeat and positive about ourselves. Uppers aren't necessarily unconditionally positive in their communication. A true friend can be an upper by recognizing our weaknesses and helping us work on them. Instead of putting us down, an upper believes in us and helps us believe in ourselves and our capacity to change. Identify two uppers in your life.

People act as **downers** when they communicate negatively about us and our self-worth. They call attention to our flaws, emphasize our problems, and put down our dreams and goals. When we're around downers, we tend to feel down about ourselves. Reflecting their perspectives, when we're around downers, we're more aware of our weaknesses and are less confident of what we can accomplish. Identify two downers in your life.

Vultures are extreme downers. When people act as vultures, they not only communicate negative images of us but also attack our self-concepts just as actual vultures prey on their victims (Simon, 1977). Sometimes vultures initiate harsh criticism. They say, "You don't measure up to the other people hired when you were," or

"You'll never look professional at your weight." Vultures pick up on our own self-doubts and magnify them. They find our weak spots and exploit them; they pick us apart by focusing on sensitive areas in our self-concept. For example, a friend of mine manages his time inefficiently and is very sensitive about it. I once observed a co-worker pick him apart just as a vulture picks apart its prey. The co-worker said, "I can't believe this is all you've done. You're the most unproductive person I've ever known. What a waste! Your output doesn't justify your salary." That harangue typifies the sort of attack on self-worth that vultures enjoy. By telling us we are inadequate, vultures demolish our self-esteem. Can you identify vultures in your life?

Reflect on how you feel about yourself when you're with people who act as uppers, downers, and vultures. Can you see how powerfully others' communication affects your self-concept? You might also think about the people for whom you act as an upper, a downer, or a vulture. *Student Companion:* Activity 2.1.

Reflected appraisals are not confined to childhood but continue throughout our lives. Sometimes, teachers are the first to see potential in students that the students have not recognized in themselves. When teachers communicate that students are talented in a particular area, the students may come to see themselves that way. Later, as you enter professional life, you will encounter co-workers and bosses who reflect their appraisals of you: You're on the fast track, average, or not suited to your position. The appraisals of us that others communicate shape our sense of ourselves.

One particularly powerful way in which reflected appraisals can affect our self-concept is through **self-fulfilling prophecies,** which is acting in ways that embody our internalization

Communication in Everyday Life
Internalizing Racial Stereotypes

DIVERSITY

According to Stanford University researcher Claude Steele, groups that are negatively stereotyped by others may internalize those negative stereotypes, thereby creating a self-fulfilling prophecy. Steele says that groups that are victims of widely held negative perceptions often fear that the stereotypes about them are true (Woo, 1995).

To test his idea, Steele designed an experiment. He told undergraduate students that they would be taking a test to measure their verbal reasoning. Half the students were asked to identify their race before taking the test. The other half were not asked to identify their race. Steele's results were dramatic. When students were required to state their race, blacks tested significantly lower than whites. When students weren't asked to identify their race, scores for blacks and whites were equivalent.

of others' expectations or judgments about us. If you have done poorly in classes where teachers didn't seem to respect you, and you have done well with teachers who thought you were smart, then you know what a self-fulfilling prophecy is. The prophecies we act to fulfill usually are first communicated by others. However, because we internalize others' perspectives, we may allow their definitions and prophecies for us to become our own.

Many of us believe things about ourselves that are inaccurate. Sometimes, labels that were once true aren't any longer, but we continue to believe them. In other cases, the labels may never have been valid, but we believe them anyway. Unfortunately, children often are called "slow" or "stupid" when they have physiological difficulties, such as impaired vision or hearing, or when they are struggling with a second language. Even when the real source of difficulty is discovered, the children already may have internalized a destructive self-fulfilling prophecy.

RENEE I now see that I labeled myself because of others' perspectives. Since I was in first grade, my grandmother said I was fat and that I would never lose weight. Well, you can imagine what this did to my self-esteem. I felt there was nothing I could do about being fat. At one point, I weighed 181 pounds—pretty heavy for a girl who's 5 feet 5 inches tall. Then, I got with some other people who were overweight, and we convinced ourselves to shape up. I lost 50 pounds, but I still thought of myself as fat. That's only started to change lately as friends and my family comment on how slim I am. Guess I'm still seeing myself through others' eyes. *Student Companion:* Activity 2.2.

Identity Scripts   Psychologists define **identity scripts** as rules for living and identity (Berne, 1964; Harris, 1969). Like the scripts for plays, identity scripts define our roles, how we are to play them, and the basic elements in the plots of our lives. Think back to your childhood, and identify some of the principal scripts that operated in your family. Did you hear any of these scripts from family members: "We are responsible people," "Our family always helps those in need," "A good education is the key to success," or "Live by God's word." These are examples of identity scripts people learn in families.

Most psychologists believe that the basic identity scripts for our lives are formed very early, probably by age 5. This means that fundamental understandings of who we are and how we are supposed to live are forged when we have almost no control. Adults have the power, and children unconsciously internalize the scripts that others write. As adults, however, we have the capacity to review the identity scripts that were given to us and to challenge and change those that do not fit the selves we now choose to be.

Attachment Styles   Finally, parents and others who care for young children communicate through **attachment styles,** which are patterns of caregiving that teach us who we and others are and how to approach relationships. From extensive studies of interaction between parents and children, John Bowlby (1973, 1988) developed a theory that we learn attachment styles in our earliest relationships. In these formative relationships, caregivers communicate how they see us, others, and relationships.

© Bill Aron/PhotoEdit

Most children form their first human bond with a parent—usually the mother, because women typically take primary care of children. Clinicians who have studied attachment styles believe that the first bond is especially important because it forms the child's expectations for later relationships (Ainsworth, Blehar, Waters, & Wall, 1978; Bartholomew & Horowitz, 1991; Miller, 1993). Four distinct attachment styles have been identified, as shown in Figure 2.2.

A **secure attachment style** is the most positive. This style develops when the caregiver responds in a consistently attentive and loving way to the child. In response, the child develops a positive sense of self-worth ("I am lovable") and a positive view of others ("People are loving and can be trusted"). People with secure attachment styles tend to be outgoing, affectionate, and able to handle the challenges and disappointments of close relationships without losing self-esteem. Equally important, people who have secure attachment styles usually are comfortable with themselves when they are not involved in close relationships. Their security enables them to engage in intimacy with others without depending on relationships for their self-worth.

A **fearful attachment style** is cultivated when the caregiver in the first bond communicates in negative, rejecting, or even abusive ways to the child. Children who are treated this way often infer that they are unworthy of love and that others are not loving. Thus, they learn to see themselves as unlovable and others as rejecting. Not surprisingly, people with a fearful attachment style tend to be apprehensive about relationships. Although they often want close bonds with others, they sometimes fear others will not love them and that they are not lovable. Thus, as adults they may avoid others or feel insecure in relationships.

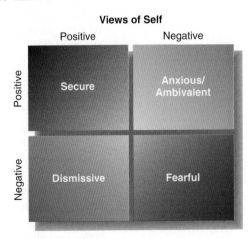

FIGURE 2.2

Styles of Attachment

In South Africa, where I was born, I learned that I was not important. Most daughters learn this. My name is Zondomini, which means "between happiness and sadness." The happiness is because a child was born. The sadness is because I am a girl, not a boy. I am struggling now to see myself as worthy.

A **dismissive attachment style** is also promoted by caregivers who are disinterested in, rejecting of, or abusive toward children. Yet people who develop this style do not accept the caregiver's view of them as unlovable. Instead, they typically dismiss others as unworthy. Consequently, children develop a positive view of themselves and a low regard for others and relationships. Those with a dismissive attachment style often develop a defensive view of relationships and regard them as unnecessary or undesirable.

A final pattern is the **anxious/ambivalent attachment style,** which is the most complex of the four. Each of the other three styles results from a consistent pattern of treatment by a caregiver. The anxious/ambivalent style, however, is fostered by inconsistent treatment from the caregiver. Sometimes the person who cares for a child is loving and attentive; at other times, the caregiver is indifferent or rejecting. The caregiver's communication is not only inconsistent but also unpredictable. He or she may respond positively to something a child does on Monday but react negatively to the same behavior on Tuesday. Naturally, this unpredictability can cause anxiety for the child who depends on the caregiver (Miller, 1993). Because children tend to assume that adults are always right, they believe themselves to be the source of any problem—that they are unlovable or deserve abuse.

NOREEN When I was little, my father was an alcoholic, but I didn't know that then. All I knew was that sometimes he loved me and played with me, and sometimes he would shout at me for nothing. Once he told me I was his sunshine, but later that same night he told me he wished I'd never been born. Even though now I understand the alcohol made him act that way, it's still hard to feel I'm okay.

In adult life, people who have anxious/ambivalent attachment styles tend to be preoccupied with relationships. On one hand, they know others can be loving and affirming. On the other hand, they realize that others can hurt them and be unloving. Reflecting the pattern displayed by the caregiver, people with an anxious/ambivalent attachment style often are inconsistent themselves. One day, they invite affection; the next day, they rebuff it and deny needing or wanting closeness.

The likelihood of developing a particular attachment style is affected by socio-economic class, as clinical psychiatrist Robert Karen reports (in Greenberg, 1997). Whereas nearly two thirds of middle-class children in the United States are securely attached, the numbers are much lower for children from poor families because poor families face serious hardships brought on by poverty: lack of adequate and nutritious food, poor shelter or homelessness, and inadequate medical care. These hardships can preoccupy and depress parents, making it difficult for them to be as consistently responsive and loving to children as parents who have more material resources (Greenberg, 1997).

The attachment styles we learned in our first close relationship tend to persist (Bartholomew & Horowitz, 1991; Belsky & Pensky, 1988; Bowlby, 1988; Guerrero, 1996). However, this is not inevitable. We can modify our attachment styles by challenging the disconfirming self-perceptions communicated in our early years and by forming relationships that foster secure connections. A study by Beth LePoire, Carolyn Shepard, and Ashley Duggan (1999) provides evidence that attachment styles can change. They found that the influence of parental attachment style was modified by romantic partners later in life. In 2002, Franz Neyer added support to this finding by reporting that adult attachment styles are influenced by romantic partners. In other words, the people we choose to have relationships with affect our attachment styles.

THE GENERALIZED OTHER

The perspectives of the **generalized other** reflect the views generally held by others in a society. Every society and social group has a generalized other, which reflects the shared values, experiences, and understandings of the particular society or social group (Sorrentino, Cohen, Olson, & Zanna, 2005). The perspectives of the generalized other are revealed to us in two ways. First, we learn them as we interact with others, who have internalized cultural values and pass them on to us. For instance, most of us are exposed to the generalized other's perspective on gender in the process of playing with childhood friends. A recent study by Carol Martin, Richard Fabes, Stephanie Evans, and Heidi Wyman (2000) showed that children 3$^1/_2$ to 7 years old have strong preferences for playing with other children of the same sex. This study also showed that young boys and girls thought peers were more likely to approve of their behavior if they played with others of the same sex.

Broadly shared social perspectives are also communicated to us through media and institutions that reflect cultural values. In many Asian societies, families and other cultural institutions teach children to value cooperation and teamwork over competition and individual achievement (Yum, 2000). In the United States, popular

Communication in Everyday Life
Attachment Styles and Relationships with Television Characters

Do you feel you have a relationship with TV characters that you particularly like? How you answer this question may be related to your attachment style. In 1999, communication researchers Tim Cole and Laura Leets investigated the relationship between attachment styles and the tendency to form relationships with TV personalities. They found that people with fearful attachment styles were least likely to form relationships with television characters, which is consistent with fearful people's reluctance to form actual relationships with others. On the other hand, people with an anxious/ambivalent attachment style were the most likely to form relationships with characters on television. Cole and Leets reasoned that people with anxious/ambivalent attachment styles may feel safe forming relationships with characters on television, whose personalities remain stable and thus predictable.

To learn more about how attachment styles affect children, go to: http://www.casel.org/home/index.php. Type "attachment styles" into the Google search bar to find information on current research.

Everyday Application
Identifying Social Values in Media

Select four popular magazines. Record the focus of their articles and advertisements. What do the articles and ads convey about what is valued in the United States? Identify themes and types of people that are emphasized.

What cultural values about gender do the magazines communicate? What do articles convey about how women or men are regarded and what they are expected to be and to do? Ask the same questions about advertisements.

How many ads aimed at women focus on being beautiful, looking young, losing weight, taking care of others, and attracting men? How many ads aimed at men emphasize strength, virility, success, and independence?

To extend this exercise, identify cultural values conveyed by television, films, and news stories. Pay attention to who is highlighted and how different genders, races, and professions are represented.

magazines and movies inundate us with messages about how women and men are supposed to look and act (Brown & Cantor, 2000; Holtzman, 2000).

The institutions that organize our society also communicate the generalized other's perspective by the values they uphold. For example, our judicial system reminds us that, as a society, we value laws and punish those who break them. In Western culture, the institution of marriage communicates society's view that, when people marry, they become a single unit, which is why joint ownership of property is assumed for married couples. Our institutions inevitably reflect prevailing social prejudices. For instance, we may be a lawful society, but wealthy defendants often can buy better "justice" than poor ones can. These and other values are woven into the fabric of our culture, and we learn them with little effort or awareness.

The generalized other in modern Western culture emphasizes race, gender, sexual orientation, and socioeconomic class as central to personal identity (Andersen & Collins, 1998).

Race   In Western society, race is considered a primary aspect of personal identity. In the United States, the race that has been historically favored and privileged is Caucasian. Although much progress has been made toward racial equality, white privilege still exists today. Often, white children have better access to good schools than children of other races do; and the upper levels of government, education, and most businesses are dominated by white men, whereas people of color and women continue to fight overt and covert discrimination in admission, hiring, and advancement.

Communication in Everyday Life
The Construction of Race

The word *white* wasn't used to describe race or identity until Europeans colonized the United States. They invented the label *white* as a way to increase solidarity among European settlers, who actually had diverse ethnic backgrounds. By calling themselves white, these diverse groups could gloss over differences between them and use their common skin hue to distinguish themselves from people of color. And who was considered white varied. Irish immigrants experienced stinging discrimination when they first came to the United States. The first generations of Irish immigrants were not considered white. As they internalized the mainstream values of whites, they came to be regarded as white (Bates, 1994).

When slavery was an institution in the United States, Southern plantation owners invented a system of racial classification known as "the one drop rule." According to this system, a person with as little as one drop of African blood was classified as black. Thus, racial divisions in the United States were established firmly although arbitrarily (Bates, 1994; Manning, 2000).

Beyond the borders of the United States, race is constructed in other ways. For example, South Africa recognized three major racial categories: white, colored, and black. Under apartheid, Japanese were classified as white, and Chinese were classified as colored.

Social demographer William Petersen (1997) says that ethnicity is incredibly difficult to measure reliably. One problem is that increasing numbers of people have multiple racial and ethnic identities. For example, if a man is one-fourth black, one-fourth Chinese, one-fourth Thai, one-eighth white, and one-eighth American Indian, what race is he?

DERRICK   If my mama told me once, she told me a million times: "You got to work twice as hard to get half as far because you're black." I knew that my skin was a strike against me in this society since I can remember knowing anything. When I asked why blacks had to work harder, Mama said, "Because that's just how it is." I guess she was telling me that's how this society looks on African Americans.

SUE   The media call Asian Americans the "ideal minority." That's a stereotype that's really hard for some of us to live up to. I'm a good student, but I'm not excellent, especially not at math and computers, which people of my heritage are supposed to be naturally good at. So it's like I'm always not living up to the image of me that people have just because I'm Chinese American.

Gender   Gender is another important category in Western culture. Despite significant progress toward equal rights for the sexes, there are still inequities in the opportunities available to women and men. From the pink and blue blankets hospitals wrap around newborns to the differences in salaries earned by women and men, gender is a major facet of identity. Given the importance our society places on gender, it is no wonder that one of the first ways children learn to identify themselves is by their sex. When my niece Michelle was 4 years old, I asked her who she was. Her immediate response was, "I'm a girl." Only after naming her sex did she describe her family, her likes and dislikes, and other aspects of her identity.

Western cultures have strong gender prescriptions. Girls and women are expected to be caring, supportive of others, and cooperative, whereas boys and men are supposed to be more independent, self-assertive, and competitive (Kerr, 1999; Pollack, 2000). Consequently, women who assert themselves or compete sometimes experience social disapproval for violating gender prescriptions. Men who depart from broadly held social views of masculinity and who are gentle and caring risk being labeled "wimps." Our gender makes a great deal of difference in how others view us and how we come to see ourselves.

Reprinted by permission of the author.

ALLISON   When I was real young, I was outside playing in a little swimming pool one day. It was hot, and my brothers had their shirts off, so I took mine off, too. When my mother looked up and saw me, she went berserk. She told me to get my shirt back on and act like a lady. That's when I knew that girls have to hide and protect their bodies, but boys don't.

Sexual Orientation   A third aspect of identity that is salient in our culture is sexual orientation. Historically and today, heterosexuality is viewed as the normal sexual orientation, and some people regard lesbians, bisexuals, transsexuals, transgenders, intersexed people, and gay men as abnormal.

The generalized other's perspective is communicated through privileges given to heterosexuals but denied to people with other sexual orientations (Wood, in press). For example, a woman and a man who love each other can have their commitment recognized religiously and legally. Heterosexuals can cover their partners on insurance policies and inherit from them without paying taxes. Although the normalization of

Communication in Everyday Life
A GLAAD Self-Concept

Sexual orientation is an important influence on self-concept, as are the opportunities and material conditions of our lives. Yet, it is difficult to find good sources of information on how gay men, lesbians, transsexuals, and bisexuals view themselves and society. One useful source is the website of the Gay & Lesbian Alliance Against Defamation (GLAAD). This website offers extensive information on self-concept and other issues that affect individuals. To visit the website, go to http://www.glaad.org/.

DIVERSITY

Communication in Everyday Life
Bruce, Brenda, and David

Imagine being born a boy but being raised as a girl. Imagine discovering at age 14 that your sex had been changed right after your birth and you were never told. That's exactly what happened to one person.

In *As Nature Made Him*, John Colapinto (2000) tells this extraordinary story. Bruce was born a normal male child. However, during his circumcision, doctors erred tragically and cut off most of his penis. Telling the young parents that Bruce could never be a normal male, the doctors advised the parents to allow them to make him like a female anatomically and to give him estrogen treatments to enhance his femininity. The confused parents relied on the doctors, renamed their child Brenda, and brought him up as a girl. Brenda was never told she had been born a boy, but she resisted being treated as a girl. At age 14, Brenda learned of the botched circumcision.

Brenda decided then to live as a male, renamed herself David, and ceased estrogen treatments. As an adult, David had strong relationships with family members and friends and was married to a woman.

heterosexuality continues, some religions now perform same-sex union ceremonies, some localities recognize domestic partnerships, and many organizations provide insurance and other benefits to domestic partners of employees.

DEL I'm gay, and many people think that gay is all I am. Once they find out I'm gay, nothing else about me seems relevant to them. They can't see all the ways in which we are alike and that we have more similarities than differences. They don't see that, once they find out I'm gay. They don't see that I am a student (just like them), that I am working my way through school (just like them), that I am Christian (just like them), that I worry about tests and papers (just like them), that I love basketball (just like them). All they see is that I am gay, and that is not like them.

Socioeconomic Class A fourth important aspect of the generalized other's view of identity is socioeconomic class. Even though the United States is less rigid than many societies with regard to class, the socioeconomic class we belong to affects everything from how much money we make to the kinds of schools, jobs, and lifestyle choices

© Rick Gomez/CORBIS

we see as possibilities for ourselves. Socioeconomic class affects which stores, restaurants, and schools are part of our lives. It influences who our friends are, where we live and work, and even the kind of car we drive (Langston, 1992).

In a 1995 book edited by Barney Dews and Carolyn Law and titled *This Fine Place So Far from Home: Voices of Academics from the Working Class,* a number of academics say that they have entered a middle-class world where they don't feel at ease or fully accepted. Many report wrenching identity conflicts as they interact with their working-class families and their middle-class colleagues. "Torn between two worlds and two identities" is how they describe themselves. The values and self-concepts that they grew up endorsing are at odds with the values and identities regarded as appropriate where they now live and work.

Socioeconomic class influences which needs we focus on in Maslow's hierarchy. For example, people with economic security have the resources and leisure time to focus on therapy, yoga, spiritual development, and spas to condition their bodies. These are not feasible for people who are a step away from poverty. Members of the middle and upper classes assume they will attend college and enter good professions, yet often these options are not realistic for working-class people (Langston, 1992).

GENEVA   I don't fit with most of the folks here. That hits me in the face every day. I walk across campus and see girls wearing shoes that cost more than all four pairs I own. I hear students talking about restaurants and trips that I can't afford. Last week, I heard a guy complaining about being too broke to get a CD player for his car. I don't own a car. I don't know how to relate to these people who have so much money. I do know they see the world differently than I do.

It's important to realize that these aspects of identity intersect. Race interacts with gender, so women of color experience double oppression and devaluation in our culture (Lorde, 1992; McIntosh, 1995). Socioeconomic class and sexual orientation also interact: Homophobia, or fear of homosexuals, is particularly pronounced in the working class, so a lesbian or gay person in a poor community may be socially ostracized (Langston, 1992). Socioeconomic class and gender also are interlinked; women are far more likely to live at the poverty level than men (Ehrenreich, 1995; Roux, 2001). Gender and race intersect, so black men have burdens and barriers not faced by white men (Dyson, 1995). All facets of our identity interact.

Communication in Everyday Life
Caste Counts

Societies around the world have created systems of classifying people (Ferrante, 1992). One of the most rigid is the caste system in India. Within this system, a person's class is hereditary: One is born into a particular caste and cannot move out of it in the current life. The Brahmans are the highest caste; they are priests and lawmakers. Next are the Kshatriyas, the warriors. The third caste, the Vaisyas, are farmers and merchants. Sudras, or laborers, make up the fourth caste. Until very recently, there was a fifth caste: Harijans, also known as untouchables, who were considered to be entirely outside the social order. This caste was abolished by a specific clause added to India's constitution. The remaining four classes are progressively subdivided, producing finer and finer distinctions among people (Human Rights Watch, 1999).

Rigid class distinctions are also part of South Africa's history (Wren, 1990). *Apartheid,* an Afrikaans word that means "apartness," has prevailed in South Africa for hundreds of years and was made the official policy of the country in 1948. Once the Nationalists, a conservative white political party, seized power, they passed hundreds of laws to enforce rigid racial separation in almost every area of life and to support domination of the country by the white minority. In 1990, South Africa abolished the Separate Amenities Act, which had mandated separate and unequal cemeteries, parks, trains, hotels, hospitals, and so forth for whites and blacks. Other discriminatory practices and laws are gradually being dismantled in South Africa.

Visit the Human Rights Watch website to learn more about the caste system and other ways people are restricted by class memberships: http://www.hrw.org.

Communication in Everyday Life
Language and Class

For years, Herbert Gans (1995) has studied urban poverty in the United States. After all his research, he advances this conclusion: The real war is not the war against poverty, but the war of words. Gans's point is that the language widely used to talk about the poor creates negative labels and stereotypes that harm the very people being discussed. Gans particularly objects to two terms: *the culture of poverty* and *underclass*. He thinks both terms suggest that poor people are morally inferior to those who aren't poor.

Another respected scholar, Jonathan Kozol (1995), joins Gans in criticizing language that creates a false sense of enormous differences between the character of poor and nonpoor people. Kozol rejects terms such as *underclass* and *the culture of poverty* because they suggest that the differences between poor and nonpoor people are so great that nothing would change the lives of the poor.

Both Gans and Kozol believe that it is misguided to divide people into categories that imply different degrees of moral worth. According to Gans and Kozol, it's time for all of us to mind and mend how we talk about those who are poor.

Social Comparison As we learn the generalized other's perspective, we come to ask how we measure up to others. **Social comparison** is assessing ourselves in relation to others to form judgments of our own talents, abilities, qualities, and so forth. Whereas reflected appraisals are based on how we think others view us, social comparisons are our own use of others as measuring sticks for ourselves. We gauge ourselves in relation to others in two ways.

First, we compare ourselves with others to decide whether we are like them or different from them. Are we the same sex, age, color, religion? Do we hang out with the same people? Do we have similar backgrounds, political beliefs, and social commitments? Assessing similarity and difference allows us to decide with whom we fit. Research shows that most people are more comfortable with others who are like them, so we tend to gravitate toward those we regard as similar (Pettigrew, 1967; Whitbeck & Hoyt, 1994). However, this can deprive us of the perspectives of people whose experiences and beliefs differ from our own.

> **SANDI** I babysit three children. A big thing for them is when the mail comes each day. The older two children sometimes get letters, but the youngest one, Harrison, never does. He always asks if there are any letters for him, and when I tell him no, he just looks so disappointed. So I've started writing him once a week. It's helped him feel more equal to his older brother and sister.

We also use social comparison to measure ourselves and our abilities in relation to others. Am I as good a guard as Hendrick? Do I play the guitar as well as Chris? Am I as smart as Serena? Am I as attractive as Leigh? Comparing ourselves to others is normal, and it helps us develop realistic self-concepts. However, we should be wary of using inappropriate standards of comparison. It isn't realistic to judge our attractiveness in relation to stars and models or our athletic ability in relation to professional players.

We have seen that the self arises in communication. From interaction with family members, peers, and society as a whole, we are taught who we are. We are also taught the prevailing values of our culture and of particular others who are significant in our lives. These perspectives become part of who we are. We now discuss other premises about the self.

THE SELF IS MULTIDIMENSIONAL

There are many dimensions, or aspects, of the human self. You have an image of your physical self: how large, attractive, and athletic you are. In addition, you have perceptions of your cognitive self, including your intelligence and aptitudes. You also have an emotional self-concept. Are you sensitive or not? Are you easily hurt? Are you generally upbeat or cynical? Then there is your social self, which involves how you are with others. Some of us are extroverted and joke around a lot or dominate interactions, whereas others prefer to be less prominent.

Our social selves also include our social roles: daughter or son, student, worker, parent, or partner in a committed relationship. Each of us also has a moral self that consists of our ethical and spiritual beliefs, the principles we believe in, and our overall sense of morality. Although we use the word *self* as though it referred to a single entity, in reality the self is made up of many dimensions. For an interesting exploration of how others present and reveal their "self" online, complete *Student Companion:* Activity 2.8.

The multiple dimensions of self are shaped by direct definitions, reflected appraisals, identity scripts, attachment styles, social comparisons, and the perspectives of the generalized other.

THE SELF IS A PROCESS

The self develops gradually and changes throughout our lives. We do not enter the world with fully formed identities. Newborn babies have no **ego boundaries,** which define where an individual stops and the rest of the world begins (Chodorow, 1989). To an infant, nursing is a single sensation in which the boundary between itself and the mother is blurred. A baby perceives no boundaries between its foot and the tickle by a father. Over time, infants gradually begin to distinguish themselves from the external environment. This is the beginning of a self-concept: the realization that one is a separate entity.

Within the first year or two of life, as infants start to differentiate themselves from the rest of the world, the self begins to develop. Babies, then toddlers, then children devote enormous energy to understanding who they are. They actively seek to define themselves and to become competent in the identities they claim (Kohlberg, 1958; Piaget, 1932/1965). For instance, early on little girls and boys start working to be competent females and males, respectively. They scan the environment, find models of females and males, and imitate and refine their performances of gender (Levy, 1999). In like manner, children figure out what it takes to be smart, strong, attractive, and responsible, and they work to become competent in each area. Throughout our lives, we continue the process of defining and presenting our identities. The ways we define ourselves vary as we mature. Struggling to be a swimmer at age 4 gives way to striving to be popular in high school and being a successful professional and partner in adult life. The fact that we change again and again during our lives is evidence of our capacity for self-renewal and continual growth.

SOCIAL PERSPECTIVES ARE SUBJECT TO CHANGE

As we interact with particular others and the generalized other, we learn what and whom our society values, and we learn how others view us. However, social perspectives do not remain outside of us. We internalize many of them, and we thus come to share the views and values generally endorsed in our society. In many ways, this is useful, even essential, for collective life. If we all made up our own rules about when to stop and go at traffic intersections, the number of car accidents would skyrocket. If each of us operated by our own code for lawful conduct, there would be no shared standards regarding crime. Life would be chaotic.

Yet, not all social views are as constructive as traffic rules and criminal law. The generalized other's unequal valuing of different races, genders, socioeconomic classes, and sexual orientations fosters discrimination against whole groups of people whose only fault is not being what society defines as normal or good. Each of us has a responsibility to exercise critical judgment about which social views we personally accept and use as guides for our own behaviors, attitudes, and values. We also have an ethical responsibility to challenge social views and values that we consider harmful or wrong.

Socially Constructed Views   Social perspectives are constructed in particular cultures at specific times. What a society values does not reflect divine law, absolute truth, or the natural order of things. The values that are endorsed in any society at a specific time reflect the prevailing values in that era and place. For example, denying women the right to vote preserved men's power to control the laws of the land. By approving of heterosexuality and not homosexuality, the culture supports a particular family ideal. Defining certain races as inferior protects the interests of races defined as superior (Manning, 2000). When we reflect on widely endorsed social values, we realize that they tend to serve the interests of those who are privileged by the status quo. In addition, we realize that currently endorsed social views could be otherwise.

Variable Social Views   The constructed and arbitrary nature of social values becomes especially obvious when we consider how widely values differ from culture to culture. For example, in Sweden, Denmark, and Norway, same-sex marriages are given full legal recognition. Members of Japanese culture are expected to fit in with the group and not to stand out as individuals (Gudykunst & Lee, 2002). In some cultures, men are typically emotional and dependent, and women tend to be assertive and emotionally controlled. In many countries south of the United States, race is emphasized less than in North America, and mixed-race marriages are common and accepted. *Student Companion:* Activity 2.6.

HANNAH Because I'm an older student, I have a good understanding of how much views change in society. Twenty years ago, when I first started college, women were not taken very seriously. I had no female professors, and there wasn't a women's studies department at my school. Our professors and all of us just expected that most women at the school would become wives and mothers who either worked little part-time jobs or didn't work outside the home. Any woman who said she wanted to pursue a full-time career was considered kind of strange. Attitudes on campus are so different today. There are a number of female professors. A majority of the female students I know have serious career ambitions, and most of the male students seem to assume their female classmates and girlfriends will work full time for most of their lives. What a difference 20 years has made in how women are viewed.

Communication in Everyday Life
A Cross-Cultural Look at Sexual Identity

The Navajo and Mojave Indian tribes gave special respect to *nadles*, who were considered neither male nor female but a combination of the two sexes (Olien, 1978). The identity of nadle sometimes was conferred at birth on babies born with ambiguous genitals. People could also adopt the nadle identity later in life. When working on weaving or other tasks assigned to women, nadles dressed and acted as women. When engaged in activities assigned to men, nadles dressed and acted as men. Nadles could marry either women or men. Within their tribes, nadles were regarded as very wise and were given special privileges and deference.

Find out more about the impact of gender on self-concept by visiting Alan Liu's page on gender studies, the Voice of the Shuttle. Go to http://vos.ucsb.edu.

Social meanings also vary across time within single cultures. For example, in the 1700s and 1800s women in the United States were defined as too delicate to engage in hard labor. During World Wars I and II, however, women were expected to do "men's work" while the men were at war. When the men returned home, society once again decreed that women were too weak to perform in the labor market, and they were reassigned to homes. The frail, pale appearance considered feminine in the 1800s gave way to robust, fleshy ideals in the mid-1900s, as embodied by Marilyn Monroe. The photos on this page illustrate the difference between Monroe and Nicole Richie as images of ideal femininity.

Kevin Winter/Getty Images

Hulton Archive/Getty Images

Social prescriptions for men have also varied. The rugged he-man who was the ideal in the 1800s disposed of unsavory rustlers and relied on his physical strength to farm wild lands. After the Industrial Revolution, physical strength and bravado gave way to business acumen, and money replaced muscle as a sign of manliness. Today, as our society struggles with changes in women, men, and families, the ideals of manhood are being revised yet again. Increasingly, men are involved in caring for children and are sensitive as well as independent and strong.

Other socially constructed views are also variable. Even a decade ago, most people regarded online relationships as poor substitutes for "real" relationships. In contrast, today many people meet and form relationships—sometimes lasting ones—through online interaction (Baym, 2002; Carl, 2006; Clement & McLean, 2000; Maheu & Subotnik, 2001). In the 1950s and 1960s, people with disabilities often were kept in their homes or put in institutions. Today, many schools endorse mainstreaming, which places students who have physical or mental disabilities in regular classrooms. Sensitivity to people who have special problems grows as nondisabled students interact with people who have disabilities.

The meaning of age has also varied throughout U.S. history. In the 1800s, the average life span was less than 60 years, and it was not uncommon for people to die in their forties or fifties. Then, 50 was considered old, but few people today would regard 50 as old. In the 1800s, people typically married in their teens, and they often had five or more children before reaching 30. Today many people wait until their thirties to begin having children, and people in their forties aren't considered "too old" to become parents.

As we have seen, social perspectives are fluid and respond to individual and collective efforts to weave new meanings into the fabric of social life. Each of us has the responsibility to speak out against social perspectives that we perceive as wrong or harmful. Reflecting carefully on social values allows us to make conscious choices about which ones we will accept for ourselves. By doing so, we participate in the ongoing process of refining who we are as a society. *Student Companion:* **Activity 2.3.**

JENNIFER   My parents are pretty straitlaced and conservative. They brought me up to think homosexuals are sinners and whites are better than any other race. But I don't think like that now, and I've been speaking my mind when I'm home to visit my folks. At first, they got angry and said they didn't send me to college to get a bunch of crazy liberal ideas, but gradually they are coming around a little. I think I am changing how they think by voicing my views.

●●●●●●●●●●●

Guidelines for Improving Self-Concept

So far, we have explored how we form our self-concepts as we interact with particular others and as we encounter the perspective of the generalized other. Now, we want to know how we can enhance our self-concepts.

MAKE A FIRM COMMITMENT TO PERSONAL GROWTH

The first principle for changing self-concept is the most difficult and the most important. You must make a firm commitment to cultivating personal growth. This isn't as easy as it might sound. A firm commitment involves more than saying, "I want to be more open to others." Saying this sentence is simple. What is more difficult is investing energy and effort to bring about change. From the start, realize that changing how you think of yourself is a major project.

There are two reasons why it is challenging to change our self-concept. First, doing so takes continual effort. Because the self is a process, it is not formed in one fell swoop, and it cannot be changed in a moment of decision. We must realize at the outset that there will be setbacks, and we can't let them derail our resolution to change. Last year, a student said she wanted to be more assertive, so she began to speak up more often in class. When a professor criticized one of her contributions, her resolution folded. Changing how we see ourselves is a long-term process, so we can't let setbacks undermine our commitment to change.

A second reason it is difficult to change self-concept is that the self resists change. Morris Rosenberg (1979), a psychologist who has studied self-concept extensively, says that most humans tend to resist change and that we also seek esteem or a positive view of ourselves. The good news is that we want esteem or a positive self-image; the bad news is that we find it difficult to change, even in positive directions. Interestingly, Rosenberg and others have found that we are as likely to hold on to negative self-images as we are positive ones. Apparently, consistency itself is comforting. If you realize in advance that you may struggle against change, you'll be prepared for the tension that accompanies personal growth.

GAIN AND USE KNOWLEDGE TO SUPPORT PERSONAL GROWTH

Commitment alone is insufficient to bring about constructive changes in your self-concept. In addition, you need several types of knowledge. First, you need to understand how your self-concept was formed. In this chapter, we've seen that much of how we see ourselves results from socially constructed perspectives. Based on what you've learned, you can exercise critical judgment about which social perspectives to accept and which to reject. For instance, you should critically reflect on the generalized other's views of race, gender, sexual orientation, and socioeconomic class to decide whether you want to accept these views as part of your own perspective.

> **TINA** One social value I do not accept is that it's good to be as thin as a rail if you're female. A lot of my girlfriends are always dieting. Even when they get weak from not eating enough, they won't eat, because they'll gain weight. I know several girls who are bulimic, which is really dangerous, but they are more scared of gaining a pound than of dying. I refuse to buy into this social value. I'm not fat, but I'm not skinny either. I'm not as thin as models, and I'm not aiming to be. It's just stupid to go around hungry all the time because society has sick views of beauty for women.

Second, you need information about yourself. One way to get this information is through **self-disclosure,** which is revealing information about ourselves that others are unlikely to discover on their own. Self-disclosure is an important way to learn about ourselves. As we reveal our hopes, fears, dreams, and feelings, we get responses from others that give us new perspectives on who we are. In addition, we gain insight into ourselves by seeing how we interact with others in new situations.

A number of years ago, Joseph Luft and Harry Ingham (Luft, 1969) created a model of different sorts of knowledge that affect self-development. They called the model the **Johari Window** (Figure 2.3), which is a combination of their first names, Joe and Harry.

Four types of information are relevant to the self. Open, or public, information is known both to us and to others.

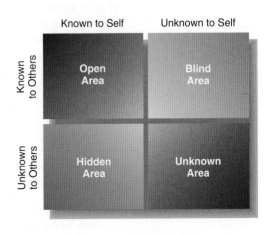

FIGURE 2.3

The Johari Window

Your name, height, major, and tastes in music probably are open information that you share easily with others. The blind area contains information that others know about us but we don't know about ourselves. For example, others may see that we are insecure even though we think we've hidden that well. Others may also recognize needs or feelings that we haven't acknowledged to ourselves. The third area includes hidden information, which we know about ourselves but choose not to reveal to most others. You might not tell many people about your vulnerabilities or about traumas in your past because you consider this private information. The unknown area is made up of information about ourselves that neither we nor others know. This consists of your untapped resources, your untried talents, and your reactions to experiences you've never had. You don't know how you will manage a crisis until you've been in one, and you can't tell what kind of parent you would be unless you've had a child.

It is important to gain access to information in our blind and unknown areas. One way to do this is to expand our experiences by entering unfamiliar situations, trying novel things, and experimenting with new kinds of communication. Another way to increase self-knowledge is to interact with others to learn how they see us. We can gain insight into ourselves by reflecting on their perceptions. Others are likely to offer us insights into ourselves only if we make it safe for them to do so. If a friend states a perception of you that you dislike, and you become defensive, the friend may not risk sharing other perceptions in the future. If we learn to respond nondefensively to others' perceptions of us, including criticism, then we pave the way for honest appraisals from them. To apply the Johari Window to your life and to discover content in the different windows of yourself, complete Activity 2.4 in your *Student Companion*.

Although self-disclosure has many potential values, it is not always advisable. Self-disclosure necessarily involves risks, such as the risk that others will not accept what we reveal or that they might use it against us. Appropriate self-disclosure minimizes these risks by proceeding slowly and in relationships in which trust has been established. It's wise to test the waters gradually before plunging into major self-disclosures. Begin by revealing information that is personal but not highly intimate or damaging if exploited. Before disclosing further, observe how the other person responds to your communication and what she or he does with it. You might also pay attention to whether the other person reciprocates by disclosing personal information to you. Because self-disclosures involve risk, we need to be cautious about when and to whom we reveal ourselves. Table 2.1 lists key benefits and risks of self-disclosing communication.

In addition to reading this book and learning from your class, there are other ways to gain knowledge to help you set and achieve personal goals. There are books and websites that focus on personal growth. Other people are another source of knowledge. Talking with others is a way to learn about relationships and what people want in them. Others can also provide useful feedback about your interpersonal skills and your progress in the process of change. Finally, others can serve as models. If someone you

Table 2.1 Benefits and Risks of Self-Disclosing Communication

BENEFITS	RISKS
May increase trust.	Others may reject us.
May increase closeness.	Others may think less of us.
May enhance self-esteem.	Others may violate our confidences.
May increase security.	
May enhance self-growth.	

know is particularly skillful in supporting others, observe her or him carefully to identify particular communication skills. You may not want to imitate this person exactly, but observing will make you more aware of concrete skills involved in supporting others. You can then tailor some of the skills others display to suit your personal style.

SET GOALS THAT ARE REALISTIC AND FAIR

Efforts to change how we see ourselves work best when we set realistic and fair goals. In a culture that emphasizes perfectionism, it's easy to be trapped into expecting more than is humanly possible.

Western society urges us to expect more, more, more of ourselves—more successes, more productivity, more possessions, more everything (Lacher, 2005). Peter Whybrow (2005), who is the director of a neuroscience center, believes that Americans relentlessly seek possessions and status. He argues that the perspective of the generalized other is unrealistic in urging us never to be satisfied, never to say we have or are enough. Whybrow gave a telling title to his book on this topic: *American Mania: When More Is Not Enough.* He argues that the American addiction to having more of everything is futile because more is never enough; if we get more, we want even more! This is unrealistic and can only make us unhappy, because we can never achieve or have or be enough.

If you define a goal as becoming a totally perfect communicator in all situations, you are setting yourself up for failure. It's more reasonable and constructive to establish a series of realistic small goals that you can meet. You might focus on improving one of the skills of communication competence we discussed in Chapter 1. When you are satisfied with your ability at that skill, you can move on to a second one.

Remembering our discussion of social comparison, it's also important to choose reasonable people to whom to compare yourself. It isn't realistic to compare your artistic talent to that of Georgia O'Keeffe or other renowned artists. It is reasonable to measure your artistic ability in relation to other people who have talent and training similar to your own.

KENDRICK   I really got bummed out my freshman year. I had been the star on my high school basketball team, so I came to college expecting to be a star here, too. The first day of practice, I saw a lot of guys who were better than I was. They were incredible. I felt like nothing. When I got back to my room, I called my mom and told her I was no good at basketball here. She told me I couldn't expect to compete with guys who had been on the team for a while and who had gotten coaching. She asked how I stacked up against just the other first-year players, and I said pretty good. She told me they were the ones to compare myself to.

Kendrick's reflection reminds us that we should be fair in judging ourselves. We often judge our abilities and set our goals with reference to unfair standards. For

example, my friend Meg is a very accomplished writer, but she faults herself constantly for not doing as much volunteer work as her neighbor. Meg's neighbor doesn't work outside the home, so she has more time for volunteer work. It might be reasonable for Meg to acknowledge that she doesn't volunteer a great deal of time if she also recognizes her impressive achievements in writing. However, when judging her writing, she compares herself to writers of national stature. Meg's self-assessment is unfair to her because she compares herself with people who are extremely successful in particular spheres of life, yet she doesn't notice that her models are not especially impressive in other areas. As a result, she mistakenly feels that she is inadequate in most ways. We should be fair to ourselves by acknowledging our strengths and virtues as well as our limitations and aspects of ourselves we want to change.

TIMOTEO   I've really struggled with my academic goals. It's very important to me and my whole family that I do well in school. I am the first in my family to go to college, so I must succeed. I've felt bad when I make Bs and Cs and others in my classes make As. For a long time, I said to myself, "I am not as smart as they are if they make better grades." But I work 35 hours a week to pay for school. Most of the others in my classes either don't have to work or work fewer hours than I do. They have more time to spend writing papers and studying for tests. I think better of my academic abilities when I compare myself to other students who work as much as I do. That is a more fair comparison than comparing myself to students who don't work.

Being fair to yourself also requires you to accept that you are in process. Earlier in this chapter, we saw that one characteristic of the human self is that it is continually in process, always becoming. This implies several things. First, it means you need to accept who you are now as a starting point. You don't have to like or admire everything about yourself, but it is important to accept who you are now as a basis for going forward. The self that you are results from all the interactions, reflected appraisals, and social comparisons you have made during your life. You cannot change your past, but you do not have to let it define your future.

Accepting yourself as in process also implies that you realize you can change. Who you are is not who you will be in 5 or 10 years. Don't let yourself be hindered by defeating, self-fulfilling prophecies or the false idea that you cannot change (Rusk & Rusk, 1988). You can change if you set realistic goals, make a genuine commitment, and then work for the changes you want.

SEEK CONTEXTS THAT SUPPORT PERSONAL CHANGE

Just as it is easier to swim with the tide than against it, it is easier to change our views of ourselves

Communication in Everyday Life
If at First You Don't Succeed

Achieving goals for self-development is hard. If you don't succeed at first, it's easy to be discouraged and to quit trying. One way to keep yourself motivated to work toward your goals is to remember that a lot of people we consider very successful weren't always so:

- Isaac Newton did so poorly in his early school years that his teachers labeled him "unpromising."
- One of Ludwig van Beethoven's early music teachers said that he was hopeless as a composer.
- Michael Jordan was cut from his high school basketball team. The same is true of Boston Celtics Hall of Famer Bob Cousy.
- One of Thomas Jefferson's grade school teachers told him he was stupid and should go into some line of work where his pleasant personality, not his mind, might allow him to succeed.
- Walt Disney was fired from his job on a newspaper because, according to his editor, he "lacked imagination and had no good ideas."
- Winston Churchill failed sixth grade and had to repeat it.
- Babe Ruth struck out 1,300 times, which remains the record for strikeouts in the major leagues.

when we have some support for our efforts. You can do a lot to create an environment that supports your growth by choosing contexts and people who help you realize your goals. First, think about settings. If you want to become more extroverted, put yourself in social situations rather than in libraries. But libraries are a better context than parties if your goal is to improve your academic performance.

BOB I never drank much until I got into this one group at school. All of them drank all the time. It was easy to join them. In fact, it was pretty hard not to drink and still be one of the guys. This year, I decided I was drinking too much, and I wanted to stop. It was hard enough not to keep drinking, because the guys were always doing it, but what really made it hard was the ways the guys got on me for abstaining. They let me know I was being uncool and made me feel like a jerk. Finally, to stop drinking, I had to get a different apartment.

Second, think about the people whose appraisals of you will help you move toward changes you desire. You can put yourself in supportive contexts by consciously choosing to be around people who believe in you and encourage your personal growth. It's equally important to steer clear of people who pull us down or say we can't change. In other words, people who reflect positive appraisals of us enhance our ability to improve.

Others aren't the only ones whose communication affects our self-concepts. We also communicate with ourselves, and our own messages influence our esteem. One of the most crippling kinds of self-talk we can engage in is **self-sabotage.** This involves telling ourselves we are no good, we can't do something, there's no point in trying to change, and so forth. We may be repeating judgments others have made of us, or we may be inventing our own negative self-fulfilling prophecies. Either way, self-sabotage defeats us because it undermines belief in ourselves. Self-sabotage is poisonous; it destroys our motivation to change and grow. We can act as downers or even vultures, just as others can. In fact, we can probably do more damage to our self-concepts than others can because we are most aware of our vulnerabilities and fears. This may explain why vultures originally were described as people who put themselves down.

We can also act as uppers for ourselves. We can affirm our strengths, encourage our growth, and fortify our sense of self-worth. Positive self-talk builds motivation and belief in yourself. It is also a useful strategy to interrupt and challenge negative messages from yourself and others. The next time you hear yourself saying, "I can't do this" or someone else says, "You'll never change," challenge the negative message with self-talk. Say out loud to yourself, "I can do it. I will change." Use positive self-talk to resist counterproductive communication about yourself.

Before leaving this discussion, we should make it clear that improving your self-concept is not facilitated by uncritical positive communication. None of us grows and improves when we listen only to praise, particularly if it is less than honest. The true uppers in our lives offer constructive criticism to encourage us to reach for better versions of ourselves.

In sum, to improve your self-concept, you must find contexts that support growth and change. Seek out experiences and settings that foster belief in yourself and the changes you desire. Also, recognize uppers, downers, and vultures in yourself and others, and learn which people and which kinds of communication assist you in achieving your own goals for self-improvement. A guide through the process of changing yourself is available in *Student Companion:* Activity 2.8 and online under "Chapter Resources for Chapter 2" at the Everyday Connections website.

Everyday Application
Improving Your Self-Concept

1. Define one change you would like to make in yourself. It might be a behavior or a self-fulfilling prophecy or anything about yourself you would like to alter.

2. Write down the change you want to make. Use strong, affirmative language to motivate yourself: "I will listen more carefully to friends" or "I will start speaking up in classes," for example.

3. Refine your general goal by making sure it is realistic and fair. Write out your refined goal using specific language: "I want to show my two best friends that I am paying attention when they talk to me" or "I want to make one comment in each meeting of one class this week," for example.

4. Place the card or paper where you will see it often. Each time you see it, repeat the message aloud to yourself. This should help sustain your commitment to making the change.

5. Observe others who are models for what you want to be. Write down what they do. Use specific language to describe how they communicate: "Tracy nods a lot and repeats back what others say so they know she is listening" or "James provides examples of concepts in class so that the ideas are more concrete," for example.

6. Select contexts that assist you in reaching your goal: "I will talk with my friends in private settings where there are no distractions that interfere with listening well" or "I will begin speaking up in class in my Communication 100 course because it is the most discussion oriented and because other students make a lot of comments there. Later, I will speak up in my sociology course, which is more lecture oriented," for example.

To learn more about the self and ways of changing yourself, visit this website:
http://mentalhelp.net.

Case Study: Continuing the Conversation

The following conversation is featured at the Everyday Connections website under "Chapter Resources for Chapter 2." Click on the link "Does He Treat You Right?" in the left-hand menu to launch the video and audio scenario scripted below.

Amy met Hailley at the beginning of the school year. Amy was drawn to Hailley because she seemed confident and positive. Over several months, the two of them became good friends, sharing high and low points about school, family, and dates.

Two months ago, Hailley started dating Dan, a man who dropped out of college after 2 years and who now works as a waiter. At first Hailley seemed happy with Dan, but then she started changing. She's become less extroverted and a lot less positive.

Often, when Amy suggests doing something together, Hailley says she can't because Dan might come over or call, and he doesn't like her not to be available to him. When Amy sees them together, she notices that Dan doesn't treat Hailley with respect and often criticizes her harshly. For example, when Hailley said something to

Case Study: Continuing the Conversation

Dan when he was on his cell phone, he shouted:

Dan: Don't talk to me. I'm on the phone.

Later, when Hailley dropped some papers, Dan spoke harshly to her:

Dan: You are so clumsy!

Amy is concerned that Hailley may be in a relationship that is verbally and physically abusive. Amy thinks that Dan is damaging Hailley's self-concept, and she wants to help.

Amy: I'm just worried about you. I don't like the way he treats you.

Hailley: Because he called me clumsy? I am clumsy, and besides, if I do something stupid, I can't expect him not to notice.

Amy: But he doesn't show any respect for you at all.

Hailley: Well, he's a guy. He says what he's thinking. I know a lot of people's boyfriends like that. Besides, I don't think there's anything wrong with Dan. I think I just have to stop doing things that make him mad.

1. Thinking about what you've read in this chapter, what might you say or do for Hailley?

2. How do social comparisons affect her view of the relationship with Dan?

3. Can you think of ways in which you might be a constructive looking-glass self for Hailley?

4. What could you do to help create a context that would foster positive change in Hailley's self-concept?

5. What would it mean to be an upper for Hailley right now? How could you communicate with her to be an upper in her life without endorsing her relationship with Dan?

You can critique and analyze this encounter based on the principles you learned in this chapter by responding to the questions included under "Conversation Analysis" at the website. By clicking on the "Submit" button at the end of the form, you can compare your work to my suggested responses. Let's continue the discussion online!

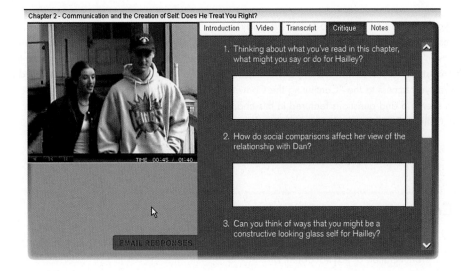

Chapter Summary

In this chapter, we explored the self as a process that evolves over the course of our lives. We saw that the self is not present at birth but develops as we interact with others. Through communication, we learn and import social perspectives—those of particular others and those of the generalized other, or society as a whole. Reflected appraisals, direct definitions, and social comparisons are communication processes that shape how we see ourselves and how we change over time. The perspective of the generalized other includes social views of aspects of identity, including race, gender, sexual preference, and class. However, these are arbitrary social constructions that we may challenge once we are adults. When we resist counterproductive social views, we promote change in society.

The final section of the chapter focused on ways to improve self-concept. Guidelines for doing this are to make a firm commitment to personal growth, to acquire knowledge about desired changes and concrete skills, to set realistic goals, to assess yourself fairly, and to create contexts that support the changes you seek. Transforming how we see ourselves is not easy, but it is possible. We can make amazing changes in who we are and how we feel about ourselves when we embrace our human capacity to make choices.

Everyday Connections Online

Now that you've read Chapter 2, go to the Everyday Connections premium website at academic.cengage.com/communication/woodinterpersonal5plus for quick access to the electronic study resources that accompany this text. The website gives you access to the "Continuing the Conversation" video scenario and questions featured in this chapter, to InfoTrac College Edition, to maintained and updated Web links, and to the study aids for this chapter, including a digital glossary, review quizzes, and the chapter activities. For more information about this text's electronic learning resources, consult the **1pass card** that came with each new copy of this book, or visit academic.cengege.com/communication/woodinterpersonal5.

Key Concepts

Audio flash cards of the following key terms are available on the Everyday Connections website. Use the flash cards to improve your pronunciation of text vocabulary.

anxious/ambivalent attachment style	ego boundaries	reflected appraisal	social comparison
attachment style	fearful attachment style	secure attachment style	upper
direct definition	generalized other	self	vulture
dismissive attachment style	identity script	self-disclosure	
downer	Johari Window	self-fulfilling prophecy	
	particular others	self-sabotage	

For Further Thought and Discussion

1. Set a specific, fair, realistic goal for improving your interpersonal communication. For the next 2 weeks, focus on making progress toward that goal, following the guidelines in this chapter. Share the results of your work with others in your class.

2. Talk with one man and one woman who are 20 years older than you. Talk with one man and one woman who are 40 years older than you. In each conversation, ask them to explain how men and women were expected to be when they were 20 years old. Ask them to describe how women and men were expected to act and dress. Ask them to explain what behaviors, goals, and attitudes were considered inappropriate for women and men when they were 20 years old. Compare their responses with views held by 20-year-olds today.

3. Use your InfoTrac College Edition to access the last four issues of *Sex Roles: A Journal of Research*. Select two articles that focus on self-concept (also look for words in the titles such as *identity, self, self-esteem,* and *personality*), and read both articles. How does what you learn expand the discussion of self-concept presented in this chapter?

4. Discuss the idea of race with members of your class. You may want to reread the section on race and identity in this chapter. What is race? Is race a useful way to classify people? Why or why not? Do you think the Census Bureau should allow people to check multiple races to define themselves?

5. Think about a time when you tried to create some change in yourself and were not successful. Review what happened by applying the four principles for improving self-concept presented in the last section of this chapter. Now that you understand these principles, how might you be more effective if you wanted to create that same change in yourself today?

6. Use your InfoTrac College Edition to read "Race and Gender as Components of Working Self-Concept" by Elizabeth Aries and her colleagues. Are their findings consistent with your own experiences in being aware of your race and gender?

7. George Herbert Mead was a philosopher and scholar who first developed many of the ideas about self presented in this chapter. To learn more about Mead's life and work, visit http://home.att.net/~escavileer/mead.html.

Perception and Communication

"The social world that we share with others is a world we have imagined together and agreed with each other to believe in."

Elizabeth Janeway

This chapter focuses on meaning, which is the heart of communication. To understand how humans create meanings for themselves and their activities, we need to understand how perception and communication interact. As we will see, perception shapes how we understand others' communication and how we ourselves communicate. At the same time, communication influences our perceptions of people and situations. Before reading further, try to connect the nine dots at the right without lifting your pencil from the paper. You may use no more than four lines, the lines must be straight, and the lines must be connected to one another.

To understand how perception and communication interact, we'll first discuss the three-part process of perception. Next, we'll consider factors that affect our perceptions. Finally, we'll identify guidelines for improving perception so we can communicate more effectively.

Before we explore those topics, let's return to the nine dots problem. Could you solve it? Most people have trouble solving the problem because they label the nine dots a square, and they try to connect the dots staying within the boundaries of a square. However, it's impossible to connect the dots with four straight lines if you define the dots as a square. One solution (there are several) appears at the end of the chapter, on page 99.

This exercise makes an important point about the relationship between labels and human perception. The label *square* affects how you perceive the nine dots. In everyday communication, our words affect how we perceive others, situations, events, behaviors, and ourselves. At the same time, our perceptions, which are always incomplete and subjective, shape what things mean to us and hence the labels we use to name them. As long as we perceive the nine dots as a square, we can't solve the problem. Similarly, we communicate with others according to how we perceive and define them, and we may miss opportunities when our labels limit what we perceive. In the pages that follow, we want to unravel the complex relationships between perception and communication.

● ● ● ● ● ● ● ● ● ● ●

The Process of Human Perception

Perception is the active process of creating meaning by selecting, organizing, and interpreting people, objects, events, situations, and other phenomena. Note that perception is defined as an active process. We do not passively receive what is "out there" in the external world. Instead, we actively work to make sense of ourselves, others, and interactions. To do so, we select only certain things to notice, and then we organize and interpret what we have selectively noticed. What anything means to us depends on the aspects of it we notice and on our organization and interpretation of those aspects. Thus, perception is not a simple matter of recording external reality. Instead, we invest a lot of energy in constructing the meanings of phenomena.

Perception consists of three processes: selecting, organizing, and interpreting. (See Figure 3.1.) These processes are continuous, so they blend into one another. They are also interactive, so each of them affects the other two. For example, what we select to perceive in a particular situation affects how we organize and interpret the situation. At the same time, how we organize and interpret a situation affects our subsequent selections of what to perceive in the situation.

SELECTION

Stop for a moment and notice what is going on around you right now. Is there music in the background? Is the room warm or cold, messy or neat, large or small,

Selection
Qualities of the phenomena
Self-indication
Culture

Organization
Cognitive schemata

Interpretation
Attributions

FIGURE 3.1

The Process of Human Perception

light or dark? Is there laundry in the corner waiting to be washed? Can you smell anything—food being cooked, the stale odor of last night's popcorn, traces of cologne? Can you hear muted sounds of activities outside? Now, think about what's happening inside you: Are you sleepy, hungry, comfortable? Do you have a headache or an itch anywhere? On what kind of paper is your book printed? Is the type large, small, easy to read? How do you like the size of the book, the colors used, the design of the pages?

Probably you weren't conscious of most of these phenomena when you began reading the chapter. Instead, you focused on understanding the material in the book. You narrowed your attention to what you defined as important, and you were unaware of other aspects of the book and your surroundings. This is typical of how we live our lives. We can't attend to everything in our environment, because there is far too much going on in and around us, and we don't view most of it as relevant to us in any given moment.

We select to attend to certain stimuli based on a number of factors. First, some qualities of phenomena draw attention. For instance, we notice things that **STAND OUT,** because they are larger, more intense, or more unusual than other phenomena. So we're more likely to hear a loud voice than a soft one and to notice someone in a bright shirt than someone in a drab one. In the photo on this page, your eyes are probably drawn to the figure wearing the white shirt, because it stands out from all of the others. Change also compels attention, which is why we may take for granted all the pleasant interactions with a friend and notice only the tense moments.

Sometimes, we deliberately influence what we notice by indicating things to ourselves (Mead, 1934). In fact, in many ways education is a process of learning to point out to ourselves things we hadn't seen before. Right now, you're learning to be more conscious of the selectivity of your perceptions, so in the future you will notice this more on your own. In English courses, you learn to notice how authors craft characters and use words to create images. In science courses, you learn to attend to molecular structures and chemical reactions. Classes in business teach you to notice assets, liabilities, and gross and net profits. Look at the vase in Figure 3.2. Look again at Figure 3.2, knowing that it is not a vase but profiles of two faces. Do you see the faces now?

What we select to notice is also influenced by who we are and what is going on within us. Our motives and needs affect what we see and don't see. If you have recently ended a romantic relationship, you're more likely to notice attractive people at a party than if you are committed to someone. Motives also explain the oasis phenomenon, in which thirsty people stranded in the desert see water although none really exists. Our expectations also affect what we notice (Bargh, 1999). This explains the self-fulfilling prophecy we discussed in Chapter 2. A child who is told she is unlovable may notice rejecting, but not affirming, communication from others. An employee who is told he has leadership potential is likely to notice all his professional successes and strengths and to be less aware of his shortcomings.

Cultures also influence what we select to perceive. Assertiveness and competitiveness are encouraged and considered good in the United States, so we don't find it odd when people compete and try to best one another. By contrast, because some traditional Asian cultures emphasize group loyalty, cooperation, and face saving, competitiveness is noticed and judged negatively (Gudykunst & Lee, 2002). In Korea, age is a very important aspect of identity: The older a person is, the more he or she is respected. Many Koreans also place priority on family relations. Consequently, Koreans are more likely than Westerners to perceive the ages and family roles of people with whom they communicate. The Korean language reflects the cultural value of age and family ties through its different word forms used for people of different ages and different family status: *Gahndah,* meaning "to go," is used when speaking to a teenage peer, *gah* to a parent, and *gahneh* to a grandparent (Ferrante, 1995).

FIGURE 3.2
Perception

ORGANIZATION

Once we have selected what to notice, we must make sense of it. We organize what we have noticed and attribute meaning to it. A useful theory for explaining how we organize experience is **constructivism,** which states that we organize and interpret experience by applying cognitive structures called *schemata.* (See Figure 3.3.) We rely on four schemata to make sense of interpersonal phenomena: prototypes, personal constructs, stereotypes, and scripts (Kelly, 1955; Hewes, 1995).

Prototypes   A **prototype** defines the clearest or most representative examples of some category (Fehr, 1993). For example, you probably have a prototype of the great teacher, the excellent supervisor, the true friend, and the perfect romantic partner. Each of these categories is exemplified by a person who is the ideal; that's the prototype. For example, if Jane is the best friend you've ever known, then Jane is your prototype of a good friend. The prototype (Jane) helps you decide who else fits in a particular category (friend). You get to know Burt, and ask how closely he resembles Jane. If you view him as resembling her, then you would put Burt in the category Jane exemplifies: friend. Prototypes organize our perceptions by allowing us to place people and other phenomena in broad categories. We then consider how close they are to our prototype, or exemplar, of that category.

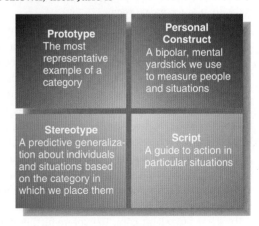

FIGURE 3.3
Cognitive Schemata

DAMION   The person who is my ideal of a friend is my buddy Jackson. He stood by me when I got into a lot of trouble a couple of years ago. I got mixed up with some guys who used drugs, and I started using them, too. Pretty soon the coach figured out what was going on, and he suspended me from the team. I felt like I was finished when he did that, and then I really got into drugs. But Jackson wouldn't give up on me, and he wouldn't let me give up either.

HMMM... COLDHEARTED, SERVES NO APPARENT FUNCTION, AND CAN'T MAKE A MOVE WITHOUT ASSISTANCE... GOOD LORD, HE'S *PERFECT!*

THE DISCOVERY OF THE EXECUTIVE PROTOTYPE

1-3

©1997 Washington Post Writers Group

E-mail: Wileytoon@aol.com
www.washingtonpost.com/wiley

He took me to a drug center and went there with me every day for 3 weeks. He never turned away when I was sick or even when I cried most of one night when I was getting off the drugs. He just stood by me. Once I was straight, Jackson went with me to see the coach about getting back on the team.

We also have prototypes of relationships (Fehr, 1993; Fehr & Russell, 1991; Hasserbrauck & Aaron, 2001). Most Americans' prototypes of romantic relationships emphasize trust, caring, honesty, friendship, and respect. Although passion may come to mind when we think of love, it seems less central to our prototype of love than companionship and caring.

Personal Constructs   A **personal construct** is a "mental yardstick" we use to measure a person or situation along a bipolar dimension of judgment (Kelly, 1955). Examples of personal constructs are *intelligent–*

Communication in Everyday Life
I'm Cablinasian!

DIVERSITY

Tiger Woods firmly but politely rejects it when others label him "African American" or "Asian." He's both and more, he says. As a young boy, he made up the term *Cablinasian* to symbolize his ethnic heritage. He is part Caucasian (*Ca*), part black (*bl*), part Indian (*in*), and part Asian (*asian*) (Strege, 1997; Woods, McDaniel, & Woods, 1998).

Tiger's not alone in embracing his multiracial identity. Keanu Reeves defines his ethnicity as Hawaiian, Chinese, and white. Mariah Carey identifies herself as black, Venezuelan, and white. Johnny Depp is Cherokee and white (Leland & Beals, 1997).

We can expect more and more people to have multiple ethnic heritages (Chideya, 1999). Interracial marriages are increasing in the United States, so we can expect to see more children who have mixed ethnic heritages. In the 1990s, more than 400,000 marriages in the United States were between Asians or Pacific Islanders and whites, more than 300,000 between Native Americans and whites, and nearly 100,000 between blacks and whites. After touring the country and talking with young men and women, Farai Chideya (1999) concluded that the rising generation is breaking down many stereotypes and prejudices about race.

Visit Tiger's official website at http://www.seeq.com/educationcentral/directory.jsp?domain= educationcentral-int.com. To explore further how race and ethnicity are organized into categories and whether or not they are sufficient to account for an individual's sense of racial and ethnic identity, complete *Student Companion: Activity 3.5.* This activity utilizes the World Wide Web.

AP/Wide World Photos

unintelligent, kind–unkind, responsible–irresponsible, assertive–unassertive, and *attractive–unattractive.* We rely on personal constructs to size up people and other phenomena. How intelligent, kind, or attractive is this person? Whereas prototypes help us decide into which broad category a phenomenon fits, personal constructs let us make more detailed assessments of particular qualities of people and other phenomena.

> **NAI LEE**   One of the ways I look at people is by whether they are independent or related to others. That is one of the first judgments I make of others. In Korea, we are not so individualistic or independent as people in the United States. We think of ourselves more as members of families and communities than as individuals. The emphasis on independent identity was the first thing I noticed when I came to this country, and it is still an important way I look at people.

The personal constructs we rely on shape our perceptions because we define things only in the terms of the constructs we use. Notice that we structure what we perceive and what it means by the constructs we choose to use. Thus, we may not notice qualities of people that aren't covered by the constructs we apply.

Stereotypes   A **stereotype** is a predictive generalization about a person or situation. Based on the category in which we place someone or something and how that person or thing measures up against the personal constructs we apply, we predict what he, she, or it will do. For instance, if you define someone as a liberal, you might stereotype her or him as likely to vote Democratic, to support social legislation, to be pro-environment, and so forth. You may have stereotypes of fraternity and sorority members, military personnel, athletes, and people from other cultures. Stereotypes don't necessarily reflect actual similarities between people. Instead, stereotypes are based on our perceptions of similarities between people or on social perspectives that we've internalized. We may perceive similarities that others don't, and we may fail to perceive commonalities that are obvious to others.

Everyday Application
Changing Constructs, Changing Perceptions

Use the left-hand column below to list five constructs that are important in your assessment of potential romantic partners.

1. _____   1. _____
2. _____   2. _____
3. _____   3. _____
4. _____   4. _____
5. _____   5. _____

Now, use the right-hand column to list five other constructs that you could use in your assessment of potential romantic partners. How would using the constructs on the right alter or enlarge your perceptions of people you consider as romantic partners?

SHANNON I hate the way people stereotype me because of my accent. I grew up in Alabama, and I have a pretty heavy Southern accent—at least that's what people at this school say. They act like I'm stupid because of my "Southern drawl." And then, some of them ask me to talk—I mean, really—they ask me to talk, and then say, "Isn't that the cutest accent you ever heard?" It's like they're so busy listening to my accent they don't listen to WHAT I have to say. I knew, when I decided to attend a college halfway across the country, I'd run into some differences. But I didn't know that the way I talk would lead others to label me slow and unintellectual.

Racial and ethnic stereotypes can lead us not to see differences among people we place in a particular category. The broad label *Asian* doesn't distinguish among people from varied cultures, including Japan, Malaysia, Nepal, and China. Even the U.S. Census Bureau is struggling with how to create categories that can provide useful and accurate information on social groups (Liang, 1997). *Native American* is a very broad category that includes diverse Native American tribes (Vickers, 1999). A student of mine, Winowa, thinks that the term *Native American* leads people not to notice differences among tribes.

Communication in Everyday Life
"I can't understand the teacher's accent."

DIVERSITY

It's not unusual to hear American students complain that international teachers are hard to understand because of heavy accents, faulty pronunciation of English words, and so forth. In response to student complaints, more than a dozen states have passed laws to establish standards for English for international teaching assistants. According to John Gravois (2005), who writes for the *Chronicle of Higher Education,* such laws may be solving the wrong problem.

Gravois asks whether the problem is that some international teaching assistants don't speak English clearly or that some American students don't listen well because they stereotype international teaching assistants as lacking proficiency in English. Don Rubin, a professor of communication, designed an experiment to answer that question.

Rubin audiotaped an American man from central Ohio delivering a lecture. He then played that lecture to students. To half the students, the lecturer was identified as "John Smith from Portland," and the image of an American man was projected in the classroom. The same tape was played to the other half the students, but the lecturer was identified as "Li Wenshu from Beijing," and the image of an Asian man was projected in the classroom.

After hearing the lecture, students were asked to fill in the missing words from a printed transcript of the lecture. The students who thought the lecturer was Asian made 20% more errors than students who thought the lecturer was American. Rubin concluded that students stereotype international teachers as less proficient at English than American teachers. They heard Li Wenshu as less proficient in English than John Smith even though the two were the same person giving the same lecture.

WINOWA People have a stereotype of Native Americans. People who are not Native American think we are all alike—how we look, how we act, what we believe, what our traditions are. But that isn't true. The Crow and Apache are as different as people from Kenya and New York. Some tribes have a history of aggression and violence; others have traditions of peace and harmony. We worship different spirits and have different tribal rituals and customs. All of these differences are lost when people stereotype us all into one group.

Stereotypes may be accurate or inaccurate. In some cases, we have incorrect understandings of a group, and in other cases individual members of a group don't conform to the behaviors typical of a group as a whole. Although we need stereotypes to predict what will happen around us, they can be harmful if we forget that they are based not on objective reality but instead on our prototypes and our application of personal constructs.

Scripts The final cognitive schema we use to organize perceptions is the script. A **script** is a guide to action. Scripts consist of sequences of activities that are expected of us and others in particular situations. They are based on our experiences and observations of interaction in various contexts. Many of our daily activities are governed by scripts, although we're typically not aware of them. We have a script for greeting casual acquaintances on campus ("Hey, what's up?" "Not much"). You also have scripts for dating, managing conflict, talking with professors, dealing with clerks, and interacting with coworkers on the job.

Scripts organize perceptions into lines of action. Prototypes, personal constructs, stereotypes, and scripts are cognitive schemata that we use to organize our perceptions of people and other phenomena. These cognitive schemata reflect the perspectives of particular others and the generalized other. As we interact with people, we internalize our culture's ways of classifying, measuring, and predicting phenomena and its norms for acting in various situations.

Scripts are useful in guiding us through many of our interactions. However, they are not always accurate or constructive, so we shouldn't accept them uncritically. For instance, if your parents often engaged in bitter, destructive quarreling, you may have learned a script for conflict

Communication in Everyday Life
A Script for Romance

Researchers Christine Bachen and Eva Illouz (1996) wanted to know to what extent mass media influence young people's ideas about romance. To find out, they asked students in the fourth, seventh, tenth, and eleventh grades to pick three out of six photos shown to them that represented a man and a woman in love. They then asked the students to select the single photo that best exemplified a man and a woman in love. Next, the researchers asked the students to use their own words to describe a romantic dinner and a typical first date. Finally, the researchers asked the students to tell an ideal love story.

There was a high rate of agreement among students. For the first task, they overwhelmingly chose pictures of couples in exotic locales who were looking directly at each other and touching or kissing. For the second task, the majority of students selected a photo showing a couple on a boat, the most exotic of the pictures they had been shown. Descriptions of romantic dinners emphasized atmosphere and the visual features of settings: soft lighting, music, exquisite food. Students also agreed on the script for a first date: going out to dinner, although not necessarily a romantic dinner, or to a movie. Most interesting to the researchers was what students offered as ideal love stories: The stories involved falling in love and getting married, but that wasn't the end. The final focus of students' stories was having children and acquiring material goods to give them comfortable lives.

After analyzing the data, Bachen and Illouz concluded that students' perceptions of love and romance reflect media ideals. Advertising and broadcast media link romance to leisure, consumption, and exotic places and activities—the very things the students in their study associated with love and romance.

Everyday Application
Sizing Up Others

Pay attention to the cognitive schemata you use the next time you meet a new person. First, notice how you classify the person. Do you categorize her or him as a potential friend, date, co-worker, or neighbor? Next, identify the constructs you use to assess the person. Do you focus on physical characteristics (attractive–unattractive), mental qualities (intelligent–unintelligent), psychological features (secure–insecure), or interpersonal qualities (friendly–unfriendly)? Would different constructs be prominent if you used a different prototype to classify the person? Now, note how you stereotype the person. What do you expect him or her to do based on the prototype and constructs you've applied? Finally, identify your script, or how you expect interaction to unfold between you.

Extend your thinking about how our classifications of people affect our perceptions of them by reading Nancy Shute's brief 2001 article, "A Black and White World," available in your InfoTrac College Edition.

that will undermine your relationships. Similarly, if you grew up in a community that treated people of certain races negatively, you may want to assess that script critically before using it to direct your own activities.

INTERPRETATION

Even after we have selectively perceived phenomena and organized our perceptions, what they mean to us is not clear. There are no intrinsic meanings in phenomena. Instead, we assign meaning by interpreting what we have noticed and organized. **Interpretation** is the subjective process of explaining our perceptions in ways that make sense to us. To interpret the meaning of another's actions, we construct explanations for them.

Attributions   An **attribution** is an explanation of why something happened or why someone acts a certain way (Heider, 1958; Kelley, 1967). Attributions have four dimensions, as shown in Figure 3.4. The first is locus, which attributes a person's actions to internal factors ("He has no patience with people who are late") or external factors ("The traffic jam frustrated him"). The second dimension is stability, which explains actions as the result of stable factors that won't change over time ("She's a Type A personality") or unstable factors that may or will be different at another time ("She acted that way because she has a headache right now").

Specificity is the third dimension, and it explains behavior in terms of whether the behavior has global implications that apply in most or all situations ("He's an introvert") or specific implications that apply only in certain situations or under certain conditions ("He gets quiet whenever he needs to think"). Many people think stability and specificity are similar, but really they are distinct dimensions. Stability concerns time (whether the reason is temporary or enduring), whereas specificity concerns the breadth of the explanation (all situations, events, and places, or particular or limited situations and places). Here are examples of how we might combine these two dimensions to explain why Angela yelled at Fred:

··· Stable and specific: She yelled at Fred (specific) because she is short tempered (stable).
··· Stable and global: She yells at everyone (global) because she is short tempered (stable).
··· Unstable and specific: She yelled at Fred (specific) because she was in a hurry that day (temporary, unstable factor that could change).
··· Unstable and global: She yells at everyone (global) when she is in a hurry (unstable).

The dimensions of stable–unstable, global–specific, and internal–external lead us to explain phenomena on a fourth dimension, which is responsibility. Do we hold a person responsible for a particular behavior? We're more likely to hold someone responsible if we think she or he could control the behavior. If we attribute Angela's yelling to her lack of effort to control her temper, we're more likely to judge her harshly than if we attribute her yelling to lack of sleep or to a medication she's taking for a short time

Dimension

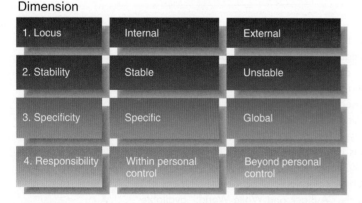

1. Locus	Internal	External
2. Stability	Stable	Unstable
3. Specificity	Specific	Global
4. Responsibility	Within personal control	Beyond personal control

FIGURE 3.4

Dimensions of Attributions

(unstable). How we account for others' actions affects our feelings about them and our relationships with them. We can be more or less positive toward others, depending on how we explain what they do.

Our attributions influence the meanings we attach to others and to their communication. For example, how do you account for the fact that your supervisor at work shouts orders gruffly? Does she have an authoritarian personality? Or is she insecure because she is new in the role of supervisor? Or is she reacting to a medication? Each of the three attributions invites a distinct understanding of why the supervisor shouts.

Attributional Errors   Researchers have identified two common errors people make in their attributions. The first is the **self-serving bias.** As the term implies, this is a bias toward ourselves and our interests. Research indicates that we tend to construct attributions that serve our personal interests (Hamachek, 1992; Sypher, 1984). Thus, we are inclined to make internal, stable, and global attributions for our positive actions and our successes. We're also likely to claim that good results come about because of personal control we exerted. For example, you might say that you did well on a test because you are a smart (internal and stable) person who is always responsible (global) and studies hard (personal control).

> **CHICO**   When I do badly on a test or paper, I usually say either the professor was unfair or I had too much to do that week and couldn't study like I wanted to. But when my friends do badly on a test, I tend to think they're not good in that subject or they aren't disciplined or whatever.

The self-serving bias also works in a second way. We tend to avoid taking responsibility for negative actions and failures by attributing them to external, unstable, and specific factors that are beyond personal control (Schutz, 1999). To explain a failing grade on a test, you might say that you did poorly because the professor (external) put a lot of tricky questions on that test (unstable, specific factor), so all your studying didn't help (outside of personal control). In other words, our misconduct results from outside forces that we can't help, but all the good we do reflects our personal qualities and efforts. This self-serving bias can distort our perceptions, leading us to take excessive personal credit for what we do well and to abdicate responsibility for what we do poorly. When the self-serving bias shapes how we interpret our behaviors, we form an unrealistic image of ourselves and our activities.

In a 1996 interview with *Newsweek*'s John McCormick and Sharon Begley, Tiger Woods described how his father taught him to accept responsibility for his bad shots in golf. When he was a preschooler and hit a bad shot, he slammed his club on the ground. His father would ask him, "Who's responsible for that bad shot? The crow that made the noise

Communication in Everyday Life
Self-Serving Attributions and Sports

Our team is always better, right? If the other team wins, it's due to luck, right? It turns out that the self-serving bias shows up not just in judgments of people but also in judgments of sports. Curious to know whether sports fans would fall victim to the fundamental attributional error, Daniel Wann and Michael Schrader (2000) designed an experiment. They asked 59 undergraduate women and 55 undergraduate men to view athletic contests and explain why their teams won or lost. Consistently, students who identified strongly with their teams attributed their teams' victories to internal, controllable, and stable causes. Just as consistently, they attributed their teams' losses to external factors for which the teams couldn't be blamed.

Read the full text of Wann and Schrader's article in your InfoTrac College Edition. Go to the key word search and enter *attributions.* You may want to read some of the other articles your search produces.

Communication in Everyday Life
Thinking Your Way to a Good Relationship

What makes a relationship work? Obviously, lots of things are involved, but one that most people don't recognize is how we think about what our friends and romantic partners do and don't do (Bradbury & Fincham, 1990; Fletcher & Fincham, 1991; Friesen, Fletcher, & Overall, 2005; Seligman, 2002). Partners in happy relationships tend to think in positive ways about each other. People attribute nice things a partner does to internal, stable, and global reasons. "He got the film for us because he is a good person who always does sweet things for us." Happy couples attribute unpleasant things a partner does to external, unstable, and specific factors. "She yelled at me because all the stress of the past few days made her not herself."

In contrast, unhappy couples tend to think negatively. They tend to attribute a partner's nice actions to external, unstable, and specific factors. "She got the tape because she had some extra time this particular day." Negative actions are seen as stemming from internal, stable, and global factors. "He yelled at me because he is a nasty person who never shows any consideration to anybody else." Negative attributions fix pessimistic views and undermine motivation to improve a relationship. Whether positive or negative, attributions may be self-fulfilling prophecies.

Related research demonstrates that attributional patterns are linked to marital quality and forgiveness. We are less likely to forgive a partner if we attribute his or her transgression to personal irresponsibility (Fincham, 2000; Fincham, Paleari, & Regalia, 2002; Findel, Rusbult, Kumashiro, & Hannon, 2002; McCullough & Hoyt, 2002).

during your backswing? The bag somebody dropped? Whose responsibility was that?" (McCormick & Begley, 1996, p. 55). Tiger learned to say it was his responsibility. As he took responsibility for his bad shots, Tiger Woods learned that he could control his skill.

The second kind of attributional error is so common it is called the **fundamental attribution error.** This involves how we use the dimension of locus. We tend to overestimate the internal causes of others' undesirable behaviors and underestimate the external causes. Conversely, we are likely to underestimate the internal causes of our own misdeeds and failures and overestimate the external causes (Schutz, 1999; Sedikides, Campbell, Reeder, & Elliott, 1998).

The fundamental attributional error was obvious in a legal case on which I consulted a few years ago. A woman sued her employer for transferring her. She alleged that he did so because her boss was biased against women. Her boss denied being biased against women. He claimed that he transferred her because her poor performance made her the most expendable person in his department. Written records, such as yearly performance reviews, and the woman's own testimony revealed that she had not met all of her job responsibilities, and she had been told this repeatedly. Furthermore, her boss's record of hiring and promotions showed that nearly 50% of his hires and promotions over the past decade had been women and minorities.

At the trial, the plaintiff was asked whether it was possible that her performance had influenced her boss's decision to transfer her. "No, he did it because he doesn't want to work with women," she replied. Thus, she totally discounted external factors that could explain his decision and placed full responsibility on internal qualities (his alleged sex bias). When asked whether she thought her performance might have made her more expendable than others who worked in her former department, she said, "No, the only problems with my performance were due to interruptions and lack of cooperation from others." Thus, she rejected any personal responsibility for errors in her work and laid full responsibility on circumstances beyond her control. In court, I explained the fundamental attribution error to the jury and showed how it surfaced in the woman's testimony. The jury found in favor of the woman's boss.

We've seen that perception involves three interrelated processes. The first of these, selection, involves noticing certain things and ignoring others out of the total complexity of what is going on. The second process is organization, whereby we use prototypes, personal constructs, stereotypes, and scripts to organize what we have selectively perceived. Finally, we engage in interpretation to make sense of the perceptions we have gathered and organized. Attributions are a primary way we explain what we and others do.

Although we've discussed selection, organization, and interpretation separately, in reality they may occur in a different order or simultaneously. Thus, our interpretations shape the cognitive schemata we use to organize experiences, and the ways we organize perceptions affect what we notice and interpret. For instance, in her commentary earlier in this chapter, Nai Lee's interpretations of Westerners' individualism were shaped by the schemata she learned in her homeland of Korea. Also, reliance on the individualistic–communal construct shaped what she noticed about Americans.

Now that we understand the complex processes involved in perception, we're ready to consider a range of factors that influence what and how we perceive.

· · · · · · · · · · ·

Influences on Perception

Individuals differ in how they perceive situations and people. In this section, we consider some of the influences on our perceptions.

PHYSIOLOGY

One reason perceptions vary among people is that we differ in our sensory abilities and physiologies. I have a keener sense of hearing than Robbie does; he can barely hear music at the volume I find comfortable. The hot, spicy foods I perceive as delicious are painful to Robbie. Such differences in sensory abilities affect our perceptions.

Our physiological states also influence perception. If you are tired or stressed, you're likely to perceive things more negatively than you normally would. For instance, a playful insult from a co-worker might anger you if you were feeling down but wouldn't bother you if you were feeling good. Each of us has our own biorhythm, which influences the times of day when we tend to be alert and fuzzy. I'm a morning person, so that's when I prefer to teach classes and write. I am less alert and less creative later in the day. Thus, I perceive things in the morning that I simply don't notice when my energy level declines.

Medical conditions are another physiological influence on perceptions. If you've ever taken drugs that affected your thinking, you know how dramatically they can alter perceptions. People may become severely depressed, paranoid, or uncharacteristically happy under the influence of hormones or drugs. Changes in our bodies caused by medical conditions may also affect what we selectively perceive. I have a back disorder that periodically renders me immobile or dependent on canes. When my back is out of order, I am far more aware of stairs, uneven ground, and any activities that require me to bend. When my back is working well, I don't notice these things any more than someone without back problems does.

AGE

Age is another factor that influences our perceptions. Compared with a person of 20, a 60-year-old has a more complex fund of experiences to draw on in perceiving

situations and people. When I was 22 years old and in graduate school, I mentioned to my father that it was hard to get by on the salary from my teaching assistantship. He said that, during the early 1930s, he would have been very happy to have had enough money just to eat. Because my father had lived through the Great Depression, he had a broader perspective than I did on how hard life can be.

Age also influences our perceptions of time. My 7-year-old nephew perceives a year as much longer than I do. A year is a full seventh of his life but less than a fiftieth of mine; a year really is longer in his life than mine. As we grow older and have more experiences, our perspective on many things changes. For example, I used to feel down if my teaching didn't go well on a given day or if I had an unexpected expense. When my father died when I was 36, I gained a wholly new perspective on what is bad and what is worth feeling down about.

Age and the wealth of experiences it brings can also change our perceptions of social issues. The extent of discrimination still experienced by women and minorities understandably frustrates many college students. I am more hopeful than some of them because I have seen many changes in my lifetime. When I attended college, women were not admitted on an equal basis with men, and almost all students of color attended minority colleges. When I entered the job market, few laws protected women and minorities against discrimination in hiring, pay, and advancement. The substantial progress made during my lifetime leads me to perceive substantial progress in lessening discrimination and to perceive current inequities as changeable.

CULTURE

A **culture** is the totality of beliefs, values, understandings, practices, and ways of interpreting experience that are shared by a number of people. Culture forms the pattern of our lives and guides how we think, feel, and communicate (Lee, 2000). The influence of culture is so pervasive that it's hard to realize how powerfully it shapes our perceptions.

Consider a few aspects of modern Western culture that influence our perceptions. Western culture emphasizes technology and its offspring, speed. Most Westerners expect things to happen fast, almost instantly. Whether it's instant photos, accessing websites, or 1-hour dry cleaning, we live at an accelerated pace (Wood, 2000a). We send letters by express mail, we jet across the country, and we microwave meals. In countries such as Nepal and Mexico, life often proceeds at a more leisurely pace, and people spend more time talking, relaxing, and engaging in low-key activity.

How do values in Western culture affect your everyday perceptions and activities? See whether you can trace concrete implications of these cultural values.

Example: Competition—This value is evident in concrete practices such as competitive sports, grading policies, and attempts to have the last word in casual conversations.

Productivity _____

Individualism _____

Speed _____

Youth _____

Wealth _____

Discuss with classmates the impact of cultural values on your day-to-day perceptions and activities.

The United States is also a highly individualistic culture in which personal initiative is expected and rewarded. In more collectivist cultures, identity is defined in terms of membership in a family rather than as an individual quality. Because families are more valued in collectivist cultures, elders are given greater respect and care than they often receive in the United States. More communal countries also have policies that reflect the value they place on families. In every developed country except the United States, new parents, including adoptive parents, are given at least 6 weeks of paid parental leave, and some countries provide nearly a year's paid leave.

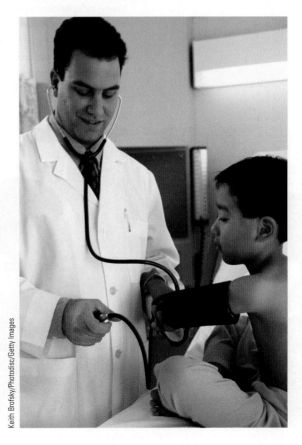

Keith Brofsky/Photodisc/Getty Images

Many doctors in the United States now are encouraged to attend workshops that teach them about the cultural practices and folk beliefs of immigrants from other countries (Anders, 1997; Mangan, 2002). One doctor, Jeffrey Syme, found immediate application for what he learned in a workshop. A number of his patients had emigrated from Cape Verde, a string of islands off West Africa. Many of these patients asked him for Valium but refused to discuss their problems with him. According to Syme's training as well as United States drug policy, Valium is a medication that should be prescribed only for specific conditions. In the workshop, Syme learned that, in Cape Verde, Valium is an over-the-counter treatment people routinely take for everyday blues. Thus, they perceived Valium as a mild medication that they could take as casually as many Americans take aspirin. In another case, ignorance of folk beliefs led a doctor to faulty perceptions of a patient. A folk belief among many Guatemalans is that giant worms in the stomach govern well-being. One doctor attending the workshop said, "I just had a patient like that." What had the doctor done when her patient complained that giant worms in his stomach were making him feel bad? She referred him to mental health specialists because she perceived his statement to indicate that he was mentally unbalanced. In both cases, the doctors misperceived patients by not taking into account the patients' cultural customs and beliefs.

Standpoint   In recent years, scholars have realized that we are affected not only by the culture as a whole but by particular social groups to which we belong (Hallstein, 2000; Haraway, 1988; Harding, 1991). A **standpoint** is a point of view shaped by awareness of the material, social, and symbolic conditions common for members of a social group. People who belong to powerful, high-status social groups have a vested interest in preserving the system that gives them privileges; thus, they are unlikely to perceive its flaws and inequities. On the other hand, those who belong to less privileged groups are able to see inequities and discrimination (Collins, 1998; Harding, 1991).

Women and men often have different standpoints, although not every individual man and woman shares the standpoint that is typical of his or her sex. For instance, the caregiving we generally associate with women results less from any maternal instinct than from the social role of mother, which teaches women to care for others, to notice who needs what, and to defer their own needs (Ruddick, 1989). Other researchers have discovered that men who are in caregiving roles become nurturing, accommodative, and sensitive to others' needs as a consequence of being in the social role of caregiver (Kaye & Applegate, 1990).

JANICE   I'll vouch for the idea of standpoint affecting how we communicate. I was always a pretty independent person. Some people even thought I was kind of selfish, because I really would prioritize myself. Then I had my first baby, and I stayed home with him for a year. I really changed—and I mean in basic ways. I believed that my most important job was to be there for Timmy, and so my whole day focused on him. He was the person I thought about first, not myself. I learned to hear the slightest difference in his cries, so I could tell when he was hungry or needed his diapers changed or wanted company. When I went back to work after a year, a lot of my former colleagues said I was different—much more attentive and sensitive to what they said and more generous with my time than I had been. I guess I developed new patterns of communicating as a result of mothering.

© Bob Daemmrich/The Image Works

Gendered standpoints also are evident in marital conflict. Researchers have found that conflict lessens wives' love for husbands more than it lessens husbands' love for wives (Huston, McHale, & Crouter, 1985; Kelly, Huston, & Cate, 1985). From early childhood, many young girls are socialized to attend to relationships, preserve interpersonal harmony, and avoid conflict. In contrast, young boys typically are socialized to engage in conflict, resolve it, then go on with their activities. It makes sense that, in general, conflict with a spouse might be more upsetting and disruptive to women than men.

Gendered standpoints also are obvious in the effort women and men in general invest in maintaining relationships. Socialized into the role of relationship expert, many women are expected by others and themselves to take care of relationships (Tavris, 1992; Wood, 1993, 1994d, 1998). They are supposed to know when something is wrong and to resolve the tension. This may explain why women tend to be more aware than men of problems in relationships (Brehm, 1992; Wood, 1998).

Standpoints are also cultivated by membership in particular racial–ethnic groups. Stan Gaines (1995), who studies minority groups in the United States, reports that African Americans and Latinos and Latinas tend to perceive family and extended community as more central to their identities than most European Americans do. Perceiving self as a part of larger social groups also is characteristic of many Asian cultures. Our membership in an overall culture, as well as our standpoint as members of particular social groups, shape how we perceive people, situations, events, and ourselves.

ROLES

Our perceptions also are shaped by roles. Both the training we receive to fulfill a role and the actual demands of the role affect what we notice and how we interpret and evaluate the role. I perceive classes in terms of how interested students seem, whether they appear to have read the material, and whether what they're learning is useful in their lives. Students have told me that they perceive classes in terms of time of day, number and difficulty of tests, whether papers are required, and whether the professor is interesting. We have different perceptions of classes.

The professions people enter influence what they notice and how they think and act. Before her professional training, my sister Carolyn did not have highly developed analytical thinking skills. However, after she completed law school, she was extremely analytic; her conversational style changed, becoming more analytical, logical, and probing. Here is another example: Physicians are trained to be highly observant of physical symptoms. Once, at a social gathering, a friend of mine who is a physician asked me how long I had had a herniated disk. Shocked, I told him I didn't have one. "You do," he insisted, and, sure enough, a few weeks later a disk ruptured. His medical training had enabled him to perceive subtle changes in my posture and walk that I hadn't noticed.

Social roles can also influence how we perceive communication about our feelings. Professions that call for detachment and objectivity may encourage members not to express their emotions and to be uncomfortable when others do. We'll discuss the relationship between social roles and communication about emotions more fully in Chapter 7.

COGNITIVE ABILITIES

In addition to physiological, cultural, and social influences, perception is also shaped by cognitive abilities. How elaborately we think about situations and people, and our personal knowledge of others, affect how we select, organize, and interpret experiences.

Cognitive Complexity People differ in the number and type of cognitive schemata they use to perceive, organize, and interpret people and situations. **Cognitive complexity** refers to the number of personal constructs used (remember, these are bipolar dimensions of judgment), how abstract they are, and how elaborately they

© Louise Gubb/The Image Works

interact to shape perceptions. Most children have fairly simple cognitive systems: They rely on few personal constructs, focus more on concrete categories than abstract and psychological ones, and often are unaware of relationships between different perceptions.

In general, adults are more cognitively complex than children. However, adults have different degrees of cognitive complexity, and this affects perceptions. If you think of people only as nice or mean, you have a limited range for perceiving others. Similarly, people who focus on concrete data tend to have less sophisticated understandings than people who also perceive psychological data. For example, you might notice that a person is attractive, tells jokes, and talks to others easily. These are concrete perceptions. At a more abstract, psychological level, you might reason that the concrete behaviors you observe reflect a secure, self-confident personality. This is a more sophisticated perception because it offers an explanation of why the person acts as she or he does.

What if you later find out that the person is very quiet in classes? Someone with low cognitive complexity would have difficulty integrating the new information into prior observations. Either the new information would be dismissed because it doesn't fit, or it would replace the former perception, and the person would be redefined as shy (Crockett, 1965; Delia, Clark, & Switzer, 1974). A more cognitively complex person would integrate all the information into a coherent account. Perhaps a cognitively complex person would conclude that the person is very confident in social situations but less secure in academic ones.

Person-Centeredness Person-centeredness is related to cognitive complexity because it entails abstract thinking and use of a wide range of schemata. As discussed in Chapter 1, person-centeredness is the ability to perceive another as a unique individual. Our ability to perceive others as unique depends, first, on how well we make cognitive distinctions. People who are cognitively complex rely on more numerous, more abstract schemata to interpret others. Second, person-centered communicators use knowledge of particular others to guide their communication. Thus, they tailor vocabulary, nonverbal behaviors, and language to the experiences, values, and interests of others. The result is person-centered communication.

Recalling the discussion of I–Thou relationships in Chapter 1, you may remember that these are relationships in which people know and value each other as unique individuals. To do so, we must learn about another, and this entails much time and interaction. As we get to know another better, we gain insight into how she or he differs from others in a group ("Rob's not obsessive like other political activists I've known," "Ellen's more interested in people than most computer science majors"). The more we interact with another and the greater the variety of experiences we have together, the more insight we gain into the other's motives, feelings, and behaviors. As we come to understand others as individuals, we fine-tune our perceptions of them. Consequently, we're less likely to rely on stereotypes.

This is why we often communicate more effectively with people we know well than with strangers or casual acquaintances.

Person-centeredness is not empathy. **Empathy** is the ability to feel with another person, to feel what she or he feels in a situation. Feeling with another is an emotional response that some scholars believe we cannot fully achieve. Our feelings tend to be guided by our own emotional tendencies and experiences, so it may be impossible to feel exactly what another person feels. What we can do is realize that another is feeling something and connect as well as we can based on our own, different experiences. With commitment and effort, we can learn a lot about how others see the world, even if that differs from how we see it. This knowledge, along with cognitive complexity, allows us to be person-centered communicators.

When we take the perspective of another, we try to grasp what something means to that person and how he or she perceives things. This involves suspending judgment at least temporarily. We can't appreciate someone else's perspective when we're imposing our evaluations of whether it is right or wrong, sensible or crazy. Instead, we must let go of our own perspective and perceptions long enough to enter the world of another person. Doing this allows us to understand issues from the other person's point of view so that we can communicate more effectively. At a later point in interaction, we may choose to express our own perspective or to disagree with the other. This is appropriate, but voicing our own views is not a substitute for the equally important skill of recognizing others' perspectives.

SELF

A final influence on our perceptions is ourselves. Consider how differently people with the four attachment styles we discussed in Chapter 2 would perceive and approach close relationships. People with secure attachment styles assume that they are lovable and that others are trustworthy. Thus, they tend to perceive others and relationships in positive ways. In contrast, people with fearful attachment styles perceive themselves as unlovable and others as not loving. Consequently, they may perceive relationships as dangerous and potentially harmful. The dismissive attachment style inclines people to perceive themselves positively, others negatively, and close relationships as undesirable. People who have anxious/ambivalent attachment styles often are preoccupied with relationships and perceive others in unpredictable ways.

The concept of the **implicit personality theory** helps explain how the self influences interpersonal perceptions. An implicit personality theory is a collection of unspoken and sometimes unconscious assumptions about how various qualities fit together in human personalities. Most of us think certain qualities go together in people. For instance, you might think that people who are outgoing are also friendly, confident, and fun. The assumption that outgoing people are friendly, confident, and fun is not based on direct knowledge; instead, it is an inference based on your implicit personality theory of the qualities that accompany outgoingness.

In sum, physiology, culture and standpoint, social roles, cognitive abilities, and we ourselves affect what we perceive and how we interpret others and experiences.

In the final section of the chapter, we'll consider ways to improve the accuracy of our perceptions.

·········

Guidelines for Improving Perception and Communication

Because perception is a foundation of interpersonal communication, it's important to form perceptions carefully and check their accuracy. Here, we discuss seven guidelines for improving the accuracy of perceptions and, ultimately, the quality of interpersonal communication.

RECOGNIZE THAT ALL PERCEPTIONS ARE PARTIAL AND SUBJECTIVE

Our perceptions are always partial and subjective. They are partial because we cannot perceive everything. They are subjective because they are influenced by factors such as culture, physiology, roles, standpoint, and cognitive abilities.

Objective features of reality have no meaning until we notice, organize, and interpret them. It is our perceptions that construct meanings for the people and experiences in our lives. Each of us perceives from a particular perspective that is shaped by our physiology, culture, standpoint, social roles, cognitive abilities, and personal experiences. An outfit perceived as elegant by one person may appear cheap to another. A teacher one student regards as fascinating may put another student to sleep.

THALENA   So this girl I met a few weeks ago said she was having a party, and it would be lots of fun with some cool people. She asked if I wanted to come, so I said, "Sure—why not?" When I got there everybody was drinking—I mean seriously drinking. They were playing this weird music—sort of morbid—and they had the tape of *Rocky Horror Picture Show* going nonstop. They got so loud that the neighbors came over and told us to hold it down. In a couple of hours, most of the people there were totally wasted. That's not my idea of fun. That's not my idea of cool people.

"May I suggest that in today's group-therapy session we all work on our contact with reality."

The subjective and partial nature of perceptions has implications for interpersonal communication. One implication is that, when you and another person disagree about something, neither of you is necessarily wrong. It's more likely that you have attended to different things and that there are differences in your personal, social, cultural, cognitive, and physiological resources for perceiving.

A second implication is that it's wise to remind ourselves that our perceptions are based at least as much on ourselves as on anything external to us. If you perceive another person as domineering, there's a chance that you are feeling insecure in your ability to interact. If you perceive others as unfriendly toward you, it may be that you think of yourself as unworthy of friends. Remembering that perceptions are partial and subjective curbs the tendency to think that our perceptions are the only valid ones or that they are based exclusively on what lies outside us.

AVOID MIND READING

Mind reading is assuming we understand what another person thinks, feels, or perceives. When we mind read, we act as though we knew what was on another's mind, and this can get us into trouble. Marriage counselors and communication scholars say mind reading contributes to conflict between people (Dickson, 1995; Gottman, 1993; Gottman, Notarius, Gonso, & Markman, 1976). The danger of mind reading is that we may misinterpret others.

Consider a few examples. One person says to her partner, "I know you didn't plan anything for our anniversary because it's not important to you." A supervisor notices that an employee is late for work several days in a row and assumes the employee isn't committed to the job. Gina is late meeting her friend Alex, who assumes she is late because Gina's still mad about what happened. Alex is guessing reasons for Gina's tardiness and could well be wrong.

Mind reading also occurs when we say or think, "I know why you're upset" (Has the person said she or he is upset? What makes you think you know why he or she is upset if he or she actually is?) or "You don't care about me anymore" (maybe the other person is too preoccupied or worried to be as attentive as usual). We also mind read when we tell ourselves we know how somebody else will feel or react or what he or she will do. The truth is that we don't really know; we're only guessing. When we mind read, we impose our perspectives on others instead of allowing them to say what they think. This can cause misunderstandings and resentment because most of us prefer to speak for ourselves.

CONSUELA Mind reading drives me crazy. My boyfriend does it all the time, and he's wrong as often as he's right. Last week, he got tickets to a concert because he "knew" I'd want to go. Maybe I would have if I hadn't already planned a trip that weekend, but he never checked on my schedule. A lot of times, when we're talking, he'll say something, then before I can answer, he says, "I know what you're thinking." Then, he proceeds to run through his ideas about what I'm thinking. Usually he's off base, and then we get into a sideline argument about why he keeps assuming what I think instead of asking me. I really wish he would ask me what I think.

CHECK PERCEPTIONS WITH OTHERS

The third guideline follows directly from the first two. Because perceptions are subjective and partial, and because mind reading is an ineffective way to figure out what others think, we need to check our perceptions with others. In the anniversary example mentioned earlier, an effective communicator might ask, "Did you forget our anniversary?" If the partner did forget, then the speaker might ask, "Why do you think you forgot?" The person may not know why, or the reasons may not be satisfactory, but asking is more likely to open a productive dialogue than attributing bad motives is.

Perception checking is an important communication skill because it helps people arrive at mutual understandings of each other and their relationships. To check perceptions, you should first state what you have noticed. For example, a person might say to a co-worker, "Lately, I've thought you were less talkative in team meetings." Then, the person should check to see whether the other perceives the same thing: "Do you feel you've been less talkative?" Finally, it's appropriate to ask the

Everyday Application
Checking Perceptions

To gain skill in perception checking (and all communication behaviors), you need to practice. Try these exercises:

··· Monitor your tendencies to mind read, especially in established relationships in which you feel you know the other person well.
··· The next time you catch yourself mind reading, stop. Instead, tell the other person what you are noticing and invite her or him to explain how she or he perceives what's happening. First, find out whether the other person agrees with you about what you noticed. Second, if the two of you agree, find out how the other person interprets and evaluates the issue.
··· Engage in perception checking for 2 or 3 days so that you have lots of chances to see what happens. When you're done, reflect on the number of times your mind reading was inaccurate.
··· How did perception checking affect interaction with friends, co-workers, and romantic partners? Did you find out things you wouldn't have known if you'd engaged in mind reading?

To examine some of the perception mistakes we can make and to test the guidelines for making more accurate perceptions, complete *Student Companion: Activity 3.4.*

other person to explain her or his behavior. In the example, the person might ask, "Why do you think you're less talkative?" (If the other person doesn't perceive that she or he is less talkative, the question might be, "Why have you been reading memos and not saying much during our team meetings?")

When checking perceptions, it's important to use a tentative tone rather than a dogmatic or accusatory one. This minimizes defensiveness and encourages good discussion. Just let the other person know you've noticed something and would like him or her to clarify his or her perceptions of what is happening and what it means. To increase your awareness of the influence of language, complete *Student Companion:* Activity 3.1.

DISTINGUISH BETWEEN FACTS AND INFERENCES

Competent interpersonal communication also depends on distinguishing facts from inferences. A fact is an objective statement based on observation. An inference involves an interpretation that goes beyond the facts. For example, suppose that a person is consistently late reporting to work and sometimes dozes off during discussions. Co-workers might think, "That person is lazy and unmotivated." The facts are that the person comes in late and sometimes falls asleep. Defining the person as lazy and unmotivated is an inference that goes beyond the facts. It's possible that the co-worker is tired because he or she has a second job or is taking medication that induces drowsiness.

It's easy to confuse facts and inferences because we sometimes treat the latter as the former. When we say, "That employee is lazy," we've made a statement that sounds factual, and we may then perceive it as factual. To avoid this tendency, substitute more tentative words. For instance, "That employee seems unmotivated" or "That employee may be lazy" are more tentative statements that keep the speaker from treating an inference as a fact. We must make inferences to function in the world. Yet we risk misperceptions and misunderstandings if we don't distinguish our inferences from facts. To increase your skill in distinguishing between facts and inferences, complete Activity 3.2 in the *Student Companion* or online under "Chapter Resources for Chapter 3" on the Everyday Connections website.

GUARD AGAINST THE SELF-SERVING BIAS

Because the self-serving bias can distort perceptions, we need to monitor it carefully. Monitor yourself to see whether you attribute your failures or your adverse

---

Everyday Application
Using Tentative Language

To become more sensitive to our tendencies to confuse facts and inferences, for the next 24 hours, pay attention to the language you use to describe people and interactions. Listen for words such as *is* and *are* that imply factual information. Do you find instances in which tentative language would be more accurate?

Now, extend your observations to other people and the language they use. When you hear others say, "she is," "they are," or "he is," are they really making factual statements, or are they making inferences?

behaviors to factors beyond your control and whether you attribute your accomplishments to your own efforts. The self-serving bias also inclines us to notice what we do and to be less aware of what others do. Obviously, this can affect how we feel about others, as Janet illustrates in her comments.

> **JANET** For years, my husband and I have argued about housework. I am always criticizing him for not doing enough, and I have felt resentful about how much I do. He always says to me that he does a lot, but I just don't notice. After studying the self-serving bias in class, I did an "experiment" at home. I watched him for a week and kept a list of all the things he did. Sure enough, he was—is—doing a lot more than I thought. I never noticed that he sorted laundry or walked the dog four times a day or wiped the kitchen counters after we'd finished fixing dinner. I noticed everything I did but only the big things he did, like vacuuming. I simply wasn't seeing a lot of his contributions to keep our home in order.

Monitoring the self-serving bias also has implications for how we perceive others. Just as we tend to judge ourselves generously, we may also be inclined to judge others too harshly. Monitor your perceptions to see whether you attribute others' successes and admirable actions to external factors beyond their control and their shortcomings and blunders to internal factors they can (should) control. If you do this, substitute more generous explanations for others' behaviors, and notice how that affects your perceptions of them.

GUARD AGAINST THE FUNDAMENTAL ATTRIBUTION ERROR

We've also discussed a second error in interpretation: the fundamental attribution error. This occurs when we overestimate the internal causes of others' undesirable behavior and underestimate the external causes, and when we underestimate the internal causes of our own failings or bad behaviors and overestimate the external causes. We need to guard against this error because it distorts our perceptions of ourselves and others.

To reduce your chances of falling victim to the fundamental attribution error, prompt yourself to look for external causes of others' behaviors that you may not have thought of or appreciated. Instead of assuming that the unwanted behavior reflects another's motives or personality, ask yourself, "What factors in the person's situation might lead to this behavior?" You can ask the converse question to avoid underestimating internal influences on your own undesirable actions. Instead of letting yourself off the hook by explaining a misdeed as caused by circumstances you couldn't control, ask yourself, "What factor inside of me, that is my responsibility, influenced what I did?" Looking for external factors that influence others' communication and internal factors that influence your own communication checks our tendency to make fundamental attribution errors.

MONITOR LABELS

In giving names to our perceptions, we clarify them to ourselves. But just as words crystallize experiences, they can also freeze thought. Once we label our perceptions, we may respond to our own labels rather than to actual phenomena. If this happens, we may communicate in insensitive and inappropriate ways.

Consider this situation. Suppose you get together with five others in a study group, and a student named Andrea monopolizes the whole meeting with her questions and concerns. Leaving the meeting, one person says, "Gee, Andrea is so selfish and immature! I'll never work with her again." Another person responds, "She's not really selfish. She's just insecure about her grades in this course, so she was hyper in the meeting." Chances are that these two people will perceive and treat Andrea differently depending on whether they've labeled her "selfish" or "insecure." Once the two people have labeled Andrea's behavior based on their subjective and partial perceptions, they may act toward Andrea based on their labels.

When we engage in interpersonal communication, we abstract only certain aspects of the total reality around us. Our perceptions are one step away from reality because they are always partial and subjective. We move a second step from reality when we label a perception. We move even farther from the actual reality when we respond not to behaviors or our perceptions of them but instead to the label we impose. This process can be illustrated as a ladder of abstraction (see Figure 3.5), a concept emphasized by one of the first scholars of interpersonal communication (Hayakawa, 1962, 1964).

We should also monitor our labels to adapt our communication to particular people. Competent interpersonal communicators are sensitive to others and their preferences and choose their words accordingly. This is especially important when we are talking with or about identities. Many adult females resent being called *girls* and prefer to be called *women*. Most gays and lesbians reject the label *homosexual*, and they may resent hearing themselves labeled as such. Many people who have

Communication in Everyday Life
The Truth, the Whole Truth, and Nothing but the Truth

Ronnie Bullock was serving a 60-year sentence for kidnapping and raping a woman, when DNA tests revealed that he could not have committed the crime. Like a number of other prisoners, Bullock was convicted largely on the basis of eyewitness testimony. "That's the man; I'll never forget his face" tends to be highly convincing to jurors. The problem is that eyewitness testimony isn't always accurate.

Based on extensive studies, Brian Cutler and Steven Penrod (1995) estimate that eyewitness testimony may have led to the conviction and imprisonment of more than 4,500 innocent people.

Why is eyewitness testimony not always reliable? One reason is that witnesses' perceptions are shaped by the language attorneys use. In one experiment, viewers were shown a film of a traffic accident and then were asked, "How fast were the cars going when they smashed into each other?" Other viewers were asked how fast the cars were going when they "bumped" or "collided." Viewers testified to significantly different speeds depending on which word was used.

Attorneys' language can also influence jurors' perceptions (Feigenson, 2000). In a separate experiment (Trotter, 1975), viewers were shown a film of a traffic accident, after which they filled out a questionnaire that included questions about things that had not actually been in the film. Viewers who were asked, "Did you see the broken headlight?" more frequently testified that they had seen it than did viewers who were asked, "Did you see a broken headlight?" Roy Malpass, a psychologist at the University of Texas, notes another reason for inaccurate eyewitness testimony: selective perception. Research shows that witnesses focus selectively on weapons, a phenomenon scholars call "weapon focus." When perception is riveted on a weapon, it's not focused on the person holding the weapon (Miller, 2000). Thus, recall of that person's appearance may be flawed.

Eyewitness Evidence: A Guide for Law Enforcement (1999), a Department of Justice publication, summarizes research on eyewitness testimony and offers guidelines for improving its reliability. Learn more about eyewitness evidence by going to the Department of Justice's website at http://www.usdoj.gov. Go to "publications and reports," then type "eyewitness evidence" at the search prompt.

disabilities feel that the term *disabled people* suggests that they are disabled as people simply because they have some physical or mental condition. They prefer to the term *person with disabilities* to the term *disabled person* (Braithwaite, 1996).

In 1995, the U.S. Department of Labor surveyed 60,000 households to learn what identity labels different ethnic groups prefer. Not surprisingly, the survey revealed that members of various racial groups do not have uniform preferences. Among blacks, 44% wanted to be called *black*, 28% wanted to be called *African American*, 12% wanted to be called *Afro-American*, and 16% preferred other labels or had no preference. Nearly half of American Indians preferred to be called *American Indian*, yet 37% wanted to be called *Native American*. A majority of Hispanics wanted to be called *Hispanic*, not *Latino* or *Latina*. Whites overwhelmingly preferred to be called *white;* only 3% wanted to be called *European-American* ("Politically correct," 1995).

Is effective, sensitive communication possible when there are no universal guidelines for what to call people? Yes, if we are willing to invest thought and effort in our interactions. We begin by assuming that we may not know how others want to be labeled and that not all members of a group have the same preferences. Just because my friend Marsha wants to be called *black*, I shouldn't assume that others share that preference. It's appropriate to ask others how they identify themselves. Asking shows that we care about their preferences and want

to respect them. This is the heart of person-centered communication. To enhance your awareness of person-centered communication and the arbitrariness of categories societies use to define people, complete *Student Companion: Activity 3.3.*

Perceiving accurately is neither magic nor an ability that some people naturally possess. Instead, it is a communication skill that can be developed and practiced. Following the seven guidelines we have discussed will allow you to perceive more carefully and more accurately in interpersonal communication.

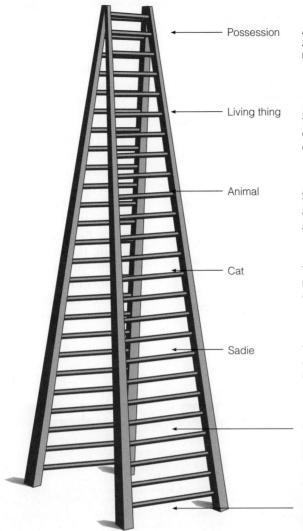

Possession — A very abstract way of describing the particular cat Sadie. At this level of abstraction, we've left out almost all references to the features of the specific cat.

Living thing — *Living thing* is an even more abstract term than *animal*. This label calls attention to what Sadie has in common with all living phenomena but fails to specify how she differs from dogs, people, trees, or flowers.

Animal — At this level of abstraction, the label is even more general. The word *animal* recognizes what Sadie has in common with all other animals but fails to note what is distinctive about her or even her species.

Cat — This species label abstracts what is common to all members of the species known as cats. Thus, it is a more abstract, or less specific, designation of Sadie.

Sadie — The name we give to the particular cat. The name captures only some of the qualities that we perceive in her and obscures other features of her that we could notice.

The cat Sadie as we perceive her. Out of the totality that she is, we abstract only certain features that we identify as Sadie.

The chemical, biological, and physical creature that is Sadie has specific qualities and makeup that cannot be fully appreciated by the human eye.

FIGURE 3.5
The Ladder of Abstraction

Case Study: Continuing the Conversation

The following conversation is featured at the Everyday Connections website under "Chapter Resources for Chapter 3." Click on the link "College Success" in the left-hand menu to launch the video and audio scenario scripted below.

Your friend Jim tells you about a problem he's having with his par-

ents. According to Jim, his parents have unrealistic expectations of him. He tends to be an average student, usually making Cs, a few Bs, and an occasional D in his courses. His parents are angry that his grades aren't better.

Jim tells you that, when he went home last month, his father said this:

Jason Harris/© 2001 Wadsworth

Jim's father: I'm not paying for you to go to school so you can party with your friends. I paid my own way and still made Phi Beta Kappa. You have a free ride, and you're still just pulling Cs. You just have to study harder.

Jim: I mean, I like to hang out with my friends, but that's got nothing to do with my grades. My dad's this brilliant guy, I mean, he just cruised through college, he thinks it's easy. I don't know how it was back then, but all my classes are hard. I mean, no matter how much studying I do I'm not gonna get all As. What should I do? I mean, how do I convince them that I'm doing everything I can?

1. Both Jim and his parents make attributions to

explain his grades. Describe the dimensions of Jim's attributions and those of his parents.

2. How might you assess the accuracy of Jim's attributions? What questions could you ask him to help you decide whether his perceptions are well-founded or biased?

3. What constructs, prototypes, and scripts seem to operate in how Jim and his parents think about college life and being a student?

4. What could you say to Jim to help him and his parents reach a shared perspective on his academic work?

You can critique and analyze this encounter according to the principles you learned in this chapter by responding to the questions included under "Conversation Analysis" at the website. By clicking on the "Submit" button at the end of the form, you can compare your work to my suggested responses. Let's continue the discussion online!

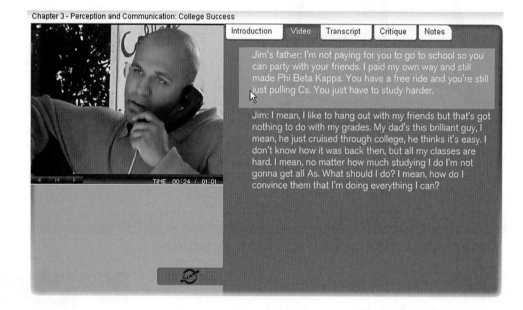

Chapter Summary

In this chapter, we've explored human perception, a process that involves selecting, organizing, and interpreting experiences. These three processes are not separate in practice; instead, they interact such that each one affects the others. What we selectively notice affects what we interpret and evaluate. At the same time, our interpretations become a lens that influences what we notice in the world around us. Selection, interpretation, and evaluation interact continuously in the process of perception.

We have seen that perception is influenced by many factors. Our sensory capacities and our physiological condition affect what we notice and how astutely we recognize stimuli around us. In addition, our cultural backgrounds and standpoints in society shape how we see and interact with the world. Social roles, cognitive abilities, and who we are also influence perception. Thus, interpersonal perceptions reflect both what is inside of us and what is outside of us.

Understanding how perception works provides a foundation for improving our perceptual capacities. We discussed seven guidelines for improving the accuracy of perceptions. First, realize that all perceptions are subjective and partial, so there is no absolutely correct or best understanding of a situation or a person. Second, because people perceive differently, we should avoid mind reading or assuming that we know what others perceive or what their actions mean. Third, it's a good idea to check perceptions, which involves stating how you perceive something and asking how another person does.

A fourth guideline is to distinguish facts from inferences. Avoiding the self-serving bias is also important because it can lead us to perceive ourselves too charitably and to perceive others too harshly. We should also guard against the fundamental attribution error, which can undermine the accuracy of our explanations of our own and others' communication. Finally, it's important to monitor the labels we use. This involves awareness that our labels reflect our perceptions of phenomena, and sensitivity to the language others prefer, especially when we describe their identities. Just as we can't see how to solve the nine dots problem if we consider the dots a square, so we cannot see aspects of ourselves and others when our labels limit our perceptions. Here is one solution to the nine dot problem on page 73.

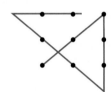

Everyday Connections Online

Now that you've read Chapter 3, go to the Everyday Connections premium website at academic.cengage.com/communication/woodinterpersonal5plus for quick access to the electronic study resources that accompany this text. The website gives you access to the "Continuing the Conversation" video scenario and questions featured in this chapter, the InfoTrac College Edition, maintained and updated web links, and the study aids for this chapter, including a digital glossary, review quizzes, and the chapter activities. For more information about this text's electronic learning resources, consult the **1pass card** that came with each new copy of this book, or visit academic.cengage.com/communication/woodinterpersonal5.

Key Concepts

Audio flash cards of the following key terms are available on the Everyday Connections website. Use the flash cards to improve your pronunciation of text vocabulary.

attribution	fundamental attribution	perception	standpoint
cognitive complexity	error	personal construct	stereotype
constructivism	implicit personality theory	prototype	
culture	interpretation	script	
empathy	mind reading	self-serving bias	

For Further Thought and Discussion

1. To understand how your standpoint influences your perceptions, visit a social group that is different from your own. If you are white, you might attend services at a black church or go to a public meeting of Native Americans on your campus. If you are Christian, you could go to a Jewish synagogue or a Buddhist temple. In the unfamiliar setting, what stands out to you? What verbal and nonverbal communications do you notice? Do they stand out because they are not present in your usual settings? What does your standpoint highlight and obscure?

2. Think of two situations, one in which you perceive that the majority of people are like you (same sex, race, sexual orientation, age) and one in which you perceive that you are a minority. How does your sense of being a majority or minority influence your perceptions of the others present?

3. Identify an example of the self-serving bias in your interpersonal perceptions. Describe how you explained your own behavior and and that of others. Then, revise your explanation in such a way that the self-serving bias is eliminated.

4. Identify an example of the fundamental attribution error in your interpersonal perceptions. Describe how you explained your own behavior and that of others. Then, revise your explanation in such a way that it no longer reflects the fundamental attribution error.

5. Use your InfoTrac College Edition to read David De-Cremer's 2000 article, "Effect of Group Identification on the Use of Attributions," published in the *Journal of Social Psychology*. Describe what DeCremer means by the "group-serving bias" and who is most likely to have it. Does DeCremer's finding of a group-serving bias fit your personal experiences?

6. Conduct a survey to find out how students on your campus prefer to define their identities. Ask blacks whether they prefer *black, African American, Afro-American,* or another label. Ask whites how they identify their race. Ask Hispanic students what term they use to describe their ethnicity. Compare your findings to those of the U.S. Department of Labor discussed on page 96. Do students on your campus reflect national preferences?

7. Use the ladder of abstraction to describe the relationships between perception, communication, and action in one interpersonal encounter in your life. First, describe the total situation as fully as you can (your descriptions won't be absolutely complete—that's impossible). Next, describe the behaviors and environmental cues you noticed. Then, identify the way you labeled what was happening and others who were present. Finally, describe how you acted in the situation. Now, consider alternative selective perceptions you might have made and how they might have influenced your labels and actions.

The World of Words

"The limits of my language mean the limits of my world."

Ludwig Wittgenstein

© Jeff Greenberg/The Image Works

n Poland in the 1980s, the trade union Solidarity was born. The birth was not a dramatic event. There were no fireworks. There was no grand announcement of a powerful new union. Instead, the union grew out of words—simple, face-to-face conversations among ten or so workers in a Gdansk shipyard. They talked with each other about wanting freedom from oppressive conditions, about the need for change. Then, this handful of individuals talked with other workers and others and others. Within just a few months, the Solidarity trade union had more than 9 million members (Wheatley, 2002). Language is powerful. It can create enormous changes in all spheres of life—personal, interpersonal, professional, social, and political.

The human world is a world of words and meanings. Just as weavers intertwine individual threads together to create fabric, so do we weave words together to create meaning in our lives. We use words to express ourselves and to give meaning to our identities, relationships, and activities. This chapter focuses on the verbal dimension of communication and its impact on our lives. We begin by defining symbols and symbolic abilities. Next, we explore different communication communities to appreciate differences in how distinct social groups use language. We close the chapter by discussing guidelines for effective verbal communication.

The Symbolic Nature of Language

Symbols are arbitrary, ambiguous, abstract representations of other phenomena. For instance, your name is a symbol that represents you. *House* is a symbol that stands for a particular kind of building. *Love* is a symbol that represents certain intense feelings. All language is symbolic, but not all symbols are language. Art, music, and much nonverbal behavior are symbolic representations of feelings, thoughts, and experiences. To better understand symbols, we'll consider three characteristics of symbols: arbitrariness, ambiguity, and abstraction. (See Figure 4.1.)

LANGUAGE IS ARBITRARY

Language is **arbitrary,** which means that words are not intrinsically connected to what they represent. For instance, the word *book* has no necessary or natural connection to what you are reading now. All our symbols are arbitrary because we could easily use other symbols as long as we all agreed on their meanings. Certain words seem right because members of a particular society or social group agree to use them in particular ways, but they have no natural correspondence with their referents. The arbitrary nature of language becomes obvious—sometimes humorously so—when we discover that our words don't mean the same thing in another culture. The manufacturer of Dr. Pepper learned this lesson when marketing the soft drink didn't work in the United Kingdom. There, "I'm a pepper" means "I'm a prostitute" (Leaper, 1999).

Because language is arbitrary, the meanings of words can change over time. In other words, language is dynamic. In the 1950s, *gay* meant "lighthearted" and "merry"; today it is generally understood to refer to homosexuals. The words *geek* and *nerd* used to be insults, but today they often convey admiration of someone's technological expertise. Our language also changes as we invent new words. Some African Americans began using *disrespect* as a verb to describe behaviors that demean someone. Now, the term *disrespect* and its abbreviated form, *dis*, are widely used. In the 1996 Random House *College Dictionary*, *dis* appears, along with the definition "to show disrespect for; affront; disparage; belittle" (Kilpatrick, 1996).

Qualities of
Symbols

Arbitrariness
Ambiguity
Abstraction

FIGURE 4.1

Symbols

Language is **ambiguous** because the meanings of words aren't clear-cut or fixed. To one person, a *good friend* is someone to hang out with; to another, it is someone to confide in. The term *affordable clothes* means different things to people who earn the minimum wage and to people who are affluent. The words are the same, but their meaning varies according to people's unique experiences and circumstances.

Although words don't mean exactly the same thing to everyone, within a culture many symbols have an agreed-upon range of meanings. Thus, all of us know that dogs are four-footed creatures, but *dog* has personal meanings for each of us that are based on dogs we have known and our experiences with them. In learning language, we learn not only words but also the meanings and values attributed to them by our society. In the United States, most children learn not only that dogs are four-footed creatures but also that they are friends, members of the family, or useful in guarding, herding, and so forth. In some other countries, children learn that dogs are four-footed creatures that can be killed and eaten. We tend to assume that words mean the same thing to others that they do to us. Because symbols are ambiguous, however, there is no guarantee that people will agree on meanings.

RON A while ago, I told my girlfriend I needed more independence. She got upset because she thought I didn't love her anymore and was pulling away. All I meant was that I need some time with the guys and some for just myself. She said that the last time a guy said he wanted more independence, she found out he was dating other girls.

Ambiguous language is a common problem between friends and romantic partners (Beck, 1988). A wife asks her husband to be more sensitive, but she and he have different understandings of what "being more sensitive" means. Martina tells her friend that he's not being attentive, meaning that she wants him to listen more closely to what she says. However, he infers that she wants him to call more often and open doors for her.

Ambiguity in language can also create confusion in the workplace. When the CEO of a company tells employees to restrict computer usage to their jobs, the CEO means employees should not use their computers to chat with family and friends. However, employees interpret the message as telling them not to send or respond to e-mails about company issues that are outside their specific job descriptions. Similarly, telling a supervisor that you'd appreciate feedback on your job performance doesn't identify the kind of feedback you want or which aspects of your job performance you want your supervisor to assess. It would be more effective to say, "I would like you to give me your assessment of the thoroughness of my written reports."

Communication in Everyday Life
Technospeak

TECHNOLOGY

In 1991, Random House published the first *Computer and Internet Dictionary*. In 1999, the third edition appeared, and it includes 3,000 new terms. Editor Philip Margolis (1999) says it's almost impossible to keep up with all the new words that are invented to refer to our computerized lives. New words spawned to refer to computer-related activities include *blog, cybering, cyberspace, cybernaut, cyperpunk, chat room, fan site, hyperlink, URL, instant message, real-time quote, real-time chat, netiquette,* and *netlet.*

As technology races ahead, no doubt more new words will enter the language. Yet, not all will survive the test of time. Mechanical transit invigorated the English language in the early 20th century much as the computer is doing today. New means of transit gave us some words that have survived, such as *dashboard, speedometer,* and *carsick.* Yet many words that were coined in response to new modes of transportation did not endure; *aerodrome* was replaced by *airport,* for example (Ayto, 1999).

James Kilpatrick (2000), who studies and writes about the use of English, notes that "the English language functions in the fashion of a great tree. It sheds dead limbs, and it produces green shoots" (p. 11A).

LARRY, I'D LIKE YOU TO MEET SUSAN, MY...ERRR...MATE... UHHH...MY COMPANION.... YOU KNOW, MY PARTNER... ACTUALLY, MY CLOSEST FRIEND.... ERRR, UH, MY LOVER...MY SOULMATE ...MY SIGNIFICANT OTHER, IF YOU WILL...

OH, YOU'RE AN ITEM? GOING TOGETHER? A COUPLE? ROMANTICALLY INVOLVED? A MONOGAMOUS PAIR? DOMESTIC PARTNERS? IS THAT IT?

Reprinted with permission of John Grimes. © John Grimes. grimescartoons.com.

LANGUAGE IS ABSTRACT

Finally, language is **abstract,** which means that it is not concrete or tangible. Words stand for ideas, people, events, objects, feelings, and so forth, but they are not the things they represent. In Chapter 3, we discussed the process of abstraction, whereby we move farther and farther away from concrete reality. As our symbols become increasingly abstract, the potential for confusion mushrooms. One way this happens is through overgeneralization. Couple counselor Aaron Beck (1988) reports that overly general language distorts how partners think about a relationship. They may make broad, negative statements, such as, "You always interrupt me." In most cases, such statements are overgeneralizations and hence not accurate. Yet, by symbolizing experience this way, partners frame how they think about it.

Researchers have shown that we are more likely to recall behaviors that are consistent with our labels for people than behaviors that are inconsistent (Fincham & Bradbury, 1987). When we say that a friend is always insensitive, we cue ourselves to remember all the occasions in which the friend was insensitive and to overlook times when she or he was sensitive. When we call a co-worker uncooperative, we're likely to notice uncooperative behaviors rather than cooperative ones.

We can lessen the potential for misunderstanding by using specific language. It's clearer to say, "I wish you wouldn't interrupt when I'm talking" than to say, "Don't be so dominating." It's clearer to say, "On Fridays, men don't need to wear ties, and women don't need to wear heels" than to say, "Casual dress is okay on Fridays."

Everyday Application
Communicating Clearly

To express yourself clearly, it's important to learn to translate ambiguous words into concrete language. Practice translating with the statements below.

Example:

Ambiguous language: You are rude.
Clear language: I don't like it when you interrupt me.

Ambiguous Language	Clear Language
You're conceited.	_____
I want more freedom.	_____
Casual dress is okay on Fridays.	_____
I want us to be closer.	_____
Your work is sloppy.	_____

For an additional activity on recognizing ambiguity in verbal language, complete Activity 4.3 in the *Student Companion* or online under "Chapter Resources for Chapter 4" at the Everyday Connections website.

Principles of Verbal Communication

We've seen that language is arbitrary and ambiguous and that words are abstract representations of other phenomena. We're now ready to explore how language works. We'll discuss four principles of verbal communication.

LANGUAGE AND CULTURE REFLECT EACH OTHER

Communication reflects cultural values and perspectives. It also creates or reproduces culture by naming and normalizing practices valued by the culture. The words of a language reflect what the mainstream in a culture regards as worth naming. The dominant values of a culture are reflected in calendars, in which important days are named. Look at a calendar. Are Christmas, Thanksgiving, New Year's Day, and Passover recognized? Are Kwanzaa, Saka, Seleicodae, Elderly Day, and Ramadan on the calendar? Most Western calendars reflect the Judeo-Christian heritage of the mainstream culture.

To understand further how cultural values are woven into language, consider the cultural values that adages express. What is meant by the common American saying, "Every man for himself"? Does it reflect the idea that men, and not women, are the standard? Does it reflect individualism as a value? What is meant by "The early bird gets the worm"?

Different values are expressed in adages from other cultures. What values are expressed in the Mexican proverb, "He who lives a hurried life will soon die"? How is this view of time different from dominant views of time in the United States? In Africa, two popular adages are "The child has no owner" and "It takes a whole village to raise a child," and in China a common saying is "No need to know the person, only the family" (Samovar & Porter, 2000). A Japanese adage states that "it is the nail that sticks out that gets hammered down" (Gudykunst & Lee, 2002). What values are expressed by these sayings? How are they different from mainstream Western values and the language that embodies them?

The power of naming is dramatically clear in the case of Rose Marie Augustine, a resident of Tucson, Arizona. For years, Augustine had tried to get local officials to recognize that polluted wells in her community were making residents ill, but officials refused to acknowledge that there was a problem. At a meeting of environmentalists, Augustine heard language that named the problem. She said, "I heard words like 'economic blackmail,' 'environmental racism.' Somebody put words, names, on what our community was experiencing" (in Cox, in press).

Many Asian languages include specific words to describe numerous particular relationships, such as "my grandfather's sister," "my mother's uncle," or "my youngest son." These words reflect traditional Asian cultures' emphasis on family relationships (Ferrante, 1995). The English

Communication in Everyday Life
Our Multicultural Language

Although the term *multicultural* has only recently come into popular usage, our society and our language have always been multicultural (Carnes, 1994). Do you know the cultural origins of the following everyday words?

1. brocade	6. silk
2. chocolate	7. skunk
3. cotton	8. gingham
4. klutz	9. noodle
5. khaki	10. zombie

Answers: 1, Spanish; 2, Nahuatl (Native American); 3, Arabic; 4, Yiddish; 5, Hindi; 6, Greek; 7, Algonquian (Native American); 8, Malay; 9, German; 10, Congo.

language has far fewer words to represent specific kinship bonds, which suggests that Western culture places less priority on ties beyond those in the immediate family.

Imagine this scenario: An American businessman travels to Japan to negotiate a deal. After the American has made his proposal, the Japanese businessman responds, "I see you have put much thought into this idea." Assuming that this indicates the Japanese executive is pleased with the proposal, the American says, "Then, shall we sign the contract and be on our way?" The Japanese executive replies, "I think we have much to talk about on your good proposal." What's happening here? If you are unfamiliar with Japanese communication styles, you might assume that the Japanese businessman is being evasive or is not putting his cards on the table. However, Japanese culture prioritizes cooperation, politeness, and not causing others to lose face. The Japanese businessman's communication reflects the rules of his speech community that require him not to say "no" directly to another person (Cathcart & Cathcart, 1997; Dolan & Worden, 1992).

Scholars of language and culture maintain that the language we learn shapes how we categorize the world and even how we perceive and think about our world (Fantini, 1991; Hakuta, 1986; Lim, 2002). For example, Hopi Indians have one word for "water in open space" and another word for "water in a container." The English language has only the one noun, *water*. In the United States, we perceive saying good-bye to guests as a single event. In contrast, in Japan saying good-bye is a process. Hosts and guests typically say good-bye in the living room and again at the front door. Guests walk a distance from the house, then turn and wave good-bye to the hosts, who are waiting at their gate or door to wave the third good-bye.

Communication also changes cultures, as is clear from the example of the Solidarity trade union that opened this chapter. A primary way in which communication changes cultural values and perspectives is by naming things in ways that alter understandings. For example, the term *date rape* was coined in the late 1980s. Although probably many women had been forced to have sex with their dates before that

Communication in Everyday Life
The Whorf–Sapir View of Language

Linguist Benjamin Whorf and anthropologist Edwin Sapir (Whorf, 1956) advanced the theory of **linguistic determinism,** which states that language determines what we can perceive and think (Hoijer, 1994). According to this theory, we cannot perceive or think about things for which we don't have words. Initially, this theory was widely accepted. Examples from languages of non-Western cultures were used to support the theory. For instance, the language of the Hopi Indians makes no distinction between stationary objects and moving processes, whereas English uses nouns and verbs, respectively. The language that Hopi Indians learn and use teaches them to perceive people and events as highly processual rather than static.

Over time, however, linguistic determinism has been discredited. Numerous examples show that members of a culture can perceive phenomena that have no specific names. For example, Geoff Nunberg (2003) notes that, although Arabic does not have a single word for *compromise,* the language has many phrases that capture the idea of compromise.

Although linguistic determinism is no longer accepted by most scholars, there is acceptance of the less extreme claim that language reflects and shapes perception and thought. This notion helps us understand why some words and phrases can't be translated into other languages without losing meaning. *Tsuris* is a Yiddish word that is best translated as "trouble upon trouble." For instance, *tsuris* might describe a homeowner who experiences drenching rains followed by the breaking of a dam that floods the property. The language of the Muskogee–Creek tribe includes a word that designates the unique kind of love between parents and children (Seay, 2004), and Pacific Islanders' language, which is now disappearing, includes names for many species of fish that are unnamed in the languages of cultures less dependent on fish for survival (Nettle & Romaine (2000).

time, until the term was coined there was no way to describe such an occurrence as a violent and criminal act (Wood, 1992b). Cultural understandings of other sexual activities have been similarly reformed by the coining of terms such as *sexual harassment* and *marital rape*, both of which characterize activities previously perceived as acceptable. As society has become more aware and accepting of gay and lesbian relationships, the term *domestic partnership* has gained acceptance.

> **MARY**   It was 15 years ago, when I was just starting college, that a professor sexually harassed me, only I didn't know what to call it then. I felt guilty, like maybe I'd done something to encourage him, or I felt maybe I was overreacting to his kissing and touching me. But after the Clarence Thomas–Anita Hill hearings in 1991, I had a name for what happened—a name that said he was wrong, not me.

Language is a primary tool of social movements in their efforts to change cultural life and meanings. In the 1960s, the civil rights movement in the United States relied on communication to transform public laws and, more gradually, public views of blacks. Powerful speakers, such as the Reverend Martin Luther King Jr. and Malcolm X, praised black Americans' heritage and identity. Language has also been influential in altering social views of persons with disabilities. Whereas *disabled person* was a commonly accepted phrase for many years, most people are now aware that this label can offend, and they know that the preferred phrase is *person with a disability* (Braithwaite, 1996). The gay rights movement has increased awareness of multiple sexual orientations by increasing use of words such as *transsexual* and *transgender*. Social views of deaf people have also been altered in recent times. The term *deaf*, a medical condition, is distinguished from *Deaf*, a culture with rich linguistic resources (Carl, 1998).

THE MEANINGS OF LANGUAGE ARE SUBJECTIVE

© Grant LeDuc

Because symbols are abstract, ambiguous, and arbitrary, the meanings of words are never self-evident or absolute. Instead, we construct meanings in the process of interacting with others and through dialogues we carry on in our own heads (Duck, 1994a, 1994b; Shotter, 1993). The process of constructing meaning is itself symbolic because we rely on words to think about what words and other things mean.

For humans, words are layered with multiple meanings. Although we're usually not conscious of the effort we invest to interpret words, we continuously engage in the process of constructing meanings. When somebody says, "Get lost," you have to think about the comment and the person who made it to decide whether it's an insult, friendly needling, or a demand that you leave. You might take it as a joke from a friend but as criticism from an employer. What the words mean to you also depends on your self-esteem and previous experiences. People who are secure and have high self-esteem are not as likely to be hurt as people who have less self-confidence. *Student Companion:* Activity 4.2.

Verbal communication is patterned by unspoken but broadly understood rules (Argyle & Henderson, 1985; Schiminoff, 1980). **Communication rules** are shared understandings of what communication means and what kinds of communication are appropriate in particular situations. For example, we understand that people take turns speaking, that flaming can get us kicked out of some chat rooms, and that we should speak softly in libraries. In the course of interacting with our families and others, we unconsciously absorb rules that guide how we communicate and how we interpret others' communication. According to Judi Miller (1993), children begin to understand and follow communication rules as early as 1 to 2 years of age.

Two kinds of rules govern communication (Cronen, Pearce, & Snavely, 1979; Pearce, Cronen, & Conklin, 1979). **Regulative rules** regulate interaction by specifying when, how, where, and with whom to talk about certain things. For instance, Westerners know not to interrupt when someone else is speaking in a formal setting, but in more casual situations, interruptions may be appropriate. In other cultures, there are strong rules against interrupting in any context. Some families have a rule that people cannot argue at the dinner table. Families also teach us rules about how to communicate in conflict situations (Honeycutt, Woods, & Fontenot, 1993; Jones & Gallois, 1989; Yerby, Buerkel-Rothfuss, & Bochner, 1990). Regulative rules vary across cultures and social groups, so what is acceptable in one context may be regarded as inappropriate elsewhere.

> **YUMIKO** I try to teach my children to follow the customs of my native Japan, but they are learning to be American. I scold my daughter, who is 7 this year, for talking loudly and speaking when she has not been addressed, but she tells me all the other kids talk loudly and talk when they wish to talk. I tell her it is not polite to look directly at others, but she says everyone looks at others here. She communicates as an American, not a Japanese.

Constitutive rules define what communication means by specifying how to count, or interpret, specific kinds of communication. We learn what counts as respect (paying attention), friendliness (smiles or smiley emoticons in online communication), affection (kisses, hugs), and professionalism (dressing well, working overtime). We also learn what communication is expected if we want to be perceived as a good friend (showing support, being loyal), a responsible employee (meeting deadlines, making confident oral presentations), and a desirable romantic partner (showing respect and trust, being faithful, sharing confidences). We learn constitutive and regulative rules from particular others and the generalized other. Like regulative rules, constitutive rules are shaped by cultures. Among traditional Arabs, smelling another person's cheeks counts as a customary form of greeting (Almany & Alwan, 1982).

Communication rules tell us when to speak, what to say, and how to interpret others' communication. Social interactions, which involve I–It and I–You relationships, tend to adhere to rules that are widely shared in our society. Interaction between intimates also follows

Communication in Everyday Life
Chat Room Etiquette

TECHNOLOGY

What are the rules and norms for communicating online? At the moment, that's uncharted water. Many people think chat rooms and discussion newsgroups are uncivil: One person can flame another with angry, demeaning insults. People can ignore others and even block their communication. Another kind of problem is that people can misrepresent themselves by saying they are Asian when they are Hispanic, male when they are female, and so forth. Who regulates what is allowable on the Internet?

To think further about rules for communicating online, go to http://ga.essortment.com/chatroomsetiqu_rixx.htm.

rules, but intimates often negotiate private rules to guide how they communicate and what certain things mean (Beck, 1988; Fitzpatrick, 1988; Wood, 1982, 2000a).

It's important to understand that we don't have to be aware of communication rules to follow them. For the most part, we're not conscious of the rules that guide how, when, where, and with whom we communicate about various things. We may not realize we have rules until one is broken, and we become aware that we had an expectation. A study by Victoria DeFrancisco (1991) revealed a clear pattern between spouses, in which husbands interrupted wives and were unresponsive to topics wives initiated. Both husbands and wives were unaware of the rules, but their communication nonetheless sustained the pattern. Becoming aware of communication rules empowers you to change those that don't promote good interaction.

© David Young-Wolff/PhotoEdit

EMILY My boyfriend and I had this really frustrating pattern about planning what to do. He'd say, "What do you want to do this weekend?" And I'd say, "I don't know. What do you want to do?" Then, he'd suggest two or three things and ask me which of them sounded good. I would say they were all fine with me, even if they weren't. And this would keep on forever. Both of us had a rule not to impose on the other, and it kept us from stating our preferences, so we just went in circles about any decision. Well, two weekends ago, I talked to him about rules, and he agreed we had one that was frustrating. So we invented a new rule that says each of us has to state what we want to do, but the other has to say if that is not okay. It's a lot less frustrating to figure out what we want to do since we agreed on this rule.

Everyday Application
Communication Rules

Think about the regulative and constitutive rules you follow in your communication. For each item, identify two rules you have learned.

After you've identified your rules, talk with others in your class about the rules they follow. Are there commonalities among your rules that reflect broad cultural norms? What explains differences in people's rules? *Student Companion:* Activity 4.6 provides an additional opportunity to increase your awareness of communication rules.

REGULATIVE RULES

List rules that regulate how you

- Talk with elders
- Interact at dinner time
- Have first exchanges in the morning
- Respond to criticism from your supervisor
- Greet casual friends on campus
- Talk with professors

CONSTITUTIVE RULES

How do you communicate to show

- Respect
- Love
- Disrespect
- Support
- Professional ambition
- Contempt

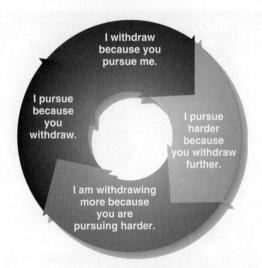

FIGURE 4.2

The Demand-Withdraw Pattern

In writing, we use commas, periods, and semicolons to define where ideas stop and start and where pauses are needed. Similarly, in interpersonal communication, **punctuation** defines beginnings and endings of interaction episodes (Watzlawick, Beavin, & Jackson, 1967). *Student Companion: Activity 4.5.*

To determine what communication means, we must define when interaction began or who started it. When we don't agree on punctuation, problems may arise. If you've ever heard children arguing about who started a fight, you understand the importance of punctuation.

A common instance of conflicting punctuation is the demand–withdraw pattern (Bergner & Bergner, 1990; Caughlin & Vangelisti, 2000; Christensen & Heavey, 1990; James, 1989). In this pattern, one person tries to create closeness with personal talk, and the other strives to maintain autonomy by avoiding intimate discussion (Figure 4.2). The more the first person pushes for personal talk ("Tell me what's going on in your life"), the further the second withdraws ("There's nothing to tell"). Each partner punctuates interaction as starting with the other's behavior. Thus, the demander thinks, "I pursue because you withdraw," and the withdrawer thinks, "I withdraw because you pursue."

In 2005, Harry Wegner conducted a study to learn how the demand–withdraw pattern affects conflict between spouses. He found that husbands and wives both feel less confirmed when their partners withdraw from conflict. They feel less understood by partners, and feeling understood is directly related to marital satisfaction, especially for wives.

There is no objectively correct punctuation. Punctuation depends on subjective perceptions. When communicators don't agree on punctuation, they don't share meanings for what is happening between them. To break out of unconstructive cycles such as demand–withdraw, communicators need to realize that they may punctuate differently and should discuss how each of them experiences the pattern.

> **HAL** Punctuation helps me understand what happens with me and my girlfriend a lot of times. Sometimes, when we first get together, she's all steamed, and I can't figure out why. I'm like, what's going on? How can you be mad at me when we haven't even started talking? But she's steamed about something that happened the night before or even longer ago. For me, whatever argument we might have had is over—it ended when we separated the last time. But for her, it may not be over—we're still in that episode.

Everyday Application
Punctuating Interaction

The next time you and another person get into an unproductive cycle, stop and discuss how each of you punctuates interaction.
1. What do you define as the start of interaction?
2. What does the other person define as the beginning?
3. What happens when you learn about each other's punctuation? How does this affect understanding between you?

The meaning of verbal communication arises out of cultural teachings, subjective interpretations, communication rules, and punctuation. These four principles highlight the creativity involved in constructing meaning. We're now ready to probe how verbal communication affects us and our relationships.

Symbolic
Abilities

Definition
Evaluation
Organization
Hypothetical thought
Self-reflection

Symbolic Abilities

FIGURE 4.3
Symbolic Abilities

Our ability to use symbols allows us to live in a world of ideas and meanings. Instead of just reacting to our concrete environments, we think about them and sometimes transform them. Philosophers of language have identified five ways symbolic abilities affect our lives (Cassirer, 1944; Langer, 1953, 1979). As we discuss each one, think about how you can realize the constructive power of language and minimize the problems it can cause. (See Figure 4.3.)

LANGUAGE DEFINES

The most basic symbolic ability is definition. We use symbols to define experiences, people, relationships, feelings, and thoughts. As we saw in Chapter 3, the definitions we impose shape what things mean to us.

Language Shapes Perceptions   When we label someone, we focus attention on particular aspects of that person and her or his activities, and we neglect or overlook other aspects of the person. We might define a person as an environmentalist, a teacher, a gourmet cook, our boss, or a father. Each definition directs our attention to certain aspects of the person. We might talk with the environmentalist about wilderness legislation, discuss class assignments with the teacher, swap recipes with the chef, restrict ourselves to work topics with the boss, and exchange stories about children with the father. If we define someone as an Asian American or a Latina, then that may be all we notice about the person, although there are many other aspects. We tend to perceive and interact with people according to how we define them.

The impact of labels is evident in language about AIDS (Best, 1989). Calling it a "moral problem" defines people with AIDS as sinful and suggests that the solution is to change behavior. By contrast, calling AIDS a "health problem" defines people as having a disease that should be managed through medical care.

Language Can Totalize   Totalizing occurs when we respond to a person as if one label (one we have chosen or accepted from others) totally represented who he or she is. We fix on one symbol to define someone and fail to recognize many other aspects of that person. Some people totalize gay men and lesbians as if sexual orientation were the only facet of their identities. Yet, we don't totalize heterosexuals on the basis of their sexuality. Totalizing is not the same as stereotyping. When we stereotype someone, we define him or her in terms of characteristics of a group. When we totalize others, we negate most of who they are by focusing on a single aspect of their identity.

> **JAMAL**   I know all about totalizing. A lot of people relate to me as black, like that's all I am. Sometimes in classes, teachers ask me to explain the "African American perspective" on something, but they don't ask me to explain my perspective as a premed major or a working student. I am an African American, but that's not all I am.

Julia T. Wood

Language Affects Relationships The symbols we use to define experiences in our relationships affect how we think and feel about those relationships. My colleagues and I asked romantic couples how they defined differences between themselves (Wood, Dendy, Dordek, Germany, & Varallo, 1994). We found that some people define differences as positive forces that energize a relationship and keep it interesting. Others defined differences as problems or barriers to closeness. There was a direct connection between how partners defined differences and how they dealt with them. Partners who viewed differences as constructive approached them with curiosity, interest, and a hope for growth through discussion. On the other hand, partners who labeled differences as problems tended to deny differences and to avoid talking about them.

The language we use to think about relationships affects what happens in them. People who consistently use negative labels to describe their relationships heighten awareness of what they don't like (Cloven & Roloff, 1991). It's also been shown that partners who focus on good facets of their relationships are more conscious of virtues in partners and relationships and less bothered by imperfections (Bradbury & Fincham, 1990; Fletcher & Fincham, 1991; Seligman, 2002; Duck & Wood, in press). This suggests that we might want to reconsider language that overemphasizes problems in relationships.

LANGUAGE EVALUATES

Language isn't neutral or objective. It is laden with values. This is an intrinsic quality of language. It's difficult, if not impossible, to find words that are completely neutral or objective. Thus, the particular words that we use shape our perceptions and those of others.

Language Reflects and Shapes Perceptions We tend to describe people we like with language that accents their good qualities and downplays their flaws. Just the reverse is true of our descriptions of people we don't like. Restaurants use positive words to heighten the attractiveness of menu entrees. A dish described as "tender London broil gently sautéed in natural juices and topped with succulent mushrooms" sounds more appetizing than one described as "cow carcass cooked in blood and topped with fungus grown in compost."

Perhaps you've seen humorous illustrations of how we describe the same behaviors enacted by ourselves, by people we like, and by people we don't like. I am casual; you are messy; she's a slob. I am organized; you are methodical; he is obsessive–compulsive. I am assertive; you are aggressive; she's a bully. These examples reflect our tendency to use language that reflects our values and views.

In recent years, we have become more sensitive to different groups' preferences for names. The term *African American* emphasizes cultural heritage, whereas *black* focuses on skin color. People with roots in Spanish-speaking Caribbean countries usually refer to themselves as Latinas and Latinos, whereas people with roots in Mexico and Central and South America generally define themselves as Hispanic (Glascock, 1998). Designations for homosexuals are currently in transition. The term *homosexual* has negative connotations; even more do words such as *fairy, dyke,* and *faggot.* Some gays and lesbians use the term *sexual orientation* to suggest they didn't choose their sexuality. Others use the term *sexual preference* to indicate that their sexuality is a matter of choice, not genetics.

Communication in Everyday Life
The First Jewish Candidate for Vice President

When Al Gore chose Senator Joe Lieberman as his vice presidential running mate in 2000, the media immediately labeled Lieberman "the first Jew to run for vice president." In the 1960s, media dubbed presidential candidate John Fitzgerald Kennedy "the first Catholic ever to run for president." Kennedy chastised the media for totalizing him that way. He said "I am the Democratic candidate for president, and I happen to be Catholic."

Filmmaker Spike Lee has been totalized as a black filmmaker. Lee says, "I want to be known as a talented young filmmaker. That should be first. But the reality today is that no matter how successful you are, you're black first" (McDowell, 1989, p. 92).

John Hope Franklin is a distinguished historian who has gained national stature for his books on the South. He is sometimes introduced as a man who has written twelve books on black history. Franklin says that, because he is black, many people assume he knows and writes only about blacks. Actually, his books—like the region they describe—are about both whites and blacks (McGurl, 1990).

Language Can Be Loaded **Loaded language** is words that strongly slant perceptions and thus meanings. Terms such as *geezer* and *old fogey* incline us to regard older people with contempt or pity. Alternatives such as *senior citizen* and *older person* reflect more respectful attitudes.

> **MAYNARD** I'm as sensitive as the next guy, but I just can't keep up with what language offends what people anymore. When I was younger, *Negro* was an accepted term, then it was *black,* and now it's *African American.* Sometimes I forget and say *black* or even *Negro,* and I get accused of being racist. It used to be polite to call females *girls,* but now that offends a lot of the women I work with. Just this year, I heard that we aren't supposed to say *blind* or *disabled* anymore; we're supposed to say *visually impaired* and *differently abled.* I just can't keep up.

Many of us probably sympathize with Maynard, who was 54 years old when he took a course with me. It is hard to keep up with changes in language, and it's inevitable that we will occasionally irritate or offend someone unintentionally. Nonetheless, we should try to learn what terms hurt or insult others and avoid using them. It's also advisable for us to tell others when they've referred to us with a term that we don't prefer. As long as we speak assertively but not confrontationally, it's likely that others will respect our ideas.

Language Can Degrade Others Haig Bosmajian is a scholar of communication and ethics. Throughout his career, he has been concerned with the ways in which language is used to degrade and dehumanize others. Bosmajian (1974) notes that how we see ourselves is profoundly influenced by the names we are called. One form of degrading language is **hate speech,** which is language that radically dehumanizes members of particular groups. A few years ago, Brown University student Dennis Hann made national news because of the way he chose to celebrate turning 21. After drinking heavily, Hann went to a central quad on campus and spewed out

Communication in Everyday Life
Reappropriating Language

An interesting communicative phenomenon is the reappropriation of language. This happens when a group reclaims terms used by others to degrade it and treats those terms as positive self-descriptions.

Reappropriation intends to take the sting out of a term that others use pejoratively. Some feminists and women musicians have reappropriated the term *girl* to define themselves and to resist the general connotations of childishness. Some gays have reappropriated the term *queer* and are using it as a positive description of who they are.

Writer Reynolds Price developed cancer of the spine that left him paralyzed. He scoffs at terms such as *differently abled* and *physically challenged* and refers to himself as a "cripple" and others as "temporarily able-bodied."

curse words and epithets, including *niggers, Jews,* and *faggots.* Hann was promptly and permanently expelled from Brown.

Unfortunately, Hann's actions are not an isolated incident. Around the nation, hate speech erupts both on and off campus. Malicious and abusive messages are scrawled on the cars and homes of minority citizens. Graffiti in bathrooms and on public buildings disparages gays, lesbians, and other groups. People post vicious gossip and hateful messages online (Abelson, 2001), and numerous Internet hate groups target children as well as adults (Waltman, 2003). Hate speech has become so prevalent that nine out of ten Americans in a 1996 poll said they thought incivility was a serious problem in the United States (Morris, 1997). Not all hate speech is direct. Often, it is veiled in indirect language. Laura Leets (1999) found that many Asian Americans find indirect racist messages more offensive than direct ones, probably because in traditional Asian cultures people tend to avoid direct criticism and instead convey negative judgments indirectly through nonverbal cues, hints, and so forth.

Language is powerful. It shapes our perceptions and those of others. This implies that each of us has an ethical responsibility to recognize the impact of language and to guard against engaging in uncivil speech ourselves as well as refusing to tolerate it from others.

LANGUAGE ORGANIZES PERCEPTIONS

We use symbols to organize our perceptions. As we saw in Chapter 3, we rely on cognitive schemata to classify and evaluate experiences. How we organize experiences affects what they mean to us. For example, your prototype of a good friend affects how you judge particular friends. When we place someone in the category *friend,* the category influences how we interpret the person and his or her communication. An insult is likely to be viewed as teasing if made by a friend but a call to battle if made by an enemy. The words don't change, but their meaning varies depending on how we organize our perceptions of words and those who speak them.

Language Allows Abstract Thought   The organizational quality of language also allows us to think about abstract concepts, such as justice, integrity, and healthy family life. We use broad concepts to transcend specific, concrete activities and to enter the world of conceptual thought and ideals. Because we think abstractly, we don't have to consider every specific object and experience individually. Instead, we can think in general terms.

Language Can Stereotype   Our capacity to abstract can also distort thinking. A primary way this occurs is through stereotyping, which is thinking in broad generalizations about a whole class of people or experiences. Examples of stereo-types are "sorority women are preppy," "teachers are smart," "jocks are dumb," "feminists hate men," "religious people are kind," and "conflict is bad." Notice that stereotypes can be positive or negative.

Common to all stereotypes is classifying an experience or person based on general perceptions of some category. When we use terms such as *athletes, African Americans, lesbians, men,* and *blue-collar workers,* we may see what members of each group have in common and may not perceive differences between individuals.

Stereotyping is related to totalizing because, when we stereotype someone, we may not perceive other aspects of the person, aspects not represented in the stereo-type. For example, if we stereotype someone as a fraternity man, we may see only what he has in common with other members of fraternities. We may not notice his political stands, individual values, commitment to family, and so forth.

Clearly, we have to generalize. We simply cannot think about everything in our lives as a unique phenomenon. However, stereotypes can blind us to important differences between phenomena we lump together. Thus, it's important to reflect on stereotypes and to stay alert to differences between phenomena we place in any category. We should also remind ourselves that we place others in categories; the categories are our tools. They are not objective descriptions.

LANGUAGE ALLOWS HYPOTHETICAL THOUGHT

Where do you hope to be 5 years from now? What is your fondest memory from childhood? Do you think you'll have an e-mail note from your friend when you go online tonight? To answer these questions, you must think hypothetically, which means thinking about experiences and ideas that are not part of your concrete, present situation. Because we can think hypothetically, we can plan, dream, remember, set goals, consider alternative courses of action, and imagine possibilities.

We Can Think Beyond Immediate, Concrete Situations   Hypothetical thought is possible because we use symbols. When we symbolize, we name ideas so that we can hold them in our minds and reflect on them. We can contemplate things that currently have no real existence, and we can remember ourselves in the past and project ourselves into the future. Our ability to imagine possibilities that do not exist in the moment explains why we can set goals and work toward them (Dixson & Duck, 1993). For example, you've invested many hours studying and writing papers because you imagine yourself as someone with a college degree. The degree is not real now, nor is the self that you will become once you have the degree. Yet, the idea is sufficiently real to motivate you to work hard for many years.

We Live in Three Dimensions of Time   Hypothetical thought also allows us to live in more than just the present moment. We infuse our present lives with knowledge of our histories and plans for our futures. Both past and future affect our experience in the present. In the context of work, we often remember past interactions with a colleague and anticipate future ones, and both of these affect how we communicate in the present.

Close relationships rely on ideas of past and future. One of the strongest "glues" for intimacy is a history of shared experiences (Bellah, Madsen, Sullivan, Swindler, & Tipton, 1985; Bruess & Hoefs, 2006; Wood, 2006). Just knowing that they have weathered rough times in the past helps partners get through trials in the present.

Belief in a future also sustains intimacy. With people we don't expect to see again, we interact differently from the way we interact with people who are continuing parts of our lives. Talking about the future also knits intimates together because it makes real the idea that more lies ahead (Acitelli, 1993; Duck, 1990; Wood, 2006).

> **RACHAEL** During the first week of my freshman year, I went to a mixer and got plowed. I'd never drunk in high school, so I didn't know what alcohol could do to me. I was a mess—throwing up, passing out. The next morning, I hated myself for how I'd been. But in the long run, I think it was good that it happened. Whenever I feel like having more to drink than I should, I just remember what I was like that night and how much I hated myself that way, and that stops me from having anything more to drink.

We Can Foster Personal Growth Thinking hypothetically helps us grow personally. In Chapter 2, we noted that one guideline for improving self-concept is to accept yourself as in process. This requires you to remember who you were at an earlier time, to appreciate progress you've made, and to keep an ideal image of the person you want to become to fuel continued self-improvement. If you want to become more outgoing, you imagine yourself talking easily to others, going to parties, and so forth. If you want to be more effective in presenting ideas to members of your work team, you imagine yourself preparing your ideas, speaking confidently, and responding to questions from colleagues.

> **DUK-KYONG** Sometimes, I get very discouraged that I do not yet know English perfectly and that there is much I still do not understand about customs in this country. It helps me to remember that, when I came here 2 years ago, I did not speak English at all, and I knew nothing about how people act here. Seeing how much progress I have made helps me not to be discouraged with what I do not know yet.

LANGUAGE ALLOWS SELF-REFLECTION

Just as we use language to reflect on what goes on outside of us, we also use it to reflect on ourselves. According to Mead (1934), there are two aspects to the self. First, there is the *I*, which is the spontaneous, creative self. The *I* acts impulsively in response to inner needs and desires, regardless of social norms. The *Me* is the socially conscious part of the self that monitors and moderates the *I*'s impulses. The *Me* reflects on the *I* from the social perspectives of others. The *I* is impervious to social conventions and expectations, but the *Me* is keenly aware of them. In an argument, your *I* may want to hurl a biting insult at someone you don't like, but your *Me* censors that impulse and reminds you that it's impolite to put others down.

The *Me* reflects on the *I* by analyzing the *I*'s actions. This means we can think about who we want to be and set goals for becoming the self we desire. The *Me* can feel shame, pride, and regret for the *I*'s actions, an emotion that is possible because we self-reflect. We can control what we do in the present by casting ourselves forward in time to consider how we might later feel about our actions. Elyse makes this point in her commentary.

> **ELYSE** I volunteer at the homeless shelter. Sometimes, when I'm talking to the people who come there for food or to sleep, I feel like shaking them and telling them to get their lives in order. I get so frustrated with the ones who don't seem to make any effort to change their situations. But I know that everybody puts them down all the time—the last thing they need is to hear more of that from a college kid who probably never experienced real hardships. So I keep my frustration to myself. I guess that's the Me part of me controlling my I.

Self-Reflection Allows Us to Monitor Communication   Self-reflection also empowers us to monitor ourselves, a skill we discussed in Chapter 1. For instance, during a discussion with a friend, you might say to yourself, "Gee, I've been talking nonstop about me and my worries, and I haven't even asked how she's doing." Based on your monitoring, you might inquire about your friend's life. When interacting with people from different cultures, we monitor by reminding ourselves that they may have different values and communication rules from ours. Self-reflection allows us to monitor our communication and adjust it to be effective.

Self-Reflection Allows Us to Manage Our Image   Most of us work hard to present ourselves in certain ways and not others. We want to present a particular "face" in our interpersonal encounters (Ting-Toomey, 1988). Because we reflect on ourselves from social perspectives, we are able to adapt our communication so that we appear positively in others' eyes. When talking with teachers, you may present yourself as respectful, attentive, and studious. When interviewing for a job, you may work to appear especially confident and hardworking. When talking with someone you'd like to date, you may choose to be more attentive than you are in other circumstances. We continuously adjust our communication to fit particular situations and people.

We use symbols to define, classify, and evaluate experiences; to think hypothetically; and to self-reflect. Each of these abilities helps us create meaning in our personal and interpersonal lives. Each of them also carries with it ethical responsibilities for how we use communication and the impact it has on ourselves and others.

• • • • • • • • • • •

Speech Communities

Although all humans use language, we don't all use it in the same way. As we have seen, language is arbitrary, abstract, and ambiguous. in the process of interacting with others, we learn what particular words and language rituals mean. For this reason, people from different social groups use communication in different ways and attach different meanings to particular communicative acts.

A **speech community** exists when people share norms about how to use talk and what purposes it serves (Labov, 1972). Members of speech communities share perspectives on communication that outsiders do not have. Conversely, members of particular speech communities may not understand how communication is used in other speech communities. This explains why misunderstandings often arise between members of different social groups.

Speech communities are defined not by countries or geographic locations but by shared understandings of how to communicate. In Western society, there are numerous speech communities, each of which has some distinct understandings of communication and ways of using it. For example,

Julia T. Wood

in traditional Native American communities, silence expresses respect and thoughtfulness (Braithwaite, 1990). African American scholars report that African Americans generally communicate more assertively (Johnson, 2000; Hamlet, 2000; Orbe & Harris, 2001; Ribeau, Baldwin, & Hecht, 1994) and place greater emphasis on verbal wit (Kelley, 1997) than most European Americans. Traditional Korean, Japanese, and some other South Asian cultures emphasize communication more as a means of building community than as a means of asserting individual selves (Diggs, 1998, 2001).

GENDER SPEECH COMMUNITIES

Of the many speech communities that exist, gender has received particularly extensive study. Because we know more about it than about other speech communities, we'll explore gender as a specific example of speech communities and the misunderstandings that surface between members of different speech communities. Researchers have investigated both the way in which women and men are socialized into some different understandings of how communication functions and the way their communication differs in practice.

Socialization into Gender Speech Communities   One of the earliest studies showed that children's games are a primary agent of gender socialization (Maltz & Borker, 1982). Since that landmark study, many other researchers have studied gender socialization in children's play groups (Clark, 1998; Leaper, 1994, 1996; Martin, Fabes, Evans, & Wyman, 2000). They report that children's play usually is sex segregated, and there are notable differences between the games the sexes tend to play. These differences seem to teach boys and girls some distinct rules for using communication and interpreting the communication of others.

Games that are traditionally favored by girls, such as house and school, involve few players, include talk to negotiate how to play (because there aren't clear-cut guidelines), and depend on cooperation and sensitivity between players. Baseball and war, which are typical boys' games, involve more players and have clear goals and rules, so less talk is needed to play. Most boys' games are highly competitive both between teams and for individual status within teams. Interaction in games teaches boys and girls distinct understandings of why, when, and how to use talk.

Gendered Communication in Practice   Research on women's and men's communication reveals that the rules taught through childhood play are evident in adult interaction. For instance, women's talk generally is more expressive and focused on feelings and personal issues, whereas men's talk tends to be more instrumental and competitive (Aries, 1987; Beck, 1988; Coates & Cameron, 1989; Johnson, 1989; Martin, Fabes, Evans, & Wyman, 2000; Treichler & Kramarae, 1983; Wood, 1994c, 1994d, 1998).

Another general difference between the sexes involves what members of each sex tend to perceive as the primary foundation of close relationships. For most men, activities tend to be the primary foundation of close friendships and romantic relationships (Metts, 2006; Swain, 1989; Wood & Inman, 1993; Inman, 1996). Thus, men typically cement friendships by doing things together and for one another. For many women, communication usually is a primary foundation of relationships. Women also do things with and for people they care about, yet most women see talk as an essential foundation for intimacy. For many women, communicating is the essence of building and sustaining closeness (Aries, 1987; Becker, 1987; Braithwaite & Kellas, 2006; Metts, 2006; Riessman, 1990).

Notice that differences between men and women are matters of degree. They are not absolute dichotomies (MacNeil & Byers, 2005). Men sometimes use talk expressively, and women sometimes use talk instrumentally. Also, keep in mind that not all women follow rules of feminine communication communities, and not all men follow rules of masculine ones.

Misunderstandings between Gender Speech Communities   Socialization in different gender communities accounts for some common misunderstandings between women and men. One such misunderstanding occurs when women and men discuss problems. Often, when a woman tells a man about something that is troubling her, he offers advice or a solution (Duck, 2006; Tannen, 1990; Wood, 1994d, 1996, 1998). His view of communication as primarily instrumental leads him to show support by doing something. Because feminine communities see communication as a way to build connections with others, however, women often want empathy and discussion of feelings before advice is useful. Thus, women sometimes feel that men's responses to their concerns are uncaring and insensitive. On the other hand, men may feel frustrated when women offer empathy and support instead of advice for solving problems.

Research also indicates that men tend to be less comfortable than women about making personal disclosures (Aries, 1987; Wood & Inman, 1993). Another conundrum in interaction between men and women concerns different styles of listening. Socialized to be responsive and expressive, women tend to make listening noises such as "um hm," "yeah," and "I know what you mean" when others are talking (Tannen, 1990; Wood, 1996, 1998). This is how they show that they are attentive and interested. Yet, masculine communities don't emphasize using communication responsively, so men tend to make fewer listening noises when another is talking. Thus, women sometimes feel that men aren't listening to them because men don't symbolize their attention in the ways women have learned and expect. Notice that this does not mean that men don't listen well. Rather, the ways in which many men

The World of Words   **119**

listen aren't perceived as listening carefully by some women, because women and men tend to have different regulative and constitutive rules for listening. Recall from Chapter 3 that perception shapes meaning.

A very common misunderstanding occurs when a woman says, "Let's talk about us." To many men, this often means trouble because they interpret the request as implying that there is a problem in the relationship. For women, however, this is not the only—or even the main—reason to talk about a relationship. Feminine speech communities regard talking as the primary way to create relationships and build closeness (Riessman, 1990). In general, women view talking about a relationship as a way to celebrate and increase intimacy. Socialized to use communication instrumentally, however, men tend to think talking about a relationship is useful only if there is some problem to be resolved (Acitelli, 1988, 1993). For many men, the preferred mode of enhancing closeness is to do things together. Suzie's commentary illustrates this gender difference. To increase your awareness of how gender socialization shapes your verbal communication and to gain insight into others' perception of verbal communication that is and is not appropriate for each sex, complete *Student Companion: Activity 4.1.*

SUZIE My boyfriend and I have dated for 3 years, and we're pretty serious, so I wanted our anniversary to be really special. I suggested going out for a romantic dinner where we could talk about the relationship. Andy said that sounded dull, and he wanted to go to a concert where there would be zillions of people. At the time, I thought that meant he didn't care about us like I do, but maybe he feels close when we do things together instead of when we just are together.

Gender is just one example of many speech communities. Communication patterns vary among people from different social groups, even if they live in the same society (Johnson, 2000). Online communi-

Communication in Everyday Life
Which Blacks' Black English?

"Every time I hear the phrase *Black English*, I shudder. I am black, and I don't speak like that. I was raised in an upper-middle-class family, and I was taught to speak correct English. I don't want to be stigmatized as someone who doesn't use good English. I'm black, but I do not use Black English." A student of mine made this statement after reading African American linguist Geneva Smitherman's book *Black Talk* (1994). In her book, Smitherman offers examples of what she calls "Black Talk":

Chill: Relax

Sweet: Outstanding

Amen corner: Place in black churches where elders sit

Drop a dime: Tell on someone who is doing something wrong or illegal

Scared of you: A compliment, acknowledging that another is very accomplished

My student's response to Smitherman's work reminds us that not all African Americans use "Black Talk" or "Black Vernacular English" (Johnson, 2000). Another black student wrote me that he loved reading about black English and traditional African American speech patterns because he felt his language and his culture were acknowledged. He wrote, "Too often, I feel like a speck of pepper on a mountain of salt at this white school." Unlike the first student, the second one identified with traditional African American speech communities.

Within any community, there is great variation. Not all women or men speak in the same way, and not all of them conform to all the features typical of feminine and masculine speech communities. Not all Asian Americans or even Asians communicate in ways wholly consistent with the attributes typical of Asian communities. And not all European Americans speak according to the general norms of European American communication. Thus, when we refer to speech communities, we are describing only broad, general patterns that may not apply to all members of a particular social group.

To learn more about different attitudes toward social communities and their communication patterns, visit http://www.diasporalinks.com/Social/Communities/. You can join one of the online communities to articulate your views and learn about others' views.

If you'd like to learn more about what are classified as traditional "African American speech patterns," go to http://www.melanet.com/clegg_series/ebonics.html.

ties also have particular communication patterns, which new members must learn if they are to participate effectively. Recognizing and respecting different speech communities increases our ability to participate competently in a diverse culture.

Guidelines for Improving Verbal Communication

Building on what we've learned about language, we will now consider guidelines for improving effectiveness in verbal communication.

ENGAGE IN DUAL PERSPECTIVE

A critical guideline for effective verbal communication is to engage in dual perspective. This involves recognizing another person's perspective and taking that into account as you communicate. Effective interpersonal communication is not a solo performance but a relationship between people. Awareness of others and their viewpoints should be reflected in how we speak. For instance, it's advisable

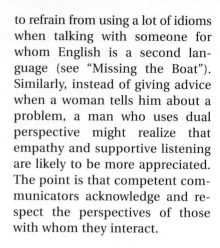
to refrain from using a lot of idioms when talking with someone for whom English is a second language (see "Missing the Boat"). Similarly, instead of giving advice when a woman tells him about a problem, a man who uses dual perspective might realize that empathy and supportive listening are likely to be more appreciated. The point is that competent communicators acknowledge and respect the perspectives of those with whom they interact.

SPANKY For so long, my mother and I have argued with each other. I have always felt she was overly protective of me and tried to intrude in my life with all the questions she asked about what I'm doing, who I'm seeing, and everything. For years, almost any discussion between us wound up in an argument. I would just resist and challenge her. But for the last month, I've been trying to understand where she's coming from. When she asks who I'm seeing, I don't just say, "None of your business" or "Get off my case" like I used to. Now, I ask her why she wants to know. What she says is she's interested in who I hang with and why I like them. That's kind of cool—that my mom is really interested in my life. That's a lot different than seeing her questions as coming from a mother hen who wants to run my life. Trying to understand her perspective has been really, really tough, but it has made an incredible difference in our relationship.

We don't need to abandon our own perspectives to accommodate those of others. In fact, it would be as unhealthy to stifle your own views as to ignore those of others. Dual perspective, as the term implies, consists of two perspectives. It requires honoring both our own point of view and another's when we communicate. Most of us can accept and grow from differences, but we seldom feel affirmed if we are unheard or disregarded. Acknowledging others' viewpoints in your communication paves the way for affirming relationships.

OWN YOUR FEELINGS AND THOUGHTS

We often use language in ways that obscure our responsibility for how we feel and what we think. For instance, we say, "You made me mad" or "You hurt me," as if what we feel had been caused by someone else. On a more subtle level, we sometimes blame others for our responses to what they say. "You're so demanding" really means that you are irritated by what someone else wants or expects. The irritation is *your* feeling.

Although how we interpret what others say may lead us to feel certain ways, others do not directly cause our responses. In certain contexts, such as abusive relationships, others may powerfully shape how we think and feel. Yet, even in these extreme situations, we need to remember that we, not others, are responsible for our feelings. Telling others they make you feel some way denies your responsibility for your own feelings and is likely to arouse defensiveness, which doesn't facilitate healthy interpersonal relationships.

Effective communicators take responsibility for themselves by using language that owns their thoughts and feelings. They claim their feelings and do not blame

YOU LANGUAGE	I LANGUAGE
You make me nervous on the job.	When you watch me work, I feel nervous.
You hurt me.	I feel hurt when you ignore what I say.
You make me feel small.	I feel small when you tell me that I'm selfish.
You're so domineering.	When you shout, I feel dominated.
You humiliated me.	I felt humiliated when you mentioned my problems in front of our friends.

others for what happens in themselves. To take responsibility for your own feelings, rely on **I language** rather than **you language.** *I* language owns thoughts and feelings and does not blame them on others. Table 4.1 gives examples of the difference. There are two differences between *I* language and *you* language. First, *I* language takes responsibility, whereas *you* language projects it onto another person. Second, *I* language is more descriptive than *you* language. *You* language tends to be accusatory and abstract. This is one of the reasons it's ineffective in promoting change. *I* language, on the other hand, provides concrete descriptions of behaviors we dislike without directly blaming the other person for how we feel.

Some people feel awkward when they first start using *I* language. This is natural because most of us have learned to rely on *you* language. With commitment and practice, however, you can learn to communicate with *I* language.

Once you feel comfortable using *I* language, you will find that it has many advantages. First, it is less likely than *you* language to make others defensive, so *I* language opens the doors for dialogue. *You* language is particularly likely to arouse defensiveness or anger when it is used to express criticism or dissatisfaction. In a recent study, Amy Bippus and Stacy Young (2005) found that some people reacted positively when they were targets of positive *you* language (e.g., "You make me feel wonderful.").

Second, *I* language is more honest. We misrepresent our responsibility when we say "You made me feel . . ." because others don't control how we feel. Finally,

○ ## Everyday Application
Using I *Language*

For the next 3 days, whenever you use *you* language, try to rephrase what you said or thought in *I* language. How does this change how you think and feel about what's happening? How does using *I* language affect interaction with others? Are others less defensive when you own your feelings and describe, but don't evaluate, their behaviors? Does *I* language facilitate working out constructive changes?

Now that you're tuned into *I* and *you* language, monitor how you feel when others use *you* language about you. When a friend or romantic partner says "You make me feel . . .," do you feel defensive or guilty? Try teaching others to use *I* language so that your relationships can be more honest and open. For additional experience using *I* language, complete Activity 4.7 in your *Student Companion* or online under "Chapter Resources for Chapter 4" on the Everyday Connections website.

© Bryce Flynn/Stack Boston, LLC

I language is more empowering than *you* language. When we say you did this or you made me feel that, we give control of our emotions to others. This reduces our personal power and, by extension, our motivation to change what is happening. Using *I* language allows you to own your own feelings while explaining to others how you interpret their behaviors.

NEELY I thought that the idea of *I* language was kind of silly, but I did the exercise assigned in class anyway. Surprise. I found out I was using a lot of *you* language, and it had the effect of letting me off the hook for what I felt and did. Like, I would say, "You pushed me to say that," when really I had control over whether to say it or not. But when I said, "You pushed me," I could dismiss what I said as not my fault.

RESPECT WHAT OTHERS SAY ABOUT THEIR FEELINGS AND THOUGHTS

Has anyone ever said to you, "You shouldn't feel that way"? If so, you know how infuriating it can be to be told that your feelings aren't valid, appropriate, or acceptable. It's equally destructive to be told our thoughts are wrong. We feel disconfirmed when someone says, "How can you think something so stupid?" Effective communicators don't dispute or disparage what others say about what they feel and think. Even if you don't feel or think the same way, you can still respect another person as the expert on her or his own thoughts and emotions.

One of the most disconfirming forms of communication is speaking for others when they are able to speak for themselves. We shouldn't assume we understand how they feel or think. As we have seen, our distinct experiences and ways of interpreting life make each of us unique. We seldom, if ever, completely grasp what another person feels or thinks. Although it is supportive to engage in dual perspective, it isn't supportive to presume we fully grasp what's happening in someone else and can speak for them.

It's particularly important not to assume we understand people from other cultures and distinct communities within our society. Recently, a Asian Indian woman in one of my classes commented on discrimination she faces, and a white man in the class said, "I know what you mean. Prejudice really hurts." Although he meant to be supportive, his response angered the woman, who retorted, "You have no idea how I feel, and you have no right to act like you do until you've been female and nonwhite."

Respecting what others say about what they feel and think is a cornerstone of effective interpersonal communication. We also grow when we open ourselves to perspectives, feelings, and thoughts that differ from our own. If you don't understand what others say, ask them to elaborate. This shows you are interested and respect their expertise or experience. Inviting others to clarify, extend, or explain their communication enlarges understanding between people.

STRIVE FOR ACCURACY AND CLARITY

Because symbols are arbitrary, abstract, and ambiguous, the potential for misunderstanding always exists. In addition, individual and cultural differences foster varying interpretations of words. Although we can't completely eliminate misunderstandings, we can minimize them.

Communication in Everyday Life
Respecting Others' Experiences

Marsha Houston, an accomplished communication scholar, explains how claiming understanding can diminish a person. She writes that white women should never tell African American women that they understand black women's experiences. Here's Houston's (2004) explanation:

> I have heard this sentence completed in numerous, sometimes bizarre, ways, from "because sexism is just as bad as racism," to "because I watch the 'Cosby Show,'" to "because I'm also a member of a minority group. I'm Jewish . . . Italian . . . overweight." Similar experiences should not be confused with the same experience; my experience of prejudice is erased when you identify it as "the same" as yours (p. 124).

Be Aware of Levels of Abstraction   Misunderstanding is less likely when we are conscious of levels of abstraction. Much confusion results from language that is excessively abstract. For instance, suppose a professor says, "Your papers should demonstrate a sophisticated conceptual grasp of material and its pragmatic implications." Would you know how to write a paper to satisfy the professor? Probably not, because the language is abstract. Here's a more concrete description: "Your papers should include definitions of the concepts and specific examples that show how they apply in real life." With this more concrete statement, you would have a clear idea of what the professor expected.

Everyday Application
Using Concrete Language

Rewrite each statement, replacing abstract language with more concrete language.
Example: I want to be more responsible.
Rewrite: I want to be on time for work and classes, and I want to live within my budget each month and not run up charges on my credit card.

1. I get really angry when people are rude.
2. I like teachers who are flexible and open minded.
3. My roommate is such a slob.
4. I believe intimate relationships are based on unconditional love and acceptance.
5. I resent it when my supervisor has unrealistic expectations of me.
6. I think the media in this country are irresponsible.

   To increase your ability to recognize highly abstract language and increase your skill in reducing the abstractness of language, complete Activity 4.8 in your *Student Companion* or online under "Chapter Resources for Chapter 4" at the Everyday Connections website.

Sometimes, however, abstract language is appropriate. As we have seen, abstract language allows us to generalize, which is necessary and useful. The goal is to use a level of abstraction that suits particular communication objectives and situations. Abstract words are appropriate when speakers and listeners have similar concrete knowledge about what is being discussed. For example, an established couple might talk about "lighthearted comedies" and "heavy movies" as shorthand ways to refer to two kinds of films. Because they have seen many movies together, they have shared referents for the abstract terms *lighthearted* and *heavy,* so confusion is unlikely. Similarly, long-term friends can say "Let's just hang out" and understand the activities implied by the abstract term *hang out.* More concrete language is useful when communicators don't have shared experiences and interpretations. For example, early in a friendship the suggestion to "hang out" would be more effective if it included specifics: "Let's hang out today—maybe watch the game and go out for pizza." In a new dating relationship, saying "Let's have a casual evening" would be less clear than "Let's rent a movie and fix dinner at your place tonight."

Abstract language is particularly likely to lead to misunderstandings when people talk about changes they want in one another. Concrete language and specific examples help people have similar understandings of which behaviors are unwelcome and which ones are wanted. For example, "I want you to be more helpful around the house" does not explain what would count as being more helpful. Is it vacuuming and doing laundry? Shopping for groceries? Fixing half the meals? It won't be clear what the speaker wants unless more concrete descriptions are supplied. Saying, "I want our team to be more efficient" could mean that the person wants meetings to start promptly, wants all members of a team to be on time for meetings, or wants more accomplished at each meeting. Likewise, "I want to be closer" could mean that the speaker wants to spend more time together, to talk about the relationship, to do things together, to have a more adventurous sex life, or any number of other things.

Qualify Language   Another strategy for increasing the clarity of communication is to qualify language. Two types of language should be qualified. First, we should qualify generalizations so that we don't mislead ourselves or others into mistaking a general statement for an absolute one. "Politicians are crooked" is a false statement because it overgeneralizes. A more accurate statement would be "A number of politicians have been shown to be dishonest." Qualifying reminds us of the limitations of what we say.

We should also qualify language when describing and evaluating people. A **static evaluation** is an assessment that suggests that something is unchanging or static. These are particularly troublesome when applied to people: "Ann is selfish," "Don is irresponsible," "Bob is generous," "Vy is dependent." Whenever we use the word *is*, we suggest that something is inherent and fixed. In reality, we aren't static but continuously changing. A person who is selfish at one time may not be at another. A person who is irresponsible on one occasion may be responsible in other situations. *Student Companion:* Activity 4.10.

KEN   Parents are the worst for static evaluations. When I first got my license 7 years ago, I had a fender bender and then got a speeding ticket. Since then, I've had a perfect record, but you'd never know it from what they say. Dad's always calling me "hot-rodder," and Mom goes through this safety spiel every time I get ready to drive somewhere. You'd think I was the same now as when I was 16.

Indexing is a technique developed by early communication scholars to remind us that our evaluations apply only to specific times and circumstances (Korzybski, 1958). To index, we would say "Ann$_{\text{June 6, 1997}}$ acted selfishly," "Don$_{\text{on the task committee}}$ was irresponsible," "Bob$_{\text{in college}}$ was generous," and "Vy$_{\text{in high school}}$ was dependent on others for self-esteem." See how indexing ties description to a specific time and circumstance? Mental indexing reminds us that we and others are able to change in remarkable ways.

Case Study: Continuing the Conversation

The following conversation is featured on the Everyday Connections website under "Chapter Resources for Chapter 4." Click on the link "Ed Misses the Banquet" in the left-hand menu to launch the video and audio scenario scripted below.

Ed recently began working at a new job. Although he's been there only 5 weeks, he likes it a lot and sees a real future for himself with the company. Last week, Ed was invited to the annual company banquet and awards ceremony. The invitation to the banquet stated only "Hope to see you there" and had no RSVP, so Ed didn't mention to anyone that he wouldn't be attending because his daughter was in a play the same night. When he arrived at work the next Monday morning, however, his manager spoke to him.

Manager: Hey, Ed, you missed the banquet Saturday night. I thought you were really committed to our company.

Ed is confused by the comment and tries to explain why he was absent.

Ed: My daughter was in a play that night.

Manager: I don't care why you didn't come. We really pay attention to who's with us and who isn't.

Later, when Ed talks with several co-workers who have been around a few years, he discovers that top management sees the annual banquet as a "command performance" that signifies company unity and loyalty.

1. How does the concept of constitutive rules help explain the misunderstanding between Ed and his manager?

2. How might Ed learn the normative practices of the company so that he can understand the meanings longtime employees have?

3. How do the ambiguity and abstraction inherent in language explain the misunderstanding between Ed and his manager?

4. How would you suggest that Ed repair the damage done by his absence from the company banquet? What might he say to his manager? How could he use *I* language, indexing, and dual perspective to guide his communication?

5. Sign onto InfoTrac College Edition. Use the PowerTrac author search to find articles by Jeanette W. Gilsdorf. Read "Organizational Rules

Jason Harris/© 2001 Wadsworth

on Communicating: How Employees Are—Or Are Not—Learning the Ropes," which was published in the *Journal of Business Communication* in April 1998. What light does her study shed on Ed's situation? Does Gilsdorf's research suggest that not understanding organizational rules is common for new employees? Does her research suggest ways to minimize the problem?

You can critique and analyze this encounter based on the principles you learned in this chapter by responding to the questions included under "Conversation Analysis" at the website. By clicking on the "Submit" button at the end of the form, you can compare your work to my suggested responses. Let's continue the conversation online!

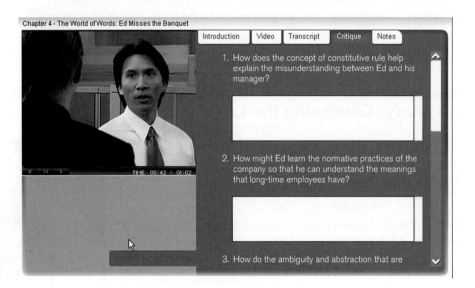

Chapter 4 - The World of Words: Ed Misses the Banquet

| Introduction | Video | Transcript | Critique | Notes |

1. How does the concept of constitutive rule help explain the misunderstanding between Ed and his manager?

2. How might Ed learn the normative practices of the company so that he can understand the meanings that long-time employees have?

3. How do the ambiguity and abstraction that are

TIME 00:42 / 01:02

Chapter Summary

In this chapter, we discussed the world of words and meaning, the uniquely human universe that we inhabit because we are symbol users. Because symbols are arbitrary, ambiguous, and abstract, they have no inherent meanings. Instead, we actively construct meaning by interpreting symbols based on perspectives and values that are endorsed in our culture and social groups and based on interaction with others and our personal experiences. We also punctuate to create meaning in communication.

Instead of existing only in the physical world of the here and now, we use language to define, evaluate, and classify ourselves, others, and our experiences in the world. In addition, we use language to think hypothetically, so we can consider alternatives and simultaneously inhabit all three dimensions of time. Finally, language allows us to self-reflect so that we can monitor our own behaviors.

Although members of a society share a common language, we don't all use it the same way. Different groups, or speech communities, which exist both within and between countries, teach us rules for talking and for interpreting communication. Because communication rules vary between social groups, we shouldn't assume that others use words just as we do. Likewise, we shouldn't assume that others share our rules for communicating.

The final section of this chapter discussed principles for improving effectiveness in verbal communication. Because words can mean different things to various people and because different social groups instill some distinct rules for interacting, misunderstandings are always possible. To minimize them, we should engage in dual perspective, own our thoughts and feelings, respect what others say about how they think and feel, and monitor abstractness, generalizations, and static evaluations. In Chapter 5, we will continue our discussion of the world of human communication by exploring the fascinating realm of nonverbal behavior.

Everyday Connections Online

Now that you've read Chapter 4, go to the Everyday Connections premium website at academic.cengage.com/communication/woodinterpersonal5plus for quick access to the electronic study resources that accompany this text. The website gives you access to the "Continuing the Conversation" video scenario and questions featured in this chapter, to InfoTrac College Edition, to maintained and updated Web links, and to the study aids for this chapter, including a digital glossary, review quizzes, and the chapter activities. For more information about this text's electronic learning resources, consult the **1pass card** that came with each new copy of this book, or visit academic.cengage.com/communication/woodinterpersonal5.

Key Concepts

Audio flash cards of the following key terms are available on the Everyday Connections website. Use the flash cards to improve your pronunciation of text vocabulary.

abstract	hate speech	punctuation	totalizing
ambiguous	*I* language	regulative rules	*you* language
arbitrary	indexing	speech community	
communication rules	linguistic determinism	static evaluation	
constitutive rules	loaded language	symbols	

For Further Thought and Discussion

1. Think about different metaphors for American society. For many years, the country was described as a melting pot, which suggests that differences between citizens are supposed to melt down and blend into one unified character. Recently, some have criticized this melting pot metaphor because it emphasizes wiping out differences, not respecting them. The Reverend Jesse Jackson refers to the United States as both a rainbow and a family quilt. Both of Jackson's metaphors emphasize recognizing and appreciating differences. What metaphor would you propose?

2. Use your InfoTrac College Edition to read "When Situations Call for Instrumentality and Expressiveness: Reason Appraisal, Coping Strategy Choice, and Adjustment" by Jayne Stake. When does Stake claim masculine communication style (more instrumental) is effective, and when

does she claim feminine communication style (more expressive) is effective? Do you agree?

3. To appreciate the importance of hypothetical thought enabled by symbols, try to imagine living only in the present with no memories and no anticipations of the future, having no goals for yourself, and knowing only the concrete, immediate reality. How would not having hypothetical thought affect your life?

4. In this chapter, we learned that language changes. We coin new words when we feel the need to represent something that is not currently named in our language. Can you think of experiences, situations, or relationships that are not currently named? What names would you give them?

5. Check out the graffiti on your campus. Do you see examples of loaded language, stereotyping, and hate speech? Share your findings with your classmates.

6. Visit http://www.spectacle.org/freespch/musm/hate.html. What do you learn about how hate speech is defined, who engages in it, and efforts to regulate hate speech on the Web? What should be done about hate speech on the Web and off it? Should we censor it? Would doing so violate our constitutional right to freedom of speech? Are there other, perhaps less formal, ways to reduce hate speech?

7. What labels that you dislike have been applied to you or to groups to which you belong? Explain how the labels affect you.

8. Notice how media describe black people and white people in the news. Do television programs, newspapers, and other media spotlight race when the person is not white? How often are minorities described in terms of their races (black, Asian, Hispanic, and so on)? Are people ever described as white?

The World Beyond Words

"The eyes have one language
everywhere."

George Herbert

*J*ay and Emma gaze into each other's eyes as they nibble their beautifully prepared salads topped with marinated mushrooms and herb croutons. They can hear only muffled sounds from people at the other tables spread sparsely throughout the lavish dining area. The comfortable upholstered chairs, subtle lighting, and soft music add to the leisurely, intimate mood of the evening. Fifteen minutes after bringing the salads, the server returns with their entrees and asks whether they would like anything else.

Amy's and Ted's eyes meet across the Formica table in the diner. They speak loudly to be heard above the clamor of rock music, conversations at other tables crowded around them in the bright room, and order announcements shouted from the grill. Less than 5 minutes after they order, the server plops loaded plates in front of them and leaves the check. Ted and Amy eat their burritos quickly and leave, spending less than 20 minutes on the entire meal.

These two couples had very different dining experiences. The restaurant where Jay and Emma dined featured low lighting, carefully arranged spaces, soft music, and a gracious pace of service that encouraged lingering and intimate conversation. In contrast, Ted's and Amy's restaurant was crowded, bright, and loud, and the service was fast and functional, all of which discouraged lingering or intimate conversation. These aspects of nonverbal communication account for much of the difference in the dining experiences.

In Chapter 4, we explored verbal communication. To complement that focus, this chapter examines the fascinating world beyond words that is central to interpersonal communication. To launch our discussion, we define nonverbal communication and note how it is similar to and different from verbal communication. Next, we identify four principles of nonverbal communication. The third section of the chapter discusses different types of nonverbal behavior. We complete the chapter with guidelines for improving personal effectiveness in nonverbal communication.

•••••••••••

Defining Nonverbal Communication

Nonverbal communication is all aspects of communication other than words themselves. It includes not only gestures and body language but also how we utter words: inflection, pauses, tone, volume, and accent. These nonverbal features affect the meanings of our words. Nonverbal communication also includes features of environments that affect interaction, personal objects such as jewelry and clothes, physical appearance, and facial expressions.

Scholars estimate that nonverbal behaviors account for 65% to 93% of the total meaning of communication (Birdwhistell, 1970; Hickson, Stacks, & Moore, 2004; Mehrabian, 1981). To understand verbal and nonverbal dimensions of communication, we identify similarities as well as differences between verbal and nonverbal communication.

SIMILARITIES BETWEEN VERBAL AND NONVERBAL COMMUNICATION

Nonverbal communication is similar to verbal communication in four respects: it is symbolic, it is rule guided, it may be intentional or nonintentional, and it reflects culture.

Nonverbal Communication Is Symbolic Like verbal communication, much non-verbal communication is symbolic, which means that it represents other things. To represent different moods, we shrug our shoulders, lower our eyes, and move away from or toward others. We smile to symbolize pleasure in seeing a friend, frown to show anger or irritation, and widen our eyes to indicate surprise.

Because nonverbal communication is symbolic, it is arbitrary, ambiguous, and abstract. Thus, we cannot be sure what a wink or a hand movement means. Depending on the context and the people involved, a wink might express romantic interest, signal that the person winking is joking, or mean that the person winking has something in her or his eye. Also, we can't guarantee that others will perceive the meanings we intend to communicate with our nonverbal actions. You might move closer to someone to indicate that you like the person, but he or she may feel that you are rude and imposing.

Nonverbal Communication Is Rule Guided Within particular societies, we share general understandings of what specific nonverbal behaviors are appropriate in various situations and what they mean. For example, in the United States and many other countries, the handshake is the conventional way to begin and end a business meeting. Smiling generally is understood to express friendliness, and scowling generally is perceived as indicating displeasure of some type.

We follow rules (often unconsciously) to create different interaction climates. For instance, people dress differently to attend a funeral and to attend a soccer game. A formal speaking occasion might call for a podium placed at a distance from listeners' chairs, which are arranged in neat rows. Flags, banners, or other ceremonial symbols might be displayed near the podium. To symbolize a less formal speaking occasion, a podium might be omitted, chairs might be arranged in a circle, and the person speaking might be seated. The different spatial arrangements symbolize different moods and set the stage for distinct kinds of interaction.

Nonverbal Communication May Be Intentional or Unintentional Both verbal and nonverbal communication may be deliberately controlled or unintentional. For example, you may carefully select clothes to create a professional impression when you are going to a job interview. You may also deliberately control your verbal language in the interview to present yourself as assertive, articulate, and respectful. We exert conscious control over much of our nonverbal communication.

© Image100/SuperStock

Sometimes, however, both nonverbal and verbal communication are unconscious and unplanned. Without awareness, you may wince when asked a tough question by the interviewer. Without knowing it, you may use incorrect grammar when speaking. Thus, both nonverbal and verbal communication are sometimes controlled and sometimes inadvertent.

Nonverbal Communication Reflects Culture
Like verbal communication, nonverbal behavior is shaped by cultural ideas, values, customs, and history (Emmons, 1998; Andersen, Hecht, Hoobler, & Smallwood, 2002). Just as we learn our

culture's language, we also learn its nonverbal codes. For example, in the United States most people use knives, forks, and spoons to eat. In Korea, Japan, China, Nepal, and other Asian countries, chopsticks often are the primary eating utensil. Western women wear slacks or jeans, shirts, dresses, and suits, whereas women in India may wear saris. In the United States, it is common for friends and romantic partners to sample food from each other's plates, but many Germans consider this extremely rude. Later in this chapter, we look more closely at cultural influences on nonverbal behavior as one of the principles of the nonverbal communication system.

DIFFERENCES BETWEEN VERBAL AND NONVERBAL COMMUNICATION

There are also differences between verbal and nonverbal communication and the meanings we attach to each. We consider three distinctions between the two kinds of communication.

Nonverbal Communication Is Perceived as More Believable   One major difference is that most people believe that nonverbal communication is more reliable than verbal communication in expressing true feelings (Andersen, 1999). This is especially the case when verbal and nonverbal messages are inconsistent. If someone glares and says, "I'm glad to see you," you are likely to believe the nonverbal message, which communicates that the speaker is *not* pleased to see you. If you say you feel fine, but you are slumping and the corners of your mouth are turned down, others probably will not believe your verbal message.

The fact that people tend to believe nonverbal behaviors doesn't mean that nonverbal behaviors actually are honest or that we really can interpret them reliably. It's also possible for people to manipulate nonverbal communication, just as we manipulate our verbal communication. Politicians are coached not only in how to speak but in how to use nonverbal communication to bolster images. Atlanta nonverbal trainer Patti Wood (Basu, 2004) analyzed nonverbal communication of the candidates in the 2004 presidential election. She thinks George W. Bush's frequent smiles and winks established connections with voters and that vice presidential candidate John Edwards's thumbs-up gesture helped him appear confident and positive.

Nonverbal Communication Is Multichanneled   Nonverbal communication often occurs simultaneously in two or more channels, whereas verbal communication tends to take place in a single channel. Nonverbal communication may be seen, felt, heard, smelled, and tasted, and we may receive nonverbal communication through several of these channels at the same time. If you touch a person while smiling and whispering an endearment, nonverbal communication occurs in three channels at once. In contrast, vocal verbal communication is received through hearing, whereas written verbal communication and American Sign Language are received through sight—in each case, a single channel.

One implication of the multichanneled nature of nonverbal communication is that selective perception is likely to operate. If you are visually oriented, you may tune in more to visual cues than to smell or touch. On the other hand, if you are touch oriented, you may pay particular attention to tactile cues.

Nonverbal Communication Is Continuous   Finally, nonverbal communication is more continuous than verbal communication. Verbal symbols start and stop. We say something or write something, and then we stop talking or writing. However, it is difficult, if not impossible, to stop nonverbal communication. We continuously adjust our posture and facial expressions. Furthermore, nonverbal features of environment, such as lighting or temperature, are ongoing influences on interaction and meaning.

Principles of Nonverbal Communication

We're now ready to explore how nonverbal communication works. Four principles enhance insight into how nonverbal communication influences meaning in human interaction.

NONVERBAL COMMUNICATION MAY SUPPLEMENT OR REPLACE VERBAL COMMUNICATION

Communication researchers have identified five ways in which nonverbal behaviors interact with verbal communication (Andersen, 1999; Malandro & Barker, 1983). First, nonverbal behaviors may repeat verbal messages. For example, you might say "yes" while nodding your head. Second, nonverbal behaviors may highlight verbal communication. For instance, you can emphasize particular words by speaking louder. Third, we use nonverbal behavior to complement or add to words. When you see a friend, you might say, "I'm glad to see you" and underline the verbal message with a warm embrace. Lyrics (verbal) and music (nonverbal) often work together (Sellnow & Sellnow, 2001). Fourth, nonverbal behaviors may contradict verbal messages, as when someone says, "Nothing's wrong!" in a hostile tone of voice. Finally, we sometimes substitute nonverbal behaviors for verbal ones. For instance, you might roll your eyes to indicate that you disapprove of something. In all these ways, nonverbal behaviors supplement or replace verbal communication.

NONVERBAL COMMUNICATION MAY REGULATE INTERACTION

More than verbal cues, nonverbal behaviors regulate the flow of communication between people. In conversations, we generally know when someone else is through speaking and when it is our turn to talk. We also sense when a professor welcomes discussion from students and when the professor is in a lecture mode. Seldom do explicit verbal cues tell us when to speak and when to keep silent. When talking, friends typically don't say, "Your turn to talk," or hold up signs saying "I am through now." Instead, turn taking in conversation usually is regulated nonverbally (Malandro & Barker, 1983). We signal that we don't want to be interrupted by averting our eyes or by maintaining a speaking volume and rate that thwarts interruption. When we're through talking, we look back to others to signal, "Okay, now somebody else can speak." We invite specific people to speak by looking directly at them. Although we aren't usually aware of nonverbal actions that regulate interaction, we rely on them to know when to speak and when to remain silent.

NONVERBAL COMMUNICATION OFTEN ESTABLISHES RELATIONSHIP-LEVEL MEANINGS

You'll recall that, in Chapter 1, we discussed two levels of meaning in communication. To review, the content level of meaning is the literal message. The relationship level of meaning defines communicators' identities and relationships between them. Nonverbal communication often acts as "relationship language" that expresses the overall feeling of relationships (Burgoon, Buller, Hale, & deTurck, 1984; Keeley & Hart, 1994; Sallinen-Kuparinen, 1992). Nonverbal communication can convey three dimensions of relationship-level meanings (Mehrabian, 1981).

Responsiveness One dimension of relationship-level meaning is responsiveness. Through eye contact, facial expressions, and body posture, we indicate our interest in others' communication. Online, we may communicate responsiveness by responding immediately to an instant message or to comments in a chat room. In face-to-face interaction, Westerners signal interest by holding eye contact and assuming an attentive posture. To express lack of interest or boredom, we may slouch or decrease visual contact.

Synchronicity, or harmony, between people's postures and facial expressions may reflect how comfortable they are with each other (Berg, 1987; Burgoon, Stern, & Dillman, 1995; Capella, 1991). We're more likely to perceive co-workers as interested in our ideas if they look at us, nod, and lean forward than if they gaze around the room, look bored, and fiddle with papers as we speak (Miller & Parks, 1982).

> **ALLAN** The most useful professional development seminar I've ever taken taught me how to sit and look at people to show I am interested. Our instructor told us that a lot of times men don't show their interest with head nods and eye contact. That explained to me why some of the women I supervise complained that I never seemed interested when they came to talk to me. It wasn't that I wasn't interested. I just didn't show it with my nonverbal behavior.

As Allan's commentary illustrates, different speech communities teach members distinct rules for showing responsiveness. Because feminine speech communities tend to emphasize building relationships by expressing interest in others, women generally display greater nonverbal responsiveness than men (Montgomery, 1988; Ueland, 1992). In addition to communicating their own feelings nonverbally, women generally are more skilled than men in interpreting others' emotions (Hall, 1978; Hall, Carter, & Horgan, 2000; Noller, 1986). Prisoners, another subordinate group, also show strong decoding capacity (Wood, 1994d), which suggests that decoding may be a learned survival strategy for people with limited power. The well-being and sometimes physical safety of those with low power depend on being able to decipher the feelings and intentions of those with more power.

Liking A second dimension of relationship meaning is liking. Nonverbal behaviors often are keen indicators of how positively or negatively we feel toward others. Smiles and friendly touching tend to indicate positive feelings, whereas frowns and belligerent postures express antagonism (Keeley & Hart, 1994). Opening your arms to someone signals affection and welcome, whereas turning your back on someone indicates dislike.

In addition to these general rules shared in Western society, more specific rules are instilled by particular speech communities. Masculine speech communities tend to emphasize emotional control and independence, so men are less likely than women to use nonverbal behaviors to reveal how they feel. Reflecting the values of feminine socialization, women, in general, sit closer to others, smile more, and engage in greater eye contact than men (Hall, et al., 2000; Montgomery, 1988; Reis, Senchak, & Solomon, 1985). With intimate partners, women are more likely than men to initiate hand holding and touch. Women also tend to be more nonverbally expressive of their inner feelings because that is encouraged in feminine speech communities.

Nonverbal behaviors also tend to reflect feelings between marriage partners. Happy couples tend to sit closer together and engage in more eye contact than unhappy couples do. Furthermore, people who like each other tend to touch often and to orient their body postures toward each other (Burgoon et al., 1995; Miller & Parks, 1982; Noller, 1986).

© Anne Dowie

> **WILL** One of the neatest things about my parents is how they are always connecting with each other. I don't mean with words. It's more like looks and touching. If Mom says something, Dad looks at her. Whenever either of them comes in a room the other's in, they have to touch—just brush a shoulder or scratch the other's back or whatever. It's like they're always reaching out to each other.

Power The third dimension of relationship-level meaning is power. We use nonverbal behaviors to assert dominance and to negotiate for status and influence (Burgoon & LePoire, 1999; Henley, 1977; Remland, 2000). Given what we have learned about gender socialization, it is not surprising that men generally assume greater amounts of space than women and use greater volume and more forceful gestures to assert themselves (Hall, 1987; Henley, 1977; Leathers, 1986; Major, Schmidlin, & Williams, 1990).

Status also affects tendencies to communicate power nonverbally. The prerogative to touch another reflects power, so people with power tend to touch those with less power. For instance, bosses touch secretaries far more often than secretaries touch bosses (Spain, 1992). Time is also linked to people's status. People who are considered important can keep others waiting. How often have you waited for your appointment at a doctor's office? People with high status can also be late to appointments and events without risking serious repercussions. Yet, if someone with lower power is late, she or he may suffer disapproval, penalties, or cancellation of the appointment.

> **JERRY** Last summer, I had an internship with a big accounting firm in Washington, and space really told the story on status. Interns like me worked in two large rooms on the first floor with partitions to separate our desks. New employees worked on the second floor in little cubicles. The higher up you were in the hierarchy of the firm, the higher up your office was—literally. I mean, the president and vice presidents—six of them—had the whole top floor, while there were forty or more interns crowded onto my floor.

As Jerry's observations indicate, space also expresses power relations. People who have power usually have more space than those who have little or no power. Most executives have large, spacious offices, whereas their secretaries often have smaller offices or workstations. As people move up the organizational ladder, they tend to have larger offices. Homes also reflect power differences among family members. Adults usually have more space than children, and men more often than women have their own rooms, chairs, or other special spaces.

Responsiveness, liking, and power are dimensions of relationship-level meanings that are often expressed through nonverbal communication. This is why communication researchers Judee Burgoon and Beth LePoire (1999) conclude that "nonverbal cues are laden with relationship meaning" (p. 121). *Student Companion: Activity 5.1.*

Like verbal communication, nonverbal patterns reflect specific cultures. This implies that most nonverbal behavior is not instinctive but learned in the process of socialization.

Have you ever seen the bumper sticker "If you can read this, you're too close"? That slogan proclaims North Americans' fierce territoriality. We prize private space, and we resent—and sometimes fight—anyone who trespasses on what we consider our turf. The German culture also emphasizes private space. Germans often build walls and hedges to insulate themselves from neighbors. In other cultures—called *high-contact* cultures—people are less territorial. For instance, many Brazilians stand close together in shops, buses, and elevators, and when they bump into one another, they don't apologize or draw back (Andersen et. al, 2002; Wiemann & Harrison, 1983). In many Middle Eastern countries, men often walk with their arms around other men, but in the United States touching between male friends is uncommon except during sports events.

Norms for touching also reflect cultural values. In one study, North Americans, who are relatively reserved, were observed engaging in an average of only two touches an hour. The emotionally restrained British averaged zero touches an hour. Parisians, long known for their emotional expressiveness, touched 110 times an hour. Puerto Ricans touched most, averaging 180 touches an hour (Knapp, 1972). Iraqis don't want or expect the amount of personal space that most Americans do. To help American soldiers stationed in Iraq, the Marine Corps distributes Iraq Culture Smart Cards, which include advice such as the fact that Iraqis consider it offensive to step or lean away from a male, never touch another person with your left hand, and do not expose the soles of shoes or feet (Word for Word, 2005).

Patterns of eye contact also reflect cultural values. In North America, frankness and assertion are valued, so meeting another's eyes is considered appropriate and a demonstration of personal honesty. Eye contact is also valued among most Hispanics. Yet, in many Asian and northern European countries, direct eye contact is considered abrasive and disrespectful (Axtell, 1990a, 1990b; Hall, 1968; Samovar & Porter, 2000). On the other hand, in Brazil eye contact often is so intense that many Americans consider it rude. Imagine the confusion this causes in intercultural business negotiations.

Cultural training also influences which emotions we express and how we express them (Matsumoto, Franklin, Choi, Rogers, & Tatani, 2002). For example, many people raised in traditional Italian and Jewish communities are more emotionally expressive than people raised in English or German communities. In Japan and many other Asian cultures, it is generally considered rude to express negative feelings toward others. In the United States, the display of negative feelings is less constrained.

Cultures also differ in their orientations toward time. Anthropologist Edward Hall (1976) dis-

Communication in Everyday Life

INSIGHT

"I'll Move When I'm Ready and Not Before!"

Have you ever felt that a driver was really slow in pulling out of a parking space for which you were waiting? It turns out that your imagination may not be playing tricks on you. A recent study of 400 drivers in a shopping mall found that drivers took longer to pull out of a space if someone was waiting than if nobody was there to claim the space (Raphael, 1997). On average, if nobody was waiting for the space, drivers took 32.2 seconds to pull out of a spot after opening a car door. If someone was waiting, drivers took about 39 seconds. And woe to the person who honks to hurry a driver: Drivers took 43 seconds to pull out of a space when the waiting driver honked!

tinguishes between cultures that have monochronic orientations toward time and those with polychronic orientations. Monochronic (one time) cultures, such as the United States, view time as a valuable commodity to be saved, scheduled, and carefully guarded. Within monochronic cultures, punctuality and efficiency are valued. Thus, people are expected to be on time for appointments and classes, and they are expected to complete work quickly (Honoré, 2004, 2005).

In contrast, polychronic (many times) cultures take a more holistic, systemic view of time. Members of these cultures assume that many things are happening simultaneously. Thus, punctuality is seldom stressed. Meetings may start late, with people joining in after discussions begin. Tangential discussions and social conversations are part of normal meetings in polychronic cultures. People may even cancel meetings without the dramatic reasons expected for cancelling in monochronic cultures.

Communication in Everyday Life
Multitasking Time

Technology is shifting our sense of time (Potter, 2001; Urgo, 2000). Computers encourage multitasking, which is engaging in multiple tasks simultaneously or in overlapping and interactive ways. Windows technology was designed to make it possible for a user to do multiple tasks at once. As I am writing this chapter, the e-mail program running behind my word-processing program alerts me when new messages arrive. As I type, the office assistant pops up occasionally to offer me formatting options; my program alerts me when a diskette is full and asks me to turn from what I'm doing to put in a new diskette or remove files from the present one.

Multitasking goes beyond what we do with computers. People interrupt conversations or other activities to answer cell phones and check pagers. Drivers talk on phones while navigating traffic. Students bring laptops to class and, when not taking notes, check e-mail or work on other tasks. The buzz of call waiting prompts a person to suspend the present telephone conversation.

So what's wrong with multitasking? One obvious problem is that, when we attend to several tasks at once, we're likely to do each one less well than if we concentrated on one thing at a time (Brooks, 2001). Another problem is that overtime multitasking may diminish our ability to give sustained attention to any single topic or activity (Honoré, 2005; Healy, 1990). It appears that the continuously shifting images and messages in computer games and online communication shape our neural maps such that we expect new images or stimulation frequently, so we learn to hold attention for only short spans of time.

JOSH Last year, my wife and I had our house painted. The company we hired had a lot of Hispanic workers. They were never on the job at 8 A.M. when the other workers were. They'd usually arrive around 8:30 or even 9, and they would take breaks and talk during the workday. But I'll have to say that they also stayed past 5 when they were working on a part of the house. They weren't in any hurry to leave—just weren't going by the clock to do their work. The white workers were out of there at 5 on the dot.

The belief that time is holistic leads members of polychronic cultures to assume that the rhythms of life—working, socializing, attending to personal matters—are interrelated and often overlapping. A faculty member at a U.S. university discovered how differently cultures view time when he accepted a teaching position in Brazil (Levine, 1988). Some of his students didn't show up until halfway through the class period, and many students were in no hurry to leave when the class ended. Instead, they wanted to stay to ask questions and discuss ideas.

In sum, four principles provide a foundation for understanding nonverbal communication. First, nonverbal behavior may supplement or replace verbal communication. Second, nonverbal behaviors may regulate interaction. Third, nonverbal behavior is more powerful than verbal behavior in expressing relationship-level meanings. Finally, nonverbal communication reflects and expresses cultural values. We're now ready to explore the types of nonverbal behavior that make up this intricate communication system.

Types of Nonverbal Communication

In this section, we consider nine forms of nonverbal behavior and point out how we use each to establish relationships and express personal identity and cultural values.

KINESICS

Kinesics refers to body position and body motions, including those of the face. Clearly, we signal a great deal about how we feel and see ourselves by how we hold our bodies. Someone who stands erectly and walks confidently is likely to be perceived as self-assured, whereas someone who slouches and shuffles may be seen as lacking confidence. A person who walks quickly with a resolute facial expression will be perceived as more determined than someone who saunters along with an unfocused gaze.

An interesting example of using body motions to sculpt others' perceptions comes from Ted Conover's book, *Coyotes: A Journey Through the Secret World of America's Illegal Aliens* (1987). Conover helped many Mexican workers illegally enter the United States. Critical to the workers' success in not getting caught was learning how to avoid calling attention to themselves. Conover taught the workers how to walk nonchalantly, control furtive eye movements, and sit with a relaxed posture. All these behaviors communicate "I've done this hundreds of time. No need to pay any special attention to me."

Body postures may signal whether we are open to interaction. In classes, students often look downward to dissuade teachers from calling on them. To invite interaction, Westerners look at others and smile, signaling that conversation is welcome. Yet, in many traditional Asian societies, direct eye contact and smiling at someone who is not an intimate might be considered disrespectful.

Gestures are important nonverbally. Humans communicated

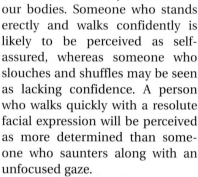

Communication in Everyday Life
Cultural Differences in Workplace Nonverbal Communication

WORK

More and more companies are becoming international, but not all workers who get transferred or who do business with international colleagues find it easy to understand and adapt to the nonverbal norms of their new cultures (Axtell, 1990a, 1990b). For instance, in Germany it is considered very rude to cough in concerts and in many other public areas. In India, whistling tunes is highly offensive.

Gift giving holds many opportunities for misunderstandings. A gift wrapped in blue and black might offend many Asians because those colors symbolize death in many Asian cultures.

An American might take offense if a Japanese person does not open a presented gift. In Japan, however, it is customary not to open gifts in front of the giver. An American might bring an extravagant gift to make a good impression on a Singaporean manager with whom he hopes to do business. Unfortunately for the American, the Singaporean manager probably would view an extravagant gift as an attempt at bribery—not exactly a good impression (Axtell, 1990a, 1990b).

How much time does a good worker invest in his or her work? That may depend on where one works. The typical job in Germany requires 37 hours a week, and stores close on weekends and four of five weeknights so that workers can have leisure time. Personal time is considered so precious in Germany that it is illegal to work more than one job during holidays, which are meant to allow people to restore themselves (Benjamin & Horwitz, 1994; Robinson, 2000).

In the United States, jobs typically require 44 to 80 hours a week. Vacation time is also limited to 2 weeks per year for most United States workers. Many other countries have laws that ensure more vacation time for workers. According to the Economic Policy Institute (Robinson, 2000), laws guarantee the following numbers of vacation days: Spain, 30; France, 30; Ireland, 28; Japan, 25; Portugal, 25; Belgium, 24; Norway, 21; Germany, 18; United States, 0.

Go to http://www.executiveplanet.com/community/. Select "articles," and read about what is appropriate in various cultures for business dress, gifts, and interaction norms.

by gesture long before they learned to communicate verbally (Corballis, 2002). Many people "talk with their hands," which psychology professor Susan Goldin-Meadow (2004) says actually helps us think. We use gestures to emphasize verbal language and to express feelings. We use a hand gesture to indicate "okay" and a different hand gesture to communicate contempt. But gestures don't always translate across cultures. For example, the hand gesture that stands for "okay" in the United States is the gesture for worthlessness in France and is regarded as obscene in Iraq (Word for Word, 2005).

Our faces are intricate messengers. The face alone is capable of more than a thousand distinct expressions that result from variations in tilt of the head and movements of the eyebrows, eyes, and mouth (Eckman, Friesen, & Ellsworth, 1971). Our eyes can shoot daggers of anger, issue challenges, or radiate feelings of love. With our faces, we can indicate disapproval (scowls), doubt (raised eyebrows), admiration (warm eye gazes), and resistance (stares). The face is particularly powerful in conveying responsiveness and liking (Keeley & Hart, 1994; Patterson, 1992).

One of the most important aspects of kinesics concerns how we position ourselves relative to others and what our positions say about our feelings toward them. Couples communicate dissatisfaction by increasing distance between them and by smiling less and looking away from each other (Miller & Parks, 1982). We also use nonverbal behaviors such as smiles, close seating, and warm gazes to signal that we like others and are happy with them (Gueguen & De Gail, 2003; Walker & Trimboli, 1989).

For good reason, poets call the eyes "the windows to the soul." Our eyes communicate some of the most important and complex messages about how we feel about others. If you watch infants, you'll notice that they focus on others' eyes. Even as adults, we tend to look at eyes to judge others' honesty, interest, friendliness, and self-confidence. Virginia Richmond and James McCroskey (2000) found that eye contact, along with other nonverbal behaviors, affects relationships between supervisors and subordinates. Supervisors who look at subordinates, smile, and incline their heads toward subordinates are perceived by subordinates as more credible and interpersonally attractive. Furthermore, these nonverbal behaviors from supervisors are positively related to subordinates' motivation and job

Everyday Application
Communicating Closeness

To become more aware of nonverbal cues of intimacy, watch a television show that features interaction between characters, and keep a record of characters' kinesic communication.

··· How close to each other do characters who are intimate stand or sit? How close do characters who are antagonistic stand or sit? What is the distance between characters who are just meeting or who have casual relationships?

··· What patterns of eye contact do you notice between characters who are intimates, characters who are enemies, and characters who are casual acquaintances? How often do they look at each other? How long is eye gaze maintained in each type of relationship?

··· What facial expressions signal characters who do and don't like each other? How often do they smile or stare?

What your do observations reveal about kinesics and relationship-level meanings?

Communication in Everyday Life
Kinesics to Discourage Assault

Many criminals are highly skilled at interpreting nonverbal behavior. Their success in getting away with crimes depends on their ability to read others. Convicted thieves report that they don't pick victims randomly. They carefully select their victims. They look for people whose walk signals uncertainty and whose posture and face suggest passivity. To avoid being picked as a victim, walk confidently, hold your head upright, and meet others' eyes without staring. Above all, never appear unsure or lost, particularly if you are.

satisfaction. It's also the case that customers leave larger tips for servers who maintain eye contact than for servers who don't (Davis & Kieffer, 1998).

For years, many attorneys have used body language to sway jurors' feelings and impressions of cases. For example, to suggest that a witness is lying, an attorney might roll his or her eyes in full sight of jurors. The attorney's standing farther away from witnesses during questioning enhances the witnesses' credibility with jurors. Some attorneys look conspicuously at their watches to signal jurors that the opposition's arguments are boring or ridiculous. Recently, some judges have tried to set limits on allowable nonverbal behavior by attorneys. A growing number of judges now require attorneys to stand at lecterns and limit face and body motions that might influence jurors. Perhaps the most stringent restriction of attorneys' nonverbal behavior comes from Samuel Kent, a U.S. District Court judge in Galveston, Texas. In his courtroom, Judge Kent says, "Facial gestures, nods of the head, audible signs, anything along those lines is strictly prohibited" (Schmitt, 1997, p. B7).

Gestures are the special interest of David McNeill, a professor of linguistics and psychology at the University of Chicago. According to McNeill (1992), much of what we want to communicate involves imagery, and imagery is not well conveyed by words. Thus, to communicate the images we have, we rely heavily on gestures, especially hand movements. In an interview (Mahany, 1997), McNeill offered the interesting observation that the gesture of the extended middle finger, which some Westerners use to convey contempt, was used for the same message more than 2,000 years ago by ancient Romans.

© David Young-Wolff/Stone/Getty Images

HAPTICS

Haptics, the sense of touch, is the first of our five senses to develop (Leathers, 1976), and many scholars believe that touching and being touched are essential to a healthy life (Benjamin & Werner, 2004). Research on dysfunctional families reveals that mothers touch babies less often and less affectionately than mothers in healthy families. In disturbed families, mothers tend to push children away, nonverbally signaling rejection (Birdwhistell, 1970). In contrast, babies who are held closely and tenderly tend to develop into self-confident adults who have secure attachment styles (Main, 1981; Mwakalye & DeAngelis, 1995).

Touching also communicates power and status. People with high status touch others and invade others' spaces more than people with less status do (Henley, 1977). Cultural views of women as more touchable than men are reflected in gendered patterns of contact. In general, parents touch sons less often and more roughly than they touch daughters (Condry, Condry, & Pogatshnik, 1983). Exposure to these patterns early in life teaches the sexes different rules for using touch and interpreting touches from others. As adults, women tend to use touch to show liking and intimacy (Montgomery, 1988), whereas men are more likely than women to use touch to assert power and control (Henley, 1977; Jhally & Katz, 2001; Leathers, 1986).

PHYSICAL APPEARANCE

Western culture places an extremely high value on physical appearance. For this reason, in face-to-face interactions, most of us notice how others look, and we often base our initial evaluations of others on their appearance, over which they have limited control. The excessive emphasis Western culture places on physical attractiveness and youthful appearance contributes to eating disorders, abuse of steroids and other drugs, and the popularity of cosmetic surgery.

Does physical appearance affect what people earn? It may. A study of 2,500 male and female lawyers revealed a relationship between physical attractiveness and earning power. The attorneys who were judged more attractive earned as much as 14% more than attorneys who were judged less attractive ("Good-Looking Lawyers," 1996).

Cultures stipulate ideals for physical form. Currently, Western cultural ideals emphasize thinness and youth in women and muscularity and height in men. Heterosexual women and gay men seem particularly vulnerable to cultural pressures to be thin because they are judged so keenly by their attractiveness, whereas heterosexual men are judged primarily by their accomplishments (Spitzack, 1990, 1993). Reflecting the increasing value placed on thinness in women in the United States is the fact that in the 1950s the average Miss America weighed 134 pounds, but by the early 1980s her weight had dropped to 117. Also, in 1962 leading fashion models weighed only 8% less than average women; by 1992, they weighed 25% less ("The Wrong Weight," 1997). The cultural emphasis on thinness is so great that many people consider being seriously overweight a greater social stigma than a criminal record, cancer, a facial scar, or a missing hand (Harris, Walters, & Waschall, 1991).

Thinness in women is not prized or encouraged in all cultures and social communities. In traditional African societies, full-figured bodies are perceived as symbolizing health, prosperity, and wealth, which are all desirable (Villarosa, 1994). African Americans who embrace this value accept or prefer women who weigh more than the current ideal for Caucasians (Root, 1990; Molloy &

Communication in Everyday Life
Help with Eating Disorders

INSIGHT

Preoccupation with weight can rob you of vitality and, in its extreme form, endanger your life. If you are obsessed with weight or have an eating disorder, help is available from the health center on your campus or from the following national organizations:

··· American Anorexia Bulimia Association, 418 E. 76th Street, New York, NY 10021.

··· Center for the Study of Anorexia and Bulimia, 1 West 91st Street, New York, NY 10024.

··· National Anorexic Aid Society, 1925 East Dublin–Granville Road, Columbus, OH 43229.

There are also good online sources of information. One is the site for the National Association of Anorexia Nervosa and Associated Disorders (ANAD) at http://www.anad.org.

Communication in Everyday Life
Beauty for Sale

Sander Gilman (1999a, 1999b) studies people who have surgery that is strictly cosmetic. People want larger or smaller breasts, noses, and chins. They want less fat here and more there. They want hair put on their bald heads and varicose veins removed from legs. They want skin tightened, eyelids lifted, wrinkles removed.

Aesthetic surgery isn't just for women or Americans. In the United States, the most popular cosmetic surgeries for men are hair implants, face lifts, and, increasingly, penis enlargements (Bordo, 1999). In the Far East, "eye straightening" is nearly as common as nose surgery is in the United States. And cosmetic surgery is no longer restricted to wealthy people—65% of people who have plastic surgery in the United States have annual family incomes of less than $50,000 (Gross, 2000; Sharlet, 1999).

Trends in plastic surgery tend to mirror trends in cultural views of physical attractiveness. When fuller body styles were idealized in women, there were few surgeries to reduce fat and many to increase breast size. As thinner, more athletic bodies have become cultural ideals for women, liposuction and breast reduction surgeries have increased. Likewise, as the culture increasingly emphasizes leanness and muscularity as masculine ideals, more men are having pectoral implants and liposuction.

Herzberger, 1998; Thomas, 1989; Vobejda & Perlstein, 1998).

TYRA I don't see anything beautiful about a body like a pencil. Why do white girls want to have stick figures? I sure don't, and neither do the girls I hang out with. Guys don't like it either. The guys I know like a girl to have some curves, some substance. It's more feminine.

Class membership further modifies ethnic values concerning weight. African American women who are either affluent or poor are likely to have strong black identities that reject the preoccupations with thinness that many whites endorse. On the other hand, middle-class, upwardly mobile African American women are more susceptible to eating disorders and obsession with weight (Villarosa, 1994).

ARTIFACTS

Artifacts are personal objects we use to announce our identities and heritage and to personalize our environments. Many people use avatars to symbolize identities in online communication. In face-to-face communication, we craft our image by how we dress and what objects we carry and use. Nurses and physicians wear white and often drape stethoscopes around their necks; professors travel with briefcases, whereas students more often tote backpacks. White-collar professionals tend to wear tailored outfits and dress shoes, whereas blue-collar workers more often dress in jeans or uniforms and boots. The military requires uniforms that define individuals in terms of the group; in addition, stripes and medals signify rank and accomplishments. A recent study (Morris, Gorham, Cohen, & Huffman, 1996) showed that undergraduate students tend to perceive graduate teaching assistants as having greater expertise if the teaching assistants dress professionally than if they dress casually. However, the same study showed that the undergraduate students perceived casually dressed teaching assistants as more extroverted and sociable than those dressed formally.

Artifacts may also define personal territories. To claim our spaces, we fill them with objects that matter to us and that reflect our experiences and values. Lovers of art adorn their homes with paintings and sculptures that announce their interests and personalize their private space. Religious families often express their commitments by displaying pictures of holy scenes and the Bible, the Koran, or other sacred texts. Lohmann, Arriga, and Goodfriend (2003) studied artifacts in homes. They found that couples with more objects depicting the couple as couple than as individuals—wedding photos, for example—have greater closeness than couples who have fewer artifacts that define them as a couple. The researchers concluded that "the environment in which much of a couple's joint life unfolds—their home—is imbued with their couple identity" (p. 447).

In our homes and other personal spaces, we exhibit artifacts that symbolize important relationships and experiences in our lives (Wood, 2006). On my desk, I have a photograph of my sister, Carolyn; an item that belonged to my father; the first card my partner, Robbie, ever gave me; and a jar of rocks from a beach to which I retreat whenever possible. These artifacts personalize my desk and remind me of people and experiences I cherish.

JENETTA   Whenever I move, the first thing I have to do is get out the quilt that my grandmother made. Even if it is summer and I won't use the quilt, I have to unpack it first and put it out where I can see it. She brought me up, and seeing that quilt is my way of keeping her in my life.

In her book *Composing a Life,* Mary Catherine Bateson (1990) comments that we turn houses into homes by filling them with what matters to us. We make impersonal spaces familiar and comfortable by adorning them with artifacts that express our experiences, relationships, values, and personalities. We use mugs given to us by special people, surround ourselves with books and magazines that announce our interests, and sprinkle our world with objects that reflect what we care about.

Artifacts are used to express identity from an early age. Many hospitals still swaddle newborns in blue and pink blankets to designate sex, and even though many parents today try to be nonsexist, many still send gender messages through the toys they give their children. In general, parents (especially fathers) give sons toys that encourage rough and active play (balls, trains) and competitiveness (baseball gloves, toy weapons), whereas they give daughters toys that cultivate nurturing (dolls, toy kitchens) and attention to appearance (makeup kits, frilly clothes) (Caldera, Huston, & O'Brien, 1989; Lytton & Romney, 1991; Pomerleau, Bolduc, Malcuit, & Cossette, 1990).

Although clothing has become more unisex in recent years, once you venture off campus, gendered styles are evident. Thus, women sometimes wear makeup, dresses with lace or other softening touches, skirts, high-heeled shoes, jewelry, and hosiery, all of which conform to the cultural ideal of femininity. Typically, men wear less jewelry, and their clothes and shoes tend to be more functional and less decorative. Flat shoes allow a person to walk comfortably or run if necessary; high heels don't. Men's clothing is looser and less binding, and it includes pockets for wallets, change, keys, and so forth. In contrast, women's clothing tends to be more tailored and often doesn't include pockets, making a purse necessary. Clothing is also used to reflect ethnic identity. In recent years, marketers have offered more ethnic clothing and jewelry so people can more easily acquire artifacts that express their distinctive cultural heritages.

We use artifacts to announce our identities and to project a particular image to others. Jeans

PEPPER AND SALT © Mike Shapiro. *Wall Street Journal,* August 21, 1997.
Reprinted by permission of Cartoon Features Syndicate.

"I suggest you get yourself a real briefcase, Miller. A tote bag just doesn't say vice president."

Communication in Everyday Life
Identity Symbols in Military Life

On May 16, 1996, Admiral Jeremy M. Boorda, the Navy's most senior officer, killed himself by shooting a .38-caliber bullet into his chest.

Why did he commit suicide? A widely read magazine had disclosed that Admiral Boorda had never earned two of the war decorations he wore. Bernard Trainor, a retired Marine Corps lieutenant general, explains that "when service people meet for the first time they immediately look at the ribbons each wears. In a way, it establishes a hierarchy of respect. . . . For a soldier, sailor, airman or Marine a decoration is the symbol of status within the military fraternity" (Trainor, 1996, p. A8). When Admiral Boorda's artifacts were revealed to be unearned, he lost his status and perhaps his identity.

and a grungy shirt convey one image; a silk business suit conveys a very different one. Body piercings are increasingly popular, but not everyone appreciates them (Forbes, 2001). Customers in some restaurants have been offended by waitstaff with multiple piercings, so management has policies that regulate piercings (Business Bulletin, 1996). Tattoos are also used to announce identity. In his amusing (but also serious) book *The T-Shirt,* Scott Fresener (1995) profiles people who own thousands of T-shirts, each important for defining some aspect of who they are or have been.

Cultures, as well as social groups within a single culture, have artifacts that are especially important reflections of heritage and values. For example, many Jewish people light candles in a menorah to symbolize sacred values. Christians rely on crosses and manger replicas to symbolize reverence for Jesus.

ENVIRONMENTAL FACTORS

Environmental factors are elements of settings that affect how we feel and act. For instance, we respond to architecture, colors, room design, temperature, sounds, smells, and lighting. Rooms with comfortable chairs invite relaxation, whereas rooms with stiff chairs induce formality. Dimly lit rooms can set a romantic mood,

Everyday Application
Artifacts and Identity

How did artifacts in your childhood contribute to your gender identity? What kinds of toys did your parents give you? Did they ever discourage you from playing with particular kinds of toys? Did you ask for toys that aren't the ones society prescribes for your gender (boys asking for dolls, girls for train sets)? Did your parents let you have the toys?

Now, think about the clothing your parents gave you. If you're a woman, did your parents expect you to wear frilly dresses and stay clean? If you're a man, did your parents give you clothes meant for rough play and getting dirty?

Do you have artifacts that reflect your ethnic identity? What objects are part of your celebrations and spiritual observances? Do you have any jewelry or clothes that reflect your ethnic heritage? To increase your awareness of the ways in which you use artifacts to personalize your environment, complete Activity 5.3 in your *Student Companion* or online under "Chapter Resources for Chapter 5" at the Everyday Connections website. This activity utilizes InfoTrac College Edition.

although dark rooms can be depressing. We feel solemn in churches and synagogues with their somber colors and sacred symbols.

We tend to feel more lethargic on sultry summer days and more alert on crisp fall ones. Delicious smells can make us hungry, even if we weren't previously interested in food. Our bodies synchronize themselves to patterns of light, so we feel more alert during daylight than during the evening. In settings where people work during the night, extra lighting and even artificial skylights are used to simulate daylight so that workers stay alert. Even Wal-Mart wants to bring natural light into its stores because a test showed that workers were more productive and customers bought more when natural light was used instead of artificial light (Pierson, 1995).

As the examples that opened this chapter illustrate, the environments of most fast-food restaurants encourage customers to eat quickly and move on, whereas more expensive restaurants are designed to promote longer stays and extra spending on wines and desserts. Even background music can affect diners' behavior. Studies show that people eat faster when fast music is played in an eating area ("Bites," 1998; Bozzi, 1986).

An interesting illustration of the relationship between culture and environmental factors is *feng shui* (which means "wind and water" and is pronounced "fung shway"). Dating back more than 3000 years, feng shui is rooted in Taoism and aims to balance life energy, or *chi* (Spear, 1995). Feng shui consultants help homeowners and businesspeople arrange spaces to promote a smooth flow of energy and a harmony with nature. Some of the feng shui principles are consistent with Western research on nonverbal communication: Don't put large furniture in the path to the front door; you should never see a stairway from the front door; use green to increase good fortune; use

© A. Ramey/Stock Boston, LLC

Communication in Everyday Life
Kwanzaa

Rituals allow people to acknowledge and celebrate important values (Otnes & Lowrey, 2004). One relatively new ritual is associated with Kwanzaa, which in 1966 was designated a time for African Americans to honor their African heritage and the everyday activities of keeping a home. In this way, Kwanzaa symbolizes the centrality of home and family to African Americans historically and today (Bellamy, 1996; George, 1995).

The *kinara* is a branched candleholder that holds seven candles, one to be lit on each day of the Kwanzaa observance. Three red candles, which symbolize struggles, are placed on the left for days two, four, and six of the celebration. The day two candle symbolizes the principle of *kujichagulia,* or self-determination. The day four candle symbolizes *ujamma,* cooperative economics within communities. The day six candle represents *kuumba,* or creativity. On the right side of the kinara are placed three green candles to symbolize the future. The day three candle on the far right represents *ujima,* collective work and responsibility. The day five candle symbolizes *nio,* or purpose. The day seven candle represents *imani,* or faith. The middle candle is black to stand for *umoja,* unity among black people.

On the sixth day of Kwanzaa, there is a feast called Karamu. During the feast, traditional African foods and family favorites are featured. Thus, Kwanzaa celebrates foods that have been passed down through generations of Africans and African Americans.

© Paul Barton/CORBIS Stock Market

Communication in Everyday Life
Environmental Racism

DIVERSITY

According to a former president of the Sierra Club (Cox, 2005), the term *environmental racism* was coined to describe a pattern whereby toxic waste dumps and hazardous industrial plants are disproportionately located in low-income neighborhoods and communities of color.

Whether this is deliberately planned or not, many industries expose our most vulnerable communities to pollutants and carcinogens that seldom affect middle- and upper-class neighborhoods. Even when an affluent neighborhood is initially considered as a location for an environmentally hazardous operation, citizens have the resources and the influence to fight and, usually, to win to keep their communities safe. The pattern is very clear: The space of minorities and poor people can be invaded and contaminated, but that of more affluent citizens cannot.

mirrors where you want to stimulate creativity (Cozart, 1996; O'Neill, 1997). *Student Companion:* Activity 5.8 and Activity 5.9.

PROXEMICS AND PERSONAL SPACE

Proxemics refers to space and how we use it (Hall, 1968). Every culture has norms that prescribe how people should use space, how close people should be to one another, and how much space different people are entitled to have. In the United States, we generally interact with social acquaintances from a distance of 4 to 12 feet but are comfortable with 18 inches or less between ourselves and close friends and romantic partners (Hall, 1966). When we are angry with someone, we tend to move away and to resent it if the person approaches us. Nonverbal expectancy theory shows that societies establish norms for how closely people should come to one another and that violating those norms can affect others' responses to us (Afifi & Burgoon, 2000; Burgoon & Hale, 1988; Mongeau, Carey, & Williams, 1998).

> **GARY** Part of our training for management was to learn how to manage turf. We were taught we should always try to get competitors into our offices—not to go to theirs. This gives us the advantage, just like playing on the home court gives a team an advantage. We also learned that we should go to subordinates' offices if we needed to criticize them so that they would feel less threatened and more willing to improve performance. The trainers also stressed the importance of meeting on neutral ground when we had to negotiate a deal with another company. They warned us never to meet on the other guys' turf, because that would give them the advantage.

The amount of space with which people feel comfortable differs among cultures. In 1994, nearly half of the homes that were built in the United States exceeded 3000 square feet and were owned by couples without children (Templin, 1994). In contrast, in collectivist cultures people require little personal space in homes, workplaces, or public areas (Andersen, 2003).

Space also announces status, with greater space assumed by those with higher status (Henley, 1977). Substantial research shows that women and minorities generally take up less space than white men in Western society (Spain, 1992). The prerogative to invade someone else's personal space is also linked to power; those having greater power are the most likely to trespass into others' territory. Responses to invasions of space also reflect power, with men likely to respond aggressively when their space is invaded (Fisher & Byrne, 1975).

How people arrange space reflects how close they are and whether they want interaction. Couples who are very interdependent tend to have greater amounts of common space and less individual space in their homes than do couples who are more independent (Fitzpatrick, 1988; Fitzpatrick & Best, 1979; Werner, Altman, & Oxley, 1985; Werner & Haggard, 1985). Similarly, families that value interaction arrange furniture to invite conversation and eye contact. Families that are less inclined to interact arrange furniture to discourage conversation. Chairs may be far apart and may face televisions instead of one another (Burgoon, Buller, & Woodhall, 1989; Keeley & Hart, 1994). *Student Companion:* Activity 5.2.

The effects of proxemics on behavior have not gone unnoticed by companies that make money by moving people quickly. At McDonald's restaurants around the world, seats tilt forward at a 10-degree angle to discourage customers from lingering. The fast-food giant further fosters quick eating by making seats at the two-person tables only 2 feet 2 inches apart, when it has been established that the distance most people find comfortable for interaction is about 3 and one half feet (Eaves & Leathers, 1991). *Student Companion:* Activity 5.4.

CHRONEMICS

Chronemics refers to how we perceive and use time to define identities and interaction. In Western culture, there is a norm that important people with high status can keep others waiting (Hickson, et al., 2004). Conversely, people with low status are expected to be punctual. It is standard practice to have to wait, sometimes a good while, to see a physician, even if you have an appointment. This carries the message that the physician's time is more valuable than yours. Professors can be late to class and students are expected to wait, but students may be reprimanded if they appear after a class has begun. Subordinates are expected to report punctually to meetings, but bosses are allowed to be tardy.

In Western societies, time is valuable, so speed is highly valued (Honoré, 2005; Keyes, 1992; Schwartz, 1989). Linguists (Lakoff & Johnson, 1980) have noted many everyday American phrases that reflect the cultural view that time is very valuable: "Don't waste time," "Save time," "Spend time," "Can't spare time," "Invest time," "Run out of time," "Budget time," "Borrowed time," "Lose time," "Use time profitably."

Many other cultures have more relaxed attitudes toward time (Levine & Norenzayan, 1999). In many South American countries, it's not impolite to come late to meetings or classes, and it's not assumed that people will leave at the scheduled ending time.

The length of time we spend with different people reflects our interpersonal priorities. When possible, we spend more time with people we like than with those we don't like or who bore us. Researchers report that increasing contact is one of the most important ways college students intensify relationships, and reduced time together signals decreasing interest (Baxter, 1985; Dindia, 1994; Tolhuizen, 1989).

In work settings, time is also related to status. Bankers spend more time with important clients who have major accounts, brokers spend more time with clients who have a lot of money than with clients who have less, architects meet more often and for longer periods with companies that are building a series of large structures than with individuals who want to build a single home, and fund-raisers invest greater amounts of time in generous donors than in moderate contributors.

Communication in Everyday Life
The Time Bind

WORK

Sociologist Arlie Hochschild claims that time is the central issue in American corporate life today. In her recent book *The Time Bind: When Work Becomes Home and Home Becomes Work* (1997), Hochschild reports that many professionals today feel compelled to force home and family time into an industrial, time-saving model that, ironically, is less and less endorsed in workplaces. Children often are allotted 20 or 30 minutes of time at the end of the day when two working parents get home. Dinner is restricted to 15 minutes so that there is enough time to drive the kids to their soccer game. Breakfasts are made and eaten assembly-line style. Tasks that families used to share are increasingly outsourced as busy parents hire a birthday party service, a personal shopper, and a cleaning service. There just isn't enough time for parents to do all the homemaking and child-rearing activities themselves.

Where has the time gone? Hochschild says it goes more and more into paid jobs. Many professionals work 9, 10, or more hours a day, including weekends. Perhaps most disturbing is Hochschild's conclusion that many people prefer to be in the workplace than at home; they stretch their on-the-job hours and condense their time at home. Why? Because for many people, the workplace is more pleasant, less frenzied and rushed, with time to socialize and relax on breaks. The bottom line, according to Hochschild, is that home and work have switched places; for many, work is a sanctuary, and home is a site of stress and agitation.

But, says Hochschild, that is not acceptable. She urges people to demand a workplace that doesn't compromise their families. She also encourages businesses to encourage workers to leave at the end of a reasonable work day and to reward employees who do that.

PARALANGUAGE

Paralanguage is communication that is vocal but does not use words. It includes sounds, such as murmurs and gasps, and vocal qualities, such as volume, pitch, and inflection. Paralanguage also includes accents, pronunciation, and the complexity of sentences.

Our voices are versatile instruments that give others cues about how to interpret us. Whispering, for instance, signals secrecy and intimacy, whereas shouting conveys anger. Negative paralanguage, such as sneering and ridiculing by tone of voice, is closely associated with dissatisfaction in marriage (Gottman, Markman, & Notarius, 1977; Noller, 1987). A derisive or sarcastic tone communicates scorn or dislike more emphatically than words.

Our voices affect how others perceive us. To some extent, we control vocal cues that influence image. For instance, we can deliberately sound firm and sure of ourselves in job interviews when we want to project self-confidence. Similarly, we can consciously make ourselves sound self-righteous, seductive, and unapproachable when those images suit our purposes. In addition to the ways we intentionally use our voices to project an image, vocal qualities we don't deliberately manipulate affect how others perceive us. For instance, people with accents often are stereotyped: Someone with a pronounced Bronx accent may be perceived as brash, and someone with a Southern drawl may be stereotyped as lazy. People with foreign accents often are falsely perceived as less intelligent than native speakers.

Paralanguage also reflects cultural heritage and may signal that we are members of specific communication communities. For example, in general African American speech has more vocal range, inflection, rhythmic variation and emphasis, and tonal quality than Caucasian speech (Garner, 1994; Ribeau, Baldwin, & Hecht, 1994).

SILENCE

A final type of nonverbal behavior is silence, which can communicate powerful messages. "I'm not speaking to you" actually speaks volumes. We use silence to communicate different meanings. For instance, it can symbolize contentment when intimates are so comfortable they don't need to talk. Silence can also communicate awkwardness, as you know if you've ever had trouble keeping conversation going on a first date. In some cultures, including many Eastern (Lim, 2002) and Native American (Braithwaite, 1990) ones, silence indicates respect and thoughtfulness.

Silence soothes seriously ill babies. Hospital intensive care nurseries have found that special headphones that block noise reduce the stress caused by the sounds of respirators, ventilators, and other hospital machinery. Within the headphones is a mini-microphone that detects irritating low-frequency noises and eliminates them by generating anti-noise waves. In trials of the headphones, babies who wore them had fewer sleep disturbances and less change in blood pressure ("Cyberscope," 1996).

Yet, silence isn't always comforting. It is sometimes used to disconfirm others. In some families, children are disciplined by being ignored. No matter what the child says or does, parents refuse to acknowledge his or her existence. In later life, the silencing strategy may also surface. You know how disconfirming silence can be if you've ever said "hello" to someone and gotten no reply. Even if the other person didn't deliberately ignore you, you feel slighted. We sometimes deliberately freeze out intimates and refuse to answer e-mails from friends with whom we're angry. In some military academies, such as West Point, silencing is a recognized method of stripping a cadet of personhood if he or she is perceived as having broken the academy code.

> **GINDER** Silencing is the cruelest thing you can do to a person. That was how my parents disciplined all of us. They told us we were bad and then refused to speak to us—sometimes for several hours. I can't describe how awful it felt to get no response from them, to be a nonperson. I would have preferred physical punishment. I'll never use silencing with my kids.

The complex system of nonverbal communication includes kinesics, haptics, physical appearance, artifacts, environmental features, space, chronemics, paralanguage, and silence. In the final section of this chapter, we consider guidelines for improving the effectiveness of our nonverbal communication.

●●●●●●●●●●

Guidelines for Improving Nonverbal Communication

Following two guidelines should decrease the chance that you will misunderstand others' nonverbal behaviors or that others will misperceive yours.

MONITOR YOUR NONVERBAL COMMUNICATION

Think about the previous discussion of ways we use nonverbal behaviors to announce our identities. Are you projecting the image you desire? Do friends ever tell you that you seem uninterested or far away when they are talking to you? If so, you can monitor your nonverbal actions so that you convey greater involvement and interest in conversations. *Student Companion:* Activities 5.6 and 5.7.

Have you set up your spaces so that they invite the kind of interaction you prefer, or are they arranged to interfere with good communication? Paying attention to nonverbal dimensions of your world can empower you to use them more effectively to achieve your interpersonal goals.

Although stores are filled with popular advice books that promise to show you how to read nonverbal communication, there really aren't any surefire formulas. It's naive to think we can precisely decode something as complex and ambiguous as nonverbal communication.

In this chapter, we've discussed findings about the meanings people attach to nonverbal behaviors. It's important to realize that these are only generalizations. We have not and cannot state what any particular behavior ever means to specific people in a given context. For instance, we've said that satisfied couples tend to sit closer together than unhappy couples. As a general rule, this is true in Western society. However, sometimes very contented couples prefer to keep distance between them. In work settings, people who don't look at us may be preoccupied with solving a problem and do not intend to ignore us. Different cultures teach members different rules for expressing and interpreting nonverbal behavior (Matsumoto et al., 2002). Because nonverbal communication is ambiguous and personal, we should not assume we can interpret it with absolute precision. Effective communicators qualify interpretations of nonverbal communication with awareness of personal and contextual factors. *Student Companion:* Activity 5.5.

Personal Qualifications   Generalizations about nonverbal behavior tell us only what is generally the case. They may not apply to particular people. Although eye contact generally indicates responsiveness in Western culture, some people close their eyes to concentrate when listening. Similarly, people who cross their arms and have a rigid posture often are expressing hostility or lack of interest in interaction. However, the same behaviors might mean a person feels cold and is trying to conserve body heat. Most people use less inflection, fewer gestures, and a slack posture

---

Everyday Application
Using I *Language about Nonverbal Behaviors*

I language makes communication about nonverbal behaviors more responsible and clear. Practice the skill of translating *you* language into *I* language to describe nonverbal behavior.

Example: You language: You're staring at me.
    I language: When you look at me so intensely, I feel uneasy.

You Language	I Language
I hate it when you give me that know-it-all look.	_____
I can tell you don't believe me by your expression.	_____
Don't crowd me.	_____
Your T-shirt is offensive.	_____

© E. Williamson/Index Stock Imagery

when they're not really interested in what they're talking about. However, we exhibit these same behaviors when we are tired.

Because nonverbal behaviors are ambiguous and vary among people, we need to be cautious about how we interpret others. Meaning is something we construct and assign to behaviors. A good way to keep this distinction in mind is to rely on *I* language, not *you* language, which we discussed in Chapter 4. *You* language might lead us to inaccurately say of someone who doesn't look at us, "You're communicating lack of interest." A more responsible statement would use *I* language to say, "When you don't look at me, I feel you're not interested in what I'm saying." Using *I* language reminds us to take responsibility for our judgments and feelings. In addition, it reduces the likelihood of making others defensive by inaccurately interpreting their nonverbal behavior.

Contextual Qualifications   Our nonverbal communication reflects not only how we see ourselves and how we feel. In addition, it reflects the various settings we inhabit. Most people are more at ease on their own turf than on someone else's, so we tend to be friendlier and more outgoing in our homes than in business meetings and public places. We also dress according to context. Students who see me in professional clothing on campus often are surprised to find me in jeans or a running suit when they come to my home or see me in town.

Immediate physical setting is not the only context that affects nonverbal communication. As we have seen, all communication, including the nonverbal dimension, reflects the values and understandings of particular cultures (Andersen et al., 2002). We are likely to misinterpret people from other cultures when we impose the norms and rules of our own.

> **MEI-LING**   I often have been misinterpreted in this country. My first semester here, a professor told me to be more assertive and to speak up in class. I could not do that, I told him. He said I should put myself forward, but I have been brought up not to do that. In Taiwan, that is very rude and ugly, and we are taught not to speak up to teachers. Now that I have been here for 3 years, I sometimes speak in classes, but I am still more quiet than Americans. I know my professors think I am not so smart because I am quiet, but that is the teaching of my country.

Even within our own country, we have diverse speech communities, and each has its own rules for nonverbal behavior. We run the risk of misinterpreting men if we judge them by the norms of feminine speech communities. A man who doesn't make "listening noises" may well be listening intently according to the rules of masculine speech communities. Similarly, men often misperceive women as agreeing when they nod and make listening noises while another is talking. According to feminine speech communities, ongoing feedback is a way to signal interest, not necessarily approval. We should try to adopt a dual perspective when interpreting others, especially when different social groups are involved.

We can become more effective nonverbal communicators if we monitor our own nonverbal behaviors and qualify our interpretation of others by keeping personal and contextual considerations in mind.

Case Study: Continuing the Conversation

The following conversation is featured on the Everyday Connections website under "Chapter Resources for Chapter 5." Click on the "Doctor and Patient" link in the left-hand menu to launch the video and audio scenario scripted below.

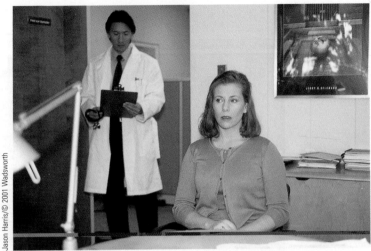

Jason Harris/© 2001 Wadsworth

You have been hired to help doctors learn to listen more effectively when interacting with patients. You observe the following interaction between Dr. Zhug and Ms. Ryder, who came in to find out why she is so tired.

Dr. Zhug: Ms. Ryder, there's good news. All the tests we did show you are normal.

Ms. Ryder: If I'm normal, why do I feel so tired all the time?

Dr. Zhug: Perhaps you need to get more sleep at night.

Ms. Ryder: I've been getting more sleep than I've ever needed before, and in the last 6 months I've felt tired. I feel that way no matter how many hours I sleep. I know this isn't normal.

Dr. Zhug: According to the tests, you have no medical problems. Perhaps your fatigue is emotional. This is common in women your age. Would you like a referral for counseling?

Ms. Ryder: Fatigue has nothing to do with my age. I'm only 35, and I felt fine 6 months ago.

I'm telling you, this isn't normal.

Dr. Zhug: Well, you might also try

sleeping more than you used to; our bodies change, you know.

Ms. Ryder: I just told you I am sleeping more, and it's not helping. What I need to know is . . .

Dr. Zhug: Ms. Ryder, there's no need to get hysterical. I assure you I know how to read test results, and physically you are quite normal.

Ms. Ryder: Doctor, I know this isn't normal for me. I can't do my work well. I don't have the energy I need for my family. This isn't normal. I need to get my energy back.

Dr. Zhug: I wish I could help you.

1. Identify nonverbal behaviors of Dr. Zhug that Ms. Ryder could interpret as a lack of attentiveness or interest in her.

2. How does Ms. Ryder's nonverbal communication change during her conversation with Dr. Zhug? To what would you attribute the changes?

3. Based on what you have learned about effective interpersonal communication from this and previous chapters, what feedback would you give Dr. Zhug so that he can communicate more effectively with patients?

You can critique and analyze this encounter based on the principles you learned in this chapter by responding to the questions included under "Conversation Analysis" at the website. By clicking on the "Submit" button at the end of the form, you can compare your work to my suggested responses. Let's continue the conversation online!

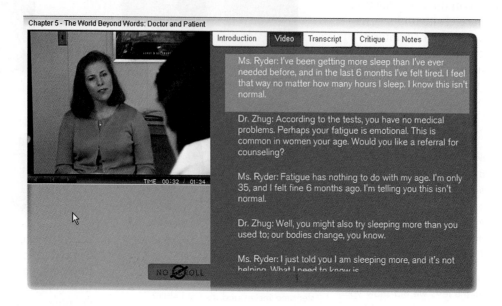

Chapter 5 - The World Beyond Words: Doctor and Patient

| Introduction | Video | Transcript | Critique | Notes |

TIME 00:32 / 01:34

Ms. Ryder: I've been getting more sleep than I've ever needed before, and in the last 6 months I've felt tired. I feel that way no matter how many hours I sleep. I know this isn't normal.

Dr. Zhug: According to the tests, you have no medical problems. Perhaps your fatigue is emotional. This is common in women your age. Would you like a referral for counseling?

Ms. Ryder: Fatigue has nothing to do with my age. I'm only 35, and I felt fine 6 months ago. I'm telling you this isn't normal.

Dr. Zhug: Well, you might also try sleeping more than you used to; our bodies change, you know.

Ms. Ryder: I just told you I am sleeping more, and it's not helping. What I need to know is

Chapter Summary

In this chapter, we've explored the fascinating world beyond words. We began by noting both the similarities and the differences between verbal and nonverbal communication. Next, we discussed how nonverbal communication functions to supplement or replace verbal messages, to regulate interaction, to reflect and establish relationship-level meanings, and to express cultural values.

We discussed nine types of nonverbal communication. These are kinesics (face and body motion), proxemics (use of space), physical appearance, artifacts, environmental features, haptics (use of touch), chronemics (use of and orientations to time), paralanguage, and silence. Each type of nonverbal communication reflects cultural understandings and values and also expresses our personal identities and feelings toward others. In this sense, nonverbal communication has a theatrical dimension because it is a primary way we create and present images of ourselves.

Because nonverbal communication, like its verbal cousin, is symbolic, it has no inherent meaning. Instead, its meaning is something we construct as we notice, organize, and interpret nonverbal behaviors that we and others enact. Effectiveness requires that we learn to monitor our own nonverbal communication and to exercise caution in interpreting that of others.

Everyday Connections Online

Now that you've read Chapter 5, go to the Everyday Connections premium website at academic.cengage.com/ communication/woodinterpersonal5plus for quick access to the electronic study resources that accompany this text. The website gives you access to the "Continuing the Conversation" video scenario and questions featured in this chapter, to InfoTrac College Edition, to maintained and updated web links, and to the study aids for this chapter, including a digital glossary, review quizzes, and the chapter activities. For more information about this text's electronic learning resources, consult the **1pass card** that came with each new copy of this book, or visit academic.cengage.com/ communication/woodinterpersonal5.

Key Concepts

Audio flash cards of the following key terms are available on the Everyday Connections website. Use the flash cards to improve your pronunciation of text vocabulary.

artifacts	haptics	nonverbal communication	proxemics
chronemics	kinesics	paralanguage	

For Further Thought and Discussion

1. Think about the information on lawyers' nonverbal communication (page 142). What ethical issues are involved in lawyers' use of nonverbal behaviors in an effort to influence jurors? What ethical issues are involved in judges' restrictions of lawyers' nonverbal communication? Is this a violation of the right to free speech?

2. Visit six restaurants near your campus. Describe the seats, lighting, music (if any), distance between tables, and colors of decor. Do you find any relationship between nonverbal communication patterns and expensiveness of restaurants?

3. Read an online journal that is devoted exclusively to research on haptic communication. Visit Haptics-E at http://www.haptics-e.org.

4. Use your InfoTrac College Edition to skim articles and advertisements in *Better Homes and Gardens,* which has a predominantly white readership, and *Essence,* which has a predominantly black readership. How many articles and advertisements that focus on weight (losing it, controlling it) do you find in each of these magazines? What can you conclude about different racial groups' views of weight?

5. Founded in 1997, the Center for Nonverbal Studies is located in Spokane, Washington, and La Jolla, California. It publishes *The Nonverbal Dictionary of Gestures, Signs, and Body Language Cues* and presents essays on nonverbal behaviors by anthropologists, archeologists, biologists, linguists, and communication scholars. You can read the dictionary, news files, and essays by going to http:// members.aol.com/nonverbal2/index.htm.

6. For thousands of years, colors have been used in oriental rugs to represent important religious and cultural ideas. For instance, blue symbolizes truth, green healing, and yellow the intellect. Learn more about the significance of color and symbols in oriental rugs by visiting http://www.travelchinaguide.com/shopping/silk_ carpet/style.htm.

7. Use your InfoTrac College Edition to read B. Bower's 2002 article, "Abused Kids Face Up to Angry Expressions," published in *Science News.* What relationship do you see between our discussion in Chapter 4 of communication communities and Bower's finding that abused children develop keen abilities to read nonverbal cues of anger?

Mindful Listening

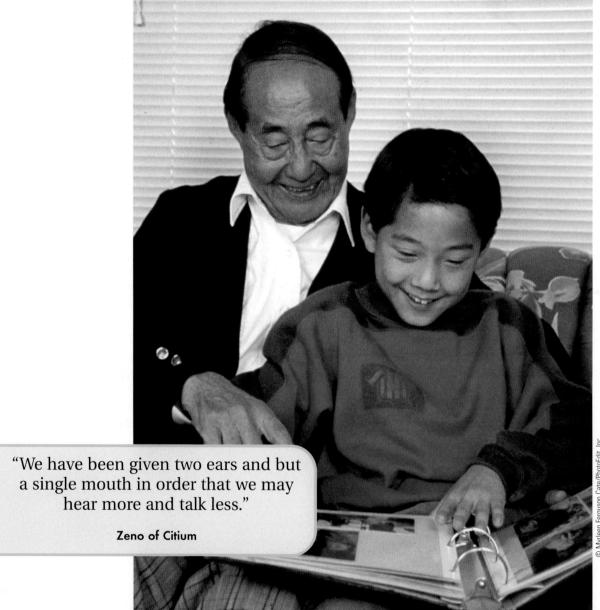

"We have been given two ears and but a single mouth in order that we may hear more and talk less."

Zeno of Citium

eet Anna Deavere Smith. She's a playwright, an artist in residence at MTV, a recipient of the MacArthur Foundation "genius" award, a performance studies teacher at Tisch School of the Arts, and a professor at NYU. She's won high praise for her one-woman shows, *Fires in the Mirror,* which dealt with ethnic turmoil in Crown Heights, Brooklyn, and *Twilight: Los Angeles,* which focused on the riots that erupted following the acquittal of the police officers accused of beating Rodney King. She also played the president's secretary in *The American President* and a paralegal in *Philadelphia,* and she has a continuing role on the television series *The West Wing.*

Anna Deavere Smith just added another title to her résumé—teaching medical students at Yale and law students at New York University. You might wonder what qualifies her to instruct medical and law students. After all, she's not a doctor or lawyer.

Anna Deavere Smith is a virtuoso listener. That's why she was hired to teach medical and law students. "No one listens better . . . than Anna Deavere Smith," says Dr. Ralph Horat, Chair of the Department of Internal Medicine at Yale's School of Medicine (Arenson, 2002, p. 34). Doctors and lawyers need to listen, and conventional medical and legal training doesn't teach them how to listen well. That's why the school turned to Anna Deavere Smith. She says, "Listening is not just hearing what someone tells you word for word. You have to listen with a heart. . . . It's very hard work" (Arenson, 2002, p. 35). In teaching prospective doctors and attorneys how to listen well to patients and clients, Smith emphasizes the need to be "wide awake" (2005).

Doctors and attorneys aren't the only ones who need to listen well. We all do. If you think about your normal day, you'll realize that listening—or trying to—takes up at least half your waking time. Attending to others' communication—by listening, reading lips, or using American Sign Language—takes up more of our time than any other communication. We spend more time listening than talking, reading, or writing. This point is well made by Marilyn Buckley, who says, "Students listen to the equivalent of a book a day; talk the equivalent of a book a week; read the equivalent of a book a month; and write the equivalent of a book a year" (1992, p. 622).

Studies of a range of people from college students to professionals indicate that the average person spends at least 50% of waking time listening to others (Barker, Edwards, Gaines, Gladney, & Holley, 1981; Wagner, 2001). You listen in classes, listen to acquaintances in casual conversation, listen to your parents during phone calls, listen to clerks in stores, listen to your supervisor and customers when you're at work, and listen to friends when they talk to you about important concerns or issues in their lives. If we don't attend to others' communciation effectively, we're communicating poorly about half of the time. This point was well made in an advertisement sponsored by the Unisys Corporation: "How can we expect him to learn when we haven't taught him how to listen?" (cited in Berko, Wolvin, & Wolvin, 1995, p. 81). If

we can't listen, we can't learn. *Student Companion:* Activity 6.5.

The costs of poor listening can be very high. Doctors who don't listen fully to patients may

© Corbis Sygma

Communication in Everyday Life
"The spirit catches you, and you fall down."

That's how the parents of three-month-old Lia Lee explained why she fainted. Doctors diagnosed the problem as epilepsy, but Lia's Hmong parents disagreed. They told the doctors that the soul can temporarily disappear from the body. When it does, evil spirits catch you and make you fall down (Fadiman, 1997). The doctors didn't listen to the Lees, dismissing their ideas as superstitious folklore. And the Lees didn't listen to the doctors, dismissing them as not understanding why their daughter fainted. The doctors prescribed anti-seizure medications, but the Lees didn't give Lia the medication regularly. Instead, they treated her with sacred amulets and visits to a shaman, and they changed her name to fool the evil spirits. Lia suffered a massive seizure that left her in a vegetative state, where she has been for 18 years (Underwood & Adler, 2005). Had the doctors and the Lees listened more mindfully, Lia's situation might be totally different.

Or consider the case of Mohammad Kochi, an Afghan immigrant, who developed stomach cancer. Kochi had the recommended surgery but refused to undergo the recommended chemotherapy. The doctors assumed that Kochi refused because he didn't want to endure the unpleasantness of chemotherapy, so they didn't communicate with him about his reasons for refusing. Later—too late to help Kochi—the doctors learned that he refused because, as a Muslim, he could not allow fluids to enter his body after he had cleansed himself for prayer. A continuous IV drip, which the doctors had proposed, would have required him to disrespect his religion (Underwood & Adler, 2005). If the doctors had asked Kochi why he refused, and then had listened to his answer, they could have told him about other ways that chemotherapy can be administered.

misdiagnose or mistreat medical problems (Nyquist, 1992; Underwood & Adler, 2005). For this reason, an increasing number of medical practices hire communication specialists to provide listening workshops for medical practitioners. They'd rather pay the consultants' fees than the legal fees for malpractice suits that can result from poor listening (Crossen, 1997).

In this chapter, we explore listening and how to listen effectively. First, we consider what's involved in listening (it's more than most of us realize). Next, we discuss obstacles to effective listening and how we can minimize them. We also consider some common forms of nonlistening. The fourth section of the chapter explains different types of listening and the distinct skills needed for each. To wrap up the chapter, we identify guidelines for improving listening effectiveness.

The Listening Process

Listening is a complex process that involves far more than our ears. To listen well, we rely on our ears, minds, and hearts. Although we often use the words *listening* and *hearing* as if they were synonyms, actually they are different. **Hearing** is a physiological activity that occurs when sound waves hit our eardrums. People who are deaf or hearing impaired receive messages visually through lip reading or sign language.

Listening is far more complex than hearing or otherwise physically receiving messages. Listening has psychological and cognitive dimensions that mere hearing, or physically receiving messages, does not. The multifaceted aspects of listening are reflected in the Chinese character in Figure 6.1, which includes the symbols for the eyes, ears, and heart. We can define **listening** as an active, complex process that consists of being mindful; hearing, selecting and organizing information; interpreting communication; responding; and remembering.

Listening, then, is more than hearing. It also requires us to interpret, remember, and respond to what others com-

Eyes

Ears

Heart

Listening

FIGURE 6.1
The Chinese Character
for the Word Listening

municate. The International Listening Association (1995; see the ILA website at http://listen.org) emphasizes that listening is an active process, which means we must exert effort to listen well. We must be involved with our ears and hearts and minds if we want to listen effectively. Figure 6.2 outlines the listening process.

| Being Mindful |
| Physically Receiving Messages |
| Selecting and Organizing Information |
| Interpreting Communication |
| Responding |
| Remembering |

FIGURE 6.2
The Listening Process

MINDFULNESS

The first step in listening is to make a decision to be mindful. **Mindfulness** is being fully present in the moment. It's what Anna Deavere Smith calls "wide awakeness." When we are mindful, we don't let our thoughts drift to what we did yesterday or plan to do this weekend, nor do we focus on our own feelings and responses. Instead, when we listen mindfully, we tune in fully to another person and try to understand what that person is communicating, without imposing our own ideas, judgments, or feelings. Mindfulness starts with the decision to attend fully to another. Physically, this is signified by paying attention, adopting an involved posture, keeping eye contact, and indicating interest in what the other person says (Bolton, 1986).

Because mindful listening involves taking the perspective of another, it fosters dual perspective—a cornerstone of effective communication. In addition, mindfulness enhances the effectiveness of another's communication. When people sense we are really listening, they tend to elaborate on their ideas and express themselves in more depth.

Mindfulness is a choice. It is not a talent that some people have and others don't. No amount of skill will make you a good listener if you don't make a commitment to attend to another person fully and without diversion. Thus, effective listening begins with the choice to be mindful.

MARISA I always thought I was a good listener, until I spent 2 years living in Japan. In that culture there is a much deeper meaning to listening. I realized that most of the time I was only hearing others. Often, I was thinking of my responses while they were still talking. I had not been listening with my mind and heart.

PHYSICALLY RECEIVING MESSAGES

The second process involved in listening is physically receiving messages. As we noted earlier, hearing is a physiological process in which sound waves hit our eardrums so that we become aware of noises, such as music, traffic, or human voices. For people who have hearing impairments, messages are received in other ways, such as writing, lip reading, and ASL.

Receiving messages is a prerequisite for listening. For most of us, hearing is automatic and unhindered. However, people with hearing impairments may have difficulty receiving oral messages. When we speak with someone who has a hearing disability, we should face the person and ask if we are coming across clearly.

Communication in Everyday Life
Good Listening = Career Advancement

What monetary value would you attach to good listening? It turns out that effective listening can be worth a lot in your paycheck. Listening skill is ranked as the single most important feature of effective managers (Winsor, Curtis, & Stephens, 1997). It's also the top-ranked communication skill for accountants (Morreale, 2004). Just as listening skill is associated with career advancement, poor listening is a leading reason that some people don't advance in careers (Deal & Kennedy, 1999; Waner, 1995).

WORK

Hearing impairments are not the only restriction on physically receiving messages. Hearing ability tends to decline when we are fatigued from concentrating on communication. You may have noticed that it's harder to pay attention in classes that run 75 minutes than in classes that run 50 minutes. Background noise can also interfere with hearing. It's difficult to hear well if loud music is playing, a television is blaring, cell phones are beeping, or others are talking nearby.

Women and men seem to differ somewhat in their listening. As a rule, women are more attentive than men to the whole of communication. Thus, many men tend to focus their hearing on specific content aspects of communication, whereas women generally are more likely to attend to the whole of communication, noticing details, tangents, and relationship-level meanings. Judy Pearson (1985), a prominent communication scholar, suggests that this could result from the brain's hemispheric specializations. Women usually have better-developed right lobes, which govern creative and holistic thinking, whereas men typically have better-developed left lobes, which control analytic and linear information processing.

> **MARK** My girlfriend amazes me. We'll have a conversation, and then later one of us will bring it up again. What I remember is what we decided in the talk. She remembers that, too, but she also remembers all the details about where we were and what was going on in the background and particular things one of us said in the conversation. I never notice all of that stuff, and I sure don't remember it later.

SELECTING AND ORGANIZING MATERIAL

The third element of listening is selecting and organizing material. As we noted in Chapter 3, we don't perceive everything around us. Instead, we selectively attend only to some messages and elements of our environments. What we attend to depends on many factors, including our interests, cognitive structures, and expectations. Selective listening is also influenced by culture; as early as age 1, babies distinguish the sounds of their language, but they don't learn to recognize sounds in other languages. Thus, people who learn a second language later in life may not be able to recognize sounds that weren't in their first language (Monastersky, 2001).

We can monitor our tendencies to attend selectively by remembering that we are more likely to notice stimuli that are intense, loud, or unusual or that otherwise stand out from the flow of communication. This implies that we may overlook communicators who speak quietly and don't call attention to themselves. Intan, an Asian American student, once told me that Caucasians often ignore what she says because she speaks softly and unassertively. Westerners accustomed to assertive speaking styles may not attend to speaking styles that are less bold. If we're aware of the tendency not to notice people who speak quietly, we can guard against it so that we don't miss out on people and messages that may be important.

> **CHAD** I had to have outpatient surgery on my knee last year. My doctor told me to bring an adult with me for the surgery. I said my friend Jake was going to bring me and come back to pick me up. The doctor said, "No, he must stay here with you the whole time." The doctor explained that I wouldn't be able to listen carefully to instructions because of anxiety and the anesthesia. I thought he was wrong, but he wasn't. After the surgery, I thought I was alert and normal when the doctor explained how to take care of the knee and what was normal and not normal after this surgery. By the time Jake drove me home, I couldn't remember a thing the doctor had said.

Once we've selected what to notice, we then organize the stimuli to which we've attended. As you'll recall from Chapter 3, we organize our perceptions by relying on cognitive schemata, which include prototypes, personal constructs, stereotypes, and scripts. As we listen to others, we decide how to categorize them by asking which of our prototypes they most closely resemble: good friend, person in trouble, student, teacher, and so forth. We then apply personal constructs to define in more detail others and their messages. We evaluate whether they are upset or calm, open to advice or closed to it, and so on. Based on our construction of others, we then apply stereotypes that predict what they will do. When friends are clearly distraught, we can reasonably predict that they will want to vent and that they may not want advice until after they have had a chance to express their feelings. Finally, we apply scripts, which specify how interaction should proceed, including how we should act.

The schemata we use to organize our perceptions (see Chapter 2) help us figure out how to respond to others. It's important to remember that *we construct others and their communication* when we use our schemata to make sense of situations and people. In other words, we create meaning by how we select and organize communication. Remembering this reminds us to keep perceptions tentative and open to revision. In the course of interaction, we may want to modify perceptions.

INTERPRETING COMMUNICATION

The fourth step in listening is interpreting others' communication. The most important principle for effective interpretation is to engage in dual perspective so that you interpret others on their terms. Certainly, you won't always agree with other people or how they see themselves, others, and situations. Engaging in dual perspective doesn't require you to share, or agree with, others' perspectives; however, it does require you to make an earnest effort to understand them.

To interpret someone on her or his own terms is one of the greatest gifts we can give another. Too often, we impose our meanings on others, try to correct or argue with them about what they feel, or crowd out their words with our own. As listening expert Robert Bolton (1986, p. 167) observes, good listeners "stay out of the other's way" so they can learn what others think and feel.

BART I'd been married and working for years when I decided I wanted to come back to school and finish my degree. When I mentioned it to the guys I worked with, they all came down hard on me. They said I was looking for an easy life as a college Joe and trying to get above them. My dad said it would be irresponsible to quit work when I had a wife and child, and he said no self-respecting man would do that. It seemed like everyone had a view of what I was doing and why, and their views had nothing to do with mine. The only person who really listened to me was Elaine, my wife. When I told her I was thinking about going back to school, the first thing out of her mouth was, "What would that mean to you?" She didn't presume she knew my reasons, and she didn't start off arguing with me. She just asked what it meant to me, then listened for a long, long time while I talked about how I felt. She focused completely on understanding me. Maybe that's why we're married.

© Chabruken/The Image Bank/Getty Images

RESPONDING

Effective listening also involves **responding,** which is communicating attention and interest. As we noted in Chapter 1, interpersonal communication is a transactional process in which we simultaneously listen and speak. Skillful listeners show that they are following and interested. In the United States, signs of responsive listening include eye contact, nodding, attentive posture, and questions and comments that invite others to elaborate. These behaviors signal that we are involved in what is happening in the moment. We all tend to communicate more clearly and interestingly when we feel that others are committed to us and our communication (Deal & Kennedy, 1999).

We don't respond only when others have finished speaking; rather, we respond throughout interaction.

The next time a friend or co-worker starts to talk with you, express disinterest by slouching, avoiding eye contact, and withholding vocal feedback. You might want to look at something else, such as a paper or book, while your friend is talking. Note what happens as you communicate a lack of interest. How does the other person act? What happens to her or his communication? Does she or he criticize you for not listening? Now, reverse the experiment. When somebody starts to talk to you, show interest. Put aside what you were doing, incline your body slightly forward, make eye contact, and give vocal feedback to indicate that you are following. Note what happens as you listen responsively. Does the other person continue talking? Does she or he become more engaging?

Finally, try varying your listening style during a single conversation. Begin by listening responsively, then lapse into a passive mode that expresses disinterest. What happens when you vary your listening style?

This is what makes listening such an active process. Good listeners let others know they are interested throughout interaction by adopting attentive postures, nodding their heads, making eye contact, and giving vocal responses such as "um hmm," and "go on." These nonverbal behaviors demonstrate engagement. On the relationship level of meaning, responsiveness communicates that we care about the other person and what she or he says.

REMEMBERING

The final aspect of listening is **remembering,** which is the process of retaining what you have heard. According to communication teachers Ron Adler and Neil Towne (1993), we remember less than half of a message immediately after we hear it. As time goes by, retention decreases further; we recall only about 35% of a message 8 hours after hearing it. Because we forget about two thirds of what we hear, it's important to make sure we retain the most important third. Effective listeners let go of a lot of details to retain the more important content (Cooper, Seibold, & Suchner, 1997; Fisher, 1987). By being selective about what to remember, we enhance our listening competence. Later in this chapter, we discuss strategies for retaining material.

Obstacles to Mindful Listening

We've seen that a lot is involved in mindful listening. Adding to the complexity are hindrances to effective listening. There are two broad types of barriers to mindful listening: obstacles in the communication situation and obstacles in the communicators. (Did you notice that this series of ideas to be discussed was organized into two broad classes to aid your retention of the basic content?)

EXTERNAL OBSTACLES

Many barriers to mindful listening are present in communication situations. Although we can't always control external obstacles, knowing what situational factors hinder effective listening can help us guard against them or compensate for the noise they create.

Message Overload   The sheer amount of communication we engage in makes it difficult to listen fully all the time. Think about your typical day. You go to classes for 3 hours. How much you learn and how well you do on examinations depend on your ability to listen mindfully to material that is often difficult. After listening for 50 minutes in a history class, you listen for 50 minutes in a communication class and 50 more minutes in a business class. A great deal of information comes your way in those three lectures. After class, you check your voice mail and find three messages from friends—you need to remember them and respond before the day ends. You start doing research on the Web and find more than 300 sites for your topic—how can you possibly process all the information they offer? Then, you go to work, and your supervisor informs you of new procedures. Feeling a need to get on to other matters, your supervisor describes the procedure quickly, and you are expected to understand and follow it.

Naturally, we feel overwhelmed by the amount of information we are supposed to understand and retain. To deal with the overload, we often screen the talk around us, much as we screen calls on our answering machines, to decide when to listen carefully.

> **RAYMOND**   I've been married nearly 30 years, so I've figured out when I have to listen sharply to Edna and when I can just let her talk flow in one ear and out the other. She's a talker, but most of what she talks about isn't important. But if I hear code words, I know to listen up. If Edna says, "I'm really upset about such and such," or if she says, "We have a problem," my ears perk up.

Message Complexity   The more detailed and complicated the message, the more difficult it is to follow and retain it. People for whom English is a second language often find it hard to understand English speakers who use complex sentences with multiple clauses or slang expressions (Lee, 1994, 2000). Even native speakers of English often feel overwhelmed by the complexity of some messages. It's tempting to tune out messages that are filled with technical words, detailed information, and complex sentences. If we let message complexity overwhelm us, however, we may perform poorly in school or on the job, and we may let down friends and intimates.

There are ways to manage complex messages to maximize how much we understand and retain. When we have to listen to messages that are dense with information, we should summon up extra energy. In addition, taking notes and asking questions for clarification may help us understand and retain difficult information. A third strategy is to group material as you listen, organizing the ideas in ways that make later recall easier.

Noise   A third impediment to effective listening is physical noise. Perhaps you've been part of a crowd at a rally or a game. If so, you probably had to shout to the person next to you just to be heard. Although most noise is not as overwhelming as the roar of crowds, there is always some noise in communication situations. It might be music or television in the background, other conversations nearby, pagers that are beeping, or thunder or traffic sounds from outside.

> **GREGORY**   I've been a salesman for a long time, and I know when clients are really interested and when they're not. If someone answers a phone when I'm in his or her office, I know they aren't focused on what I'm saying. Taking calls or leaving the door open for people to drop in communicates that they're not interested in me or the service I represent.

Gregory reminds us that allowing distractions communicates, on the relationship level of meaning, that we're not responsive. Good listeners do what they can to minimize environmental distractions. It's considerate to turn off a television or lower the volume of music if someone wants to talk with you. Likewise, it is courteous to turn off the ringers of cell phones and pagers when attending lectures, concerts, or other events in which a buzzing phone could distract others who have come to listen. Professionals often ask that their calls be held when they want to give undivided attention to a conversation with a client or business associate. It's also appropriate to move from a noisy area to cut down on distractions. Even if we can't always eliminate noise, we can usually reduce it or change our location to one that is more conducive to mindful listening.

Communication in Everyday Life
Technological Overload

TECHNOLOGY

Our era is dominated by technologies of communication. We can reach others faster than ever before. We can find people we want to talk with in their homes, offices, or cars or when they're in meetings or at restaurants, movies, or the beach. Many people feel overloaded by the relentless stream of information that technology makes possible (Hymowitz, 2000; Imperato, 1999; Salopek, 1999; Shenk, 1997).

You don't have to be hopelessly outdated to wonder whether communication technologies impede meaningful communication between people. Does being wired all the time diminish how we interact with people we are with in any given moment? Author Jonathan Coleman (2000) recalls a summer evening when he attended his daughter's lacrosse practice. He writes, "Standing next to me was a father more intent on the cell-phone conversation he was having than on watching his daughter play. Time and again she would look toward him, craving his attention, but he never saw her. Nor, for that matter, did another girl's mother see her child, focused as she was on her laptop, merrily tapping away." Can we really engage others if we have a cell phone handy and will answer it if it rings? Can we listen well to any conversation—in person or on a phone—if we are actually or potentially involved in more than one conversation? If we can't, then does technology, as Coleman suggests, "create the illusion of intimacy" while it actually "makes us intimate strangers"?

INTERNAL OBSTACLES

In addition to external obstacles, five barriers inside us can hinder listening: preoccupation, prejudgment, reacting to emotionally loaded language, lack of effort, and not recognizing and adapting to diverse listening styles.

Preoccupation   When we are absorbed in our own thoughts and concerns, we can't focus on what someone else is saying. Perhaps you've attended a lecture right before you had a test in another class and later realized you got almost nothing out of the lecture. That's because

© Sepp Seitz/Woodfin Camp & Associates

you were preoccupied with the upcoming test. Or maybe you've been in conversations with co-workers and realized that you weren't listening at all because you were thinking about your own concerns.

> **DAWN** I think my biggest problem as a listener is preoccupation. Like my friend Marta came to me the other day and said she wanted to talk about her relationship with her boyfriend. I followed her for a few minutes, but then I started thinking about my relationship with Ted. After a while—I don't know how long—Marta said to me, "You're not listening at all. Where is your head?" She was right. My head was in a totally different place.

When we are preoccupied with our own thoughts, we aren't fully present for others. We're not being mindful. In describing how she stays mindful in intense interviews, Anna Deavere Smith says, "I empty out myself. While I'm listening, my own judgments and prejudices certainly come up. But I know I won't get anything unless I get those things out of the way" (Arenson, 2002, p. 35). It's natural for our thoughts to wander occasionally. When they do, we should note that our focus has wandered and actively call our minds back to the person who is speaking and the meaning of his or her message.

Prejudgment Another reason we may not listen effectively is that we prejudge others or their communication. Sometimes we think we already know what is going to be said, so we don't listen carefully. At other times, we decide in advance that others have nothing to offer us, so we tune them out. When we prejudge others' communication, we sacrifice learning new perspectives that might enlarge our thinking (Van Styke, 1999).

> **MELEA** My parents are so busy prejudging what I'm going to say that they absolutely cannot listen to me. Like last weekend, I went home and was trying to explain why I am having difficulty with my physics class. My dad interrupted before I'd even described the problem with his take on it: He said I couldn't help it because girls have trouble with the sciences. Thanks a lot, but that's not the problem. I've done fine in other science classes, but he conveniently forgets that. The problem here is the teacher, but dad will never know that because he won't listen.

Melea's commentary demonstrates that we prejudge when we impose our preconceptions about a message. When this happens, we assume we know what another feels, thinks, and will say, and we then assimilate her or his message into our preconceptions. In the workplace, we may not pay close attention to what a co-worker says because we think we already know what is being expressed. Recalling our earlier discussion of mind reading, you'll realize that it's unwise to assume we know what others think and feel. When we mind read, misunderstandings are likely. We may misinterpret what the person means because we haven't really listened on her or his terms.

When we prejudge, we disconfirm others because we deny them their own voices. Instead of listening openly to others, we force their words into our own preconceived mind-set. This devalues them. Prejudgments also reduce what we learn in communication with others. If we decide in advance that others have nothing worthwhile to say, we foreclose the possibility of learning something new. Melea's father foreclosed learning what was troubling her about her physics class.

Reacting to Emotionally Loaded Language A fourth internal obstacle to effective listening is the tendency to react to emotionally loaded language—words that evoke very strong responses, positive or negative. You may find some words and phrases very soothing or pleasant. Certain other words and phrases may summon up negative feelings and images for you. When we react to words that are emotionally loaded for us, we may fail to grasp another person's meaning (Wagner, 2001).

One of my closest friends responds very negatively and emotionally to any statement that begins, "You should. . . ." As soon as she hears that phrase, my friend feels that the speaker is judging her and telling her what she should feel, think, or do. And she stops listening. Politicians often rely on voters to respond emotionally to particular words. One person who was nominated for high office was labeled the "quota queen" by those who opposed her appointment. Although the charge was not grounded in the nominee's record, the word *quota* resonated so negatively with so many people that her appointment was halted. In recent years, politicians have also used the term *family values* frequently because so many voters respond to it with strong positive emotion. Some politicians count on voters not to think critically about what they mean by *family values* but instead to vote for them, because the term itself evokes positive feelings.

When we react to emotionally loaded language, we don't learn what another person has to say. We give up our responsibility to think critically about what others say, to consider their words carefully instead of reacting unthinkingly to particular words. One way to guard against this is to be aware of words and phrases that tend to trigger strong emotional reactions in us. If we bring these to a conscious level, then we can monitor our tendencies to respond unthinkingly.

Lack of Effort It is hard work to listen mindfully—to focus closely on what others are saying, to grasp their meanings, to ask questions, and to give responses so that they know we are interested and involved. It's also hard to control situational noise and perhaps fight fatigue, hunger, or other physiological conditions that can impede listening (Isaacs, 1999).

Because active listening takes so much effort, we can't always do it well. We may want to listen but have trouble marshaling the energy needed. When this happens, you might ask the other person to postpone interaction until a time when you will have the energy to listen mindfully. If you explain that you want to defer communication because you really are interested and want to be able to listen well, she or he is likely to appreciate your honesty and commitment to listening.

Failure to Adapt Listening Styles A final internal hindrance to effective listening is not recognizing and adjusting to the need for different listening styles. How we listen should vary, for two reasons. First, different skills are needed when we listen for information, to support others, and for pleasure. We discuss these kinds of listening later in the chapter. A second reason for having diverse listening styles is differences between cultures and speech communities. In some cultures, listening means quietly attending to others. In other cultures, listening means participating while others are talking. In the United States, it is considered polite to make frequent, but not constant, eye contact with someone who is speaking. In other cultures, continuous eye contact is normative, and still other cultures severely restrict eye contact.

Even in the United States, there are differences in listening rules based on membership in gender, racial, and other speech communities. Because feminine socialization emphasizes conversation as a way to form and develop relationships, women tend to maintain eye contact, give substantial vocal and verbal feedback, and use nods and facial expressions to signal interest (Tannen, 1990; Wood, 1994d, 1998). Masculine speech communities, with their focus on emotional control, teach

Communication in Everyday Life
Listening in a World Dominated by Sight

Does the visual orientation of Western culture make listening more difficult? Writer William Isaacs thinks it does. In his 1999 book *Dialogue and the Art of Thinking Together*, Isaacs notes that light moves at 186,000 miles per second, whereas sound moves at 1,088 feet per second. If we watch television for a few minutes, we're exposed to thousands of images. We see at least as many images if we spend the same amount of time on the Internet or the Web. Isaacs thinks that we've become habituated to the pace of visual stimuli such that we are impatient with the pace of aural stimuli. His advice? If you want to listen better, slow down!

most men to provide fewer verbal and nonverbal signs of interest and attentiveness. If you understand these general differences, you can adapt your listening style to provide appropriate responses to women and to men.

> **JENIFER** I used to get irritated at my boyfriend because I thought he wasn't listening to me. I'd tell him stuff, and he'd just sit there and not say anything. He didn't react to what I was saying by showing emotions in his face or anything. Several times, I accused him of not listening, and he said back to me exactly what I'd said. He was listening, just not my way. I've learned not to expect him to show a lot of emotions or respond to what I say as I'm talking. That's just not his way, but he is listening.

Race also shapes listening style. Most whites follow the communication rule that one person shouldn't speak while another is talking, especially in formal speaking situations. In some African American communities, however, talking while others are talking is a form of showing interest and active participation (Houston & Wood, 1996). Thus, some African Americans may signal that they are listening intently to a speaker by interjecting comments such as "Tell me more" or "I know that's right." Many black churches are more participatory than most white churches, with members of the congregation routinely calling out responses to what a preacher is saying. When the Reverend Martin Luther King Jr. delivered his "I Have a Dream" speech to a crowd of thousands, his words were echoed and reinforced by the listeners during the speech.

Because speech communities cultivate different communication styles, we shouldn't automatically impose our rules and interpretations on others. Instead, we should try to understand and respect their styles and listen effectively to them on their terms, not ours.

© SuperStock, Inc.

Forms of Nonlistening

Now that we've discussed obstacles to effective listening, let's consider forms of nonlistening. We call these patterns *nonlistening* because they don't involve real listening. We discuss six kinds of nonlistening that may seem familiar to you because most of us engage in them at times.

PSEUDOLISTENING

Pseudolistening is pretending to listen. When we pseudolisten, we appear to be attentive, but really our minds are elsewhere. We engage in pseudolistening when we want to appear conscientious, although we really aren't interested. Sometimes we pseudolisten because we don't want to hurt someone who is sharing experiences.

> **RENEE** Pseudolistening should be in the training manual for flight attendants. I had that job for 6 years, and you wouldn't believe the kinds of things passengers told me about—everything from love affairs to family problems. At first I tried to listen, because I wanted to be a good attendant. After a year, though, I learned just to appear to be listening and to let my mind be elsewhere.

We also pseudolisten when communication bores us but we have to appear engaged. Superficial social conversations and dull lectures are two communication situations in which we may consciously choose to pseudolisten so that we seem polite even though we really aren't interested. Although it may be appropriate to decide to pseudolisten in some situations, there is a cost: We run the risk of missing information because we really aren't attending.

> **BELLINO** I get in a lot of trouble because I pseudolisten. Often, I slip into pretending to listen in classes. I'll start off paying attention and then just drift off and not even realize I've stopped listening until the teacher asks me a question, and I don't even know what we're discussing.

Pseudolisteners often give themselves away when their responses reveal that they weren't paying attention. Common indicators of pseudolistening are responses that are tangential or irrelevant to what was said. For example, if Martin talks to Charlotte about his job interviews, she might respond tangentially by asking about the cities he visits: "Did you like New York or Atlanta better?" Although this is related to the topic of Martin's job interviews, it is tangential to the main issue. An irrelevant response would be, "Where do you want to go for dinner tonight?" That response is completely unrelated to what Martin said.

MONOPOLIZING

Monopolizing is continuously focusing communication on ourselves instead of listening to the person who is talking. Two tactics are typical of monopolizing. One is conversational rerouting, in which a person shifts the topic back to himself or herself. For example, Ellen tells her friend Marla that she's having trouble with her roommate, and Marla reroutes the conversation with this response: "I know what you mean. My roommate is a real slob. And that's just one of her problems. Let me tell you what I have to live with. . . ." Rerouting takes the conversation away from the person who is talking and focuses it on the self.

Another monopolizing tactic is interrupting to divert attention from the speaker to ourselves or to topics that interest us. Interrupting can occur in combination with rerouting—a person interrupts and then directs the conversation to a new topic. In other cases, diversionary interrupting involves questions and challenges that disrupt the speaker. For example, Elliot says that the war in Iraq will continue for at least five years, and Paul responds by saying, "What makes you think that?" "How can you be sure?" "Bush says we'll be out in a year." Having interrupted Elliot, Paul might then reroute the conversation to topics that interest him more: "Speaking of Bush, do you think he'll manage to get Congress to approve the changes he wants to make in Social Security?" Both rerouting and diversionary interrupting are techniques for monopolizing a conversation. They are the antithesis of good listening. The following conversation illustrates monopolizing and also shows how disconfirming of others it can be:

Chuck: I'm really bummed about my Econ class. I just can't seem to get the stuff.

Sally: Well, I know what you mean. Econ was a real struggle for me too, but it's nothing compared to the stat course I'm taking now. I mean, this one is going to destroy me totally.

Chuck: I remember how frustrated you got in Econ, but you finally did get it. I just can't seem to, and I need the course for my major. I've tried going to review sessions, but . . .

Sally: I didn't find the review sessions helpful. Why don't you focus on your other classes and use them to pull up your average?

Chuck: That's not the point. I want to get this stuff.

Sally: You think you've got problems? Do you know that right now I have three papers and one exam hanging over my head?

Chuck: I wonder if I should hire a tutor.

Sally shows no interest in Chuck's concerns, and she pushes her own conversational agenda. Chances are good that she doesn't even understand what he is feeling, because she isn't really focusing on what he says; she isn't really listening.

Monopolizing is costly not only to those who are neglected but also to the monopolizers. A person who dominates communication has much less opportunity to learn from others than does a person who listens to what others think and feel. We already know what we think and feel, so there's little we can learn from hearing ourselves!

It's important to realize that not all interruptions are attempts to monopolize. We also interrupt to show interest, to voice support, and to ask for elaboration. Interrupting for these reasons doesn't divert attention from the person speaking; instead, it affirms that person and keeps the focus on her or him. Research indicates that women are more likely than men to interrupt to show interest and support (Anderson & Leaper, 1998; Aries, 1987; Beck, 1988; Mulac, Wiemann, Widenmann, & Gibson, 1988; Stewart, Stewart, Friedley, & Cooper, 1990). Some studies suggest that men are more likely than women to interrupt to gain control of conversations, but more research is needed to verify or disconfirm this (Aries, 1996; Goldsmith & Fulfs, 1999).

SELECTIVE LISTENING

A third form of nonlistening is **selective listening,** which involves focusing on only particular parts of communication. As we've noted, all listening is selective to an extent because we can't attend to everything around us. With selective listening, however, we screen out parts of a message that don't interest us and rivet attention on topics that do interest us. For example, Robbie tends to selectively tune out anything I say about financial matters, because that topic doesn't interest him. Students become highly attentive when a teacher says, "This will be on the test." Employees zero in on communication about raises, layoffs, and holidays. People who own beach property become highly attentive to information about hurricanes. The other night, I fixed cream of broccoli soup for dinner. When Robbie saw it, he said, "Just last week, I told you I hated broccoli." I had no recollection of his having said that—perhaps because broccoli is a favorite of mine, and I didn't want to hear that he wouldn't enjoy it at our meals.

Selective listening also occurs when we reject communication that makes us uneasy. For instance, smokers may selectively not attend to a radio report on the dangers of smoking and secondhand smoke. We may also screen out communication that is critical of us. You may not take in a friend's comment that you are really judgmental; you may selectively tune out your boyfriend's or girlfriend's observation that you can be selfish. We all have subjects that bore us or disturb us, yet it's unwise to listen selectively when doing so could deprive us of information or insights that could be valuable.

DEFENSIVE LISTENING

After taking cooking lessons, Thelma bakes a cake for her friend Louise's birthday. When Louise sees the cake, she says, "Wow, that's so sweet. My Mom always made a special cake for my birthday, and she would decorate it so elaborately." Thelma replies, "Well I'm sorry that I didn't decorate the cake extravagantly. I guess I still have a lot to learn about cooking." Thelma's response illustrates **defensive listening,** which is perceiving personal attacks, criticism, or hostility in communication that is not critical or mean-spirited. When we listen defensively, we assume others don't like, trust, or respect us, and we read these motives into whatever they say, no matter how innocent their communication may be.

Some people are generally defensive, expecting criticism from all quarters. They perceive negative judgments in almost anything said to them. In other instances, defensive listening is confined to specific topics or vulnerable times when we judge ourselves to be inadequate. A man who is was laid off from work and hasn't found another job may listen defensively to phone solicitations for contributions; a worker who fears she is not performing well may hear criticism in benign comments from co-workers; a student who fails a test may hear doubts about his intelligence in an innocent question about how school is going. Defensive listening can deprive us of information and insights that might be valuable even if not pleasant. In addition, responding defensively to honest feedback may discourage others from being honest with us.

AMBUSHING

Ambushing is listening carefully for the purpose of attacking a speaker. Unlike the other kinds of nonlistening we've discussed, ambushing involves very careful listening, but it isn't motivated by a genuine desire to understand another. Instead, ambushers listen intently to gather ammunition they can use to attack a speaker. Krista listens very carefully to her teammate Carl as he describes a marketing campaign. When Carl finishes, Krista pounces: "You said we could get a rough draft of the whole campaign by the end of the month. You forgot that we lose two work days for the annual retreat next week. Besides, your plan calls for some outsourcing. Where are you getting the funds for that?" Krista's response shows that she listened to Carl's ideas not to understand them and work with him but to identify weak spots and attack them.

> **KRALYN**   My first husband was a real ambusher. If I tried to talk to him about a dress I'd bought, he'd listen just long enough to find out what it cost and then attack me for spending money. Once, I told him about a problem I was having with one of my co-workers, and he came back at me with all of the things I'd done wrong and didn't mention any of the things the other person had done. Talking to him was like setting myself up to be assaulted.

Not surprisingly, people who engage in ambushing tend to arouse defensiveness in others. Few of us want to speak up when we feel we are going to be attacked. In Chapter 8, we look more closely at communication that fosters defensiveness in others.

LITERAL LISTENING

The final form of nonlistening is **literal listening,** which involves listening only for content and ignoring the relationship level of meaning. As we have seen, all communication includes content or literal meaning as well as relationship meaning, which pertains to power, responsiveness, and liking between people. When we listen literally, we attend only to the content level and overlook what's being communicated on the relationship level. When we listen only literally, we are insensitive to others' feelings and to our connections with them. Lindsay's commentary provides a good illustration of literal listening that deals only with content-level meaning.

Everyday Application
Identifying Your Nonlistening Habits

Apply the material we've just discussed by identifying times when you've engaged in nonlistening.

··· Describe a situation in which you pseudolistened.
··· Describe an instance in which you monopolized communication.
··· Describe a time when you listened defensively.
··· Describe an example of ambushing someone else.
··· Describe an instance when you listened selectively.
··· Describe a time when you listened literally.

Now, repeat this exercise, but this time focus on examples of others who engage in each of the six types of ineffective listening.

For additional practice in recognizing forms of ineffective listening in everyday situations, complete Activity 6.2 in your *Student Companion* or online under "Chapter Resources for Chapter 6" at the Everyday Connections website.

LINDSAY When I found out I had to have wrist surgery, I told my boss and said I'd be needing some time off. He listened and then explained the policy on sick leave. He didn't say he was sorry, ask if I was worried, tell me he hoped the surgery was successful, nothing.

Literal listening may disconfirm others. When we listen literally, we don't make the effort to understand how others feel about what they say or to endorse them as people.

We have seen that there are many obstacles to effective listening. Situational obstacles include message overload, message complexity, and noise. In addition to these, there are five potential interferences inside of us: preoccupation, prejudgment, unthinking reactions to emotionally loaded language, lack of effort, and failure to adapt our style of listening. The obstacles to effective listening combine to create six types of nonlistening: pseudolistening, monopolizing, selective listening, defensive listening, ambushing, and literal listening. What you've learned prepares you to think now about how you can listen more mindfully.

· · · · · · · · · · ·

Adapting Listening to Communication Goals

The first requirement for listening effectively is to determine your reason for listening. We listen differently when we listen for pleasure, to gain information, and to support others. We'll discuss the particular attitudes and skills that contribute to each type of effective listening.

LISTENING FOR PLEASURE

Often, we engage in **listening for pleasure.** We listen to music for pleasure. We may listen to some radio programs for enjoyment. Because listening for pleasure doesn't require us to remember or respond to communication, the only guidelines are to be mindful and control distractions. Just as being mindful in lectures allows us to gain information, being mindful when listening for pleasure allows us to derive full enjoyment from what we hear. Controlling interferences is also important when we are listening for pleasure. A beautifully rendered Mozart concerto can be wonderfully satisfying but not if a television is on in the background.

LISTENING FOR INFORMATION

Much of the time, we are **listening for information.** At such times, our goal is to gain and evaluate information. We listen for information in classes, at political debates, when important news stories are reported, and when we need guidance on everything from medical treatments to directions to a new place. In each case, we listen to gain and understand information in order to act appropriately. To do this, we need to use skills for critical thinking and for organizing and retaining information.

Be Mindful First, it's important to choose to be mindful. Don't let your mind wander when information gets complicated or confusing. Instead, stay focused on the information, and take in as much as you can. Later, you may want to ask questions about material that wasn't clear even when you listen mindfully.

© Doug Menuez/Iconica/Getty Images

Control Obstacles You can also minimize noise in communication situations. You might shut a window to mute traffic noises or adjust a thermostat so that the room's temperature is comfortable. You should also try to minimize psychological distractions by emptying your mind of concerns and ideas that can divert your attention. Let go of preoccupations and prejudgments that can interfere with effective listening. In addition, it's important to monitor the tendency to react to emotionally loaded language. As William Isaacs (1999) notes, we must make a very deliberate effort to cultivate an inner silence that allows us to listen thoughtfully to others.

Ask Questions Also important is posing questions to speakers. Asking a speaker to clarify or elaborate the message may help you understand information you didn't grasp at first; it also enhances insight into content that you did comprehend. "Could you explain what you meant by . . . ?" and "Can you clarify the distinction between . . . ?" are questions that allow you to deepen your grasp of content. Questions compliment a speaker because they indicate that you are interested and want to know more.

Use Aids to Recall To understand and remember important information, we can apply the principles of perception we discussed in Chapter 3. For instance, we learned that we tend to notice and recall stimuli that are repeated. To use this principle in everyday communication, repeat important ideas to yourself immediately after hearing them (Estes, 1989). Repetition can save you the embarrassment of having to ask people you've just met to repeat their names.

Everyday Application
Improving Your Retention

Apply the principles we've discussed to enhance memory.

••• The next time you meet someone, repeat his or her name to yourself three times in a row after you are introduced. Do you remember the name better when you do this?
••• After your next interpersonal communication class, take 15 minutes to review your notes. Try reading them aloud so that you hear as well as see the main ideas. Does this increase your retention of material covered in class?
••• Invent mnemonics to help you remember basic information in communication.
••• Organize complex ideas by grouping them into categories. Try this first in relation to material presented in classes. To remember the main ideas of this chapter, you might use major subheadings to form categories: the listening process, obstacles to listening, forms of nonlistening, listening goals, and guidelines. The mnemonic PONGG (process, obstacles, nonlistening, goals, guidelines) could help you remember those categories.

Another way to increase retention is to use mnemonic (pronounced "knee-monic") devices, which are memory aids that create patterns for what you've heard. You probably already do this in studying. For instance, you could create the mnemonic MR SIRR, which is made up of the first letter of each of the six parts of listening (mindfulness, receiving, selecting and organizing, interpreting, responding, remembering). If your supervisor asks you to code and log in all incoming messages, you might remember the instruction by inventing CLAIM, a word that uses the first letter of each part of your supervisor's instructions. If you meet someone named Kit and want to remember something about the person, you might associate something about Kit with each letter of the name: Kit from Iowa is going to be a teacher.

Organize Information   A third technique for increasing retention is to organize what you hear. For example, suppose a friend tells you he's concerned about a current math course that he's finding difficult. Then, he wonders what kind of jobs his history major qualifies him for and whether graduate school is necessary to get a good job, and says he needs to line up an internship for this summer. You could reduce the complexity of this message by regrouping the stream of concerns into two categories: short-term issues (the course, setting up an internship) and long-term issues (jobs for history majors, graduate school). Remembering those two categories allows you to retain the essence of your friend's concerns even if you forget many of the specifics. Repetition, mnemonics, and regrouping are ways to enhance what we remember.

Poor listening causes mistakes and problems, which explains why many companies now require employees to attend listening workshops. Starbucks, for instance, requires employees to learn to listen to orders and rearrange customers' requests in the sequence of size, flavoring, milk, and caffeine. That's helpful when customers often spurt out "double-shot decaf grande" or "iced, skim, cappuccino, small" (Crossen, 1997).

LISTENING TO SUPPORT OTHERS

We engage in relationship listening, **listening to support others,** when we listen to a friend's worries, hear a romantic partner discuss our relationship, or help a co-worker sort through a problem. Specific attitudes and skills enhance relationship listening.

Be Mindful   The first requirement for effective relationship listening is mindfulness. You'll recall that this was also the first step in listening for information and pleasure. When we're interested in relationship-level meanings, however, a different kind of mindfulness is needed. Instead of focusing on information, we concentrate on what lies between and behind the content in order to understand what another is feeling, thinking, needing, or wanting in a conversation.

Be Careful of Expressing Judgments   When listening to help another person, it's usually wise to avoid judgmental responses, at least initially. Imposing our own judgments separates us from others and their feelings. We've inserted something between us. Yet, there are times when it is appropriate and supportive to offer opinions and to make evaluative statements. Sometimes, people we care about genuinely want our judgments, and in those cases we should be honest about how we feel. Particularly when others are confronting ethical dilemmas, they may seek the judgments of people they trust.

Once, my friend Cordelia was asked to work for a presidential candidate, but she had agreed to take a job. She talked to me about her quandary and asked me what I thought she should do. Although it was clear to me that she wanted to join the campaign, I couldn't honestly tell her I approved of that. I told her that, for me, it would be wrong to go back on my word. I then offered to think with her about ways she might approach her future employer about starting at a later date. After a long talk, Cordelia thanked me for being honest. Part of being a real friend in this instance was making a judgment. That's appropriate only if someone invites our evaluation or if we think another person is in danger of making a serious mistake.

If someone asks our opinion, we should try to present it in a way that doesn't disconfirm the other person. I could have said to Cordelia, "How can you even think of breaking your word? That would be immoral." Whew—pretty disconfirming. Many times, people excuse cruel comments by saying, "Well, you asked me to be honest" or "I mean this as constructive criticism." Too often, however, the judgments are harsher than candor requires. If we are committed to supporting others, we use honesty to support them, not to tear them down.

LOGAN   I hate the term *constructive criticism*. Every time my dad says it, what follows is a put-down. By now, I've learned not to go to him when I have problems or when I'm worried about something in my life. He always judges what I'm feeling and tells me what I ought to feel and do. All that does is make me feel worse than I did before.

Understand the Other Person's Perspective   We can't respond effectively to others until we understand their perspective and meanings. To do this, we must focus on the words and nonverbal behaviors that give us clues about how others feel and think.

Paraphrasing is a method of clarifying others' meaning or needs by reflecting our interpretations of their communication back to them. For example, a friend might confide, "I think my kid brother is messing around with drugs." We could paraphrase this way: "So you're really worried that your brother's experimenting with drugs." This allows us to clarify whether the friend has any evidence of the brother's drug involvement and also whether the friend is, in fact, worried about the possibility.

The response might be, "No, I don't have any real reason to suspect him, but I just worry, because drugs are so pervasive in high schools now." This clarifies by telling us the friend's worries are more the issue than any evidence that the brother is experimenting with drugs. Paraphrasing also helps us figure out what others feel. If a friend screams, "This situation is really getting to me," it's not clear whether

Everyday Application
Learning to Paraphrase

Practice effective listening by paraphrasing the following statements:

··· I've got so many pressures closing in on me right now.
··· I'm worried about all the money I've borrowed to get through school.
··· I'm nervous about telling my parents I'm gay when I see them next weekend.
··· I don't know whether Pat and I can keep the relationship together once she moves away to her new job.

Student Companion: Activity 6.3.

your friend is angry, hurt, upset, or frustrated. We could find out which emotion prevails by saying, "You seem really angry." If anger is the emotion, your friend would agree; if not, she would clarify what she is feeling.

Another strategy for increasing understanding of others is to use **minimal encouragers,** which gently invite others to elaborate by expressing interest in hearing more. Examples of minimal encouragers are "Tell me more," "Really?" "Go on," "I'm with you," "Then what happened?" and "I see." We can also use nonverbal minimal encouragers, such as a raised eyebrow, a head nod, or widened eyes. Minimal encouragers indicate that we are listening, following, and interested. They encourage others to keep talking. Keep in mind that these are *minimal* encouragers. They should not interrupt or reroute conversation. Instead, effective minimal encouragers are brief interjections that prompt, rather than interfere with, another's talk.

A third way to enhance your understanding of another person's perspective is to ask questions that yield insight into what a speaker thinks or feels. For instance, we might ask, "How do you feel about that?" or "What do you plan to do?" Another reason we ask questions is to find out what a person wants from us. Sometimes, it isn't clear whether someone wants advice, a shoulder to cry on, or a safe place to vent feelings. If we can't figure out what's wanted, we can ask the other person, "Are you looking for advice or a sounding board?" Asking direct questions signals that we want to help and allows others to tell us how we can best do that.

© Bob Daemmrich/The Image Works

Express Support Once we understand another's meanings and perspective, it's important to communicate support. This doesn't necessarily require us to agree with the other person's perspective or feelings, but it does require that we express support for the person. We may express support in a number of ways without agreeing. For example, you can say that you appreciate the difficulty of a friend's situation, you realize what a tough decision this is, you understand your friend's feelings (even if your feelings are different). Perhaps the most basic way to support another is by listening mindfully, which shows that you care enough to attend fully to the other person. *Student Companion:* Activity 6.4.

> **SHERYL**   I think the greatest gift my mother ever gave me was when I told her I was going to marry Bruce. He isn't Jewish, and nobody in my family has ever married out of the faith before. I could tell my mother was disappointed, and she didn't try to hide that. She asked me if I understood how that would complicate things like family relations and rearing kids. We talked for a while, and she realized I had thought through what it means to marry out of the faith. Then she sighed and said she had hoped I would find a nice Jewish man. But then she said she supported me whatever I did, and Bruce was welcome in our family. She told me she'd raised me to think for myself, and that's what I was doing. I just felt so loved and accepted by how she acted.

●●●●●●●●●●●

Guidelines for Effective Listening

Three guidelines summarize our discussion and foster effective listening.

BE MINDFUL

By now, you've read this suggestion many times. Because it is so central to effective listening, however, it bears repeating. Mindfulness is a choice to be wholly present in an experience. It requires that we put aside preoccupations and preconceptions to attend fully to what is happening in the moment. Mindful listening is one of the highest compliments we can pay to others because it conveys the relationship-level meaning that they matter to us. Being mindful requires discipline and commitment. We have to discipline our tendencies to judge others, to dominate the talk stage, and to let our minds wander. Mindfulness also requires commitment to another person and to the integrity of the interpersonal communication process. Being mindful is the first and most important principle of effective listening.

ADAPT LISTENING APPROPRIATELY

Like all communication activities, listening varies according to goals, situations, and people. What's effec-

Communication in Everyday Life
More on Developing Listening Skills

Many good resources can help you improve your listening skills. One good book is Madelyn Burley-Allen's *Listening: The Forgotten Skill* (1995), which offers a self-teaching guide for recognizing listening styles, including your own, and learning to listen more effectively. In addition, the Web offers a number of sites that provide concrete, practical suggestions for improving your skill at listening. Many of the sites elaborate on guidelines offered in this chapter, including those on creating and using mnemonics and taking notes effectively.

To learn more about taking good notes to improve recall, visit the Web page created by the Department of Academic Advising Services at the College of St. Benedict/St. John's University: http://www.csbsju.edu/academicadvising.html.

To develop skill in creating and using mnemonics and other techniques for improving recall, visit http://www.mindtools .com/memory.html.

tive depends on our purpose for listening, the context in which we are listening, and the needs and circumstances of the person to whom we are listening.

When we listen for pleasure, we should be mindful and minimize distractions so that we derive as much enjoyment as possible from listening. When we listen for information, a critical attitude, evaluation of material, and a focus on the content level of meaning enhance listening. Yet when we engage in relationship listening, very different skills are needed. We want to communicate openness and caring, and the relationship level of meaning is at least as important as the content level of meaning. Thus, we need to adapt our listening styles and attitudes to different goals.

Effective listening is listening that is adapted to others. Some people need prompting and encouragement to express themselves, whereas others need us only to be silent and attentive. Paraphrasing helps some people clarify what they think or feel, whereas others don't need that kind of assistance. We need to be skilled in a variety of listening behaviors and to know when each is appropriate. Recall from Chapter 1 that the ability to use a range of skills and to exercise judgment about which ones are called for is fundamental to interpersonal communication competence.

LISTEN ACTIVELY

When we realize all that's involved in listening, we appreciate what an active effort it is. To listen effectively, we must be willing to focus our minds, to organize and interpret others' ideas and feelings, to express our interest on both the content level and the relationship level of meaning, and to retain what a speaker says. In some situations, we also become active partners by listening collaboratively and engaging in problem solving. Doing this is hard work! Recognizing that mindful listening is an active process prepares us to invest the effort needed to do it effectively.

Case Study: Continuing the Conversation

The following conversation is featured on the Everyday Connections website under "Chapter Resources for Chapter 6." Click on the link "Online Dating" in the left-hand menu to launch the video and audio scenario scripted below. www

Christina is visiting her family for the holidays. One evening after dinner, her mother comes into her room, where Christina is typing at her computer. Her mother sits down, and the following conversation takes place.

Mom: Am I disturbing you?

Chris: No, I'm just signing off on e-mail. [She finishes at the keyboard and turns to face her mom.]

Mom: E-mailing someone?

Chris: Just a guy.

Mom: Someone you've been seeing at school?

Chris: Not exactly.

Mom: [laughs] Well, either you are seeing him or you're not, honey. Are you two dating?

Chris: Sort of. Yeah, you could say we're dating.

Mom: [laughs] What's the mystery? What's he like?

Chris: He's funny and smart and so easy to talk to. We can talk for hours, and it never gets dull. I've never met anyone who's so easy to be with. We're interested in the same things,

Jason Harris/© 2001 Wadsworth

and we share so many values. Brandon's just super. I've never met anyone like him.

Mom: Sounds great. When do I get to meet this fellow?

Chris: Well, not until I do. [laughs] We met online, and we're just starting to talk about getting together in person.

Mom: Online? You met this man online? And you act as if you know him!

Case Study: Continuing the Conversation

Chris: I do know him, Mom. We've talked a lot—we've told each other lots of stuff, and . . .

Mom: How do you know what he's told you is true? For all you know, he's a 50-year-old mass murderer!

Chris: You've been watching too many movies on Lifetime, Mom. Brandon's 23, he's in college, and he comes from a family a lot like ours.

Mom: How do you know that? He could be lying about every part of what he's told you.

Chris: So? A guy I meet at school could lie too. Meeting someone in person is no guarantee of honesty.

Mom: Haven't you read about all of the weirdos that go to these online matching sites?

Chris: Mom, Brandon's not a weirdo, and we didn't meet in a matching site. We met in a chat room where people talk about politics. He's as normal as I am. After all, I was in that chat room too!

Mom: But, Chris, you can't be serious about someone you haven't met.

Chris: I have met him, Mom, just not face to face. Actually, I know him better than lots of guys I've dated for months. You can get to know a lot about a person from talking.

Mom: This makes me really nervous, honey. Please don't meet him by yourself.

Chris: Mom, you're making me feel sorry I told you how we met. This is exactly why I didn't tell you about him before. Nothing I say is going to change your mind about dating online.

Mom: [pauses, looks away, then looks back at Chris] You're right. I'm not giving him—or you—a chance. Let's start over. [smiles] Tell me what you like about him.

Chris: [tentatively] Well, he's thoughtful.

Mom: Thoughtful? How so?

Chris: Like, if I say something one day, he'll come back to it a day or so later, and I can tell he's thought about it, like he's really interested in what I say.

Mom: So he really pays attention to what you say, huh?

Chris: Exactly. So many guys I've dated don't. They never return to things I've said. Brandon does. And another thing, when I come back to things he's said with ideas I've thought about, he really listens.

Mom: Like he values what you think and say?

Chris: Exactly! That's what's so special about him.

1. Identify examples of ineffective and effective listening on the part of Chris's mother.

2. What do you perceive as the key obstacle to listening for Chris's mom during the early part of this conversation?

3. Identify specific listening skills that Chris's mother uses once she chooses to listen mindfully.

4. Is Chris's mother being unethical not to continue expressing her concerns about Chris's safety?

You can critique and analyze this encounter based on the principles you learned in this chapter by responding to the questions included under "Conversation Analysis" at the website. By clicking on the "Submit" button at the end of the form, you can compare your work to my suggested responses. Let's continue the conversation online!

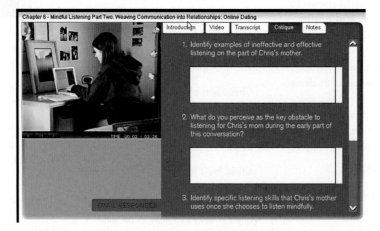

Chapter Summary

This chapter opened with a quote from Zeno of Citium, an ancient philosopher. His wry observation is as relevant today as it was thousands of years ago. Similar wisdom came from Mother Theresa in an interview with Dan Rather (Bailey, 1998, p. C5):

Rather: What do you say to God when you pray?

Mother Theresa: I listen.

Rather: Well, what does God say?

Mother Theresa: He listens.

In this chapter, we've explored the complex and demanding process of mindful listening. We began by distinguishing hearing and listening. Hearing is a physiological process that doesn't entail effort on our part. Listening, in contrast, is a complicated process involving physically receiving messages, selecting, organizing, interpreting, responding, and remembering. To do it well takes commitment and skill.

There are many obstacles to effective listening. External obstacles include message overload, complexity of material, and external noise in communication contexts. In addition, listening can be hampered by preoccupations and prejudgments, reactions to emotionally loaded language, lack of effort, and failure to adapt listening to fit situations. These obstacles give rise to various types of nonlistening, including pseudolistening, monopolizing, selective listening, defensive listening, ambushing, and literal listening.

We've identified skills and attitudes appropriate to different listening goals. Listening for pleasure is supported by mindfulness and efforts to minimize distractions and noise. Informational listening requires us to adopt a mindful attitude and to think critically, organize and evaluate information, clarify understanding by asking questions, and develop aids for retention of complex material. Relationship listening also involves mindfulness, but it calls for different listening skills: Suspending judgment, paraphrasing, giving minimal encouragers, and expressing support enhance the effectiveness of relationship listening.

The ideas we've discussed yield three guidelines for effective listening. First, we must be mindful. Second, we should adapt our listening skills and style to accommodate differences in listening purpose and individuals. Finally, we should remember that listening is an active process and be prepared to invest energy and effort in doing it skillfully. Because listening is important in all speech communities, in later chapters we'll revisit some of the ideas covered here as we discuss dynamics in relationships.

Everyday Connections Online

Now that you've read Chapter 4, go to the Everyday Connections premium website at academic.cengage.com/communication/woodinterpersonal5plus for quick access to the electronic study resources that accompany this text. The website gives you access to the "Continuing the Conversation" video scenario and questions featured in this chapter, to InfoTrac College Edition, to maintained and updated Web links, and to the study aids for this chapter, including a digital glossary, review quizzes, and the chapter activities. For more information about this text's electronic learning resources, consult the **1pass card** that came with each new copy of this book, or visit academic.cengage.com/communication/woodinterpersonal5.

Key Concepts

Audio flash cards of the following key terms are available on the Everyday Connections website. Use the flash cards to improve your pronunciation of text vocabulary.

ambushing	listening for information	mindfulness	pseudolistening
defensive listening	listening for pleasure	minimal encouragers	remembering
hearing	listening to support others	monopolizing	responding
listening	literal listening	paraphrasing	selective listening

For Further Thought and Discussion

1. Review the six types of nonlistening discussed in this chapter. Are any of them common in your communication? Select one of your nonlistening practices and work to reduce its occurrence.

2. What ethical principles can you identify to guide the three kinds of listening? Are different ethical principles appropriate when listening for information and listening to support others?

3. Keep a record of your listening for the next 2 days. How much time do you spend listening for information, listening to support others, and listening for pleasure?

4. Use your InfoTrac College Edition to read Eileen Brill Wagner's 2001 article, "Listening: Hear Today, Probably Gone Tomorrow," published in the *Business Journal*. Are the barriers to listening that she identifies consistent with those discussed in this chapter?

5. Apply the strategies for remembering what we discussed in this chapter. Create mnemonics, organize material as you listen, and review material immediately after listening. Do you find that using these strategies increases your listening effectiveness?

6. Who is your prototype, or model, of an effective listener? Describe what the person does that makes him or her effective. How do the person's behaviors fit with guidelines for effective listening discussed in this chapter?

7. The International Listening Association (ILA) is a rich resource for learning more about listening and networking with others who recognize its importance in everyday life. Its website features exercises to test and improve listening, factoids about listening, Internet discussion groups, quotes about the nature and value of listening, and a bibliography for those who want to read more. Visit the site at http://www.listen.org.

Emotions and Communication

© Lew Long/CORBIS

"The doors we open and close each day decide the lives we live."

Flora Whittemore

My sister Carolyn and I, shown in the photo on this page, had been very close for years when her first child, Michelle, was born. I shared Carolyn's delight in the new baby, yet I also felt pushed out of her life. Carolyn was so entranced with her daughter that she had little time for me. Phone calls from her, which had been frequent, almost ceased. When I called Carolyn, she often cut our conversation short because it was time to feed Michelle or get her up or change her diaper. Over lunch with my friend Nancy, I complained, "Carolyn never has time for me anymore. I am so angry with her!"

"Sounds to me more like you're hurt than angry," Nancy remarked.

What was I feeling? Was it anger or hurt or both? Emotions, or feelings, are part of our lives. We feel happiness, sadness, shame, pride, embarrassment, envy, disappointment, and a host of other emotions. And we communicate to express our emotions. We may express emotions nonverbally (smiling, trembling, blushing) or verbally ("I'm excited," "I feel anxious about the interview"), or both. Sometimes we express emotions through complex verbal messages, such as metaphors and similes (Kovecses, 1990). For instance, you might say, "I feel like a plane that's soaring" or "I am a bomb just waiting to explode."

Although we experience and express feelings, we don't always do so effectively. There are times when we aren't able to identify exactly what we feel, as I wasn't when trying to describe my feelings about reduced time with Carolyn. Even when we do recognize our emotions, we aren't always sure how to express them clearly and effectively. Do we want to vent, or do we want another person to comfort us, apologize to us, empathize with us, or behave differently toward us? To communicate well, we need to develop skill in identifying and expressing our emotions.

To open this chapter, we'll discuss *emotional intelligence,* which is distinct from cognitive intelligence. Next, we define emotions and examine different theories that attempt to explain emotions and their causes. Then, we explore why we sometimes fail to express our feelings and how we can learn to express them effectively. Finally, we discuss guidelines for communicating emotions in ways that foster our individual growth and the quality of our relationships with others.

Julia T. Wood

Emotional Intelligence

In his 1995 book *Emotional Intelligence,* Daniel Goleman (1995a) explored a kind of intelligence distinct from the type that standard IQ tests measure. In 2002, Goleman and his colleagues Richard Boyatzis and Annie McKee co-authored *Primal Leadership: Realizing the Power of Emotional Intelligence.* Goleman highlighted the critical role that emotional intelligence plays in organizational leadership.

Goleman popularized an idea that Carol Saarni (1990) originated. In her early work, Saarni emphasized a quality she called "emotional competence," which involves awareness of our own emotions, including multiple emotions experienced simultaneously, the ability to recognize and empathize with others' emotions, awareness of the impact of our expression of emotions on others, and sensitivity to cultural rules for expressing emotions.

Emotional intelligence is the ability to recognize feelings, to judge which feelings are appropriate in which situations, and to communicate those feelings effectively. According to Goleman (1995a, 1995b, 1998; Goleman, Boyatzis, & McKee, 2002), people who have high emotional intelligence quotients (EQs) are more likely than people with lower EQs to create satisfying relationships, to be comfortable with themselves, and to work effectively with others.

Emotional intelligence consists of qualities that aren't assessed by standard intelligence tests:

- ⋯ Being aware of your feelings
- ⋯ Dealing with emotions without being overcome by them
- ⋯ Not letting setbacks and disappointments derail you
- ⋯ Channeling your feelings to assist you in achieving your goals
- ⋯ Being able to understand how others feel without their spelling it out
- ⋯ Listening to your feelings and those of others so you can learn from them
- ⋯ Having a strong yet realistic sense of optimism

Emotional intelligence includes more than identifying your feelings. You also need skill in expressing them constructively. To illustrate this, let's return to my conversation with

Communication in Everyday Life
Emotional Intelligence on the Job

The value of emotional intelligence is not limited to intimate relationships. It is equally relevant to the workplace and job success. Psychologist Daniel Goleman (1998; Goleman et al., 2002) reports that EQ, or emotional intelligence, is a critical factor in career advancement. To reach this conclusion, Goleman collected data from 150 firms to learn what distinguishes mediocre employees from superstars. He reports that conventional IQ accounts for no more than 25% of success on the job, whether the job is copier repairperson, CEO, or scientist. The greater difference comes from EQ. Furthermore, claims Goleman, the importance of conventional IQ decreases, and the importance of EQ increases, as jobs become more difficult and higher in company rank.

Goleman is careful to point out that cognitive abilities, including those measured by IQ tests, are important to getting a job—most people get jobs because they have the necessary cognitive qualifications. But advancement depends on other factors, including EQ.

EQ is not just being nice to others. In the workplace, EQ is the ability to manage your own emotions and handle relationships with others constructively. Among the emotional competencies Goleman sees as critical to career advancement are self-control, initiative, empathy, political savvy, and supportive, cooperative communication.

Several websites offer additional materials on emotional intelligence. One is the Consortium for Emotional Intelligence in the Workplace at http://www.eiconsortium.org. This site provides background information on EQ, resources that discuss EQ's relevance to specific topics such as the workplace and parenting, and answers to frequently asked questions about EQ.

Another site is the EQ institute at http://eqi.org. This site provides definitions of EQ, self-tests for EQ, references, and suggestions for college students writing papers on emotional intelligence.

Nancy. After we had talked a while, I said, "I think I'll call Carolyn and tell her I resent being pushed out of her life."

"Well, when my friend Penny had a child and was totally preoccupied with him, I felt what I think you're feeling," Nancy disclosed.

"And what did you do?" I asked.

"I told her I missed her."

"Missed her?" I thought it over. I did miss Carolyn. Telling her that would be an honest and affirming way to express my feelings. Telling Carolyn I missed her might open the door to restore our closeness. Telling her I was angry or resentful probably wouldn't enhance our relationship.

Through the conversation with Nancy, I discovered that anger was a defensive reaction I was using to avoid realizing how vulnerable and hurt I felt. Later that day, I called Carolyn and told her I missed her. Her response was immediate and warm: "I miss you too. I'll be so glad when we get adjusted enough to Michelle that we have time for us again." I was effective in communicating my feelings to Carolyn, thanks to Nancy's insight into emotions and her skill in helping me figure out what I was feeling and how to express it effectively.

•••••••••••

Understanding Emotions

Although emotions are basic to human beings and communication, they are difficult to define precisely. Some researchers assert that humans experience two kinds of emotions: some that are based in biology and thus instinctual and universal, and others that we learn in social interaction (Kemper, 1987). Yet, scholars don't agree on which emotions are basic (Izard, 1991; Shaver, Schwartz, Kirson, & O'Connor, 1987; Shaver, Wu, & Schwartz, 1992). Also, many scholars don't think it's useful to distinguish between basic emotions and learned emotions (Ekman & Davidson, 1994).

Many scholars think that most or all emotions are socially constructed to a substantial degree. For example, we learn when and for what to feel guilty or proud. We learn from particular others and the generalized other when to feel gratitude, embarrassment, and so forth. In her 1989 book *Anger: The Misunderstood Emotion*, Carol Tavris argues that anger is not entirely basic or instinctual. She shows that our ability to experience anger is influenced by social interaction, through which we learn whether and when we are supposed to feel angry.

Everyday Application
What's Your EQ?

Answer the following four questions, which are adapted from Goleman's EQ test.

1. Imagine you're on an airplane and it suddenly begins rolling dramatically from side to side. What would you do?
   a. Keep reading your book, and ignore the turbulence.
   b. Become vigilant in case there is an emergency. Notice the flight attendants and review the card with instructions for emergencies.
   c. A little of a and b.
   d. Not sure—I never noticed an airplane's motion.

2. Imagine that you expect to earn an A in a course you are taking, but you get a C on your midterm exam. What would you do?
   a. Develop a specific plan to improve your grade, and resolve to implement the plan.
   b. Resolve to do better in the future.
   c. Nurture your self-concept by telling yourself that the grade doesn't really matter and focus on doing well in your other courses.
   d. Go to see the professor and try to talk him or her into raising your midterm grade.

3. While riding in a friend's car, your friend becomes enraged at another driver who just cut in front of him. What would you do?
   a. Tell your friend to let it slide—that it's no big deal.
   b. Put in your friend's favorite CD and turn up the volume to distract him.
   c. Agree with him and show rapport by talking about what a jerk the other driver is.
   d. Tell him about a time when someone cut in front of you and how mad you felt, but explain you then found out that the other driver was on her way to the hospital.

4. You and your girlfriend or boyfriend have just had an argument that became a heated shouting contest. By now, you're both very upset, and each of you has started making nasty personal attacks on the other. What do you do?
   a. Suggest that the two of you take a 20-minute break to cool down and then continue the discussion.
   b. Decide to put an end to the argument by not talking anymore. Just be silent and don't speak, no matter what the other person says.
   c. Apologize to your partner, and ask him or her to say "I'm sorry" too.
   d. Pause to collect your thoughts, then explain your views and your side of the issue clearly.

Scoring your EQ: Award yourself the following points for each response:

1. a = 20, b = 20, c = 20, d = 0
   D is the only poor answer to this question. Answer D indicates you are unaware of feelings.
2. a = 20, b = 0, c = 0, d = 0
   One aspect of emotional intelligence is being able to motivate yourself to form an action plan to tackle obstacles.
3. a = 0, b = 5, c = 5, d = 20
   B is helpful because it distracts your friend. C is helpful because it shows empathy and support. D is the most emotionally intelligent response because it distracts, shows empathy, and suggests a perspective on the other driver that is less likely to generate anger.
4. a = 20, b = 0, c = 0, d = 0
   The most emotionally intelligent response is A because research shows that we need at least 20 minutes to calm physiological reactions to strong emotion (heart rate, blood pressure). Until you calm down, perception is distorted, and it's difficult to exercise self-control.

Higher scores indicate greater emotional intelligence. To learn more about EQ and to take the original test, go to http://www.utne.com/azEQ.tmpl.

For additional practice in examining your emotional intelligence and how socialization affects it, complete Activity 7.2 in your *Student Companion* or online under "Chapter Resources for Chapter 7" at the Everyday Connections website.

Most scholars also agree that we experience emotions holistically, not individually. In many instances, what we feel is not a single emotion but several mingled together, as I felt in the situation with Carolyn. Paul Ekman and Richard Davidson (1994) surveyed research on emotions and concluded that blends of emotion are common. For instance, you might feel both sad and happy at your graduation or both grateful and resentful when someone helps you.

KENNETH Last year, my daughter got married, and I've never felt so many things in one moment. As I walked her down the aisle and took her arm from mine and placed it on the arm of her future husband, I felt sadness and happiness, hope and anxiety about her future, pride in the woman she'd become and her confidence in starting a new life, and loss because we would no longer be her primary family.

We can define **emotions** as our experience and interpretation of internal sensations as those are shaped by physiology, perceptions, language, and social experiences. It's important to realize that emotions are processes rather than fixed states of being. Physiological, perceptual, linguistic, and social influences are not independent. Instead, they interact continuously to shape our experience of emotions. Although researchers vary in the degree to which they emphasize each of these influences, most people who have studied emotions agree that physiology, perceptions, social experience, and language all play parts in our emotional lives.

PHYSIOLOGICAL INFLUENCES ON EMOTIONS

Have you ever felt a knot in your stomach when you got back an exam with a low grade? If so, you experienced a physiological reaction. Early theorists believed that we experience emotion when external stimuli cause physiological changes in us. This is the **organismic view of emotions,** and it is shown in Figure 7.1.

Advanced by philosopher William James and his colleague Carl Lange, the organismic view, also called the James–Lange view, asserts that, when an event occurs, we first respond physiologically, and only after that do we experience emotions (James, 1890; James & Lange, 1922). This perspective assumes that emotions are reflexes that follow from physiological arousal. In other words, from the organismic outlook, emotions are both the product and the expression of occurrences in our bodies. For example, Chris Kleinke, Thomas Peterson, and Thomas Rutledge (1998) found that, when people smile, their moods are more positive, and when people frown, their moods are more negative.

James wrote that emotional expression begins with a perception of something, perhaps seeing a gift with your name on it or noticing that someone with a weapon is running toward you. After the perception, James

FIGURE 7.1

The Organismic View of Emotions

believed, we experience changes in our bodies: We smile on seeing the gift; adrenaline surges when we are approached by someone with a weapon. Finally, said James, we experience emotion: We feel joy at the gift, fear at the aggressor.

The organismic view regards emotions as instinctual responses to physiological arousal caused by external stimuli. James specifically discounted what he called "intellectual mind stuff" (Finkelstein, 1980) as having nothing to do with our perceptions of stimuli and, by extension, our emotions. For James and others who shared his view, emotions result from physiological factors that are instinctual and beyond conscious control.

PERCEPTUAL INFLUENCES ON EMOTIONS

James's view of the relationship between bodily states and feelings is no longer widely accepted (Ekman & Davidson, 1994; Frijda, 1986; McLemee, 2003; Reisenzaum, 1983). Today, most researchers think the physiological influences are less important than other factors in shaping emotions.

The **perceptual view of emotions,** which is also called *appraisal theory,* asserts that subjective perceptions shape what external phenomena mean to us. External objects and events, as well as physiological reactions, have no intrinsic meaning. Instead, they gain meaning only as we attribute significance to them. We might interpret trembling hands as a symbol of fear, a raised fist as a threat, and a knot in the stomach as anxiety. Alternatively, we might interpret trembling hands as signifying joy on graduation day; a raised fist as power and racial pride, as it was during the civil rights movement of the 1960s and 1970s; and a knot in the stomach as excitement about receiving a major award. These different interpretations would lead us to define our emotions quite distinctly. That's the key to the perceptual view of emotions: We act on the basis of our interpretation of phenomea, not the actual phenomena (trembling hands, raised fist, a knot in the stomach).

The ancient Greek philosopher Epictetus observed that people are disturbed not by things but by the views we take of them. Buddha observed that we are what we think; with our thoughts we make the world. In other words, how we view things leads us to feel disturbed, pleased, sad, joyous, afraid, and so forth. Thus, our perceptions filter our experiences, and it is the filtered experiences that influence what we feel and how we respond.

HARIHAR   Buddhism teaches us that our feelings arise not from things themselves but from what we attach to them. In my life, this is true. If I find myself upset about how a conversation is going, I ask myself, "Harihar, what is it that you were expecting to happen? Can you let go of that and enter into what is actually happening here?" That helps me realize and let go of my attachment to certain outcomes of the conversation.

We respond differently to the same phenomenon depending on the meaning we attribute to it. For example, if you earn a low score on a test, you might interpret it as evidence that you are not smart. This interpretation could lead you to feel shame or disappointment or other unpleasant emotions. On the other hand, you might view the low score as the result of a tricky or overly rigorous exam, an interpretation that might lead you to feel anger at the teacher or resentment at the situation. Anger is very different from shame. Which one you feel depends on how you perceive the score and the meaning you attribute to it. The perceptual view of emotions is represented in Figure 7.2.

A slight modification of the perceptual view is the **cognitive labeling view of emotions,** which claims that our labels for our physiological responses influence our interpretations of and reposes to events (Schachter, 1964; Schachter & Singer,

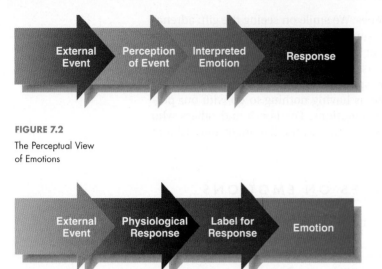

FIGURE 7.2

The Perceptual View of Emotions

FIGURE 7.3

The Cognitive Labeling View of Emotions

1962). Phrased another way, what we feel may be shaped by how we label physiological responses. For example, if you feel a knot in your stomach when you see that you received a low grade on an exam, you might label the knot as evidence of anxiety. Thus, what you felt would not result directly from either the event itself (the grade) or your perceptions of the event. Instead, it would be shaped by how you labeled your physiological response to the event. This view of emotions is represented in Figure 7.3.

I witnessed how our labels for events and our responses to them influence what we feel. When my niece, Michelle, was 2 years old and weighed less than 30 pounds, she and my sister Carolyn visited Robbie and me. As they came into our home, our 65-pound dog, Madhi, ran out to greet them and started licking Michelle. Immediately, Michelle started crying. I got Madhi to lie down across the room, and Michelle said, "Mommy, Mommy, I'm scared. My heart is going fast because she came after me and made me scared." Carolyn cuddled Michelle and said, "Your heart isn't going fast because you're scared, sweetheart. It's because Madhi surprised you and you were startled. Madhi was telling you how much she loves you. Dogs are our friends." Carolyn and I then petted Madhi and let her lick us and said repeatedly, "Oh, Madhi licked me because she loves me. She startled me."

Michelle quickly picked up our language and began to laugh, not cry, when Madhi bowled her over. By the end of the day, Michelle and Madhi were fast friends. Before she went to bed that night, Michelle told us, "Madhi makes my heart beat faster because I love her." What happened here? Madhi's exuberance didn't diminish, nor did Michelle's physiological response of increased heart rate. What did change was how Michelle labeled her physiological response. Carolyn and I taught her to interpret Madhi's behavior as friendly and exciting instead of threatening. Michelle's label for her emotion also changed: *scared* became *startled*.

> **ARMANO**   The most important lesson I learned when my family first moved to the United States was that a bad grade on a test is not a judgment that I am stupid. It is a challenge for me to do better. My ESL teacher taught me that. He said if I saw a bad grade as saying I am dumb or a failure that I would never learn English. He taught me to see grades as challenges that I could meet. That attitude made it possible for me not to give up and to keep learning.

There is probably some validity to each view of emotions that we've explored. The organismic view calls our attention to the physiological aspects of emotions; we do have bodily responses to what happens around us. The perceptual view reminds us that how we perceive external events and our physiological reactions influences the meanings we attach to experiences and the emotions we think are appropriate. Finally, the cognitive labeling view emphasizes the role of language in shaping our interpretation of events, our physiological responses, appropriate emotions, or all three. Each of the models we've considered so far gives us insight into emotions. Yet, none of these models is complete, because none adequately accounts for the critical influence of culture in shaping emotions and how we communicate them.

As we learned in Chapter 3, perception is influenced by the culture and the social groups to which we belong. Historian Barbara Rosenwein (1998) considers the groups we identify with "emotional communities" because they teach us how to understand and express emotions. Examples of emotional communities are families, neighborhoods, gangs, monasteries, and religious groups. The society and communities in which we live influence our beliefs about which emotions are good or bad, which emotions we should express or repress, and with whom we can appropriately communicate which emotions. For example, the emotion of shame is emphasized much more in traditional Asian societies than in Western societies. This may explain why 95% of Chinese parents report that their children understand the meaning of shame by age 3, whereas only 10% of American parents report this (Sedgwick, 1995; Shaver, Schwartz, Kirson, & O'Connor, 1987; Shaver, Wu, & Schwartz, 1992).

Insight into social influences on emotions and our expression of them is fairly new. Beginning in the 1970s, some scholars began to advance the **interactive view of emotions,** which proposes that social rules and understandings shape what people feel and how they do or don't express their feelings. Arlie Hochschild (1979, 1983, 1990) pioneered in this area by investigating the ways that people experience, control, and express feelings. The interactive view of emotions rests on three key concepts: framing rules, feeling rules, and emotion work.

Framing Rules **Framing rules** define the emotional meaning of situations. For instance, Western culture defines funerals as sad and respectful occasions and weddings as joyful events. Within any single culture, however, there are multiple social groups and resulting standpoints. Different social groups may teach members distinct framing rules for the same situations. For example, many Irish Americans hold wakes when a person dies. A wake is a festive occasion during which people tell stories about the departed person and celebrate his or her life. Other groups define funerals and the receptions following them as somber occasions at which any mirth or festivity would be perceived as disrespectful and inappropriate. During the Jewish practice of sitting *shiva,* family members do not engage others in routine ways such as talking on the phone.

Feeling Rules **Feeling rules** tell us what we have a right to feel or what we are expected to feel in particular situations. Feeling rules reflect and perpetuate the values of cultures and social groups. For example, cultures that emphasize individuality promote the feeling rule that it is appropriate to feel pride in personal accomplishments, whereas cultures that emphasize collectivism teach members that accomplishments grow out of membership in groups and reflect well on those groups, not on individuals (Johnson, 2000). Thus, in such cultures a feeling rule might be that it is appropriate for a person to feel gratitude to family and community for personal accomplishments.

A few years ago, I read a newspaper story that shows how feeling rules differ between cultures. Teachers didn't realize that parents

Robert A. Sabo/Getty Images

Communication in Everyday Life
The Social Shaping of Grief

Cultures have distinct framing rules about death (Lofland, 1985; Miller, 1993, 1998). In some African tribes, death is regarded as cause to celebrate a person's passage to a better form of life. Buddhists do not regard the death of a body as the end of a person, because the person is assumed to continue in other forms. In some cultures, people feel deep grief over the loss of cousins to whom they have deep and lasting attachments. In contrast, other cultures define cousins as distant relations whose death seldom provokes deep sadness.

Framing rules about death also vary over time in a single culture. Modern Western cultures enjoy a low infant mortality rate (approximately 9 deaths per 1,000 infants) and a long life expectancy. In earlier times, the infant mortality rate in Western societies ranged from 50 to 400 deaths per 1,000 infants, and the life expectancy was decades shorter than it is today. Scholars who have studied historical and diary research from earlier times report that death was viewed as a normal, routine part of life that did not call for intense and prolonged mourning.

and students from collectivist cultures are dismayed when report cards state that students "speak up in class." Because collectivist cultures emphasize the overall community, an individual who stands out may be perceived as showing off and inappropriately calling attention to himself or herself ("Teachers' Words," 2000). All social communities have rules that specify acceptable and unacceptable ways to feel.

Feeling rules are sometimes explicated in terms of rights and duties. The following common phrases highlight the language of duty and rights that infuses feeling rules:

I'm entitled to feel sad.
You have no right to feel unhappy.
She should be grateful to me for
    what I did.
My disappointment in you is
    justified.
I ought to feel happy my friend got
    a job.
I shouldn't feel angry at my father.

Everyday Application
Religions and Feeling Rules

Religions urge people to follow particular feeling rules. For example, Judeo-Christian commandments direct people to "honor thy father and thy mother" and to "not covet thy neighbor's house, nor his wife." Buddhism commands people to feel compassion for all living beings and to do what they can to alleviate suffering. Hinduism commands followers to accept their place (caste) in this life.

Make a list of all the feeling rules you can identify that are proposed by your spiritual or religious affiliation. Be sure to list both what you are supposed to feel and what you are not supposed to feel.

1. _____
2. _____
3. _____
4. _____
5. _____
6. _____

Compare your responses with those of students who have different religious or spiritual beliefs. What similarities and differences in feeling rules can you identify?

© Michael Kagan

Hochschild perceives a strong connection between feeling rules and social order. She (1990) claims that one way a society attempts to control people is through feeling rules that uphold broad social values and structures. For example, teaching people that they should feel pride in their personal accomplishments reinforces the value that Western culture places on individualism and ambition. Teaching people to regard accomplishments as communal, not individual, upholds the value that many non-Western cultures place on groups. Philosopher Jerome Kagan (1998) points out that morality is not innate but learned as people internalize the moral values of their cultures.

A second way in which feeling rules uphold social structure is by permitting the expression of negative feelings and of bad-mannered means of expressing them toward people with limited power. Hochschild's (1983) studies of people in service industries reveal that the less power employees have, the more they tend to be targets of negative emotional expressions from others. People who have more power may learn they have a right to express anger, offense, frustration, and so forth, whereas people who have less power may learn that it isn't acceptable for them to express such emotions. To test the validity of this idea, ask yourself who is the target of more complaints and greater hostility: servers or restaurant

DIVERSITY

Communication in Everyday Life
Cultural Codes for Anger

Suppose you felt extremely angry and wanted to express your feeling. What would you do? Would you go for a long, hard run? Would you work out in the gym? Would you kick a wall or closet door? Would you hit someone? Would you yell at friends? Would you go on a shooting rampage?

Anthropologists tell us that how we express anger is influenced by the society in which we live. In the United States and many other Western cultures, anger is viewed as healthy and something we express so that it doesn't fester inside us (Nanda & Warms, 1998). In some societies, however, anger is almost absent. For example, the Semai of Malaysia are a nonviolent people who do not perceive anger as a healthy or appropriate emotion. Semais believe that a person who stays angry will have misfortune. Because it is the angry person who gets hurt, Semais try to avoid anger. Not a single murder among Semais has ever been recorded (Robarchek & Dentan, 1987; Dentan, 1995).

Other societies view anger differently. For instance, one group that lives in the New Guinea highlands has a well-established custom for venting aggression. People who feel aggressive are defined as wild pigs, who are out of control. Because they are out of control, they are allowed to behave in bizarre ways that would never be condoned in a normal person. Wild pigs are said to "run amok." They are able to vent aggression without being judged as deviant. After all, when they are in the agitated state, they aren't people— they're wild pigs. By running amok, the person expresses aggressive feelings and can then return to normal identity. Thus, these New Guinea communities have created a safety valve for people who feel overcome by unruly impulses (Newman, 1964; Shott, 1979; Winzeler, 1990).

Communication in Everyday Life
Faking It

"It happened again today: I was bluffing my way through material in my Property class [a standard course in law school], about which I knew no more than what the teaching manual told me . . ." (2003, p. 1). That's how law professor William Miller begins his book *Faking It*. This isn't Miller's first foray into the world of self-presentation. For years, he has studied emotions—those of the Vikings, particularly Viking warriors (Miller, 1993, 1998). Now, Miller turns his attention to modern-day warriors like you and me as we bluff and fake our way through surface acting: pretending to be happy for a colleague who wins a major award, feigning pleasure when someone you dislike enters your space, acting informed when we know little. His 2003 book *Faking It* takes note of how we bluff our way through life and work. The book is not only informative but also wonderfully funny and interesting.

managers, flight attendants or pilots, receptionists or CEOs?

Parents differ in how they teach children to deal with feelings. Some parents encourage children to control their inner feelings through **deep acting,** which involves learning what they should and should not feel. For instance, children may be taught that they should feel grateful when given a gift even if they don't like the gift. Many children are taught that they should not feel angry when a sibling takes a toy. Deep acting requires changing how we perceive and label events and phenomena.

Other parents emphasize **surface acting,** which involves controlling the outward expression of emotions rather than controlling feelings. Parents who emphasize surface acting teach children to control their outward behaviors, not necessarily their inner feelings. For example, children learn that they should say "thank you" when they receive a gift and that they should not hit a sibling who takes a toy. Expressing gratitude is emphasized more than feeling grateful, and refraining from hitting someone who takes a toy is stressed more than being willing to share toys.

Emotion Work   The final concept is **emotion work,** which is the effort to generate what we think are appropriate feelings in particular situations. Notice that emotion work concerns our effort to fashion how we feel, not necessarily our success at squelching feelings we think are inappropriate or at generating the feelings we think we should experience. When successful, emotion work allows us to engage in deep acting.

Although we do emotion work much of the time, we tend to be most aware of engaging in it when we think our feelings are inappropriate in specific situations. For example, you might think it is wrong to feel gleeful when someone you dislike is hurt. Hochschild (1979, 1983) refers to this as "the pinch," which is a discrepancy between what we feel and what we think we should feel. If you feel gleeful about another's bad luck, you might engage in emotion work in an effort to make yourself feel sad.

Typically, what we think we should feel is based on what we've learned from our social groups and the larger culture. Social groups teach us what feelings are appropriate in particular situations. For example, Clifton Scott and Karen Meyers (2005) found that firefighters engage in emotion work to manage feelings such as fear and disgust, which can interfere with controlling damage and providing medical help to victims of fires. People who have been socialized in multiple cultures with different values may be especially vulnerable to feeling "the pinch." For example, Kimberly Gangwish (1999) describes Asian American women as "living in two worlds" in terms of their emotions and how they express them. First-generation Asian American women said they knew that, in the United States, it was acceptable to feel angry and upset, but they couldn't express those feelings because Asian cultures frown on expressing negative emotions.

In my native country, students are supposed to be respectful of teachers and never speak out in class. It has been hard for me to learn to feel I have a right to ask questions of a professor here. Sometimes I have a question or I do not agree with a professor, but I have to work to tell myself it is okay to assert myself. To me, it still feels disrespectful to speak up.

Emotion work is the effort to curb feelings we think we shouldn't have or to generate feelings we think we should have. We do emotion work to suppress or eliminate feelings we think are wrong (for example, feeling happy over the misfortune of someone we dislike). We also engage in emotion work to cultivate feelings we think we should have, such as prodding ourselves to feel joy for our friend's good fortune. As Donna Vocate (1994) notes, much of our emotion work takes place through self-talk—we try to talk ourselves into feeling what we think is appropriate and out of feeling what we think is inappropriate. In addition, we often talk to friends to figure out whether our feelings are appropriate—we rely on friends to help us reduce uncertainty about feelings (Heise, 1999; Milardo, 1986; Parks & Adelman, 1983).

Framing rules, feeling rules, and emotion work are interrelated (see Figure 7.4). Framing rules that define the emotional meaning of situations lead to feeling rules that tell us what we should feel or have a right to feel in a given context. If we don't feel what our feeling rules designate we should, we may engage in emotion work to squelch inappropriate feelings or to bring about feelings that we think suit the circumstances. We then express our feelings by following rules for appropriate expression of particular emotions in specific contexts. *Student Companion:* Activity 7.3.

The interactive view of emotions emphasizes the impact of social factors on how we perceive, label, and respond emotionally to experiences in our lives. A strength of this model is its acknowledgment of cultural differences in feelings and their expression.

How we think about emotions affects how much we believe we can control what we experience and express in everyday life. If you agree with William James that feelings are instinctual, then you will assume that feelings cannot be managed. Whatever you feel, you feel. That's it. On the other hand, if you accept the interactive view of emotions, you are

Communication in Everyday Life
The Gift of Fear

Don't ignore your fear. That's the message of Gavin de Becker's book, *The Gift of Fear* (1997). For years, de Becker has worked as a security consultant to celebrities. He notes that many people have been taught to dismiss feelings of fear by labeling them "silly" or "stupid." They invest emotion work in talking themselves out of feeling fear. Big mistake, says de Becker. If you're waiting for an elevator, and when the door opens, you have a strong, fearful reaction to a person in the elevator, what do you do? De Becker says many people try to talk themselves out of the fear with thoughts such as, "There's nothing to be afraid of." Wrong, says de Becker. He advises us to wait for the next elevator. If you have a feeling that someone is lurking in a parking lot, don't dismiss it as paranoia; heed it, and find someone to walk with you. De Becker believes that fear often arises in response to subtle cues in an environment—cues of which we are not consciously aware but to which we respond anyway.

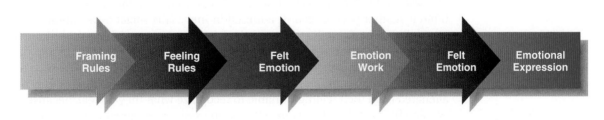

FIGURE 7.4

The Interactive View of Emotions

more likely to think you can analyze your feelings and perhaps change them and your expression of them through emotion work. The interactive view assumes we have some power over how we feel and act. If you agree with this perspective, you are more likely to monitor your feelings and to make choices about how to communicate them.

We may not have total control over what we feel, but usually we can exert some control. Furthermore, we can exercise substantial control over how we do or don't express our feelings and to whom we express them. Taking personal responsibility for when, how, and to whom you express feelings is a cornerstone of ethical interpersonal communication.

There is no clear dividing line between what we feel and how we express feelings. The two interact in the emotional process. What we feel influences how we express (or don't express) our emotions. It's equally true that how we express our feelings is echoed back to us, affecting how we interpret our feelings (Anderson & Guerrero, 1998; Fridlund, 1994; Philippot & Feldman, 2004).

• • • • • • • • • • •

Obstacles to the Effective Communication of Emotions

Skill in recognizing and expressing emotions is important to interpersonal competence, yet many of us repress feelings or express them inappropriately. Let's consider reasons we may not express emotions, and then ask how we can learn to express emotions effectively.

REASONS WE MAY NOT EXPRESS EMOTIONS

We can identify four common reasons people don't communicate emotions. As we discuss each reason, reflect on whether you rely on it in your own emotional expression.

Social Expectations As we have noted, what we feel and how we express it are influenced by the culture and social groups to which we belong. Gender socialization seems particularly important in shaping feelings and the expression of them. In the United States, men are expected to be more restrained than women in expressing emotions—at least most emotions. Men are allowed to express anger, which is often disapproved of in women. Anger and other emotions regarded as powerful are allowed and often admired in men.

In other ways, however, men in Western societies are expected to be emotionally restrained. The expression of hurt, fear, depression, and many other emotions often is neither encouraged or admired in men. This social expectation is not universal. For example, Italian men routinely express a range of emotions dramatically and openly. In Western society, however, most men learn the feeling rule that they should not feel or express a great many emotions. This can lead some men to deny feelings or avoid expressing how they feel. Over time, men who do this may become alienated from their feelings, unable to recognize what they do feel, because society has taught them that they aren't allowed to experience a great many feelings.

Women face different restrictions than men on the feelings society allows them. Women are generally taught that they should not feel or express anger. Our culture considers anger unattractive and undesirable in women (Tavris, 1989). Thus, many women are constrained by the feeling rule that they should not feel anger and that, if they do, they should not express it. This discourages women from acknowledging legitimate anger and expressing it assertively.

Other feeling rules are learned by many Western women. Most women in our society are encouraged from childhood to care about others (Eisenberg, 2002; Taylor, 2002). Many women learn the feeling rule that they should care about and for others all the time (Eichenbaum & Orbach, 1987; Rubin, 1985). Thus, many women engage in emotion work in an attempt to make themselves feel (deep acting) caring when they don't naturally feel that way.

Even more often, report researchers, women squelch feelings of jealousy toward friends and feelings of competitiveness in personal and professional relationships. Because most Western women are taught that they should support others, they often feel that they shouldn't experience or express envy or competitiveness. Not being able to express or even acknowledge such feelings can interfere with honest communication in interpersonal relationships.

Communication in Everyday Life
Sugar and Spice and Bullying!

"Sugar and spice and everything nice" is not the whole picture about girls. Recently, scholars' tracking of adolescent girls' bullying (Simmons, 2002, 2004; Underwood, 2003) shows that many young girls engage in social aggression toward other girls, and they do so using distinctly feminine rules for expressing aggression. Unlike physical aggression, which is standard in boys' aggression, social aggression is usually indirect, even covert. It takes forms such as spreading hurtful rumors, social exclusion, and encouraging others to turn against a particular girl. Why do young girls rely on indirect and social strategies of aggression? One reason appears to be that, even at young ages, girls understand that they are supposed to be nice to everyone, so they fear that being overtly mean to others would lead to disapproval or punishment. Instead of learning how to work through feelings of anger and dislike, young girls learn to hide such feelings and express them only indirectly.

> **SADIE** The other night, I got home after working the dinner shift at my restaurant. I was dead tired. The phone rang, and I almost didn't answer. Now, I wish I hadn't. It was my friend Brooke, and she was upset about a fight with her boyfriend. I tried to cut the call short, but she said, "I'm really hurting, and I need to talk." And so I reminded myself that I do care about Brooke. I told myself that my fatigue wasn't as important as Brooke's problem. So we stayed on the phone for over an hour, and we talked through what was happening. Sometimes I wish I could just say, "I'm not available for you now," but I'd feel like a real jerk if I did that.

When women squash these feelings, there can be undesirable personal and relationship effects. Denying or refusing to act on competitive feelings can limit women's career advancement. Not dealing openly with feelings of jealousy or envy

in friendships can create barriers and distance. For women, demanding of themselves that they always be emotionally available and caring to anyone who wants their help can be overwhelming.

Vulnerability   A second reason we may not express our feelings is that we don't want to give others information that could affect how they perceive us. We fear that someone will like us less if we disclose that we feel angry with him or her. We worry that someone will lose respect for us if our nonverbal behaviors show that we feel weak or scared. We fear that if we disclose how deeply we feel about another person, she or he will reject us. Furthermore, we may be concerned that others could use knowledge of our vulnerabilities against us. To protect ourselves from being vulnerable to others, we may not express feelings verbally or nonverbally.

Protecting Others   Another reason we often choose not to express feelings is that we fear we could hurt or upset others. Sometimes we make an ethical choice not to express emotions that would hurt another person without achieving any positive outcome. Choosing not to express emotions in some situations or to some people can be constructive and generous, as Tara's commentary illustrates.

> **TARA**   My best friend, Fran, is a marriage saver. When I'm really angry with my husband, I vent to her. If there's a really serious problem between me and Al, I talk with him. But a lot of times I'm upset over little stuff. I know what I'm feeling isn't going to last and isn't any serious problem in our marriage, but I may be seething anyway. Letting those feelings out to Fran gets them off my chest without hurting Al or our marriage.

The tendency to restrain emotional expression to protect others is particularly strong in many Asian cultures because they view hurting others as shameful (Johnson, 2000; Min, 1995; Ting-Toomey & Oetzel, 2002; Yamamoto, 1995). Traditional Asian cultures also view conflict as damaging to social relationships, so they discourage emotional expressions that might lead to conflict (Johnson, 2000; Servaes, 1988; Ting-Toomey & Oetzel, 2002; Yum, 1987).

Yet, Asians and people of Asian descent are not the only ones who want to protect relationships from emotional expression. If a friend of yours behaves in ways you consider irresponsible, you may refrain from expressing your disapproval because to do so might cause tension between you. Yet, it isn't healthy to consistently avoid expressing emotions. The physical and psychological impact of denying or repressing emotions can harm you and devastate your relationships (Pennebaker, 1997; Schmanoff, 1985, 1987).

Totally open and unrestrained expression of feeling isn't necessarily a good idea. Sometimes it is both wise and kind not to express feelings. It's often not productive to vent minor frustrations and annoyances. If someone we care about is already overburdened with anxiety or emotional problems, we may choose to monitor our communication so that the other person doesn't have to respond to our feelings at the moment. Thus, there can be good reasons not to show or discuss feelings or not to show or discuss them at a given time.

> **ISHMAEL**   Last week, I got rejected by the law school that was my top choice. Normally, I would have gone over to Jason's apartment to hang out with him and let him boost me up. Ever since we met freshman year, we've been tight friends, and we talk about everything in our lives. But right now, Jason's struggling with his own stuff. His mother just got diagnosed with cancer, and his father is out of work. I know we'll talk about my disappointment some time, but I figured it could wait until he gets into a better place.

Ishmael's commentary provides a good example of an instance in which it is caring not to express feelings. Yet, we would be mistaken to think it's always a good idea to keep feelings to ourselves. Avoiding the expression of negative or upsetting feelings can be harmful if such feelings directly affect relationships with others or if doing so may threaten our own health. Susan Schmanoff (1987) found that intimacy wanes when couples' communication consistently lacks emotional disclosures, even unpleasant ones. If not expressing feelings is likely to create barriers in relationships or to cause us serious personal distress, then we should try to find a context and mode of expression that allow us to communicate our emotions.

Social and Professional Roles   A final reason we may not express some feelings is that our roles make it inappropriate. The Queen of England, for example, must always monitor her expression of feelings so that she does not act in ways that are incongruent with her role as the Queen. An attorney who cried when hearing a sad story from a witness might be perceived as unprofessional. A doctor or nurse who expressed anger toward a patient might be regarded as unprofessional. Police officers and social workers might be judged out of line if they expressed animosity instead of objective detachment when investigating a crime.

When I testify as an expert witness in trials, the attorneys questioning me often try to rattle me with personal attacks, trick questions, or by deliberately twisting what I've said. These are routine, normal tactics in cross-examinations. If I were to respond emotionally—perhaps with an angry outburst—I would lose credibility with the jury. To be effective in the role of an expert witness, I must restrain highly emotional reactions.

We've identified four common reasons we may not express our emotions. Although we can understand all of them, they are not equally constructive in their consequences. There is no simple rule for when to express feelings. Instead, we must exercise judgment. We have an ethical obligation to make thoughtful choices about whether, when, and how to express our feelings. As a responsible communicator, you should strive to decide when it is necessary, appropriate, and constructive to express your feelings, keeping in mind that you, others, and relationships will be affected by your decision. *Student Companion:* Activity 7.7.

THE INEFFECTIVE EXPRESSION OF EMOTIONS

We don't always deny or repress our emotions. Sometimes, we realize we have feelings, and we try to express them, but we don't do so effectively. We'll look at three of the most common forms of ineffective emotional expression.

Speaking in Generalities   "I feel bad." "I'm happy." "I'm sad." Statements such as these do express emotional states, but they do so ineffectively. Why? Because they are so general and abstract that they don't clearly communicate what the speaker feels. Does "I feel bad" mean the person feels depressed, angry, guilty, ashamed, or anxious? Does "I'm happy" mean the speaker is in love, pleased with a grade, satisfied at having received a promotion, delighted to be eating chocolate, or excited about an upcoming vacation? When we use highly general, abstract emotional language, we aren't communicating effectively about what we feel.

Also, our nonverbal repertoire for expressing emotions may be limited. Withdrawing from interaction may be an expression of sadness, anger, depression, or fear. Lowering our head and eyes may express a range of emotions, including reverence, shame, and thoughtfulness. We are capable of experiencing many, many emotions. Yet, most of us recognize or express only a small number. In *Anger: The Struggle for Emotional Control in America's History* (1986), Carol Stearns and Peter Stearns report that people in the United States recognize only a few of the emotions humans can experience, and they express those emotions whenever they feel something. An acquaintance of mine says, "I'm frustrated" when he is angry, confused, hurt, anxious, disappointed, and so forth. In the example that opened this chapter, I said I felt angry when *hurt* would have more accurately described my feeling. A limited emotional vocabulary restricts our ability to communicate clearly with others (Saarni, 1999).

Not Owning Feelings Stating feelings in a way that disowns personal responsibility for the feeling is one of the most common obstacles to effective expression of emotions (Proctor, 1991). Our discussion of *I* language and *you* language in Chapter 4 is relevant to learning to express emotions effectively.

"You make me angry" states a feeling (although the word *angry* may be overly general). Yet, this statement relies on *you* language, which suggests that somebody other than the speaker is the source or cause of the angry feeling. Others certainly say and do things that affect us; they may even do things to us. But we—not anyone else—decide what their actions mean, and we—not anyone else—are responsible for our feelings.

How could we use *you* language to revise the statement, "You make me angry"? We could change it to this: "I feel angry when you don't call when you say you will." The statement would be even more effective—clearer and more precise—if the speaker said, "I feel hurt and insecure when you don't call when you say you will." And the statement would be still more effective if it included information about what the speaker wants from the other person: "I feel hurt and insecure when you don't call when you say you will. Would you be willing to call if we agree that it's okay for calls to be short sometimes?" This statement accepts responsibility for a feeling, communicates clearly what is felt, and offers a solution that could help the relationship.

Counterfeit Emotional Language   A third ineffective form of emotional communication is relying on **counterfeit emotional language.** This is language that seems to express emotions but does not actually describe what a person is feeling. For example, shouting "Why can't you leave me alone?" certainly reveals that the speaker is feeling something, but it doesn't describe what she or he is feeling. Is it anger at the particular person, frustration at being interrupted, stress at having to meet a deadline, or the need for time alone? We can't tell what feeling the speaker is experiencing.

Effective communicators provide clear descriptions of their feelings and the connection between their feelings and others' behaviors. "I feel frustrated because when I'm working and you walk in, I lose my train of thought" is a more constructive statement than "Why can't you leave me alone?" The first statement communicates what is troubling you and states that it is situation-specific.

It's also counterfeit and unproductive not to explain feelings. "That's just how I feel" doesn't tell a person how her or his behavior is related to your feelings or what you would like her or him to do. Sometimes, we say, "That's just how I feel" because we haven't really figured out why we feel as we do or what we want from another person. In such cases, we should take responsibility for understanding what's going on inside ourselves before we ask others to understand. Only when you can identify situations and your emotional reactions to them can you communicate clearly to others (Planalp, 1997).

Another form of counterfeit emotional language uses feeling words but really expresses thoughts: "I feel this discussion is getting sidetracked." The perception that a discussion is going off on a tangent is a thought, not a feeling. Maybe the speaker feels frustrated that the discussion seems to be wandering, but that feeling is not communicated by the statement.

The three types of ineffective emotional communication we've considered give us insight into some of the more common ways we may evade—consciously or not—clear and honest communication about our feelings. In the final section of this chapter, we consider specific ways to communicate our feelings effectively and constructively and to respond sensitively to others' communication about their emotions.

· · · · · · · · · · ·

Guidelines for Communicating Emotions Effectively

What we've explored so far in this chapter suggests several guidelines for becoming skilled at communicating our feelings. In this section, we extend our discussion to

Everyday Application
Avoiding Counterfeit Emotional Language

Listed here are five statements that include counterfeit emotional language. Rewrite each statement so that it describes a feeling or an emotional state. Make sure you also rely on *I* language, not *you* language, and offer precise, clear descriptions, not vague ones.

1. Shut up! I don't want to hear anything else from you.
2. You're a wonderful person.
3. I feel like we should get started on our group project.
4. I can't believe you were here all day and didn't ever clean up this mess.
5. Can't you see I'm working now? Leave me alone.

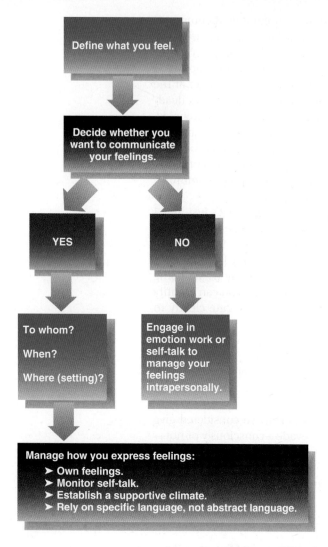

Define what you feel.

↓

Decide whether you want to communicate your feelings.

YES / **NO**

YES → To whom? When? Where (setting)?

NO → Engage in emotion work or self-talk to manage your feelings intrapersonally.

Manage how you express feelings:
➤ Own feelings.
➤ Monitor self-talk.
➤ Establish a supportive climate.
➤ Rely on specific language, not abstract language.

FIGURE 7.5

Effective Communication of Emotions

identify six guidelines for effective communication of emotions. This process is summarized in Figure 7.5.

IDENTIFY YOUR EMOTIONS

Before you can communicate emotions effectively, you must be able to identify what you feel. As we have seen, this isn't always easy. For reasons we've discussed, people may be alienated from their emotions or unclear about what they feel, especially if they experience multiple emotions at once. To become more aware of your emotions, give mindful attention to your inner self. Just as we can learn to ignore our feelings, we can teach ourselves to notice and heed them.

Sometimes, identifying our emotions requires us to sort out complex mixtures of feeling. For example, we sometimes feel both anxious and hopeful. To recognize only that you feel hopeful is to overlook the anxiety. To realize only that you feel anxious is to ignore the hope you also feel. Recognizing the existence of both feelings allows you to tune in to yourself and to communicate accurately to others what you are experiencing.

When sorting out intermingled feelings, it's useful to identify the primary or main feeling—the one or ones that are dominant in the moment. Doing this allows you to communicate clearly to others what is most important in your emotional state. Think back to the example that opened this chapter. I said I felt angry that Carolyn didn't seem to have time for me. I did feel anger, but that wasn't my primary emotion. Hurt and sadness were the dominant feelings, and they were the ones I communicated to Carolyn. This gave her an understanding of what I felt that was more accurate than if I'd told her I felt angry.

CHOOSE HOW TO EXPRESS EMOTIONS

Once you know what you feel, you'll want to consider how to express your emotions. The first choice facing you is whether you want to communicate your emotions to particular people. As we noted in the previous section, sometimes it is both wise and compassionate not to tell someone what you feel. You may decide that expressing particular emotions would hurt others and would not accomplish anything positive. This is not the same thing as not expressing emotions just to avoid tension, because tension between people can foster growth in individuals and relationships.

We may also decide not to communicate emotions because we prefer to keep some of our feelings private. This is a reasonable choice if the feelings we keep to ourselves are not ones that others need to know in order to understand us and to be in satisfying relationships with us. We don't have a responsibility to bare our souls to everyone, nor are we required to tell all our feelings, even to our intimates.

If you decide you do want to communicate your emotions, then you should assess the different ways you might do that and select the one that seems likely to be most effective. Four guidelines can help you decide how to express emotions. First, evaluate your current state. If you are really upset, you may not be able to express yourself clearly and fairly. In moments of extreme emotion, our perceptions may be distorted, and we may say things we don't mean. Remember that communication is irreversible—we cannot unsay what we have said. According to Daniel Goleman (1995b), it takes about 20 minutes for us to cleanse our minds and bodies of anger. Thus, if you are really angry, you may want to wait until you've cooled down so that you can discuss your feelings more fruitfully.

The second step is to decide to whom you want to express your feelings. Often, we want to communicate our emotions to the people they concern—the person with whom we are upset or whose understanding we seek. Yet, sometimes we don't want to talk to the person who is the target of our feelings. You might be too upset to talk productively, or you might not think the person can help you. In cases such as these, it may be useful to find someone to whom you can safely express your feelings without harming the person about whom you have them. Venting can be healthy because it allows us to acknowledge strong feelings without imposing them on others who might be hurt. A good friend can be a safety valve when we want to vent.

BOB When I didn't get a promotion, I was ready to blow my top. But I knew better than to blow it around my boss or anyone at the company. Nope, I said I was sick and left for the day and called a friend who works at home. We met for lunch, and she let me just blow off steam with her in a place that wouldn't hurt me on the job.

Next, select an appropriate time to discuss feelings. Most of us are better able to listen and respond when we are not preoccupied, defensive, stressed, rushed, or tired. Generally, it's not productive to launch a discussion of feelings when we lack the time or energy to focus on the conversation. It may be better to defer discussion until you and the other person have the psychological and physical resources to engage mindfully.

Finally, select an appropriate setting for discussing feelings. Many feelings can be expressed well in a variety of settings. For instance, it would be appropriate to tell a friend you felt happy while strolling with him through a shopping mall, walking on campus, or in a private conversation. However, it might not be constructive to tell a friend you feel angry or disappointed in her in a public setting. Doing so could make the other person feel on display, which is likely to arouse defensiveness, making it less likely that the two of you can have a constructive, open discussion of feelings. Many people report that they feel freer to express emotions honestly online than in face-to-face communication (Baym, 2002). However, some people really dislike communicating about personal topics online. So, before choosing to discuss emotions in cyberspace, make sure the other person is comfortable with that.

OWN YOUR FEELINGS

We noted the importance of owning your emotions in Chapter 4 and again in this chapter's discussion of ineffective ways of communicating feelings. Owning your feelings is so important to effective communication that the guideline bears repeating. Using *I* language to express feelings reminds us that we—not anyone else—have responsibility for our feelings. When we rely on *you* language ("You hurt me"), we risk misleading ourselves about our accountability for our emotions.

I language also reduces the potential for defensiveness by focusing on specific behaviors that we would like changed ("I feel hurt when you interrupt me") instead

Communication in Everyday Life
Virtual Emotions

Most of the time, we're not highly conscious of our need to express emotions, because most communication media don't constrain our ability to do so. But when we enter cyberspace, things change. Have you ever had a friend misunderstand an e-mail message because the text you typed didn't covey that you were being sarcastic, ironic, or just plain joking?

The potential for misunderstanding because nonverbal cues of emotion are missing on the Internet probably is why emoticons are so popular (Netspeak, 2000). The word *emoticon* is a combination of two words: *emotion* and *icon.* Thus, emoticons are icons that represent facial expressions that show what feeling we mean to convey with our written message.

:D grin	;) wink	: > devilish grin	:/ frustrated
:*) kiss	:) smile	{name} hug	:O surprise
:(frown	:'(crying/sad	::(::):: Band-Aid	

of criticizing another's basic self ("You are so rude"). Criticisms of specific behaviors are less face threatening than criticisms of our personality or self (Cupach & Carlson, 2002). Thus, when we use *I* language to describe how we feel when another behaves in particular ways, the other person is more able to listen thoughtfully and respond sensitively to our expression of emotion.

MONITOR YOUR SELF-TALK

A fourth guideline is to monitor your self-talk. You'll recall from Chapter 2 that the ways we communicate with ourselves affect how we feel and act. **Self-talk** is communication with ourselves. We engage in self-talk when we do emotion work. We might say, "I shouldn't feel angry" or "I don't want to come across as a wimp by showing how much that hurt." Thus, we may talk ourselves out of or into feelings and out of or into ways of expressing feelings.

Psychologist Martin Seligman (1990) believes that "our thoughts are not merely reactions to events; they change what ensues" (p. 9). In other words, the thoughts we communicate to ourselves affect what happens in our lives. Self-talk can work for us or against us, depending on whether we manage it or it manages us. This point is stressed by Tom Rusk and Natalie Rusk in their book *Mind Traps* (1988). They point out that many people have self-defeating ideas that get in the way of their effectiveness and happiness. According to the Rusks, unless we learn to manage our feelings effectively, we cannot change patterns of behavior that leave us stuck in ruts. Tuning in to your self-talk and learning to monitor it helps you manage your emotions.

ADOPT A RATIONAL–EMOTIVE APPROACH TO FEELINGS

Monitoring your self-talk allows you to appreciate the connections between thoughts and feelings. As Sally Planalp and Julie Fitness (2000) point out, "Cognition relies on emotion, emotion relies on cognition" (p. 732). Thus, how we think about feelings affects our feelings. The relationship between thoughts and feelings led a therapist named Albert Ellis to develop the **rational–emotive approach to feelings.** This approach uses rational thinking and self-talk to challenge debilitating thoughts about emotions that undermine healthy self-concepts and relationships. The rational–emotive approach to feelings proceeds through four steps, as shown in Figure 7.6.

The first step is to monitor your emotional reactions to events and experiences that distress you. Notice what's happening in your body; notice your nonverbal behavior. Does your stomach tighten? Are you clenching your teeth? Is your heart racing? Do you feel nauseated?

The second step is to identify the events and situations to which you have unpleasant responses. Look for commonalities between situations. For example, perhaps you notice that your heart races and your palms get clammy when you talk with professors, supervisors, and academic advisers, but you don't have these physiological responses when you interact with friends, co-workers, or people whom you supervise. You label your emotions as insecurity in the former cases and security in the latter ones. One commonality between the situations in which you feel insecure is the greater power of the other person. This could suggest that you feel insecure when talking with someone who has more power than you.

The third step is to tune in to your self-talk (Vocate, 1994). Listen to what's happening in your head. What is your *Me* saying? Is it telling you that you shouldn't feel certain emotions ("It's stupid to feel anxious," "Don't be a wimp")? Is it telling you to stuff your feelings ("Don't let on that you're insecure")? Is it telling you that you should feel something you don't ("You're supposed to feel confident and in command")? We need to identify and challenge debilitating ways of thinking about our emotions and, by extension, ourselves. These irrational beliefs, or fallacies, hinder our ability to manage and express emotions effectively. Figure 7.7 lists some of the most common fallacies that sabotage realistic appraisals of ourselves and our feelings.

We can use our self-talk to challenge the debilitating fallacies. For example, assume that Tyronne has been working well at his job and thinks his boss should give him a raise. He tunes in to his self-talk (step 3) and hears himself saying, "Well, maybe I shouldn't ask for a raise, because, after all, I have made some mistakes. I could do better." This self-talk reflects the fallacy of perfectionism. Tyronne listens further to himself and hears this message: "If I ask him for a raise, and he gets angry, he might fire me, and then I wouldn't have a job and couldn't stay in school. Without a degree, I have no future." This self-talk exemplifies the fear of catastrophic failure.

Step 4
Use self-talk to dispute fallacies.

Step 3
Tune into your self-talk; notice irrational beliefs and fallacies.

Step 2
Identify commonalities in events and experiences to which you respond emotionally.

Step 1
Monitor emotional reactions.

FIGURE 7.6

The Rational–Emotive Approach to Feelings

Fallacy	Typical Effects
Perfectionism	Unrealistically low self-concept Stress Chronic dissatisfaction with self Jealousy and envy of others
Obsession with shoulds	Saps energy for constructive work Can make others defensive Can alienate self from feelings Unrealistic standards set the self up for failure
Overgeneralization	Perceive one failure as typical of self Generalize inadequacies in some domains to total self
Taking responsibility for others	Thinking you are responsible for others' feelings Guilt for how others feel Deprives others of taking responsibility for selves
Helplessness	Believing that there is nothing you can do to change how you feel Resignation; depression
Fear of catastrophic failure	Extreme negative fantasies and scenarios of what could happen Inability to do things because of what might happen

FIGURE 7.7

Common Fallacies about Emotions

Communication in Everyday Life
Talking Yourself into—or out of—a Job

WORK

Imagine that you have a really important job interview coming up. It's kind of scary to think about, isn't it? Now, imagine that you are someone who is generally anxious in communication situations, and you have a big job interview coming up. That's even scarier.

Research shows that communication anxiety affects people before, during, and after job interviews (Ayres, Keereetaweep, Chen, & Edwards, 1998). People with communication anxiety fuel their anxiety with negative self-talk. In addition, these people create self-fulfilling prophecies that undermine their effectiveness in job interviews. Examples of negative self-talk that impairs interviewing competence are, "There's not a chance I'll get an offer," "I should have stayed home," or "There's no point in being here." When people repeat these messages to themselves before and during interviews, they tend to talk themselves into ineffectiveness.

How might Tyronne dispute these fallacies? To challenge the perfectionism fallacy, he could say, "True, I'm not perfect, but I'm doing more and better work than the other employees hired at the same time I was." To dispute the fallacy of catastrophic failure, Tyronne might say to himself, "Well, he's not likely to fire me, because I do my job well, and training someone new would be a lot of trouble. And what if he does fire me? It's not like this is the only job in the world. I could get another job pretty fast." Instead of letting debilitating fallacies defeat us, we can use our self-talk to question and challenge the irrational thinking that undermines us.

RESPOND SENSITIVELY WHEN OTHERS COMMUNICATE EMOTIONS

A final guideline is to respond sensitively when others express their feelings to you. Learning to communicate your emotions effectively is only half the process of communicating about emotions. You also want to become skilled in listening and responding to others when they share feelings with you.

Communication in Everyday Life
Albert Ellis in Action

INSIGHT

Albert Ellis was not a mild-mannered sort of therapist, nor did he want to be. He was known for his dramatic style and for pushing, pushing, pushing his clients. He firmly believed that people whom many clinicians diagnosed as neurotics were not neurotic but only suffering from irrational thinking. He often described this as stupid thinking on the part of nonstupid people. And Ellis was convinced that we can unlearn stupid behaviors and function more effectively (Ellis, 1962; Ellis & Harper, 1975; Seligman, 1990).

In dealing with clients, Ellis berated them for stupid thinking, all the while insisting that they were not stupid people. He wanted his clients to learn new and better ways of thinking. "You're living under a tyranny of *shoulds.* Stop *shoulding* yourself to death," he demanded. "Quit thinking wrong and start thinking right," he urged. And clients responded to Ellis's unorthodox style and therapy. Many learned to think differently, and this led them to feel and act differently and more effectively in their lives.

Visit the Albert Ellis Institute at http://www.rebt.org. The site provides background information on rational–emotive therapy and features Albert Ellis's answers to questions from visitors to the site.

When others express feelings, our first tendency may be to respond with general statements, such as "Time heals all wounds," "You shouldn't feel bad," "You'll be fine," or "You'll feel better once you get this in perspective." Although such statements may be intended to provide reassurance, in effect they tell others that they aren't allowed to feel what they feel or that they will be okay (right, normal) once they stop feeling what they are feeling.

Another common mistake in responding to others' expression of feelings is to try to solve the other person's problem so the feelings will go away. Research suggests that the tendency to try to solve others' problems is more common in men than women (Swain, 1989; Tannen, 1990). Helping another solve a problem may be appreciated, but usually it's not the first support a person needs when she or he is expressing strong emotions. What many people need first is just the freedom to say what they are feeling and have those feelings accepted by others. Probably because of socialization, women are generally more skilled than men at providing solace, comfort, and emotional support (Basow & Rubenfeld, 2003; MacGeorge, Gillihan, Samter, & Clark, 2003; MacGeorge, Graves, Feng, Gillihan, & Burleson, 2004).

When others express emotions to you, it's supportive to begin by showing you are willing to discuss emotional topics (Steiner-Pappalardo & Gurung, 2002). Next, accept where they are as a starting place (Goldsmith & Fitch, 1997). You don't have to agree or approve to accept what another is feeling. While listening, it's helpful to interject a few minimal encouragers, which we discussed in Chapter 6. Saying "I understand" or "Go on" conveys that you accept the other person's feelings and want him or her to continue talking. It's appropriate to mention your own experiences briefly to show that you empathize. However, it's not supportive to refocus the conversation on you and your experiences.

Paraphrasing, which we discussed in Chapter 6, is another way to show that you understand what another

Communication in Everyday Life
Managing Anger

In their book *Anger Kills* (1998), Redford Williams and Virginia Williams summarize years of research and clinical studies that show that anger harms our physical and mental health. Convinced by evidence that anger is dangerous, the Williamses developed a test to measure how dangerous a person's level of anger is. Here are a few items adapted from the test:

1. When I get stuck in a traffic jam,
   a. I am usually not particularly upset.
   b. I start to feel irritated and annoyed quickly.
2. When someone treats me unfairly,
   a. I usually forget the incident fairly quickly.
   b. I tend to keep thinking about the incident for hours.
3. When I am caught in a slow-moving line at the grocery store,
   a. I seldom notice or mind the wait.
   b. I fume at people who dawdle ahead of me.
4. When I hear or read about another terrorist attack,
   a. I wonder why some people are so cruel to others.
   b. I feel like lashing out.

The more Bs a person has, the more anger she or he feels. The authors recommend strategies for controlling anger that include the communication skills we've discussed.

- Use self-talk to reason with yourself about your anger.
- Learn to assert yourself firmly but not aggressively.
- Develop your ability to empathize with others.
- Develop one or more strong friendships in which you can confide feelings.
- Listen!
- Use the rational–emotive approach to feelings to stop angry thoughts.

The test items are adapted from the test on pages 5–11 of *Anger Kills*.

feels. When you mirror back not just the content but the feeling of what another says, it confirms the other and what he or she feels. "So, it sounds as if you were really surprised by what happened. Is that right?" "What I'm hearing is that you are more hurt than angry. Does that sound right to you?" These examples of paraphrasing allow you to check on your perception of the speaker's feelings and also show that you are listening actively.

The guidelines we've identified may not always make emotional communication easy and comfortable. However, following them will help you understand and express your feelings and respond effectively when others discuss their feelings. To practice expressing emotions effectively and to identify ineffective expressions of emotion, complete Activity 7.4 in your *Student Companion* or online under "Chapter Resources for Chapter 7" at the Everyday Connections website.

Case Study: Continuing the Conversation

The following conversation is featured on the Everyday Connections website under "Chapter Resources for Chapter 7." Click on the link "Damien & Chris" in the left-hand menu to launch the video and audio scenario scripted below.

You work with a person who is generally friendly and talkative during breaks; the two of you have often enjoyed casual conversation about issues related to the job as well as ones outside of the job. For the past week, Chris hasn't initiated any talk in the break room and has made only minimal responses to your efforts to strike up a conversation. You think Chris may be upset, and you decide to explore this. The next time you find Chris alone in the break room, this conversation occurs:

You: Hey, Chris, you've been kind of quiet lately. Is anything wrong?

Chris: No, not really, well, not anything I know how to talk about.

You: Sounds like something is bothering you.

Chris: Yeah, well, I guess that's life, right? I'm just down.

You: Down can cover a lot of territory. Sometimes it helps me if I talk to somebody when I'm feeling down. Want to tell me what's getting to you?

Chris: Well, okay. It's Mr. Brewster. He's been on my case for the past 3 weeks.

You: What about? Is he criticizing your job performance?

Chris: Yeah. He says I'm sloppy when I write reports and that I am not always nice to our clients. I mean, what am I supposed to be—Little Mary Sunshine?

You: Sounds like you're angry.

Chris: Darned right I am. I come in to work here every day, and I do my job, and I don't complain. It's not like they're paying us big bucks, so they shouldn't expect us to be all charm and cheer to every client—some of those folks are real jerks.

You: I agree. Some of them are difficult and rude. What exactly does Mr. Brewster say about how you deal with clients?

Chris: He says stuff about not being nice. I feel like he's biased against me just because I'm not as pleasant and smiley as I should be.

You: He may be biased against anyone who isn't super nice to clients. Remember how he really drilled it into all of us when we were hired that we are supposed to be polite and smile and all that.

Chris: Well, I don't always feel like smiling. And I don't think Mr. Brewster has any right to tie my job to whether I am a beacon of sunshine for every client who walks in here! I need this job.

You: Sounds as if you may be feeling a little worried about the job too. Am I reading you right?

Chris: Sure, I'm worried. I need this job. I've got a child and nobody but me to support him.

You: Has Mr. Brewster said anything about your losing this job?

Chris: No, not yet, he hasn't, but I know I'm not perfect, and I know he can fire me any time he wants. If he does, I'm finished. But I'm just not cheerful all the time, even if I should be. I know I should be nicer sometimes, but I can't.

1. What has happened so far in this conversation? Has Chris changed at all in terms of identifying emotions?

2. Do you perceive any examples of counterfeit emotional language in Chris's communication?

3. If you wanted to help Chris keep the job, would you advise deep acting, surface acting, or some combination of the two? Explain your reasons.

4. Does Chris seem to be operating on any irrational beliefs?

5. How would you want the conversation to progress now? What would you say next to support and help Chris?

6. Would you communicate differently if Chris were a woman or man? Do you think Chris's sex would affect how he or she communicates?

You can critique and analyze this encounter based on the principles you learned in this chapter by responding to the questions included under "Conversation Analysis" at the website. By clicking on the "Submit" button at the end of the form, you can compare your work to my suggested responses. Let's continue the conversation online!

Chapter Summary

In this chapter, we explored the complex world of emotions and our communication about them. We considered different views of what's involved in experiencing and expressing emotions. From our review of theories, we learned that emotions have physiological, perceptual, linguistic, and social dimensions. We also examined some of the reasons people don't express feelings or express them ineffectively. The final focus of our attention was on guidelines for effective communication about emotions.

We identified six guidelines that can help us be effective in expressing our feelings and responding to the feelings of others. Because these guidelines are critical to interpersonal communication, we'll close the chapter by restating them:

1. Identify your emotions.
2. Choose how to communicate your emotions.
3. Own your feelings.
4. Monitor your self-talk.
5. Adopt a rational–emotive approach to emotions.
6. Respond sensitively when others communicate emotions.

Everyday Connections Online

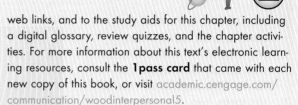

Now that you've read Chapter 7, go to the Everyday Connections premium website at academic.cengage.com/communication/woodinterpersonal5plus for quick access to the electronic study resources that accompany this text. The website gives you access to the "Continuing the Conversation" video scenario and questions featured in this chapter, to InfoTrac College Edition, to maintained and updated web links, and to the study aids for this chapter, including a digital glossary, review quizzes, and the chapter activities. For more information about this text's electronic learning resources, consult the **1pass card** that came with each new copy of this book, or visit academic.cengage.com/communication/woodinterpersonal5.

Key Concepts

Audio flash cards of the following key terms are available on the Everyday Connections website. Use the flash cards to improve your pronunciation of text vocabulary.

cognitive labeling view of emotions

counterfeit emotional language

deep acting

emotional intelligence emotions

emotion work

feeling rules

framing rules

interactive view of emotions

organismic view of emotions

perceptual view of emotions

rational–emotive approach to feelings

self-talk

surface acting

For Further Thought and Discussion

1. Use your InfoTrac College Edition to read Sherri Widen's and James Russell's 2002 article, "Gender and Preschoolers' Perception of Emotion," published in the *Merrill-Palmer Quarterly*. What do the authors report about differences in emotions attributed to males and females? How might you explain their findings based on Chapter 3's discussion of influences on perception?

2. Review the fallacies discussed in the last section of this chapter. Do any of these fallacies show up in your intrapersonal communication? After reading about the fallacies and ways to challenge them, can you monitor and revise your intrapersonal communication?

3. We discussed different perspectives on emotions. Which perspective—or what combination of several—makes the most sense to you? Why? Explain how the perspective you favor gives you insight into emotions that you don't get from other perspectives.

4. What ethical principles can you identify to guide when and how people express emotions to others? Is honesty always the best policy? Is it ethical for one person to decide what another should know or can handle? How might ethical principles vary across cultures?

Communication Climate: The Foundation of Personal Relationships

Photonica/Getty Images

> "In a full heart there is room for everything, and in an empty heart there is room for nothing."
>
> **Antonio Porchia**

Do you feel foggy-headed or down when the sky is overcast, and upbeat when it's sunny? Does your mood ever shift as the weather changes? Most of us respond to climate. We feel more or less positive depending on the conditions around us. In much the same way that we react to physical climates, we also respond to interpersonal climates.

Interpersonal climate is the overall feeling or emotional mood between people—warm or cold, safe or anxious, comfortable or awkward, accepting or rejecting, open or guarded. Understanding interpersonal climates will give you insight into why you feel relaxed and comfortable in some of your relationships and uneasy and defensive in others. Further, learning how communication shapes interpersonal climates will empower you to create and sustain the climates that you want in your relationships.

This chapter explores communication as a primary influence on building and sustaining interpersonal climates in personal, social, and professional relationships. We begin by discussing features of satisfying interpersonal relationships. Next, we examine the kinds of communication that build confirming, supportive interpersonal climates. Finally, we discuss guidelines for creating and sustaining healthy interpersonal climates. In the next chapter, we'll see how confirming, supportive climates assist us in managing conflict when it arises.

●●●●●●●●●●

Features of Satisfying Personal Relationships

As we saw in Chapter 1, we relate to others to fulfill human needs for survival, safety, belonging, esteem, and self-actualization in a diverse social world. When we are involved in satisfying relationships, we feel more positive about our lives and ourselves.

FIONA   The worst time in my whole life was my first semester here. I felt so lonely being away from my family and all my friends at home. Back home, there was always somebody to be with and talk to, but I didn't know anybody on this campus. I felt all alone and like nobody cared about me. I became depressed and almost left school, but then I started seeing a guy, and I made a couple of friends. Everything got better once I had some people to talk to and hang out with.

Many people feel as Fiona does. Research indicates that, in the United States, loneliness during the first year of college depends more on whether a person has friends than on whether a person has good family ties (Cutrona, 1982). Americans rely more on friends than do Russians, Koreans, or Turks (Ryan, La Guardia, Solky-Butzel, Chirkov, & Kim, 2005). We rely on friends to satisfy our needs for belonging and acceptance, especially after we have moved away from home.

Personal relationships are very complex and are shaped by numerous factors. Of the many influences, four are particularly critical for building and sustaining satisfying close relationships: investment, commitment, trust, and comfort with relational dialectics. As we discuss each of these influences, realize that members of different speech communities may have distinct rules for what each feature includes and how it is communicated. For example, in general, Westerners rely heavily on verbal disclosures to build trust, whereas most traditional Asians are less verbally revealing and depend on actions to build trust. Caucasians tend to regard commitment as a tie between two people, whereas for many Asians, Hispanics, Latina/os, and African Americans, commitment includes links between families and communities (Gaines, 1995).

INVESTMENT

Investments are what we put into relationships that we could not retrieve if the relationship were to end. When we care about another person, we invest time, energy, thought, and feelings in interaction. We may also invest materially by spending money, giving gifts, and so forth. In workplace relationships, we also invest time, energy, thought, and feeling and often give material assistance to co-workers.

Investments cannot be recovered, so the only way to reap the benefits of your investments is to stick with a relationship (Brehm, 1992). We can't get back the time, feelings, and energy we invest in a relationship. We cannot recover the history we have shared with another person. Thus, to leave is to lose the investment we've made.

Perceived equality of investment affects satisfaction with romantic relationships. The happiest dating and married partners feel that they invest equally (Fletcher, Fincham, Cramer, & Heron, 1987; Hecht, Marston, & Larkey, 1994). When we perceive ourselves as investing more than our partner, we tend to be dissatisfied and resentful. When we perceive our partner as investing more than we are, we may feel guilty. Thus, perceived inequity erodes satisfaction (Brehm, 1992) and communication. Partners who feel they are investing unequally tend to have limited disclosures and engage in little supportive communication (Brehm, 1992).

SIBBY   I dated this one guy for a long time before I finally had to cut my losses. He said he loved me, but he wouldn't put anything in the relationship. I gave so much—always accommodating him, doing things for him, loving him—but there just wasn't any reciprocity. It was a one-way street with him, and I felt like he didn't value me very much at all.

Everyday Application
Your Investment in Relationships

What have you invested in your closest friendship, romantic relationship, and workplace relationship?

··· How much time have you spent in each relationship?
··· How many decisions have you made to accommodate the other person?
··· How much money have you spent?
··· To what extent is your history entwined with that of the other person?
··· How much trust have you given each person?
··· How much support have you given each person?
··· Do the other person's investments roughly equal yours?
··· What would be lost if these relationships ended? Could you recover your investments?

Communication in Everyday Life
What Keeps Relationships Together?

Imagine that the person you have been seeing for a long time says, "I love you." Would you assume that meant that the person wants to spend his or her life with you? You wouldn't if you were familiar with research on what holds relationships together over time.

To find out what holds a relationship together, Mary Lund (1985) studied heterosexual college seniors. She measured their love for partners by asking how they felt about their partners. To measure commitment, Lund asked them to rate the strength of their intention to stay in the relationship. She found that the continuation of relationships depended more on commitment than on love. Couples who had high levels of love but low commitment to a shared future were less likely to remain together than couples who were highly committed to a joint future. Thus, the intention to stay together is a more powerful glue than positive feelings between partners.

It seems that, once people decide to stay in a relationship, they are more likely to invest in it. In turn, their investments enrich the relationship so that staying is rewarding. Summarizing her findings, Lund said that, although love usually accompanies commitment, commitment and investment have more to do with whether a relationship lasts than do love and rewards.

Lund's findings provide insight into one reason arranged marriages often are strong and enduring (Nanda & Warms, 1998). In societies where marriages are arranged, bride and groom enter the marriage without love (sometimes they have not even met) but with a steadfast commitment to the permanence of the marriage. Love may come later.

COMMITMENT

Commitment is a decision to remain in a relationship. Notice that commitment is defined as a decision, not a feeling (Etcheverry & Le, 2005). The hallmark of commitment is the intention to share the future. In committed relationships, partners assume that they will continue together. Unlike passion or attraction, which arise in the present, commitment links partners together in the future. Because partners in committed relationships view their connection as continuing, they are unlikely to bail out during the inevitable rough times. Problems and tensions aren't seen as reasons to end the relationship. To increase your understanding of the difference between love and commitment, complete Activity 8.7 in your *Student Companion* or online under "Chapter Resources for Chapter 8" at the Everyday Connections website.

Whereas love is a feeling we can't control, commitment is a decision. It is a choice to maintain a relationship. Counselor Aaron Beck (1988) believes that the decision to commit injects responsibility into relationships. When partners make a commitment, they take responsibility for continuing to invest in and care for their bond. Without responsibility, relationships are subject to the whims of feeling and fortune, which are not a stable basis for the long term.

> **PHILLIP** When Denny and I decided to go out on our own, we'd worked together in a tech firm for 2 years, and neither of us felt like that was where we wanted to be for life, or even in another 3 years. So we started our own company. It was really scary because we didn't have any guarantees or any safety net. All we had was each other, and that really changed our relationship. We spent a lot more time together, talked for hours about every detail of our business, traveled together to evaluate new software and business-to-business companies. We took risks with each other, learned to trust each other to the max. And we spent a lot of time dreaming about what could happen with our company and how we could bring that about. In a way, I think the dreaming and planning together was like a real cement for us. After a year of working together that closely, we were more like brothers than partners in a business.

TRUST

A third cornerstone of satisfying personal relationships is a high degree of trust between partners (Brehm, 1992; Steiner-Pappalardo & Gurung, 2002; Veroff, 1999).

Trust involves believing in another's reliability (that he or she will do as promised) and emotionally relying on another to look out for our welfare and our relationship. Trust doesn't come automatically in relationships. Usually, it is earned over time: We learn to trust others as they prove that they are reliable, show that they care, and make the investments to enrich the relationship. When trust is established, we feel psychologically safe in the relationship. One reason trust is so important to relationships is that it allows us to take risks with others. We open ourselves to others only if we feel we can count on them to protect our confidences and to care about us and our well-being.

This is such a dumb time, Jack, to start talking about whether or not something is written in stone.

Self-Disclosure   Self-disclosure can both build and reflect trust between people. **Self-disclosure** is the revelation of personal information about ourselves that others are unlikely to discover in other ways. According to researchers who have studied communication between intimates, self-disclosure is a key gauge of closeness, at least among Westerners (Derlega & Berg, 1987; Hansen & Schuldt, 1984; Meeks, Hendrick, & Hendrick, 1998).

Self-disclosure should take place gradually and with appropriate caution. We begin by disclosing superficial information ("I'm worried that I won't find a job," "I'm afraid of heights"). If a person responds with empathy to early and limited disclosures, we're likely to reveal progressively more intimate information ("My father served time in prison," "I was fired from my last job," "I take medication for depression"). If these disclosures are also met with understanding and confidentiality, trust continues to grow.

In the early stages of relationship development, reciprocity of disclosures is important. We're willing to disclose our private feelings only as long as the other person also reveals personal information (Cunningham, Strassberg, & Haan, 1986). When a relationship is just beginning, we feel vulnerable; the other could betray a confidence or reject us because we disclose something negative. Our feeling of vulnerability is reduced if the other person is also allowing vulnerability by making self-disclosures to us.

Reciprocity of disclosures becomes less important as a relationship grows and stabilizes. In most stable relationships, people don't feel the need to reciprocate disclosures immediately. Unlike new acquaintances, they have the time to reciprocate on a more leisurely schedule. Thus, in established relationships disclosure is more likely to be greeted with a response to what has been revealed than with an immediate, equivalent disclosure.

Although all of us disclose some personal information in close relationships, not everyone discloses equally

Communication in Everyday Life
Dialogue and Doing: Alternate Paths to Closeness

Research indicates that women and men generally place equal value on closeness, but they tend to differ somewhat in how they create and express it. Many researchers trace these differences to childhood play (Benenson, Apostoleris, & Parnass, 1997; Rose & Asher, 2000).

Young boys typically interact with their friends by doing things in groups (playing sports or engaging in rough-and-tumble play). As a result, boys tend to bond with others by doing things together. Carrying the lessons of childhood play into adult friendships, many men do not regard intimate or emotional conversation and self-disclosure as the only, or even the primary, path to closeness. Instead, their preferred path to intimacy is activity (doing things with and for others). This mode is called *closeness in the doing*.

Young girls tend to interact with friends through dialogue (socializing in dyads or triads in which face-to-face communication is central). As a result, many girls learn to form intimate connections through talking. As adults, women tend to favor dialogue (sharing personal disclosures and intimate communication) as a path to intimacy. This is called *closeness in dialogue*.

Both women and men travel both paths to intimacy. What differs is the degree of emphasis that women and men, in general, place on each path. Recent studies indicate that both women and men do things for people they care about. Instrumental shows of affection, or closeness in the doing, are part of most women's friendships, although they are usually not as central as in men's friendships (Floyd & Parks, 1995). Research also indicates that men sometimes express closeness through dialogue, just not as frequently as most women (Canary & Dindia, 1998; Inman, 1996; Metts, 2006; Wood & Inman, 1993). Both ways of expressing and experiencing closeness are valid, and both should be respected.

Different modes of expressing closeness are not confined to personal relationships. They also show up in the workplace. Women generally rely more than men on talk to form and sustain close working relationships, whereas men generally rely more than women on doing things for and with co-workers to establish and develop close working relationships (Tannen, 1995).

To learn more about gender and other sources of diversity in workplace interactions, visit http://www.diversityinc.com.

or in the same ways. People vary in how much they want to self-disclose, so an absolute amount of disclosure is not a surefire measure of trust or relationship health. Also, cultural differences shape our tendencies to self-disclose. People raised in traditional Chinese society tend to disclose less personal information than most Westerners do. Among Pakistanis, disclosures between parents and children are much rarer than among native-born Americans. Gender also seems to affect how and how much people disclose. In general, women—particularly Western women—make more verbal disclosures and place greater value on verbal disclosures than do most men (Floyd & Parks, 1995). Men generally talk less about personal feelings, especially their shortcomings or self-doubts (Johnson, 2000). Many men self-disclose more often with actions than with words.

> **RUSSELL** When I really need some support from my girlfriend, I don't just come out and say, "I need you." What I do is go over to her place or call her to see if she wants to come to my place. Sometimes, we just sit together watching TV or something. And that helps. I know she knows that I am down and need her, but I don't have to say it. I do the same thing when I think she is feeling low. It's hard for me to say, "I love you and am sorry you feel bad." But I can be with her, and I can hug her and let her know through my actions that I care.

Although self-disclosing is important early in the process of developing intimacy, for most relationships it is not a primary communication dynamic over the long haul. Although disclosure wanes over time, partners continue to reap the benefits of the trust and depth of personal knowledge created by early disclosures. Radical decreases in disclosures may signal trouble in a relationship (Baxter, 1987).

> **CRAIG** I think what first clued me in that Shelby was losing interest was that she stopped telling me private stuff about herself. For the first couple of months we dated, she shared so

much about her dreams, plans, and fears. The more she told me about herself and the more I told her, the closer I felt. But then, she seemed to withdraw and not want to share her private thoughts. That was really the start of the end.

COMFORT WITH RELATIONAL DIALECTICS

A final quality of healthy relationships is understanding and being comfortable with **relational dialectics,** which are opposing forces, or tensions, that are normal in relationships. Although these tensions are normal, they can be frustrating if we don't understand them and if we don't label them as normal. Table 8.1 illustrates three relational dialectics that have been identified by researchers (Baxter, 1988, 1990, 1993; Baxter & Simon, 1993; Erbert, 2000).

Autonomy/Connection   All of us experience tension between the desire to be autonomous, or independent, and the desire to be close, or connected to others. Friends and romantic partners want to spend time with each other, to have joint interests, and to talk personally. At the same time, they need to feel that their individuality is not swallowed up by relationships. Tension between the need for autonomy and the need for connection also marks relationships on the job. We may enjoy being part of teams and like the sense of community in our workplace. At the same time, we may want to do some solo projects and work independently.

Relationship counselors agree that the most central and continuous friction in most close relationships arises from the opposing needs for autonomy and for connection (Beck, 1988; Scarf, 1987). When Robbie and I take vacations, we eat all meals together, engage in shared activities, and sleep and interact in confined spaces where privacy is limited. Typically, when we return home after a vacation, we interact less than usual for several days. Having been immersed in togetherness, we both seek distance to reestablish our autonomous identities. Both autonomy and closeness are natural human needs. The challenge is to preserve individuality while also nurturing connection in a relationship.

> **KEN**   Dialectics explains something that has really confused me. I've never understood how I could want so much to be with Ashley for a while and then feel suffocated and need to get away. I've worried that it means I don't love her anymore or there is something wrong between us. But now, I see how both needs are normal and okay.

Novelty/Predictability   The second dialectic is the tension between wanting routine or familiarity and wanting novelty in a relationship. All of us like a certain amount of routine to provide security and predictability in our lives. For example,

Table 8.1   Relational Dialectics

AUTONOMY/CONNECTION	NOVELTY/PREDICTABILITY	OPENNESS/CLOSEDNESS
I want to be close. I need my own space.	I like the familiar rhythms and routines of our relationship. We need to do something new and different.	I like sharing so much with you. There are some things I don't want to talk about with you.

my friend Nancy and I long ago agreed to get together on Sundays for lunch and visiting. We count on that as a steady, habitual time to see each other. Yet, too much routine becomes boring, so it's also natural to seek novel experiences. Every so often, Nancy and I decide to explore a new restaurant or make a day trip just to introduce variety into our friendship.

On-the-job relationships also feel the tension between the desire for predictability and the desire for novelty. We want enough routine at work to feel competent and familiar with our responsibilities. But we also want enough novelty, or change, to keep us stimulated. However, as Dennis points out, too much novelty in the workplace can be overwhelming.

> **DENNIS**   Last year was extremely difficult for my wife, Katie. It seemed like everything at her job changed at once. First, the company was bought up by a large corporation. Then, the CEO Katie had worked under for 10 years was fired and a new one brought on board. The new guy implemented all kinds of changes in company policies and procedures. A lot of the staff got frustrated and quit, so that led to changes in Katie's coworkers.

Openness/Closedness   The third dialectic is a tension between wanting open communication and needing a degree of privacy, even with intimates. With our closest partners, we self-disclose in ways we don't with co-workers and casual acquaintances. Yet, we also desire some privacy, and we want our intimates to respect that. Completely unrestrained expressiveness would be intolerable (Baxter, 1993; Petronio, 1991). There is nothing wrong with seeking privacy; it doesn't mean that a relationship is in trouble. It means only that we have normal needs for both openness and closedness.

> **ANDY**   My girlfriend has trouble accepting the fact that I won't talk to her about my brother Jacob. He died when I was 8, and I still can't deal with all my feelings, especially with feeling guilty that he died and I'm alive. I just can't talk about that to anybody. With my girlfriend, I talk about lots of personal stuff, but Jacob is just too private and too hard.

The three dialectics create ongoing tensions in healthy relationships. This is a problem only if partners don't understand that dialectics and the tension they generate are natural parts of relational life. Once we realize that dialectics are normal in all relationships, we can accept and grow from the tensions they generate (Baxter & Montgomery, 1996; Metts, 2006).

Dialectics are interrelated. For instance, friends who are highly open are also likely to be very connected, whereas more closed friends tend to favor greater autonomy (Aries, 1987). Relational dialectics also interact with other facets of interpersonal communication. For instance, partners who prefer a high degree of individuality tend to create more individual spaces and fewer common ones in their homes than do partners who favor greater connection (Fitzpatrick, 1988; Fitzpatrick & Best, 1979). Likewise, some workplaces have lots of open spaces and few doors (or few closed doors), whereas other work sites feature separate offices, closed doors, and few common spaces for interaction.

Negotiating Dialectical Tensions Baxter (1990) has identified four ways partners handle the tension generated by opposing needs. One response, called *neutralization*, is to negotiate a balance between two dialectical needs. Each need is met to an extent, but neither is fully satisfied. A couple might have a fairly consistent equilibrium between the amount of novelty and the amount of routine in their relationship.

A second response is *selection*, in which we give priority to one dialectical need and neglect the other. For example, co-workers might be very closed about all topics. Some partners cycle between dialectical needs, favoring each one alternately. A couple could be continuously together for a period and then autonomous for a time.

> **BEVERLY** My folks are so funny. They plod along in the same old rut for ages and ages, and my sister and I can't get them to do anything different. Mom won't try a new recipe for chicken, because "we like ours like I always fix it." Dad won't try a new style of shirt because "that's not the kind of shirt I wear." Dynamite wouldn't blow them out of their ruts. But then, all of a sudden, they'll do a whole bunch of unusual things. Like once they went out to three movies in a day, and the next day they went for a picnic at the zoo. This kind of zaniness goes on for a while, then it's back to humdrum for months and months. I guess they get all of their novelty in occasional bursts.

A third way to manage dialectics is *separation*. When we separate dialectics, we assign one dialectical need to certain spheres of interaction and the opposing dialectical need to other aspects of interaction. For instance, friends might be open about many topics but respect each other's privacy in one or two areas. Employees might work independently on most tasks but operate very interactively and openly on specific teams. Many dual-career couples are autonomous professionally, relying little on each other for advice, although they are very connected about family matters.

The final method of dealing with dialectics is *reframing*. This is a complex and transformative strategy in which partners redefine contradictory needs as not in opposition. In other words, they reframe their perceptions by redefining what is happening. My colleagues and I found an example of this when we studied differences

Everyday Application
Applying Relational Dialectics

How do relational dialectics operate in your life? To find out, select three of your relationships: a close friendship, a current or past romantic relationship, and an on-the-job relationship. For each relationship, answer these questions:

··· How are needs for autonomy expressed and met?
··· How are needs for connection expressed and met?
··· How are needs for novelty expressed and met?
··· How are needs for predictability expressed and met?
··· How are needs for openness expressed and met?
··· How are needs for closedness expressed and met?

Now, think about how you manage the tension between opposing needs in each dialectic. When do you rely on neutralization, selection, separation, and reframing? How satisfied are you with your responses? Experiment with new ways to manage dialectical tensions.

For further practice in identifying relational dialects in everyday situations, complete Activity 8.9 in your *Student Companion* or online under "Chapter Resources for Chapter 8" at the Everyday Connections website.

between intimate partners (Wood, Dendy, Dordek, Germany, & Varallo, 1994). Some partners transcended the opposition between autonomy and connection by defining differences and disagreements (which emphasize individuals) as enhancing intimacy (which emphasizes the relationship). Another example of reframing is deciding that novelty and predictability are not opposites but allies. A couple I know says their routines make novelty interesting, and novelty makes routines comforting.

Research indicates that, in general, the least effective and least satisfying response is selection, in which one dialectical need is neglected (Baxter, 1990). Squelching any natural human impulse diminishes us. The challenge is to find ways to accommodate all our needs, even when they seem contradictory. To help you understand the basis of satisfaction in two important relationships in your life, complete Activity 8.1 in your *Student Companion* or online under "Chapter Resources for Chapter 8" at the Everyday Connections website.

Healthy relationships exist when the people in them create a satisfying interpersonal climate by investing, making a commitment, developing trust, and learning to understand and negotiate dialectical tensions. Underlying these four features is *confirmation,* which we discuss in the next section of the chapter.

Confirming and Disconfirming Climates

We first encountered philosopher Martin Buber in Chapter 1 when we discussed I–It, I–You, and I–Thou relationships. Buber (1957) believed that all of us need confirmation to be healthy and to grow. The essence of confirmation is feeling known and valued as an individual. In relationships that have a confirming climate, we feel personally cherished and respected.

Interpersonal climates exist on a continuum from confirming to disconfirming (Figure 8.1). Few relationships are purely confirming or disconfirming; most fall somewhere between the two extremes. Some interactions are confirming, and others are disconfirming; or communication cycles between basically confirming and basically disconfirming.

Relationships usually don't move abruptly from one spot on the continuum to a different spot. Usually, one level of confirmation flows into the next in a gradual way. You might not feel very confirmed by a person you have just met. As the two of you talk and interact, the other person may communicate that he or she values you, so you begin to feel more confirmed. Over time, you move on to feeling that the relationship is basically confirming.

LEVELS OF CONFIRMATION AND DISCONFIRMATION

Building on Buber's ideas as well as those of psychiatrist R. D. Laing (1961), communication scholars have extended insight into confirming and disconfirming climates (Cissna & Sieburg, 1986). They have identified three levels of communication that confirm or disconfirm others. As we discuss these, you'll notice that confirming communication involves person-centeredness, which we discussed in Chapter 1. Highly person-centered communication recognizes another's feelings and ideas as legitimate. Low person-centered communication denies, ignores, or challenges another's feelings and ideas (Burleson, 1994; Jones & Burleson, 2003).

Confirming Climate	Mixed Climate / Cycling Climate	Disconfirming Climate

FIGURE 8.1

The Continuum of Interpersonal Climates

The most basic form of confirmation is *recognizing that another person exists*. We do this with nonverbal behaviors (a smile or touch) and verbal communication ("Hello," "Good to meet you"). We disconfirm others at a fundamental level when we don't acknowledge their existence. For example, you might not speak or look up when a co-worker enters your office. A parent who punishes a child by refusing to speak to her or him disconfirms the child.

RYAN I hate it when my girlfriend gives me the silent treatment. I'd rather she shout or scream or tell me off—at least, doing that would let me know she knows I'm there. When she gives me the silent treatment, I feel totally invisible, like I'm not there at all.

The second level of confirmation is *acknowledgment of what another feels, thinks, or says*. Nonverbally, we acknowledge others by nodding our heads or by making eye contact to show we are listening. Verbal acknowledgments are direct responses to others' communication. If a friend says, "I'm really worried that I blew the LSAT exam," you could acknowledge that by paraphrasing: "So you're scared that you didn't do well on it, huh?" This paraphrasing response acknowledges both the thoughts and the feelings of the other person.

We disconfirm others when we don't acknowledge their feelings or thoughts. Reponses that are tangential, irrelevant, or impersonal don't acknowledge what another has said. For instance, a tangential response to your friend's statement about the LSAT would be, "Yeah, the LSAT's a killer. The people who design those standardized tests must be real sadists. Have you ever wondered what kind of person would do that for a living?" "Want to go out and shoot some darts tonight?" would be an irrelevant response that ignores the friend's comment. An impersonal response that fails to acknowledge your friend individually would be, "Everybody feels that after taking the test." A denial response would be, "You did fine on the LSAT." Notice that each type of disconfirmation is not person-centered.

LORI You'd be amazed by how often people refuse to acknowledge what differently abled people say. A hundred times, I've been walking across campus, and someone has come up and offered to guide me. I tell them I know the way and don't need help, and they still put an arm under my elbow to guide me. I may be blind, but there's nothing wrong with my mind. I know if I need help. Why won't others acknowledge that?

Lori makes an important point. It is fundamentally disconfirming to have others ignore what we say and think. Especially when we deal with people who differ from us in important ways, we should take time to learn what they perceive as confirming and disconfirming. The "Communication in Everyday Life" feature on page 224 offers advice for confirming communication with people who have disabilities.

The strongest level of confirmation is *endorsement*. Endorsement involves accepting another's feelings or thoughts. For example, you could endorse by saying, "It's natural to be worried about the LSAT when you have so much riding on it. I know how much going to law school means to you." We disconfirm others when we don't accept their thoughts and feelings. If you respond to the friend by saying, "How can you worry about the LSAT when the country is on the verge of war?" you reject the validity of the expressed feelings.

Endorsement isn't always possible if we are trying to be honest with others. Sometimes we cannot accept what another feels or thinks, so we can't give an endorsing response. A few years ago, I spent a lot of time with a 15-year-old. Bobby and I found many things to do and talk about, and I continually looked for ways to confirm him. Gradually, trust between us grew, and Bobby and I shared more and more personal information. One day, he told me that he had tried acid and was looking forward to doing more acid in the future. I couldn't endorse what Bobby

Communication in Everyday Life
Guidelines for Communicating with People with Disabilities

Like all of us, people with disabilities value confirming communication that demonstrates that we respect them and their abilities. The following guidelines provide advice for communicating confirmation when interacting with people who have disabilities.

··· When you talk with someone who has a disability, speak directly to the person, not to a companion or interpreter.

··· When you are introduced to a person with a disability, offer to shake hands. People who have limited hand use or who have artificial limbs usually can shake.

··· When you meet a person who has a visual impairment, identify yourself and anyone who is with you. If a person with a visual impairment is part of a group, preface your comments to that person with his or her name.

··· You may offer assistance, but don't provide it unless your offer is accepted. Then, ask the person how you can best assist (ask for instructions).

··· Treat adults as adults. Don't patronize people in wheelchairs by patting them on the shoulder or head; don't use childish language when speaking to people who have no mental disability.

··· Respect the personal space of people with disabilities. It is rude to lean on a wheelchair, because that is part of someone's personal territory.

··· Listen mindfully when you talk with someone who has difficulty speaking. Don't interrupt or supply words to others. Just be patient and let them finish. Don't pretend to understand if you don't. Instead, explain what you didn't understand, and ask the person to respond.

··· When you talk with people who use a wheelchair or crutches, try to position yourself at their eye level and in front of them to allow good eye contact.

··· It is appropriate to wave your hand or tap the shoulder of people with hearing impairments as a way to get their attention. Look directly at the person and speak clearly, slowly, and expressively. Face those who lip-read, place yourself in a good light source, and keep hands, cigarettes, and gum away from your mouth.

··· Relax. Don't be afraid to use common expressions, such as "See you later" to someone with a visual impairment, or "Did you hear the news?" to someone with a hearing difficulty. They're unlikely to be offended and may turn the irony into a joke.

Adapted from AXIS Center for Public Awareness of People with Disabilities, 4550 Indianola Avenue, Columbus, OH 43214. Visit their website at http://www.axiscenter.org.

had done, and I couldn't support his desire to continue using acid. I told Bobby that I cared about him but couldn't approve of this behavior. I informed him of some of the long-term consequences of acid and the dangers of its being mixed with other drugs. Bobby hadn't been aware of this information. In this situation, I was able to confirm him as a person without endorsing a particular behavior. The trust we had built up and the confirming climate we had established allowed us to talk honestly about the dangers of drugs.

Disconfirmation is not mere disagreement. After all, disagreements can be productive and healthy, and they imply that people matter enough to each other to argue. What is disconfirming is to be told that we are crazy, wrong, stupid, or unimportant. If you think about what we've discussed, you'll probably find that the relationships in which you feel most valued and comfortable are those with high levels of confirmation. Table 8.2 on p. 225 illustrates the different levels on which confirmation and disconfirmation occur.

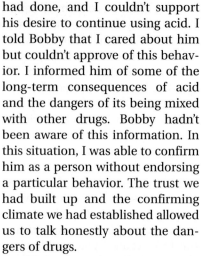

WAYNE I've gotten a lot of disconfirmation since I came out. When I told my parents I was gay, Mom said, "No, you're not." I told her I was, and she and Dad both said I was just confused, but I wasn't gay. They refuse to acknowledge I'm gay, which means they reject who I am. My older brother isn't any better. His view is that I'm sinful and headed for hell. Now, what could be more disconfirming than that?

DEFENSIVE AND SUPPORTIVE CLIMATES

Communication researcher Jack Gibb (1961, 1964, 1970) studied the relationship between communication and interpersonal climates. He began by noting that with some people we feel disconfirmed and on guard, so we are unlikely to communicate

	CONFIRMING MESSAGES	DISCONFIRMING MESSAGES
Recognition	"You exist."	"You don't exist."
	"Hello."	Silence.
Acknowledgment	"You matter to me."	"You don't matter."
	"We have a relationship."	"We are not a team."
	"I'm sorry you're hurt."	"You'll get over it."
Endorsement	"What you think is true."	"You are wrong."
	"What you feel is okay."	"You shouldn't feel what you do."
	"I feel the same way."	"Your feeling doesn't make sense."

openly with them. Gibb called these _defensive climates_. Gibb also noted that with other people we feel supported and confirmed, so we are likely to communicate freely with them. Gibb called these _supportive climates_. Even in the healthiest and most supportive relationships, there are usually some defensive moments and some situations in which we don't feel comfortable. Yet, in most satisfying relationships, the overall climate is generally supportive and confirming.

Gibb believed that the different interpersonal climates result largely from communication that promotes feeling defensive or feeling supported. Gibb identified six types of communication that promote defensive climates and six opposite types of communication that foster supportive climates, as shown in Table 8.3. For practice in identifying communication that tends to foster defensive and supportive climates, complete Activity 8.8 in your *Student Companion* or online under "Chapter Resources for Chapter 8" at the Everyday Connections website.

Evaluation Versus Description   Few of us feel what Gibb called "psychologically safe" when we are the targets of judgments. Communication researchers report that evaluative communication evokes defensiveness (Conrad & Poole, 2002; Eadie, 1982; Stephenson & D'Angelo, 1973). We are also less likely to self-disclose to someone we think is judgmental (Caughlin, Afifi, Carpenter-Theune, & Miller, 2005). As we noted in Chapter 6, even positive evaluations can sometimes make us defensive

Table 8.3 Communication and Climate

DEFENSIVE COMMUNICATION	SUPPORTIVE COMMUNICATION
Evaluation	Description
Certainty	Provisionalism
Strategy	Spontaneity
Control	Problem orientation
Neutrality	Empathy
Superiority	Equality

because they carry the relationship-level meaning that another person feels entitled to judge us (Cupach & Carlson, 2002). Here are several examples of evaluative statements: "It's dumb to feel that way," "You shouldn't have done that," "I approve of what you did," "That's a stupid idea."

Descriptive communication doesn't evaluate others or what they think and feel. Instead, it describes behaviors without passing judgment. *I* language, which we learned about in Chapter 4, describes what the person speaking feels or thinks, but it doesn't evaluate another. (*You* language does evaluate). Descriptive language may refer to another, but it does so by describing, not evaluating, the other's behavior: "You seem to be sleeping more lately" versus "You're sleeping too much," "You seem to have more stuff on your desk than usual" versus "Your desk is a mess."

Everyday Application
Using Descriptive Language

To develop skill in supportive communication, translate the following evaluative statements into descriptive ones.

Example:

Evaluative: This report is poorly done.

Descriptive: This report doesn't include relevant background information.

Evaluative: You're lazy.

Descriptive:_____

Evaluative: I hate the way you dominate conversations with me.

Descriptive:_____

Evaluative: Stop obsessing about the problem.

Descriptive:_____

Evaluative: You're too involved.

Descriptive:_____

Certainty Versus Provisionalism We communicate certainty by using language that is absolute and often dogmatic. This kind of language suggests that there is one and only one answer, valid point of view, or reasonable course of action. Because certainty proclaims one absolutely correct position, it slams the door on further discussion. There's no point in talking with people whose minds are made up and who demean any point of view other than their own. Sometimes, certainty is expressed by restating a position over and over instead of responding to alternative ideas from others (Alexander, 1979).

Perhaps you've been in a conversation with someone who says, "I don't want to hear it," "You can't change my mind," or "I've already figured out what I'm going to do, so just save your breath." These comments reflect certainty and an unwillingness to consider other points of view. When confronted with such statements, we're likely to feel disconfirmed and to follow the advice to "save our breath."

One form of certainty communication is **ethnocentrism,** which is the assumption that our culture and its norms are the only right ones. For instance, someone who says, "It is just plain rude to speak out loud during a sermon" doesn't understand the meaning of the call–response pattern in traditional African culture. Dogmatically asserting, "It's disrespectful to be late" reveals a lack of awareness of cultures that place less value on speed and efficiency than American culture does.

RELATIONSHIP TIP # 42: TRY TO SEE THE BEAUTY IN LIFE'S LITTLE IRONIES.

SELF-CENTERED? MOI? HOW DO YOU THINK THAT MAKES ME FEEL?

Reprinted by permission of Jennifer Berman

MONIKA My father is a classic case of closed-mindedness. He has his ideas, and everything else is crazy. I told him I was majoring in communication studies, and he hit the roof. He said there was no future in learning to write speeches, and he told me I should go into business so that I could get a good job. He never even asked me what communication studies is. If he had, I would have told him it's a lot more than speech writing. He starts off sure that he knows everything about whatever is being discussed. He has no interest in other points of view or learning something new. He just locks his mind and throws away the key. We've all learned just to keep our ideas to ourselves around him—there's no communication.

An alternative to certainty is provisionalism, which communicates openness to other points of view. When we speak provisionally, or tentatively, we suggest that our minds aren't sealed. We signal that we're willing to consider what others have to say, and this encourages others to voice their ideas. Provisional communication includes statements such as "The way I tend to see the issue is . . . ," "One way to look at this is . . . ," and "Probably what I would do in that situation is . . .". Notice how each of these comments signals that the speaker realizes there could be other positions that are also reasonable. Tentativeness signals an open mind, which is why it invites continued communication.

Strategy Versus Spontaneity   Most of us feel on guard when we think others are manipulating us or being less than open about what's on their minds. An example of strategic communication is this: "Would you do something for me if I told you it really mattered?" If the speaker doesn't tell us what we're expected to do, it feels like a setup. We're also likely to feel that another is trying to manipulate us with a comment such as, "Remember when I helped you with your math last term and when I did your chores last week because you were busy?" With a preamble like that, we can smell a trap. When employees think supervisors are trying to manipulate them, they become defensive (Conrad & Poole, 2002). Nonverbal behaviors may also convey strategy, as when a person pauses for a long time before answering or refuses to look at us when he or she speaks. A sense of deception pollutes the communication climate.

> **JANA**   Last year, I worked for someone who was always using strategies on me. She'd come to my work station on Monday and ask, "How does your week look?" At first, I'd give her a straight answer, but after a few times I realized she was setting me up. If I said, "Not too bad," she'd give me another assignment. I wouldn't have minded if she'd just asked me straight up if I could do a particular thing.

Spontaneity is the counterpoint to strategy. Spontaneous communication feels open, honest, and unpremeditated. "I really need your help with this computer glitch" is a more spontaneous comment than "Would you do something for me if I told you it really matters?" Likewise, it is more spontaneous to ask for a favor in a straightforward way ("Would you help me?") than to preface a request by reciting all we have done for someone else. Strategic communication is contrived and devious, whereas spontaneous interaction is authentic.

Control Versus Problem Orientation   Like strategies, controlling communication attempts to manipulate others. Unlike strategies, controlling communication tends to be relatively overt. A common instance of controlling communication is a person's insistence that her or his solution or preference should prevail. Whether the issue is trivial (what movie to see) or serious (whether to move to a new part of the country), controllers try to impose their point of view on others. This disconfirms and disrespects others.

Defensiveness arises because the relationship level of meaning is that the person exerting control thinks she or he has greater power, rights, or intelligence than others. It's disconfirming to be told our that opinions are wrong, that our preferences don't matter, or that we aren't smart enough to have good ideas. Supervisors who micromanage subordinates communicate that they don't trust others to do the job right (Conrad & Poole, 2002). A wife who earns a higher salary might say to her husband, "Well, I like the Honda more than the Ford you want, and it's my money that's going to pay for it." The speaker not only pushes her preference but also tells her husband that she has more power than he does because she makes more money.

> **PAT**   My roommate freshman year was a real jerk. Her goal in life was to control me and everyone else around her. Sometimes, she'd say she felt like going out for dinner, and I'd agree, and then she'd ask me where I wanted to go. Even if I picked her favorite place, she would insist on going somewhere else. She just had to be in charge. Once I moved things around in the room, and she fussed a lot and moved them back. Later, she moved things the way I had, but then it was her choice. She didn't care about issues or working things through. All she cared about was being in control.

Problem-oriented communication tends to cultivate supportive, confirming interpersonal climates. Problem-oriented communication focuses on finding a solution that all parties find acceptable. Here's an example of problem-oriented communication between co-workers: "It seems that we have really different ideas about how to tackle this new project. Let's talk through what each of us has in mind and see how we can connect our goals." Notice how this statement invites collaboration and emphasizes the goal of meeting both people's needs. Problem-oriented behaviors tend to reduce conflict and keep lines of communication open (Alexander, 1979; Civickly, Pace, & Krause, 1977; McKinney, Kelly, & Duran, 1997).

Paul Barton/CORBIS

One of the benefits of problem-oriented communication is that the relationship level of meaning emphasizes the importance of the relationship between communicators. When we convey that we want to collaborate with another person to resolve some mutual problem, we let the other know that we care more about the relationship than about getting our own way. In contrast, controlling behaviors aim for one person to triumph over the other, an outcome that undercuts the other person and the relationship.

Neutrality Versus Empathy People tend to become defensive when others respond to them in a neutral or detached manner. Research on interview climates indicates that defensiveness arises when an interviewer appears withdrawn and distant (Civickly, Pace, & Krause, 1977). Neutral communication implies a lack of regard and caring for others. Consequently, it disconfirms their worth.

> **NEL** My brother never responds to what I say. He listens, but he just gives me nothing back. Sometimes I push him and ask, "What do you think?" or "Does what I'm saying make sense to you?" All he does is shrug or say, "Whatever." He simply won't show any involvement. So I say, why bother talking to him?

In contrast to neutrality, empathic communication confirms the worth of others and our concern for their them. Empathic communication is illustrated by these examples: "I can understand why you feel that way. It's an entirely reasonable way to feel in your situation" and "Wow, it must have really stung when your supervisor said that to you." Empathy doesn't necessarily mean agreement; instead, it conveys acceptance of other people and respect for their perspectives. Especially when we don't agree with others, it's important to communicate that we value them as people.

Superiority Versus Equality Like many of the other communication behaviors we've discussed, the final pair of behaviors that affect climate is the one most pertinent to the relationship level of meaning. Communication that conveys superiority says, "I'm better." Understandably, we feel on guard when people act as if they are better than we are.

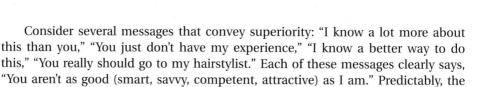

Everyday Application
Assessing Communication Climates

Use the behaviors we've discussed as a checklist for assessing communication climates.

The next time you feel defensive, ask whether communication reflects superiority, control, strategy, certainty, neutrality, or evaluation. Chances are that one or more of these are present in communication.

For a communication climate you find supportive and open, check to see whether the communication reflects spontaneity, equality, provisionalism, problem orientation, empathy, and description.

To improve defensive climates, try modeling supportive communication. Resist the normal tendencies to respond defensively when a climate feels disconfirming. Instead, focus on being empathic, descriptive, and spontaneous, showing equality and tentativeness, and solving problems. For experience in transforming communication that fosters supportive climates, complete Activity 8.5 in your *Student Companion* or online under "Chapter Resources for Chapter 8" at the Everyday Connections website.

Consider several messages that convey superiority: "I know a lot more about this than you," "You just don't have my experience," "I know a better way to do this," "You really should go to my hairstylist." Each of these messages clearly says, "You aren't as good (smart, savvy, competent, attractive) as I am." Predictably, the result is that we protect our self-esteem by trying to avoid people who belittle us.

Communication that conveys equality is confirming and fosters a supportive interpersonal climate. We feel more relaxed and comfortable communicating with people who treat us as equals. At the relationship level of meaning, expressed equality communicates respect and equivalent status. We can have exceptional experience or ability in certain areas and still show regard for others and their contribution to interaction. Creating a climate of equality allows everyone to be involved without fear of being judged inadequate. *Student Companion:* Activity 8.4.

We've seen that confirmation, which may include recognizing, acknowledging, and endorsing others, is the basis of healthy communication climates. Our discussion of defensive and supportive forms of communication enlightens us about the specific behaviors that tend to make us feel confirmed or disconfirmed.

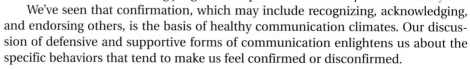

Guidelines for Creating
and Sustaining Healthy Climates

Now that we understand how communication creates interpersonal climates, we're ready to identify five guidelines for building and sustaining healthy climates.

ACTIVELY USE COMMUNICATION
TO BUILD CONFIRMING CLIMATES

The first principle is to use what you've learned in this chapter to enhance the climates in your relationships. Now that you know what generates defensive and supportive climates, you can identify and curb disconfirming patterns of talk, such as evaluation and superiority. In addition, you can actively use supportive communication, such as problem orientation and tentativeness.

You can also enhance interpersonal climates by accepting and growing from the tension generated by relational dialectics. Growth in individuals and relationships depends on honoring our needs for autonomy and connection, novelty and routine, and openness and closedness. Thus, the friction between contradictory needs keeps us aware of our multiple needs and the importance of fulfilling each of them.

ACCEPT AND CONFIRM OTHERS

Throughout this chapter, we've seen that confirmation is central to healthy climates and fulfilling relationships. Although we can understand how important it is, it isn't always easy to give confirmation. Sometimes we disagree with others or don't like certain things they do. Being honest with others is important because we expect real friends to be sources of honest feedback, even if it isn't always pleasant to hear (Rawlins, 1994). This implies that we should express honest misgivings about our friends and their behaviors. We can offer honest feedback within a context that assures others that we value and respect them, as Houston's commentary explains.

> **HOUSTON** The best thing my friend Jack ever did for me was to light into me about experimenting with drugs. He told me it was stupid to play with my mind and to risk my health just for kicks, and he kept at me until I tapered off. What made it work was that Jack was clear that he thought too much of me to stand by when I was hurting myself. A lot of my other so-called friends just stood by and said nothing. Jack is the only one who was a real friend.

For a relationship to work, people in it must feel confirmed. Confirmation begins with acknowledging others and accepting the validity of their needs and preferences. Dual perspective is a primary tool for accepting others because it calls on us to consider them on their own terms. Although intimate talk may be what makes you feel closest to another person, that person may experience greater closeness when you do things together. To meet the needs of both of you, you could take turns honoring each other's preferred paths to closeness. Alternatively, you might combine the two styles of intimacy by doing things together that invite conversation. For example, backpacking is an activity in which talking naturally occurs.

AFFIRM AND ASSERT YOURSELF

It is just as important to affirm yourself as it is to affirm others. You are no less valuable, your needs are no less important, and your preferences are no less valid than those of others. It is a misunderstanding to think that the interpersonal communication principles we've discussed concern only how we behave toward others. Equally, they pertain to how we should treat ourselves. Thus, the principle of confirming people's worth applies just as much to oneself as to others. Likewise, we should respect and honor both our own and others' needs, preferences, and ways of creating intimacy.

Although we can't always meet the needs of all parties in relationships, it is possible to give voice to everyone, including yourself. If your partner favors greater autonomy than you do, you need to recognize that preference and also assert your own. If you don't express your feelings, there's no way others can confirm you. Thus, you should assert your feelings and preferences while simultaneously honoring different ones in others.

LAQUANDA   It took me a long time to learn to look out for myself as well as I look out for others. I was always taught to put others first, probably because I'm a girl. I mean, neither of my brothers had that drilled into them. But I did, and for years I would just muffle my needs and whatever I wanted. I concentrated on pleasing others. I thought I was taking care of relationships, but really I was hurting them, because I felt neglected, and I resented that. What I'm working on now is learning to take care of myself and others at the same time.

Unlike aggression, assertion doesn't involve putting your needs above those of others. At the same time, assertion doesn't subordinate your needs to those of others as does deference. **Assertion** is a matter of clearly and nonjudgmentally stating what you feel, need, or want (see Table 8.4). You can do this without disparaging others or what they want. You should simply state your feelings clearly in an open, descriptive manner.

The meaning of assertion varies between cultures. For instance, directly asserting your own ideas is considered disrespectful by many Koreans and Chinese. Because African Americans are generally more assertive than European Americans, an African American may have a more direct, more pointed style of asserting him- or herself (Houston, 2004; Orbuch & Veroff, 2002).

To communicate effectively with others, we need to learn how they affirm themselves and how they express their feelings directly or indirectly. When each person states his or her feelings and expresses awareness of the other's perspective, the parties are likely to find a way to acknowledge both viewpoints. Eleanor's commentary illustrates acknowledging another's needs.

ELEANOR   About a year after George and I married, he was offered a promotion if he'd move to Virginia. We were living in Pennsylvania at the time, and that's where our families and friends were. I didn't want to move, because I was rooted with my people, but we could both see how important the move was to George's career. The week before we moved, George gave me the greatest present of our lives. He handed me two tickets: one for a round-trip flight from Virginia to Pennsylvania so that I could visit my family, and a second ticket he'd gotten for my best friend so that she could visit me after we moved. I felt he really understood me and had found a way to take care of my needs. I still have the ticket stubs in my box of special memories.

RESPECT DIVERSITY IN RELATIONSHIPS

Just as individuals differ, so do relationships. There is tremendous variety in what people find comfortable, affirming, and satisfying in interpersonal interaction. For exam-

---

Table 8.4   Aggression, Assertion, and Deference

AGGRESSIVE	ASSERTIVE	DEFERENTIAL
We're going to spend time together.	I'd like to create more time for us.	It's okay with me not to spend time with each other.
Tell me what you're feeling; I insist.	I would like to understand more of how you feel.	If you don't want to talk about how you feel, okay.
I don't care what you want; I'm not going to a movie.	I'm really not up for a movie tonight.	It's fine with me to got to a movie if you want to.

To increase your awareness of distinctions among aggressive, assertive, and deferential styles of communication, complete Activity 8.6 in your *Student Companion* or online under "Chapter Resources for Chapter 8" at the Everyday Connections website.

ple, you might have one friend who enjoys a lot of verbal disclosure and another who prefers less. There's no reason to try to persuade the first friend to disclose less or the second one to be more revealing. Similarly, you may be comfortable with greater closeness in some of your relationships and with more autonomy in others. Differences between people create a rich variety of relationships.

DORZIUS Communication has a lot to do with climate in work relationships, too. When I first came here from Haiti, I had many job interviews. People would say to me, "We've never hired one of you," like Haitians are not normal people. They also would say I would have to work hard and was I ready to do that, which told me they assumed I was lazy. When I did get a job, my supervisor watched me much more closely than he watched American workers. He was always judging.

Even a single relationship varies over time. Because dialectics generate constant tension, people continuously shift their patterns and ways of honoring contradictory needs in their relationships. It's natural to want more closeness at some times and more distance at other times over the life of a relationship. It's also advisable to experiment with different responses to dialectical tensions. You may find that it's effective to compromise between closeness and autonomy and to satisfy your desire for openness by sharing certain topics while meeting your need for privacy by not discussing other topics. *Student Companion: Activity 8.3.*

Because people and relationships are diverse, we should strive to respect a range of communicative choices and relationship patterns. In addition, we should be cautious about imposing our meaning on others' communication. People from various cultures, including ones within the United States, have learned different communication styles. What Westerners consider openness and healthy self-disclosure may feel offensively intrusive to people from some Asian societies. The dramatic, assertive speaking style of many African Americans can be misinterpreted as abrasive

Everyday Application
Communicating Assertively

The following statements are deferential or aggressive. Revise each one so that it is assertive.

1. I guess your preference for going to the party is more important than my studying.
2. I don't need your permission to go out. I'll do what I please.
3. I suppose I could work extra next week if you really need a loan.
4. I don't like it when you spend time with Tim. Either stop seeing him, or we're through.

Student Companion: **Activity 8.11.**

or confrontational from a Western, Caucasian perspective (Orbuch & Veroff, 2002). The best way to understand what others' behavior means is to ask. This conveys the relational message that they matter to you, and it allows you to gain insight into the interesting diversity around us.

RESPOND CONSTRUCTIVELY TO CRITICISM

A fifth guideline is to learn to respond effectively when others offer constructive criticism. Sometimes, others communicate criticism in language that fosters defensiveness: "You are so inconsiderate!" "You're selfish." We tend to react defensively to such judgmental language, and we may dismiss the criticism (think that it isn't true) or just think that the other person is being mean. These are natural and understandable responses, but they aren't necessarily constructive ways to deal with criticism. The problem with denying or dismissing criticism is that it deprives us of a chance to learn more about how others see us and to reevaluate our own actions. Refusing to acknowledge others' criticism is also likely to erect barriers in relationships.

A more constructive response to criticism is to begin by seeking more information: "What do you mean, I'm inconsiderate?" "What do I do that you see as selfish?" Asking these questions allows you to get concrete information. Remember that others may not have your understanding of how to communicate effectively. Thus, they may use abstract terms that you can help them translate into specifics to be addressed. They may also use *you* language ("You hurt me") that you can explore to determine whether there is something you do to which they respond by feeling hurt.

A second step in responding constructively to criticism is to consider it thoughtfully. Is the criticism valid? Are you inconsiderate in some ways? Are you selfish in some respects? If, after reflection, you don't think the criticism is accurate, offer your interpretation of the behaviors the other perceived as inconsiderate or selfish. You might say, "I can see how you might feel it's selfish of me to go out with my friends so often, but to me it's because I care about them, just like I spend time with you because I care about you." Notice that this response not only offers an alternative interpretation of particular behavior but also affirms the other person.

If you decide that the criticism is valid, then consider whether you want to change how you act. Do you want to be perceived by others as inconsiderate or self-ish? If not, you can choose to change how you act. For suggestions on how to bring about changes in yourself, you may want to review the guidelines offered at the end of Chapter 2.

BETSY I didn't appreciate it when my roommate called me a slob. But because of what I've learned in this course, I didn't just ignore what Marie said or fire back an insult to her. Instead, I asked her what she meant. She told me she hated coming home to our apartment and finding my clothes on the bathroom floor and dishes in the sink. Well, I could deal with that. So I resolved to pick my clothes up and wash my dishes before I left each day. Before, if this had happened, I would have felt hurt and probably wouldn't have done anything different. But I felt less hurt and more in control because of how I responded to Marie's criticism, and I know she's a lot happier living with me now!

© Gary A. Conner/PhotoEdit

A final suggestion is to thank the person who offered the criticism. At first, this may seem absurd. After all, criticism doesn't feel good, so it's hard to be grateful. But on second thought, you may realize that criticism is a gift. It offers us opportunities to see ourselves through others' eyes. In addition, it gives us insight into how others feel about us and what we do. Both of these effects of criticism can foster personal growth and healthy relationships that allow honest expression of feelings. Even if we disagree with a criticism, we should let others know we appreciate their willingness to share their perceptions with us. This keeps the door open for communication in the future.

The guidelines we've discussed combine respect for self, others, and relationships with communication that fosters healthy, affirming climates for connections with others. We can transform our relationships when we take responsibility for shaping interpersonal climates and when we develop the knowledge and communication skills to do so.

Case Study: Continuing the Conversation

The following conversation is featured on the Everyday Connections website under "Chapter Resources for Chapter 8." Click on the link "Alan O'Connor: Manager" to launch the video and audio scenario scripted below.

Alan O'Connor dreads this time of year. It's his job to conduct performance interviews with the people who work directly under his supervision, and he's always felt inadequate to this task. He tries to be honest with

Jason Harris/© 2001 Wadsworth

Case Study: Continuing the Conversation

his employees about what they need to improve, but usually the employees seem to resent his honesty instead of appreciating his efforts to help them. He also feels very awkward when employees bring up personal issues and doesn't feel it's his place to deal with them. O'Connor remembers an interview a few years ago that went badly. After greeting Gretchen Bennett, he focused on a problem that was hindering her progress.

O'Connor: Uh, Gretchen, your work pace is too slow. You've gotta turn the work around more quickly so that you don't slow the rest of the team down.

Bennett: I take the time because I want to do it right. You know, I can flip stuff out really fast, if that's what you want, but it's not going to be top quality.

O'Connor: Ah, look, I don't want to lose you, but you've got to work more quickly.

Bennett: So, you're threatening my job.

Bennett left the company 2 months later, and O'Connor felt partly responsible. He recalls another performance interview that also turned sour. In this one, he tried to start the discussion less bluntly. Andrews is in the hot seat now. He is in his early forties.

O'Connor: How do you feel about your work over the last 6 months since we last reviewed it?

Andrews: I guess I've done okay. Uh, I'm not sure what you're after here.

O'Connor: Well, I'd just like to know your own appraisal before we

talk about my perceptions of your work.

Andrews: Like I said, I guess I've done pretty good work.

O'Connor: You've missed a lot of days. And you're often late getting in.

Andrews: Well, there have been some family issues. My son developed a serious medical condition, and we had to go through testing with several doctors and then some treatments. It took a lot of time.

O'Connor: Look, I don't want to get into your family issues. Can we just focus on the work for now? I need to know that you're not going to be absent much more from now on and that you can be here on time.

Andrews: Not if my son needs help. I mean, he comes first. I'm sure you can understand that. But when I'm here, I do my best, and sometimes I stay late if I had to come in late.

This interview also ended tensely. O'Connor isn't sure what he's doing wrong. He's even less sure how to conduct performance interviews that are more effective, productive, and motivating to employees.

1. Describe how O'Connor's views of his job, noted in the opening paragraph of this case, may affect his approach to performance interviews. How does his definition of his role and his goals influence the kind of climate he is likely to foster?

2. Identify specific comments by O'Connor that exemplify confirming and disconfirming communication. How

could disconfirming comments be modified or replaced to create more confirming communication?

3. Identify specific comments by O'Connor that are likely to cultivate defensive or supportive climates between him and his employees. What changes could be made in O'Connor's communication to increase the supportiveness of the climate?

4. What suggestions can you make that would allow O'Connor to fulfill his responsibility to provide employees with critical feedback about performance and to establish a more supportive climate?

5. Focus on framing the performance interviews. What advice would you give O'Connor about how to start interviews in ways that might establish a supportive foundation for interaction?

You can critique and analyze this encounter based on the principles you learned in this chapter by responding to the questions included under "Conversation Analysis" at the website. By clicking on the "Submit" button at the end of the form, you can compare your work to my suggested responses. Let's continue the conversation online!

Case Study: Continuing the Conversation

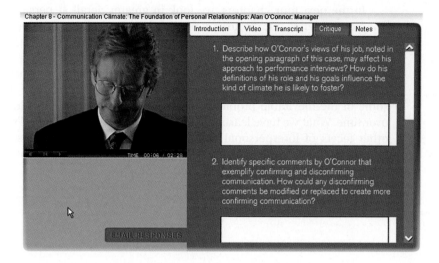

Chapter 8 - Communication Climate: The Foundation of Personal Relationships: Alan O'Connor: Manager

Introduction | Video | Transcript | Critique | Notes

1. Describe how O'Connor's views of his job, noted in the opening paragraph of this case, may affect his approach to performance interviews? How do his definitions of his role and his goals influence the kind of climate he is likely to foster?

2. Identify specific comments by O'Connor that exemplify confirming and disconfirming communication. How could any disconfirming comments be modified or replaced to create more confirming communication?

TIME 00:06 / 02:23

E-MAIL RESPONSES

Chapter Summary

In this chapter, we've explored personal relationships and the communication climates that make them more or less satisfying. The four elements of healthy interpersonal relationships are investment, commitment, trust, and comfort with relational dialectics.

Perhaps the most basic requirement for healthy communication climates is confirmation. Each of us wants to feel valued, especially by those who matter most to us. When partners recognize, acknowledge, and endorse each other, they communicate, "You matter to me." We discussed particular kinds of communication that foster supportive and defensive climates in relationships. Defensiveness is bred by evaluation, certainty, superiority, strategies, control, and neutrality. More supportive climates arise from communication that is descriptive, provisional, equal, spontaneous, empathic, and problem oriented.

To close the chapter, we considered five guidelines for building healthy communication climates. The first is to use your communication to enhance the mood of a relationship. Second, we should accept and confirm our friends and romantic partners, communicating that we respect them, even though we may not always agree with them or feel as they do. The third guideline is a companion to the second one: We should accept and confirm ourselves just as fully as we do others. Each of us is entitled to assert his or her own thoughts, feelings, and needs. Doing so allows us to honor ourselves and to help our partners understand us. Fourth, we should realize that diversity in relationships is a source of personal and interpersonal growth. People vary widely, as do the relationship patterns and forms they prefer. By respecting differences among us, we all expand our insights into the fascinating array of ways that humans form and sustain intimate relations. Finally, personal growth and healthy relationships are fostered by dealing constructively with criticism.

In the next four chapters, we look in greater detail at personal relationships. Chapter 9 extends our discussion of climate by examining how we can create constructive relationship contexts for dealing effectively with conflict. Chapter 10 discusses friendships, Chapter 11 considers romantic relationships, and Chapter 12 focuses on communication in families. In each chapter, we consider what these relationships are, how communication affects them, and how we might cope with some of the inevitable problems and challenges of sustaining close relationships over time. What we have learned about climate, as well as what we've learned about other facets of interpersonal communication in earlier chapters, will serve as a foundation for a deeper look at the dynamics of close relationships.

Everyday Connections Online

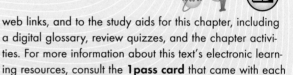

Now that you've read Chapter 8, go to the Everyday Connections premium website at academic.cengage.com/communication/woodinterpersonal5plus for quick access to the electronic study resources that accompany this text. The website gives you access to the "Continuing the Conversation" video scenario and questions featured in this chapter, to the InfoTrac College Edition, to maintained and updated web links, and to the study aids for this chapter, including a digital glossary, review quizzes, and the chapter activities. For more information about this text's electronic learning resources, consult the **1pass card** that came with each new copy of this book, or visit academic.cengage.com/communication/woodinterpersonal5.

Key Concepts

Audio flash cards of the following key terms are available on the Everyday Connections website. Use the flash cards to improve your pronunciation of text vocabulary.

assertion	ethnocentrism	investment	self-disclosure
commitment	interpersonal climate	relational dialectics	trust

For Further Thought and Discussion

1. Have you found it difficult to confirm others when you disagree with them? If so, does reading this chapter help you distinguish between recognition, acknowledgment, and endorsement? Can you distinguish between confirming others as people and endorsing particular ideas or behaviors?

2. What ethical principles are implied in communication that confirms and disconfirms others? Is it wrong to disconfirm others? All others? Intimates?

3. To what extent do you honor yourself and others in communication situations? Do you give equal attention to both your needs and those of others? If not, focus on balancing your efforts to confirm yourself and others in future interactions.

4. Think of an interaction in which you felt disconfirmed or defensive. Describe how others in the situation communicated toward you. How many of Gibb's defensiveness-producing communication behaviors can you identify as present in the situation?

5. How often are you deferential, assertive, and aggressive in your communication? What are the situations and relationships in which each kind of behavior is most likely for you? Do the behaviors you select advance your own goals and your relationships?

6. Use the PowerTrac option on your InfoTrac College Edition to find and read Donna Pawlowski's 1998 article, "Dialectical Tensions in Marital Partners' Accounts of Their Relationships." What does Pawlowski report as differences between husbands and wives' perceptions of dialectical tensions? How do her findings extend what we've discussed in this chapter?

7. Practice applying this chapter's guidelines for responding to criticism. What happens when you listen to criticism without becoming angry and when you express appreciation to others for their feedback?

Managing Conflict in Relationships

"Sometimes it's worse to win a fight than to lose."

Billie Holiday

© Peter Chapman

Joseph: You really made me angry when you flirted with other guys at the party last night.

Carmen: I'm surprised you could even see I was flirting, as much as you were drinking.

Joseph: Maybe I was drinking because my girlfriend was too busy dancing with other guys to pay any attention to me.

Carmen: Did it ever occur to you that maybe I'd pay more attention to you if you'd clean up your act? Why don't you get serious about graduate school and start acting responsibly?

Joseph: I'll do that right after you quit smoking and spend some time with me instead of always burying yourself in readings for your classes.

Carmen: You just say that because you're jealous that I'm in a graduate program and you're not.

Joseph: I wouldn't exactly call social work much of a graduate program.

Carmen: It's more than you have. At least I'm planning for a profession. Why don't you?

Joseph: You never do anything but complain, complain, complain. You really are a drag.

Carmen: It takes one to know one.

Joseph and Carmen have a problem, and it isn't just the issues they're discussing. Their larger problem is that they are not handling their conflict constructively. From previous chapters, we've learned enough to understand how negative communication fuels discord between them. For example, Joseph launched the conversation with *you* language. Instead of owning his anger, he blamed Carmen for it. In turn, she didn't own her anger. Joseph may also have misidentified what he was feeling. Is he really feeling angry at Carmen, or is he hurt or jealous that she spent more time with others than with him?

Both Joseph and Carmen disconfirmed the other with personal attacks. Furthermore, neither of them engaged in dual perspective: Neither recognized and acknowledged the other's point of view. Each of them listened defensively and ambushed the other. Carmen and Joseph pursued their individual agendas and failed to connect with each other. As a result, Carmen and Joseph clash. Their argument did nothing for either of them or for the climate of their relationship.

Let's start the conversation again, and see how positive communication might improve things.

Joseph: I felt hurt when you flirted with other guys at the party last night, and then I felt angry. [Joseph identifies hurt as the more basic feeling. He also owns his feelings.]

Carmen: I can understand that. I know you don't like me to pay attention to other men. [She acknowledges Joseph's feelings.] I got upset when you drank a lot, and I want you to understand how I feel about that. [Carmen owns her feelings and asserts her needs in the situation.]

Joseph: You're right about my drinking and your talking with other men. I know you hate it when I drink too much. [He acknowledges her concern.]

Carmen: Well, I guess neither of us was at our best last night. I was really tired, so I probably got more irritated than I usually would. [She shares responsibility for what happened.]

Joseph: And I've been feeling kind of down because you're so focused on your graduate program, and I can't seem to get started. [Because an affirming climate has been created, Joseph can disclose his deeper worries to Carmen.]

Carmen: I know you feel discouraged right now. [She again acknowledges his feelings.] I would too. [She shows empathy.] But you're so smart, and you'll do great once you settle on a course of action. [She confirms him by showing that she believes in him. She focuses their discussion on a single issue, which may allow them to address it effectively.] Why don't we put our heads together to sort through some of the options and try to figure out how you can proceed? [She offers support and shows commitment to his welfare.]

Joseph: That would really help me. I just need to talk through a lot of possibilities. [He acknowledges her offer of help.] I'd really like to get your perspective on some ideas I've got. [He shows he values her viewpoint.]

Carmen: I've got all the time you want. [She confirms his value and her commitment to the relationship. Her comment also addresses Joseph's relationship-level concern that she may not want to spend time with him.]

Joseph: (smile) Okay, and I promise I won't drink while we're talking. [He uses humor to restore good climate. On the relationship level of meaning, he is asking, "Are we okay now?"]

Carmen: (smile) And I promise I won't flirt with other guys while we're talking. [She reciprocates his relationship-level message by signaling that she, too, feels friendly again.]

The conflict proceeded very differently in the second instance. Both Carmen and Joseph owned their feelings and confirmed each other by acknowledging expressed feelings and concerns. The supportive climate they established enabled Joseph to reveal deeper worries that lay below his opening complaint about Carmen's flirting, and Carmen responded supportively to his disclosure. They also came up with a plan to address Joseph's worries. Especially important, they communicated effectively at the relationship level of meaning. Their relationship would be strengthened by how they managed their conflict in the second scenario.

Unlike Carmen and Joseph, we usually don't get a chance to go back and redo a conflict we've already had. Instead, we have to live with the consequences, which may be unpleasant. Because we can't hit an instant replay button for our conflicts, it's wise to learn how to manage conflict effectively so we're ready to do so when the need arises.

There is no magic bullet for handling conflict constructively. However, communication is one of the most important influences on conflict and its effect on relationships. Research shows that communication problems contribute to dissatisfaction with relationships and to breakups (Dindia & Fitzpatrick, 1985). We also know that positive, supportive communication is one of the strongest influences on long-term satisfaction with relationships (Gottman & Silver, 2000; Markman, 1981).

In this chapter, we explore conflict in interpersonal relationships. We begin by defining conflict. Next, we consider principles of conflict to add depth to our understanding of it. Third, we discuss different ways to approach conflict. The fourth section of the chapter focuses on specific communication patterns that affect the process of conflict and its impact on individuals and relationships. We conclude by identifying guidelines for communicating effectively when engaging in conflict.

Defining Interpersonal Conflict

Interpersonal conflict exists when people who depend on each other express different views, interests, or goals that they perceive as incompatible or opposed. Let's look more closely at each part of this definition.

EXPRESSED DISAGREEMENT

Interpersonal conflict is expressed disagreement, struggle, or discord. Thus, it is not conflict if we don't recognize disagreement or anger or if we repress it so completely that it is not expressed directly or indirectly. Conflict exists only if disagreements or tensions are expressed in some way.

We express disagreement in various ways. Shooting daggers with your eyes nonverbally communicates anger and discord just as clearly as saying, "I'm angry with you." Walking out on a conversation and slamming a door express hostility, as does refusing to talk to someone. Sometimes, we express disagreement overtly or directly, such as by saying, "I'm furious with you." Other modes of communicating conflict are more covert or indirect, such as deliberately not answering the phone because you are angry with the caller. In both cases, people realize they are in conflict, and they express their conflict, although in different ways.

INTERDEPENDENCE

Interpersonal conflict can occur only between people who depend on each other in the area of the conflict. Differences need not be resolved between people who don't affect each other. My food preferences differ from those of most of my colleagues. Because my colleagues and I don't need to agree about food, we are not in conflict over this issue. We may disagree with others and even judge them negatively, but that alone doesn't mean conflict will occur. Interpersonal conflict exists only when it is expressed by people who affect one another.

> **LENORE** It's kind of strange, but you really don't fight with people who don't matter. With a lot of guys I dated, if I didn't like something they did, I'd just let it go because they weren't important enough for the hassle. But Rod and I argue a lot, because we do affect each other. Maybe fighting is a sign that people care about each other. If you don't, why bother?

THE FELT NEED FOR RESOLUTION

Conflict is more than just having differences. We differ with people about many things, but this doesn't invariably lead to conflict. For example, my in-laws don't like large dogs, and we don't like small ones; my best friend dislikes cats, and I adore them. These differences don't spark conflict: My in-laws tolerate our Labrador, and we accept their Boston terrier. As my friend and I don't live together, we don't have to agree on whether we want cats in a shared home. In these cases, differences don't result in conflict. Conflict involves tensions between goals, preferences, or decisions that we feel we need to reconcile. In other words, conflict involves two perceptions: the perception that our concerns are at odds with those of another person, and the perception that we and that other person must resolve our differences.

Principles of Conflict

Many people view conflict as inherently negative (Turner & Shutter, 2004), but that is a misunderstanding. To address this misunderstanding as well as others, we discuss five principles of conflict.

PRINCIPLE 1: CONFLICT IS NATURAL IN RELATIONSHIPS

Conflict is a normal, inevitable part of most interpersonal relationships. When people matter to each other and affect each other, disagreements are unavoidable. You like meat, and your friend is a strict vegetarian. You like to work alone, and your co-workers like to interact in teams. You think money should be enjoyed, and your partner believes in saving for a rainy day. You want to move to a place where there's a great job for you, but the location has no career prospects for your partner. Again and again, we find ourselves at odds with people who matter to us. When this happens, we have to resolve the differences, preferably in a way that doesn't harm the relationship.

The presence of conflict does not indicate that a relationship is unhealthy or in trouble, although how partners manage conflict does influence relational health. Actually, engaging in conflict indicates that people are involved with each other. If they weren't, there would be no need to resolve differences. This is a good point to keep in mind when conflicts arise, because it reminds us that a strong connection underlies even disagreement.

> **RON** It sounds funny, but the biggest thing my fiancée and I fight about is whether it's okay to fight. I was brought up not to argue and to think that conflict is bad. In her family, people did argue a lot, and she thinks it is healthy. What I'm coming to realize is that there is a lot of conflict in my family, but it's hidden, so it never gets dealt with very well. I've seen her and her parents really go at it, but I have to admit they work through their differences, and people in my family don't.

Most of us have attitudes about conflict that reflect scripts we learned in our families. Like Ron, some of us were taught that conflict is bad and should be avoided, whereas others learned that airing differences is healthy. Because conflict is inevitable in interpersonal relationships, we should develop constructive ways to deal with it.

PRINCIPLE 2: CONFLICT MAY BE OVERT OR COVERT

When we defined conflict, we noted that disagreement can be expressed either overtly or covertly. Overt conflict is out in the open and explicit. It exists when people deal with their differences in a direct, straightforward manner. They might calmly discuss their disagreement, intensely argue about ideas, or engage in a shouting match. Overt conflict can also involve physical attacks, although of course that's neither healthy nor constructive. Physical violence is never acceptable in an enduring relationship with someone whom you care about, and it is rarely appropriate even in less close relationships.

Yet, conflict isn't always overt. Covert conflict exists when people express their feelings about disagreements indirectly. When angry, a person may deliberately do something to hurt or upset another person. Angry that his supervisor is requiring employees to make up a day missed for snow, Andy spends half the day surfing the net. Knowing that Elliott hates to be kept waiting, his wife intentionally arrives 20 minutes late for a dinner date because he chose a restaurant she doesn't like. These people are expressing their anger indirectly, and the conflict is covert.

A common form of covert conflict is **passive aggression,** which is acting aggressively while denying feeling or acting aggressive. If Dedra doesn't call her mother every week, her mother "forgets" to send Dedra a check for spending money. When Arlene won't forgo studying to go out dancing, Clem coincidentally decides to play music at high volume in the room adjacent to Arlene. Passive aggression punishes another person without accepting responsibility for the punishment. It undercuts the possibility of honest, healthy relationships.

> **STACI**   I was recently in a relationship that I thought was the greatest ever strictly because we never fought. I've had relationships with lots of arguments, so I thought it was fabulous that Steve and I never fought. I grew up with a twice-divorced mom, and I've seen her and my father and stepfather really go at it. All I ever wanted was a conflict-free relationship because I thought that would be a good relationship. One time, Steve called me to say he had to break our date to cover at work for another guy. All I did was sigh and say, "Fine, if that is what you need to do." But it wasn't fine with me; I resented his putting the other guy ahead of me. A little later, he called me back to say he'd changed his mind and would join me and two friends of ours. So, what happened? He sat at the table all night and barely said two words. I was so mad, but I didn't say a word about the evening, and neither did he. Just a month later, we broke up. Even then, there was no overt conflict.

Much covert conflict takes place through **games,** highly patterned interactions in which the real conflicts are hidden or denied and a counterfeit excuse created for arguing or criticizing (Berne, 1964). Games also involve cooperation between players.

The nature of games will become clear if we discuss a few specific ones. In a game called "Blemish," one person pretends to be complimentary but actually puts another down. Ann asks her friend whether she looks okay for an important interview. The friend, who is angry that she herself doesn't have any interviews lined up, responds, "The new suit looks really great. There's just this one little thing. You seem to have gained weight. Your stomach and hips look big, and that suit doesn't hide the extra pounds." The friend is playing "Blemish"; she focuses on one thing that is wrong and downplays all that is right. Her anger or resentment is expressed indirectly.

Another game is "NIGYYSOB" ("Now I've Got You, You Son of a B——"). In this one, a person deliberately sets another person up for a fall. Knowing that her husband is not a good cook, Ellie asks him to fix dinner one evening. When he overcooks the main dish, and the sauce is lumpy, she criticizes him for preparing a bad meal. Ellie worked to find a way to make him fail and then pounced on him when he did.

"Mine Is Worse Than Yours" is another commonly played game. Suppose you tell a friend that you have two tests and a paper due next week, and your friend says, "You think that's bad? Listen to this: I have two tests, three papers, and an oral report all due in the next two weeks." Your friend expressed no concern for your plight; rather, he told you that his situation is worse. In this game, people try to monopolize rather than listen and respond to each other.

> **CHUCK** My parents specialize in games. Dad likes to set Mom up by asking her to take care of some financial business or get the car fixed. Then he explodes about what she does. I think he is just trying to find excuses for blessing her out. Mom also plays games. Her favorite is Blemish. She always finds something wrong with an idea or a paper I've written or a vacation or whatever. Then she just harps and harps on the defect. Sometimes being around them is like being in a minefield.

"Yes, But" is a game in which a person pretends to be asking for help but then refuses all help that's offered. Doing this allows the person who initiates the game to attempt to make the other person feel inadequate for being unable to help. Lorna asks her boyfriend to help her figure out how to better manage her money. When he suggests that she should spend less, Lorna says, "Yes, but I don't buy anything I don't need." When he suggests she might work extra hours at her job, she responds, "Yes, but that would cut into my free time." When he mentions she could get a better-paying job, Lorna says, "Yes, but I really like the people where I work now." When he points out that she could save a lot by packing lunches instead of buying them, she replies, "Yes, but I'd have to get up earlier." "Yes, But" continues until the person trying to help finally gives up in defeat. Then, the initiator of the game can complain, "You didn't help me."

Games and passive aggression are dishonest, ineffective ways to manage conflict. They are dishonest because they camouflage the real issues. They are ineffective because, as long as conflict remains hidden or disguised, it's almost impossible for people to recognize and resolve it.

PRINCIPLE 3: SOCIAL GROUPS SHAPE THE MEANING OF CONFLICT BEHAVIORS

Our cultural membership and socialization in particular social communities affect how we view and respond to conflict.

Cultural Differences Regarding Conflict   The majority of Mediterranean cultures regard conflict as a normal, valuable part of everyday life. Within these cultures, people routinely argue and wrangle, and nobody gets upset or angry. In France and

---

Everyday Application
Identifying Games in Your Communication

Apply what you've read about covert conflict to your own life. Describe an instance when you or someone you have a relationship with played each of these games:

Blemish	NIGYYSOB
Mine Is Worse Than Yours	Yes, But

What was accomplished by playing the games? Were the real conflicts addressed?

in Arabic countries, men debate one another for the sheer fun of it. It doesn't matter who wins the debate—the argument itself is enjoyable (Copeland & Griggs, 1985). Many Hispanic cultures also regard conflict as both normal and interesting. Because Hispanic cultures tend to value emotions, conflicts are opportunities for emotional expression.

Chinese people have a very different view of conflict. Yan Bing Zhang, Jake Harwood, and Mary Hummert (2005) asked Chinese adults to evaluate transcripts in which an older worker criticized a younger worker. Older participants favored an accommodating style. Younger adults preferred a problem-solving style (assertive and cooperative) to an accommodating style (emphasizes relational harmony) or perceived the two styles as equally desirable. Older and younger participants alike had less positive perceptions of the avoiding style, which was perceived as disrespectful of others, and the competing (driven by self-interest) style of dealing with conflict. In contrast, many Westerners prefer the competing style (Bergstrom & Nussbaum, 1996).

Mainstream culture in the United States emphasizes assertiveness and individuality, so many Westerners are competitive and reluctant to give in to others. In more communal societies, people have less individualistic perspectives and are less likely to focus on winning conflicts (Ting-Toomey, 1991; Vanyperen & Buunk, 1991). Similarly, in Japan and many other Asian cultures, open disagreement is strongly condemned (Gangwish, 1999). Great effort is made to avoid winning at the cost of causing another person to lose face (Rowland, 1985; Weiss, 1987). In Japanese sports, the ideal is not for one team to win but for a tie to occur so that neither team loses face. When there is to be a winner, Japanese athletes try to win by only a slim margin so that the losing team is not humiliated ("American Games, Japanese Rules," in Ferrante, 1992).

VALAYA One of the hardest adjustments for me has been how Americans assert themselves. I was very surprised that students argue with their teachers. We would never do that in Taiwan. It would be extremely disrespectful. I also see friends argue, sometimes very much. I understand this is a cultural difference, but I have trouble accepting it. I learned that disagreements hurt relationships.

Differences among Social Communities Our orientations toward conflict are influenced not only by culture but also by social communities based on gender, sexual orientation, and race/ethnicity. There are some general differences in how women and men respond to conflict, although the generalizations don't apply to all women and men (Stafford, Dutton, & Haas, 2000; Wood, 2005). In general, women are more likely to want to discuss conflictual issues, whereas many men tend to avoid conflict. Women are also more likely than men to defer and compromise, both of which reflect gendered prescriptions for women to accommodate others.

Men are more likely than women to feel overwhelmed when asked to engage in communication about differences. Women sometimes feel that men are unwilling to discuss anything about relationships. Of course, these are broad generalizations that overstate how men and women act. Nonetheless, women and men often find themselves responding very differently to relationship tensions and not understanding each other's perspective.

NICK My girlfriend drives me crazy. Any time the slightest thing is wrong in our relationship, she wants to have a long, drawn-out analysis of it. I just don't want to spend all that time dissecting the relationship.

GINA My boyfriend is a world-class avoider. When something is wrong between us, I naturally want to talk about it and get things right again. But he will evade, tell me everything's fine when it's not, say the problem is too minor to talk about, and use any other tactic he can come up with to avoid facing the problem. He thinks if you don't deal with problems, they somehow solve themselves.

Masculine socialization places less emphasis on talk as a means to intimacy; as a group, men are less likely than women to see discussion as a good way to handle conflict in personal relationships. In professional situations and athletics, men may be very vocal in dealing with conflict. Yet, in their personal lives, men often deny or minimize problems rather than deal openly with them. Long-term studies of marriage indicate that husbands are more inclined than wives to withdraw from conflict and that stonewalling by husbands is a strong predictor of divorce (Bass, 1993). Men are more likely than women to use coercive tactics, both verbal and physical, to avoid discussing problems and to force their resolutions on others (Johnson, in press; Snell, Hawkins, & Belk, 1988; White, 1989).

Before leaving our discussion of gender, we should note one other important finding. Psychologist John Gottman (1993; Jacobson & Gottman, 1998) reports that, in general, men experience greater and longer-lasting physical responses to interpersonal conflict than women do. Compared with women, during conflict men's heart rates rise more quickly and to higher levels and stay elevated for a longer period of time. Because conflict tends to be more physically and psychologically painful to men than to women, men may be motivated to deny, avoid, or minimize issues that could cause conflict.

© Anne Dowie

Sexual orientation doesn't seem to be a major influence on how people see and deal with conflict. Caryl Rusbult and her colleagues (Rusbult, Johnson, & Morrow, 1986; Rusbult, Zembrodt, & Iwaniszek, 1986; Wood, 1986, 1994b) report that, in their responses to conflict, gay men are much like heterosexual men, and lesbians are similar to heterosexual women. Similarly, a major national study reported that gender explains far more of the differences between partners than does sexual orientation (Blumstein & Schwartz, 1983). Most children, regardless of sexual orientation, are socialized on the basis of their sex. Thus, boys, both gay and heterosexual, tend to learn masculine orientations toward interaction, whereas lesbian and heterosexual girls are socialized toward feminine styles of interaction.

Recent research indicates that race–ethnicity is related to conflict styles and to interpretations of them. Terri Orbuch and Joseph Veroff and their colleagues (Orbuch & Eyster, 1997; Orbuch & Veroff, 2002; Orbuch, Veroff, & Hunter, 1999) report that open, verbal arguing is destructive for white couples but not necessarily for black couples. They also report that black wives are more likely than white wives to believe that airing conflicts can lead to positive resolution.

PRINCIPLE 4: CONFLICT CAN BE MANAGED WELL OR POORLY

People respond to conflict in a variety of ways, from physical attack to verbal aggression to collaborative problem solving. Although each method may resolve differences, some are clearly preferable to others. Depending on how we handle disagreements, conflict can either promote continuing closeness or tear a relationship apart.

© Audrey Gottlieb

One of the main reasons conflict is handled poorly is that it often involves intense feelings, which many people do not know how to identify or express. We may feel deep disappointment, resentment, or anger toward someone we care about, and this is difficult to manage. Our discussion in Chapter 7 should help you identify your feelings and choose effective ways to communicate your emotions in conflict situations. Other skills we've discussed—such as using *I* language and monitoring the self-serving bias—will also help you manage the feelings that often accompany conflict.

Learning how different kinds of communication affect relationships, individuals, and conflict resolution empowers you to make informed choices about dealing with conflict in your relationships. The ideas and skills we cover in this chapter and throughout this book will help you manage interpersonal conflict to cultivate personal growth and relationship maturity.

PRINCIPLE 5: CONFLICT CAN BE GOOD FOR INDIVIDUALS AND RELATIONSHIPS

Although we tend to think of conflict negatively, it can be beneficial in a number of ways. (See Figure 9.1.) When managed constructively, conflict provides opportunities for us to grow as individuals and to strengthen our relationships. We deepen insight into our ideas and feelings when we express them and get responses from others. Conflict also allows us to consider points of view different from our own. Based on what we learn, we may change our own views.

Danger   Opportunity

JALEH A while back, I was arguing with a buddy of mine about quotas. I've always supported them because I think that's the only way minorities have a chance of getting the education and jobs they deserve. Without quotas, people of color will still be shut out no matter how skilled or smart or achieving they are. But the guy I was debating is against quotas because he thinks they hurt us. He said that, as long as quotas are used, any minority person in a good school or with a status job will be regarded as there because of quota, not merit. What really made me think was when he said that quotas can be used against minorities— like if a school has a quota for 10 percent minorities, it can refuse to admit more than 10 percent minorities even if more are qualified. Arguing with him has pushed me to rethink my position.

FIGURE 9.1
The Chinese Character for *Crisis*

Conflict can also enhance relationships by enlarging partners' understandings of each other. What begins as a discussion of a particular issue usually winds up providing broader information about why partners feel as they do and what meanings they attach to the issue. In the example that opened this chapter, the original complaint about Carmen's flirting led to the discovery that Joseph felt insecure about his identity and Carmen's respect for him because she was succeeding in graduate work, and he wasn't advancing in school or a career. Once his concern emerged, the couple could address deeper issues in their relationship.

Lack of conflict isn't necessarily a symptom of a healthy relationship (Arnett, 1986). Low levels of conflict could reflect limited emotional depth between partners or unwillingness to engage in communication about differences. Researchers report that there is no direct association between marital happiness and the number of arguments spouses have (Howard & Dawes, 1976; Muehlhoff & Wood, 2002). Instead, the key is to have a greater number of positive, affirming interactions than negative ones. One group of researchers refers to this as "keeping a positive balance in the marital bank account" (Gottman & Silver, 2000; Gottman, Notarius, Markman, Banks, Yoppi, & Rubin, 1976).

> **JANA**   Geoff and I have a pretty intense relationship. We fight a lot, and we fight hard. Some of my friends think this is bad, but we don't. Nothing is swept under the carpet in our relationship. If either of us is angry or upset about something, we hash it out then and there. But we are just as intense in positive ways. Geoff lets me know all the time that he loves me, and I am always hugging and kissing him. I guess you could just say our relationship is passionate—in bad moments and good ones.

To review, we've discussed five principles of interpersonal conflict. First, we noted that conflict is both natural and inevitable in interpersonal relationships. Second, we discovered that conflict can be directly communicated or covertly expressed through indirect communication or games that camouflage real issues. Third, we saw that conflict styles and meanings are shaped by social location—membership in cultures and social communities. Fourth, we emphasized that how we manage conflict influences its resolution and its impact on interpersonal climates. Finally, we saw that conflict can be constructive for individuals and relationships. We can now build on these principles by discussing diverse ways people approach and respond to conflict.

Orientations to Conflict

We've noted that conflict can be managed in various ways, some more effective than others. We now look at three basic orientations that affect how we approach conflict situations. In the next section of the chapter, we'll see how these different approaches shape our patterns of responding during conflict. Each way of approaching conflict is appropriate in some relationships and situations; the challenge is to know when a particular approach is constructive.

LOSE–LOSE

A **lose–lose** orientation assumes that conflict results in losses for everyone and that it is unhealthy and destructive for relationships. A wife might feel that conflicts about money hurt her, her husband, and the marriage. Similarly, a person may refrain from arguing with a friend, believing the result would be wounded pride for both of them. Because the lose–lose orientation assumes that conflict is inevitably negative, people who adopt it typically try to avoid conflict at all costs. Yet, seeking to avoid conflict at all costs may be very costly indeed. We may have to defer our own needs or rights, and we may feel unable to give honest feedback to others.

> **THEO** I hate to fight with friends. I do just about anything to avoid an argument. But sometimes, what I have to do is sacrifice my preferences or even my rights just to avoid conflict. And sometimes, I have to go along with something I don't believe in or think is right. I'm starting to think that maybe conflict would be better than avoiding it—at least in some cases.

Although the lose–lose orientation is not usually beneficial in dealing with conflicts in close relationships, it has merit in some circumstances. Some issues aren't worth the energy and the discomfort that conflict arouses. A couple may have different preferences for dining out but feel that the issue isn't worth an argument.

WIN–LOSE

Win–lose orientations assume that one person wins at the expense of the other. A person who sees conflict as a win–lose matter thinks that disagreements are battles that can have only one victor. What one person gains, the other loses; what one person loses, the other gains. Disagreements are seen as zero-sum games in which there is no possibility for everyone to benefit. The win–lose orientation is cultivated in cultures that place value on individualism, self-assertion, and competition. If you guessed that the United States emphasizes those values, you're right. A win–lose approach to conflict is not common in cultures that place priority on cooperation, keeping others from failing, and finding areas of agreement.

Partners who disagree about whether to move to a new location might adopt a win–lose orientation. In turn, this would lock them into a yes–no view in which only two alternatives are seen: move or stay put. The win–lose orientation almost guarantees that the partners won't work to find or create a mutually acceptable solution, such as moving to a third place that meets both partners' needs, or having a long-distance relationship so that each person can have the best location. The more person A argues for moving, the more person B argues for not moving. Eventually one of them "wins" but at the cost of the other and the relationship. A win–lose orientation toward conflict tends to undermine relationships because someone has to lose.

A win–lose approach can be appropriate when we have a high desire for our position to prevail, low commitment to a relationship, and little desire to take care of the person with whom we disagree. When you're buying a car, for instance, you want the best deal you can get, and you probably have little concern for the dealer's profit and little commitment to continuing the relationship. I adopted a win–lose approach to conflict with doctors when my father was dying. The doctors weren't doing all they could to help him, because they saw little value in investing in someone who was dying. On the other hand, I wanted the doctors to do everything possible to help my father. The doctors and I had opposing views, and I cared less about whether the doctors were happy and liked me than about winning the best medical care for my father.

© Fotostudio FM/zefa/CORBIS

Communication in Everyday Life
Japanese and American Styles of Negotiation

The differences between Japanese and American views of conflict shape specific communication patterns during business negotiations (McDaniel & Quasha, 2000; Weiss, 1987). Consider how each of the following negotiation strategies reflects values typical of Japanese or American society.

Japanese Style

··· Understate your own initial position or state it vaguely to allow the other room to state his or her position.
··· Find informal ways to let the other person know your bottom line to move agreement forward without directly confronting the other with your bottom line.
··· Look for areas of agreement, and focus talk on them.
··· Avoid confrontation or explicit disagreement.
··· Work to make sure that neither you nor the other person fails.
··· Plan to spend a long time discussing issues before even moving toward a decision.

American Style

··· Overstate initial position to establish a strong image.
··· Keep your bottom line secret from the other person to preserve your power and gain the most.
··· Where there are differences, assert your position and attempt to win the other's assent.
··· Be adversarial.
··· Work to win all you can.
··· Push to reach decisions as rapidly as possible.

Win–win orientations assume that there are usually ways to resolve differences so that everyone gains. A good solution is one that everyone finds satisfactory. When all people are committed to finding a solution that satisfies everyone, a win–win resolution is often possible. Sometimes, people can't find or create a solution that is each person's ideal. In such cases, each person may make some accommodations to build a solution that lets the other win as well. When partners adopt win–win views of conflict, they often discover solutions that neither had thought of previously. This happens because they are committed to their own and the other's satisfaction. Sometimes, win–win attitudes result in compromises that satisfy enough of each person's needs to provide confirmation and to protect the health of the relationship.

In Chapter 3, we learned that how we perceive things has a powerful impact on what they mean to us and on the possibilities of resolution that we imagine. Remember how you couldn't solve the nine dots problem in Chapter 3 if you perceived it as a square? In a similar way, we're unlikely to find a win–win solution if we perceive conflict as win–lose or lose–lose.

> **TESS** One of the roughest issues for Jerry and me was when he started working most nights. The time after dinner had always been "our time." When Jerry took the new job, he had to stay in constant contact with the California office. Jerry and I used to do something together at 6 P.M., but because of the time difference, it's only 3 P.M. on the West Coast, and the business day is still going. I was hurt that he no longer had time for us, and he was angry that I wanted time he needed for business. We kept talking and came up with the idea of spending a day together each weekend, which we'd never done. Although my ideal would still be to share evenings, this solution keeps us in touch with each other.

•••••••••••

Responses to Conflict

> **WAYNE** One thing I learned when I was serving in the military is that a fist will stop an argument a lot faster than words. You can talk all day long and never reach resolution, but a good pop in the face ends conflict real fast.

Wayne is correct that physical violence can sometimes stop an argument—at least temporarily. Physical force may be an unfortunate necessity in some situations, such as combat or self-protection. In interpersonal relationships, however, it is a very poor way to deal with conflict. A great deal of research demonstrates that violence in families harms both perpetrators and victims, and it violates the trust on which close relationships are built (Jacobson & Gottman, 1998; Johnson, in press). In Chapter 11, we'll look more closely at the dynamics of violence between intimate partners. In this section, we'll consider ways of responding to conflict other than with violence.

Our approach to conflict shapes how we respond when conflict occurs. A series of studies identified four distinct ways North Americans respond to relational distress (Rusbult, 1987; Rusbult, Johnson, & Morrow, 1986; Rusbult & Zembrodt, 1983; Rusbult, Zembrodt, & Iwaniszek, 1986). These are represented in Figure 9.2. According to this model, responses to conflict can be either active or passive, depending on how overtly they address problems. Responses can also be constructive or destructive in their capacity to resolve tension and to preserve relationships.

THE EXIT RESPONSE

The **exit response** involves physically walking out or psychologically withdrawing. Refusing to talk about a problem is an example of psychological exit. Ending a relationship and leaving when conflict arises are examples of literal exit. Because exit doesn't address problems, it tends to be destructive. Because it is a forceful way to avoid conflict, it is active.

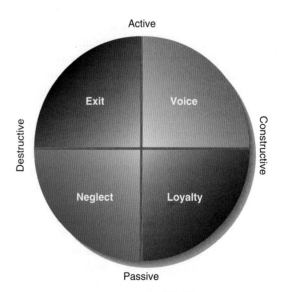

FIGURE 9.2

Responses to Conflict

Exit responses are associated with lose–lose and win–lose orientations toward conflict. People who have a lose–lose orientation assume that nobody can benefit if conflict takes place, so they see no point in engaging in conflict and prefer to avoid it. For different reasons, the win–lose orientation may promote the exit response. People who see conflicts as win–lose situations may exit physically or psychologically if they think they will lose should the conflict become overt.

THE NEGLECT RESPONSE

The **neglect response** denies or minimizes problems, disagreements, anger, tension, or other matters that could lead to overt conflict. People communicate that they prefer to neglect conflicts by saying, "There isn't a disagreement here," "You're creating a problem where none exists," or "You're making a mountain out of a molehill." These statements deny that a problem exists or that a problem is important. Neglect generally is destructive because it doesn't resolve tension. It is passive because it avoids discussion. In some situations, however, neglect may be an effective response to conflict. For instance, if an issue can't be resolved, discussing it may further harm a relationship. Also, if a conflict isn't important to a relationship's health, it may be appropriate not to deal with it.

The lose–lose and win–lose orientations may prompt the neglect response for the same reasons that each of those orientations is associated with the exit response. Either the person thinks that escalating the disagreement will harm everyone, or the person thinks that she or he will lose if the conflict is allowed to progress.

THE LOYALTY RESPONSE

The **loyalty response** is staying committed to a relationship despite differences. In other words, the person who adopts loyalty as a response to conflict decides to stay in a relationship and tolerate the differences. Loyalty may be desirable if tolerating differences isn't too costly, but in some instances deferring your own needs and goals may be too high a price for harmony. The loyalty response may also take the form of focusing on what is good and desirable about the relationship and minimizing its problems. Loyalty is silent allegiance that doesn't actively address conflict, so it is a passive response. Because it preserves the relationship, loyalty tends to be constructive, at least in the short term.

Loyalty is most likely to spring from a lose–lose orientation toward conflict. Believing that engaging in overt disagreement only hurts everyone, people may choose to remain loyal to the relationship and not try to work through differences.

Finally, the **voice response** addresses conflict directly and attempts to resolve it. People who respond with voice identify problems or tensions and assert a desire to deal with them. Voice implies that people care enough about a relationship to notice when something is wrong and to want to do something to improve the situation. Thus, voice often is the most constructive way of responding to conflict in enduring intimate relationships.

The voice response is most likely to be fostered by a win–win orientation toward conflict. It takes belief in yourself and the other person to give voice to problems and disagreements. Voicing concerns also expresses belief in the relationship. We're unlikely to voice disagreements unless we believe that a relationship can withstand our doing so. Voice may also take the form of genuine apology for behavior that has hurt another, or explicit acceptance of a partner's apology (Fincham & Beach, 2002; Vangelisti & Crumley, 1998).

Although each of us has developed a preferred response, we can become skillful in other responses if we so choose. Constructive strategies (voice and loyalty) are advisable for relationships that matter to you and that you want to maintain. Exit may be useful as an interim strategy when partners need time to reflect or cool off before dealing with conflict directly. Loyalty may be appropriate in situations where conflict is temporary and provoked by external pressures. Developing skill in a range of responses to conflict increases your ability to communicate sensitively and effectively. *Student Companion:* Activity 9.2.

Communication Patterns during Conflict

Communication skills shape the process and outcomes of conflict. Thus, we want to understand specific kinds of communication that foster or impede effective conflict.

Everyday Application
Enlarging Your Repertoire of Responses to Conflict

Identify two responses to conflict that you do not often use. For each one, specify two strategies to increase your skill in using that response.

Example

Voice Response to Conflict: I have trouble talking about conflict.
Strategies for Achieving Competence:

1. When I feel like avoiding conflict, I will remind myself that avoiding has never made problems go away.
2. When friends ask what's wrong, I will stop saying "Nothing's wrong."

To further explore your preferred responses to interpersonal conflict, complete Activity 9.1 in your *Student Companion* or online under "Chapter Resources for Chapter 9" at the Everyday Connections website.

Ineffective communication can hurt individuals, damage relationships, and undermine the possibility of resolving problems. Unproductive communication patterns in managing conflict reflect a preoccupation with self and a disregard for the other. Table 9.1 identifies behaviors that foster constructive and unproductive conflict communication (Gottman, 1993; Gottman, Notarius, Gonso, et al., 1976; Gottman, Notarius, Markman, et al., 1976; Vangelisti, 1993).

The Early Stages   The foundation of unproductive conflict is established by communication that fails to confirm individuals. If John says, "I want us to spend more time together," Shannon may reply, "That's unreasonable." This disconfirms John's feeling and request. Shannon could also disconfirm him by not replying at all, which would be a refusal to acknowledge him. During the early stages of conflict, people tend to listen poorly. They may listen selectively, taking in only what they expect or want to believe. They may communicate disdain nonverbally. For instance, Shannon could roll her eyes to tell John his request is outrageous, or she might shrug and turn away to signal that she doesn't care what he wants.

Cross-complaining occurs when one person's complaint is met by a counter-complaint. Shannon could respond to John's request for more time by saying, "Yeah, well, what I want is a little more respect for what I do." That response doesn't address John's concern; it is an attempt to divert the conversation and to switch the fault from Shannon to John. Poor listening and disconfirmation establish a climate in which dual perspective is low and defensiveness is high.

Negative climates tend to build on themselves. As parties in conflict continue to talk, mind reading is likely. Instead of offering an explicit apology, John assumes Shannon knows he is sorry (Vangelisti & Crumley, 1998). Instead of asking John to clarify or explain his feelings, Shannon assumes she knows his motives. Perhaps she thinks he wants to divert her from her work so that she won't succeed. If Shannon makes this assumption, she discounts what John wants. Mind reading in distressed relationships has a distinctly negative tone. The negative assumptions and attributions reflect and fuel hostility and mistrust.

Table 9.1   Summary of Constructive and Unproductive Communication

CONSTRUCTIVE	UNPRODUCTIVE
Validation of each other	Disconfirmation of each other
Sensitive listening	Poor listening
Dual perspective	Preoccupation with self
Recognition of other's concerns	Cross-complaining
Asking for clarification	Hostile mind reading
Infrequent interruptions	Frequent interruptions
Focus on specific issues	Kitchen-sinking
Compromises and contracts	Counterproposals
Useful metacommunication	Excessive metacommunication
Summarizing the concerns	Self-summarizing by both partners

The Middle Stages Once a negative climate has been set, it is stoked by other unconstructive communication. People often engage in **kitchen-sinking,** in which everything except the kitchen sink is thrown into the argument. John may add to his original complaint by recalling all sorts of other real and imagined slights from Shannon. She may reciprocate by hauling out her own laundry list of gripes. The result is such a mass of grievances that John and Shannon are overwhelmed. They can't solve all the problems they've dragged into the discussion, and they may well forget what the original issue was. Kitchen-sinking is particularly likely to occur when people have a host of concerns they've repressed for some time. Once a conflict begins, everything that has been stored up is thrown in.

The middle stages of unproductive conflict tend to be marked by frequent interruptions that disrupt the flow of talk. Interruptions may also be attempts to derail a partner's issues and reroute discussion: "I don't want to find more time together until we discuss your responsibility for this house." Cross-complaining often continues in this middle stage of the syndrome. Because neither person is allowed to develop thoughts fully (or even to finish a sentence), discussion never focuses on any topic long enough to make headway in resolving it.

The Later Stages Even if people make little progress in solving their problems, limited time and energy guarantee an end to an episode of conflict. Unfortunately, preceding stages didn't lay the groundwork for effective discussion of solutions. As a result, each person's proposals tend to be met with counterproposals. The self-preoccupation that first surfaced in the early phase persists now, so each person is more interested in pushing his or her solution than in considering the other person's. John proposes, "Maybe we could spend two nights together each week." Shannon counterproposes, "Maybe you could assume responsibility for half the chores around here." Her counterproposal fails to acknowledge his suggestion, so her

communication does not confirm him. Compounding self-preoccupation is self-summarizing, which occurs when a person keeps repeating what she or he has already said. This egocentric communication ignores the other person and simply restates the speaker's feelings and perspective.

Excessive metacommunication is a final form of negative communication in unproductive conflict. Metacommunication, which we discussed in Chapter 1, is communication about communication. For example, John might say, "I think we're avoiding talking about the real issue here." This is a comment about the communication that is happening. Metacommunication is used by couples in both unproductive conflict and constructive conflict, but it is used in very different ways (Gottman, Notarius, Gonso, et al., 1976; Gottman, Notarius, Markman, et al., 1976; Gottman et al., 1977).

In constructive conflict communication, people use metacommunication to keep the discussion on track, and then they return to the topics at hand. For instance, during a disagreement, Aaron might comment that Norma doesn't seem to be expressing her feelings and invite her to do so. Then, he and Norma would return to their discussion.

In contrast, people who manage conflict unproductively often become embroiled in metacommunication and can't get back to the issues. For example, Norma and Aaron might get into extended metacommunication about the way they deal with conflict and never return to the original topic of conflict. Excessive metacommunication is more likely to block partners than to resolve tensions satisfactorily.

The communication that makes up the unproductive conflict reflects and promotes egocentrism and dogmatism because negative communication tends to be self-perpetuating. Egocentrism leads to poor listening, which promotes disconfirmation, which fuels defensiveness, which stokes dogmatism, which leads to hostile mind reading and kitchen-sinking, which pave the way for self-summarizing. Each negative form of communication feeds into the overall negative system. Unproductive communication fosters a defensive, negative climate, which makes it almost impossible to resolve conflicts, confirm individuals, or nurture a relationship.

CONSTRUCTIVE CONFLICT COMMUNICATION

Constructive communication during conflict creates a supportive, positive climate that increases the possibility of resolving differences without harming the relationship. Let's look at how constructive communication plays out in the three phases of conflict.

The Early Stages The foundation of constructive management of conflict is established long before a specific disagreement is aired. Climate, which is the foundation both of conflict and of the overall relationship, sets the tone for communication during conflict.

To establish a good climate, communicators confirm each other by recognizing and acknowledging each other's concerns and feelings. Returning to our example, when John says, "I want us to spend more time together," Shannon could confirm him by replying, "I wish we could, too. It's nice that you want us to have more time together." Shannon's statement communicates to John that she is listening and that she cares about his concerns and shares them. After she says that, their discussion might go like this:

John: Yeah, it just seems that we used to spend a lot more time together, and we felt closer then. I miss that.

Shannon: I do, too. It sounds as if what's really on your mind is how close we are, not specifically the amount of time we spend together. Is that right?

John: Yeah, I guess that is more what's bothering me, but I kind of think they're connected, don't you?

Shannon: To an extent, but we won't feel closer just by spending more time together. I think we also need some shared interests like we used to have.

John: I'd like that. Do you have any ideas?

Let's highlight several things in this conversation. First, notice that, when Shannon responds directly to John's opening statement, he elaborates and clarifies what is troubling him. Instead of time per se, the issue is closeness. Listening sensitively, Shannon picks up on this and refocuses their conversation on closeness. We should also notice that Shannon doesn't mind read; instead, she asks John whether she has understood what he meant. When he asks Shannon whether she thinks time and closeness are related, John shows openness to her perceptions; thus, he confirms her and doesn't mind read. The openness they create clears the way for effective discussion of how to increase their closeness. Once a supportive climate is established, the couple can proceed to the middle stages of conflict knowing they are not fighting each other but working together to solve a problem.

The Middle Stages   The positive groundwork laid in the early phase of conflict supports what happens as people dig into issues. The middle stages of constructive conflict are marked by what Gottman (1993) calls *agenda building*, which involves staying focused on the main issues. When partners keep communication on target, kitchen-sinking is unlikely to derail discussion.

Side issues may come up, as they do in unproductive conflict, but people who have learned to communicate effectively control digressions and stay with their agenda. One useful technique is **bracketing,** which is noting that an issue arising in the course of conflict should be discussed later. Bracketing allows partners to confirm each other's concerns by agreeing to deal with them later. In addition, bracketing topics peripheral to the current discussion allows partners to make progress in resolving the immediate issue.

During the middle stage of constructive conflict, communicators continue to show respect for each other by not interrupting except to get clarification ("Before you go on, could you explain what you mean by closeness?") or to check perceptions ("So you think time together leads to closeness?"). Unlike disruptive interruptions, those that clarify ideas and check perceptions confirm the person speaking by showing that the listener wants to understand the meaning.

Parties in conflict continue to recognize and acknowledge each other's point of view. Rather than the cross-complaining, they acknowledge each other's feelings, thoughts, and concerns. This doesn't mean they don't put their own concerns on the table. Constructive conflict includes asserting our own feelings and needs as part of an honest dialogue. Honoring both ourselves and others is central to good interpersonal communication.

The Later Stages   In the culminating phase, attention shifts to resolving the tension. Whereas in unproductive conflict this involves meeting proposals with counterproposals, in constructive conflict people continue to operate collaboratively.

Keeping in mind that they share a relationship, they continue using dual perspective to remain aware of each other's perspectives. Instead of countering each other's proposals, they engage in **contracting,** which is building a solution through negotiation and the acceptance of parts of proposals. The difference between counterproposals and contracting is illustrated in this example:

Counterproposals

John: I want us to spend 3 nights a week doing things together.

Shannon: I can't do that right now because we're short-handed at work, and I am filling in nights. Get a hobby so you aren't bored nights.

John: Not being bored isn't the same as our being close. I want us to spend time together again.

Shannon: I told you, I can't do that. Don't be so selfish.

John: Aren't we as important as your job?

Shannon: That's a stupid question. I can't take 3 nights off. Let's take more vacations.

Contracting

John: I want us to spend 3 nights a week doing things together.

Shannon: I'm all for that, but right now we're short-handed at work. How about if we use your idea but adjust it to my job? Maybe we could start with 1 night each week and expand that later.

John: Okay, that's a start, but could we also reserve some weekend time for us?

Shannon: That's a good idea. Let's plan on that. I just can't be sure how much I'll have to work on weekends until we hire some new people. What if we promise to give ourselves an extra week's vacation to spend together when we have full staff?

John: Okay, that's a good backup plan, but can we take weekend time when you don't work?

Shannon: Absolutely. How about a picnic this Sunday? We've haven't gone on a picnic in so long.

In the counterproposal scenario, John and Shannon were competing to get their own way. Neither tried to identify workable parts of the other's proposals or to find common ground. Because each adopts a win–lose view of the conflict, it's likely that both of them and the relationship will be losers. A very different tone shows up in the contracting scenario. Neither person represses personal needs, and each is committed to building on the other's proposals.

> **BETTINA**   My son and I used to argue all the time, and we never got anywhere, because we were each trying to get our own way, and we weren't paying attention to the other. Then, we went into family counseling, and we learned how to make our arguments more productive. The most important thing I learned was to be looking for ways to respond to what my son says and wants. Once I started focusing on him and trying to satisfy him, he was more willing to listen to my point of view and to think about solutions that would satisfy me. We still argue a lot—I guess we always will—but now it's more like we're working things through together instead of trying to tear each other down.

Specific differences between unproductive and productive conflict can be summarized as the difference between confirming and disconfirming communication. Communication characteristic of unproductive conflict disconfirms both individuals and the relationship. On the other hand, the communication in constructive conflict consistently confirms both people and the relationship.

CONFLICT MANAGEMENT SKILLS

Our discussion of constructive and unproductive conflict communication highlights communication skills and attitudes we've emphasized in previous chapters. This is a good time to explicate eight conflict management skills that rely on effective interpersonal communication.

Attend to the Relationship Level of Meaning   Conflict situations, like all other communication encounters, involve both the content level and the relationship level of meaning. Yet, many of us tend to focus on the content level of meaning: the issues or the problem.

Focusing on the content level of meaning is understandable, but it's not enough, because it neglects a major dimension of communication. We need to tune into relationship-level meanings also. Who is she saying she is (my friend, my superior, my teacher)? Is he being responsive, showing liking, demonstrating power? What does this suggest about the relationship between us (it is not in jeopardy, its continuation depends on how we resolve this conflict)? It's equally important to monitor the relationship level of your own communication. Are you saying you care about getting your way more than you care about the relationship or other person? Are you communicating respect, attentiveness, or superiority? Are you attacking a co-worker personally instead of arguing about issues? Are you affirming the relationship, even though there is a difference at the moment? During conflict, it's critical to think carefully about relationship-level messages and meanings.

Communicate Supportively   An important conflict management skill is to monitor your communication to ensure that it encourages a supportive climate that is likely to build a win–win approach to conflict. From our discussion in Chapter 8, you'll recall that supportive interpersonal climates are cultivated by communication that is descriptive, provisional, spontaneous, problem oriented, empathic, and egalitarian. It's also useful to remind ourselves of the kinds of communication that tend to generate defensive climates: evaluation, certainty, strategies, control orientation, neutrality, and superiority. In conflict situations, we may be especially likely to engage in communication that fosters defensiveness and reduces the possibilities for resolving the conflict and sustaining the relationship.

Listen Mindfully   You already know that mindful listening is a very important interpersonal communication skill. This is especially true in conflict because we may not want to consider the other person's ideas or criticisms of our ideas. Even when you disagree with someone's thoughts, actions, goals, or values, you should show respect for the person by paying attention and seeking to understand him or her. That can be really difficult if the other person is not practicing effective communication skills. For example, imagine this scene: One evening, the person you've been dating greets you by griping, "You're late again. Why can't you ever be on time?" That kind of attack tends to make us feel defensive, so a natural reply might be, "What's your problem? Don't make a big deal out of 5 minutes. Get off my case." However, this kind of retort is likely to fan the flames of discord. A more effective reply would be, "I'm sorry I kept you waiting. I didn't know being on time was so important to you." This response acknowledges your lateness, shows respect for the other person's feelings, and opens the door to a conversation.

Take Responsibility for Your Thoughts, Feelings, and Issues *I* language is a cornerstone of effective conflict management. Own your feelings: "I feel angry when you are late" instead of "You make me angry with your lateness." It's also important to own your thoughts and your issues. "We need to keep this apartment cleaner" is a statement that you want the apartment cleaner. The other person may not care, in which case it's not accurate to say, "*We* need to keep this apartment cleaner." The issue is yours, so you should own it by saying, "I am uncomfortable with how messy this place is. Can we figure out a way to deal with this?"

Check Perceptions Perceptions are easily distorted when conflict is afoot. You may see another person's position as more extreme than it is; you may think someone is immature or unreasonable; you may be inclined to engage in self-serving bias, which we discussed in Chapter 3. During conflict, we need to check our perceptions. Paraphrasing is one effective way to do this: "So you think we should spend every weekend cleaning our apartment?" "Does it seem to you that I'm always late?" We can also check perceptions by asking direct questions, being careful to avoid communication that fosters defensiveness: "What would be clean enough for you?" "Is it the 5 minutes I'm late that's bothering you, or does lateness mean something else to you?"

Checking perceptions is particularly important in online communication. I recently read a colleague's paper and e-mailed a response in which I suggested she strengthen one part of her analysis. She replied: "Okay." I wondered if the short reply meant I had offended her with my suggestions, so I called her and said, "I don't know what your 'okay' means. Are you angry about my suggestion?" She replied that she had been rushed and so had typed only a quick response. Paraphrasing and asking questions say, "You matter to me. I'm trying to understand you."

Look for Points of Agreement During conflict, we tend to focus on disagreements or ways we differ from another person. Although we should acknowledge and deal with real differences, we should also look for points of agreement. You and a friend may disagree on goals, values, or courses of action, but you probably agree on other matters related to a conflict episode. Returning to the previous example, you and your date may disagree on whether being 5 minutes late is important. However, you may also share a belief that people who care about each other respect each other's feelings. This shared belief is common ground that may help you work out a resolution to the conflict. If we are looking for common ground, we can usually find it. When we do, we're likely to deal with conflict effectively without harming the relationship.

Look for Ways to Preserve the Other's Face In Japan and some other Asian cultures, *face* is a central concept. Your face is the image of yourself that you want others to see and believe (McDaniel & Quasha, 2000). We are embarrassed or ashamed when we lose face. Whereas Western cultures tend to emphasize protecting one's own face, many Asian cultures emphasize the importance of protecting others' faces (Ting-Toomey, 1988; Ting-Toomey & Oetzel, 2001, 2002). The goal is for no one to feel defeated, stupid, or embarrassed.

Protecting others' faces is part of managing conflict effectively. If your point or idea is accepted in an argument, be gracious toward the other person. He or she is likely to feel face is lost if you say, "I knew you'd come around." If you are committed to protecting the other person's face, you might say, "I appreciate your generosity in understanding how important this is to me." This statement allows the person who may have lost the argument to retain dignity and save face.

Imagine How You'll Feel in the Future   Recall that, in Chapter 4, we noted that one of our symbolic abilities is hypothetical thought. Among other things, this capacity allows us to imagine ourselves in the future and to respond to the future self that we imagine. You can use this ability to help you manage conflict effectively. To illustrate, consider this scenario: A friend has just told you that he borrowed your car without asking and had a minor accident. You feel like shouting and attacking the friend verbally.

Before you say anything, you imagine how you would feel tomorrow or next week or next year if you launched a scathing attack on your friend. Then, you imagine how you would feel tomorrow or next week or next year if you expressed your anger calmly yet not aggressively, showed concern about whether your friend was hurt in the accident, and found a way to help your friend save face. You probably prefer the you who behaved considerately to the you who was combative. Taking a moment to imagine yourself after the conflict ends can help you choose to communicate in ways that are ethical, that foster self-respect, and that support the continuation of the relationship.

The eight skills we've discussed translate general communication skills and principles into the specific context of interpersonal conflict. Developing competence in these eight skills will empower you to manage conflict competently, graciously, and effectively. Figure 9.3 summarizes skills for managing conflict productively.

Guidelines for Effective Communication during Conflict

Our study of conflict, along with many of the ideas we've considered in previous chapters, suggests five guidelines for dealing with conflict constructively.

FOCUS ON THE OVERALL COMMUNICATION SYSTEM

As we noted in Chapter 1, communication is systemic, which means it occurs in contexts, and it is composed of many interacting parts. Applying the principle of systems to conflict, we can see that how we deal with conflict is shaped by the overall systems of relationships and communication.

Attend to relationship-level meanings.

Communicate supportively.

Listen mindfully.

Own your feelings, thoughts, and issues.

Check perceptions.

Look for points of agreement.

Look for ways to preserve the other's face.

Imagine how you will feel in the future.

FIGURE 9.3
Conflict Management Skills

People who have developed negative interpersonal climates cannot argue constructively simply by practicing "good conflict techniques" such as focusing talk and not interrupting. Those techniques occur within larger contexts that affect how they are interpreted. People who have learned to be generally defensive and distrustful are unlikely to respond openly to even the best conflict resolution methods. By the same reasoning, in climates that are generally supportive and confirming, even unconstructive conflict communication is unlikely to derail relationships. Conflict, like all interaction, is affected by larger contexts in which it takes place.

In other words, conflict is part of a larger whole, and we must make that whole healthy to create a context in which conflict can be resolved without jeopardizing partners or relationships. Keep in mind that conflict always has implications for three parties: you, another person, and the relationship between the two of you. Healthy conflict communication honors all three.

TIME CONFLICT PURPOSEFULLY

Timing affects how we communicate about conflicts. There are three ways to use chronemics so that conflicts are most likely to be effective. First, try not to engage in serious conflict discussions at times when one or both people will not be fully present psychologically.

Most of us are less attentive, less mindful listeners when we are tired. It's generally more productive to discuss problems in private rather than in public settings (Cupach & Carlson, 2002). If time is limited or if we are rushing, we're less likely to take the time to deal constructively with differences. It's impossible to listen well and respond thoughtfully when a stopwatch is ticking in our minds.

It's also considerate and constructive to deal with conflict when each person is ready to talk constructively about a problem. Of course, this works only if the person who isn't ready agrees to talk about the issue at a later time. Because research indicates that men are more likely than women to avoid discussing relationship conflicts, they may be especially reluctant to talk about disagreements without first gaining some distance (Beck, 1988; Rusbult, 1987). Some people prefer to tackle problems as soon as they arise, whereas others need time to percolate privately before interacting. It's generally a good idea not to discuss conflict in the heat of anger. For the same reason, it's wise to save an e-mail reply you write when angry to see if that's what you want to send when you've cooled down. Constructive, healthy conflict communication is more likely when tempers aren't flaring.

> **STEPHANIE** I have a really hot temper, so I can cut someone to pieces if I argue when I'm mad. I have hurt a lot of friends by attacking them before I cooled off, and I hate myself when I act like that. I have finally figured out that I can handle fights constructively if I cool down. Now when I'm hot, I tell my friends or my boyfriend that I can't discuss it right then. Later, when I'm calm, I can talk without saying things that hurt them and that I feel bad about.

A third use of chronemics to promote positive conflict is bracketing, which we discussed earlier in this chapter. It is natural for a variety of issues needing attention to come up in the course of conflict. If we try to deal with all the sideline problems that arise, however, we can't focus on the immediate problem. Bracketing other concerns for later discussion lets us keep conflict focused productively. Keep in mind, however, that bracketing works only if partners return to the issues they set aside.

AIM FOR WIN–WIN CONFLICT

How you approach conflict shapes what will happen in communication. When conflict exists between two people who care about each other and want to sustain a good relationship, however, the win–win style is usually the best choice. If you enter conflict with the assumption that you, the other person, and the relationship can all benefit from conflict, it's likely that you will bring about a resolution that benefits everyone. Adopting a win–win orientation to conflict reflects a commitment to honoring yourself, the other person, and the integrity of your shared relationship.

To maximize the chance of a win–win conflict resolution, begin by identifying your feelings and your needs or desires in the situation. You may want to review Chapter 7 to remind yourself of ways to clarify your emotions. Understanding what your feelings and desires are is essential to productive conflict communication. Once you figure out what you feel and need, express yourself in clear language. It's not effective to make vague or judgmental statements such as, "I don't like the way you ignore me, and I want you to be more sensitive." It would be more effective to say, "I feel hurt when you don't call, and I want us to find some way that I can be assured of your love without making you feel handcuffed."

The second step is to figure out what the other person feels, needs, and wants. If you don't already know what the other person wants and feels, don't mind read. Instead, ask the other person what she or he is feeling and what she or he needs or wants in terms of a resolution to the conflict. When the other person expresses feelings and preferences, listen mindfully. Resist the temptation to countercomplain. Just listen, and try to understand the other person's perspective as fully as you can. Minimal encouragers and paraphrasing let the other person know you are listening closely and are committed to understanding her or his perspective.

Third, focus on language that promotes cooperation and mutual respect. To do this, rely on supportive communication, and try to avoid communication that fosters a defensive climate. You should also use *I* language to own your thoughts and feelings. Throughout conflict communication, mindful listening allows you to gain the maximum understanding of the other person's perspective and feelings.

Finally, keep reminding yourself that win–win solutions are most likely when both people balance concern for themselves and concern for each other. On the relationship level of meaning, you want to communicate this message: "I care about you and your feelings and desires, and I know you care about me and how I feel and what I want." If that message underlies your conflict communication, chances are good that you will attain a win–win resolution.

HONOR YOURSELF, YOUR PARTNER, AND THE RELATIONSHIP

Throughout this book, we've emphasized the importance of honoring yourself, others, and relationships. It's important to keep all three in balance, especially when conflicts arise.

Constructive conflict communication is impossible if we disregard or demean the other person's needs and feelings. Doing so disconfirms the other and sets a win–lose tone for conversation. It is equally undesirable to muffle your own needs and feelings. In fairness to yourself and the other person, you should express your feelings and needs clearly.

Reprinted from *The Chronicle of Higher Education* with the permission of Carole Cable.

*"Look, instead of constantly grading one another,
let's make this a simple pass/fail relationship."*

In addition to attending to ourselves and others, we must remember that relationships are affected by how we handle conflict. For this reason, win–lose orientations toward conflict should really be called win–lose–lose, because when only one person wins, both the other person and the relationship lose. Win–win orientations and constructive forms of communication make it possible for both individuals and the relationship to win.

© David Bitters/Index Stock Imagery

SHOW GRACE WHEN APPROPRIATE

Finally, an important principle to keep in mind during conflict is that grace is sometimes appropriate. **Grace** is granting forgiveness or putting aside our own needs when there is no standard that says we should or must do so. Grace is not forgiving when we *should* (for instance, excusing people who aren't responsible for their actions).

Also, grace isn't allowing others to have their way when we have no choice. Instead, grace is unearned, unrequired kindness. For instance, two roommates agree to split chores, and one doesn't do her share, because she has three tests in a week. Her roommate might do all the chores even though there is no agreement or expectation of this generosity. This is an act of grace. It's also an act of grace to defer to another person's preference when you could hold out for your own. Similarly, when someone hurts us and has no right to expect forgiveness, we may choose to forgive anyway. We do so not because we have to but because we want to. Grace is a matter of choice.

Grace involves letting go of anger, blame, and judgments about another and what she or he did. When we let go of these feelings, we release both ourselves and others from their consequences. Sometimes, we tell a friend that we forgive him for some offense, but then later we remind him of it. When we hang on to blame and judgment, we haven't really let go, so we have not really shown grace. There's no grace when we blackmail others for our kindness or hang on to hostile feelings.

Grace is given without strings. Arthur Osborne (1996), who believes grace is essential in loving relationships, makes this point clearly when he says, "The person who asks for a reward is a merchant, not a lover" (p. 6). We show kindness, defer our needs, or forgive a wrong without any expectation of reward. Grace isn't doing something nice to make a friend feel grateful or indebted to us. Nor do we act in grace when we do something with the expectation of a payback. To do a favor because you want a reciprocal favor is bargaining, not showing grace. For an act to be one of grace, it must be done without conditions or expectations of return.

Grace is not always appropriate. People can take advantage of grace and kindness. Some people repeatedly abuse and hurt others, confident that pardons will be granted. When grace is extended and then exploited, it may be unwise to extend it again to the same person. However, if you show grace in good faith, and another abuses it, you should not fault yourself. Kindness and a willingness to forgive are worthy ethical values. The richest and most enduring relationships allow room for grace occasionally.

It is important to honor and assert ourselves, as we've emphasized throughout this book. However, self-interest and self-assertion alone are insufficient ethical principles for creating rich interpersonal relationships. None of us is perfect. We all make mistakes, wound others with thoughtless acts, and occasionally do things we know are wrong and hurtful. Sometimes, there is no reason others should forgive us when we wrong them; we have no right to expect exoneration.

R. Walters (1984) offers a moving insight about the role of grace in human relationships. He says, "When we have been hurt we have two alternatives: be destroyed by resentment, or forgive. Resentment is death; forgiving leads to healing and life" (p. 366). For human relationships to live and thrive, there must be some room for redemption, for forgiveness, and for grace. *Student Companion:* Activity 9.5.

INSIGHT

Communication in Everyday Life
The Communication of Forgiveness

What do you do when you feel betrayed by someone with whom you are close? What do you do when you betray someone you love? These questions come up in most relationships that endure over time.

Douglas Kelley (1998) is a communication scholar and a relationship counselor. In both his research and clinical work, he emphasizes forgiveness as a major influence on how—or whether—relationships progress. Kelley assumes that transgressions both minor and major are inevitable in relationships, so the question becomes, How do couples go forward after harm has been done?

Kelley reports that one crucial dynamic in the forgiveness process is motivations, those of both the transgressor and the forgiver.

Forgiveness is most likely to occur and to allow relationship continuity when both parties are motivated by a desire to restore the well-being of themselves, each other, and the relationship. How willing a person is to forgive a wrong depends in part on what the offender communicates. People are more likely to grant forgiveness to a person who apologizes, expresses remorse, or takes responsibility for the wrong. Kelley also finds that the capacity to forgive is enhanced if the forgiver can reframe the hurtful event by gaining understanding into it, attributing it to factors beyond the offender's control, or viewing it as unintentional.

Finally, Kelley emphasizes that forgiving is a process, not an event that occurs in a single moment. He emphasizes that, even after forgiveness is granted, time is needed to heal a relationship, restore trust, and return to healthy, comfortable interaction.

Adding to Kelley's work is a study by William Cupach and Christine Carlson (2002). They found that forgiveness is more than a set of behaviors and more than efforts to overcome negative feelings, such as wanting revenge. At least as important, they report, is a readiness to forgive—a desire to accept and confirm another, even—or especially—after a transgression of some sort.

The Forgiveness Institute has a website that includes a reading room, message boards, related links, and information about upcoming conferences and workshops: http://www.forgivenessweb.com/.

Case Study: Continuing the Conversation

The following conversation is featured on the Everyday Connections website under "Chapter Resources for Chapter 9." Click on the link "Jan & Ken" to launch the video and audio scenario scripted below.

Jason Harris/© 2001 Wadsworth

Ken: Jan, we need to talk. Why'd you tell Shannon about what happened between Katie and me? Now, Shannon doesn't want to talk to me.

Jan: Ken, I'm sorry, I didn't mean to tell her. It just kind of slipped out when we were talking.

Ken: Sorry? Sorry is not enough. I told you that in private, and you promised that you'd keep it just between you and me.

Jan: Ken, I told her that long before the two of you started dating. You know, Shannon and I, we've been friends for a long time. We were just talking about guys and cheating and stuff. It wasn't about you specifically.

Ken: It wasn't about me? It was totally about me. You had no right to tell anyone that, under any circumstances. Now, Shannon doesn't trust me. She thinks I'm a low-life who sleeps around.

Jan: Well, I'm sorry, but the two of you weren't even dating yet.

Ken: That's irrelevant. You know, it would be irrelevant even if Shannon and I weren't dating. But the point is that I thought I could trust you and tell you anything and that it would go no further.

Jan: Yeah, like the time I told you I was thinking about dropping out of school for a semester and you just happened to tell my dad?

Ken: Ah, that's not the same thing.

Jan: You know what, it's exactly the same! I trusted you, and you squealed. My dad lit into me big time. He should have never known I was thinking about that. I trusted you, and you betrayed me!

Ken: Don't change the subject. Are you saying that you telling Shannon is some sort of payback for me telling your dad?

Jan: No, I'm just trying to point out that you've got no right to throw stones!

Ken: You know what? Maybe neither of us can trust the other. Maybe we just shouldn't tell each other anything that we don't want broadcast to the world, huh?

Jan: Don't be such a jerk. I'm sorry, okay?

Ken: Well, that's not good enough. You ruined any chance I had with her.

1. Can you think of ways Ken might open this conversation more productively? Review the chapters on language and emotions to suggest ways he might more clearly express his feelings and might rely more on *I* language.

2. Identify communication by both Ken and Jan that fosters defensiveness between them. How could they change their communication to create a more supportive climate for discussing this issue?

3. Identify examples of countercomplaints.

4. How do you perceive Jan's effort to convince Ken to forgive her? Based on what you've learned in this chapter, can you suggest ways she might more effectively seek Ken's forgiveness?

5. How might bracketing help Jan and Ken deal with their conflict?

6. The conversation—as it has progressed so far—seems to be framed in a win–lose format. Each person wants to be right, to prevail. How might Ken and Jan move their conflict discussion into a win–win framework?

7. Review the eight conflict management skills discussed in this chapter. Identify examples of these skills in the dialogue between Jan and Ken. Identify places in the dialogue where Ken and Jan missed opportunities to manage conflict skillfully.

You can critique and analyze this encounter based on the principles you learned in this chapter by responding to the questions included under "Conversation Analysis" at the website. By clicking on the "Submit" button at the end of the form, you can compare your work to my suggested responses. Let's continue the conversation online!

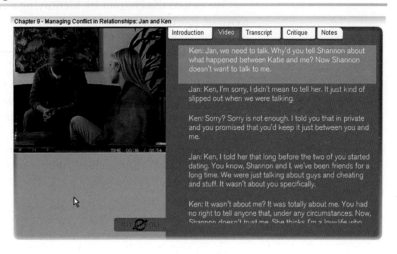

Chapter 9 - Managing Conflict in Relationships: Jan and Ken

| Introduction | Video | Transcript | Critique | Notes |

Ken: Jan, we need to talk. Why'd you tell Shannon about what happened between Katie and me? Now Shannon doesn't want to talk to me.

Jan: Ken, I'm sorry, I didn't mean to tell her. It just kind of slipped out when we were talking.

Ken: Sorry? Sorry is not enough. I told you that in private and you promised that you'd keep it just between you and me.

Jan: Ken, I told her that long before the two of you started dating. You know, Shannon and I, we've been friends for a long time. We were just talking about guys and cheating and stuff. It wasn't about you specifically.

Ken: It wasn't about me? It was totally about me. You had no right to tell anyone that, under any circumstances. Now, Shannon doesn't trust me. She thinks I'm a lowlife who...

Chapter Summary

Because conflicts are normal and unavoidable in any relationship of real depth, the challenge is to learn to manage conflicts effectively. Patterns of conflict are shaped by how people view conflict. We discussed lose–lose, win–lose, and win–win approaches to conflict and explored how each affects interaction. In addition, conflict patterns are influenced by how people respond to tension. Inclinations to exit, neglect, show loyalty, or voice conflict vary in how actively they deal with tension and how constructive they are for relationships. In most cases, voice is the preferred response because only voice allows partners to intervene actively and constructively when conflicts arise.

Communication is a particularly important influence on interpersonal conflict. Communication skills that promote constructive conflict management include being mindful, confirming others, showing dual perspective, listening sensitively, focusing discussion, contracting solutions, and avoiding mind reading, interrupting, self-summarizing, and cross-complaining.

We closed the chapter by identifying five guidelines for increasing the productivity of interpersonal conflict. First, we need to remember that conflicts occur within overall systems of communication and relationships. To be constructive, conflict must take place within supportive, confirming climates in which good interpersonal communication is practiced. Second, it's important to time conflicts so that all people have the time they need for private reflection and for productive discussion. A third principle is to aim for win–win solutions to conflict. Consistent with these three guidelines is working to balance commitments to yourself, others, and relationships when conflict arises.

Although grace can be exploited, it can also infuse relationships with kindness and make room for inevitable human errors. It's important to balance the tensions inherent in the notion of grace so that we recognize both its potential values and its dangers.

Everyday Connections Online

Now that you've read Chapter 9, go to the Everyday Connections premium website at academic.cengage.com/communication/woodinterpersonal5plus for quick access to the electronic study resources that accompany this text. The website gives you access to the "Continuing the Conversation" video scenario and questions featured in this chapter, to InfoTrac College Edition, to maintained and updated

Web links, and to the study aids for this chapter, including a digital glossary, review quizzes, and the chapter activities. For more information about this text's electronic learning resources, consult the **1pass card** that came with each new copy of this book, or visit academic.cengage.com/communication/woodinterpersonal5.

Key Concepts

Audio flash cards of the following key terms are available on the Everyday Connections website. Use the flash cards to improve your pronunciation of text vocabulary.

bracketing	grace	loyalty response	win–lose
contracting	interpersonal conflict	neglect response	win–win
exit response	kitchen-sinking	passive aggression	
games	lose–lose	voice response	

For Further Thought and Discussion

1. What ethical principles are implicit in lose-lose, win–lose, and win–win orientations to conflict? Some styles of conflict emphasize fairness, whereas other styles place greater value on cooperation. Do you identify more strongly with either of these value emphases?

2. Think about the ways you typically respond to conflict. Do you tend to rely on one or two of the four responses we discussed (exit, voice, loyalty, neglect)? Are your response tendencies consistent with research findings about women and men, in general?

3. Have you ever been in a relationship in which conflict was stifled? Using the concepts you learned in this chapter, can you now describe how the conflict was repressed? Can you now think of ways you might have engaged in more effective conflict communication in that relationship?

4. Identify one situation in your life in which each orientation to conflict was, or would have been, appropriate. When would lose-lose have been appropriate? When would win-lose have been a reasonable approach? When would win-win have been the best approach?

5. Use your InfoTrac College Edition to read Esin Tezer's and Ayhan Demir's 2001 article, "Conflict Behaviors Toward Same-Sex and Opposite-Sex Peers Among Male and Female Late Adolescents," published in *Adolescence*. Are the reported differences in males' and females' conflict orientations consistent with your personal experiences and observations?

6. This chapter emphasizes aiming for a win-win approach to conflict in personal relationships. Do you believe that, in most cases, both people can benefit (or win) if each is committed to honoring self and other?

7. Have you been in relationships in which you felt there was grace? How was grace communicated? What was the impact of grace? Have you extended grace to others? Use your InfoTrac College Edition to review recent issues of *Religious Studies*. Do authors address issues such as grace, forgiveness, and kindness toward others? How do their views correspond with those in this chapter?

8. To learn about common conflicts in families and ways people deal with them, go to http://www.suite101.com/welcome.cfm/family_conflict_resolution. The site provides articles, discussions, and links to other websites.

Friendships in Our Lives

"The most holy bond of society is friendship."

Mary Wollstonecraft

Image Source RF/Getty Images

For most of us, friends are important. Friends help us pass time, figure out problems, grow personally, celebrate moments of joy, and get through hard times. Across differences in race, gender, class, and sexual orientation, most of us expect friends to provide intimacy, acceptance, trust, practical assistance, and support. These are common threads in diverse friendships. However, people differ in how they express trust, intimacy, acceptance, and support in friendship.

In this chapter, we explore what friendships are, how they work, and how they differ among people. To launch our discussion, we identify common features of friendship and then point out variations across cultures and social communities. Second, we explore the typical developmental path of friendships and some of the common rules for friendships. Next, we consider pressures on friendship and how we can deal with them. Guidelines for effective communication between friends conclude the chapter.

· · · · · · · · · ·

The Nature of Friendship

Friendship is a unique relationship. Unlike most relationships, friendship is voluntary. Biology or legal procedures establish relationships between family members, and proximity defines neighbors and co-workers. However, friends come together voluntarily. Unlike marital and family relationships, friendships lack institutionalized structure or guidelines. There are legal and religious ceremonies for marriage, social and legal rules that govern family relationships. We have no parallel ceremonies to recognize friendships and no formal standards to guide interaction between friends.

WILL It's funny. Kids have ways to symbolize friendship, but adults don't. I remember when Jimmy down the block and I became blood brothers. It was a big, big deal for me at 8. My sister and her best friend bought matching friendship rings and wore them until their fingers turned green. But what do we have to symbolize friendships when we grow up?

Even though there are no formal standards for friendship, people within a culture hold some fairly consistent ideas about what a friend is and what happens between friends. Regardless of race, sexual orientation, gender, age, and class, Westerners share basic expectations of friends and friendship.

WILLINGNESS TO INVEST

Friendships are built on personal investments, which we discussed in Chapter 8 (Duck & Wright, 1993; Monsour, 1992). We expect to invest time, effort, thought, and feeling in our friendships. Regardless of sexual orientation, women and men say that friends are important in their lives (Mazur, 1989; Nardi & Sherrod, 1994; Parks & Floyd, 1996b; Sherrod, 1989).

LAKISHA I don't know what I'd do without my friends. More than once, they've held me together when I had a fight with my mom or broke up with a guy. When something good happens, it's not quite real until I share it with my friends. I don't think I could be happy without friends.

DENNIS I really count on my buddies to be there for me. Sometimes, we talk or do stuff, but a lot of times we just hang out together. That might not sound important, but it is. Hanging out with friends is a big part of my life.

Everyday Application
Your Style of Friendship

Before reading further, answer the following questions about how you experience and express closeness with friends. With your closest or best friends, how often do you do the following things?

1. Talk about family problems
2. Exchange favors (provide transportation, lend money)
3. Engage in sports (shoot hoops, play tennis, and so forth)
4. Try to take their minds off problems with diversions
5. Disclose your personal anxieties and fears
6. Talk about your romantic relationships and family relationships
7. Do things together (camp, go to a game, shop)
8. Confide secrets you wouldn't want others to know
9. Just hang out without a lot of conversation
10. Talk about small events in your day-to-day life
11. Provide practical assistance to help friends
12. Talk explicitly about your feelings for each other
13. Discuss and work through tensions in your friendship
14. Physically embrace or touch to show affection
15. Ignore or work around problems in the friendship

Items 1, 5, 6, 8, 10, 12, 13, and 14 have been found to be more prominent in women's friendships. Items 2, 3, 4, 7, 9, 11, and 15 tend to be more pronounced in men's friendships.

To recognize different styles of experiencing and expressing closeness in friendship, complete Activity 10.1 in your *Student Companion* or online under "Chapter Resources for Chapter 10" at the Everyday Connections website.

© Roy Morsch/CORBIS Stock Market

EMOTIONAL CLOSENESS

With friends, we want to feel emotionally close. Emotional intimacy grows out of investments, such as time, talk, and shared experiences, and out of becoming familiar and comfortable being together. Although most people agree that closeness is central to close friendships, we have different ideas about what intimacy is. Research on friendship suggests that sex and gender influence how we experience and express intimacy with friends.

Closeness through Dialogue If you found items 1, 5, 6, 8, 10, 12, 13, and 14 in the "Everyday Application" above more true of your friendships, then you regard communication as the centerpiece of friendship. This is especially true for people socialized in feminine speech communities, which emphasize talk as a primary path to intimacy. In general, women see talking and listening as the main activities that create and sustain closeness (Aries, 1987; Becker, 1987; Rubin, 1985). Talk between women friends tends to be disclosive and emotionally expressive (Maccoby, 1998). Women discuss not only major issues but also day-to-day activities. This small talk isn't really small at all, because it allows friends to understand the rhythms of each other's lives (Braithwaite & Kellas, 2006; Metts, 2006). Out of intimate conversation, friends build a deep sense of connection.

A majority of women expect to know and be known intimately by close friends (Johnson, 1996). This is also true of androgynous men, who incorporate both feminine and masculine values into their identities (Jones & Dembo, 1989; Williams, 1985). They want friends to know and understand their inner selves, and they want to know their friends in the same emotional depth.

> **LORI ANN** My girlfriends and I know everything about each other. We tell all our feelings and don't hold anything back. I mean, it's total knowledge. We give updates on each new episode in our relationships, and we talk about what it means. There's just nothing I wouldn't tell my friends.

Reflecting feminine socialization, communication between women friends typically is responsive and supportive (Chatham-Carpenter & DeFrancisco, 1998; Wright & Scanlon, 1991). Animated facial expressions and head movements convey involvement and emotional response. In addition, women friends ask questions and give feedback to signal that they are following and want to know more. Women friends also tend to give emotional support to one another. They do this by accepting one another's feelings and staying involved in the other's dreams, problems, and lives.

Closeness through Doing A second way to create and express closeness is by sharing activities. Friends enjoy doing things together and doing things for one another. Items 2, 3, 4, 7, 9, 11, and 15 in the "Everyday Application" on page 274 reflect this approach to intimacy. Closeness through doing often is the primary, but not the only, emphasis in men's friendships (Harris, 1998; Inman, 1996; Metts, 2006; Monsour, in press; Swain, 1989; Wood & Inman, 1993). Given the focus on doing things together, it's not surprising that male friends are more likely to negotiate activities ("Are we going to play racquetball or go skating?") than female friends or male and female friends (Samter & Cupach, 1998). Sharing activities and working toward common goals (winning the game, getting the contract) build a sense of camaraderie (Inman, 1996; Sherrod, 1989).

> **JOSH** The thing I like about my buddies is that we can just do stuff together without a lot of talk. Our wives expect us to talk about every feeling we have, as if that's required to be real. I'm tight with my buddies, but we don't have to talk about feelings all the time. You learn a lot about someone when you hunt together or coach the Little League.

Josh has a good insight. We reveal ourselves and learn about others by doing things together. In the course of playing football or soccer, teammates learn a lot about one another's courage, reliability, willingness to take risks, and security. Soldiers who fight together also discover one another's strengths and weaknesses. Strong emotional bonds and

© Larry Williams/CORBIS

© Amy Etra/PhotoEdit, Inc.

personal knowledge can develop without verbal interaction (Rubin, 1985). Intimacy through doing also involves expressing care by doing things for friends. Scott Swain (1989) says men's friendships typically involve a give-and-take of favors. Jake helps Matt move into his new apartment, and Matt later helps Jake install a new program on his computer. Perhaps because masculine socialization emphasizes instrumental activities, men are more likely than women to see doing things for others as a primary way to say they care.

It would be a mistake to conclude that women and men are radically different in how they create intimacy. They are actually more alike than we often think (Canary & Dindia, 1998; Parks & Floyd, 1996b). Although women generally place a special priority on communication, men obviously talk with their friends. Like women, men disclose personal feelings and vulnerabilities. They simply do it less, as a rule, than women. Similarly, although men's friendships may be more instrumental, women friends also do things with and for one another and count these as important in friendship (Duck & Wright, 1993).

Everyday Application
Appreciating Talking and Doing in Friendships

For each of the following scenarios, write out one thing you might say and one thing you might do to show you care about the person described.

1. Your best friend has just broken up with his/her long-term boyfriend/girlfriend. Your friend calls you and says, "I feel so lonely."
   You say_____
   You do _____
2. A good friend of yours tells you he/she has been cut from the team and won't get to play this year.
   You say_____
   You do _____
3. Your best friend from high school calls and says she/he thinks about you often even though the two of you no longer maintain much contact.
   You say_____
   You do _____
4. A close friend stops you on campus and excitedly says, "I just found out I've been accepted into the law school here. Can you believe it?"
   You say_____
   You do _____

To learn more about similarities and differences between women's and men's friendships, use your InfoTrac College Edition. Into the EasyTrac subject search, type the word *friendship*. Scroll down until you find the article by Roseanne Roy, Joyce Benenson, and Fray Lilly that appeared in 2000 in the *Journal of Psychology*, Volume 134.

Sometimes, different emphases on instrumental and expressive behaviors lead to misunderstandings. If Myra sees intimate talk as the crux of closeness, she may not interpret Ed's practical help in fixing her computer as indicating that he cares about her.

> **KAYA** My husband's life centers on doing things for me and our kids. He looks for things to do for us. Like when our son came home over break, he tuned up his car and replaced a tire. I hadn't even noticed the tire was bad. When I wanted to return to school, he took a second job to make more money. One day, he came home with a microwave to make cooking easier for me. All the things he does for us are his way of expressing love.

ACCEPTANCE

We expect friends to accept us, including our flaws. Each of us has shortcomings and vices, but we count on friends to accept us in spite of them. With people we don't know well, we often feel we need to put on our best face to impress them. With friends, however, we don't want to put up false fronts. If we feel low, we can act that way instead of faking cheerfulness. If we are upset, we don't have to hide it. We expect friends to accept us as we are and as we change over time (Adams & Allan, 1999; Yager, 1999).

As we saw with Maslow's hierarchy of human needs in Chapter 1, being accepted by others is important to our sense of self-worth. Most of us are fortunate enough to gain acceptance from family and friends. However, this is not always true. Some parents of gays and lesbians, for example, refuse to validate their children's basic worth.

> **MARTIN** It isn't just the homosexual who is outed. Everyone in that person's life is affected when he comes out. My ex-wife was devastated when I told her I was gay. She felt it said something about her as a woman. My father and stepmother are homophobic. They are more fearful of how friends and family will judge them than they are concerned with my issues. My coming out was all about their embarrassment and fear.

Because social and familial acceptance sometimes is lacking for them, gay men and lesbians may count on friends for acceptance even more than heterosexuals do (Nardi & Sherrod, 1994; Roberts & Orbe, 1996). Friendships may have heightened importance because they often substitute for families, as reflected in the title of Kath Weston's 1991 book, *Families We Choose*. Although lesbians and gay men may depend more heavily than heterosexuals on friends for acceptance, research has not identified major differences in how their friendships operate. Like heterosexuals, gay men and lesbians value friendship and rely on both talking and doing as paths to intimacy.

> **MATTIE** I knew my parents wouldn't be pleased that I was seeing someone of another race, but I didn't think they'd go totally into orbit. When I finally got the nerve to tell them about Sheldon, they went nuts. You would have thought I had told them I'd grown a third leg or was hooked on drugs. They yelled at me that they hadn't raised me to "be like that." They threatened to disown me if I didn't stop seeing Sheldon. They said I was immoral and was bringing shame on my whole family. They never even asked what Sheldon is like or what he wants to do or anything about him.

Mattie and Martin feel their parents totalize them by focusing on a single aspect of their lives and ignoring everything else about them. They are still students, loving children, people who have dreams, ambitions, hopes, and fears. Yet, they feel that their parents see them only in terms of sexual orientation or interracial dating and disregard everything else about them.

TRUST

A key component of close friendships is trust, which has two dimensions. First, trust involves confidence that others will be dependable. We count on them to do what they say and not to do what they promise they won't. Second, trust assumes emotional reliability, which is the belief that a friend cares about us and our welfare. When we feel both dimensions of trust, we feel safe sharing private information with friends, secure in the knowledge that they will not hurt us.

> **SARINI** Trust is the bottom line for friends. It's the single most important thing. It takes me a long time to really trust someone, but when I do, it's complete. I was so hurt when a friend told another person something I told her in confidence. We still get together, but the trust is gone. I don't tell her private things, so there's no depth.

Like most qualities of friendship, trust develops gradually and in degrees. We learn to trust people over time as we interact with them and discover that they do what they say they will and that they don't betray us. As trust develops, friends increasingly reveal themselves to one another. When a high level of trust develops, friends feel less of the uncertainty and insecurity that are natural in early stages of relationships (Boon, 1994).

The level of trust that develops between friends depends on a number of factors. First, our individual histories influence our capacity to trust others. Recalling the discussion of attachment styles in Chapter 2, you'll remember that early interactions with caregivers shape our beliefs about others. For those of us who got consistently loving and nurturing care, trusting others is not especially difficult. On the other hand, some children do not receive that kind of care. If caring is absent or inconsistent, the capacity to trust others is jeopardized.

> **JAMES** It's tough for me to really trust anybody, even my closest friends or my girlfriend. It's not that they aren't trustworthy. The problem's in me. I just have trouble putting full faith in anyone. When my parents had me, Dad was drinking, and Mom was thinking about divorce. He got in Alcoholics Anonymous, and they stayed together, but I wonder if what was happening between them meant they weren't there for me. Maybe I learned from the start that I couldn't count on others.

Family scripts also influence how much and how quickly we trust others. Did your parents have many friends? Did you see them enjoying being with their friends? Were their friends often in your home? How many friends your parents had and how much they seemed to value them may have taught you an early lesson about the importance of friendship in our lives. Basic scripts from families, although not irrevocable, often affect the ease and extent of our ability to trust and our interest in investing in friendships.

Willingness to take risks also influences trust in relationships. In this sense, trust is a leap into the unknown. To emphasize the risk in trusting, it has been said that "trust begins where knowledge ends" (Lewis & Weigert, 1985, p. 462). The risk involved may explain why we trust only selected people.

SUPPORT

Communication scholars Brant Burleson and Wendy Samter (1994) report that support is a basic expectation of friendship. We expect friends to support us in times of personal stress. Once people leave home for college, friends often become the primary people to whom they turn for help and comfort (Adelman, Parks, & Albrecht, 1987).

There are many ways to show support. Common to the various types of support is the relationship message, "I care about you." Often, we support friends by listening to their problems. The more mindfully we listen, the more support we provide. How we respond also shows support. For example, it's supportive to offer to help a friend with a problem or to talk through options. Another way we support friends is by letting them know they're not alone. When we say, "I've felt that way too" or "I've had the same problem," we signal that we understand their feelings. Having the grace to accept friends when they err or hurt us is also a way to show support and validate their worth (Burleson, 1984).

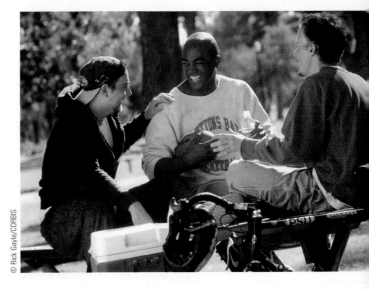
© Rick Gayle/CORBIS

Another important form of support is availability. Sometimes we can't do or say much to ease a friend's unhappiness. However, we can be with friends so that at least they have company in their sadness. In one study, young adults said the essence of real friendship was "being there for each other" (Secklin, 1991). Increasingly, people rely on friends for online support—being there for them when they can't be there physically (Baym, 2002; Carl, 2006). *Student Companion: Activity 10.2.*

> **JOSÉ** Last year, my father died, back in Mexico, and I wasn't with him when he died. I felt terrible. My friend Alex spent a lot of time with me after my father died. Alex didn't do anything special, and we didn't even really talk much about my father or how I felt. But he was there for me, and that meant everything. I knew he cared even though he never said that.

Women and men tend to differ somewhat in how they support friends. Because feminine socialization emphasizes personal communication, women generally provide more verbal emotional support than men do (Aries, 1987; Becker, 1987; Duck & Wright, 1993; Johnson, 2000). They are likely to talk in detail about feelings, dimensions of emotional issues, and fears that accompany distress. By talking in depth about emotional troubles, women help one another identify and vent feelings and work out problems.

> **RICH** If I don't want to think about some problem, I want to be with a guy friend. He'll take my mind off the hassle. If I'm with a girl, she'll want to talk about the problem and wallow in it, and that just makes it worse sometimes. But when I really need to talk or get something off my chest, I need a girl friend. Guys don't talk about personal stuff.

Men often provide support to friends through "covert intimacy," a term Swain (1989) coined to describe the indirect ways men support one another. Instead of an intimate hug, men are more likely to clasp a shoulder or playfully punch an arm. Instead of engaging in direct and sustained emotional talk, men tend to communicate support more instrumentally. This could mean giving advice on how to solve a problem, or offering assistance, such as a loan or transportation. Finally, men are more likely than women to support friends by coming up with diversions (Cancian, 1987; Tavris, 1992). If you can't make a problem any better, at least you can take a friend's mind off it. "Let's throw some darts" provides a diversion.

BELLINO   A year ago, a friend of mine from back home called me up to ask for a loan. I said, "Sure," and asked what was up. He told me his hours had been cut back and he couldn't buy groceries for his family. I knew the problem was more than paying for groceries. I figured he also couldn't pay for lights and rent and everything else. So I talked with several of his friends in our church, and we took up a collection to help him. Then, I took it over and left it at his house without any note and without saying anything. He didn't have to ask for help, and I didn't have to say anything. What I and the others in our congregation did was to do what was needed to help him.

Culture also influences orientations toward friendship. In a study of Japanese and American friendships, Dean Barnlund (1989) found that both groups preferred friends who were similar to them in age and ethnic heritage. Yet, Japanese respondents said togetherness, trust, and warmth were the most important qualities in friendship, whereas Americans listed understanding, respect, and sincerity as the top qualities. The differences in rankings reflect distinctions between Japanese and American culture. Interpersonal harmony and collective orientation are central values in Japan, whereas American culture emphasizes individuality, candor, and respect.

A more recent study by Mary Jane Collier (1996) identified different priorities for friendship in four ethnic groups. European Americans give priority to sincerity and freedom to express ideas. Consistent with traditional Asian cultural values, many Asian Americans especially value courtesy, restraint, and respect for families. Among African Americans in Collier's research, problem solving and respect for ethnic heritage were primary criteria in selecting friends. Collier also found that Latinas and Latinos see relationship support and emotional expressiveness as priorities.

In sum, friendship grows out of investments, intimacy, acceptance, trust, and support. Our membership in different cultures and social communities may lead to variations in how we experience and express these aspects of friendship. However, it seems that these five common expectations (willingness to invest, emotional closeness, acceptance, trust, and support) transcend differences between us.

• • • • • • • • • •

The Development of Friendship

Although intense bonds sometimes are formed quickly, the majority of friendships evolve through a series of stages. Bill Rawlins (1981), an interpersonal communication researcher who focuses on communication between friends, developed a six-stage model of how friendships develop (see Figure 10.1). Although not every friendship follows the sequence in Rawlins's model, many do.

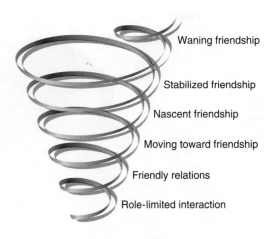

FIGURE 10.1
The Developmental Course of Friendship

The spiral labels from top to bottom read:
- Waning friendship
- Stabilized friendship
- Nascent friendship
- Moving toward friendship
- Friendly relations
- Role-limited interaction

ROLE-LIMITED INTERACTION

We might meet a person at work, through membership on an athletic team, in a club, or by chance in an airport, store, or class. We also might encounter new people in chat rooms or newsgroups (Parks & Floyd, 1996a). The initial meeting is the first stage of interaction and possibly of friendship. During this stage, we tend to rely on standard social rules and roles. We are polite and limit our disclosures.

Because new acquaintances don't have enough personal knowledge of each other to engage in dual perspective, they rely on general scripts and stereotypes. Also, early interactions often are awkward and laced with uncertainty because people haven't worked out patterns for relating to each other.

FRIENDLY RELATIONS

The second stage of friendship is friendly relations, in which each person checks out the other to see whether common ground and interests exist (Weinstock & Bond, 2000). After class, Jean makes a comment about the teacher to Paula. If Paula responds with her impressions of the teacher, she conveys the relationship-level message that she's interested in interacting. A businessperson may joke or engage in small talk to see whether an associate wants to move beyond the acquaintance level of relating. One person in an Internet newsgroup invites another member of the group to engage in individual exchanges.

MOVING TOWARD FRIENDSHIP

In this stage, we start moving beyond social roles. We might make a small self-disclosure to signal that we'd like to personalize the relationship. We also move toward friendship when we meet outside of contexts that naturally occur. Emily might ask her associate Sam whether he wants to get a cup of coffee after work. Ben might ask his classmate Drew to get together to study. Sometimes, we involve others to lessen the potential awkwardness of being with someone we don't yet know well. For instance, Amy might invite Stuart to a party where others will be present.

Many friendships never move beyond this phase (Knapp & Vangelisti, 2005). They stabilize as pleasant but casual friendships. The friends enjoy interacting but generally don't invest a lot of effort to arrange times together. Disclosures tend to be limited, as are investments and expectations of support.

NASCENT FRIENDSHIP

If people continue to interact and to like what they discover in each other, they begin to think of themselves as friends or as becoming friends. This is the stage of nascent, or embryonic, friendship. As we interact more personally with others, we progress to sharing feelings, values, concerns, interests, and so forth.

© Larry Williams/zefa/CORBIS

At this point, friends begin to work out their private rules for interacting. When my friend Nancy and I were in this stage, each Sunday we asked if the other wanted to get together the next Sunday. This was a private rule we generated to accommodate our schedules and to make sure we got together regularly. Some friends settle into patterns of getting together for specific things (watching games, shopping, racquetball, going to movies) and never expand those boundaries. Other friends share a wider range of times and activities. Although during the nascent stage friends are working out rules for their relationship, often they aren't aware of the rules until later. The milestones of this stage are that people begin to think of themselves as friends and to work out their own patterns for interaction.

STABILIZED FRIENDSHIP

The touchstone of this stage is the assumption of continuity. Whereas in earlier stages the people didn't count on getting together unless they made a specific plan, stabilized friends assume they'll continue to see each other even if they don't have specific dates reserved. We take future interaction for granted because we consider the relationship ongoing. Once Nancy and I reached this stage in our friendship, we didn't need to check with each other about getting together—we just assumed that we would.

Another criterion of this stage is trust, which cements friendship. A close friendship is unlikely to stabilize until there is a mutually high level of trust. Once friends have earned each other's trust, many of the barriers to fully interpersonal communication dissolve, and they communicate more openly. Stabilized friendships may continue indefinitely, in some cases lasting a lifetime.

Internet discussions are an increasingly popular way to meet new friends, and e-mail exchanges are a key way in which many people maintain established friendships (Carl, 2006). Nearly two-thirds of the people that Malcolm Parks and Kory Floyd (1996a) surveyed reported that they had a good friendship with someone they first had met in an Internet newsgroup. Parks and Floyd also found that friendships maintained largely through e-mail and Internet communication were as personal and committed as those maintained through face-to-face contact.

Communication in Everyday Life
Maintaining Friendships

Do we spend more time with casual friends or with best friends? The answer might surprise you. Research indicates that frequent interaction is more important for casual friendships than for best friendships (Rose & Serafica, 1986). When casual friends don't see each other, they aren't sure the friendship still exists.

Lack of interaction doesn't appear to threaten relationships between best friends. Close and best friendships depend on assurances of affection, although these need not be frequent. The best explanation is that close and best friends feel more secure in their connection than do casual friends. Because they assume they're continuing parts of each other's lives, best friends don't need regular interaction.

MARLENE Martha and I go way, way back—all the way to childhood, when we lived in the same housing complex. As kids, we made mud pies and ran a lemonade stand together. In high school, we double-dated and planned our lives together. Then we both got married and stayed in touch, even when Martha moved away. We still sent each other pictures of our children, and we called a lot. When my last child entered college, I decided it was time for me to do that, too, so I enrolled in college. Before I did that, though, I had to talk to Martha and get her perspective on whether I was nuts to go to college in my thirties. She thought it was a great idea, and she's thinking about that for herself now. For nearly 40 years, we've shared everything in our lives.

Friendships generally follow rules that specify what is expected and what is not allowed. (Argyle & Henderson, 1985). Most of the time, we're not consciously aware of relationship rules, even though we may be following them. Typically, **relationship rules** are unspoken understandings that regulate how people interact. For instance, most friends have a tacit understanding that they can be a little late for get-togethers but won't keep each other waiting long. A delay of 5 minutes is within the rules, but a 40-minute delay is a violation. Most friends have an unspoken understanding that private information they share is to be kept confidential. The case study at the end of Chapter 9 illustrates what can happen when friends violate the unspoken rule to keep disclosures confidential.

Many rules concern what friends want and expect of each other, such as support, time, and acceptance. Equally important are "shalt not" rules that define what won't be tolerated. For example, friends don't tell others private information we share with them. Most of our "shalt nots" for friendship are inverted forms of the rules for sustaining good friendships. Although friends may never explicitly discuss their rules, the rules matter, as we discover when one is violated.

JUANITA   Celia and I had been friends for 3 years before we decided to share an apartment. After a while, I noticed that my best pair of earrings was missing, and then a gold necklace my father gave me disappeared. Money I was sure I had in my wallet was gone a couple of times. I thought this was strange, but it never occurred to me that Celia would steal from me. Then, one day I needed one of Celia's purses that went with my outfit. She wasn't there, but since we borrowed each other's clothes all the time, I didn't think anything about getting it from her closet. When I opened the purse, I saw my earrings and necklace. I never felt so betrayed in all my life. I asked her to move out that day.

Rules regulate both trivial and important aspects of interaction. Not interrupting may be a rule, but breaking it probably won't destroy a good friendship. However, stealing money, jewelry, or romantic partners may be the death knell of a friendship. Although friends often develop some very unique rules, many of our friendship rules reflect cultural perspectives, as the "Communication in Everyday Life" feature on p. 284 demonstrates.

WANING FRIENDSHIP

When one or both friends stop investing in a friendship, it is likely to wane. Sometimes, friends drift apart because one moves or because the two are pulled in different directions by career or family demands. In other cases, friendships deteriorate because they've run their natural course and have become boring. Many, perhaps most, friendships fade slowly rather than abruptly (Schappell, 2005). A third reason friendships end is violations of trust or other rules friends establish for themselves. Saying "I don't have time for you now" may violate friends' tacit agreement always to make room for each other. Criticizing a friend or not sharing confidences may also breach unspoken rules between friends.

Communication in Everyday Life
Friendships around the World

Like most things, friendship is shaped by culture (Atsumi, 1980; Mochizuki, 1981; Feig, 1989; Goodwin & Plaza, 2000; Lustig & Koester, 1999). In Thailand, friendship is all or nothing. People raised in the United States may be friends with people even if they differ in personal values or political allegiances. Not so in Thailand. Thais generally don't develop friendships with anyone of whom they disapprove in any way. Among Thais, a friend is totally accepted and approved.

The Japanese distinguish between two types of friendships. *Tsukiai* are friendships based on social obligation. These usually involve neighbors or work associates and tend to have limited life spans. Friendships based on affection and common interests usually last a lifetime; personal friendship is serious business. The number of personal friends is very small and stable, in contrast to friendship patterns in the United States. Friendships between women and men are rare in Japan. Before marriage, only 20% of Japanese say they have close friends of the opposite sex.

In Spain, friends are very important both for personal support and to anchor people in the collectivist Spanish culture. In a recent study, Spanish respondents reported that they counted on friends more than on family members to provide emotional support. Friendship support was also linked to self-esteem for Spanish respondents in the study.

CARY Janet and I had been friends since our first year at school. We told each other everything and trusted each other totally. When I told her that Brad had cheated on me, I knew she would not tell anyone else. She knew I felt bad about it, plus Brad and I got back together, so I didn't want anyone to know about that incident. One day, I was talking with another girl, and she asked me how I'd been able to trust Brad again after he cheated on me. I hadn't told her about that! I knew she was friends with Janet, so I figured that's how she knew. To me, that was the ultimate betrayal. I'm still on friendly terms with Janet, but she's not a close friend, and I don't tell her anything private.

When friendships deteriorate or suffer serious violations, communication changes in predictable ways. Defensiveness and uncertainty rise, causing people to be more guarded, less spontaneous, and less disclosive than they were. Communication may also become more controlling and strategic as waning friends try to protect themselves from further exposure and hurt. Yet, the clearest indicator that a friendship is fading may be decreased quantity and quality of communication. As former friends drift apart or are hurt by each other, they are likely to interact less often and to talk about less personal and consequential topics.

Even when serious violations occur between friends, relationships sometimes can be repaired. Sometimes, friends hurt us when they are under serious stress. If we attribute something we don't like to factors beyond their control, we may be willing to forgive them and continue the friendship. We may also be more willing to stay with a friend who has hurt us unintentionally than with one who deliberately harmed us. For a friendship that has waned to be revived, however, both friends must be committed to rebuilding trust and intimacy. *Student Companion:* Activity 10.4.

Pressures on Friendships

Like all human relationships, friendships are subject to internal tensions and external pressures.

INTERNAL TENSIONS

Friendships are vulnerable to tensions inherent in being close. **Internal tensions** are relationship stresses that grow out of people and their interactions. We consider three of these.

Relational Dialectics In Chapter 8, we discussed relational dialectics, which are opposing human needs that create tension and propel change in close relationships. The three dialectics of connection/autonomy, openness/privacy, and novelty/familiarity punctuate friendship, prompting us to adjust continually to natural yet contradictory needs.

Digital Vision RF/Getty Images

Friendships can be strained when people have different needs. There could be tension if Joe is bored and wants novelty but his friend Andy is overstimulated and needs calming routines. Similarly, if Andy has just broken up with a woman, he may seek greater closeness with Joe at a time when Joe has a strong need to feel independent of others. When needs collide, friends should talk. It's important to be up front about what you need and to be sensitive to what your friend needs. Doing this simultaneously honors yourself, your friend, and the relationship. Friends usually can work out ways to meet each person's needs or at least to understand that differing needs don't reflect unequal commitment to the friendship. Student Companion: Activity 10.3.

> **LANA** My girlfriends and I are so often in different places that it's hard to take care of each other. If one of my friends isn't seeing anyone special, she wants more time with me and wants to do things together. If I'm in a relationship with a guy, her needs feel demanding. But when I've just broken up, I really need my friends to fill time and talk with. So I try to remember how I feel and use that to help me accept it when my friends need my time.

Diverse Communication Styles Friendships may also be strained by misunderstandings that arise from diverse cultural backgrounds. Because our communication reflects the understandings and rules of our culture, misinterpretations are likely between friends from different cultures. For instance, in many traditional Asian societies, people are socialized to be unassuming and modest, whereas American culture encourages assertion and celebration of ourselves. Thus, a native Japanese might perceive a friend from Milwaukee as arrogant for saying, "Let's go out to celebrate my acceptance to law school." A Thai woman might not get the support she wants from a friend from Brooklyn, because she was taught not to assert her needs, and the Brooklyn friend was taught that people should speak up for themselves.

Misunderstandings also arise from differences between social groups in the United States. Aaron, who is white, might feel hurt if Markus, an African American friend, turns down Aaron's invitation to a concert to go home to care for an ailing aunt. Aaron might interpret this as a rejection by Markus because he thinks Markus is using the aunt as an excuse to avoid going out with him. Aaron would interpret Markus differently if he realized that many African Americans are more communal than European Americans, so taking care of extended family members is a priority (DeFrancisco & Chatham-Carpenter, 2000; Gaines, 1995; Orbe & Harris, 2001). Ellen may feel that her friend Jed isn't being supportive when, instead of empathizing with her problems, he offers advice or suggests that they go out to take her mind off her troubles. Yet, he is showing support according to masculine rules of communication. Jed, on the other hand, may feel that Ellen is intruding on his autonomy when she pushes him to talk about his feelings. According to feminine rules of communication, however, Ellen is showing interest and concern.

Communication in Everyday Life
Just Friends?

Recent research suggests that being "just friends" often includes sexual activity. Walid Afifi and Sandra Faulkner (2000) surveyed 315 women and men in college about their cross-sex friendships. They found that 51% of respondents reported having had sex with a friend of the other sex at least once. One-third of respondents said they had repeatedly engaged in sexual activity with friends. Most of the respondents said that sexual activity increased the quality of their friendships, but a few said it harmed the friendships. Perhaps most interesting is the finding that engaging in sexual activity with friends doesn't necessarily—or even usually—change a friendship into a romantic relationship.

At least for the people in Afifi and Faulkner's study, sex was seen as a way to enrich—not recast—the existing relationship. Lee West, Jennifer Anderson, and Steve Duck (1996) emphasize that, if people agree that they have a friendship, not a romance, then specific activities don't necessarily change the definition of the relationship.

Your InfoTrac College Edition provides the text of a number of articles about sex and friendship. Find these by typing friendship into the subject search, then accessing the subdivision analysis.

Differences themselves usually aren't the cause of problems in friendship. Instead, how we interpret and judge others' communication is the root of tension and hurt. What Jed and Ellen did wasn't the source of their frustrations. Jed interpreted Ellen according to his communication rules, not hers, and she interpreted Jed according to her communication rules, not his. Notice that the misunderstandings result from our interpretations of others' behaviors, not the behaviors themselves. This reminds us of the need to distinguish between facts and inferences.

Sexual Attraction Sexual attraction can cause difficulty between friends. Friendships between heterosexual men and women or between gay men or lesbians often include sexual tensions. Because Western culture so strongly emphasizes gender and sex, it's difficult not to perceive people in sexual terms (Johnson, Stockdale, & Saal, 1991; O'Meara, 1989). Even if there is no actual sexual activity, sexual undertones may ripple beneath the surface of friendships.

> **SHASHA** It is so hard to be just friends with guys. When I try to be friends with a guy, he'll hit on me at some point. I tell guys if friendship is all I'm interested in, and they agree, but they hit on me anyway. It's happened so much that by now I feel on guard with guys even before they start anything.

Sexual attraction or invitations can be a problem between friends who have agreed not to have a sexual relationship (O'Meara, 1989). Tension over sexual attraction or interest can be present in friendships between heterosexual women and men (O'Sullivan & Gaines, 1998; West, Anderson, & Duck, 1996) as well as in friendships between lesbians and between gay men (Nardi & Sherrod, 1994). Trust may be damaged if a friend makes a pass.

Guidelines for effective communication that we've discussed in other chapters help us deal with tensions in our friendships. For example, it's important to be clear and to rely on *I* language so that you communicate what you feel and want without deflecting responsibility. Sensitive listening and supportive communication are also helpful in keeping a friendship intact while partners address sexual tensions.

EXTERNAL PRESSURES

In addition to internal tensions, friendships may encounter pressures from outside sources. Three such pressures are competing demands, changes, and geographic distance.

Competing Demands Friendships exist within larger social systems that affect how they function (Allan, 1994). Our work and our romantic relationships tend to be woven into our everyday lives, ensuring that they get daily attention. The early stages of a career take enormous amounts of energy and time. We may not have enough time or energy left to maintain friendships, even those that matter to us (Duck, Rutt, Hurst, & Strejc, 1991).

We sometimes neglect established friends because of other relationships, especially new ones. When a new romance is taking off, we may be totally immersed in it. We may also neglect friends when other important relationships in our lives are in crisis. If one of our parents is ill or another friend is having trouble, we may need all our energy to cope with the acute situation. To avoid hurting friends, we should let them know when we have to focus elsewhere, and assure our friends that we are still committed to them.

Personal Changes Our friendships change as our lives do. Although a few friendships are lifelong, most are not. If you think about your experiences, you'll realize that many of your friends changed as you made major transitions in your life (Allan, 1994; Yager, 1999). The people you spent time with and counted as friends shifted when you started high school, entered college, or moved to a new town. They'll change again when you leave college, move for career or family reasons, and perhaps have children. Because one base of friendship is common interests, established friends may not be able to share new interests we develop.

Communication in Everyday Life
Friendships across the Life Span

Friendships vary during the course of life (Blieszner & Adams, 1992; Monsour, 1997; Yager, 1999). Most children begin forming friendships around age 2, when they start learning how to communicate with others. Toddlers play primarily side by side, and each is focused more on his or her activity than on the other person. At the same time, toddlers work to sustain friendships that matter to them, and they sometimes grieve when a friend moves away (Whaley & Rubenstein, 1994).

Children under age 6 tend to think of friendships primarily in terms of their own needs. As children mature, they develop awareness of norms of friendship, including reciprocity. First-grade friends are less likely to share equally. By the time friends are in third grade, however, they tend to rely on communal norms that lead them to strive for equity with friends (Pataki, Shapiro, & Clark, 1994).

During adolescence, friendship assumes great importance for most people. Having friends is very important, and belonging to friendship cliques is a measure of self-worth. Adolescent boys tend to define their friends as groups of people, usually other boys. Girls, on the other hand, tend to name only one or two peers as close friends.

Sharing personal information and activities are primary criteria for friendships among young adults, who are the group most likely to form and maintain friendships with people of the other sex (Werking, 1997).

In adulthood, friendships are more difficult to sustain. People marry, have children, move, and focus on careers. Despite these complications, most adults consider friendships important in their lives.

Later in life, people tend to value longtime friends with whom they can relive events that are part of their shared lives and the era in which they have lived (McKay, 2000). Many friendships between older people were formed between couples or between whole families when each family had young children. Because many older adults are retired and no longer have children at home, friends become an increasingly important source of emotional and instrumental support.

RUTH Sandi and I had been friends for years when I had my first baby. Gradually, we saw less of each other and couldn't find much to talk about when we did get together. She was still doing the singles scene, and I was totally absorbed in mothering. I got to know other mothers in the neighborhood, and soon I thought of them as my friends. What's funny is that last year Sandi had a baby, and it was so good to get together and talk. We reconnected with each other.

Lee West, Jennifer Anderson, and Steve Duck (1996) point out that friendships vary over our life spans. Peer friendships are very important to most children and adolescents. During their twenties, many people are starting careers and families, and they have less time and energy to devote to friends. Later in life, many people once again have time to invest in friendships.

We're most likely to become friends with people we see regularly, so where we live and work influences our choice of friends (Wellman, 1985). Similarly, unemployment can alter friendships because it takes people out of their usual social networks (Allen, Waton, Purcell, & Wood, 1986). Socioeconomic class affects friendships because it shapes our interests and tastes in everything from music to lifestyle. In addition, our economic status affects where we live and work and how much money we have for socializing with friends (O'Connor, 1992).

Geographic Distance   Most friendships face the challenge of distance, and many don't survive it. A majority of North Americans have at least one long-distance friendship (Rohlfing, 1995). Whether distance ends friendship depends on several factors. Perhaps the most obvious influence is how much people care about continuing to be friends. The greater the commitment, the more likely a friendship is to persist despite separation. Geographic distance is the reason the majority of high school friendships dissolve when students begin college (Rose, 1984).

The likelihood of sustaining a long-distance friendship also depends on other factors, such as socioeconomic class and sex. Friendships that survive distance involve frequent e-mail contact, phone calls, letters, and visits. It takes money to finance trips and long-distance calls and to pay for computers and Internet access. Thus, friends with greater economic resources are better able to maintain their relationships than are friends with less discretionary income (Willmott, 1987). A second way in which socioeconomic class affects the endurance of long-distance friendships is flexibility in managing work and family. Middle- and upper-class people usually have considerable flexibility in work schedules, so they can make time to travel. Working-class citizens tend to have less personal control over when they work and how much vacation time they get. Income also affects our ability to pay for babysitters, who may make it possible to visit a friend for a weekend.

Everyday Application
Maintaining Friendship over Distance

Do you have a long-distance friendship? If so, which of the following strategies do you use to maintain it?

- Call at least once a week
- Call at least once a month
- Communicate by e-mail at least weekly
- Call once or twice a year
- Write letters
- Visit weekly
- Visit monthly
- Visit occasionally
- Have conversations in your head with the friend

Now, identify three ways you might strengthen the closeness between you and your friend. *Student Companion:* Activity 10.5 and Activity 10.7.

Sex and gender also affect the endurance of long-distance friendships. There appear to be two reasons why women are more likely than men to sustain ties with friends who live at a distance. First, compared to women, men place less value on their same-sex relationships and invest less in them (Duck & Wright, 1993). This is especially true of married men, who often consider their wives their best friends (Rubin, 1985). Thus, women are more willing than men to adjust schedules and priorities to make time for friends (Rubin, 1985), and they are more willing to tolerate less than ideal circumstances for being with friends. For example, mothers who sustain long-distance friendships report that, when they visit, they are seldom alone because their children need attention and care. Even though these mothers say they miss the intimacy of uninterrupted conversations, they value each other enough to sustain friendships under the terms that are possible (Rohlfing, 1995). Women also report getting more out of their friendships with women than men report getting out of their friendships with men (Duck & Wright, 1993).

CASS My parents are so different from each other in their approaches to friendship. When I was growing up, Dad was on a career roll, so we were always moving to better neighborhoods or new towns. Each time we moved, he'd make a whole new set of friends. Even if his old friends lived nearby, he would want to be with the people he called his new peers. Mom is 180 degrees different. She still talks with her best friend in the town where I was born. She has stayed close to all of her good friends, and they don't change with the season like Dad's do. Once, I asked him if he missed his old friends, and he said that friends were people you share common interests with, so they change as your job does. That doesn't make sense to me.

Another reason women and men differ in how likely they are to maintain long-distance friendships is that the sexes tend to have different views of the nucleus of closeness. As we've seen previously, shared interests and emotional involvement are the crux of closeness for many women. Both of these are achieved primarily through communication, especially personal talk (Aries, 1987; Becker, 1987). The focus of men's friendships tends to be activities, which are difficult to share across distance (Swain, 1989; Wood & Inman, 1993). Women can and do sustain ties with important friends by talking on the phone and writing. Men, on the other hand, are more likely to replace friends who have moved away with others who can share activities they enjoy (Rohlfing, 1995).

Lillian Rubin's (1985) studies led her to say that women tend to develop **friends of the heart,** who remain close regardless of distance and circumstances. Rubin also noted that many men have **friends of the road,** who change as they move along the road of life and develop new interests and find themselves in new situations. It is easier to replace a friend who was a tennis partner than one with whom we shared intimate feelings and details of our life.

BLYTHE I think the person who invented digital cameras was in a long-distance friendship and felt pictures would help keep the connection. I love it when Vicky sends me photos, and I can keep them in a file and look at them whenever I want to feel close to her and what's going on in her life. And I love sending her pictures of me and Mike and my campus. They say, "One picture is worth a thousand words," and I think that's true when it comes to staying in touch with friends.

Guidelines for Communication between Friends

Satisfying communication between friends follows the principles of good interpersonal communication that we've discussed in preceding chapters. For instance, it is important to create a confirming climate by being open, spontaneous, empathic, equal, and nonevaluative. In addition, you should keep in mind what you have learned about using verbal and nonverbal communication effectively, including ways to discuss emotions. Finally, managing conflict constructively is important in friendships, as in all relationships. In addition to these general principles, we can identify four specific guidelines for satisfying communication between friends.

ENGAGE IN DUAL PERSPECTIVE

As in all interpersonal relationships, dual perspective is important in friendship. To be a good friend, we must understand our friends' perspectives, thoughts, and feelings. As we've noted before, accepting another person's perspective is not the same as agreeing with it. The point is to understand what friends feel and think and to accept that as their reality.

To exercise dual perspective, we distinguish between our judgments and perceptions and what friends say and do. Keep in mind the abstraction ladder we discussed in Chapter 3. When we feel hurt or offended by something a friend says, we should remember that our perceptions and inferences do not equal their behavior. The process goes like this:

A friend acts.
We perceive the action(s) selectively.
We then interpret and evaluate what happened.
We assign meaning to it and make inferences from what we've labeled.

Notice how far from the original act we move in the process of trying to make sense of it. There's lots of room for slippage as we ascend the abstraction ladder. Let's consider a concrete example. Shereen tells her friend Kyle that she's upset and needs support; she shouldn't assume he's uninterested if he suggests they go out for the evening. As we have learned, men often support friends by trying to divert them from problems.

Two communication principles help us avoid misinterpreting our friends. First, it's useful to ask questions to find out what others mean. Shereen might ask Kyle, "Why would you want to go out when I said I needed support?" This would allow Kyle to explain that he was trying to support her in his own way: by coming up with an activity to distract her from her problems. Consequently, Shereen could grasp his meaning and interpret what he did in that light.

Second, we should explain, or translate, our own feelings and needs so the friend understands what would feel supportive to us. Shereen could say, "What would help me most right now is to have a sympathetic ear. Could we just stay in and talk about the problem?" If we make our needs clear, we're more likely to get the kind of support we value.

COMMUNICATE HONESTLY

A few years ago, I confronted an ethical choice when my close friend Gayle asked me for advice. Several months earlier, she had agreed to give the keynote speech at a professional conference, and now she had an opportunity to travel to Italy with her partner at the time of the conference. She wanted to accompany her partner to Italy but wondered whether it was ethical to renege on her agreement to give the keynote address. Following principles we've discussed in this book, I first asked a number of questions to find out how Gayle felt and what her perspective was. It became clear that she really wanted me to tell her it was okay to retract her agreement to give the speech.

Because I love Gayle, I wanted to support her preference and to encourage her to do what she wanted. Yet I didn't think it would be right for her to go back on her word, and I didn't think Gayle would respect herself in the long run if she didn't keep her word. Also, I knew that I wouldn't respect myself if I wasn't honest with Gayle. Ethically, I was committed both to being honest and to supporting my friend.

I took a deep breath and told her three things: First, I told her I would love her whatever she decided to do. Second, I told her that I didn't think it would be right not to give the speech. And, third, I suggested we look for more options. At first, she was quiet, clearly disappointed that I hadn't endorsed her dream. As we talked, we came up with the idea of her making the keynote speech and then joining her partner, who would already be in Italy. Even with this plan, Gayle was dejected when she left, and I felt I'd let her down by not supporting her dream. Later that night, she called to thank me for being honest with her. After we'd talked, she'd realized it went against her own values to renege on her word, and nobody else had helped her see that.

Honesty is one of the most important gifts friends can give each other. Even when honesty is less than pleasant or is not what we think we want to hear, we count on it from friends. In fact, people believe that honest feedback is what sets real friends apart from others (Burleson & Samter, 1994). Sometimes it's difficult to be honest with friends, as it was for me with Gayle. Yet, if we can't count on our friends for honest feedback, then where can we turn for truthfulness?

Many people make the mistake of thinking that support is saying only nice things that others want to hear. This is not the essence of support. The key is to care enough about a person to look out for her or his welfare. Parents discipline children and set limits because they care about their children's long-term welfare. Colleagues who want to help each other give honest, often critical feedback so that others can improve.

Romantic partners who are committed tell each other when they perceive problems or when the other isn't being his or her best self. We can be supportive and loving while being honest, but to be less than honest is to betray the trust placed in us. Although it may be easier to tell friends what they want to hear or only nice things, genuine friendship includes honest feedback and candid talk.

MILANDO   I can count on one hand (with three fingers left over!) the people who will really shoot straight with me. Most of my friends tell me what I want to hear. Yeah, that's kind of nice in the moment, but it doesn't wear well over the long haul. If I just want reinforcement for what I'm already feeling or doing, then why would I even talk to anyone else? Real friends tell you straight-up what's what.

GROW FROM DIFFERENCES

A third principle for forming rich friendships is to be open to diversity in people. Western culture encourages us to think in either–or terms: Either he acts like I do, or he's wrong; either she's like me, or she's odd. The problem with either–or thinking is that it sharply limits interpersonal growth.

Most of us tend to choose friends who are like us. We feel more immediately comfortable with friends who share our values, attitudes, backgrounds, and communication rules. But if we limit our friendships to people like us, we miss out on the fascinating variety of people who can be our friends. It does take time and effort to understand and become comfortable with people who differ from us, but the rewards of doing so can be exceptional.

DON'T SWEAT THE SMALL STUFF

© Tom & Dee Ann McCarthy/CORBIS

The 18th-century writer Samuel Johnson once remarked that most friendships die not because of major violations and problems but because of small slights and irritations that slowly destroy closeness. Johnson's point is well taken. Certainly, we will be irritated by a number of qualities and habits of others. If you are a punctual person, you might be annoyed by a friend who is chronically late. If you don't like prolonged telephone conversations, you may be irritated by a friend who likes to talk for hours on the phone. Feeling annoyance is normal. What we do with that feeling can make the difference between sustaining a friendship and suffocating it.

What we learned about perception in Chapter 3 gives us insight into how to let go of small irritations. Knowing that perceptions are subjective, you might remind yourself not to focus on aspects of a friend that you dislike or find bothersome. There's a big difference between acknowledging irritations and letting them preoccupy us. Is the lateness really more significant than all that you value in your friend? Do your friend's good qualities compensate for the long phone conversations that you dread? You can exercise some control over your perceptions and the weight you attach to them.

BERNADETTE I grew up with a single mother, but our home was always full. She had so many friends, and somebody was visiting all the time. I used to tell her that I didn't like Mrs. Jones's language or Mrs. Perry's political attitudes or the way Mr. Davis slurped his coffee. One day, when I was telling her what was wrong with one of her friends, my mother said, "Keep going like that, girl, and you won't ever have any friends. If you want to have friends, don't sweat the small stuff. Just keep your eye on what's good about them."

All of us want to be accepted and valued despite our flaws. You want that from your friends. And they want that from you. Acceptance doesn't mean you like everything about your friends. It does mean you accept friends and don't try to change them to suit your personal preferences.

Communication in Everyday Life
A Both–And Approach to Relationships

Many Westerners have been socialized to think in either–or terms. Using this mind-set, they divide the world into opposing categories: in-groups and out-groups, right and wrong, good and bad. Most of us were taught that either one way, idea, answer or the other is valid, but not both.

When we apply the either–or mind-set to our relationships, we are likely to diminish them (Campbell, 1986). According to the either–or mind-set, we can focus on your needs or my needs; we can adopt your perspective or my perspective; we can do things your way or mine. In reality, a relationship is not two separate, totally independent people. It is the two people and the connections between them, connections that can be unraveled by imposing an either–or mindset. Why should we limit ourselves to one perspective or the other, one way of doing things or another, when incorporating both partners' perspectives and ways enlarges both the individuals and their relationship?

Case Study: Continuing the Conversation

The following conversation is featured on the Everyday Connections website under "Chapter Resources for Chapter 10." Click on the link "Sean & Bart" in the left-hand menu to launch the video and audio scenario scripted below.

Bart and Sean have been friends and co-workers at Capital Bank for 10 years. Over the years, they've been through a lot together, including Bart's divorce 3 years after they met and Sean's wedding, where

Bart was his best man. They've kept each other informed about other employees and the everyday office gossip. Both Bart and Sean felt that their friendship was solid until Sean got promoted 2 months ago. The promotion made Sean Bart's boss, although both of them try to minimize that. But Bart feels that Sean doesn't share information about Capital with him anymore, and he won't talk about other employees the way they used to. Sean feels he can't talk about work topics with Bart because it would be unfair to

Jason Harris/© 2001 Wadsworth

Case Study: Continuing the Conversation

Bart's peers, who are also under his supervision. Sean also misses the closeness he and Bart had for so long. He wishes there were a way to keep the friendship as it was but separate it from their work relationship.

Bart: So, I heard that Jack is being courted by Jefferson Financial. What's the story?

Sean: I don't know the details on that.

Bart: I mean, is Capital going to match the offer to keep Jack?

Sean: (silence)

Bart: Because a lot of us would be upset if he got a raise and we didn't. It would be like encouraging us to go job hunting just to get a counteroffer.

Sean: Hey, look, you know that it's not Capital's policy to make counteroffers to match the competition's offers.

Bart: Well, sure, I know the official policy. I also know Capital ignores it when they want to keep someone who has a good offer. I just want to know where Jack stacks up.

Sean: I can't talk to you about that, Bart, you know that.

Bart: Damn it, Sean, you can trust me. Nothing you say is going any further. I just want to know myself.

Sean: Well, what about all the other managers who are not my best friend? How is it fair to them?

Bart: Best friend? You could have fooled me. I thought best friends told each other things.

Sean: Look, when are you going to realize that, because of my new job, there's just some things that I can't

talk to you about? It's impossible. For instance, this situation that you're talking about with Jack, it's creating nothing but tension between the two of us. I can't talk to you about anything right now.

1. What relational dialectics do you see operating in the friendship between Sean and Bart?

2. Review the ways people respond to relational dialectics, and assess how effective each response might be in this situation. How would separation, segmentation, and so forth affect interaction?

3. How is the trust between Bart and Sean affected by the changes in their relationship? In what ways might each man feel less able to trust the other?

4. Think about the systemic nature of relationships. Identify how the one change (Sean's promotion) affects other aspects of this relationship and interaction within it.

5. If you could rewrite the conversation between Bart

and Sean, how would you revise it? What would you want to happen that isn't happening? What that is happening would you want not to happen? In revising the conversation, think about ways in which Sean and Bart might use communication to build a good interpersonal climate and express emotions effectively. How might each man listen more actively and effectively?

6. Can you envision ways in which Sean's ideal scenario might be realized, so that he and Bart could stay close friends and keep the friendship separate from their working relationship?

You can critique and analyze this encounter based on the principles you learned in this chapter by responding to the questions included under "Conversation Analysis" at the website. By clicking on the "Submit" button at the end of the form, you can compare your work to my suggested responses. Let's continue the conversation online!

Chapter 10 - Friendships in Our Lives: Sean and Bart

| Introduction | Video | Transcript | Critique | Notes |

Bart and Sean have been friends and coworkers at Capital Bank for 10 years. Over the years, they've been through a lot together, including Bart's divorce three years after they met and Sean's wedding, where Bart was his best man. They've kept each other informed about other employees and the everyday office gossip. Both Bart and Sean felt that their friendship was solid until Sean got promoted two months ago. The promotion made Sean Bart's boss, although both of them try to minimize that. But Bart feels that Sean doesn't share information about Capital with him anymore, and he won't talk about other employees the way they used to. Sean feels he can't talk about work topics with Bart because it would be unfair to Bart's peers, who are also under his supervision. Sean also misses the closeness he and Bart had for so long. He wishes there were a way to keep the friendship as it was but to separate it from their work relationship.

Chapter Summary

In this chapter, we explored how friendships form and how they function and change over time. We began by considering common expectations for friends, including investment, intimacy, acceptance, and support. Into our discussion of these common themes, we wove insights about differences between us. We discovered that there are some differences in how women and men and people in different cultures and social communities create and express intimacy, invest in friendships, and show support.

Most friendships evolve gradually, moving from role-governed interactions to stable friendship and sometimes to waning friendship. Both social rules and private rules lend regularity and predictability to interaction so that friends know what to expect from one another.

Like all other relationships, friendships encounter challenges and tensions that stem from the relationship itself and from causes beyond it. Internal tensions of friendship include managing relational dialectics and misunderstandings and dealing with sexual attraction. External pressures on friendship are competing demands, changing personal needs and interests of friends, and geographic distance. Principles of interpersonal communication covered throughout this book suggest how we can manage these pressures and the day-to-day dynamics of close friendships. In addition, communication between friends is especially enhanced by engaging in dual perspective, being honest, being open to diversity and the growth it can prompt in us, and not sweating the small stuff.

Everyday Connections Online

Now that you've read Chapter 10, go to the Everyday Connections premium website at academic.cengage.com/communication/woodinterpersonal5plus for quick access to the electronic study resources that accompany this text. The website gives you access to the "Continuing the Conversation" video scenario and questions featured in this chapter, to InfoTrac College Edition, to maintained and updated Web links, and to the study aids for this chapter, including a digital glossary, review quizzes, and the chapter activities. For more information about this text's electronic learning resources, consult the **1pass card** that came with each new copy of this book, or visit academic.cengage.com/communication/woodinterpersonal5.

Key Concepts

Audio flash cards of the following key terms are available on the Everyday Connections website. Use the flash cards to improve your pronunciation of text vocabulary.

friends of the heart   friends of the road   internal tensions   relationship rules

For Further Thought and Discussion

1. Think about a friendship you have with a person of your own sex and a friendship you have with a person of the other sex. To what extent does each friendship conform to the gender patterns described in this chapter?

2. Review the rules of friendship presented in this chapter. Do these rules show up in your friendships? Are there other rules that you would add based on your personal experiences with friendship?

3. Do you have any long-distance friends? How far away are they? How often do you see them in person? How do you manage to maintain the friendship across the distance?

4. Use your InfoTrac College Edition to read Marianne Dainton's and Brooks Aylar's 2001 article, "A Relational Uncertainty Analysis of Jealousy, Trust, and Maintenance in Long-Distance Versus Geographically Close Relationships," published in *Communication Quarterly*. What does this study tell us about the relationship between relationship uncertainty and trust?

5. Write out typical topics of talk for each stage in the evolution of friendships. How do topics change as friendships wax and wane?

6. Think about someone who is a very close or best friend. Describe the investments you and your friend have made in the relationship. Describe how you build and communicate trust, acceptance, and closeness. Are the dynamics of your friendship consistent with those identified by researchers as discussed in this chapter?

7. Use the PowerTrac option on your InfoTrac College Edition to read Jennifer Thomas's and Kimberly A. Daubman's 2001 article, "The Relationship Between Friendship Quality and Self-Esteem in Adolescent Boys and Girls." How would you explain the differences in how friendships affect boys' and girls' self esteem?

8. To learn how others view friendships and what issues arise in their friendships, visit the Friendship Page at http://www.friendship.com.au/. This site offers songs, poetry, and quotes about friendship, as well as chat rooms and an advice forum. To what extent do the issues raised in the advice forum reflect challenges to friendship discussed in this chapter?

Committed Romantic Relationships

© Donna Day/Getty Images/Stone

"A loving person lives in a loving world.
A hostile person lives in a hostile world.
Everyone you meet is your mirror."

Ken Keys

I n this chapter, we explore communication in committed romantic relationships. We begin by defining committed romantic relationships and the different styles of loving that people bring to romance. Next, we discuss the developmental pattern that many romantic relationships follow as they grow, stabilize, and sometimes dissolve. To close the chapter, we identify guidelines for communicating effectively to meet challenges that often arise in romantic relationships.

Committed Romantic Relationships

Committed romantic relationships are relationships between unique individuals who assume they will be primary and continuing parts of each other's lives. These relationships are voluntary, at least in Western culture. We don't pick our relatives, neighbors, or work associates, but we do choose our romantic intimates.

Committed romantic relationships are created and sustained by unique individuals who cannot be replaced. In many of our relationships, others are replaceable. If a colleague at work leaves, you can get another colleague, and work will go on. If your racquetball buddy moves out of town, you can find a new partner, and the games will continue. In fact, most of our social relationships are I–You connections. Committed romantic relationships, in contrast, are I–Thou bonds, in which we invest heavily of ourselves and in which each person knows the other as a completely distinct individual.

Committed romantic relationships involve romantic and sexual feelings, which are not typically part of relationships with co-workers, friends, and family members. Another distinctive quality of romantic relationships is that, in our society, they are considered primary and permanent. We expect to move away from friends and family, but we assume we'll be permanently connected to a romantic partner. Current divorce rates indicate that many of those who marry will separate. Even so, we think of romantic commitment (although not every romantic relationship) as permanent or very long lasting, and this makes romantic commitments unique.

© Najlah Feanny/CORBIS

DIMENSIONS OF ROMANTIC RELATIONSHIPS

For years, researchers have struggled to define romantic commitment. As a result of their work, we now believe that romantic love consists of three dimensions: intimacy, commitment, and passion. Although we can think about these dimensions separately, they overlap and interact (Acker & Davis, 1992; Hendrick & Hendrick, 1989). One scholar (Sternberg, 1986) arranges these three dimensions to form a triangle, representing the different facets of love (see Figure 11.1).

Passion For most of us, passion is what first springs to mind when we think about romance.

Passion is intensely positive feelings and fervent desire for another person. Passion is not restricted to sexual or sensual feelings. In addition to sexual feelings, passion may involve exceptional emotional, spiritual, and intellectual attraction. The sparks and emotional high of being in love stem from passion. It's why we feel butterflies in the stomach and fall head over heels.

As exciting as passion is, it isn't the primary foundation for most enduring romantic relationships. In fact, research consistently shows that passion is less central to how we think about love than are the dimensions of intimacy and commitment. This makes sense when we realize that passion seldom can be sustained over a long-term relationship. Like other intense feelings, it ebbs and flows. Because passion comes and goes and is largely beyond our will, it isn't a strong basis for long-term relationships. In other words, passion may set romance apart from other relationships, but it isn't what holds romance together. To build a lasting relationship, we need something more durable.

Communication in Everyday Life
The Rise of Online Romance

Ellen Fein and Sherri Schneider (2002) say that online dating is the new millennium's form of blind date. Each year, 61% of American singles look for a date on the Internet (Fagan, 2001). Many of them find dates—and more. Some people who meet online have eventually married, and others have sustained long-term romances or friendships (Clement & McLean, 2000). Online romance often includes sexual activity just as face-to-face romance does. Roughly 75 million people worldwide—about 20% of Internet users—engage in online sexual activities, called *cybering* (Maheu & Subotnik, 2001). For them, online sex allows maximum freedom with minimum dangers. Studies of people who date online identify both advantages and disadvantages of online romance.

Advantages	Disadvantages
You can choose people who match your criteria.	Identities aren't necessarily what they are claimed to be.
You can minimize risk by preserving your anonymity.	People can use outdated photos or even photos of other people. They can lie about sex, race, and other facets of identity.
You can judge someone on values and interests instead of superficial physical qualities.	It's hard to judge some aspects of "chemistry" without meeting face to face.
You can screen e-mail to check for red flags, check information, and so forth.	

Commitment   The something else needed is commitment, the second dimension of romantic relationships. As we noted in Chapter 8, **commitment** is the intention to remain with a relationship. Although often linked to love, commitment is not the same thing as love. Love is a feeling based on the rewards of our involvement with a person. Commitment, in contrast, is a choice based on our investments in the relationship (Lund, 1985; Rusbult, Drigotas, & Verette, 1994). We choose to entwine our life and future with another person's.

> **THERESA**   I'm sick of guys who say they love me but run if I try to talk about the future. They're allergic to the C-word. If you truly love someone, how can you not be committed?

> **TED**   I don't know why everyone thinks that saying "I love you" means you want to plan a life together. I love my girlfriend, but I haven't even figured out what I want to do next year, much less for the rest of my life. She thinks if I really loved her, I'd want to talk about marriage. I think love and marriage can be different things.

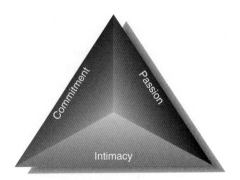

FIGURE 11.1

The Triangle of Love

Communication in Everyday Life
The Prototype of Love

Westerners have a clear prototype of love. Research repeatedly reveals that we regard feeling valued by and comfortable with another as more important than passion (Button & Collier, 1991; Fehr, 1993; Luby & Aron, 1990; Rousar & Aron, 1990). Love is typified by feelings such as closeness, caring, and friendship, and commitment is typified by trust and respect. Intimacy and commitment eclipse passion in importance. Even when people are asked what's most important for being in love, companionate features have priority.

Do women and men differ in how important they consider the dimensions of love? Although women and men don't differ significantly in what they consider typical of love in general, they do diverge in their personal ideals for love. For both sexes, passion is less salient than companionate features. However, features linked to intimacy and commitment are even more prominent in women's personal ideals of romantic love than in men's. The only feature that men rate higher than women is fantasy. No differences have been found among heterosexuals, gay men, and lesbians.

Intimacy is abiding affection and warm feelings for another person. It is why partners are comfortable with each other and enjoy being together even when there are no fireworks. When asked to evaluate various features of love, people consistently rate companionate features such as getting along and friendship as most important. Although passionate feelings also matter, they are less central to perceptions of love than caring, honesty, respect, friendship, and trust (Fehr, 1993; Hasserbrauck & Aaron, 2001; Hasserbrauck & Fehr, 2002; Luby & Aron, 1990).

Most Westerners want both passion and commitment in long-term romantic relationships (Bellah, Madsen, Sullivan, Swidler, & Tipton, 1985). We desire the exhilaration of passion, but we know that love alone won't allow a couple to weather rough times, that it won't ensure compatibility and comfort on a day-in, day-out basis. Commitment provides a sturdier foundation for a life together. Commitment is the determination to stay together despite trouble, disappointments, sporadic restlessness, and lulls in passion. Commitment involves accepting responsibility for maintaining a relationship (Beck, 1988; Swidler, 2001). Thus, it isn't surprising that commitment is positively related to willingness to sacrifice for and invest in a relationship (Rusbult et al., 1994).

> **WADE** I've been married for 15 years, and we would have split a dozen times if love was all that held us together. Lucy and I have gone through spells where we were bored with each other or where we wanted to walk away from our problems. We didn't, because we made a promise to stay together "for better or for worse." Believe me, a marriage has both.

Passion happens without effort—sometimes despite our efforts. Commitment is an act of will. Passion is a feeling; commitment is a choice. Passion may fade in the face of disappointments and troubles; commitment remains steadfast. Passion occurs in the present moment; commitment is tied to the future. Without commitment, romantic relationships are subject to the whims of transient feelings and circumstances.

Intimacy The third dimension of romantic relationships is **intimacy,** which is feelings of closeness, connection, and tenderness. Unlike passion and commitment, which are distinct dimensions of romance, intimacy seems to underlie both passion and commitment (Acker & Davis, 1992; Hasserbrauck & Fehr, 2002). Intimacy is related to passion because both involve very strong feelings. The link between intimacy and passion is commitment, which joins partners not only in the present but through the past and into the future.

STYLES OF LOVING

⋯ Does real love grow out of friendship? Can you decide to love only someone who meets your criteria for a partner?

- ··· Would you rather suffer yourself than have someone you love suffer?
- ··· Is love at first sight possible?
- ··· Is love really a game—playful, not serious?

If you were to survey everyone in your class, you'd discover different answers to these questions. For every person who thinks love grows gradually out of friendship, someone else believes that love at first sight is possible.

Whatever we have experienced as love is what we consider "real love." Anything else we discount as "just infatuation," "a fling," or "not the real thing." People differ in how they experience and express love (Lee, 1973, 1988). Just as there are three primary colors, there are three primary styles of loving. In addition, just as secondary colors are combinations of two primary colors, secondary love styles are combinations of two primary ones. Secondary styles are as vibrant as primary ones, just as purple (a secondary color) is as dazzling as red or blue (primary colors that make up purple). Figure 11.2 illustrates the colors of love.

© Royalty-Free/CORBIS

Primary Styles of Love   The three primary styles of love are *eros, storge,* and *ludus.* **Eros** is a powerful, passionate style of love that blazes to life suddenly and dramatically. It is an intense kind of love that may include sexual, spiritual, intellectual, or emotional attraction. Eros is the most intuitive and spontaneous of all styles, and it is also the fastest moving. Erotic lovers are likely to self-disclose early in a relationship, be very sentimental, and fall in love fast. Although folk wisdom claims that women are more romantic than men, research indicates that men are more likely than women to be erotic lovers (Hendrick & Hendrick, 1996).

> **MIKE**   When I fall for someone, I fall all the way—like, I mean total and all that. I can't love halfway, and I can't go gradually, though my mother is always warning me to slow down. That's just not how I love. It's fast and furious for me.

Storge (pronounced "store-gay") is a comfortable, even-keeled kind of love based on friendship and compatibility. Storgic love tends to grow gradually and to be peaceful and stable. In most cases, it grows out of common interests, values, and life goals (Lasswell & Lobsenz, 1980). Storgic relationships don't have the great highs of erotic ones, but neither do they have the fiery conflict and anger that can punctuate erotic relationships.

> **STEPHEN**   Lisa and I have been together for 15 years now, and it's been easy and steady between us from the start. I don't remember even falling in love way back when. Maybe I never did fall in love with Lisa. I just gradually grew into loving her and feeling we belonged to each other.

The final primary style of love is **ludus,** which is playful love. Ludic lovers see love as a game. It's a lighthearted adventure full of challenges, puzzles, and fun, but love is not to be taken seriously. For ludics, commitment is not the goal. Instead, they like to play the field and enjoy falling in love. Many people go through ludic periods but

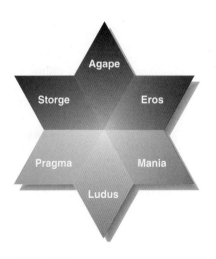

FIGURE 11.2
The Colors of Love

are not true ludics. After ending a long-term relationship, it's natural and healthy to date casually and steer clear of serious entanglements. Ludic loving may also suit people who enjoy romance but aren't ready to settle down. Research indicates that more men than women have ludic inclinations when it comes to love (Hendrick & Hendrick, 1996).

> **VIJAY** I'm not ready to settle down, and I may not ever be. I really like dating and seeing if I can get a girl to fall for me, but I'm not out for anything permanent. To me, the fun is in the chase. Once somebody falls for me, I kind of lose interest. It's just not challenging anymore.

Secondary Styles of Love   The three secondary styles of love are *pragma, mania,* and *agape*. **Pragma,** as the word suggests, is pragmatic or practical love. Pragma blends the conscious strategies of ludus with the stable, secure love of storge. Pragmatic lovers have clear criteria for partners, such as religious affiliation, career, and family background. Although many people dismiss pragma as coldly practical, pragmatic lovers aren't necessarily unfeeling or unloving. For them, though, practical considerations are the foundation of enduring commitment, so these must be satisfied before they allow themselves to fall in love. Pragmas are likely to like online matching services that allow them to specify their criteria for a desirable mate (Fagan, 2001). Pragmatic considerations also guide arranged marriages, in which families match children on economic and social criteria.

> **RANCHANA** I have to think carefully about who to marry. I must go to graduate school, and I must support my family with what I earn when I finish. I cannot marry someone who is poor, who will not help me get through school, or who won't support my family. For me, these are very basic matters.

Mania derives its name from the Greek term *theia mania,* which means "madness from the gods" (Lee, 1973). Manic lovers have the passion of eros, but they play by ludic rules—a combination that can be perilous. Typically unsure that others really love them, manics may devise tests and games (that's the ludic streak in mania) to evaluate a partner's commitment. They often experience emotional extremes, ranging from euphoric ecstasy to bottomless despair (that's the erotic streak). In addition, manics may think obsessively about a relationship and be unable to think about anyone or anything else.

> **PAT** I never feel sure of myself when I'm in love. I always wonder when it will end, when my boyfriend will walk away, when he will lose interest. Sometimes I play games to see how interested a guy is, but then I get all upset if the game doesn't work out right. Then I just wallow in my insecurities, and they get worse the more I think about them.

The final style of love is **agape,** which is a blend of storge and eros. The term *agape* comes from Saint Paul's admonition that we should love others without expectation of personal gain or return. People who love agapically feel the intense passion of eros and the constancy of storge. Generous and selfless, they put a loved one's happiness ahead of their own without any expectation of reciprocity. For them, loving and giving to another is its own reward. Many of my students say that agapic love is more possible for saints than for mere mortals. Although the original studies of love styles found no people who were purely agapic, many people have agapic tendencies.

> **KEENAN** My mother is agapic. She has moved more times than I can count because my father needed to relocate to advance. She agreed to the house he wanted and went on the vacations he wanted, even when she had other ideas. There's nothing she wouldn't do for him. I used to think she was a patsy, but I've come to see her way of loving as very strong.

When I discuss love styles with students, they want to figure out which love style they have. Since you may also be figuring out your love style, you should keep in mind four issues related to identifying your love style. First, most of us have a combination of styles (Hendrick, Hendrick, Foote, & Slapion-Foote, 1984). So you might be primarily storgic with strong agapic inclinations, or mainly erotic with an undertone of ludic mischief. Second, styles of love are not necessarily permanent. We learn how to love (Maugh, 1994), so our style of loving may change as we have more experiences in loving. Third, a love style is part of an overall interpersonal system, so it is affected by all other aspects of a relationship (Hendrick & Hendrick, 1996). Your partner's style of love may influence your own. For instance, even if you don't tend toward mania, being with a strongly ludic partner could foster manic tendencies in you. Finally, individual styles of love are not good or bad in an absolute sense; what matters is how partners' styles fit together. *Student Companion:* Activity 11.3.

The Development of Romantic Relationships

Like friendships, romantic relationships tend to follow a developmental course. Irwin Altman and Dalmas Taylor (1973, 1987) developed social penetration theory to explain how romantic intimacy progresses. The key idea in social penetration theory is that intimacy grows as interaction between people penetrates from the outer to inner layers of each person's personality. In other words, we have to move beyond the surface of another person to know him or her well enough to develop an I–Thou relationship.

Some years after Altman and Taylor introduced social penetration theory, James Honeycutt (1993) amended it to note that intimacy progresses based on our perceptions of interaction, not on interaction itself. For example, if Terry discloses personal information to Janet, and if Janet and Terry interpret self-disclosure as a move toward greater intimacy, the relationship is likely to escalate. If Janet doesn't perceive disclosure as linked to intimacy, she's unlikely to feel closer to Terry. It is the meaning they assign to self-disclosing, not the actual act of self-disclosing, that determines how they perceive their level of intimacy.

The meanings we assign to behavior in romantic relationships are not entirely individualistic. They also reflect broad cultural views, which we learn and often internalize. For this reason, there are strong consistencies in how people socialized in the same culture and social groups attribute meaning to communication in romantic relationships. Research shows that college students in the United States agree on the goals and script for first dates (Mongeau, Serewicz, & Therrien, 2004; Pryor & Merluzzi, 1985). Both women and men perceive getting to know the new person and having fun as parts of a first-date script. Women are more likely than men to perceive companionship as a goal for a first date, and men are more likely than women to perceive sexual activity as a goal (Mongeau et al., 2004).

Men and women also tend to have similar ideas about how men and women should act. The majority of college students think that men should initiate and plan dates and make decisions about most activities but that women control sexual activity (Laner & Ventrone, 2002; Rose & Frieze, 1989). However, women were more egalitarian than men in their ratings of who was responsible for paying for a first date. While only 9% of men thought either partner could pay for the date, 22% of women thought either person could (Laner & Ventrone, 2002). In other cultures, different rules prevail for first dates and the whole process of courting. For example, in parts of India, marriages often are arranged by parents; love is understood to be something that develops after marriage. In Nepal, ritualistic dancing and celebrations are an important part of courtship.

Research on the evolution of romantic relationships has focused on Western society, so we know most about the developmental course of romance in the West. Investigations show that Westerners typically perceive romantic relationships as evolving through three broad phases: growth, navigation, and deterioration. Within these three broad categories, we distinguish a number of more specific stages (see Figure 11.3).

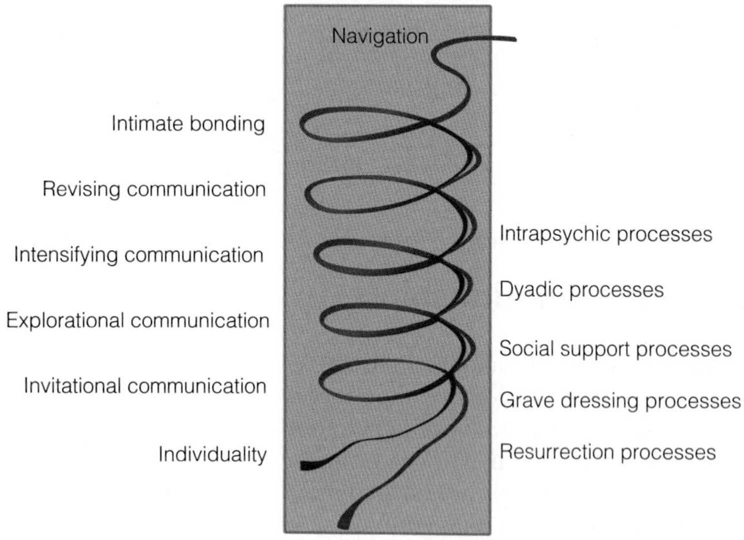

Intimate bonding
Revising communication
Intensifying communication
Explorational communication
Invitational communication
Individuality

Navigation

Intrapsychic processes
Dyadic processes
Social support processes
Grave dressing processes
Resurrection processes

FIGURE 11.3

Developmental Stages in Romantic Relationships

GROWTH STAGES

There are six stages of interaction that mark progressive intimacy. Typically, but not always, these stages occur in sequence. The first stage is *individuality;* each of us is an individual with particular needs, goals, love styles, perceptual tendencies, and qualities that affect what we look for in relationships. Our choices of people with whom to start romance may also be influenced by aspects of ourselves of which we are unaware, such as our attachment styles (Mikulincer & Shaver, 2005) and whether we give to others conditionally or unconditionally (Clark & Finkel, 2005).

EDNA   It's funny how things change as we age. When I was first dating in my teens, the topics for small talk early in the relationship were your major, career plans, and background. Now I'm 47, divorced, and dating again, and the opening topics tend to be about career achievements, past marriages, and finances.

The second growth stage is *invitational communication,* in which people signal that they are interested in interacting and respond to invitations from others. "I love this kind of music," "Where are you from?" and "Hi, my name's Shelby" are examples of bids for interaction. We may also invite interaction in chat rooms or websites that are designed for meeting new people. The most important meaning of invitational communication is found on the relationship level, not the content level. "I love this kind of music" literally means that a person likes the music. On the relationship level of meaning, however, the message is, "I'm interested in interacting. Are you?"

Of all the people we meet, we are attracted to only a few. The three greatest influences on initial attraction are self-concept, proximity, and similarity. Our self-concept affects the people we consider candidates for romance. Among members of each sexual orientation, there tend to be somewhat consistent criteria for selecting dating partners. Many gay men place priority on physical characteristics, including slimness, body conditioning, and grooming (Huston & Schwartz, 1995). Heterosexual men also place importance on physical attractiveness; they prefer women who are slim and beautiful (Sprecher, 1989; Sprecher & Regan, 2002). Heterosexual women and lesbians tend to emphasize qualities of personality, such as kindness, honesty, and integrity (Huston & Schwartz, 1995; Sprecher, 1989). Socioeconomic class also influences whom we notice and consider appropriate for us. The myth that the United States is classless is disproved by the fact that most people seek romantic partners of their own social class or above it (Sprecher & Regan, 2002; Whitbeck & Hoyt, 1994).

Proximity and similarity are major influences on initial attraction in face-to-face relationships. We can interact only with people we meet in person or in cyberspace, so where we live, work, and socialize affects the possibilities for relationships. Nearness to others doesn't necessarily increase liking. The term **environmental spoiling** denotes situations in which proximity breeds ill will. This happens when we're forced to be around others whose values, lifestyles, or behaviors conflict with our own.

For the most part, we seek romantic partners whose values, attitudes, and lifestyles are similar to ours (Buston & Emlen, 2003). Similarity of personality is also linked to the fit between people (Caspi & Harbener, 1990). People who are extroverted and who find it easy to talk with strangers often find it fun to initiate new relationships. On the other hand, people who are less outgoing or less comfortable interacting with strangers may find invitational communication very awkward and difficult. Research by Bradford Scharlott and William Christ (1995) suggests

Communication in Everyday Life
Development of Interracial Relationships

In addition to the stages generally followed in developing intimacy, partners in interracial relationships often deal simultaneously with four distinct developmental stages (Foeman & Nance, 1999).

1. **Racial awareness**—Each partner becomes conscious of his or her race and his or her views of the partner's race. In addition, partners become more aware of broad social perspectives on their own and each other's racial group.
2. **Coping**—The couple struggles with external pressures, including disapproval from family and friends, and develops strategies to protect their relationship from external damage.
3. **Identity emergence**—Partners declare their couple identity to themselves and others.
4. **Relationship maintenance**—The couple works at preserving the relationship as it incorporates new challenges, such as having children, moving to new areas, and entering new social circles.

Communication in Everyday Life
The Real Valentine's Day

Valentine's Day means love, romance, and passion. It's a time for sweethearts, a time to be mushy. If that's how you think of Valentine's Day, think again.

In 498 A.D., the Roman Catholic Church declared February 14 to be St. Valentine's Feast Day. The Church's goal in naming this holiday was to replace existing holidays that celebrated love, marriage, and fertility. At the time, on the evening of February 14, the night before the Lupercalia fertility festival, girls' names were put into a container, and each boy drew out one name. For the next year, the boy and the girl whose name he had drawn would be sexual partners. The Church thought this practice should be stopped because it had little use for passion, love, or even marriage. In fact, for the first 1,500 years of its history, the Church did not honor either love or marriage and certainly didn't suggest that the two went together (Coontz, 2005). The St. Valentine's Feast Day was meant to recognize that marriage was a necessary institution in which romance had no place.

Of course, young people disagreed and continued to think that passion and love were great and to enjoy both. By the Middle Ages, St. Valentine had become associated with romance in popular culture, but, even then, romance was not assumed to lead to or to be part of marriage. Only in the 18th century did the idea that love and marriage go together begin to gain popular acceptance in the West.

And just who was St. Valentine? He was a Christian priest in the third century A.D. Valentine was jailed (the reason is a matter of controversy); awaiting execution, Valentine wrote a sentimental goodbye letter to his jailer's daughter, with whom he had fallen in love. He signed the letter, "from your Valentine."

that computer dating services may be especially helpful to people who find it hard to launch new romantic relationships. Scharlott and Christ found that people who described themselves as shy and tense when interacting with people they don't know were more likely to join computer matchmaking services than were people who didn't describe themselves as shy or uneasy interacting with strangers.

Explorational communication is the third stage in the escalation of romance, and it focuses on exchanging information. In this stage, people fish for common interests and grounds for interaction: "Do you like jazz?" "Where have you traveled?" "Have you been following the political debates?" In this stage, we continue to try to reduce uncertainty about the other person so that we can evaluate the possibility of a more serious relationship. We may make self-disclosures, which can increase trust between people (Berger & Bell, 1988). At this early stage of interaction, reciprocity of disclosure is expected so that one person isn't more vulnerable than the other (Duck, 1998; Miell & Duck, 1986). It's also possible for this phase to be where a relationship settles—that is, stabilizes as a casual dating relationship (Knapp & Vangelisti, 2005).

AMANDA   I met Scott my first semester here. We went out a few times, and then we both let it drop. That spring, he called and asked me to a party at his fraternity, and I went, and we saw each other a few more times. Then summer came, and we went our separate ways. Same thing sophomore year and now junior year. We enjoy each other, and we both love to dance, so it's fun to get together, but there's no electricity.

The fourth growth stage is *intensifying communication*, which my students nicknamed *euphoria* to emphasize its intensity and happiness. During this stage, partners spend more time together, and they rely less on external structures such as movies or parties. They immerse themselves in the relationship and may feel that they can't be together enough. Further disclosures occur, personal biographies are filled in, and partners increasingly learn how the other feels and thinks. This further reduces uncertainty about each other and about the desirability of a long-term relationship (Berger, 1987; Berger & Gudykunst, 1991). As partners increase the depth of their knowledge of each other, they begin to develop dual perspective and to begin thinking and talking of themselves as a couple.

SUSAN I fell in love this year after being alone for 8 years after my husband died. Sometimes, I think I'm crazy because I'll miss Ben at night after spending the whole day with him. We call each other several times a day just to say hello. I feel as giddy as a teenager.

© Ariel Skelley/CORBIS

Also characteristic of the intensifying stage are idealizing and personalized communication. Idealizing involves seeing the relationship and the partner as more wonderful, exciting, and perfect than they really are (Hendrick & Hendrick, 1988; Murray, Holmes, & Griffin, 1996a, 1996b). During euphoria, partners often exaggerate each other's virtues, downplay or fail to perceive vices, and overlook problems in the relationship. It is also during euphoria that partners begin to develop private nicknames and language. Sometimes I say "*namaste*" to Robbie. This is a Nepali greeting that is roughly translated as, "I honor the spirit that is in you and the oneness of us all." Saying "*namaste*" reminds us of the month we spent trekking in the mountains of Nepal.

Revising communication, although not a stage in the development of all romantic relationships, is important when it does occur. During this stage, partners come out of the clouds to look at their relationship more realistically. Problems are recognized, and partners evaluate whether they want to work through them. Many people fall in love and move through the intensifying stage yet do not choose to stay together. It is entirely possible to love a person with whom we don't choose to share our life.

THELMA Breaking up with Ted was the hardest thing I ever did. I really loved him, and he loved me, but I just couldn't see myself living with a Christian. My whole heritage is Jewish—it's who I am. I celebrate Hanukkah, not Christmas. Seder, Passover, and Yom Kippur are very important to me. Those aren't part of Ted's heritage, and he wouldn't convert. I loved him, but we couldn't have made a life together.

The final growth stage is *commitment,* which is the decision to stay with the relationship. Before commitment, partners don't assume that the relationship will continue forever. With commitment, the relationship becomes a given, around which they arrange other aspects of their lives.

Communication in Everyday Life
E-Crushes

TECHNOLOGY

Have you ever had a crush on someone but were afraid to let the person know because you feared the feeling wasn't mutual? If that happens again, a new website may be able to help you find out whether your feelings are reciprocated. Ecrush.com lets you post a message that you have a crush on someone (Straus, 2000). Ecrush then sends the person you like an e-mail message that someone has a crush on him or her. The other person can then visit the website, and if she or he types in your name, you are revealed as the author of the original message.

Apparently, a lot of people like the Ecrush idea. Clark Benson and Karen DeMars, who cofounded Ecrush, say they have more than 400,000 users, and more than 2,000 new people sign up each day. So far, Ecrush has made more than 80,000 matches. Appropriately enough, Ecrush made its debut on Valentine's Day in 1999. *Student Companion:* Activity 11.6.

Navigating is the ongoing process of staying committed and living a life together despite ups and downs and pleasant and unpleasant surprises. Couples continually adjust, work through new problems, revisit old ones, and accommodate changes in their individual and relational lives. During navigation, partners also continually experience tension from relational dialectics, which are never resolved once and for all. As partners respond to dialectical tensions, they revise and refine the nature of the relationship itself. *Student Companion: Activity 11.5.*

To use an automotive analogy, navigating involves both preventive maintenance and periodic repairs (Dindia, 2000; Canary & Stafford, 1994). The goals of navigating are to keep intimacy satisfying and healthy and to deal with any serious problems that arise. To understand the navigating stage, we'll discuss relational culture, placemaking, and everyday interaction.

The nucleus of intimacy is **relational culture,** which is a private world of rules, understandings, meanings, and patterns of acting and interpreting that partners create for their relationship (Bruess & Hoefs, 2006; Wood, 1982, 2000a). Relational culture includes how a couple manages relational dialectics. Jan and Byron may negotiate a lot of autonomy and little togetherness, whereas Louise and Kim emphasize connectedness and minimize autonomy. Bob and Cassandra are very open, whereas Mike and Zelda preserve more individual privacy in their marriage. Satisfied couples tend to agree on how to deal with dialectical tensions (Fitzpatrick & Best, 1979).

Relational culture also includes rules and rituals. Couples develop rules, usually unspoken, about how to communicate anger, sexual interest, and so forth. Couples also develop rules for commemorating special times such as birthdays and holidays. Couples also create rituals for couple time (Duck, 2006, Wood, 2006), celebrations and play, and so forth (Bruess & Pearson, 1997). The rules and rituals that partners develop and follow provide a predictable rhythm for intimate interaction.

Placemaking is the process of creating a comfortable personal environment that reflects the values, experiences, and tastes of the couple (Bateson, 1990; Werner, Altman, Brown, & Ginat, 1993). In our home, Robbie and I have symbols of our travels: Tibetan carpets, a batik from Thailand, ancient masks from Nepal, marble dishes from Turkey, and a wood carving from Mexico. Photographs of friends and family members who matter to us are scattered throughout our home. Our CDs include much jazz, lots of Mozart, and a number of crossover artists, and we have built-in bookshelves, all overloaded, in most rooms of our home. The books, photos, music, and travel

Communication in Everyday Life
The Chemistry of Love

INSIGHT

People often talk about the chemistry they have with certain others. Research suggests there may be a factual, biological basis to the idea of chemistry between people (Ackerman, 1994).

The cuddle chemical is oxytocin, which is stimulated by physical or emotional cues. Oxytocin is released when babies nurse, making mothers nuzzle and cuddle them. Oxytocin also pours out during sexual arousal and lovemaking, making lovers want to caress and cuddle one another.

The infatuation chemical is phenylethylamine (PEA). Like amphetamines, PEA makes our bodies tremble when we're attracted to someone and makes us feel euphoric, happy, and energetic when we're in love.

The attachment chemical is a group of morphine-like opiates that calm us and create feelings of relaxed comfort. This allows couples to form more peaceful, steady relationships than the speed-like PEA does. Opiates of the mind promote abiding commitment.

souvenirs make the house into a home that reflects who we are and what we've done together.

An especially important dimension of relational culture is everyday interaction (Wood & Duck, 2006). The importance of everyday interaction for couples becomes most obvious when it's not possible. People in long-distance relationships say that being together for big moments is not what they miss most; instead, they miss sharing small talk and the trivial details of their days with each other (Gerstel & Gross, 1985). Most conversations between intimates aren't dramatic or noteworthy, yet they are at least as important in sustaining intimacy as "big" discussions (Duck, 1994b; Spencer, 1994).

© Ragnar Schmuck/zefa/CORBIS

DETERIORATION STAGES

Steve Duck (1998; Wood & Duck, in press) describes relational deterioration as happening through a sequence of five processes. First, there are *intrapsychic processes,* during which one or both partners begin to feel dissatisfied with the relationship and to focus their thoughts on its problems or shortcomings. As gloomy thoughts snowball, partners may actually bring about the failure of their relationship. During the intrapsychic phase, partners may begin to think about alternatives to the relationship.

If not reversed, the intrapsychic phase leads to *dyadic processes,* which involve the breakdown of established patterns, rules, and rituals that make up the

---

Everyday Application
Measuring the Strength of Your Relationship

Following are some of the true/false questions marriage researcher John Gottman (Gottman & Silver, 2000; Kantowitz & Wingert, 1999) uses to gauge the strength of relationships, based on his assumption that, in strong relationships, partners know each other well and share a deep understanding of the other's life, feelings, thoughts, and perceptions.

- I can name my partner's best friends.
- I can tell you what stresses my partner is currently facing.
- I know the names of some of the people who have been irritating my partner lately.
- I can tell you some of my partner's life dreams.
- I can list the relatives my partner likes least.
- At the end of the day, my partner is glad to see me.
- My partner is one of my best friends.
- We just love to talk to each other.
- I feel that my partner knows me pretty well.
- My partner appreciates the things I do in this relationship.

relational culture. Partners may stop talking after dinner, no longer call when they are running late, and in other ways neglect the little things that tie them together. As the fabric of intimacy weakens, dissatisfaction intensifies.

There are general sex differences in the causes of dyadic breakdown (Wood & Duck, in press). For many women, unhappiness with a relationship tends to arise when communication declines in quality, quantity, or both. Men, in general, are more likely to be dissatisfied when specific behaviors or activities change (Riessman, 1990). Many women regard a relationship as breaking down if "we don't really communicate with each other anymore," whereas men tend to be dissatisfied if "we don't do fun things together anymore." Another sex difference is in who notices problems in a relationship. As a rule, women are more likely than men to notice tensions and early symptoms of problems (Cancian, 1989; Tavris, 1992).

Dyadic processes may also include discussion of problems and dissatisfaction. This doesn't always occur (Duck, 1998), because many people avoid talking about problems (Baxter, 1984; Metts, Cupach, & Bejlovec, 1989). Although it is painful to talk about the decline of intimacy, avoiding discussion does nothing to resolve problems and may make them worse. The outcome of dyadic processes depends on how committed the partners are, whether they perceive attractive alternatives to the relationship, and whether they have the communication skills to work through problems. If partners lack commitment or the communication skills needed to resuscitate intimacy, they must decide how to tell outsiders that they are parting.

Social support is a phase in which partners look to friends and family for support. Partners may give self-serving accounts of the breakup to save face and to secure sympathy and support from others. Thus, Beth may portray Janine as at

fault and herself as the innocent party in a breakup. During this phase, partners often criticize their exes and expect friends to take their side (Duck, 1998; La Gaipa, 1982). Although self-serving explanations of breakups are common, they aren't necessarily constructive. It's a good idea to monitor communication during this period so that we don't say things we'll later regret.

SAMANTHA I hate it when couples in our social circle divorce. It never fails that we lose one of them as a friend because each of them wants us to take sides. They each blame the other and expect us to help them do that, and you can't do it for both spouses. One of them won't be a friend anymore.

Grave dressing processes involve burying the relationship and accepting its end. During grave dressing, we work to make sense of the relationship: what it meant, why it failed, and how it affected us. Usually, people need to mourn intimacy that has died. Even if we initiate a breakup, we are sad about the failure to realize what once seemed possible. Grave dressing processes also include explaining to others why the relationship ended.

The final part of relationship deterioration involves *resurrection processes,* during which the two people move on with their lives without the other as an intimate. We conceive of ourselves as single again, and we reorganize our lives to break the synchrony we had with our ex-partner.

The stages we have discussed describe how many romantic relationships evolve. However, not all people follow these stages in this order. For example, people with pragmatic love styles might not allow themselves to enter into euphoria until they have engaged in the very practical considerations of the revising stage. Other couples skip one or more stages in the typical sequences of escalation or deterioration, and many of us cycle more than once through certain stages. For example, a couple might soar through euphoria, work out some tough issues in revising, then go through euphoria a second time. It's also normal for long-term partners to depart navigation periodically to experience both euphoric seasons and intervals of dyadic breakdown and then move back to navigating. Furthermore, because relationships are embedded in larger systems, romantic intimacy follows different developmental paths in other cultures. *Student Companion:* Activity 11.2 and Activity 11.4.

Guidelines for Communicating in Romantic Relationships

Romantic relationships often experience unique challenges. We'll now discuss four guidelines for communicating to meet such challenges and to build and maintain a healthy, satisfying relationship.

ENGAGE IN DUAL PERSPECTIVE

In Chapter 1, we first discussed dual perspective, which is an understanding of our own perspective as well as another person's perspective, thoughts, feelings, needs, and so forth. In Chapter 1, we noted that the ability to take the perspective of others is central to interpersonal communication competence. In Chapter 10, we offered the same guideline—engage in dual perspective—in relation to maintaining friendships.

Dual perspective is especially important in serious romantic relationships. When we love someone, we want to know and be known by that person. We want to understand and to be understood by that person. And we want to feel that she or he takes our perspective into account when interacting with us. Engaging in dual perspective requires us really to get to know the other person and then to use that knowledge to guide our communicative choices.

SALLY FORTH © 1992. Reprinted with special permission of King Features Syndicate.

Communication in Everyday Life
Facts about Sexually Transmitted Diseases

Many people hold dangerous misunderstandings about sexually transmitted diseases (STDs). Let's check the facts. (American Social Health Association, 2005; Cates, Herndon, Schulz, & Darroch, 2004; Weinstock, Berman, & Cates, 2004; http://www.cdc.gov/ncidod/ diseases/hepatitis/b/fact.htm).

Misconception: If I'm tested for HIV and make sure any sexual partner is, I'm safe.

Get the Facts: HIV is not the only STD, and it's not the most common. Other STDs are genital warts, genital herpes, hepatitis B, human papillomavirus (HPV), chlamydia, gonorrhea, syphilis, and trichomoniasis. One in 20 people will get hepatitis B in his or her lifetime, and 15 to 25% of those who do will die of liver disease.

Misconception: I'm not taking much of a chance, because few people have STDs.

Get the Facts: One of 2 sexually active youths will contract an STD by age 25. Over 65 million Americans are currently living with an STD, and 15 million new cases are diagnosed each year.

Misconception: STDs affect older people.

Get the Facts: Half of all new STDs occur in people 15 to 24 years old. Each year, 1 in 4 teens contracts an STD.

Misconception: The incidence of STDs is declining.

Get the Facts: Some STDs, such as genital warts, are actually increasing.

Misconception: I can't catch an STD if I have only oral sex.

Get the Facts: Think again. You can catch STDs from oral, anal, or vaginal sexual activity. People who think oral sex is safe are mistaken.

Misconception: I could tell if someone had an STD because there are symptoms.

Get the Facts: Many STDs have no symptoms or no early ones. For instance, HPV, which 50% of sexually active people will contract at some point, often has no symptoms.

Misconception: STDs can be treated, so there aren't serious consequences even if I do get one.

Get the Facts: Some can be treated. Some are resistant to treatment. And because some have no symptoms, people may not seek treatment until it's too late.

Misconception: I see a doctor regularly, so I am tested for STDs.

Get the Facts: Most doctors do not routinely test for STDs.

Misconception: Other than HIV, STDs don't have major consequences.

Get the Facts: Because STDs often have no symptoms, they may go untreated for some time. Effects of STDs include infertility, blindness, liver cancer, increased vulnerability to HIV, and death.

AUSTIN Mandy's the first girlfriend I've ever had who understands that I need time to think things through when we have a difference of opinion. All of the girls before her pressured me to talk when *they* wanted to, with no respect for when *I* wanted to. If I refused, they accused me of avoiding conflict or something like that. Mandy gets it that I really need to work things out *before* I can talk about issues, and she respects that.

Austin's commentary is a good example of what it feels like to have someone you care about take your perspective into consideration. It feels like—and it is—a very special gift. In I-Thou relationships, dual perspective is especially important.

PRACTICE SAFER SEX

In the HIV/AIDS era, sexual activities pose serious, even deadly, threats to romantic relationships. To date, about half a million people in the United States have died of AIDS (http://www.cdc.gov), and worldwide more than 37 million people have been diagnosed as HIV positive (Ross, 2004). Many of them contracted the virus through sex with a hookup, casual date, or serious romantic partner. And HIV is not the only sexually transmitted disease. See the "Communication in Everyday Life" feature on this page for more information about STDs.

Despite vigorous public education campaigns, many people still don't practice safer sex, which includes abstaining, restricting sexual activity to a single partner who has been tested for HIV, or using latex condoms (Clements, 1994; Reel & Thompson, 1994). Failing to practice safer sex puts both partners at risk for serious medical problems and even early death.

Why don't people who know about HIV/AIDS and other STDs consistently follow safer sex techniques? One reason is that many people find it more embarrassing to talk about sex than to engage in it. They find it awkward to ask direct questions of partners ("Have you been tested for HIV?" "Are you having sex with anyone else?") or to make direct requests of partners ("I want you to wear a condom," "I would like you to be tested for HIV before we have sex"). Naturally, it's difficult to talk explicitly about sex and the dangers of HIV/AIDS. However, it is far more difficult to live with HIV or the knowledge that you have infected someone else.

Another reason people sometimes fail to practice safer sex is that they are incapacitated by alcohol or other drugs, so they don't use the good sense and caution they would otherwise. In a series of studies of college students' sexual activities, communication researchers Sheryl Bowen and Paula Michal-Johnson (1995) found that safer sex precautions often are neglected when people drink heavily. Alcohol and other drugs loosen inhibitions, including appropriate concerns about personal safety. Surveys of undergraduate students report that 60% to 84% of them have hooked up and that they most often do so after consuming alcohol (McGinn, 2004).

A third reason is that many people think they are not at risk. They hold misconceptions such as "I only go out with nice people, and they don't have STDs," "I'm not gay," "diseases aren't spread by oral sex," and "I don't date people who use needles." Kara's commentary illustrates the error of being misinformed.

KARA When I had a medical exam, the doctor told me I had herpes. "What? Me? That's impossible," I said. I only have oral sex because I don't want to risk getting diseases. Turns out you can get them from oral sex, too. Now I have oral herpes, and I will have it for the rest of my life.

A final reason people don't practice safer sex is that they find it difficult and embarrassing to talk about it with an intimate. The principles of effective interpersonal communication we've discussed can help ease the discomfort of negotiating safer sex. *I* language that owns your feelings is especially important. It is more constructive to say, "I feel unsafe having unprotected sex" than to say, "Without a condom, you could give me an STD." A positive interpersonal climate is fostered by using relational language, such as "we," "us," and "our relationship" (Reel & Thompson, 1994).

Yes, negotiating safer sex is difficult. But your health and perhaps your life depend on your willingness to engage in talk about sex. People who care about themselves and their partners are honest about their sexual histories and careful in their sex practices. Before you decide it's too hard to talk about safer sex with your boyfriend or girlfriend, consider a few facts:

- ··· Women now account for 26% of newly diagnosed AIDS cases (Cowley & Murr, 2004).
- ··· Although publicity about the danger of AIDS has decreased, new HIV and AIDS cases have actually increased since 1999 (Carey & O'Connor, 2005).
- ··· In 2003, 4.8 million people were newly infected with HIV, and 2.9 million people died from AIDS-related deaths (Ross, 2004).
- ··· 70% of women who are HIV positive contracted the disease through heterosexual sexual contact (Cowley & Murr, 2004).

U.S. National Library of Medicine

MANAGE CONFLICT CONSTRUCTIVELY

Chapter 9 was devoted to managing conflict in relationships. Doing so is important for all kinds of relationships. Yet, there are two reasons romantic relationships require special attention to effective conflict management. First, romantic bonds, particularly serious ones, are important to us, and they are fragile. Lack of skill in handling conflicts can end a relationship that really matters.

The second reason for giving special attention to managing conflict in romantic relationships is one we'll discuss in depth. Although we like to think of romantic relationships as loving, many are not. Violence and abuse are unfortunately common between romantic partners, and they cut across lines of class, race, and ethnicity (French, 1992; Jacobson & Gottman, 1998; Johnson, in press; Spitzberg & Cupach, 1998; West, 1995; Wood, 2000b, 2001). Researchers (Christopher & Lloyd, 2000) have shown that many people who engage in violence against romantic partners lack the communicative skills to constructively manage emotions and conflicts. We'll now look more closely at intimate partner violence.

Intimate partner violence occurs not only in marriage, but also between cohabiting couples. It also occurs between cohabiting heterosexual couples (Cunningham & Antill, 1995; Schwartz & DeKeseredy, 1997; Spitzberg, 1998; White & Bondurant, 1996), gay couples, and lesbian couples (Peplau & Spalding, 2000; Harvey, Wenzel, & Sprecher, 2004). And it's happening earlier and earlier in people's lives: Surveys report that 12% to 36% of high school students are or have been in violent relationships (Goode, 2001; Gray & Foushee, 1997). Stalking is increasing in dating and cohabiting couples when one person wants to end the relationship (Brownstein, 2000). In a recent national survey, 25% of women and 8% of men have been assaulted by a spouse, girlfriend, or boyfriend in the past 12 months (Tjaden & Thoennes, 1998).

Women and men alike can be targets of violence from intimates. Yet, the majority of reported violence and abuse in intimacy is committed by men against women: 95% of cases involve male abusers and female victims (Hasenauer, 1997; Johnson, in press; Tjaden & Thoennes, 1998). Furthermore, male abusers are far more likely than female abusers to inflict physical injuries, sometimes severe ones (Christopher & Lloyd, 2000). In the United States, every 12 seconds a woman is known to be beaten by a husband or intimate, and 10 women a day are known to be beaten to death (Hasenauer, 1997; Tjaden & Thoennes, 1998; Wood, 2000b, 2001).

It's important to remember that the statistics on violence between intimates are based on *reported* incidents. Many people do not report incidents. Women may not report assaults by intimate partners because they are afraid that the consequence might be even worse violence or because they want to protect their partners. Men may not report assaults by intimate partners because they feel ashamed or embarrassed that a woman is assaulting them.

Relationships in which men abuse women often reflect traditional power dynamics that structure relationships between women and men. Some men are taught to use power to assert themselves and to dominate others (Coan, Gottman, Babcock, & Jacobson, 1997; Sugarman & Frankel, 1996; Truman, Tokar, & Fischer, 1996; Wood, 2004), and some women are socialized to defer and preserve relationships (Ellington & Marshall, 1997; Steil, 2000; Wood, 2001). When these internalized patterns combine in heterosexual relationships, a foundation exists for men to abuse women and for women to tolerate it rather than to be assertive or disloyal (Goldner, Penn, Sheinberg, & Walker, 1990; West, 1995). This may explain why national surveys reveal that an alarming 25% of women and 30% of men regard violence as a normal part of relationships (Gelles, 1987; Jones, 1994).

> **MARLA** Looking back, I can't believe I stayed with Sean for so long, but at the time, I couldn't imagine leaving him. We started hanging out together in high school, and then we both came to this university. When we first started seeing each other, he was so nice to me—flowers sometimes, lots of phone calls, all the stuff. But the summer after we graduated from high school, he hit me the first time. I was shocked. He was really sorry and said he was just so stressed about the whole college thing. A little while later, it happened again, and he apologized again, and I forgave him again. But it didn't stop. It got worse. Whenever he was in a bad mood, he took it out on me—really hitting hard, even beating me at times. Finally, my roommate saw bruises and put two and two together and walked me to a counselor at student health. That was the start of getting out of the relationship.

FIGURE 11.4
The Cycle of Abuse

Violence seldom stops without intervention (Steil, 2000). Instead, it follows a predictable cycle, just as Marla described: Tension mounts in the abuser; the abuser explodes, becoming violent; the abuser then is remorseful and loving; the victim feels loved and believes the relationship will improve; and then tension mounts, and the cycle begins again (see Figure 11.4).

People who develop skill in identifying and expressing their emotions and in managing conflict are less likely to resort to violence in their romantic relationships.

ADAPT COMMUNICATION TO MAINTAIN LONG-DISTANCE RELATIONSHIPS

A majority of college students are or have been in long-distance romances (Rohlfing, 1995; Stafford, 2004). Three problems, or tensions, are commonly experienced in long-distance relationships, and each of them can be addressed with communication. Perhaps the greatest problems are the lack of daily sharing of small events, and unrealistic expectations about time together (Duck, 1994a, 1994b; Gottman, 1997). As we have seen, sharing the ordinary comings and goings of days helps partners keep their lives interwoven. Routine conversations form and continually reform the basic fabric of our relationships (Wood & Duck, 2006). As the "Communication in Everyday

© George Shelley/CORBIS

Communication in Everyday Life
Coping with Geographic Separation

Couples report the following coping strategies they use to sustain intimacy across long distances (McGrane, 2000; Rohlfing, 1995; Stafford, 2004). It's a sign of our era that many of these strategies rely on technologies of communication.

- Recognize that long-distance relationships are common; you're not alone.
- Create more social support systems (friends) while separated from a romantic partner.
- Communicate creatively; send videotapes, audiotapes, and digital pictures.
- Before separating, work out ground rules for going out with friends and for phoning, visiting, and writing each other.
- Maintain trust by setting and abiding by ground rules, phoning when you say you will, and keeping lines of communication open.
- Make sure that time when you are physically together includes affection and fun. Being serious all the time isn't good for a healthy, balanced relationship.
- Maintain honesty. Especially when partners live apart, they need to be candid with each other.
- Build an open, supportive communication climate so that you can talk about issues and feelings.
- Focus on the positive aspects of separation.
- Set up times when you can communicate simultaneously through chat rooms or instant messaging, and protect those times from infringements.
- Use Web cameras and videoconferencing to simulate face-to-face interaction.
- Have online dates by agreeing to times when you'll both be logged on and can use instant messaging.
- Cell phones are cheap. Use them to make quick calls during the day.

You can learn more about long-distance romantic relationships—the problems and ways of coping—by visiting http://www .geocities.com/lysh19. On the site, you will find stories from people in long-distance relationships, advice, and tips shared by site visitors about making long-distance relationships work.

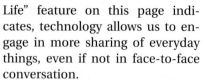

Compare what you find on this site with these strategies that researchers have identified. Can you think of other strategies that might help people involved in long-distance relationships?

Life" feature on this page indicates, technology allows us to engage in more sharing of everyday things, even if not in face-to-face conversation.

The lack of routine contact leads to the second problem faced by long-distance couples: unrealistic expectations for time together. Because partners have limited time together, they often think that every moment must be perfect. They feel that there should be no harsh words or conflict and that they should be together every moment. Yet, this is an unrealistic expectation. Conflict and needs for autonomy are natural and inevitable in all romantic relationships. They may be even more likely in reunions of long-distance couples because partners are used to living alone and have established independent rhythms that may not mesh well.

A third common problem in long-distance relationships is unequal effort invested by the two partners. According to Vicki Helgeson (1994), one of the major reasons long-distance couples break up is that one partner is doing most of the work to sustain contact and to take care of the relationship. The inequity in investment creates resentment in the person who is assuming the majority of the work to keep the relationship alive and may create guilt in the partner who is investing less.

MARIA When Miguel found a good job in another state, he moved, and both of us thought our relationship would survive. We had talked about marrying when I finished school, so we were pretty serious. At first we did okay, even though it was hard. I would write every day, and he wrote me once or twice each week. One of us called the other every week. Then, his letters got less frequent. Then, it seemed I was always the one who called him. I told him he was acting like he wasn't committed anymore, but he said he was just busy. I think that was true, but it didn't matter after a while. The upshot is that he was too busy for us, and I couldn't keep the relationship going on my own.

The good news is that these problems don't have to sabotage long-distance romance. Many people maintain satisfying commitments despite geographic separation (Rohlfing, 1995; Stafford, 2004). In fact, there are some noteworthy advantages of long-distance relationships. Because couples aren't together continually, they tend to be more loving and passionate when they are together (Blake, 1996; Reske & Stafford, 1990).

In sum, four guidelines for communication in romantic relationships are to engage in dual perspective, to practice safer sex, to manage conflict effectively to avoid intimate partner violence, and to maintain communication in long-distance relationships. Commitment, flexibility, and effective interpersonal communication help partners meet the challenges of keeping romance healthy and satisfying over the life of the relationship.

Iconica/Getty Images

Case Study: Continuing the Conversation

The following conversation is featured on the Everyday Connections website under "Chapter Resources for Chapter 11." Click on the link "Meg & Trevor" in the left-hand menu to launch the video and audio scenario scripted below.

After meeting at a New Year's party in the spring of their senior year at Agora College, Trevor and Meg quickly developed an exclusive dating relationship. Now, 4 months later, they are trying to figure out what to do about their relationship.

Trevor: Do you realize that half of our friends are planning weddings?

Jason Harris/© 2001 Wadsworth

Maybe we should start thinking about ours.

Meg: Don't start this again. You know how I feel about that. It's just too

soon. We need to know a lot more before we even think about marriage.

Trevor: Why? I'm crazy in love with you, and you are with me, right?

Case Study: Continuing the Conversation

Meg: (nods)

Trevor: So, what's too soon? What else do we need to know?

Meg: First of all, I'll be starting law school in the fall, and that's a whole new thing for me. You haven't decided on a job yet. We don't even know if we'll be in the same city!

Trevor: Sure we do. You'll be going to law school at State, and I can get a job near there. One good thing about being a business major is that I can get a job anywhere.

Meg: See, right there is a problem: I'm much more concerned about my career than you are about yours. Your whole attitude toward it is just so casual.

Trevor: I am not casual about us. I love you enough to arrange the rest of my life around our relationship. So why aren't you willing to do the same?

Meg: 'Cause it's just too soon. Law school will be very demanding, and I don't want to try starting that and a marriage at the same time.

Trevor: (grins) I'll help you study. Any other problems?

Meg: What about eating? We do okay now because we don't live together. But I'm a vegan, and you'll eat anything. I think we'd have problems if we lived together.

Trevor: Just keep your tofu away from my chicken in the refrigerator, and we'll be fine.

Meg: I'm serious, Trevor.

Trevor: So am I. I mean, just because we live together doesn't mean we have to eat the same things. That's not a problem.

Meg: You and I have different values and goals. You think I'm nuts to want a Mercedes, and I don't know how you can be happy with that old truck you drive. And you think I'm extravagant any time I buy anything for myself.

Trevor: Okay, so we'll have separate accounts, and that way each of us can decide how to spend our own money. Next problem?

Meg: What about children?

Trevor: What about children? I don't see any children. No problem there.

Meg: Quit kidding around. You know what I mean. You definitely want children; I don't know if I do. That's a big issue, one we should settle before we even think about marriage.

Trevor: Meggie, if we wait until we've settled every issue, you know, solved every problem, we'll never get married. I totally love you, and I believe in us. I think that we can resolve any issue as it comes along. That's what love is.

Meg: I'm just not comfortable with that. I'd like a lot more of these issues settled before I marry anyone. Love is great, but it's not enough.

1. What love style do you think Meg and Trevor have? What cues in the dialogue lead you to identify each person's love style?

2. Do you think Meg is "sweating the small stuff," or is she raising significant issues about the viability of the relationship?

3. Do you think Meg and Trevor would be having this conversation if they were at the close of their junior year instead of their senior year?

4. Based on the dialogue, how would you judge Trevor's and Meg's level of commitment to the relationship? How would you judge the level of their love for each other?

5. What could Trevor say or do to make Meg more willing to marry him soon? What could Meg say or do to persuade Trevor that they should wait to decide about marriage?

6. Rewrite the dialogue so that both Meg and Trevor are more affirming of each other's perspective. What might each person say to show he or she is listening and to acknowledge and confirm the other's thoughts and feelings?

You can critique and analyze this encounter based on the principles you learned in this chapter by responding to the questions included under "Conversation Analysis" at the website. By clicking on the "Submit" button at the end of the form, you can compare your work to my suggested responses. Let's continue the conversation online!

Case Study: Continuing the Conversation

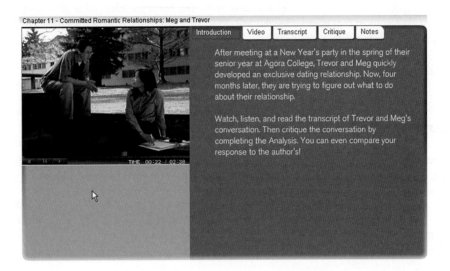

Chapter 11 - Committed Romantic Relationships: Meg and Trevor

| Introduction | Video | Transcript | Critique | Notes |

After meeting at a New Year's party in the spring of their senior year at Agora College, Trevor and Meg quickly developed an exclusive dating relationship. Now, four months later, they are trying to figure out what to do about their relationship.

Watch, listen, and read the transcript of Trevor and Meg's conversation. Then critique the conversation by completing the Analysis. You can even compare your response to the author's!

TIME 00:22 / 02:38

· · · · · · · · · ·

Chapter Summary

In this chapter, we focused on romantic relationships. Although passion may be the most dramatic dimension of romantic relationships, it is not as central as commitment (the intention to stay together) and intimacy (feelings of warmth and connection). Love comes in many forms; we considered six distinct styles of loving and how they might combine in romantic relationships.

The typical developmental course of romance begins with an escalation phase, in which communication is concentrated on gaining personal knowledge and building a private culture for the relationship. If partners decide to stay together permanently, they commit to a future of intimacy. At that point, they enter the extended phase of navigating, in which they continually adjust to small and large changes in their individual and joint lives. If a romantic bond falters, partners may enter into deterioration and eventually lay their relationship to rest.

Romantic relationships are subject to unique challenges. We discussed three guidelines for communicating to meet these challenges. Engaging in dual perspective, negotiating safer sex, and managing conflict constructively are vital to healthy, satisfying romantic relationships.

Everyday Connections Online

Now that you've read Chapter 11, go to the Everyday Connections premium website at academic.cengage.com/communication/woodinterpersonal5plus for quick access to the electronic study resources that accompany this text. The website gives you access to the "Continuing the Conversation" video scenario and questions featured in this chapter, to InfoTrac College Edition, to maintained and updated web links, and to the study aids for this chapter, including a digital glossary, review quizzes, and the chapter activities. For more information about this text's electronic learning resources, consult the **1pass card** that came with each new copy of this book, or visit academic.cengage.com/communication/woodinterpersonal5.

Key Concepts

Audio flash cards of the following key terms are available on the Everyday Connections website. Use the flash cards to improve your pronunciation of text vocabulary.

agape
commitment
committed romantic
   relationships

environmental spoiling
eros
intimacy
ludus

mania
passion
placemaking
pragma

relational culture
storge

For Further Thought and Discussion

1. If you have a current romantic partner, can you identify her or his love style? How does it fit with your own love style? Does understanding love styles give you any new insights into your relationship?

2. Have you been or are you currently involved in a long-distance relationship? If so, have you experienced one or more of the three special problems of long-distance relationships discussed in this chapter? Did you or do you follow the suggestions for maintaining contact that were presented in this chapter?

3. Have you experienced relationships in which love or commitment, but not both, were present? Describe relationships in which there was love but not commitment. Describe relationships in which there was commitment but not love. What can you conclude about the impact of each?

4. Some critics (Van Gelder, 1991, Stone, 1996) of online communities believe that there is greater potential for deceit in online relationships than in face-to-face ones. They point out that, in online relationships, people may misrepresent their appearance, sex, sexual orientation, and so forth. Do you think it is ethical for people to represent themselves inaccurately? Do you think that deception is more likely in online than in face-to-face interaction, or are different kinds of deception equally likely in the two kinds of interaction?

5. Visit the Centers for Disease Control's website at http://www.cdc.gov to learn more about HIV and AIDS. After accessing the site, select "Health Topics A–Z," then select "AIDS/HIV." Read the latest reports on the prevalence of HIV and AIDS, as well as fact sheets and FAQs.

6. The U.S. government's Violence Against Women office was recently established. Its mission, activities, and resources are summarized at http://www.ojp.usdoj.gov/vawo. Research the latest information and statistics on violence at http://www.ncadv.org. Learn about men's commitment to stopping violence against women by visiting the Men Stopping Violence website at http://www.menstoppingviolence.org.

Communication in Families

"The family is changing, not disappearing. We have to broaden our understanding of it, look for new metaphors."

Mary Catherine Bateson

Taxi/Getty Images

I n their mid-twenties, Pat and Chris decide to share their lives. They buy a home and share the responsibilities of mortgage payments, maintenance, and housekeeping. They also provide each other with emotional support, care during sickness, and financial assistance. After 7 years, Pat's unmarried sibling dies, leaving an 8-year-old child, Jamie, who moves in with Pat and Chris. During the 10 years that follow, Pat and Chris share the emotional and financial responsibilities of raising Jamie, as well as typical parental jobs, such as taking Jamie to the doctor and the dentist and attending PTA meetings, games, and school concerts. Later, Pat and Chris accompany Jamie to visit college campuses, and the three of them decide which college Jamie will attend.

Are Pat, Chris, and Jamie a family?

Does your answer depend on whether Pat and Chris are a male and a female? Does your answer depend on whether Pat and Chris are legally married and Jamie is legally adopted? Does your answer depend on whether Pat, Chris, and Jamie live in the United States, or in France, which grants legal status to unions between any two people who live together?

If this question had appeared in a textbook in 1980, most people would have counted Pat, Chris, and Jamie a family only if either Pat or Chris was male and the other female, if Pat and Chris were married, and if Jamie was legally adopted. In 1980, most people in the United States viewed "family" as a legally married man and woman who had children. Many people considered a married man and woman who did not have children a "couple" but not a "family."

Unlike the 1980s, today there is less agreement about what a family is or isn't. In the past 25 years, views of family have changed a great deal, and so have families themselves. For that reason, the first section of this chapter elaborates the opening theme by noting the enormous diversity in families in our era. The second section of the chapter discusses the importance of communication in enduring relationships, including cohabitation and marriage. Next, we consider a model of the family life cycle and explore the kinds of families it does and doesn't describe. We close the chapter with guidelines for communicating effectively to meet the challenges of family life in our era.

●●●●●●●●●●●

Diversity in Family Life

One of the most notable features of families today is their diversity. Communication scholar Kathleen Galvin (in press) uses the metaphor of a kaleidoscope to describe the proliferating types of families in our era. Think for a minute about your friends and acquaintances. How many different family forms do they represent? When I did this exercise myself, I came up with thirteen different kinds of families in my social circle:

··· A heterosexual man and woman who have been married for 12 years, who have two children, and who both work outside the home
··· A heterosexual woman and man who have cohabited for 2 years, who are child free, and who both work outside the home
··· Two gay men who have cohabited for 20 years, who both work outside the home, and who have an adopted son from another country
··· A heterosexual man and woman who are married and have three children; he works outside the home, and she is a stay-at-home mom

© Lynsey Addario/CORBIS

- Two lesbians who married in Massachusetts last year after cohabiting for 26 years and who have two adopted teenaged sons of a race different from theirs
- A single woman who adopted a daughter from Russia and who works outside the home
- A grandmother who is raising her granddaughter
- A child-free marriage between a man who lives in Pennsylvania and a woman who lives in North Carolina
- A man and a woman, both in their second marriage, who have five children from their previous marriages and who both work outside the home
- A child-free lesbian couple, both of whom work outside the home; previously, one of the women was married to a man
- A stay-at-home dad who is married to a woman who works outside the home
- A Hispanic man and a Caucasian woman who married last year, who are child free, and who are both intensely involved in careers
- A 27-year-old single mom whose mother just moved in with her

DIVERSE FORMS OF FAMILIES

The most common family forms involve marriage and cohabitation. More than 50% of people over the age of 24 are married (U.S. Bureau of the Census, 2004). For many married people, the current marriage is their second or third. On May 17, 2004, Massachusetts became the first state in the United States to allow same-sex couples to marry. Between May 17, 2004, and February 2005, 6,142 same-sex couples married in Massachusetts (Adams, 2005; Emery, 2005). Many more same-sex couples cohabit without being married, and a good number of them have children (Simmons & O'Neill, 2001).

Yet, not everyone marries, and not everyone who marries stays married. A third of births in America are to single women (Cose, 2005). In fact, women under 30 who are pregnant for the first time are more likely to be single than married, and only 40 percent of those women are cohabiting with a partner (Bumpass & Lu, 2000). Single women and single men who adopt children increase the number of single-parent families. Also adding to the number of single parent families are divorced parents who have custody of children. Over four million children live with at least one stepparent (Kreider, 2003). In 2000, 22% of children lived only with their mothers, whereas 4% of children lived only with their fathers (Simmons & O'Neill, 2001).

Stephanie Coontz (2004, 2005a, b), who studies the history of marriage, thinks the mushrooming variety of family forms makes it possible for more people to have fulfilling family lives. Because we don't all have to try to fit into one form or one model of a family, we are able to create families that suit our particular lives.

Communication in Everyday Life
Color between the Lines

What comes to mind when you hear or read the phrase *single-parent family*? If you're like the majority of Americans, you imagine a mother who is not white and one or more children. And if you're like most Americans, you're mistaken. Today, white women under 25 who have a child are more likely to be single than married (Coontz, 2005a, b; Cose, 2005). Almost 25% of white, non-Hispanic children in the United States today do not live in a two-parent household (Cose, 2005).

"And the prince and princess lived happily ever after, but not with each other."

From *The Wall Street Journal*, Nov. 6, 1996. Reprinted by permission of Cartoon Features Syndicate.

Families are diverse not only in their forms but also in their goals—the reasons people want to be involved in long-term relationships. Yet, the reasons for families have varied over time and have never been static. Historian Stephanie Coontz (2005a) notes that, historically, people didn't marry for love. During the Middle Ages, marriages functioned to forge political alliances, link families, and cement property transactions. The reverence that Christians today have for marriage and the family was absent in early church history. And the idea that passion and love are reasons to marry was not widely accepted until the 18th century. Prior to that time, the wedding day often marked the end of the bride's and groom's romances with other people and their entry into the purely practical, unemotional institution of marriage.

Beginning in the late 1700s or early 1800s, most people in the United States picked mates based on love and companionship. Although many of us assume that marriage should be based on love, there are reasons to question whether love is the most stable basis for a relationship. If marriage is based on love, shouldn't a marriage end if love dies? That's a logical conclusion. In times and places where marriage served other purposes, the waning of love—or the absence of it from the start—was not a reason to consider ending the marriage (Coontz, 2005b). If stable families are a goal, then love may not be the ideal basis for forming a family.

Historically, Americans also have viewed raising children as a primary objective of marriage (Coontz, 2005a, b). That goal often has led to a sharply gendered division of labor, particularly in white, middle-class families, in which women took responsibility for the home and family, and men took responsibility for earning the income (Cherlin, 2004).

Raising children is no longer seen as an unquestioned goal of marriage, and companionship and love are no longer the only bases for mate selection. Increasing in popularity are individualized relationships, which emphasize each partner's personal growth and self-actualization and work outside the home. In other words, a growing number of people expect marriage or long-term commitment to enhance their personal accomplishments and satisfaction. As the term implies, in individualized relationships the goals, needs, and desires of the two individuals often take priority over mutual activities and building the relationship (Cherlin, 2004).

A major reason for changes in the goals of families is that most women now work outside the home. In the mid-1970s, 60% of married women with husbands did not work outside the home. By 2000, 60% of married women were

Communication in Everyday Life
Love and Marriage Go Together Like . . .

DIVERSITY

Did you complete that song lyric with "a horse and carriage"? Many people do because we learned that little ditty when we were young. Most Westerners today assume that marriage is and should be based on love—that love and marriage naturally go together. That idea, however, is only about 200 years old and widely accepted only in Europe and North America. According to Stephanie Coontz (2005a), "Until the late 18th century, most societies around the world saw marriage as far too vital an economic and political institution to be left entirely to the free choice of the two individuals" (p. B8).

Historically, marriage has been regarded as a means to other goals, such as gaining useful in-laws and increasing financial strength or the resources to build it—for instance, an extra laborer on the farm. And that's not just history. In many societies today, marriages are arranged by family. In others, although individuals choose, their choices are guided by practical considerations at least as much as by emotional ones.

employed (Bond, Thompson, Galinsky, & Prottas, 2002; Steil, 2000). Increasingly, the breadwinner role is no longer exclusively or even primarily filled by males—only 42% of white men and 33% of black men bring in at least 70% of a family's income (Steil, 2000), and more than 30% of women in dual-worker families make more money than their male partners (Coontz, 2005b; Tyre & McGinn, 2003).

> **JOANNA**   I'd be miserable without my job. I love the sense of accomplishment that I get from teaching first graders. When a child finally catches on to reading, it's magic. Being part of that magic for so many children over the years gives me a sense of purpose in life.

As Joanna points out, many people of both sexes define their work not just as a source of income but as part of who they are. They find work personally fulfilling and rewarding. In fact, many people report that their time at work is more satisfying and affirming than their time with family (Hochschild, 1997). As we will see later in the chapter, balancing work and family responsibilities and opportunities is one of the greatest challenges facing families today.

As work increasingly provides personal fulfillment and economic support, women are becoming less dependent on family, particularly on husbands, than women have been in the past. Men are also less dependent on wives to take care of children, cook meals, wash dishes and clothes, and otherwise maintain a home. Day care and live-in babysitters are available today, and labor-saving appliances make home maintenance much less time and labor intensive than it was even 25 years ago. The same is true of food, as today's grocery stores offer many options for ready-made meals. Today's permanent-press fabrics eliminate or reduce ironing. What was a full-time job in the 1950s can be done in far less time today. Thus, men are less dependent on women to take care of homemaking. In other words, for both women and men today, marriage is more a choice than a necessity (Coontz, 2005a, b; Galvin, in press).

CULTURAL DIVERSITY OF FAMILY FORMS

Views of family vary across cultures. In some countries, marriages are arranged by families, and spouses may get to know each other only *after* the wedding ceremony. In other societies, polygamy is practiced (Werner, Altman, Brown, & Ginat, 1993). In still other cultures, marriages are so sacred that divorce is allowed only if a spouse denounces ancestors or kills someone in his or her mate's family (WuDunn, 1991). Currently, when people in Western societies marry, they begin to live relatively independently of their families of origin. In many other societies, however, marriage joins two families, and couples are intricately connected to both families, including cousins, grandparents, and great-grandparents.

> **MANSOORA**   I find it very odd that Americans marry only each other and not whole families. In South Africa, people marry into families. The parents must approve of the choice, or marriage does not happen. After marriage, the wife moves in with the husband's family. To me, this is stronger than a marriage of only two people.

Even within a single country, views of family vary over time. Despite widespread agreement among Americans that love is the basis of marriage, today the United States has a smorgasbord of families. Commuter marriages are increasingly common (Stafford, 2004), as are cohabiting arrangements (Galvin, in press). We have dual-earner couples with children, child-free marriages, single-parent families, and couples in which men are homemakers and women are the primary or sole wage earners. Social acceptance of divorce, remarriage, and single-parent families has increased (Galvin, in press). Historically, we've also thought of romantic relationships as starting with face-to-face encounters. Today, they often begin through online interaction. Now, Americans increasingly accept online romantic relationships as "real" (Carl, 2006; Clement & McLean, 2000; Fagan, 2001).

Whether our society's definition of marriage should be expanded to include same-sex commitments is one of the questions on the culture's current agenda (Wood, in press). Massachusetts now performs marriage ceremonies between lesbians and between gays, and the state recognizes those marriages as having the same legal status and rights as marriages between heterosexuals. While Massachusetts was passing its law allowing same-sex marriage, eleven other states passed laws that restrict marriage to a man and a woman. Will the marriage of two men or two women married in Massachusetts be accepted and recognized by doctors, probate courts, and insurance agents in other states? States respect and honor the laws of other states on other matters, but some states have declared that they will not respect same-sex marriages.

Compared to previous eras, today there is less bias against same-sex couples, especially among college students. In the general U.S. population, 51% of people oppose or strongly oppose same-sex marriage, and only 30% approve or strongly approve. Among college students, however, 52% approve or strongly approve of same-sex marriage, and only 26% oppose or strongly oppose it (Prime Numbers, 2004). Many churches now perform union ceremonies for gay and lesbian couples, and leading national newspapers, such as the *New York Times*, include gay and lesbian unions in the announcements section of the paper. In addition, an increasing number of municipalities grant licenses that legally recognize same-sex unions.

PEGGY   My mom and Adrienne have lived together since she and Daddy divorced when I was 2. We've always been a family. We eat together, work out problems together, vacation together, make decisions together—everything a heterosexual family does. But my mom and Adrienne aren't accepted as a legitimate couple. We've had to move several times because they were "queers," which is what a neighbor called them. Mom's insurance company won't cover Adrienne, so they have to pay for two policies. It goes on and on. I'll tell you, though, I don't know many heterosexual couples as close or stable as Adrienne and Mom.

DIVERSITY OF PATHS TO COMMITMENT

Although most people in the United States make long-term commitments, they take a variety of paths to get to the point of committing. A landmark study (Cate, Huston, & Nesselroade, 1986) identified four distinct routes to marriage. The paths to marriage that this study identified more than 20 years ago seem equally applicable to marriages today. Although we don't have relevant research on paths to nonmarital commitment, it's reasonable to believe that they would be similar to the paths to marriage.

The first path involves a gradual progression toward commitment, with a number of ups and downs and some conflict along the way. The second path is a rapid escalation toward marriage, with no downturns or serious conflict. The third path includes a medium-length courtship and progressive intimacy, followed by a hesitation and rethinking of the relationship, and then marriage and strong commitment. Finally, some couples follow a prolonged courtship period with many ups and downs and substantial, sometimes stormy, conflict.

The different pathways toward marriage may reflect partners' love styles. For example, two people with strong erotic love styles probably would follow the second pathway, which involves rapid escalation of intimacy. Two storgic people might be more likely to build their relationship more gradually, perhaps following the first or fourth pathway.

The forces that drive relationships also influence the path taken toward marriage. Some couples' decision to marry is influenced primarily by internal factors, such as love, trust, and comfort with each other. Other couples are more affected by forces external to their relationships. For instance, parents who support the relationship, and friends who are married or planning to be, are external influences that may increase the likelihood of marrying (Surra, 1987; Surra, Arizzi, & Asmussen, 1988).

© Colin Young-Wolff/PhotoEdit, Inc.

PHAEDRA It's funny how Craig and I decided to get married. We had been seeing each other for about 8 months during our senior year. My three best friends were all planning weddings in the summer following graduation, and so were a couple of the guys in Craig's crowd. One night, we were talking about our friends' marriages, and he said, "Maybe we should set a date ourselves." Of course, I'd thought about marrying him but not really seriously. But then, I thought that maybe it was a good idea. I mean, the time seemed right, since we'd both be graduating and starting to work. I love him. It's not like timing was the only reason we married, but I kind of think we wouldn't have gotten married if it had been our junior year.

Long-Term Commitments

In this section, we focus on commitment for couples. We first consider cohabitation and marriage as the two most commonly chosen ways to live as a couple. Next, we consider different styles of relationship that couples create. Third, we focus on the close link between communication and satisfaction in long-term relationships.

COHABITATION

There are many reasons why some people choose not to marry. Some don't marry because laws prohibit them from marrying. Other people don't marry because they don't want or aren't ready for a total commitment. And some people don't marry because they reject the institution of marriage and see it as incompatible with their values and identities. Let's look at several types of cohabitation.

Heterosexual Cohabitation A substantial number of heterosexual couples cohabit, and they do so for varying reasons. In the United States and Canada, cohabitation is increasingly accepted, especially among people under 30 (Cunningham & Antill, 1995). Cohabitation is also popular in other countries, including Australia, Canada, France, and India (Davis & Singh, 1989).

Although many people see cohabitation as a way to try out marriage, that may not be a realistic view. In fact, couples who cohabit before marrying are less likely to remain married than couples that do not cohabit (Bumpass & Sweet, 1989; Cunningham & Antill, 1995). One reason for this may be that marriage involves a firm commitment, whereas cohabitation is a more tentative connection that can be abandoned without great difficulty. Many people who cohabit plan to marry later but do not necessarily expect to marry the person with whom they are living currently (Cunningham & Antill, 1995; Landale & Fennelly, 1992). Cohabitation offers greater intimacy than dating but less commitment than marriage.

DIMITRI I'm crazy about Bridgette, but I'm not ready for marriage now—not even ready to think about that! There's a lot I want to do on my own before I think about settling down permanently and having a family. But I do love Bridgette, and I want to be with her now and in more than a casual way.

For some people, cohabitation is a preferred permanent alternative, not a precursor to marriage. They care enough about each other to want to live together and perhaps raise children, but they dislike the institution of marriage. For them, cohabitation is a way to make a permanent commitment on their own terms. Audrey, who has cohabited for 15 years, explains why she chooses not to marry.

AUDREY What I feel for Don isn't a matter of what's on a piece of paper or what could be said before a preacher. We don't need those formalities to know we love each other and want to spend our lives with each other. Both of us prefer to know we stay together because we love each other, not because of some legal contract.

Lesbian and Gay Cohabitation A number of countries recognize same-sex unions as marriages with all the rights associated with heterosexual marriage. Although most states in the United States do not recognize same-sex marriage, a number of U.S. clergy perform ceremonies to unite same-sex couples, and many states have passed civil rights laws to ensure that same-sex partners have legal rights.

Estimates are that at least 10% of adults in the United States are gay or lesbian (Sher, 1996). We do not have reliable estimates of the number of people who are bisexual, transsexed, or transgendered. Like heterosexuals, many gay men and lesbians seek long-term, committed relationships. Also like heterosexuals, many gay men and lesbians build relationships that are stable and enduring.

JAY There may never be a time when Joe and I can "marry" in the technical sense, but we've been married in spirit for 15 years. From the first time we got together, both of us knew the other was the one—the one for life. What we feel for each other is no different than what a man and a woman who are in love feel. We take care of each other when we're sick. We help each other out financially. We support each other emotionally. We work through problems together. We dream about the future and growing old together. If that's not a marriage, I don't know what is.

© Mark Richards/PhotoEdit, Inc.

Although some gays, lesbians, transsexuals, and transgendered people want to marry, not all do. Some see the institution of marriage as based on heterosexual values, which they reject (Butler, 2002). For them, marriage is not an idea or goal. Instead, they want long-term commitments that are based on values that confirm and cohere with their identities.

MARRIAGE

Although the number of cohabiting couples has increased over the years, marriage remains the most popular form of long-term commitment in the United States. More than 96% of men and 94% of women marry at least once (Sher, 1996). Yet, not all marriages last.

Over the course of a lifetime, a person's chance of getting divorced is roughly 50% (Notarius, 1996; Sher, 1996). However, most people who divorce intend to remarry, which is further evidence of the widespread belief in marriage.

There's great variation among marriages. Think about the marriages that you know. Do some spouses seem closer than others? Do some seem more traditional than others? Do some seem bored or even unhappy with each other? Probably you know spouses that fit each of these descriptions. Thus, you won't be surprised to learn that researchers have identified distinct kinds of marriages.

Communication in Everyday Life
Same-Sex Commitments around the World

For some years, France has instituted pacts of civil solidarity (PACS), which break the link between marriage and rights such as inheritance and insurance coverage. PACs are an option to marriage for any two people—gay, straight, lesbian, intersexed, transsexed, or transgendered—who are unrelated by blood. PACs give legal recognition on the basis of living arrangements and do not attempt to define or regulate sexual activity. They allow any two people who live together to hold property jointly, inherit, obtain health care, gain child custody, and so forth. Germany has passed similar legislation, but it restricts the unions to gays.

RELATIONSHIP TYPES

In the 1960s, a team of researchers interviewed 211 spouses (Cuber & Harroff, 1965). From their interviews, the investigators were able to distinguish five distinct types of marriage. Today, these types are useful as ways of thinking about both married and cohabiting couples. The couples studied didn't necessarily stay fixed in one type of marriage. Some couples began as one type but later changed into another type. The marital types Cuber and Harroff identified (see the "Communication in Everyday Life" feature on page 330) continue to be documented by other researchers and clinicians (Christensen & Jacobson, 1999; Gottman & Silver, 2000; Jacobson & Christensen, 1998).

Another way of classifying relationships was developed by communication scholar Mary Ann Fitzpatrick (1988; Anderson & Guerrero, 1998; Noller & Fitzpatrick, 1992). Fitzpatrick identified three distinct types of relationships: traditional, independent, and separate. The 20% of couples who fit into the traditional category are highly interdependent and emotionally expressive with each other. Traditional couples also share conventional views of marriage and family life, and they engage in conflict regularly.

Independents made up 22% of the couples in Fitzpatrick's study. Independents hold less conventional views of marriage and family life. Compared to traditionals, independents are less interdependent, more emotionally expressive, and more prone to engage in conflict. Autonomy

Communication in Everyday Life
"I do. I REALLY do."

In the traditional marriage vows in the United States, a bride and groom promise to love each other "for better or for worse, in sickness and in health, for richer or for poorer, 'til death do us part." You might think that would be a sufficient pledge. Not for some people.

Three states have adopted a covenant marriage law (Lyman, 2005). Louisiana was the first to do so, in 1998. Arizona was second, in 1998. And Arkansas, in 2001, was the third. Even in those states, couples are not required to have covenant marriages, and fewer than 2% of couples choose to have one. A covenant marriage is high-test commitment. Couples who opt for a covenant marriage agree to have premarital counseling and to have more counseling later if either one becomes dissatisfied with the marriage. The couple agrees that they will not divorce without first having counseling intended to keep the marriage together. The couple also agrees not to divorce because of "irreconcilable differences" or for many of the other reasons that cause a majority of couples to call it quits. They can only consider divorce (after counseling) for a handful of reasons, such as adultery, felony conviction, and abuse.

Communication in Everyday Life
Marital Types

In their classic study, Cuber & Harroff (1965) identified five distinct marital types:

••• Vital marriage: In this relationship, the couple is very close emotionally and wants to be together physically as much as possible. For these couples, the relationship is their primary source of satisfaction and joy.

••• Total marriage: This relationship is similar to the vital marriage except that partners are not so continuously together. Each has separate interests and sources of satisfaction, yet they look forward to being with each other and schedule their lives to maximize time together.

••• Passive–congenial marriage: In these relationships, partners are polite, and they interact, but they typically deal with superficial matters. This has been the norm for partners since they married. For partners, activities and interests outside the relationship are primary sources of pleasure and satisfaction.

••• Devitalized marriage: Partners in these relationships don't dislike each other, but they are bored with each other and the relationship. Although the relationship was vital and a source of much satisfaction earlier, it now is lifeless and characterized by apathy.

••• Conflict–habituated marriage: In these relationships, partners are incompatible. They remain tied to each other for reasons ranging from inertia to practical considerations (for example, children or finances). The primary dynamic between partners is conflict.

is moderately high for independents, so this couple type is likely to have fewer common interests and activities than traditional couples.

The third marital type is separates, who made up 17% of the couples Fitzpatrick studied. As the term implies, separates are highly autonomous. Partners give each other plenty of room, and they share less emotionally than the other two types. Separates also try to avoid conflict, perhaps because it often involves emotional expressiveness and pushes them to negotiate to reach a common decision rather than to operate separately.

In Fitzpatrick's research, 60% of couples fit into one of these three types of marriage, but 40% did not. In these mixed marriages, the husband and wife subscribe to different perspectives on marriage. The most common form of mixed marriage is the separate–traditional couple. In the couples Fitzpatrick studied, it was typically the wife who held a traditional view of marriage and wanted high interdependence and emotional closeness. Generally, husbands in mixed marriages fit the separate category.

They wanted a high degree of autonomy, and a number of them felt emotionally divorced from the marriage.

The highest levels of marital satisfaction were reported by traditional and separate–traditional couples. At first, it seems surprising that separate–traditional couples would have high satisfaction. However, it makes sense when we realize that this kind of couple embodies conventional gender roles. The traditional partner, who wants closeness and emotional expressiveness, is generally a woman, and the separate partner, who wants high independence and little emotional expressiveness, is

Everyday Application
Identifying Marital Types

Think about married or cohabiting couples you know fairly well—perhaps relatives and long-time friends of your family. They may have children or not. Using Cuber and Harroff's typology, how would you classify each of the couples? Now, describe the communication patterns you notice in each couple. Note differences among couples in communication patterns. Explain why particular communication patterns might be more and less prominent in different types of couples.

generally a man. Because their preferences are consistent with conventional femi-nine and masculine roles, they may see the relationship as complementary, with each partner contributing something the other values. The traditional partner may meet her or his needs for connection and intimacy through relationships with friends, children, and other family members. The separate partner is not expected to provide emotional intimacy and can derive his or her satisfaction from inde-pendent activities such as career or hobbies.

COMMUNICATION AND SATISFACTION IN LONG-TERM COMMITMENTS

Clifford Notarius (1996) identifies three key elements, as shown in Figure 12.1, that influence satisfaction with long-term relationships: words, thoughts, and emotions.

By *words,* Notarius means how partners talk and behave toward each other. Communication influences partners' self-esteem and feelings about the relation-ship. Happy couples tend to communicate more support, agreement, understand-ing, and interest in each other than do less happy couples. In contrast, dissatisfied and unhappy partners engage in frequent criticism, negative statements, mind reading, and egocentric communication, in which they don't rely on dual perspec-tive (Gottman & Carrère, 1994; Gottman & Silver, 2000; Notarius, 1996).

Marriage counselors (Beck, 1988; Gottman 1994a, 1994b; Markman, 1990) say that reciprocal negativity fuels dissatisfaction and conflict. Couples who engage in reciprocal negativity tend to respond to negative comments with negative mes-sages. In turn, this leads to another spiral of negative exchange, and another, and so on. Melea says, "This house is a mess. Why didn't you vacuum?" Rueben replies, "Why didn't you wash the dishes like you agreed to?" Melea then says, "I didn't wash the dishes because I knew that wouldn't matter to a slob like you." And Rueben shoots back, "Let's talk about who's a slob. Take a look at your car. It looks like a pigsty." Each negative comment is met by one equally negative or more so.

Satisfied couples generally resist the temptation to respond to negativity with reciprocal negativity. Instead, they might acknowledge a criticism or apologize. For instance, to Melea's complaint that he didn't vacuum, Rueben might reply, "I didn't get to it. I promise to before the day is over." Alternately, he might respond by meta-communicating and an expression of interest in Melea's welfare: "It's not like you to sound so critical, Melea. Are you feeling okay?" These responses to an initial nega-tive comment don't fuel negativity. Instead, they work to restore a healthy, positive interpersonal climate. Instead of having to defend her criti-cism against a negative comment from Reuben, Melea might respond by saying, "It's not a big deal—sorry I snapped," or "You're right. I'm a bit on edge about the problems at work."

The differences in the communication of satisfied and dis-satisfied spouses echo the material on climate and conflict that we discussed in Chapters 8 and 9. The differences also suggest the importance of forgiveness, at least of minor transgressions. Lorig Kachadourian, Frank Fincham, and Joanne Davila (2004) found that willingness to forgive a dating partner or spouse was positively related to satisfaction with the relationship.

By *thoughts,* Notarius means how partners think about each other and the marriage; these thoughts shape our emo-tions and words. From Chapter 3, you'll recall that, in satisfy-ing marriages, partners tend to attribute nice things the other says and does to stable, internal qualities that are within indi-vidual control (Fincham, Bradbury, & Scott, 1990). For example,

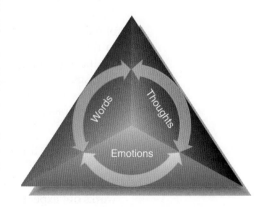

FIGURE 12.1

The Circle of Words, Thoughts, and Emotions

a wife might think, "My husband brought flowers because he is a thoughtful person who makes time to show me he cares." Likewise, in satisfying marriages partners tend to attribute negative actions and communication to unstable, external factors that are beyond individual control. If a husband forgets to run an errand, his wife might explain it by telling herself, "He forgot because he is so overwhelmed at work right now. This isn't like him; generally, he's a thoughtful person."

In less satisfying marriages, partners tend to attribute negative things the other says and does to stable, enduring qualities that are within personal control. For example, a wife might think, "My husband didn't do the errand because he is a self-ish person who never does anything to help me." Partners in unhappy marriages also tend to attribute positive thoughts and actions to unstable, external factors or to circumstances beyond personal control. To explain why her husband brought home flowers, a wife might think, "The florist must have had a sale."

A third key to marital satisfaction is *emotions,* which we discussed in detail in Chapter 7. As we saw in that chapter, emotions are affected by words and thoughts. How we feel is affected by what we say to others and what we communicate to ourselves through self-talk. For example, the attributions we make for our partners' behaviors affect how we feel about those behaviors. If a wife sees her husband's gift of flowers as evidence of his thoughtfulness and caring, she will feel closer to him than if she sees the flowers as something he bought because they were on sale.

Obviously, the words, thoughts, and actions that partners find satisfying depend on many factors, including couple type. For example, we would expect separate partners to communicate less than traditional partners. However, we would still expect that separates who are happy together and satisfied with their family would communicate supportively, make relationship enhancing attributions, and feel positive about each other and the relationship.

Words, thoughts, and emotions affect each other. What we feel affects how we communicate and how we think about ourselves, others, and our relationships. What we think influences how we feel and communicate. How we communicate shapes how we and our partners think and feel about relationships, ourselves, and each other.

The Family Life Cycle

Just as friendships and romantic relationships typically follow generalizable developmental patterns, so do many families. Figure 12.2 shows a widely accepted model of family development that includes seven stages in the life cycles of families (Olson & McCubbin, 1983). Although these stages are a useful general description of many families, they don't apply to all families. They might not apply, for instance, to the developmental paths of many cohabiting, gay, and lesbian couples. Nor do all the stages apply to all heterosexual marriages. For example, a woman who chooses to have a baby and not to have a partner would not experience stage 1. Couples who do not have children would not go through stages 2, 3, 4, and 5 because raising and launching children would not be phases of their relationship.

STAGE 1: ESTABLISHING A FAMILY

During this phase, a couple settles into marriage or a cohabiting relationship and works out expectations, interaction patterns, and daily routines for their shared life. Partners get accustomed to living together. For couples who are married, spouses get used to the labels "wife" and "husband" and to the social and legal recognition of their union.

STAGE 2: ENLARGING A FAMILY

A major change in many families' lives is the addition of children. The transition to parenthood typically brings a whole array of joys, problems, challenges, and new constraints for the couple. It also introduces new roles. A woman becomes not only a wife or partner and probably a worker but also a mother. A man becomes not only a husband or partner and probably a worker but also a father.

Furthermore, children decrease the amount of couple time and change the focus of a couple's communication. For most parents, children are a primary focus of conversation: "How are they doing?" "Which of us is taking Susie to the doctor tomorrow?" "When you had the conference with Bobby's teacher, did she have any suggestions for dealing with his behavior problems?" "How do we save money for their college education?"

Stage 1	**Establishing a family:** young couples without children
Stage 2	**Enlarging a family:** families with infants and/or preschoolers
Stage 3	**Developing a family:** families with children in elementary or high school
Stage 4	**Encouraging independence:** families with adolescents who are developing their own interests, activities, and social circles
Stage 5	**Launching children:** families who are launching children into the world
Stage 6	**Postlaunching of children:** couples after all children have left home and the couple is once again the primary unit
Stage 7	**Retirement:** couples when full-time work is no longer a part of life

FIGURE 12.2

The Typical Life Cycle of Families with Children

> **STAN** Just about everything in our lives changed when Dina was born. We had to sell our little two-door sports car because we couldn't use Dina's car seat in it. We used to enjoy a glass of wine before dinner, but now one of us fixes the dinner while the other feeds and bathes Dina. We used to sometimes decide on the spur of the moment to drive to the beach for a day trip, but now we either have to plan ahead and hire a babysitter or pack everything Dina will need, from diapers to food to toys. We're both so tired from ragged sleep because Dina wakes up several times each night. When we go to bed, neither of us is interested in sex—sleep is far more appealing.

Stan's reflection on becoming a parent is not unusual. Mari Clements and Howard Markman (1996) note that a baby can be both a bundle of joy and a home wrecker. A great deal of research shows that marital satisfaction declines after the birth of a child or children (Belsky & Rovine, 1990; Clements & Markman, 1996; Cowan, Cowan, Heming, & Miller, 1991). For many years, researchers assumed that the decline resulted from the presence of children and the demands they make. Yet, that may not be true.

A research team headed by Howard Markman (Markman, Clements, & Wright, 1991) followed 135 couples from engagement through 10 or more years of marriage. The team discovered that marital satisfaction declines after children arrive, which usually occurs after a few years of marriage. However, they also found that marital satisfaction also declines after the first few years for couples who do not have children. In other words, after the first few married years, most couples experience a dip in marital satisfaction *regardless of whether they have children.*

© Jose L. Pelaez/CORBIS Stock Market

Thus, the second stage of family life may be a time of adjusting expectations and experiencing some disappointments. It may also be that this period in family life is prone to a phenomenon known as *pileup* (Boss, 1987). Pileup occurs when many negative events occur in a short period of time and strain a family's ability to cope. A baby arrives, one partner's father is diagnosed with a serious heart condition, one partner gets a promotion that requires moving across the country. That's a lot of change and a lot of stress to handle in a short span of time.

STAGE 3: DEVELOPING A FAMILY

Most parents invest a great deal of time, thought, and energy in raising the children. Children must be taught everything from potty training to table manners, and parents are the primary teachers. During preschool years, most parents also devote themselves to instilling values in their children. This phase in the lives of families with children is one of establishing the foundations of the children's self-esteem, values, and lives.

Parent–child relationships are critical influences on children's identities. Recall from Chapter 2 that attachment styles develop in a child's first human relationship, which is usually with a parent, and that parent is more often the mother than the father. A consistently loving, attentive parent cultivates a secure attachment style in the child. Other attachment styles are fostered by other patterns of caregiving. Parents also shape children's self-concepts through labels ("such a sweet little girl," "such a big, strong boy") and identity scripts that make it clear who children are and are supposed to be.

© David Stoecklein/CORBIS

Fathers report greater stress than mothers in balancing work and family responsibilities (Milkie, Mattingly, Nomaguchi, Bianchi, & Robinson, 2004). This may be part of the reason why mothers tend to spend more time with children than fathers do (Deutsch, 2001; Hochschild with Machung, 2003). Consistent with our discussion of gendered speech communities in Chapter 4, mothers also tend to communicate more with children than fathers do. Mothers use talk to give information, advice, encouragement, and support to children (Segrin & Flora, 2005; Trad, 1995). Mothers also use communication to teach children about relating to others, building social connections, and becoming emotionally competent. Fathers' communication with children focuses more on encouraging initiative, achievement and independence (Luster & Okagaki, 2005; Popenoe, 1996; Stacey, 1996).

The sex of children also affects parent–child communication. Fathers tend to talk more with daughters and to engage in shared activities with sons (Buerkel-Rothfuss, Fink, & Buerkel, 1995). Mothers tend to talk about emotions and relationships more with daughters than with sons (Segrin & Flora, 2005; Trad, 1995). Because women as well as men talk more intimately with daughters than with sons, it's not surprising that daughters disclose significantly more information to parents than sons do (Pennington & Turner, 2004).

Although fathers spend one-third the time that mothers spend in one-on-one communication with children (LaRossa, 1998), today's fathers talk more with children than did fathers in previous generations (Silverstein, 2002). Fathers in our era say they have closer relationships with their sons than their fathers had with them (Morman & Floyd, 2002). Interestingly, sons perceive their fathers as less affectionate than their fathers perceive themselves (Floyd & Morman, 2005). Fathers' communication appears to have a particularly strong impact on children's self-esteem (Webb, Walker, Bollis, & Hebbani, 2004). This may be because fathers tend to focus communication on abilities, accomplishments, and goals. Although the number of single-father families is small, this family form seems to be highly cohesive; father–child discussions are more elaborate and less competitive than discussions between fathers and children in two-parent families (Hatfield & Abrams, 1995).

STAGE 4: ENCOURAGING INDEPENDENCE

As children enter adolescence, they seek greater autonomy. This is a natural part of their work to establish identities distinct from those of their

Communication in Everyday Life
Fathering

Fathers find it stressful to balance—or try to balance—family and work. But they are trying, and trying harder than previous generations of fathers, to make time for family. One study of men in high-pressure technology jobs (Cooper, 2000) identified three ways these men approach fathering:

··· *Superdads* try to do everything well in their careers and family lives. They don't want to slack off in either area.
··· *Traditionals* think their wives should do the vast majority of parenting whereas they themselves should be responsible for earning an income for the family.
··· *Transitionals* believe that women and men should be equally involved in parenting, but they don't enact that belief in their lives. They allow their wives to carry most of the responsibility for home maintenance and child care.

Communication in Everyday Life
Ethnicity and Parenting

Parenting varies among races. Parents whose ethnicity is not the dominant or privileged one tend to invest more energy in instilling ethnic pride in children than do parents who belong to privileged ethnic groups. African American parents were more likely to act as cultural advisors and to use more stringent discipline than European American parents (Socha, Sanchez-Hucles, Bromley, & Kelly, 1995). African American mothers were more likely than European American mothers to characterize adolescent daughters as "best friends." They also tend to set more hard-and-fast rules and to engage in more sarcasm than European American mothers (Pennington & Turner, 2004). In African American families headed by single women, daughters frequently exhibit greater self-reliance and self-esteem than their Caucasian counterparts (Diggs, 1999). African American parents also place significantly more emphasis on teaching children racial identity, history, and pride—as well as awareness of prejudice and sarcasm in the world (Mosley-Howard & Evans, 1997).

parents. Most adolescents don't want to spend a great deal of time with their parents. Instead, they have their own interests and want to pursue them with their peers. Usually, this stage involves tension between parents and children. Parents may feel hurt by the children's disinterest in being with them and with the family. Also, parents may not approve of some of their children's interests, activities, and friends. Children may feel that parents are overly protective or intrusive.

For children, this is a very important phase in personal development. They are learning to be less dependent on their families, which is essential to becoming a healthy adult. Ideally, parents realize that their children need to try their wings, and the parents encourage progressive independence—while keeping a watchful eye.

MAGGIE   After Annie arrived, Rick and I decided we wanted to attend a parenting class. It was really helpful in preparing us for the stages Annie would go through. But one thing that the teacher emphasized was that our primary job as parents was to "prepare your children not to need you." Those were her exact words. I still remember them. It just crushed me to think my job was to prepare our baby not to need me, but I knew that was good advice. Hard but good.

STAGE 5: LAUNCHING CHILDREN

The advice that Annie got was good. It prepares parents to launch their children. Launching is a time of vital change for most families. Children leave home to go to college, marry, or live on their own. When the last child leaves home, parents, who for 18 years or more have centered their lives around children, now find themselves a couple again. For parents, this can be an abrupt change. For instance, if there is only one child (or twins or triplets) in the family, when that child leaves, the parents become a couple. For parents who have more than one child, the children tend to leave home at different times, so the adjustment to being a couple again may be more gradual.

For the children, who are now young adults, this is a time of increased independence and self-discovery. As they live on their own or with peers, they begin to discover all sorts of things about themselves: what they don't know how to do because parents did it for them when they lived at home; what time they like to eat dinner, a time formerly set by parents in the home; how much emotional support they can provide for themselves.

MARK   When you have a child with special needs, the launching phase doesn't happen. We'll never have an empty nest, because Josh will never be able to live on his own. When he was born, we thought he was the most perfect baby in the world. By the time he was 1, we knew he wasn't, knew something was wrong. He is brain damaged and somewhat autistic. He's 32 and still lives in our home. I retired last year, but our nest isn't empty.

Mark makes a good point. Some parents never experience the so-called empty nest. In addition to having a child with special needs, parents may feel responsible for raising grandchildren or for letting their children live at home if they are not making it on their own. Mark's reflection also reminds us that the stage model of family life cycle doesn't describe all families. Tracy makes the same point with her story.

TRACY   It would be a real challenge to try to fit my family into the model of the family life cycle. My parents divorced when I was 6 years old. My sister and I lived with Mom until we went to college, her 4 years ago and me 2 years ago. Then, Mom started seeing this man who transferred to our town. He was a widower with 3-year-old twin boys. Last year, they got married, so my family is in the postlaunching and developing a family phases!

STAGE 6: POSTLAUNCHING OF CHILDREN

After the departure of children from the home, partners have to redefine their marriage. This period, often called the "empty nest," typically is the time of lowest satisfaction between partners (Anderson, Russell, & Schumm, 1983). This is probably because the couple is out of practice in engaging each other outside their roles as parents. The partners have more time for each other, but that may be a blessing or a curse or both.

For some couples, this is a time of renewed love—a second honeymoon—as they enjoy being able to focus on their pair relationship and not having to plan around children's schedules. For other couples, the absence of children makes obvious the distance that has arisen between them, and dissatisfaction grows. Some couples divorce after the last child has left home. Children can be the glue that holds couples together. Gretchen points out that many partners find they have to relearn how to be together with just each other and how to enjoy activities that don't involve their children.

GRETCHEN   When our last child left home for college, Brant and I realized how little we had in common as a couple. We'd centered our lives around the three children and family activities. Without any of them in the home anymore, it was like Brant and I didn't know what to do with each other. At first, it was really awkward. If we weren't Christians, maybe we would have divorced, but both of us feel marriage is forever. That meant we had to rediscover each other. We went to a weekend workshop sponsored by our church. It was called "Rediscovering Love in Your Marriage." That workshop got us started in finding our way back to each other.

Everyday Application
Your Parents' Stage in Family Life

At what stage in the family life cycle would you place your parents? If they are divorced or separated, at which stage is each of your parents? How do you perceive this stage and their happiness in it?

© Clayton Sharrard/PhotoEdit, Inc.

Retirement brings about further changes in family life. Like other changes, those ushered in by retirement can be positive or negative. For many people, retirement is a time to do what they want instead of focusing on earning a living. Many people who retire are still highly active, often volunteering in community groups, traveling, and taking up new hobbies or interests. Fran Dickson (1995) reports that people who are happy in long-lasting marriages tend to find pleasure in each other's presence and to enjoy the luxury of having more time to be together.

For other couples, retirement may evoke feelings of boredom and lack of productivity. People whose identity is strongly tied to their work may feel unanchored when they retire. Naturally, this discontent can foster tension in the marriage. Rosemary Blieszner (2000) reports that friendships in later life are very much like those in earlier life: They are important sources of emotional and instrumental support and personal growth. For many older people, friendships are a central priority and a primary way time is spent.

STUART   I looked forward to retiring for years, and I finally did it 2 years ago. For about 6 months, it was everything I had dreamed of—sleeping as late as I wanted, no pressures or deadlines, golfing any time I felt like it. Then, I got kind of bored with nothing I had to do and nobody who was counting on me for ideas or work. Every day seemed like every other day—long and empty. You can only sleep and golf for so long.

HOWARD   I retired 4 years ago, and the last 4 years have been the best years of my life! I'd always loved woodworking, but I had little time for it when I was punching the time clock. Now, I can spend as much time as I want working in my shop. I've even started selling things at the local co-op. When I was working, I always felt guilty that I didn't give anything back through civic or volunteer work. Now, I have time to contribute to my community—the Lions Club is my main volunteer activity. We raise a lot of money to help people who have vision problems and other kinds of things where they need some help. My life is more satisfying now than it has ever been.

During retirement years, the family may grow again, this time through the addition of grandchildren (Mares, 1995). Grandchildren can be welcome new members

Everyday Application
Mapping Your Family's Life Cycle

How well does your family of origin fit the family life cycle presented in this chapter? How would you modify the model presented here to make it more descriptive of your family's developmental pattern? Which stages would not be in a model for your family? Which stages would you have to add to represent how your family has evolved?

of the family who provide interest and an additional focus for grandparents' lives. The coming of grandchildren may also foster new kinds of connection and communication as grandparents talk with their children about raising grandchildren and as they interact with children for whom they don't have primary responsibility.

As we noted when introducing this discussion of family life cycle, the model doesn't apply to all families. Mark and Tracy wrote of their family experiences that do not fit well into the sequence of stages in the generic model of the family life cycle. This is another reminder of how diverse families are in our era: No one model represents all of them.

· · · · · · · · · ·

Guidelines for Effective Communication in Families

Throughout this chapter, we've noted how varied families are. They come in all sorts of shapes and sizes. For that reason, families face different challenges and find different ways to meet them. Despite this diversity, four guidelines apply to effective communication in most, if not all, families.

MAINTAIN EQUITY IN FAMILY RELATIONSHIPS

One of the most important guidelines for sustaining healthy families is to make fairness a high priority. The responsibilities of maintaining a family should not fall just or primarily on one person. Likewise, the benefits of family life should not be substantially greater for one person than for another.

Social exchange theory (Kelley & Thiabaut, 1978; Rusbult & Buunk, 1993; Thiabaut & Kelley, 1959) states that people apply economic principles to evaluate their relationships. They conduct cost-benefit analyses. Costs are undesirable things that come from being in a relationship. Perhaps a relationship costs you time, effort, and money. Rewards are desirable things that come from being in a relationship. You may value the companionship, support, and affection that come from a relationship. As long as your rewards outweigh your costs, the net outcome of the relationship is positive, so you are satisfied. If costs exceed rewards, we're dissatisfied and may move on.

Most of us are probably not as coldly calculating about relationships as social exchange theory suggests. Most of us probably don't spend our time tallying the rewards and costs of being in our families. At the same time, most of us do want relationships that are equitable, or fair, in a general sense. **Equity** is fairness, based on the perception that both people invest equally in a relationship and benefit similarly from their investments.

Equity theory does not accept social exchange theory's assumptions that people demand equality and measure rewards and costs to decide whether to stay in a relationship. Instead, it says that whether a relationship is satisfying and enduring depends on whether the people in it perceive the relationship as relatively equitable over time. This is a more flexible explanation for why relationships do or don't endure. There may be times, sometimes prolonged times, when one member of a family invests more than other members of the family. According to equity theory, this would not necessarily mean that the heavy investor feels dissatisfied. He or she might not, if in the past he or she invested less, or if in the past others in the family had given more than their fair share. As long as the relationship is perceived as relatively equitable over time, we're likely to be satisfied.

Communication in Everyday Life
The Second Shift

In the majority of dual-worker families, women leave work and come home to a **second shift** (Hochschild with Machung, 2003; Steil, 2000). Many women who work outside the home assume primary responsibility for fixing meals each night, fitting in housework in the evenings, and caring for children. Women tend to do the day-in, day-out jobs, such as cooking, shopping, and helping children with homework. Men more often do domestic work that can be scheduled flexibly. Mowing the lawn can be done morning or evening any day of the week, whereas preparing meals must be done on a tight timetable. Men also are likely to participate actively in playing with children and in fun activities, such as visiting the zoo, whereas women are more likely to take care of the routine, daily tasks, such as bathing, dressing, and feeding children.

As a rule, women assume most of the **psychological responsibility,** which involves remembering, planning, and scheduling family life. Parents may alternate who takes children to the doctor, but it is usually the mother who remembers when checkups are needed, makes appointments, and reminds the father to take the child. Birthday cards and gifts are signed by both partners, but women often assume psychological responsibility for remembering birthdays of all family members and for buying cards and gifts.

© Michael Newman/PhotoEdit

Perceived equity is very important in committed families. Although few partners demand moment-to-moment equality, most of us want our family relationships to be equitable over time. Inequity tends to breed unhappiness, which lessens satisfaction and commitment and sometimes precedes affairs or other threats to a family's survival (Anderson & Guerrero, 1998; Sprecher, 2001; Sprecher & Felmlee, 1997; Walster, Traupmann, & Walster, 1978).

Equity has multiple dimensions. We may evaluate the fairness of financial, emotional, physical, and other contributions to a relationship. Couple satisfaction seems especially affected by equity in housework and child care. Inequitable division of domestic obligations fuels dissatisfaction and resentment, both of which harm intimacy (Gottman & Carrère, 1994; White, 1998). Marital stability is closely linked to perceptions of equitable divisions of child care and housework (Fowers, 1991; Pleck, 1987; Suitor, 1991; Wilkie, 1991).

Even when both partners in heterosexual relationships work outside the home, women do the majority of child care and home-making (Chadwick & Heaton, 1999; Goldstein, 2000; Nussbaum, 1992; Okin, 1989; Risman & Godwin, 2001; Steil, 2000). In dual-worker families, wives perform two to three times more household labor than their husbands (Perry-Jenkins, Pierce, & Goldberg, 2004). Although most men in dual-worker families don't do half of the work involved in running a home and raising children, today most men assume more responsibility for running households and raising children than they did 20 or even 10 years ago. On average, among couples who earn equal incomes, men do 36% of the housework (Kamo & Cohen, 1998).

CORA MAY I said, "Either things are going to change around here, or I'm leaving." He didn't believe me, but I stood my ground. For 20 years, I had done all of the housework, the cooking, and the child care, while he did none of these. Walter just went to his job each day and came back home for me to wait on him. Well, I went to my job each day, too. I worked hard, and I was tired when I got home. It got really bad when I started taking night courses. I needed to study at night, not fix meals and do laundry, so I asked him to help out. You'd think he'd been stung by a bee. He said no, so I just quit fixing meals and left his laundry when I washed my clothes. Finally, he got with the program.

How are domestic responsibilities managed in same-sex relationships? Most gay and lesbian relationships engage in ongoing negotiation about sharing tasks or dividing them according to preference or necessity (Peplau & Beals, 2003). A majority of lesbian couples create more egalitarian relationships than do either heterosexuals or gay men (Huston & Schwartz, 1995; Kurdek, 1993). Gay men, like many heterosexual men, often use the power derived from income to authorize inequitable contributions to domestic life. In many gay couples, the man who makes more money has and uses more power, both in making decisions that affect the relationship and in avoiding housework (Huston & Schwartz, 1995).

Communication in Everyday Life
What Makes a Good Marriage?

Many people think anger is the most destructive emotion in marriage. Not so, say John Gottman and Nan Silver (2000), who have spent decades studying good and bad marriages. According to them, anger is present at times in all marriages, and all spouses fight. Happy and unhappy couples differ in the overall climate of the relationship and in how couples fight.

In all the happy couples Gottman has studied, the partners communicated frequently and with enjoyment, and this leads them to have a deep understanding of each other—the other's life, dreams, interpersonal connections, fears, and perceptions. When this kind of loving understanding exists, a relationship is not seriously harmed by occasional outbursts of anger or even vigorous arguments.

When happy couples fight, they avoid dynamics that rip apart the basic fabric of their relationship. First, they avoid what Gottman calls the "Four Horsemen of the Apocalypse": criticism (personal attacks), contempt (disrespect, sometimes accompanied by sarcasm and insults), defensiveness (focus on protecting self instead of dealing with problems or protecting the relationship), and stonewalling (refusing to discuss problems). Second, they make frequent efforts to revive intimacy and defuse tension; they reach out to each other, apologize, and use humor. The way in which happy couples deal with conflict actually strengthens their relationships.

If you would like to know more about John Gottman and his research, go to http://www.annonline.com/interviews/970122/biography.html. This site offers an audio recording of an interview with Gottman.

MAKE DAILY CHOICES THAT ENHANCE INTIMACY

A second important guideline for communication that sustains healthy families is to be aware that families are creative projects that reflect the choices made by the people in them. Although we are not always aware that we are making choices, we continuously choose who we will be and what kind of relationships we will fashion. Intimate partners choose to sustain closeness or let it wither, to build defensive or supportive climates, to rely on constructive or destructive communication to deal with conflict, to fulfill or betray trust, and to enhance or diminish each other's self-concepts.

JACKSON One of the things I love most about Meleika is the way she starts each day. Before getting out of bed, she reaches over and kisses my cheek. Then, she gets up and showers while I sneak a little more shut-eye. When I get up, the first thing she always says is "Morning, love." That is such a great way to start each day. Even after 5 years of marriage, she starts each day by letting me know I matter.

Typically, we focus on large choices, such as whether to commit or how to manage a serious conflict. As important as major choices are, they don't make up the basic fabric of family life. Instead, it is the undramatic, small choices that create or destroy families (Totten, 2006; Wood & Duck, 2006b). Do you listen mindfully to your partner or child when you are tired? Do you buy flowers or a card when there is no special reason? Do you find the energy to go to your child's game even when you've had a rough day? Do you engage in dual perspective so that you can understand your children on their terms? Do you stay in touch with your partner's concerns and dreams?

Seemingly small choices weave the basic fabric of our families. Reflecting on his own long marriage, former president Jimmy Carter (1996) wrote, "What makes a marriage? Is a personal union built or strengthened by dramatic events? I would say no. It's the year-by-year, dozen-times-a-day demonstration of the little things that can destroy a marriage or make it successful" (p. 76). Through awareness of the impact of the "small" choices we make a dozen times a day, we can make choices that continuously enhance the quality of our families.

SHOW RESPECT AND CONSIDERATION

For families to remain healthy and satisfying, family members need to demonstrate continuously that they value and respect each other. As obvious as this guideline seems, many families don't follow it. Sometimes we treat strangers with more respect and kindness than we offer our romantic partners or our children (Emmers-Sommer, 2003). It's easy to take for granted people who are continuing parts of our lives and to be less loving, respectful, and considerate than we should be.

> **MIKE** I gotta hand it to my folks on one thing. They always treated each other with respect, and it was the same with us kids. Other kids I knew had parents who wouldn't listen to them or who used that "because I said so, that's why" parent line. Not my folks. They would always listen to our side of a story or our ideas, and they'd listen thoughtfully. They always gave us reasons for decisions or rules in the family. Sometimes they let us be part of deciding how to handle something.

It's especially important to communicate respect when discussing problems and complaints. Studies of marriages reveal differences in the ways satisfied couples and dissatisfied ones talk about complaints and problems. Satisfied couples assert grievances and express anger and disagreement, but they do so in ways that don't demean each other. Dissatisfied couples communicate criticism, contempt, and sometimes disgust (Gottman & Carrère, 1994; Gottman & Silver, 2000). Family members' self-respect is at stake in how we act toward them. Because communication is irreversible, we need to be mindful of our ethical choices when communicating with family members.

DON'T SWEAT THE SMALL STUFF

We first discussed this guideline in Chapter 10 as a way to maintain healthy friendships. This guideline also pertains to family relationships. If we want them to last, we must be willing to overlook many minor irritations and frustrations that are inevitable in living with others (Carlson & Carlson, 1999; White, 1998).

When two people live together continuously, it is natural for each person's habits and qualities to annoy the other sometimes. When a family includes more than two people, the potential for irritation mushrooms. We all have quirks, habits, and mannerisms that irritate others: the toothpaste cap left off the tube, the clinking of a coffee spoon, or watching football every Sunday. At times, family members also interfere with one another's schedules and preferences. At times, families seem like nothing but a hassle! And yet, most of us would never consider giving up our families. We love them. We want them in our lives.

To reduce the tendency to make mountains out of molehills, we can take responsibility for our perceptions and our responses to them. My partner, Robbie, is hopelessly forgetful, and that isn't going to change. If I focus on that (all the things he forgets to do, the errands he forgets to run), I make myself unhappy with him and with our marriage. Notice that I am owning responsibility for how I choose to focus my perceptions and how I feel and act.

When her children were young, my sister Carolyn sometimes said to me that she found it frustrating that the children were so well behaved with others and sometimes spoiled, exasperating brats at home. She interpreted their tantrums at home as evidence that they respected her and her partner less than they respected people outside of the family. Another mother offered Carolyn the insight that children misbehave where they feel most safe, most secure that they do so without losing others' affection and love. Once Carolyn interpreted her children's occasional misbehavior at home as a compliment that they felt secure and loved, she was less

Communication in Everyday Life
Love as a Package Deal

Have you ever felt that a relationship would work better if the other person would just change—if he would stop throwing clothes on the floor; if she wouldn't be so stubborn; if he would be more interested in sex; if she would quit leaving dishes in the sink; if he would be less moody; if she would spend more money? These are the kinds of issues that cause tension and conflict in partners. Yet, change may not be the answer.

Marriage counselors Andrew Christensen and Neil Jacobson (Christensen & Jacobson, 1999; Jacobson & Christensen, 1998) say that trying to change people you love seldom works. Not only does the other person not change, but efforts to bring about change are likely to breed resentment and dissatisfaction.

Instead, they counsel couples to accept each other as package deals, to love each other despite differences and disappointments. They emphasize that to accept your partner is not to submit to her or him. It's also not to grudgingly tolerate behaviors and qualities you dislike. Rather, to accept is to realize that the person over whom you have power is not your partner but yourself. You can choose how you will respond to your partner and what judgments you will—or will not—make. Christensen and Jacobson report that partners who approach each other with genuine acceptance and empathy tend to be happier and their relationships more enduring. Ironically, partners who approach each other this way are likely to create supportive, collaborative climates in which some of the changes they want in each other may happen spontaneously.

frustrated by the behavior. She still corrected them, but she no longer interpreted their misconduct as a sign that they disrespected her and her partner.

We can also monitor the self-serving attribution that may lead us to overestimate our good qualities and behaviors and underestimate those of our partner. When I used to get angry at Robbie for being forgetful, I conveniently overlooked my own failings and his grace in accepting them. I am not as punctual as Robbie is, so he's often ready and waiting for me. Yet, he seldom criticizes me when I'm a few minutes late. Realizing that he accepts qualities in me that he doesn't like makes it easier for me to return the favor.

> **ANDY**   I used to get so mad at my parents because I thought they were harder on me than my kid sister Becky. I had to take out trash. I had to watch out for her on the playground. I had to help dad with the yard. My mother taught me a lesson. She asked me to write down everything that I had to do that Becky didn't. When I was through, she went down the list, and by each thing I listed, she listed one thing Becky did that I didn't, like cleaning the litter box, clearing the table, sweeping the porch. I'd never really noticed all Becky had to do. I just saw what I had to do.

In their book *Don't Sweat the Small Stuff in Love*, Richard Carlson and Kristine Carlson advise us to take charge of our own happiness. When we say, "I'd be happy if only she would stop doing X" or "I'd be happy if only he would do Y," we're assuming that another has control of our happiness. Of course, your happiness is affected by others, particularly intimates. However, the fact that others affect how you feel doesn't mean they are responsible for your feelings or your happiness.

When we take charge of our happiness, we can also take ownership of our issues. Ask yourself whether the issue is the other person's behavior or your own feeling about it. For years, I fussed at Robbie for not keeping our home neat. When I saw newspapers left on the table or bath towels not folded on the rack, I grumbled, "Why can't you be neater?" Robbie's response was, "Why does it matter?" He had a good point. The desire for neatness was *my* issue. My own desire for neatness—not Robbie's leaving newspapers or towels—made me displeased when things were not arranged as I wanted them to be. I couldn't and still can't control Robbie (thank goodness!), but I can control how I respond to stray newspapers and unfolded towels.

Case Study: Continuing the Conversation

The following conversation is featured on the Everyday Connections website under "Chapter Resources for Chapter 12." Click on the link "Dan & Charlotte" in the left-hand menu to launch the video and audio scenario scripted below. (Note that this scenario has two possible endings.)

Dan and Charlotte have been married for almost 5 years. They both have great careers and are very comfortable in their life and relationship. Dan is talking to his mom on the phone *while Charlotte sits in the living room working on her laptop.*

Dan: Yeah, that sounds good. We'll swing by after dinner. . . . Right. . . . No, Mom, we're still not sure. . . . Because we're still thinking about it. . . . about whether or not we're even going to have kids! I really don't want to get into right now, Mom. . . . Yeah, we'll see you then. 'Bye.

Charlotte: How's Mom?

Dan: Oh, fine. Just really wondering when her grandkids are on the way!

Charlotte: [Laughing] Your mom's funny. She's really got a one-track mind these days.

Dan: Well, we really should figure out if we're going to do it or not.

Case Study: Continuing the Conversation

Charlotte: What? Have kids?

Dan: Yeah, I mean we've been married 5 years. I'd say it's now or never.

Charlotte: Well, what do you think?

Dan: Well, it's the ultimate commitment. I mean, if we're going to do it, we have to do it right. I know so many people—friends and co-workers—who just jumped right into it and really seem to resent their kids for being a burden. I don't want to be one of those parents, you know?

Charlotte: Absolutely. And there are our careers to think about. I mean, we're both doing great right now, and we're really happy as a couple. I'd have to cut back to part-time, and I'd need help from you, too. No matter what, having a child would mean less time, money, energy for ourselves, you know?

Dan: Right. But do we really *want* to have kids?

Charlotte: I'm not against it. What about you?

Dan: Yeah, I feel the same. I'm not against it, but do we really want to give up what we have now?

Ending 1

A few months later, Dan and Charlotte attend a friend's dinner party. A lot of their friends are there, most of whom have brought their children. As Charlotte mingles, Dan plays with the younger kids, throwing them over his shoulder and tickling them. Charlotte's friend Maggie is talking about her own child.

Maggie: It's hard work, but it's so much fun. I really don't know what my family did before we had a child. I mean, we all just sit and watch her do her thing, you know? She'll dance and sing, tell us stories. It's really so funny! . . . So when are you two going start trying?

Dan approaches and hands Charlotte a drink.

Charlotte: Well, we really aren't planning on having kids.

Maggie: Haven't you guys been married for a long time? I mean, if you wait any longer, it could get complicated. There's really something to be said about having kids young, because the older you get, the less energy you'll have. I mean, how long are you going to wait?

Dan: We're not planning on having kids at all. We just decided that it's not something we want to do.

Maggie: But what about your parents? What did they say about it? I mean, aren't they expecting grandkids someday?

Dan: [A little irritated] It's really not up to them. We decided what's best for us, and that's it.

Later that night at home, Dan and Charlotte discuss the party.

Charlotte: Geez, did *everyone* there have kids? It felt like the Inquisition, you know?

Dan: Yeah, that was weird. I actually felt a bit left out, you know? I mean, I love playing with everyone's kids, but it seems like the only topic of conversation was when *we're* going to have one.

Charlotte: Do you still feel okay about our decision? You seemed to be having a lot of fun with the kids tonight.

Dan: I love playing with them! But I love where we are and what we do, and I don't want to change it. I absolutely stand by our decision. What about you?

Charlotte: Definitely. We'll just have to deal with the fact that things have changed. Our relationships with our friends are going to be different from now on since everyone else has kids.

Ending 2

A year and a half later, Dan and Charlotte have had their own child. One night, Dan is putting the baby to bed in her crib. He tickles her and smiles at her before he turns off the light and goes into the living room to sit on the couch across from Charlotte. He sighs and picks up the checkbook to balance it.

Dan: Tired?

Charlotte: I'm exhausted. She was up four times last night and wouldn't go back to sleep. I think she has a new tooth coming in, and it's keeping her up.

Dan: Well, I have tomorrow off. I'll get up with her, and you can sleep in.

Charlotte: Thanks.

Dan: You seem a little distant tonight. What is it?

Charlotte: Oh, there's just a lot happening at work that I'm missing—things I'd like to be involved with, but since I'm part-time now, I can't really take them on.

Dan: Man, we really need to watch our spending this month. We're pretty tight here.

The baby begins to cry. Dan starts to get up, but Charlotte stops him.

Charlotte: [A little irritated] Dan, didn't we agree to let her cry for a

Case Study: Continuing the Conversation

while? She has to get used to the crib sometime, right?

Dan: [Confrontational] Isn't it hard for you to hear her cry like that?

Charlotte: [Defensive] Of course, but she has to learn to calm herself down. Trust me, this is what Maggie and John did with Katie, and it worked. [She pauses before asking a question.] Did you think it would be this hard?

Dan: I don't know. It's definitely harder than I expected. I do miss just the two of us hanging out. And the tight budget is something to get used to.

Charlotte: You know, today, she was eating her oatmeal in her chair. I went outside for a second, and when I came back in, the entire bowl was on her head! [Laughing] She had dumped the whole thing on her head! She had blueberries in her nose! I wouldn't change any of

this. I don't care how tight our budget is or how exhausted we are. I love her so much.

Dan: Yeah, me too. I really love being a dad. There's nothing more important than that.

1. In their conversation about whether to have a child, to what extent do Charlotte and Dan engage in person-centered communication?

2. Dan responds somewhat defensively to Maggie's questions. Based on what you have learned about communication that fosters defensiveness, explain why Dan might have felt this when talking with Maggie.

3. In this chapter, former president Jimmy Carter is quoted as saying that it's not the big things, but

"the year-by-year, dozen-times-a-day demonstration of the little things that can destroy a marriage or make it successful." Identify some of the "little things" that Dan and Charlotte do to strengthen their relationship.

You can critique and analyze this encounter based on the principles you learned in this chapter by responding to the questions included under "Conversation Analysis" at the website. By clicking on the "Submit" button at the end of the form, you can compare your work to my suggested responses. Let's continue the conversation online!

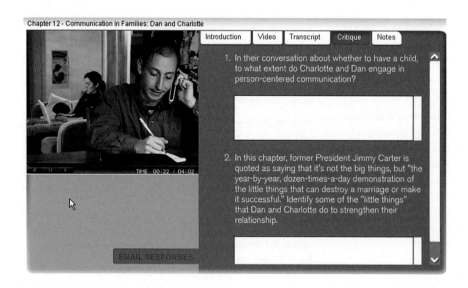

Chapter Summary

In this chapter, we focused on communication in families. We first examined many forms families take and goals they serve in our era. We then focused on long-term commitments, including marriage and cohabitation. Once again, we noted the variety in long-term relationships. In the third section of the chapter, we considered a model of the family life cycle. In our discussion, we noted ways in which the model is limited to certain kinds of families, and we considered how it might be adapted to fit other sorts of families.

The final section of the chapter identified guidelines for communicating effectively to meet the challenges of family life. First, building and maintaining equitable relationships is critical to family satisfaction and stability. Second, ongoing, daily choices enhance family relationships. Small choices can matter as much as or more than big ones in weaving the fabric of family life. Third, we pointed out the value of showing respect and consideration to family members. Too often, we save our good manners for social relationships and behave less respectfully and considerately with our partners and children. Finally, we repeated the guideline first offered in Chapter 10: Don't sweat the small stuff. Irritations are inevitable in family relationships. Focusing on them is not. Save your energy for working on big stuff.

Everyday Connections Online

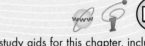

Now that you've read Chapter 12, go to the Everyday Connections premium website at academic.cengage.com/communication/woodinterpersonal5plus for quick access to the electronic study resources that accompany this text. The website gives you access to the "Continuing the Conversation" video scenario and questions featured in this chapter, to InfoTrac College Edition, to maintained and updated web links, and to the study aids for this chapter, including a digital glossary, review quizzes, and the chapter activities. For more information about this text's electronic learning resources, consult the **1pass card** that came with each new copy of this book, or visit academic.cengage.com/communication/woodinterpersonal5.

Key Concepts

Audio flash cards of the following key concepts are available on the Everyday Connections website. Use the flash cards to improve your pronunciation of text vocabulary.

equity   psychological responsibility   second shift   social exchange theory

For Further Thought and Discussion

1. How do you define *family*? What do family members do for each other? Which types of relationships discussed in this chapter do and do not fit your definition?

2. Sign onto your InfoTrac College Edition to read Susan Lang's 2000 article, "Working Couples Make Time for Their Families." What does Lang mean by a "neo-traditional" arrangement that some couples use? Does this address the problem of the second shift?

3. Use your InfoTrac College Edition to look up current information on marriages and divorces in the United States.

Access the most recent year of the *Information Please Almanac*. Can you find statistics for the number of people who married in the most recent year? What was the average age of women and men who married? How many marriages were first, second, or third marriages? How many divorces were reported in the most recent year?

4. Think about the paths to commitment discussed on pages 326-327. Can you apply this material to your own current or past relationships? If you have been in externally driven relationships, how would you describe them? How would you describe internally driven relationships?

Epilogue:
Continuing
the Conversation

> "We are all different facets of the same reality, different parts of the one whole, just as the numerous waves rising and falling in the ocean are interrelated transformations of the one ocean."
>
> **Thich Thien-An**

Although this book is drawing to a close, the conversation we've launched in these pages will continue. Interpersonal communication will be central to your life in the years ahead. As I reflect on what we've discussed since the Introduction, I see three threads that weave through the entire book.

Communication Creates and Reflects Identity

Communication is both an important influence that shapes personal identity and a primary means by which we express who we are. Our sense of personal identity grows directly out of interpersonal communication. We enter the world without any clear sense of self, and we look to others to tell us who we are. Parents, grandparents, siblings, and others who are significant in the first years of our lives express how they see us and how they value us. In turn, our own sense of self reflects our perceptions of their appraisals of us.

Family members also shape our attachment styles and the scripts we follow in dealing with conflict, expressing emotions, and engaging in other forms of interpersonal communication. As we venture beyond the confines of family, we continue to learn from others and to see ourselves through the eyes of others. Peers, teachers, friends, and romantic partners communicate their views of us, and they become part of how we see ourselves and how we define our paths of personal growth. They also give us additional scripts and perspectives that we may rely on in our interpersonal communication.

Identity not only grows out of interpersonal communication but is expressed in communication. How we communicate expresses who we are. Verbally and nonverbally, we announce that we are dominant or deferential, outgoing or introverted, caring or indifferent, emotionally expressive or reserved, self-centered or interested in others, assertive or passive, accepting or judgmental, and so forth.

Interpersonal Communication Is Central to Relationships

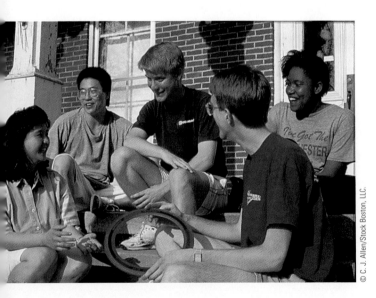

© C. J. Allen/Stock Boston, LLC.

Communication is the heart of personal relationships. The health and endurance of personal relationships depend in large measure on our ability to communicate effectively. For relationships to be satisfying, we need to know how to express our feelings, needs, and ideas in ways that others can understand. We also need to know how to listen sensitively and responsively to people in our lives so that they feel safe being open and honest with us.

Interpersonal communication skills also allow us to create climates that are supportive and affirming so that our relationships are healthy. The interpersonal climate of a relationship can facilitate or undermine constructive conflict. When we need to work through issues in our relationships, we can do so more effectively if we have built a supportive, trusting climate. Communication is the basis of meaning in human relationships, and it is the primary way we build, refine, sustain, and transform our connections with others.

Interpersonal Communication Takes Place in a Diverse World

A third theme of this book is that social diversity shapes and is reflected in communication. We've seen that our social standpoints affect how we communicate and how we interpret the communication of others. What is normal or desirable in one social group may be offensive or odd in other communities. Once we understand that standpoints shape communication, we can see that there are no absolutely right or wrong styles of communicating. Our ways of communicating, then, reflect not just our individual identities but also standpoints that are shaped by the social groups to which we belong.

Diverse cultures and the communication styles they cultivate offer rich opportunities to learn about others and ourselves. The more we interact with people whose backgrounds, beliefs, and communication styles differ from our own, the more we will grow as individuals and as members of a common world.

What you've studied about interpersonal communication should give you insight into how each of these themes applies in your current life. Let's now consider how they pertain to our personal and collective futures.

The Road Ahead

Interpersonal communication will be as important to your everyday life in the future as it is today, although it may assume different forms and functions in the years ahead. The skills and perspectives we've discussed in this book will serve you well in meeting the challenges that will accompany changes in yourself, relationships, and society.

In the coming years, your interpersonal relationships will change in anticipated and surprising ways. Some of the friends you have today will still be close in years to come, whereas others will fade away, and new people will assume importance in your life. Some romances of the moment will flourish and endure, and others will wither. New people will come into your life, and familiar ones will leave. Each person who enters or exits your life will affect your personal identity.

There will also be changes and surprises in how people go about the process of forming and sustaining relationships. The trend toward long-distance romances and friendships will grow as more people who care about each other find that they cannot live and work in the same location. Technology will also change how we communicate with friends and romantic partners. Increasingly, we will rely on electronic forms of communication to sustain important personal relationships. Currently, I use e-mail to stay in daily contact with a man who has been my friend for 20 years, and I am looking forward to meeting in person a woman with whom I've become friendly through electronic communication. Many of my students rely on e-mail to communicate daily with parents and siblings. In the future, friends, romantic partners, and family members will make increasing use of the Internet to stay in touch.

Finally, interpersonal communication and relationships will evolve in response to changes in the larger society. Medical advances will stretch the average lifespan further, so that a promise to stay together "'til death do us part" will involve a greater time commitment than it does today. Longer lives will also increase the number of older people in society and the opportunities for them to be part of our friendships and families.

Relationship forms that are not recognized or approved today may be accepted in the future. Interaction with an increasing diversity of people will change our perspective on what relationships are and how to sustain them. In addition, the horizons diversity fosters will broaden the options we recognize for creating our own relationships.

Neither you nor I can foresee what lies ahead for us and for our world. However, we can predict confidently that there will be changes in us, others, and cultural life. Whatever changes we experience, we can be sure that interpersonal communication will continue to be central to our happiness and effectiveness.

From this book and the course it accompanies, you have learned a good deal about interpersonal communication. I hope that the understandings and skills you've acquired will be valuable to you in the years ahead. If you are committed to practicing these skills in your everyday life and to building on this knowledge, then you are on the threshold of a lifelong journey that will enrich you and your relationships with others. I wish all of that and more for you.

Julia T Wood

Glossary

A

abstract Removed from concrete reality. Symbols are abstract because they are inferences and generalizations abstracted from a total reality.

agape A secondary style of loving that is selfless and based on giving to others, not on receiving rewards or returns from them. A blend of eros and storge.

ambiguous Subject to multiple meanings. Symbols are ambiguous because their meanings vary from person to person, context to context, and so forth.

ambushing Listening carefully for the purpose of attacking a speaker.

anxious/ambivalent attachment style A mode of relating characterized by preoccupation with relationships and inconsistent behavior toward the partner. Develops in childhood when a caregiver behaves inconsistently toward a child, sometimes loving and sometimes rejecting or neglectful.

arbitrary Random or not constrained by necessity. Symbols are arbitrary because there is no necessary reason for a particular symbol to stand for a particular referent.

artifact A personal object we use to announce our identity and personalize our environment.

assertion A clear, nonjudgmental statement of what we feel, need, or want. Not synonymous with aggression, which involves putting our needs ahead of others' needs, sometimes at cost to them.

attachment style A pattern of relating instilled by the way a caregiver teaches the child who he or she is, who others are, and how to approach relationships.

attribution An internal account of why something happens or why someone acted a certain way.

B

bracketing Noting an important issue that comes up in the course of discussing other matters and agreeing to discuss it at a later time. Allows partners to stay effectively focused on a specific issue but to agree to deal with the bracketed issue later.

C

chronemics The aspect of nonverbal communication that involves our perceptions and use of time to define identities and interaction.

cognitive complexity In our interpretation of experience, the number of constructs used, how abstract they are, and how elaborately they interact to create perceptions.

cognitive labeling view of emotions The theory that our feelings are shaped by the labels we apply to our physiological responses.

commitment A decision to remain with a relationship. One of three dimensions of enduring romantic relationships, commitment has greater influence on relationship continuity than does love alone. Also, an advanced stage in the escalation of romantic relationships.

committed romantic relationship A voluntary relationship between unique individuals who assume they will be primary and continuing parts of each other's lives. Committed romantic relationships include three dimensions: intimacy, passion, and commitment.

communication rules Shared understandings of what communication means and what behaviors are appropriate in various situations.

constitutive rules Rules that define what communication means by specifying how certain communicative acts are to be counted.

constructivism The theory that we organize and interpret experience by applying cognitive structures called *schemata*.

content meaning The content of, or denotative information in, communication. Content-level meanings are literal.

contracting Building a solution through negotiation and acceptance of parts of proposals for resolution. Contracting usually is present in the later stages of constructive conflict.

counterfeit emotional language Communication that seems to express feelings but doesn't actually describe what a person is feeling.

culture Beliefs, understandings, practices, and ways to interpret experience that are shared by a group of people.

D

deep acting Management of inner feelings.

defensive listening Perceiving personal attacks, criticisms, or hostile undertones in communication when none are intended.

direct definition Communication that explicitly tells us who we are by specifically labeling us and reacting to our behaviors. Usually first occurs in families, then in interaction with peers and others.

dismissive attachment style A mode of relating instilled by a disinterested, rejecting, or abusive caregiver, in which the individual dismisses others as unworthy and thus does not seek close relationships. Unlike people with fearful attachment styles, those with a dismissive style do not accept the caregiver's view of them as unlovable.

downer A person who communicates negatively about us and reflects a negative appraisal of our self-worth.

dual perspective The ability to understand both your own and another's perspective, beliefs, thoughts, and feelings.

E

ego boundaries An individual's perception of where he or she stops and the rest of the world begins.

emotional intelligence The ability to recognize which feelings are appropriate in which situations and the skill to communicate those feelings effectively.

emotions Our experience and interpretation of internal sensations as they are shaped by physiology, perceptions, language, and social experiences.

emotion work The effort we invest to make ourselves feel what our culture defines as appropriate and not to feel what our culture defines as inappropriate in particular situations.

empathy The ability to feel with another person, to feel what she or he feels.

environmental spoiling The process by which proximity breeds ill will, when we are forced to be around others whose values, attitudes, and life styles conflict with our own.

equity Fairness based on the perception that both partners invest roughly equally in a relationship and benefit similarly from their investments. Perceived equity is a primary influence on relationship satisfaction.

eros One of the three primary styles of loving, a powerful, passionate style of love that blazes to life suddenly and dramatically.

ethics The branch of philosophy that deals with moral principles and codes of conduct. Interpersonal communication involves ethical issues.

ethnocentrism The assumption that our culture and its norms are the only right ones. Ethnocentric communication reflects certainty, which tends to create defensive communication climates.

exit response To leave conflict either psychologically (by tuning out disagreement) or physically (by walking away or even leaving the relationship). One of four ways of responding to conflict, the exit response is active and generally destructive.

F

fearful attachment style A mode of relating instilled by a caregiver in the first bond who communicates to the child in consistently negative, rejecting, or even abusive ways.

feedback Responses to messages. May be verbal, nonverbal, or both; may be intentional or unintentional.

feeling rules Culturally based guidelines that tell us what we have a right to feel or are expected to feel in specific situations.

framing rules Culturally based guidelines that define the emotional meaning of situations and events.

friends of the heart Friends who remain close regardless of distance and life changes.

friends of the road Temporary friends with whom intimacy is not sustained when one of the friends moves or changes occur.

fundamental attribution error Overestimating the internal causes of others' behavior and underestimating the external causes.

G

games Interactions in which the real conflicts are hidden or denied and a counterfeit excuse is created for arguments or put-downs.

generalized other One source of social perspectives that people use to define themselves and guide how they think, act, and feel; our perception of the views, values, and perspectives that are endorsed by society as a whole.

grace Granting forgiveness or putting aside our personal need in favor of someone else's when it is not required or expected. Grace reflects generosity of spirit.

H

haptics The sense of touch and what it means. Haptics are nonverbal communication.

hate speech Language that dehumanizes others and that reflects and often motivates hostility toward the target of the speech.

hearing The physiological result of sound waves hitting our eardrums. Unlike listening, hearing is a passive process.

I

identity script A guide to action based on rules for living and identity. Initially communicated in families, scripts define our roles, how we are to play them, and basic elements in the plots of our lives.

I–It communication Impersonal communication in which people are treated as objects or as instrumental to our purposes.

I **language** Language in which one takes personal responsibility for feelings with words that own the feelings and do not project responsibility for the feelings onto others.

implicit personality theory Our often unconscious assumptions about what qualities fit together in human personalities.

indexing A technique of linking our evaluations of speech and events to specific times or circumstances, to remind ourselves that evaluations are not static or unchanging.

interactive model A model that represents communication as a feedback process, in which listeners and speakers both simultaneously send and receive messages.

interactive view of emotions The theory that social rules and understandings shape what people feel and how they express and withhold feelings.

internal tensions Relationship stresses that grow out of people and their interaction.

interpersonal climate The overall feeling, or emotional mood, of a relationship.

interpersonal communication A selective, systemic, ongoing process in which unique individuals interact to reflect and build personal knowledge and to create meanings.

interpersonal communication competence Communication that is interpersonally effective and appropriate. Competence includes the abilities to monitor oneself, to engage in dual perspective, to enact a range of communication skills, and to adapt communication appropriately.

interpersonal conflict The expressed disagreement, struggle, or discord that exists when people who depend on each other express different views, interests, or goals and perceive their differences as incompatible or as opposed by the other.

interpretation The subjective process of evaluating and explaining perceptions.

intimacy Feelings of closeness, connection, and tenderness between lovers. One of three dimensions of committed romantic relationships.

investment Something put into a relationship that cannot be recovered should the relationship end. Investment, more than rewards and love, increases commitment.

I–Thou communication Fully interpersonal communication in which people acknowledge and deal with each other as unique individuals who meet fully in dialogue.

I–You communication Communication midway between impersonal and interpersonal communication, in which the other is acknowledged as a human being but not fully engaged as a unique individual.

J

Johari Window Developed in 1969 by Joseph Luft and Harry Ingham, a model of the different sorts of knowledge that affect self-development.

K

kinesics Body position and body motions, including those of the face.

kitchen-sinking An unproductive form of conflict communication in which everything except the kitchen sink is thrown into the argument.

L

linear model A model that represents communication as a one-way process that flows in one direction, from sender to receiver. Linear models do not capture the dynamism of communication or the active participation of all communicators.

linguistic determinism The theory that language determines what we can perceive and think. This theory has been largely discredited, although the less strong claim that language shapes thought is widely accepted.

listening A complex process that consists of being mindful, hearing, selecting and organizing information, interpreting communication, responding, and remembering.

listening for information One of the three goals of listening; focuses on gaining and evaluating ideas, facts, opinions, reasons, and so forth.

listening for pleasure One of the three goals of listening; motivated by the desire to enjoy rather than to gain information or to support others.

listening to support others One of the three goals of listening; focuses more on the relationship level of meaning than on the content level of meaning. Aims to understand and respond to others' feelings, thoughts, and perceptions in affirming ways.

literal listening Listening only to the content level of meaning and ignoring the relationship level of meaning.

loaded language An extreme form of evaluative language that relies on words that strongly slant perceptions and thus meanings.

lose–lose An orientation toward conflict that assumes that nobody can win and everyone loses from engaging in conflict.

loyalty response Silent allegiance to a relationship and a person when conflict exists. One of the four ways of responding to conflict, loyalty is passive and tends to be constructive.

ludus One of the three primary styles of love, in which the goal is not commitment but to have fun at love as a game or a series of challenges and maneuvers.

M

mania Passionate, sometimes obsessive love that includes emotional extremes. One of the three secondary styles of love; made up of eros and ludus.

metacommunication Communication about communication. When excessive, as in unproductive conflict interaction, metacommunication becomes self-absorbing and diverts partners from the issues causing conflict.

mindfulness Being fully present in the moment. A concept from Zen Buddhism; the first step of listening and the foundation of all the other steps.

mind reading Assuming that we understand what another person thinks or how another person perceives something.

minimal encourager A brief phrase or sound that gently invites another person to elaborate by expressing interest in hearing more.

models Representations of what something is and how it works.

monitoring Observing and regulating your own communication.

monopolizing Continually focusing communication on ourselves instead of on the person who is talking.

N

neglect response Denial or minimization of problems. One of the four ways of responding to conflict, neglect is passive and tends to be destructive.

noise Anything that distorts communication such that it is harder for people to understand each other.

nonverbal communication All forms of communication other than words themselves. Includes inflection and other vocal qualities as well as several other behaviors.

O

organismic view of emotions The theory that external phenomena cause physiological changes that lead us to experience emotions. Also called the James–Lange view of emotions.

P

paralanguage Vocal communication that does not use words.

paraphrasing A method of clarifying another's meaning by reflecting our interpretations of his or her communication back to him or her.

particular others One source of social perspectives that people use to define themselves and guide how they think, act, and feel; people who are especially important to the self.

passion Intensely positive feelings and desires for another person. One of the three dimensions of enduring romantic relationships, passion is based on the rewards of involvement and is not equivalent to commitment.

passive aggression Attacking while denying doing so; a means of covertly expressing conflict, anger, or both.

perception The active process of selecting, organizing, and interpreting people, objects, events, situations, and activities.

perceptual view of emotions The theory that subjective perceptions shape the meanings of external phenomena and the emotions we associate with them. Also called appraisal theory.

personal constructs Bipolar mental yardsticks by which we measure people and situations along specific dimensions of judgment.

person-centeredness The ability to perceive people as unique and to differentiate them from social roles and generalizations based on their membership in social groups.

perspectives of the generalized other Our understanding of the collection of rules, roles, and attitudes endorsed by the whole social community in which we live.

placemaking The process of creating a physical environment that is comfortable and reflects one's values, experiences, and tastes. Physical environment is part of relational culture, which is the nucleus of intimacy.

pragma Pragmatic or practical love. One of the secondary styles of loving, pragma is a blend of storge and ludus.

process An ongoing, continuous, dynamic flow that has no clear-cut beginning or ending and is always evolving and changing. Interpersonal communication is a process.

prototypes Knowledge structures that define the clearest or most representative examples of some category.

proxemics An aspect of nonverbal communication that includes space and our uses of it.

pseudolistening Pretending to listen.

psychological responsibility The responsibility for remembering, planning, and coordinating domestic work and child care. In general, women assume psychological responsibility for child care and housework even though both partners may share the actual tasks.

punctuation Defining the beginning and ending of interaction or interaction episodes.

R

rational–emotive approach to feelings Using rational thinking to challenge and change debilitating emotions that undermine self-concept and self-esteem.

reflected appraisal The process of seeing and thinking about ourselves in terms of the appraisals of us that others reflect.

regulative rules Communication rules that regulate interaction by specifying when, how, where, and with whom to talk about certain things.

relational culture A private world of rules, understandings, and patterns of acting and interpreting that partners create to give meaning to their relationship; the nucleus of intimacy.

relational dialectics Opposing forces, or tensions, that are normal parts of all relationships. The three relational dialectics are autonomy and intimacy, novelty and routine, and openness and closedness.

relationship meaning What communication expresses about the relationship between communicators. The three dimensions of relationship-level meanings are liking or disliking, responsiveness, and power (control).

relationship rules Guidelines that friends or romantic partners have for their relationships. Usually, relationship rules are tacit, not explicit, understandings.

remembering The process of recalling what you have heard; the sixth element of listening.

responding Symbolizing your interest in what is being said with observable feedback to speakers during the process of interaction; the fifth of the six elements of listening.

S

script A definition of expected or appropriate sequences of action in a particular setting. Scripts are one of the four cognitive schemata; not the same as an identity script.

second shift Work that a person, usually a woman, does after coming home from working in the paid labor force outside the home, such as fixing meals, doing housework, shopping, and caring for children

secure attachment style A mode of relating that involves confidence in oneself and in relationships. Like other attachment styles, the secure mode is instilled by a caregiver who responds in a consistently attentive, loving way to a child; the most common and most positive of the four attachment styles.

selective listening Focusing only on selected parts of communication. We listen selectively when we screen out parts of a message that don't interest us or with which we disagree and when we rivet attention on parts of communication that do interest us or with which we agree.

self A multidimensional process that involves forming and acting from social perspectives that arise and evolve in communication with others and ourselves.

self-disclosure The act of revealing personal information about ourselves that others are unlikely to discover in other ways.

self-fulfilling prophecy Acting in a way that embodies our internalization of others' expectation or judgment about us.

self-sabotage Self-talk that communicates that we are no good, that we can't do something, that we can't change, and so forth. Self-sabotage undermines our belief in ourselves and our motivation to change and grow.

self-serving bias The tendency to attribute our positive actions and successes to stable, global, internal influences under our control, and to attribute our negative actions and failures to unstable, specific, external influences beyond our control.

self-talk Intrapersonal communication that affects our feelings and behaviors.

social comparison Comparing ourselves with others to form judgments of our own talents, abilities, qualities, and so forth.

social exchange theory The theory that people apply economic principles to evaluate their relationships in terms of costs and benefits and that people are satisfied only in relationships in which benefits outweigh costs.

speech community A group of people who share norms, regulative rules, and constitutive rules for communicating and interpreting the communication of others.

standpoint The knowledge and perspective shaped by the material, symbolic, and social conditions common to members of a social group.

static evaluation Assessments that suggest that something is unchanging. "Bob is impatient" is a static evaluation.

stereotypes Predictive generalizations about people and situations.

storge A comfortable, friendly kind of love, often likened to friendship. One of the three primary styles of loving.

surface acting Controlling outward expression of inner feelings.

symbol An abstract, arbitrary, and ambiguous representation of a phenomenon.

systemic Taking place within multiple systems that influence what is communicated and what meanings are constructed; a quality of interpersonal communication. Examples of systems affecting communication are physical context, culture, personal histories, and previous interactions between people.

T

totalizing Responding to a person as if one aspect were the totality of the person.

transactional model A model of communication as a dynamic process that changes over time and in which participants assume multiple roles.

trust Belief in another's reliability (that he or she will do what is prom-ised) and emotional reliance on the other to care about and protect our welfare; the belief that our private information is safe with the other person.

U

upper A person who communicates positively about us and reflects a positive appraisal of our self-worth.

V

voice response Communicating about differences, tensions, and disagreements. One of the four responses to conflict, the voice response is active and can be constructive for people and relationships.

vulture An extreme form of downer who not only communicates a negative image of us but actually attacks our self-concept.

W

win–lose An orientation toward conflict that assumes that one person wins at the expense of another person.

win–win An orientation toward conflict that assumes that everyone can win, or benefit, from engaging in conflict and that it is possible to generate resolutions that satisfy everyone.

Y

you language Language that projects responsibility for feelings or actions onto other people. Not recommended for interpersonal communication.

References

Abelson, R. (2001, April 20). Online message boards getting nasty. *Raleigh News and Observer*, pp. E1, E3.

Acitelli, L. (1988). When spouses talk to each other about their relationship. *Journal of Social and Personal Relationships, 5,* 185–199.

Acitelli, L. (1993). You, me, and us: Perspectives on relationship awareness. In S. W. Duck (Ed.), *Understanding relationship processes: 1. Individuals in relationships* (pp. 144–174). Newbury Park, CA: Sage.

Acker, M., & Davis, M. H. (1992). Intimacy, passion and commitment in adult romantic relationships: A test of the triangular theory of love. *Journal of Social and Personal Relationships, 9,* 21–51.

Ackerman, D. (1994). *A natural history of love.* New York: Random House.

Adams, R., & Allan, G. (Eds.). (1999). *Placing friendship in context.* Cambridge, England: Cambridge University Press.

Adams, W. (2005, May 23). Gay to wed. *Newsweek,* p. 8.

Adelman, M. B., Parks, M. R., & Albrecht, T. L. (1987). Supporting friends in need. In T. L. Albrecht, M. B. Adelman, & Associates (Eds.), *Communicating social support* (pp. 105–125). Beverly Hills, CA: Sage.

Adler, R., & Towne, N. (1993). *Looking out/looking in* (7th ed.). Fort Worth, TX: Harcourt Brace Jovanovich.

Afifi, W., & Burgoon, J. (2000). The impact of violations on uncertainty and the consequences for attractiveness. *Human Communication Research, 26,* 203–233.

Afifi, W., & Faulkner, S. (2000). On being "just friends": The frequency and impact of sexual activity in cross-sex friendships. *Journal of Social and Personal Relationships, 17,* 205–222.

Ainsworth, M. D. S., Blehar, M. C., Waters, E., & Wall, S. (1978). *Patterns of attachment: A psychological study of the strange situation.* Hillsdale, NJ: Erlbaum.

Alexander, E. R., III. (1979). The reduction of cognitive conflict: Effects of various types of communication. *Journal of Conflict Resolution, 23,* 120–138.

Allan, G. (1994). Social structure and relationships. In S. W. Duck (Ed.), *Understanding relationship processes: 3. Social context and relationships* (pp. 1–25). Newbury Park, CA: Sage.

Allen, S., Waton, A., Purcell, K., & Wood, S. (1986). *The experience of unemployment.* Basingstoke, UK: Macmillan.

Almany, A., & Alwan, A. (1982). *Communicating with the Arabs.* Prospects Heights, IL: Waveland.

Altman, I., & Taylor, D. (1973). *Social penetration: The development of interpersonal relationships.* New York: Holt.

Altman, I., & Taylor, D. (1987). Communication in interpersonal relationships: Social penetration processes. In M. Roloff & G. Miller (Eds.), *Interpersonal processes: New directions in communication research* (pp. 257–277). Newbury Park, CA: Sage.

American games, Japanese rules. (1988). *Frontline* [Television documentary]. National Public Television.

American Social Health Association. (2005). *State of the Nation 2005: Challenges facing STD prevention in youth.* Research Triangle Park, NC: Author.

Anders, G. (1997, September 4). Doctors learn to bridge cultural gaps. *Wall Street Journal,* pp. B1, B4.

Andersen, M. L., & Collins, P. H. (Eds.). (1998). *Race, class, and gender: An anthology* (3rd ed.). Belmont, CA: Wadsworth.

Andersen, P. (1999). *Nonverbal communication: Forms and functions.* Mountain View, CA: Mayfield.

Andersen, P. (2003). In different dimensions: Nonverbal communication and culture. In L. A. Samovar & R. E. Porter (Eds.), *Intercultural communication: A reader* (10th ed., pp. 239–252). Belmont, CA: Wadsworth.

Andersen, P., Hecht, M., Hoobler, G., & Smallwood, M. (2002). Nonverbal communication across cultures. In W. Gudykunst & B. Mody (Eds.), *The handbook of international and intercultural communication* (2nd ed., pp. 89–106). Thousand Oaks, CA: Sage.

Anderson, K., & Leaper, C. (1998). Meta-analyses of gender effects on conversational interruption: Who, when, where, and how? *Sex Roles, 39,* 225–252.

Anderson, P., & Guerrero, L. (Eds.). (1998). *Handbook of communication and emotion.* San Diego, CA: Academic Press.

Anderson, S., Russell, C., & Schumm, W. (1983). Perceived marital quality and family life cycle categories: A further analysis. *Journal of Marriage and the Family, 45,* 127–139.

Angelou, M. (1990). *I shall not be moved.* New York: Random House.

Annual report on Americans' health "a wealth of good news." (1997, September 12). *Raleigh News and Observer,* p. 8A.

Anzaldúa, G. (1987). *Borderlands/la frontera: The new mestiza.* San Francisco: Aunt Lute Books.

Arenson, K. (2002, January 13). The fine art of listening. *Education Life,* pp. 34–35.

Argyle, M., & Henderson, M. (1985). The rules of relationships. In S. W. Duck & D. Perlman (Eds.), *Understanding personal relationships: An interdisciplinary approach* (pp. 63–84). Beverly Hills, CA: Sage.

Aries, E. (1987). Gender and communication. In P. Shaver (Ed.), *Sex and gender* (pp. 149–176). Newbury Park, CA: Sage.

Aries, E. (1996). *Men and women in interaction: Reconsidering differences.* New York: Oxford University Press.

Arnett, R. C. (1986). The inevitable conflict and confronting in dialogue. In J. Stewart (Ed.), *Bridges, not walls* (4th ed., pp. 272–279). New York: Random House.

Atsumi, R. (1980). Patterns of personal relationships. *Social Analysis, 5,* 63–78.

AXIS Center for Public Awareness of People with Disabilities. *Guidelines for communicating with people with disabilities.* Retrieved July 12, 1994, from http://www.axiscenter.org

Axtell, R. (1990a). *Dos and taboos around the world* (2nd ed.). New York: Wiley.

Axtell, R. (1990b). *Dos and taboos of hosting international visitors.* New York: Wiley.

Ayres, J., Keereetaweep, T., Chen, P., & Edwards, P. (1998). Communication apprehension and employment interviews. *Communication Education, 47,* 1–17.

Ayto, J. (Ed.). (1999). *Twentieth century words.* Oxford, UK: Oxford University Press.

Bachen, C., & Illouz, E. (1996). Imagining romance: Young people's cultural models of romance and love. *Critical Studies of Mass Communication, 13,* 279–308.

Bailey, P. (1998, September 29). Daily bread. *Durham Herald Sun,* p. C5.

Bargh, J. (1999, January 29). The most powerful manipulative messages are hiding in plain sight. *Chronicle of Higher Education,* p. B6.

Barker, L., Edwards, R., Gaines, C., Gladney, K., & Holley, F. (1981). An investigation of proportional time spent in various communication activities by college students. *Journal of Applied Communication Research, 8,* 101–109.

Barnlund, D. (1989). *Communication styles of Japanese and Americans: Images and reality.* Belmont, CA: Wadsworth.

Bartholomew, K., & Horowitz, L. M. (1991). Attachment styles among young adults: A test of a four-category model. *Journal of Personality and Social Psychology, 61,* 226–244.

Basow, S., I., & Rubenfeld, K. (2003). "Troubles talk": Effects of gender and gender-typing. *Sex Roles, 48,* 183–187.

Bass, A. (1993, December 5). Behavior that can wreck a marriage. *Raleigh News and Observer,* p. 8E.

Basu, M. (2004, September 27). Experts interpret the body politic. *Raleigh News & Observer,* p. 4A.

Bates, E. (1994, Fall). Beyond black and white. *Southern Exposure,* pp. 11–15.

Bateson, M. C. (1990). *Composing a life.* New York: Penguin/Plume.

Baxter, L. A. (1984). Trajectories of relationship disengagement. *Journal of Social and Personal Relationships, 7,* 141–178.

Baxter, L. A. (1985). Accomplishing relational disengagement. In S. W. Duck & D. Perlman (Eds.), *Understanding personal relationships: An interdisciplinary approach* (pp. 243–265). Beverly Hills, CA: Sage.

Baxter, L. A. (1987). Self-disclosure and relationship disengagement. In V. Derlega & J. H. Berg (Eds.), *Self-disclosure: Theory, research, and therapy* (pp. 155–174). New York: Plenum.

Baxter, L. A. (1988). A dialectical perspective on communication strategies in relationship development. In S. W. Duck, D. F. Hay, S. E. Hobfoll, W. Iches, & B. Montgomery (Eds.), *Handbook of personal relationships* (pp. 257–273). London: Wiley.

Baxter, L. A. (1990). Dialectical contradictions in relational development. *Journal of Social and Personal Relationships, 7,* 69–88.

Baxter, L. A. (1993). The social side of personal relationships: A dialectical perspective. In S. W. Duck (Ed.), *Understanding relationship processes: 3. Social context and relationships* (pp. 139–165). Newbury Park, CA: Sage.

Baxter, L. A., & Montgomery, B. M. (1996). *Relating: Dialogues and dialectics.* New York: Guilford.

Baxter, L. A., & Simon, E. P. (1993). Relationship maintenance strategies and dialectical contradictions in personal relationships. *Journal of Social and Personal Relationships, 10,* 225–242.

Baym, N. (2002). Interpersonal life online. In L. Lievrouw & S. Livingstone (Eds.), *The handbook of new media* (pp. 62–76). Thousand Oaks, CA: Sage.

Beck, A. (1988). *Love is never enough.* New York: Harper & Row.

Becker, C. S. (1987). Friendship between women: A phenomenological study of best friends. *Journal of Phenomenological Psychology, 18,* 59–72.

Begley, S. (1997, Spring/Summer Special Issue). How to build a baby's brain. *Newsweek,* pp. 27–30.

Bellah, R., Madsen, R., Sullivan, W., Swindler, A., & Tipton, S. (1985). *Habits of the heart: Individualism and commitment in American life.* Berkeley: University of California Press.

Bellamy, L. (1996, December 18). Kwanzaa cultivates cultural and culinary connections. *Raleigh News and Observer,* pp. 1F, 9F.

Belsky, J., & Pensky, E. (1988). Developmental history, personality, and family relationships: Toward an emergent family system. In R. A. Hinde & J. Stevenson-Hinde (Eds.), *Relationships within families: Mutual influences* (pp. 193–217). Oxford, UK: Clarendon.

Belsky, J., & Rovine, M. (1990). Patterns of marital change across the transition to parenthood: Pregnancy to three years postpartum. *Journal of Marriage and the Family, 52,* 5–19.

Benenson, J., Apostoleris, N., & Parnass, J. (1997). Age and sex differences in dyadic and group interaction. *Developmental Psychology, 33,* 538–543.

Benjamin, B., & Werner, R. (2004). Touch in the Western world. *Massage Therapy Journal, 43,* 28–32.

Benjamin, D., & Horwitz, T. (1994, July 14). German view: "You Americans work too hard—and for what?" *Wall Street Journal,* pp. B1, B6.

Berg, J. H. (1987). Responsiveness and self-disclosure. In V. J. Derlega & J. H. Berg (Eds.), *Self-disclosure: Theory, research, and therapy* (pp. 87–102). New York: Plenum.

Berger, C. (1987). Communicating under uncertainty. In M. Roloff & G. Miller (Eds.), *Interpersonal processes: New directions in communication research* (pp. 39–62). Newbury Park, CA: Sage.

Berger, C., & Gudykunst, W. (1991). Uncertainty and communication. In B. Dervin & M. Voigt (Eds.), *Progress in communication sciences, 10* (pp. 21–66). Norwood, NJ: Ablex.

Berger, C. R., & Bell, R. A. (1988). Plans and the initiation of social relationships. *Human Communication Research, 15,* 217–235.

Bergner, R. M., & Bergner, L. L. (1990). Sexual misunderstanding: A descriptive and pragmatic formulation. *Psychotherapy, 27,* 464–467.

Bergstrom, M., & Nussbaum, J. (1996). Cohort differences in interpersonal conflict: Implications for older patient–younger care provider interaction. *Health Communication, 8,* 233–248.

Berko, R., Wolvin, A., & Wolvin, D. (1995). *Communicating: A social and career focus.* Boston: Houghton Mifflin.

Bernard, E. (2004). *Some of my best friends: Writings on interracial friendships.* New York: HarperCollins-Amistad.

Berne, E. (1964). *Games people play.* New York: Grove.

Bernstein, B. (Ed.). (1973). *Class, codes, and control* (Vol. 2). London: Routledge & Kegan Paul.

Bernstein, B. (1974). *Class, codes, and control: Theoretical studies toward a sociology of language* (Rev. ed.). New York: Shocken.

Best, J. (1989). *Images of issues: Typifying contemporary social problems.* New York: Aldine de Gruyter.

Bippus, A., & Young, S. (2005). Owning your emotions: Reactions to expressions of self-versus other-attributed positive and negative emotions. *Journal of Applied Communication Research, 33,* 26–45.

Birdwhistell, R. (1970). *Kinesics and context.* Philadelphia: University of Pennsylvania Press.

Bites. (1998, September 30). *Raleigh News and Observer,* p. 1F.

Blake, S. (1996). *Loving your long-distance relationship.* New York: Anton.

Blieszner, R. (2000). Close relationships in old age. In C. Hendrick & S. Hendrick (Eds.), *Close relationships: A sourcebook* (pp. 84–95). Thousand Oaks, CA: Sage.

Blieszner, R., & Adams, R. (1992). *Adult friendship.* Newbury Park, CA: Sage.

Blumstein, P., & Schwartz, P. (1983). *American couples: Money, work, and sex.* New York: William Morrow.

Bolton, R. (1986). Listening is more than merely hearing. In J. Stewart (Ed.), *Bridges, not walls* (4th ed., pp. 159–179). New York: Random House.

Bond, J. T., Thompson, C., Galinsky, E., & Prottas, D. (2002). Highlights of the national study of the changing workforce: Executive summary. Families and Work Institute, *No. 3,* pp. 1–4.

Boon, S. (1994). Dispelling doubt and uncertainty: Trust in romantic relationships. In S. W. Duck (Ed.), *Understanding relationship processes: 4. Dynamics of relationships* (pp. 86–111). Thousand Oaks, CA: Sage.

Bordo, S. (1999). *The male body: A new look at men in public and in private.* New York: Farrar, Straus & Giroux.

Bosmajian, H. (1974). *The language of oppression.* Washington, DC: Public Affairs Papers.

Boss, P. (1987). Family stress. In M. B. Sussman & S. K. Steinmerz (Eds.), *Handbook of marriage and the family* (pp. 695–723). New York: Plenum.

Bostrom, R. (1996). Aspects of listening. In O. Hargie (Ed.), *Handbook of communication skills* (2nd ed., pp. 236–259). London: Routledge.

Bowen, S. P., & Michal-Johnson, P. (1995). Sexuality in the AIDS era. In S. W. Duck & J. T. Wood (Eds.), *Understanding relationship processes: 5. Relationship challenges* (pp. 150–180). Thousand Oaks, CA: Sage.

Bowlby, J. (1973). *Separation: Attachment and loss* (Vol. 2). New York: Basic.

Bowlby, J. (1988). *A secure base: Parent–child attachment and healthy human development.* New York: Basic.

Boyd, R. (1996, October 9). Notion of separate races rejected. *Raleigh News and Observer,* pp. 1A, 15A.

Bozzi, V. (1986, February). Eat to the beat. *Psychology Today,* p. 16.

Bradbury, T. N., & Fincham, F. D. (1990). Attributions in marriage: Review and critique. *Psychological Bulletin, 107,* 3–33.

Braithwaite, C. (1990). Communicative silence: A cross cultural study of Basso's hypothesis. In D. Carbaugh (Ed.), *Cultural communication and intercultural contact* (pp. 321–327). Hillsdale, NJ: Erlbaum.

Braithwaite, D. (1996). "Persons first": Exploring different perspectives on the communication of persons with disabilities. In E. B. Ray (Ed.), *Communication and disenfranchisement: Social health issues and implications* (pp. 449–464). Hillsdale, NJ: Erlbaum.

Braithwaite, D., & Kellas, J. K. (2006). Shopping for and with friends: Everyday communication at the shopping mall. In J.T. Wood & S.

Duck (Eds.), *Composing relationships: Communication in everyday life* (pp. 86–95). Belmont, CA: Wadsworth.

Brazelton, T. B. (1997, Spring/Summer Special Issue). Building a better self-image. *Newsweek,* pp. 76–77.

Brehm, S. (1992). *Intimate relations* (2nd ed.). New York: McGraw-Hill.

Breslau, K. (2000, September 18). Tomorrowland, today. *Newsweek,* pp. 52–53.

Brooks, D. (2001, April 30). Time to do everything except think. *Newsweek,* p. 71.

Brooks, R., & Goldstein, S. (2001). *Raising resilient children.* New York: Contemporary Books.

Brown, J., & Cantor, J. (2000). An agenda for research on youth and the media. *Journal of Adolescent Health, 27,* 2–7.

Brownstein, A. (2000, December 8). In the campus shadows, women are stalkers as well as the stalked. *Chronicle of Higher Education,* pp. A40–A42.

Bruess, C., & Hoefs, A. (2006). The cat puzzle recovered: Composing relationships through family ritual. In J. T. Wood & S. Duck (Eds.), *Composing relationships: Communication in everyday life* (pp. 65–75). Belmont, CA: Wadsworth.

Bruess, C., & Pearson, J. (1997). Interpersonal rituals in marriage and adult friendship. *Communication Monographs, 64,* 25–46.

Buber, M. (1957). Distance and relation. *Psychiatry, 20,* 97–104.

Buber, M. (1970). *I and thou* (Walter Kaufmann, Trans.). New York: Scribner.

Buckley, M. (1992). Focus on research: We listen a book a day; we speak a book a week: Learning from Walter Loban. *Language Arts, 69,* 622–626.

Buerkel-Rothfuss, N. L., Fink, D. S., & Buerkel, R. (1995). Communication in the father-child dyad: The intergenerational transmission process. In T. J. Socha & G. H. Stamp (Eds.), *Parents, children, and communication: Frontiers of*

theory and research (pp. 63–85). Mahwah, NJ: Erlbaum.

Bumpass, L. L., & Lu, H. H. (2000). Trends in cohabitation and implications for children's family contexts in the United States. *Population Studies, 54,* 19–41.

Bumpass, L. L., & Sweet, J. A. (1989). National estimates of cohabitation. *Demography, 26,* 615–625.

Burgoon, J. K., Buller, D. B., Hale, J. L., & deTurck, M. A. (1984). Relational messages associated with nonverbal behaviors. *Human Communication Research, 10,* 351–378.

Burgoon, J. K., Buller, D. B., & Woodhall, G. W. (1989). *Nonverbal communication: The unspoken dialogue.* New York: Harper & Row.

Burgoon, J., & Hale, J. (1988). Nonverbal expectancy violations: Model, elaboration and application to immediacy behaviors. *Communication Monographs, 55,* 58–79.

Burgoon, J. K., & LePoire, B. (1999). Nonverbal cues and interpersonal judgments: Participant and observer perceptions of intimacy, dominance, composure, and formality. *Communication Monographs, 66,* 105–124.

Burgoon, J., Stern, L., & Dillman, L. (1995). *Interpersonal adaptation: Dyadic interaction patterns.* New York: Cambridge University Press.

Burleson, B. R. (1984). Comforting communication. In H. E. Sypher & J. L. Applegate (Eds.), *Communication by children and adults: Social cognitive and strategic processes* (pp. 63–104). Beverly Hills, CA: Sage.

Burleson, B. R. (1987). Cognitive complexity. In J. C. McCroskey & J. A. Daly (Eds.), *Personality and interpersonal communication* (pp. 305–349). Newbury Park, CA: Sage.

Burleson, B. R. (1994). Comforting messages: Features, functions, and outcomes. In J. A. Daly & J. M. Wiemann (Eds.), *Strategic interpersonal communication* (pp. 135–161). Hillsdale, NJ: Erlbaum.

Burleson, B. R., & Samter, W. (1994). A social skills approach to relationship maintenance: How individual differences in communication skills affect the achievement of relationship functions. In D. J. Canary & L. Stafford (Eds.), *Communication and relational maintenance.* Orlando: Academic Press.

Burley-Allen, M. (1995). *Listening: The forgotten skill.* New York: Wiley.

Business bulletin. (1996, July 18). *Wall Street Journal,* p. A1.

Buston, P. M., & Emlen, S. T. (2003). Cognitive processes underlying human mate choice: The relationship between self-perception and mate preference in Western society. *Proceedings of the National Academy of Sciences, 100,* 8805–8810.

Butler, J. (2002). In W. Brown & J. Halley (Eds.), *Left legalism, left critique.* Durham, NC: Duke University Press.

Butterfield, F. (1982). *China: Alive in the bitter sea.* New York: Times Books.

Button, C. M., & Collier, D. R. (1991, June). *A comparison of people's concepts of love and romantic love.* Paper presented at the Canadian Psychological Association Conference, Calgary, Alberta.

Caldera, Y. M., Huston, A. C., & O'Brien, M. (1989). Social interactions and play patterns of parents and toddlers with feminine, masculine, and neutral toys. *Child Development, 60,* 70–76.

Campbell, S. M. (1986). From either–or to both–and relationships. In J. Stewart (Ed.), *Bridges, not walls* (4th ed., pp. 262–270). New York: Random House.

Canary, D., & Dindia, K. (Eds.). (1998). *Sex differences and similarities in communication.* Mahwah, NJ: Erlbaum.

Canary, D., & Stafford, L. (Eds.). (1994). *Communication and relational maintenance.* New York: Academic Press.

Cancian, F. (1987). *Love in America.* New York: Cambridge University Press.

Cancian, F. (1989). Love and the rise of capitalism. In B. Risman & P. Schwartz (Eds.), *Gender in intimate relationships* (pp. 12–25). Belmont, CA: Wadsworth.

Capella, J. N. (1991). The biological origins of automated patterns of human interaction. *Communication Theory, 1,* 4–35.

Carey, B., & O'Connor, A. (2004, February 15). How to get those at risk to avoid risky sex? *New York Times,* pp. D1, D7.

Carl, W. (1998). A sign of the times. In J. T. Wood, *But I thought you meant . . .: Misunderstandings in human communication* (pp. 195–208). Mountain View, CA: Mayfield.

Carl, W. (2006). <where r u?. <here u?>: Everyday communication with relational technologies. In J. T. Wood & S. Duck (Eds.), *Composing relationships: Communication in everyday life* (pp. 96–109). Belmont, CA: Wadsworth.

Carlson, R., & Carlson, K. (1999). *Don't sweat the small stuff in love.* New York: Hyperion.

Carnes, J. (1994, Spring). An uncommon language. *Teaching tolerance,* pp. 56–63.

Carter, J. (1996). *Living faith.* New York: Times Books/Random House.

Caspi, A., & Harbener, E. S. (1990). Continuity and change: Assortive marriage and the consistency of personality in adulthood. *Journal of Personality and Social Psychology, 58,* 250–258.

Cassirer, E. (1944). *An essay on man.* New Haven, CT: Yale University Press.

Cate, R. M., Huston, T. L., & Nesselroade, J. R. (1986). Premarital relationships: Toward the identification of alternative pathways to marriage. *Journal of Social and Clinical Psychology, 4,* 3–22.

Cates, J. R., Herndon, N. L., Schulz, S. L., & Darroch, J. E. (2004). *Our voices, our lives, our futures: Youth and sexually transmitted diseases.* Chapel Hill: University of North Carolina at Chapel Hill School of Journalism and Mass Communication.

Cathcart, D., & Cathcart, R. (1997). The group: A Japanese context. In L. Samovar & R. Porter (Eds.), *Intercultural communication: A reader* (8th ed., pp. 329–339). Belmont, CA: Wadsworth.

Caughlin, J., Afifi, W., Carpenter-Theune, K., & Miller, L. (2005). Reasons for, and consequences of, revealing personal secrets in close relationships: A longitudinal study. *Personal Relationships, 12,* 43–59.

Caughlin, J., & Vangelisti, A. (2000). An individual difference explanation of why married couples engage in the demand/withdraw pattern of conflict. *Journal of Social and Personal Relationships, 17,* 523–551.

Chadwick, B., & Heaton, T. (1999). *Statistical handbook on the American family.* Phoenix, AZ: Oryx.

Chatham-Carpenter, A., & DeFrancisco, V. (1998). Women construct self-esteem in their own terms: A feminist qualitative study. *Feminism and Psychology, 8,* 467–489.

Cherlin, A. J. (2004). The deinstitutionalization of American marriage. *Journal of Marriage and the Family, 66,* 848–861.

Chideya, F. (1999). *The color of our future: Our multinational future.* New York: William Morrow.

Chodorow, N. (1989). *Feminism and psychoanalytic theory.* New Haven, CT: Yale University Press.

Christensen, A., & Heavey, C. (1990). Gender and social structure in the demand/withdraw pattern in marital conflict. *Journal of Personality and Social Psychology, 59,* 73–81.

Christensen, A., & Jacobson, N. (1999). *Reconcilable differences.* New York: Guilford.

Christopher, F., & Lloyd, S. (2000). Physical and sexual aggression in relationships. In C. Hendrick & S. Hendrick (Eds.), *Close relationships: A sourcebook* (pp. 330–343). Thousand Oaks, CA: Sage.

Cissna, K. N. L., & Sieburg, E. (1986). Patterns of interactional confirmation and disconfirmation. In J. Stewart (Ed.), *Bridges, not walls* (4th ed., pp. 230–239). New York: Random House.

Civickly, J. M., Pace, R. W., & Krause, R. M. (1977). Interviewer and client behaviors in supportive and defensive interviews. In B. D. Ruben (Ed.), *Communication yearbook, 1* (pp. 347–362). New Brunswick, NJ: Transaction.

Clark, M. S., & Finkel, E. J. (2005). Willingness to express emotion: The impact of relationship type, communication orientation, and their interaction. *Personal Relationships, 12,* 169–180.

Clark, R. A. (1998). A comparison of topics and objectives in a cross section of young men's and women's everyday conversations. In D. Canary & K. Dindia (Eds.), *Sex differences and similarities in communication: Critical essays and empirical investigations of sex and gender interaction* (pp. 303–319). Mahwah, NJ: Erlbaum.

Clement, C., & McLean, K. (2000). *Wired, not weird.* New York: Macmillan.

Clements, M. (1994, August 7). Sex in America today. *Parade,* pp. 4–6.

Clements, M., & Markman, H. (1996). The transition to parenthood: Is having children hazardous to marriage? In N. Vanzetti & S. W. Duck (Eds.), *A lifetime of relationships* (pp. 290–310). Pacific Grove, CA: Brooks/Cole.

Clemetson, L. (2000, September 18). Love without borders. *Newsweek,* p. 62.

Cleveland, H., Koss, M., & Lyons, J. (1999). Rape tactics from the survivors' perspective: Contextual dependence and within-event independence. *Journal of Interpersonal Violence, 14,* 532–547.

ClickZ Stats Staff. (2004, September 10). *Population explosion!* http://www.clickz.com/stats/sectors/geographics/article.php/151151

Cloven, D. H., & Roloff, M. E. (1991). Sense-making activities and interpersonal conflict: Communicative cures for the mulling blues. *Western Journal of Speech Communication, 55,* 134–158.

Coan, J., Gottman, J., Babcock, J., & Jacobson, N. (1997). Battering and the male rejection of influence from women. *Aggressive Behavior, 23,* 375–388.

Coates, J., & Cameron, D. (1989). *Women in their speech communities: New perspectives on language and sex.* London: Longman.

Colapinto, J. (2000). *As nature made him.* New York: HarperCollins.

Cole, T., & Leets, L. (1999). Attachment styles and intimate television viewing: Insecurely forming relationships in a parasocial way. *Journal of Social and Personal Relationships, 16,* 495–511.

Coleman, J. (2000, March 27). My turn: Is technology making us intimate strangers? *Newsweek,* p. 12.

Collier, M. J. (1996). Communication competence problematics in ethnic friendships. *Communication Monographs, 63,* 314–336.

Collins, P. H. (1998). *Fighting words: Black women and the search for justice.* Minneapolis: University of Minnesota Press.

Condry, S. M., Condry, J. C., & Pogatshnik, L. W. (1983). Sex differences: A study of the ear of the beholder. *Sex Roles, 9,* 697–704.

Conover, T. (1987). *Coyotes: A journey through the secret world of America's illegal aliens.* New York: Vintage.

Conrad, C., & Poole, M. S. (2002). *Strategic organizational communication* (5th ed.). Fort Worth, TX: Harcourt.

Cooley, C. H. (1912). *Human nature and the social order.* New York: Scribner.

Cooley, C. H. (1961). The social self. In T. Parsons, E. Shils, K. D. Naegele, & J. R. Pitts (Eds.), *Theories of society* (pp. 822–828). New York: Free Press.

Coontz, S. (2005a, February 14). Historically incorrect canoodling. *New York Times,* p. A. 23.

Coontz, S. (2005b). *Marriage, a history.* New York: Viking Adult.

Cooper, M. (2000). Being the "go-to guy": Fatherhood, masculinity, and the organization of work in Silicon Valley. *Qualitative Sociology, 23,* 379–405.

Cooper, L., Seibold, D., & Suchner, R. (1997). Listening in organizations: An analysis of error structures in models of listening competency. *Communication Research Reports, 14,* 3.

Copeland, L., & Griggs, L. (1985). *Going international.* New York: Random House.

Corballis, M. C. (2002). *From hand to mouth: The origins of language.* Princeton, NJ: Princeton University Press.

Cosby, P. (1973). Self-disclosure: A literature review. *Psychological Bulletin, 79,* 73–91.

Cose, E. (2000, January 1). Our new look: The colors of race. *Newsweek,* pp. 28–30.

Cose, E. (2005, March 14). Long after the alarm went off. *Newsweek,* p. 37.

Courtivron, I. (2000, July 7). Educating the global student, whose identity is always a matter of choice. *Chronicle of Higher Education,* pp. B4–B5.

Cowan, C., Cowan, P., Heming, G., & Miller, N. (1991). Becoming a family: Marriage, parenting, and child development. In P. A. Cowan & M. Hetherington (Eds.), *Family transitions* (pp. 79–109). Hillsdale, NJ: Erlbaum.

Cowley, G. (1998, March 16). Healer of hearts. *Newsweek,* pp. 50–55.

Cowley, G., & Murr, A. (2004, December 8). The new face of AIDS. *Newsweek,* pp. 76–79.

Cox, R. (2005). Personal communication.

Cox, R. (in press). *Environmental communication and the public sphere.* Thousand Oaks, CA: Sage.

Cozart, E. (1996, November 1997). Feng shui. *Raleigh News and Observer,* p. D1.

Crockett, W. (1965). Cognitive complexity and impression formation. In B. A. Maher (Ed.), *Progress in experimental personality research, 2.* New York: Academic Press.

Cronen, V., Pearce, W. B., & Snavely, L. (1979). A theory of rule-structure and types of episodes and a study of perceived enmeshment in undesired repetitive patterns ("URPs"). In D. Nimmo (Ed.),

Communication yearbook, 3. New Brunswick, NJ: Transaction.

Crossen, C. (1997, July 10). Blah, blah, blah. *Wall Street Journal,* p. 1A, 6A.

Cuber, J. F., & Harroff, P. B. (1965). *Sex and the significant Americans.* Baltimore: Penguin.

Cunningham, J. A., Strassberg, D. S., & Haan, B. (1986). Effects of intimacy and sex-role congruency on self-disclosure. *Journal of Social and Clinical Psychology, 4,* 393–401.

Cunningham, J. D., & Antill, J. K. (1995). Current trends in nonmarital cohabitation: The great POSSLQ hunt continues. In J. T. Wood & S. W. Duck (Eds.), *Understanding relationship processes: 6. Off the beaten track: Understudied relationships* (pp. 148–172). Thousand Oaks, CA: Sage.

Cupach, W. R., & Carlson, C. (2002). Characteristics and consequences of interpersonal complaints associated with perceived face threat. *Journal of Social and Personal Relationships, 19,* 443–462.

Cutler, B., & Penrod, S. (1995). *Mistaken identification: The eyewitness, psychology, and the law.* Cambridge, England: Cambridge University Press.

Cutrona, C. E. (1982). Transitions to college: Loneliness and the process of social adjustment. In L. A. Peplau & D. Perlman (Eds.), *Loneliness: A sourcebook of current theory, research, and therapy* (pp. 291–309). New York: Wiley Interscience.

Cyberscope. (1996, December 23). *Newsweek,* p. 10.

Davis, K. (1940). Extreme isolation of a child. *American Journal of Sociology, 45,* 554–565.

Davis, K. (1947). A final note on a case of extreme isolation. *American Journal of Sociology, 52,* 432–437.

Davis, S., & Kieffer, J. (1998). Restaurant servers influence tipping behaviors. *Psychological Reports, 83,* 223–236.

Davis, V. T., & Singh, R. (1989). Attitudes of university students from India toward marriage and family life. *International Journal of Sociology of the Family, 19,* 43–57.

Deal, T., & Kennedy, A. (1999). *The new corporate cultures: Revitalizing the workplace after downsizing, mergers, and reengineering.* Reading, MA: Perseus Books.

de Becker, G. (1997). *The gift of fear: Survival signals that protect us from violence.* New York: Little, Brown.

de Becker, G., McKee, A., & Boyatzis, R. (2002). *Primal leadership: Realizing the power of emotional intelligence.* Harvard University Press.

DeFrancisco, V. (1991). The sounds of silence: How men silence women in marital relations. *Discourse and Society, 2,* 413–423.

DeFrancisco, V., & Chatham-Carpenter, A. (2000). Self in community: African American women's views of self-esteem. *Howard Journal of Communication, 11,* 73–92.

Delia, J., Clark, R. A., & Switzer, D. (1974). Cognitive complexity and impression formation in informal social interaction. *Speech Monographs, 41,* 299–308.

Dentan, R. (1995). Bad day at Bukit Pekan. *American Anthropologist, 97,* 225–231.

Derlega, V. J., & Berg, J. H. (1987). *Self-disclosure: Research, theory, and therapy.* New York: Plenum.

Deutsch, F. (2001). Equally shared parenting. *Current directions in psychological Science, 10,* 25–28.

Dews, B., & Law, C. (Eds.). (1995). *This fine place so far from home: Voices of academics from the working class.* Philadelphia: Temple University Press.

Dickens, W. J., & Perlman, D. (1981). Friendship over the life-cycle. In S. W. Duck & R. Gilmour (Eds.), *Personal relationships: 2. Developing personal relationships.* London: Academic Press.

Dickson, F. (1995). The best is yet to be: Research on long-lasting marriages. In J. T. Wood & S. W. Duck (Eds.), *Understanding relationship processes: 6. Understudied relationships* (pp. 22–50). Thousand Oaks, CA: Sage.

Diggs, N. (1998). *Steel butterflies: Japanese women and the American experience.* New York: State University of New York Press.

Diggs, N. (2001). *Looking beyond the mask: When American women marry Japanese men.* New York: State University of New York Press.

Diggs, R. C. (1999). African-American and European-American adolescents' perceptions of self-esteem as influenced by parent and peer communication and support environments. In T. J. Socha & R. C. Diggs (Eds.), *Communication, race, and family* (pp. 105–146). Mahwah, NJ: Erlbaum.

Dimmitt, B. (1997, July). Chelsey's missing smile. *Reader's Digest,* 87–93.

Dindia, K. (1994). A multiphasic view of relationship maintenance strategies. In D. Canary & L. Stafford (Eds.), *Communication and relational maintenance* (pp. 91–112). New York: Academic Press.

Dindia, K. (2000). Relational maintenance. In C. Hendrick & S. Hendrick (Eds.), *Close relationships: A sourcebook* (pp. 287–300). Thousand Oaks, CA: Sage.

Dindia, K., & Fitzpatrick, M. A. (1985). Marital communication: Three approaches compared. In S. W. Duck & D. Perlman (Eds.), *Understanding personal relationships: An interdisciplinary approach* (pp. 137–157). Newbury Park, CA: Sage.

Dixson, M., & Duck, S. W. (1993). Understanding relationship processes: Uncovering the human search for meaning. In S. W. Duck (Ed.), *Understanding relationship processes: 1. Individuals in relationships* (pp. 175–206). Newbury Park, CA: Sage.

Dolan, R. E., & Worden, R. L. (Eds.). (1992). *Japan: A country study.* Washington, DC: Library of Congress.

Douthwaite, J. (2002). *The wild girl, natural man, and the monster.* Chicago: University of Chicago Press.

Duck, S. W. (1985). Social and personal relationships. In M. L. Knapp & G. R. Miller (Eds.), *Handbook of interpersonal communication* (pp. 655–686). Beverly Hills, CA: Sage.

Duck, S. W. (1990). Relationships as unfinished business: Out of the frying pan and into the 1990s. *Journal of Social and Personal Relationships, 7,* 5–24.

Duck, S. W. (1994a). *Meaningful relationships.* Thousand Oaks, CA: Sage.

Duck, S. W. (1994b). Steady as (s)he goes: Relational maintenance as a shared meaning system. In D. Canary & L. Stafford (Eds.), *Communication and relational maintenance* (pp. 45–60). New York: Academic Press.

Duck, S. W. (1998). *Human relationships* (3rd ed.). London: Sage.

Duck, S. W. (2006). The play, playfulness, and the players: Everyday interaction as improvised rehearsal of relationships. In J. T. Wood & S. Duck (Eds.), *Composing relationships: Communication in everyday life* (pp. 15–23). Belmont, CA: Wadsworth.

Duck, S. W., Pond, K., & Leatham, G. (1994). Loneliness and the evaluation of relational events. *Journal of Social and Personal Relationships, 11,* 253–276.

Duck, S. W., Rutt, D. J., Hurst, M. H., & Strejc, H. (1991). Some evident truths about conversation in everyday relationships: All communications are not created equal. *Human Communication Research, 18,* 228–267.

Duck, S. W., & Wood, J. T. (in press). What goes up may come down: Gendered dynamics in relational dissolution. In M. Fine & J. Harvey (Eds.), *Relational dissolution* (pp. 169–187). Mahwah, NJ: Erlbaum.

Duck, S. W., & Wright, P. H. (1993). Reexamining gender differences in same-gender friendships: A close look at two kinds of data. *Sex Roles, 28,* 709–727.

Dyson, M. (1995). The plight of black men. In M. L. Andersen & P. H. Collins (Eds.), *Race, class, and gender: An anthology* (2nd ed., pp. 136–146). Belmont, CA: Wadsworth.

Eadie, W. F. (1982). Defensive communication revisited: A critical examination of Gibb's theory. *Southern Speech Communication Journal, 47,* 163–177.

Eaves, M., & Leathers, D. (1991). Context as communication: McDonald's vs. Burger King. *Journal of Applied Communication, 19,* 263–289.

Eckman, P., Friesen, W., & Ellsworth, P. (1971). *Emotion in the human face: Guidelines for research and an integration of findings.* Elmsford, NY: Pergamon.

Egan, G. (1973). Listening as empathic support. In J. Stewart (Ed.), *Bridges, not walls.* Reading, MA: Addison-Wesley.

Ehrenreich, B. (1995). The silenced majority: Why the average working person has disappeared from American media and culture. In M. L. Andersen & P. H. Collins (Eds.), *Race, class, and gender: An anthology* (2nd ed., pp. 147–148). Belmont, CA: Wadsworth.

Eichenbaum, L., & Orbach, S. (1987). *Between women: Love, envy, and competition in women's friendships.* New York: Viking.

Eisenberg, N. (2002). Empathy-related emotional responses, altruism, and their socialization. In R. J. Davidson & A. Harrington (Eds.), *Voices of compassion: Western scientists and Tibetan Buddhists examine human nature* (pp. 131–164). London: Oxford University Press.

Ekman, P., & Davidson, R. (Eds.). (1994). *The nature of emotions: Fundamental questions.* New York: Oxford University Press.

Ellington, J., & Marshall, L. (1997). Gender role perceptions of women in abusive relationships. *Sex Roles, 36,* 349–369.

Ellis, A. (1962). *Reason and emotion in psychotherapy.* New York: Lyle Stuart.

Ellis, A., & Harper, R. (1975). *A new guide to rational living.* Englewood Cliffs, NJ: Prentice Hall.

Emery, T. (2005, May 17). One year later, same-sex couples find increasing acceptance. *Raleigh News & Observer,* p. 4A.

Emmers-Sommer, T. (2003). When partners falter: Repair after a transgression. In D. J. Canary & M. Dainton (Eds.), *Maintaining relationships through communication: Relational, contextual, and cultural variations* (pp. 185–205). Mahwah, NJ: Erlbaum.

Emmons, S. (1998, February 3). The look on his face: Yes, it was culture shock. *Raleigh News and Observer,* p. 5E.

Erbert, L. (2000). Conflict and dialectics: Perceptions of dialectical contradictions in marital conflict. *Journal of Social and Personal Relationships, 17,* 638–659.

Estes, W. K. (1989). Learning theory. In A. Lessold & R. Glaser (Eds.), *Foundations for a psychology of education.* Hillsdale, NJ: Erlbaum.

Etcheverry, P. E., & Le, B. (2005). Thinking about commitment: Accessibility of commitment and prediction of relationship persistence, accommodation, and willingness to sacrifice. *Personal Relationships, 12,* 103–123.

Eyewitness evidence: A guide for law enforcement. (1999, October). Washington, DC: Department of Justice.

Fadiman, A. (1997). *The spirit catches you and you fall down.* New York: Farrar, Straus & Giroux.

Fagan, E. (2001). *Cast your net.* Cambridge, MA: Harvard Common Press.

Fantini, A. E. (1991). Bilingualism: Exploring language and culture. In L. Malave & G. Duquette (Eds.), *Language, culture, and cognition: A collection of studies on first and second language acquisition* (pp. 110–119). Bristol, PA: Multilingual Matters.

Farrell, E. (2005, February 4). More students plan to work to help pay for college. *Chronicle of Higher Education,* pp. A1, A32.

Fehr, B. (1993). How do I love thee: Let me consult my prototype. In S. W. Duck (Ed.), *Understanding relationship processes: 1. Individuals in relationships* (pp. 87–122). Newbury Park, CA: Sage.

Fehr, B., & Russell, J. A. (1991). Concept of love viewed from a prototype perspective. *Journal of Personality and Social Psychology, 60,* 425–438.

Feig, J. (1989). *A common core: Thais and Americans.* Yarmouth, ME: Intercultural Press.

Feigenson, N. (2000). *Legal blame: How jurors think and talk about accidents.* Washington, DC: American Psychological Association.

Fein, E., & Schneider, S. (2002). *The rules for online dating.* New York: Simon & Schuster.

Ferrante, J. (1992). *Sociology: A global perspective.* Belmont, CA: Wadsworth.

Ferrante, J. (1995). *Sociology: A global perspective* (2nd ed.). Belmont, CA: Wadsworth.

Fincham, F. D. (2000). The kiss of the porcupines: From attributing responsibility to forgiving. *Personal Relationships, 7,* 1–23.

Fincham, F. D., & Beach, S. (2002). Forgiveness in marriage: Implications for psychological aggression and constructive communication. *Personal Relationships, 9,* 239–251.

Fincham, F. D., & Bradbury, T. N. (1987). The impact of attributions in marriage: A longitudinal analysis. *Journal of Personality and Social Psychology, 53,* 510–517.

Fincham, F. D., Bradbury, T. N., & Scott, C. K. (1990). Cognition in marriage. In F. D. Fincham & T. N. Bradbury (Eds.), *The psychology of marriage: Basic issues and applications* (pp. 118–119). New York: Guilford.

Fincham, F. D., Paleari, G., & Regalia, C. (2002). Forgiveness in marriage: The role of relationship quality, attributions, and empathy. *Personal Relationships, 9,* 27–37.

Finkel, E., Rusbult, C. E., Kumashiro, M., & Hannon, P. (2002). Dealing with betrayal in close relationships: Does commitment promote forgiveness? *Journal of Personality and Social Psychology, 82,* 956–974.

Finkelstein, J. (1980). Considerations for a sociology of emotions. *Studies in Symbolic Interaction, 3,* 111–121.

Fisher, B. A. (1987). *Interpersonal communication: The pragmatics of human relationships.* New York: Random House.

Fisher, J. D., & Byrne, D. (1975). Too close for comfort: Sex differences in response to invasions of personal space. *Journal of Personal and Social Psychology, 32,* 15–21.

Fitzpatrick, M. A. (1988). *Between husbands and wives: Communication in marriage.* Newbury Park, CA: Sage.

Fitzpatrick, M. A., & Best, P. (1979). Dyadic adjustment in relational types: Consensus, cohesion, affectional expression and satisfaction in enduring relationships. *Communication Monographs, 46,* 167–178.

Fitzpatrick, M., & Vangelisti, A. (Eds.). (1994). *Explaining family interactions.* Thousand Oaks, CA: Sage.

Fleishman, J., Sherbourne, C., & Crystal, S. (2000). Coping, conflictual social interactions, social support, and mood among HIV-infected persons. *American Journal of Community Psychology, 28,* 421–453.

Fletcher, G. J., & Fincham, F. D. (1991). Attribution in close relationships. In G. J. Fletcher & F. D. Fincham (Eds.), *Cognition in close relationships* (pp. 7–35). Hillsdale, NJ: Erlbaum.

Fletcher, G. J., Fincham, F. D., Cramer, L., & Heron, N. (1987). The role of attributions in the development of dating relationships. *Journal of Personality and Social Psychology, 59,* 464–474.

Floyd, K., & Morman, M. (2005). Fathers' and sons' reports of fathers' affectionate communication: Implications of a naïve theory of affection. *Journal of Social and Personal Relationships, 22,* 99–109.

Floyd, K., & Parks, M. (1995). Manifesting closeness in the interactions of peers: A look at siblings and friends. *Communication Reports, 8,* 69–76.

Foeman, A., & Nance, T. (1999). From miscegenation to multiculturalism: Perceptions and stages of interracial relationship development. *Journal of Black Studies, 29,* 540–557.

Forbes, G. B. (2001). College students with tattoos and piercings: Motives, family experiences, personality factors, and perception by others. *Psychological Reports, 89,* 774–786.

Fowers, B. J. (1991). His and her marriage: A multivariate study of gender and marital satisfaction. *Sex Roles, 24,* 209–221.

Fox, L., & Frankel, H. (2005). *Breaking the code: Two teens reveal the secrets of better parent-child communication.* New York: Penguin-New American Library.

French, M. (1992). *The war against women.* New York: Summit.

Fresener, S. (1995). *The T-shirt.* Layton, UT: Gibbs Smith Publishers.

Fridlund, A. J. (1994). *Human facial expression.* San Diego, CA: Academic Press.

Friesen, M., Fletcher, G., & Overall, N. (2005). A dyadic assessment of forgiveness in intimate relationships. *Personal Relationships, 12,* 61–77.

Frijda, N. H. (1986). *The emotions.* Cambridge, England: Cambridge University Press.

Gaines, S., Jr. (1995). Relationships among members of cultural minorities. In J. T. Wood & S. W. Duck (Eds.), *Understanding relationship processes: 6. Off the beaten track: Understudied relationships* (pp. 51–88). Thousand Oaks, CA: Sage.

Galvin, K. (in press). Gender and family interaction: Dress rehearsal for an improvisation? In B. Dow & J. T. Wood (Eds.), *Handbook of gender and communication.* Thousand Oaks, CA: Sage.

Gangwish, K. (1999). *Living in two worlds: Asian-American women and emotion.* Paper presented at the National Communication Convention, Chicago.

Gans, H. (1995). *The war against the poor: The underclass and antipoverty policy.* New York: Basic.

Garner, T. (1994). Oral rhetorical practice in African American culture. In A. González, M. Houston, & V. Chen (Eds.), *Our voices: Essays in culture, ethnicity, and communication* (pp. 81–91). Los Angeles: Roxbury.

Gelles, R. (1987). *Family violence* (2nd ed.). Newbury Park, CA: Sage.

George L. (1995, December 26). Holiday's traditions are being formed. *Raleigh News and Observer,* pp. C1, C3.

Gerstein, M. (1998). *Victor: A novel based on the life of Victor, the savage of Aveyron.* New York: Farrar & Straus.

Gerstel, N., & Gross, H. (1985). *Commuter marriage.* New York: Guilford.

Gibb, J. (1961). Defensive communication. *Journal of Communication, 11,* 141–148.

Gibb, J. R. (1964). Climate for trust formation. In L. Bradford, J. Gibb, & K. Benne (Eds.), *T-group theory and laboratory method* (pp. 279–309). New York: Wiley.

Gibb, J. R. (1970). Sensitivity training as a medium for personal growth and improved interpersonal relationships. *Interpersonal Development, 1,* 6–31.

Gilman, S. (1999a). *Creating beauty to cure the soul: Race and psychology in the shaping of aesthetic surgery.* Durham, NC: Duke University Press.

Gilman, S. (1999b). *Making the body beautiful: A cultural history of aesthetic surgery.* Princeton, NJ: Princeton University Press.

Glascock, N. (1998, February 22). Diversity within Latino arrivals. *Raleigh News and Observer,* p. 9A.

Goldin-Meadow, S. (2004). *Hearing gesture: How our hands help us think.* Cambridge, MA: Harvard University Press.

Goldner, V., Penn, P., Sheinberg, M., & Walker, G. (1990). Love and violence: Gender paradoxes in volatile attachments. *Family Process, 19,* 343–364.

Goldsmith, D., & Fitch, K. (1997). The normative context of advice as social support. *Human Communication Research, 23,* 454–476.

Goldsmith, D., & Fulfs, P. (1999). You just don't have the evidence: An analysis of claims and evidence in Deborah Tannen's *You just don't understand*. In M. Roloff (Ed.), *Communication Yearbook, 22* (pp. 1–49). Thousand Oaks, CA: Sage.

Goldstein, A. (2000, February 27). Breadwinning wives alter marital equation. *Washington Post*, p. A1.

Goleman, D. (1995a). *Emotional intelligence*. New York: Bantam.

Goleman, D. (1995b, November–December). What's your emotional intelligence? *Utne Reader*, pp. 74–76.

Goleman, D. (1998). *Working with emotional intelligence*. New York: Bantam.

Goleman, D., Boyatzis, R., & McKee, A. (2002). *Primal leadership: Realizing the power of emotional intelligence*. Cambridge, MA: Harvard Business School Press.

Goode, E. (2001, August 1). 20% of girls report abuse by a date. *Raleigh News and Observer*, p. 10A.

Good-looking lawyers make more money, says a study by economists. (1996, January 4). *Wall Street Journal*, p. A1.

Goodwin, R., & Plaza, S. (2000). Perceived and received social support in two cultures: Collectivism and support among British and Spanish students. *Journal of Social and Personal Relationships, 17,* 282–291.

Gottman, J. (1979). *Marital interaction: Experimental investigations*. New York: Academic Press.

Gottman, J. (1993). The roles of conflict engagement, escalation or avoidance in marital interaction: A longitudinal view of five types of couples. *Journal of Consulting and Clinical Psychology, 61,* 6–15.

Gottman, J. (1994a). *What predicts divorce? The relationship between marital processes and marital outcomes*. Hillsdale, NJ: Erlbaum.

Gottman, J. (1994b). Why marriages fail. *The Family Therapy Newsletter, 27,* 41–48.

Gottman, J. (1997, May). *Findings from 25 years of studying marriage*. Paper presented at the Conference of the Coalition of

Marriage, Family, and Couples Education, Arlington, VA.

Gottman, J., & Carrère, S. (1994). Why can't men and women get along? Developmental roots and marital inequities. In D. J. Canary & L. Stafford (Eds.), *Communication and relational maintenance* (pp. 203–229). New York: Academic Press.

Gottman, J., Markman, H. J., & Notarius, C. (1977). The topography of marital conflict: A sequential analysis of verbal and nonverbal behavior. *Journal of Marriage and the Family, 39,* 461–477.

Gottman, J., Notarius, C., Gonso, J., & Markman, H. J. (1976). *A couple's guide to communication*. Champaign, IL: Research Press.

Gottman, J., Notarius, C., Markman, H., Banks, S., Yoppi, B., & Rubin, M. E. (1976). Behavior exchange theory and marital decision making. *Journal of Experimental Social Psychology, 34,* 14–23.

Gottman, J., & Silver, N. (2000). *The seven principles for making marriage work*. Three Rivers, MI: Three Rivers Press.

Gravois, J. (2005, April 8). Teach impediment. *Chronicle of Higher Education*, pp. A10–A12.

Gray, H., & Foushee, V. (1997). Adolescent dating violence: Differences between one-sided and mutually violent profiles. *Journal of Interpersonal Violence, 12,* 126–141.

Greenberg, S. (1997, Spring/Summer Special Issue). The loving ties that bind. *Newsweek*, pp. 68–72.

Greene, J., & Burleson, B. (Eds.). (2003). *Handbook of communication and social interaction skills*. Mahwah, NJ: Erlbaum.

Gross, M. (2000, June). The lethal politics of beauty. *George*, pp. 53–59, 99–100.

Gudykunst, W., & Lee, C. (2002). Crosscultural communication theories. In W. Gudykunst & B. Mody (Eds.), *The handbook of international and intercultural communication* (2nd ed, pp. 25–50). Thousand Oaks, CA: Sage.

Gudykunst, W., & Mody, B. (Eds.). (2002). *The handbook of interna-*

tional and intercultural communication. Thousand Oaks, CA: Sage.

Gueguen, N., & De Gail, M. (2003). The effect of smiling on helping behavior: Smiling and good Samaritan behavior. *Communication Reports, 16,* 133–140.

Guerrero, L. (1996). Attachment style differences in intimacy and involvement: A test of the four-category model. *Communication Monographs, 63,* 269–292.

Hakuta, K. (1986). *Mirror of language: The debate on bilingualism*. New York: Basic.

Hall, E. (1976). *Beyond culture*. New York: Doubleday.

Hall, E. T. (1966). *The hidden dimension*. New York: Anchor.

Hall, E. T. (1968). Proxemics. *Current Anthropology, 9,* 83–108.

Hall, J. A. (1978). Gender effects in decoding nonverbal cues. *Psychological Bulletin, 85,* 845–857.

Hall, J. A. (1987). On explaining gender differences: The case of nonverbal communication. In P. Shaver & C. Hendricks (Eds.), *Sex and gender* (pp. 177–200). Newbury Park, CA: Sage.

Hall, J. A., Carter, J. D., & Horgan, T. G. (2000). Gender differences in nonverbal communication of emotion. In A. H. Fischer (Ed.), *Gender and emotion: Social psychological perspectives* (pp. 97–117). Cambridge, England: Cambridge University Press.

Hallstein, L. (2000). Where standpoint stands now: An introduction and commentary. *Women's Studies in Communication, 23,* 1–15.

Hamachek, D. (1992). *Encounters with the self* (3rd ed.). Fort Worth, TX: Harcourt Brace Jovanovich.

Hamlet, J. (2000). The reason why we sing. In A. Gonzales, M. Houston, & V. Chen (Eds.), *Our voices: Essays in culture, ethnicity, and communication* (3rd ed., pp. 93–97). Los Angeles: Roxbury.

Hansen, J. E., & Schuldt, W. J. (1984). Marital self-disclosure and marital satisfaction. *Journal of Marriage and the Family, 46,* 923–926.

Haraway, D. (1988). Situated knowledges: The science question in feminism and the privilege of partial perspective. *Signs, 14,* 575–599.

Harding, S. (1991). *Whose science? Whose knowledge? Thinking from women's lives.* Ithaca, NY: Cornell University Press.

Harris, J. (1998). *The nurture assumption.* New York: Simon & Schuster/Free Press.

Harris, M., Walters, L., & Waschall, S. (1991). Gender and ethnic differences in obesity-related behaviors and attitudes in a college sample. *Journal of Applied Social Psychology, 21,* 1545–1566.

Harris, T. J. (1969). *I'm OK, you're OK.* New York: Harper & Row.

Harvey, J. H., Wenzel, A., & Sprecher, S. (Eds.). (2004). *The handbook of sexuality in close relationships.* Mahwah, NJ: Erlbaum.

Hasenauer, H. (1997). Taking on domestic violence. *Soldiers, 52,* 34–36.

Hasserbrauck, M., & Aaron, A. (2001). Prototype matching in close relationships. *Personality and Social Psychology Bulletin, 27,* 1111–1122.

Hasserbrauck, M., & Fehr, B. (2002). Dimensions of relationship quality. *Personal Relationships, 9,* 253–270.

Hatfield, S. R., & Abrams, L. J. (1995). Interaction between fathers and their children in traditional and single-father families. In T. J. Socha and G. H. Stamp (Eds.), *Parents, children and communication* (pp. 103–112). Mahwah, NJ: Erlbaum.

Hayakawa, S. I. (1962). *The use and misuse of language.* New York: Fawcett.

Hayakawa, S. I. (1964). *Language in thought and action* (2nd ed.). New York: Harcourt, Brace & World.

Healy, J. (1990). *Endangered minds: Why children don't think and what we can do about it.* New York: Simon & Schuster.

Hecht, M. L., Marston, P. J., & Larkey, L. K. (1994). Love ways and relationship quality in heterosexual relationships. *Journal of Social and Personal Relationships, 11,* 25–44.

Heider, F. (1958). *The psychology of interpersonal relations.* New York: Wiley.

Heise, D. (1999). Controlling affective experience interpersonally. *Social Psychology Quarterly, 62,* 4–11.

Helgeson, V. (1994). Long-distance romantic relationships: Sex differences in adjustment and breakup. *Personal and Social Psychology Bulletin, 20,* 254–266.

Hendrick, C., & Hendrick, S. (1988). Lovers wear rose colored glasses. *Journal of Social and Personal Relationships, 5,* 161–184.

Hendrick, C., & Hendrick, S. (1989). Research on love: Does it measure up? *Journal of Personality and Social Psychology, 56,* 784–794.

Hendrick, C., & Hendrick, S. (1996). Gender and the experience of heterosexual love. In J. T. Wood (Ed.), *Gendered relationships.* Mountain View, CA: Mayfield.

Hendrick, C., Hendrick, S., Foote, F. H., & Slapion-Foote, M. J. (1984). Do men and women love differently? *Journal of Social and Personal Relationships, 2,* 177–196.

Henley, N. M. (1977). *Body politics: Power, sex and nonverbal communication.* Englewood Cliffs, NJ: Prentice Hall.

Hewes, D. (Ed.). (1995). *The cognitive bases of interpersonal perception.* Mahwah, NJ: Erlbaum.

Hickson, M., Stacks, D., & Moore, N. (2004). *Nonverbal communication: Studies and applications.* Los Angeles, CA: Roxbury.

Hochschild, A. (1979). Emotion work, feeling rules, and social structure. *American Journal of Sociology, 85,* 551–575.

Hochschild, A. (1983). *The managed heart.* Berkeley: University of California Press.

Hochschild, A. (1990). Ideology and emotion management: A perspective and path for future research. In T. Kemper (Ed.), *Research agendas in the sociology of emotions* (pp. 117–142). New York: State University of New York Press.

Hochschild, A. (1997). *The time bind: When work becomes home and home becomes work.* New York: Metropolitan.

Hochschild, A., with Machung, A. (2003). *The second shift.* New York: Viking.

Hoijer, H. (1994). The Sapir–Whorf hypothesis. In L. Samovar & R. Porter (Eds.), *Intercultural communication: A reader* (7th ed.). Belmont, CA: Wadsworth.

Holtzman, L. (2000). *Media messages: What film, television, and popular music teach us about race, class, gender, and sexual orientation.* New York: M. E. Sharpe.

Honeycutt, J. M. (1993). Memory structures for the rise and fall of personal relationships. In S. W. Duck (Ed.), *Understanding relationship processes: 1. Individuals in relationships* (pp. 30–59). Newbury Park, CA: Sage.

Honeycutt, J. M., Woods, B., & Fontenot, K. (1993). The endorsement of communication conflict rules as a function of engagement, marriage and marital ideology. *Journal of Social and Personal Relationships, 10,* 285–304.

Honoré, C. (2004). *In praise of slowness.* San Francisco: Harper.

Honoré, C. (2005). *In praise of slowness: Challenging the cult of speed.* San Francisco: HarperCollins.

Houston, M. (1985). Language and black woman's place: Evidence from the black middle class. In P. Treichler, C. Kramarae, & B. Stafford (Eds.), *For alma mater: Theory and practice in feminist scholarship* (pp. 177–193). Urbana: University of Illinois Press.

Houston, M. (2004). When black women talk with white women: Why dialogues are difficult. In A. González, M. Houston, & V. Chen (Eds.), *Our voices: Essays in culture, ethnicity, and communication* (4th ed., pp. 119–125). Los Angeles: Roxbury.

Houston, M., & Wood, J. T. (1996). Difficult dialogues, expanded horizons: Communicating across race and class. In J. T. Wood (Ed.), *Gendered relationships* (pp. 39–56). Mountain View, CA: Mayfield.

Howard, J. W., & Dawes, R. M. (1976). Linear prediction of marital happiness. *Personality and Social Psychology Bulletin, 2,* 478–480.

Howard, P. N., & Jones, S. (Eds.). (2004). *Society online: The Internet in context.* Thousand Oaks, CA: Sage.

Human Rights Watch. (1999). *Broken people: Caste violence against India's untouchables.* Washington, DC: Author.

Huston, M., & Schwartz, P. (1995). Relationships of lesbians and gay men. In J. T. Wood & S. W. Duck (Eds.), *Understanding relationship processes: 6. Off the beaten track: Understudied relationships* (pp. 89–121). Thousand Oaks, CA: Sage.

Huston, T. L., McHale, S. M., & Crouter, A. C. (1985). When the honeymoon is over: Changes in the marriage relationship over the first year. In R. Gilmour & S. W. Duck (Eds.), *The emerging field of personal relationships* (pp. 109–132). Hillsdale, NJ: Erlbaum.

Hymowitz, C. (2000, February 8). Racing onto the Web, one manager's secret is simple: Listening. *Wall Street Journal,* p. B1.

Imperato, G. (1999, May). The email prescription. *Fast Company,* pp. 90–92.

Inman, C. (1996). Friendships among men: Closeness in the doing. In J. T. Wood (Ed.), *Gendered relationships* (pp. 95–110). Mountain View, CA: Mayfield.

International Listening Association. (1995, April). An ILA definition of listening. *ILA Listening Post, 53,* 4.

Isaacs, W. (1999). *Dialogue and the art of thinking together.* New York: Doubleday.

Issacson, W. (1989, November 20). Should gays have marriage rights? *Time,* pp. 101–102.

Izard, C. E. (1991). *The psychology of emotions.* New York: Plenum.

Jacobson, N., & Christensen, A. (1998). *Acceptance and change.* New York: W. W. Norton.

Jacobson, N., & Gottman, J. (1998). *When men batter women.* New York: Simon & Schuster.

James, K. (1989). When twos are really threes: The triangular dance in couple conflict. *Australian and New Zealand Journal of Family Therapy, 10,* 179–186.

James, W., & Lange, C. B. (1922). *The emotions.* Baltimore: Williams & Wilkins.

Jandt, F. (2004). *An introduction to intercultural communication: Identities in a global community.* Thousand Oaks, CA: Sage.

Jhally, S., & Katz, J. (2001, Winter). Big trouble, little pond. *Umass,* pp. 26–31.

Johannesen, R. (1996). *Ethics in human communication* (4th ed.). Prospect Heights, IL: Waveland.

Johnson, C. B., Stockdale, M. S., & Saal, F. E. (1991). Persistence of men's misperceptions of friendly cues across a variety of interpersonal encounters. *Psychology of Women Quarterly, 15,* 463–465.

Johnson, F. L. (1989). Women's culture and communication: An analytic perspective. In C. M. Lont & S. A. Friedley (Eds.), *Beyond the boundaries: Sex and gender diversity in communication* (pp. 301–316). Fairfax, VA: George Mason University Press.

Johnson, F. L. (1996). Friendships among women: Closeness in dialogue. In J. T. Wood (Ed.), *Gendered relationships* (pp. 79–94). Mountain View, CA: Mayfield.

Johnson, F. L. (2000). *Speaking culturally: Language diversity in the United States.* Thousand Oaks, CA: Sage.

Johnson, M. (in press). Gendered communication and intimate partner violence. In B. Dow & J. T. Wood (Eds.), *Handbook of gender and communication.* Thousand Oaks, CA: Sage.

Jones, A. (1994). *Next time she'll be dead: Battering and how to stop it.* Boston: Beacon.

Jones, E., & Gallois, C. (1989). Spouses' impressions of rules for communication in public and private marital conflicts. *Journal of Marriage and the Family, 51,* 957–967.

Jones, G. P., & Dembo, M. H. (1989). Age and sex role differences in intimate friendships during childhood and adolescence. *Merrill–Palmer Quarterly of Behavior and Development, 35,* 445–462.

Jones, S., & Burleson, B. R. (2003). Effects of helper and recipient sex on the experience and outcomes of comforting messages: An experimental investigation. *Sex Roles, 48,* 1–19.

Jones, W. H., & Moore, T. L. (1989). Loneliness and social support. In M. Hojat & R. Crandall (Eds.), *Loneliness: Theory, research, and applications* (pp. 145–156). Newbury Park, CA: Sage.

Kachadourian, L., Fincham, F., & Davila, J. (2004). The tendency to forgive in dating and married couples: The role of attachment and relationship satisfaction. *Personal Relationships, 11,* 373–393.

Kagan, J. (1998). *Three seductive ideas.* Cambridge, MA: Harvard University Press.

Kamo, Y., & Cohen, E. (1998). Division of household work between partners: A comparison of black and white couples. *Special issue: Comparative perspectives on black family life* (Vol. 1). *Journal of Comparative Family Studies, 29,* 117–132.

Kantowitz, B., & Wingert, P. (1999, April 19). The science of a good marriage. *Newsweek,* pp. 52–57.

Kaye, L. W., & Applegate, J. S. (1990). Men as elder caregivers: A response to changing families. *American Journal of Orthopsychiatry, 60,* 86–95.

Keeley, M. P., & Hart, A. J. (1994). Nonverbal behavior in dyadic interaction. In S. W. Duck (Ed.), *Understanding relationship processes: 4. Dynamics of relationships* (pp. 135–162). Thousand Oaks, CA: Sage.

Kelley, D. (1998). The communication of forgiveness. *Communication Studies, 49,* 1–17.

Kelley, H. H. (1967). Attribution theory in social psychology. In D. Levine (Ed.), *Nebraska symposium on motivation* (Vol. 15, pp. 192–238). Lincoln: University of Nebraska Press.

Kelley, H. H., & Thiabaut, J. (1978). *The social psychology of groups.* New York: Wiley.

Kelley, R. (1997). *Yo' mama's disFUNKtional!* Boston: Beacon.

Kelly, C., Huston, T. L., & Cate, R. M. (1985). Premarital relationship correlates of the erosion of satisfaction in marriage. *Journal of Social and Personal Relationships, 2,* 167–178.

Kelly, G. A. (1955). *The psychology of personal constructs.* New York: W. W. Norton.

Kemper, T. (1987). How many emotions are there? Wedding the social and autonomic components. *American Journal of Sociology, 93,* 263–289.

Kerr, B. (1999, March 5). When dreams differ: Male-female relations on campuses. *Chronicle of Higher Education,* pp. B7–B8.

Keyes, R. (1992, February 22). Do you have the time? *Parade,* pp. 22–25.

Kilpatrick, J. (1996, June 1). An odd word or two—But don't dis the dictionary. *Raleigh News and Observer,* p. 15A.

Kilpatrick, J. (2000, June 12). Computers, et al., churn out new words. *Raleigh News and Observer,* p. 11A.

Kleinke, C., Peterson, T., & Rutledge, T. (1998). Effects of self-generated facial expressions on mood. *Journal of Personality and Social Psychology, 74,* 272–279.

Knapp, M. L. (1972). *Nonverbal communication in human interaction.* New York: Holt, Rinehart & Winston.

Knapp, M. L., & Vangelisti, A. (2005). *Interpersonal communication and human relationships* (5th ed.). Boston: Allyn and Bacon.

Kohlberg, L. (1958). *The development of modes of thinking and moral choice in the years 10 to 16.* Unpublished doctoral dissertation, University of Chicago.

Korzybski, A. (1958). *Science and sanity* (4th ed.). Lakeville, CT: International Non-Aristotelian Library Publishing Company.

Kovecses, Z. (1990). *Emotion concepts.* New York: Springer-Verlag.

Kozol, J. (1995). *Amazing grace: The lives of children and the conscience of a nation.* New York: Crown.

Kreider, R. M. (2003, October). Adopted children and stepchildren: 2000. (C2KBR-30). *Census 2000 Special Reports.* Washington, D.C.: U.S. Census Bureau, U.S. Department of Commerce.

Kupfer, D., First, M., & Regier, D. (2002). *A research agenda for DSM-V.* Washington, DC: American Psychiatric Press.

Kurdek, L. A. (1993). The allocation of household labor in gay, lesbian, and heterosexual married couples. *Journal of Social Issues, 49,* 127–139.

Labov, W. (1972). *Sociolinguistic patterns.* Philadelphia: University of Pennsylvania Press.

Lacher, I. (2005, March 3). In new book, professor sees a 'mania' in U.S. for possessions and status. *New York Times,* pp. A15, A 21.

La Gaipa, J. J. (1982). Rituals of disengagement. In S. W. Duck (Ed.), *Personal relationships: 4. Dissolving personal relationships.* London: Academic Press.

Laing, R. D. (1961). *The self and others.* New York: Pantheon.

Lakoff, G., & Johnson, M. (1980). *Metaphors we live by.* Chicago: University of Chicago Press.

Landale, N., & Fennelly, K. (1992). Informal unions among mainland Puerto Ricans: Cohabitation or an alternative to legal marriage? *Journal of Marriage and the Family, 54,* 269–280.

Lane, R. (2000). *The loss of happiness in marketplace democracies.* New Haven, CT: Yale University Press.

Laner, M. R., & Ventrone, N. A. (2002). Dating scripts revisited. *Journal of Family Issues, 21,* 488–500.

Langer, S. (1953). *Feeling and form: A theory of art.* New York: Scribner.

Langer, S. (1979). *Philosophy in a new key: A study in the symbolism of reason, rite, and art* (3rd ed.). Cambridge, MA: Harvard University Press.

Langston, D. (1992). Tired of playing monopoly? In M. L. Andersen &

P. H. Collins (Eds.), *Race, class, and gender: An anthology* (pp. 110–119). Belmont, CA: Wadsworth.

LaRossa, R. (1998). The culture and conduct of fatherhood. In K. V. Hansen & A. I. Garey (Eds.), *Family in the U.S.: Kinship and domestic policies* (pp. 377–385). Philadelphia: Temple University Press.

Lasswell, M., & Lobsenz, N. M. (1980). *Styles of loving.* New York: Doubleday.

Laswell, H. (1948). The structure and function of communication in society. In L. Bryson (Ed.), *The communication of ideas.* New York: Harper & Row.

Leaper, C. (Ed.). (1994). *Childhood gender segregation: Causes and consequences.* San Francisco: Jossey-Bass.

Leaper, C. (1996). The relationship of play activity and gender to parent and child sex-typed communication. *International Journal of Behavioral Development, 19,* 689–703.

Leaper, N. (1999). How communicators lead at the best global companies. *Communication World, 16,* 33–36.

Leathers, D. G. (1976). *Nonverbal communication systems.* Boston: Allyn & Bacon.

Leathers, D. G. (1986). *Successful nonverbal communication: Principles and applications.* New York: Macmillan.

Lee, J. A. (1973). *The colours of love: An exploration of the ways of loving.* Don Mills, Ontario, Canada: New Press.

Lee, J. A. (1988). Love-styles. In R. J. Sternberg & M. L. Barnes (Eds.), *The psychology of love* (pp. 38–67). New Haven, CT: Yale University Press.

Lee, W. S. (1994). On not missing the boat: A processual method for intercultural understanding of idioms and lifeworld. *Journal of Applied Communication Research, 22,* 141–161.

Lee, W. S. (2000). That's Greek to me: Between a rock and a hard place in intercultural encounters. In L. Samovar & R. Porter (Eds.),

Intercultural communication: A reader (9th ed., pp. 217–224). Belmont, CA: Wadsworth.

Leets, L. (1999, May). *When words wound: Another look at racist speech.* Paper presented at the annual conference of the International Communication Association, San Francisco.

Leland, J., & Beals, G. (1997, May 5). In living color. *Newsweek,* pp. 58–60.

LePoire, B. A., Burgoon, J. K., & Parrott, R. (1992). Status and privacy restoring communication in the workplace. *Journal of Applied Communication Research, 4,* 419–436.

LePoire, B. A., Shepard, C., & Duggan, A. (1999). Nonverbal involvement, expressiveness, and pleasantness as predicted by parental and partner attachment style. *Communication Monographs, 66,* 293–311.

Levine, R. (1988). The pace of life across cultures. In J. McGrath (Ed.), *The social psychology of time* (pp. 39–60). Newbury Park, CA: Sage.

Levine, R., & Norenzayan, A. (1999). The pace of life in 31 countries. *Journal of Cross Cultural Psychology, 30,* 178–205.

Levy, G. (1999). Gender-typed and nongender-typed category awareness in toddlers. *Sex Roles, 39,* 851–861.

Lewis, J. D., & Weigert, A. J. (1985). Social atomism, holism and trust. *Sociological Quarterly, 26,* 455–471.

Liang, S. (1997, Summer). Mix: A multiethnic women's dialogue. *Hues,* pp. 22–23, 56.

Lim, T. (2002). Language and verbal communication across cultures. In W. Gudykunst & B. Mody (Eds.), *The handbook of international and intercultural communication* (2nd ed., pp. 69–88). Thousand Oaks, CA: Sage.

Little girl has smile surgery. (1995, December 16). *Raleigh News and Observer,* p. 14A.

Locke, D. (1992). *Increasing multicultural understanding: A comprehensive model.* Newbury Park, CA: Sage.

Lofland, L. (1985). The social shaping of emotion: The case of grief. *Symbolic Interaction, 8,* 171–190.

Lohmann, A., Arriaga, X., & Goodfriend, W. (2003). Close relationships and placemaking: Do objects in a couple's home reflect couplehood? *Personal Relationships, 10,* 437–449.

Lorde, A. (1992). Age, race, class, and sex: Women redefining difference. In M. L. Andersen & P. H. Collins (Eds.), *Race, class, and gender: An anthology* (pp. 495–502). Belmont, CA: Wadsworth.

Luby, V., & Aron, A. (1990, July). *A prototype structuring of love, like, and being in-love.* Paper presented at the Fifth International Conference on Personal Relationships, Oxford, England.

Luft, J. (1969). *Of human interaction.* Palo Alto, CA: National Press Books.

Lund, M. (1985). The development of investment and commitment scales for predicting continuity of personal relationships. *Journal of Social and Personal Relationships, 2,* 3–23.

Luster, T., & Okagaki, L. (Eds.). (2005). *Parenting: An ecological perspective,* 2nd ed. Mahwah, NJ: Erlbaum.

Lustig, M., & Koester, J. (1999). *Intercultural competence: Interpersonal communication across cultures.* New York: Longman.

Lyman, R. (2005, February 15). Trying to strengthen an "I do" with a more binding legal tie. *New York Times,* pp. A1, A16.

Lytton, H., & Romney, D. M. (1991). Parents' differential socialization of boys and girls: A meta-analysis. *Psychological Bulletin, 109,* 267–296.

Maccoby, E. (1998). *The two sexes: Growing up apart, coming together.* Cambridge, MA: Harvard University Press.

MacGeorge, E. L., Gillihan, S. J., Samter, W., & Clark, R. A. (2003). Skill deficit or differential motivation? Accounting for sex differences in the provision of emotional support. *Communication Research, 30,* 272–303.

MacGeorge, E. L., Graves, A. R., Feng, B., Gillihan, S. J., & Burleson, B. R. (2004). The myth of gender cultures: Similarities outweigh differences in men's and women's provision of and responses to supportive communication. *Sex Roles, 50,* 143–175.

MacNeil, S., & Byers, E. S. (2005). Dyadic assessment of sexual self-disclosure and sexual satisfaction in heterosexual dating couples. *Journal of Social and Personal Relationships, 22,* 169–181.

Mahany, B. (1997, August 7). A hands-on study of language. *Raleigh News and Observer,* pp. 1E, 3E.

Maheu, M., & Subotnik, R. (2001). *Infidelity on the Internet: Virtual relationships and real betrayal.* Naperville, IL: Sourcebooks.

Main, M. (1981). Avoidance in the service of attachment. In K. Immelmann, G. Barlow, L. Petrenovich, & M. Main (Eds.), *Behavioral development: The Beilfield interdisciplinary project.* New York: Cambridge University Press.

Major, B., Schmidlin, A. M., & Williams, L. (1990). Gender patterns in social touch: The impact of setting and age. In C. Mayo & N. M. Henley (Eds.), *Gender and nonverbal behavior* (pp. 3–37). New York: Springer-Verlag.

Malandro, L. A., & Barker, L. L. (1983). *Nonverbal communication.* Reading, MA: Addison-Wesley.

Maltz, D. N., & Borker, R. (1982). A cultural approach to male–female miscommunication. In J. J. Gumperz (Ed.), *Language and social identity* (pp. 196–216). Cambridge, England: Cambridge University Press.

Mangan, K. (2002, July 5). Horse sense or nonsense? Critics decry what they consider the "softening" of medical education. *Chronicle of Higher Education,* pp. A8–A10.

Manning, A. (1996, March 6). Signing catches on as a foreign language. *USA Today,* p. 4D.

Manning, M. (Ed.). (2000). *Dispatches from the ebony tower: Intellectuals confront the African-American experience.* New York: Columbia University Press.

Mares, M. (1995). The aging family. In M. Fitzpatrick & A. Vangelisti (Eds.), *Explaining family interactions.* Thousand Oaks, CA: Sage.

Margolis, P. (Ed.). (1999). *Computer and Internet dictionary* (3rd ed.). New York: Random House.

Markman, H. (1981). Prediction of marital distress: A 5-year follow-up. *Journal of Consulting and Clinical Psychology, 49,* 760–762.

Markman, H. (1990). *Advances in understanding marital distress.* Unpublished doctoral dissertation, University of Denver, Denver, CO.

Markman, H., Clements, M., & Wright, R. (1991, April). *Why father's prebirth negativity and a first-born daughter predict marital problems: Results from a ten-year investigation.* Paper presented at a symposium at the biennial meeting of the Society for Research in Child Development, Seattle, WA.

Martin, C., Fabes, R., Evans, S., & Wyman, H. (2000). Social cognition on the playground: Children's beliefs about playing with girls versus boys and their relations to sex segregated play. *Journal of Social and Personal Relationships, 17,* 751–771.

Maslow, A. H. (1954/1970). *Motivation and personality* (3rd ed.). New York: Harper & Row.

Maslow, A. H. (1959/1970). *New knowledge in human values.* Chicago: H. Regnery.

Maslow, A. H. (1968). *Toward a psychology of being.* New York: Van Nostrand Reinhold.

Matsumoto, D., Franklin, B., Choi, J., Rogers, D., & Tatani, H. (2002). Cultural influences on the expression and perception of emotion. In W. Gudykunst & B. Mody (Eds.), *The handbook of international and intercultural communication* (2nd ed., pp. 107–126). Thousand Oaks, CA: Sage.

Maugh, T., II. (1994, November 26). Romantics seem to be bred, not born. *Raleigh News and Observer,* pp. 1A, 4A.

Mazur, E. (1989). Predicting gender differences in same-sex friendships from affiliation motive and value. *Psychology of Women Quarterly, 13,* 277–291.

McCormick, J., & Begley, S. (1996, December 9). How to raise a Tiger. *Newsweek,* pp. 52–59.

McCullough, M., & Hoyt, W. (2002). Transgression-related motivational dispositions: Personality substrates of forgiveness and their links to the big five. *Personality and Social Psychology Bulletin, 28,* 1556–1573.

McDaniel, E., & Quasha, S. (2000). The communicative aspects of doing business in Japan. In L. Samovar & R. Porter (Eds.), *Intercultural communication: A reader* (9th ed., pp. 312–324). Belmont, CA: Wadsworth.

McDowell, D. (1989, July 17). He's got to have his way. *Time,* pp. 92–94.

McGinn, D. (2004, October 4). Mating behavior 101. *Newsweek,* pp. 44–45.

McGrane, S. (2000, September 4). Absence makes the typing skills grow stronger. *New York Times* article reprinted in the *Raleigh News and Observer,* p. 5D.

McGurl, M. (1990, June 3). That's history, not black history. *The New York Times Book Review,* p. 13.

McIntosh, P. (1995). White privilege and male privilege: A personal account of coming to see correspondences through work in women's studies. In M. L. Andersen & P. H. Collins (Eds.), *Race, class, and gender: An anthology* (2nd ed., pp. 94–105). Belmont, CA: Wadsworth.

McKay, V. (2000). Understanding the co-culture of the elderly. In L. Samovar & R. Porter (Eds.), *Intercultural communication: A reader* (9th ed., pp. 180–189). Belmont, CA: Wadsworth.

McKinney, B., Kelly, L., & Duran, R. (1997). The relationship between conflict message styles and dimensions of communication competence. *Communication Reports, 10,* 185–196.

McLemee, S. (2003, February 21). Getting emotional. *Chronicle of Higher Education,* pp. A14–A16.

McLuhan, M., & Fiori, Q. (1967). *The medium is the message.* New York: Random House.

McNeill, D. (1992). *Hand and mind: What gestures reveal about thought.* Chicago: University of Chicago Press.

Meacham, J. (2000, September 18). The new face of race. *Newsweek,* pp. 38–41.

Mead, G. H. (1934). *Mind, self, and society.* Chicago: University of Chicago Press.

Meeks, B., Hendrick, S., & Hendrick, C. (1998). Communication, love and satisfaction. *Journal of Social and Personal Relationships, 15,* 755–773.

Mehrabian, A. (1981). *Silent messages: Implicit communication of emotion and attitudes* (2nd ed.). Belmont, CA: Wadsworth.

Mendenhall, M., Dunbar, E., & Oddou, G. (1987). Expatriate selection, training and career-pathing: A review and critique. *Human Resource Management, 26,* 331–345.

Metts, S. (2006). Hanging out and doing lunch: Enacting friendship closeness. In J. T. Wood & S. W. Duck (Eds.), *Composing relationships: Communication in everyday life* (pp. 76–85). Belmont, CA: Wadsworth.

Metts, S., Cupach, W. R., & Bejlovec, R. A. (1989). "I love you too much to ever start liking you": Redefining romantic relationships. *Journal of Social and Personal Relationships, 6,* 259–274.

Miell, D. E., & Duck, S. W. (1986). Strategies in developing friendship. In V. J. Derlega & B. A. Winstead (Eds.), *Friendship and social interaction* (pp. 129–143). New York: Springer-Verlag.

Mikulincer, M., & Shaver, P. (2005). Attachment theory and emotions in close relationships: Exploring the attachment-related dynamics of emotional reactions to relational events. *Personal Relationships, 12,* 149–168.

Milardo, R. (1986). Personal choice and social constraint in close relationships: Applications of network analysis. In V. Derlega & B. Winstead (Eds.), *Friendship and social interaction* (pp. 145–166). New York: Springer-Verlag.

Milkie, M. A., Mattingly, M. J., Nomaguchi, K. M., Bianchi, S. M., & Robinson, J. P. (2004). The time squeeze: Parental strategies and feelings about time with children. *Journal of Marriage and Family, 66*, 739–761.

Miller, D. W. (2000, February 25). Looking askance at eyewitness testimony. *Chronicle of Higher Education*, pp. A19–A20.

Miller, G. R., & Parks, M. R. (1982). Communication in dissolving relationships. In S. W. Duck (Ed.), *Personal relationships: 4. Dissolving personal relationships* (pp. 127–154). London: Academic Press.

Miller, J. B. (1993). Learning from early relationship experience. In S. W. Duck (Ed.), *Understanding relationship processes: 2. Learning about relationships* (pp. 1–29). Newbury Park, CA: Sage.

Miller, W. I. (1993). *Humiliation.* Ithaca: Cornell University Press.

Miller, W. I. (1998). *The anatomy of disgust.* Cambridge, MA: Harvard University Press.

Miller, W. I. (2003). *Faking it.* UK: Cambridge University Press.

Min, P. (Ed.). (1995). *Asian Americans: Contemporary trends and issues.* Thousand Oaks, CA: Sage.

Mochizuki, T. (1981). Changing patterns of mate selection. *Journal of Comparative Family Studies, 12*, 318–328.

Molloy, B., & Herzberger, S. (1998). Body image and self-esteem: A comparison of African-American and Caucasian women. *Sex Roles, 38*, 631–643.

Monastersky, R. (2001, July 6). Look who's listening. *Chronicle of Higher Education*, pp. A14–A16.

Mongeau, P., Carey, C., & Williams, M. (1998). First date initiation and enactment: An expectancy violation approach. In D. Canary & K. Dindia (Eds.), *Sex differences and similarities in communica-tion* (pp. 413–426). Mahwah, NJ: Erlbaum.

Mongeau, P., Serewicz, M., & Therrien, L. (2004). Goals for cross-sex first dates: Identification, measurement, and the influence of contextual factors. *Communication Monographs, 71*, 121–147.

Monkerud, D. (1990, October). Blurring the lines. Androgyny on trial. *Omni*, pp. 81–86.

Monsour, M. (1992). Meanings of intimacy in cross- and same-sex friendships. *Journal of Social and Personal Relationships, 9*, 277–295.

Monsour, M. (1997). Communication and cross-sex friendships across the life cycle: A review of the literature. In B. Burleson (Ed.), *Communication Yearbook, 20* (pp. 375–414). Thousand Oaks, CA: Sage.

Monsour, M. (in press). Communication and gender among adult friends. In B. Dow & J. T. Wood (Eds.), *Handbook of gender and communication.* Thousand Oaks, CA: Sage.

Montgomery, B. M. (1988). Quality communication in personal relationships. In S. W. Duck (Ed.), *Handbook of personal relationships* (pp. 343–366). New York: Wiley.

Morgan, L. (1996). When does life begin? A cross-cultural perspective on the personhood of fetuses and young children. In W. Haviland & R. Gordon (Eds.), *Talking about people: Readings in contemporary cultural anthropology* (pp. 24–34). Mountain View, CA: Mayfield.

Morgan, M. (1998). More than a mood or an attitude: Discourse and verbal genres in African-American culture. In S. S. Mufwene, J. Rickford, G. Bailey, & J. Baugh (Eds.), *African-American English: Structure, history and use* (pp. 251–281). New York: Rutledge.

Morman, M. T., & Floyd, K. (2002). A "changing culture of fatherhood": Effects on affectionate communication, closeness, and satisfaction in men's relationships with their fathers and their sons. *Western Journal of Communication, 66*, 395–411.

Morreale, S. (2001, May). Communication important to employers. *Spectra*, p. 8.

Morreale, S. (2004, December). Accounting graduates need better listening skills and correct grammar. *Spectra*, p. 7.

Morris, D. (1997, March–April). The civility wars: Is poverty more vulgar than profanity? *Utne Reader*, pp. 15–16.

Morris, T., Gorham, J., Cohen, S., & Huffman, D. (1996). Fashion in the classroom: Effects of attire on student perceptions of instructors in college classes. *Communication Education, 45*, 135–148.

Mosley-Howard, S., & Evans, C. (1997). *Relationships in the African American family.* Paper presented at the 1997 Conference of the International Network on Personal Relationships, Oxford, OH.

Muehlhoff, T. (2006). "He started it!": Communication in parenting. In J. T. Wood & S. W. Duck (Eds.), *Composing relationships: Communication in everyday life* (pp. 46–54). Belmont, CA: Wadsworth Thompson.

Muehlhoff, T., & Wood, J. T. (2002). Speaking of marriage: The marriage between theory and practice. *Journal of Social and Personal Relationships, 19*, 613–619.

Mulac, A., Wiemann, J. M., Widenmann, S. J., & Gibson, T. W. (1988). Male/female language differences and effects in same-sex and mixed-sex dyads: The gender-linked language effect. *Communication Monographs, 55*, 315–335.

Murray, S., Holmes, J., & Griffin, D. (1996a). The benefits of positive illusions: Idealization and the construction of satisfaction in close relationships. *Journal of Personality and Social Psychology, 70*, 79–98.

Murray, S., Holmes, J., & Griffin, D. (1996b). The self-fulfilling nature of positive illusions in romantic relationships: Love is not blind, but prescient. *Journal of Personality and Social Psychology, 71*, 1155–1180.

Mwakalye, N., & DeAngelis, T. (1995, October). The power of touch helps vulnerable babies survive. *APA Monitor*, p. 25.

Nanda, S., & Warms, R. (1998). *Cultural anthropology* (6th ed.). Belmont, CA: West/Wadsworth.

Nardi, P. M., & Sherrod, D. (1994). Friendship in the lives of gay men and lesbians. *Journal of Social and Personal Relationships, 11,* 185–199.

Narem, T. R. (1980). Try a little TLC. *Science, 80,* 15.

Netspeak. (2000, August–September). *bLink,* p. 19. Pasadena, CA: Earthlink.

Nettle, D., & Romaine, S. (2000). *Vanishing voices: The extinction of the world's languages.* Oxford, England: Oxford University Press.

Newman, P. (1964, February). "Wild man" behavior in New Guinea Highlands community. *American Anthropologist, 66,* 1–19.

Neyer, F. (2002). The dyadic interdependence of attachment security and dependency: A conceptual replication across older twin pairs and younger couples. *Journal of Social and Personal Relationships, 19,* 483–503.

Nicholson, J. (2006). "Them's fightin' words": Naming in everyday talk between siblings. In J. T. Wood & S. Duck (Eds.), *Composing relationships: Communication in everyday life* (pp. 55–64). Belmont, CA: Wadsworth.

Noller, P. (1986). Sex differences in nonverbal communication: Advantage lost or supremacy regained? *Australian Journal of Psychology, 38,* 23–32.

Noller, P. (1987). Nonverbal communication in marriage. In D. Perlman & S. W. Duck (Eds.), *Intimate relationships: Development, dynamics, and deterioration* (pp. 149–176). Newbury Park, CA: Sage.

Noller, P., & Fitzpatrick, M. (1992). *Communication in family relationships.* New York: Allyn & Bacon.

Notarius, C. I. (1996). Marriage: Will I be happy or will I be sad? In N. Vanzetti & S. W. Duck (Eds.), *A lifetime of relationships* (pp. 265–289). Pacific Grove, CA: Brooks/Cole.

Nunberg, G. (2003, May 29). *Fresh Air* [radio interview]. Cited in R. West & L. Turner, (2006). *Understanding interpersonal communication* (p. 164). Belmont, CA: Wadsworth.

Nussbaum, J. E. (1992, October 18). Justice for women! *New York Review of Books,* pp. 43–48.

Nyquist, M. (1992, Fall). Learning to listen. *Ward Rounds* (pp. 11–15). Evanston, IL: Northwestern University Medical School.

O'Connor, P. (1992). *Friendships between women.* London: Harvester Wheatsheaf.

Okin, S. M. (1989). *Gender, justice, and the family.* New York: Basic.

Olien, M. (1978). *The human myth.* New York: Harper & Row.

Olson, D., & McCubbin, H. (1983). *Families: What makes them work?* Thousand Oaks, CA: Sage.

O'Meara, J. D. (1989). Cross-sex friendship: Four basic challenges of an ignored relationship. *Sex Roles, 21,* 525–543.

O'Neill, M. (1997, January 12). Asian folk art of feng shui hits home with Americans. *Raleigh News and Observer,* p. 6E.

Orbe, M., & Harris, T. (2001). *Interracial communication: Theory into practice.* Belmont, CA: Wadsworth.

Orbuch, T., & Eyster, S. (1997). Divison of household labor among black couples and white couples. *Social Forces, 76,* 301–322.

Orbuch, T., & Veroff, J. (2002). A programmatic review: Building a two-way bridge between social psychology and the study of the early years of marriage. *Journal of Social and Personal Relationships, 19,* 549–568.

Orbuch, T., Veroff, J., & Hunter, A. (1999). Black couples, white couples: The early years of marriage. In E. Hetherington (Ed.), *Coping with divorce, single parenting, and remarriage* (pp. 23–43). Mahwah, NJ: Erlbaum.

Ornish, D. (1998). *Love and survival: The scientific basis for the healing power of intimacy.* New York: HarperCollins.

Ornish, D. (1999). *Love and survival: 8 pathways to intimacy and health.* New York: HarperCollins.

Osborne, A. (1996, Summer). The paradox of effort and grace. *Inner Directions,* pp. 4–6.

O'Sullivan, L., & Gaines, S. (1998). Decision-making in college students' heterosexual dating relationships: Ambivalence about engaging in sexual activity. *Journal of Social and Personal Relationships, 15,* 347–363.

Otnes, C., & Lowrey, T. (Eds.). (2004). *Contemporary consumption rituals.* Mahwah, NJ: Erlbaum.

Parks, M., & Adelman, B. (1983). Communication networks and the development of romantic relationships: An expansion of uncertainty reduction theory. *Human Communication Research, 10,* 55–79.

Parks, M., & Floyd, K. (1996a). Making friends in cyberspace. *Journal of Communication, 46,* 80–97.

Parks, M., & Floyd, K. (1996b). Meanings for closeness and intimacy in friendship. *Journal of Social and Personal Relationships, 13,* 85–107.

Parks, M., & Roberts, L. (1998). Making MOOsic: The development of personal relationships online and a comparison to their offline counterparts. *Journal of Social and Personal Relationships, 15,* 517–537.

Pataki, S., Shapiro, C., & Clark, M. (1994). Children's acquisition of appropriate norms for friendships and acquaintances. *Journal of Social and Personal Relationships, 11,* 427–442.

Patterson, M. L. (1992). A functional approach to nonverbal exchange. In R. S. Feldman & B. Rime (Eds.), *Fundamentals of nonverbal behavior* (pp. 458–495). New York: Cambridge University Press.

Pearce, W. B., Cronen, V. E., & Conklin, F. (1979). On what to look at when analyzing communication: A hierarchical model of actors' meanings. *Communication, 4,* 195–220.

Pearson, J. C. (1985). *Gender and communication.* Dubuque, IA: Brown.

Pennebaker, J. W. (1997). *Opening up: The healing power of expressing emotions* (Rev. ed.). New York: Guilford.

Pennington, B. A., & Turner, L. H. (2004). Playground or training ground?: The function of talk in African American and European American mother–adolescent daughter dyads. In P. M. Buzzanell, H. Sterk, & L. H. Turner (Eds.), *Gender in applied contexts* (pp. 275–294). Thousand Oaks, CA: Sage.

Peplau, L. A., & Beals, K. B. (2003). The family lives of lesbians and gay men. In A. Vangelisti (Ed.), *The handbook of family communication* (pp. 233–248). Mahwah, NJ: Erlbaum.

Peplau, L., & Spalding, L. (2000). The close relationships of lesbians, gay men, and bisexuals. In S. Hendrick & C. Hendrick (Eds.), *Close relationships: A sourcebook*, pp. 110–136.

Perry-Jenkins, M., Pierce, C. P., & Goldberg, A. E. (2004). Discourses on diapers and dirty laundry: Family communication about childcare and housework. In A. Vangelisti (Ed.), *Handbook of family communication* (pp. 541–561). Mahwah, NJ: Erlbaum.

Petersen, W. (1997). *Ethnicity counts.* New York: Transaction.

Petronio, S. (1991). Communication boundary management: A theoretical model of managing disclosure of private information between married couples. *Communication Theory, 1,* 311–335.

Pettigrew, T. F. (1967). Social evaluation theory: Consequences and applications. In D. Levine (Ed.), *Nebraska symposium on motivation* (pp. 241–311). Lincoln: University of Nebraska Press.

Pew Internet and American Life Project. (2004). *Internet use by region in the United States.* Retrieved December 15, 2004, from http://www.pewinternet.org.

Philippot, P., & Feldman, R. (Eds.). (2004). *The regulation of emotion.* Mahwah, NJ: Erlbaum.

Phillips, G. M., & Wood, J. T. (1983). *Communication and human relationships.* New York: Macmillan.

Piaget, J. (1932/1965). *The moral judgment of the child.* New York: Free Press.

Pierson, J. (1995, November 20). If sun shines in, workers work better, buyers buy more. *Wall Street Journal,* pp. B1, B8.

Planalp, S. (1997, September). Personal correspondence.

Planalp, S., & Fitness, J. (2000). Thinking/feeling about social and personal relationships. *Journal of Social and Personal Relationships, 16,* 731–750.

Pleck, J. H. (1987). American fathering in historical perspective. In M. S. Kimmel (Ed.), *Changing men: New directions in research on men and masculinity* (pp. 83–97). Englewood Cliffs, NJ: Prentice Hall.

Politically correct monikers are labeled incorrect. (1995, November 7). *Wall Street Journal,* p. A1.

Pollack, W. (2000). *Real boys: Rescuing ourselves from the myths of boyhood.* New York: Owl Books.

Pomerleau, A., Bolduc, D., Malcuit, G., & Cossette, L. (1990). Pink or blue: Environmental stereotypes in the first two years of life. *Sex Roles, 22,* 359–367.

Popenoe, D. (1996). *Life without father.* New York: Free Press.

Potter, W. J. (2001). *Media literacy* (2nd ed.). Thousand Oaks, CA: Sage.

Prime Numbers. (2004, July 2). The gap on gay marriage. *Chronicle of Higher Education,* p. A9.

Proctor, R. (1991). *An exploratory analysis of responses to owned messages in interpersonal communication.* Doctoral dissertation, Bowling Green University, Bowling Green, OH.

Pryor, J. B., & Merluzzi, T. V. (1985). The role of expertise in processing social interaction scripts. *Journal of Experimental Social Psychology, 21,* 362–379.

Public pillow talk. (1987, October). *Psychology Today,* p. 18.

Raphael, M. (1997, May 13). It's true: Drivers move slowly if you want their space. *Raleigh News and Observer,* p. 1A.

Rawlins, W. K. (1981). *Friendship as a communicative achievement: A theory and an interpretive analysis of verbal reports.* Unpublished doctoral dissertation, Temple University, Philadelphia.

Rawlins, W. K. (1994). Being there and growing apart: Sustaining friendships during adulthood. In D. Canary & L. Stafford (Eds.), *Communication and relational maintenance* (pp. 275–294). New York: Academic Press.

Reel, B. W., & Thompson, T. L. (1994). A test of the effectiveness of strategies for talking about AIDS and condom use. *Journal of Applied Communication Research, 22,* 127–141.

Reis, H. T., Senchak, M., & Solomon, B. (1985). Sex differences in the intimacy of social interaction: Further examination of potential explanations. *Journal of Personality and Social Psychology, 48,* 1204–1217.

Reisenzaum, R. (1983). The Schachter theory of emotion: Two decades later. *Psychological Bulletin, 94,* 239–264.

Remland, M. (2000). *Nonverbal communication in everyday life.* Boston: Houghton-Mifflin.

Reske, J., & Stafford, L. (1990). Idealization and communication in long-distance premarital relationships. *Family Relations, 39,* 274–290.

Ribeau, S. A., Baldwin, J. R., & Hecht, M. L. (1994). An African-American communication perspective. In L. Samovar & R. Porter (Eds.), *Intercultural communication: A reader* (7th ed., pp. 140–147). Belmont, CA: Wadsworth.

Richmond, V., & McCroskey, J. (2000). The impact of supervisor and subordinate immediacy on relational and organizational outcomes. *Communication Monographs, 67,* 85–95.

Riessman, C. (1990). *Divorce talk: Women and men make sense of personal relationships.* New Brunswick, NJ: Rutgers University Press.

Risman, B., & Godwin, S. (2001). Twentieth-century changes in economic work and family. In D.

Vannoy (Ed.), *Gender mosaics* (pp. 134–144). Los Angeles: Roxbury.

Robarchek, C., & Dentan, R. (1987). Blood drunkenness and the bloodthirsty Semai: Unmaking another anthropological myth. *American Anthropologist, 89,* 356–363.

Roberts, G., & Orbe, M. (1996, May). Creating that safe place: Descriptions of intergenerational gay male communication. Paper presented at the annual meeting of the International Communication Association, Chicago.

Robinson, J. (2000, September–October). 4 weeks vacation for everyone! *Utne reader,* pp. 49–54.

Rodriguez, R. (1982). *Hunger of memory: The education of Richard Rodriguez.* Toronto, Canada: Bantam.

Rohlfing, M. (1995). Doesn't anybody stay in one place anymore? An exploration of the understudied phenomenon of long-distance relationships. In J. T. Wood & S. W. Duck (Eds.), *Understanding relationship processes: 6. Off the beaten track: Understudied relationships* (pp. 173–196). Thousand Oaks, CA: Sage.

Root, M. P. P. (1990). Disordered eating habits in women of color. *Sex Roles, 22,* 525–536.

Roper poll (1999). How Americans communicate. Retrieved January 8, 2000, from http://www.natcom.org/research/Roper/how_americans_communicate.htm

Rose, A., & Asher, S. (2000). Children's friendships. In C. Hendrick & S. Hendrick (Eds.), *Close relationships: A sourcebook* (pp. 47–57). Thousand Oaks, CA: Sage.

Rose, S. (1984). How friendships end: Patterns among young adults. *Journal of Social and Personal Relationships, 1,* 267–277.

Rose, S., & Frieze, I. H. (1989). Young singles' scripts for a first date. *Gender and Society, 3,* 258–268.

Rose, S., & Serafica, F. (1986). Keeping and ending casual, close and best friendships. *Journal of Social and Personal Relationships, 3,* 275–288.

Rosenberg, M. (1979). *Conceiving the self.* New York: Basic.

Rosenwein, B. (1998). *Anger's past: The sacred uses of emotion in the Middle Ages.* Ithaca, New York: Cornell University Press.

Ross, E. (2004, July 7). New HIV infections hit record. *Raleigh News & Observer,* pp. 1A, 16A.

Rothwell, J. D. (2004). *In the company of others.* New York: McGraw-Hill.

Rousar, E. E., III, & Aron, A. (1990, July). *Valuing, altruism, and the concept of love.* Paper presented at the Fifth International Conference on Personal Relationships, Oxford, England.

Roux, A. (2001). Rethinking official measures of poverty: Consideration of race, ethnicity, and gender. In D. Vannoy (Ed.), *Gender mosaics* (pp. 290–299). Los Angeles: Roxbury.

Rowland, D. (1985). *Japanese business etiquette.* New York: Warner.

Ruberman, T. R. (1992, January 22–29). Psychosocial influences on mortality of patients with coronary heart disease. *Journal of the American Medical Association, 267,* 559–560.

Rubin, L. (1985). *Just friends: The role of friendship in our lives.* New York: Harper & Row.

Ruddick, S. (1989). *Maternal thinking: Towards a politics of peace.* Boston: Beacon.

Rusbult, C. (1987). Responses to dissatisfaction in close relationships: The exit–voice–loyalty–neglect model. In D. Perlman & S. W. Duck (Eds.), *Intimate relationships: Development, dynamics, and deterioration* (pp. 109–238). London: Sage.

Rusbult, C., & Buunk, B. (1993). Commitment processes in close relationships: An interdependence analysis. *Journal of Social and Personal Relationships, 19,* 175–204.

Rusbult, C., Drigotas, S., & Verette, J. (1994). The investment model: An interdependence analysis of commitment processes and relationship maintenance phenomena. In D. Canary & L. Stafford (Eds.), *Communication and relational maintenance* (pp. 115–140). San Diego, CA: Academic Press.

Rusbult, C. E., Johnson, D. J., & Morrow, G. D. (1986). Impact of couple patterns of problem solving on distress and nondistress in dating relationships. *Journal of Personality and Social Psychology, 50,* 744–753.

Rusbult, C. E., & Zembrodt, I. M. (1983). Responses to dissatisfaction in romantic involvement: A multidimensional scaling analysis. *Journal of Experimental Social Psychology, 19,* 274–293.

Rusbult, C. E., Zembrodt, I. M., & Iwaniszek, J. (1986). The impact of gender and sex-role orientation on responses to dissatisfaction in close relationships. *Sex Roles, 15,* 1–20.

Rusk, T., & Rusk, N. (1988). *Mind traps: Change your mind, change your life.* Los Angeles: Price, Stern, Sloan.

Ryan, R., La Guardia, J., Solky-Butzel, J., Chirkov, V., & Kim, Y. (2005). On the interpersonal regulation of emotions: Emotional reliance across gender, relationships, and cultures. *Personal Relationships, 12,* 145–163.

Saarni, C. (1990). Emotional competence: How emotions and relationships become integrated. In R. A. Thompson (Ed.), *Socioemotional development: Nebraska symposium on motivation* (pp. 115–182). Lincoln: University of Nebraska Press.

Saarni, C. (1999). *The development of emotional competence.* New York: Guilford.

Sallinen-Kuparinen, A. (1992). Teacher communicator style. *Communication Education, 41,* 153–166.

Salopek, J. (1999). Is anyone listening? *Training and Development, 53,* 58–59.

Samovar, L., & Porter, R. (Eds.) (1995). *Intercultural communication: A reader* (7th ed.). Belmont, CA: Wadsworth.

Samovar, L., & Porter, R. (Eds.) (2000). *Intercultural communication: A reader* (9th ed). Belmont, CA: Wadsworth.

Samter, W., & Cupach, W. (1998). Friendly fire: Topical variations in conflict among same- and cross-sex friends. *Communication Studies, 49,* 121–138.

Scarf, M. (1987). *Intimate partners.* New York: Random House.

Schachter, S. (1964). The interaction of cognitive and physiological determinants of emotion states. In P. Leiderman & D. Shapiro (Eds.), *Psychobiological approaches to social behavior* (pp. 138–173). Stanford, CA: Stanford University Press.

Schachter, S., & Singer, J. (1962). Cognitive, social, and physiological determinants of emotional state. *Psychological Review, 69,* 379–399.

Schappell, E. (2005). *The friend who got away.* New York: Doubleday.

Scharlott, B., & Christ, W. (1995). Overcoming relationship-initiation barriers: The impact of a computer-dating system on sex role, shyness, and appearance inhibition. *Computers in Human Behavior, 11,* 191–204.

Schiminoff, S. B. (1980). *Communication rules: Theory and research.* Newbury Park, CA: Sage.

Schmanoff, S. (1985). Expressing emotions in words: Verbal patterns of interactions. *Journal of Communication, 35,* 16–31.

Schmanoff, S. (1987). Types of emotional disclosures and request compliance between spouses. *Communication Monographs, 54,* 85–100.

Schmitt, R. (1997, September 11). Judges try curbing lawyers' body language antics. *Wall Street Journal,* pp. B1, B7.

Schneider, A. (1999, March 26). Taking aim at student incoherence. *Chronicle of Higher Education,* pp. A16–A18.

Schneider, D. (1997). Implicit personality theory: A review. *Psychological Bulletin, 27,* 294–309.

Schramm, W. (1955). *The process and effects of mass communication.* Urbana: University of Illinois Press.

Schutz, A. (1999). It was your fault! Self-serving bias in the autobio-graphical accounts of conflicts in married couples. *Journal of Social and Personal Realtionships, 16,* 193–208.

Schutz, W. (1966). *The interpersonal underworld.* Palo Alto, CA: Science and Behavior Books.

Schwartz, M., & DeKeseredy, W. (1997). *Sexual assault on the college campus: The role of male peer support.* Thousand Oaks, CA: Sage.

Schwartz, T. (1989, January–February). Acceleration syndrome: Does everyone live in the fast lane nowadays? *Utne Reader,* pp. 36–43.

Scott, C., & Meyers, K. (2005). The socialization of emotion: Learning emotion management at the fire station. *Journal of Applied Communication Research, 33,* 67–92.

Seay, E. (2004, February 11). Lost city, lost languages. *Princeton Alumni Weekly,* pp. 17, 43.

Secklin, P. (1991, November). *Being there: A qualitative study of young adults' descriptions of friendship.* Paper presented at the Speech Communication Association Convention, Atlanta, GA.

Sedgwick, E. K. (1995). *Shame and its sisters: A Silvan Tomkins reader.* Durham, NC: Duke University Press.

Sedikides, C., Campbell, W., Reeder, G., & Elliott, A. (1998). The self-serving bias in relational context. *Journal of Personality and Social Psychology, 74,* 378–386.

Segrin, C. (1998). Interpersonal communication problems associated with depression and loneliness. In P. Andersen & L. Guerrero (Eds.), *Communication and emotion: Theory, research, and applications* (pp. 215–242). San Diego, CA: Academic Press.

Segrin, C., & Flora, F. J. (2005). *Family communication.* Mahwah, NJ: Erlbaum.

Seligman, M. E. P. (1990). *Learned optimism: How to change your mind and your life.* New York: Simon & Schuster/Pocket Books.

Seligman, M. E. P. (2002). *The authentic self.* New York: Free Press.

Sellnow, D., & Sellnow, T. (2001). The "illusion of life" rhetorical perspective: An integrated approach to the study of music as communication. *Critical Studies in Media Communication, 18,* 295–415.

Servaes, J. (1988). Cultural identity in East and West. *Howard Journal of Communications, 2,* 58–71.

Shannon, C., & Weaver, W. (1949). *The mathematical theory of communication.* Urbana: University of Illinois Press.

Sharlet, J. (1999, July 2). Beholding beauty: Scholars nip and tuck at our quest for physical perfection. *Chronicle of Higher Education,* pp. A15–A16.

Shattuck, T. R. (1994). *The forbidden experiment.* New York: Farrar, Straus & Giroux.

Shaver, P., Schwartz, J., Kirson, D., & O'Connor, C. (1987). Further explorations of a prototype approach. *Journal of Personality and Social Psychology, 52,* 1061–1086.

Shaver, P., Wu, S., & Schwartz, J. (1992). Cross-cultural similarities and differences in emotion and its representation: A prototype approach. In M. S. Clark (Ed.), *Emotion* (pp. 175–212). Newbury Park, CA: Sage.

Shenk, D. (1997). *Data smog.* New York: Harper-Edge.

Sher, T. G. (1996). Courtship and marriage: Choosing a primary partner. In N. Vanzetti & S. W. Duck (Eds.), *A lifetime of relationships* (pp. 243–264). Pacific Grove, CA: Brooks/Cole.

Sherrod, D. (1989). The influence of gender on same-sex friendships. In C. Hendrick (Ed.), *Close relationships* (pp. 164–186). Newbury Park, CA: Sage.

Shott, S. (1979). Emotion and social life: A symbolic interactionist analysis. *American Journal of Sociology, 84,* 1317–1334.

Shotter, J. (1993). *Conversational realities: The construction of life through language.* Newbury Park, CA: Sage.

Silverstein, J., & Lasky, M. (2004). *Online dating for dummies.* Indianapolis, IN: Wiley.

Silverstein, L. B. (2002). Fathers and families. In J. P. McHale & W. S. Grolnick (Eds.), *Retrospect and prospect in the psychological study of families* (pp. 35–64). Mahwah, NJ: Erlbaum.

Simmons, L. (2002). *Odd girl out: The hidden culture of aggression in girls.* Orlando, FL: Harvest Books.

Simmons, L. (2004). *Odd girl speaks out: Girls write about bullies, cliques, popularity, and jealousy.* Orlando, FL: Harvest Books.

Simmons, T., & O'Neill, G. (2001, September). Households and families: 2000. (C2KBR/01-8). *Census 2000 Brief.* Washington, DC: U.S. Census Bureau, Department of Commerce.

Simon, S. B. (1977). *Vulture: A modern allegory on the art of putting oneself down.* Niles, IL: Argus Communications.

Smith, A. D. (2005, March 21). *Standing in the shadows: Wide awakeness counts.* The 2005 Weil Lecture on American Citizenship. Chapel Hill: University of North Carolina at Chapel Hill.

Smitherman, G. (1994). *Black talk: Words and phrases from the hood to the amen corner.* Boston: Houghton Mifflin.

Snell, W. E., Jr., Hawkins, R. C., II, & Belk, S. S. (1988). Stereotypes about male sexuality and the use of social influence strategies in intimate relationships. *Journal of Clinical and Social Psychology, 7,* 42–48.

Socha, T. J., Sanchez-Hucles, J., Bromley, J., & Kelly, B. (1995). Invisible parents and children: Exploring African-American parent-child communication. In T. J. Socha & G. H. Stamp (Eds.), *Parents, children and communication: Frontiers of theory and research* (pp. 127–145). Mahwah, NJ: Erlbaum.

Sorrentino, R., Cohen, D., Olson, J., & Zanna, M. (Eds.). (2005). *Culture and social behavior: The Ontario Symposium.* Mahwah, NJ: Erlbaum.

Spain, D. (1992). *Gendered spaces.* Chapel Hill: University of North Carolina Press.

Spear, W. (1995). *Feng shui made easy: Designing your life with the ancient art of placement.* New York: Harper-Collins.

Spencer, T. (1994). Transforming relationships through ordinary talk. In S. W. Duck (Ed.), *Understanding relationship processes: 4. Dynamics of relationships* (pp. 58–85). Thousand Oaks, CA: Sage.

Spitzack, C. (1990). *Confessing excess.* Albany: State University of New York Press.

Spitzack, C. (1993). The spectacle of anorexia nervosa. *Text and Performance Quarterly, 13,* 1–21.

Spitzberg, B. (1998). Sexual coercion in courtship relations. In B. Spitzberg & W. Cupach (Eds.), *The dark side of close relationships* (pp. 179–232). Mahwah, NJ: Erlbaum.

Spitzberg, B., & Cupach, W. (Eds.). (1998). *The dark side of close relationships.* Mahwah, NJ: Erlbaum.

Sprecher, S. (1989). The importance to males and females of physical attractiveness, earning potential, and expressiveness in initial attraction. *Sex Roles, 21,* 591–607.

Sprecher, S. (2001). A comparison of emotional consequences of and changes in equity over time using global and domain-specific measures of equity. *Journal of Social and Personal Relationships, 18,* 477–501.

Sprecher, S., & Felmlee, D. (1997). The balance of power in romantic heterosexual couples over time from "his" and "her" perspectives. *Sex Roles, 37,* 363–379.

Sprecher, S., & Regan, P. (2002). Liking some things (in some people) more than others: Partner preferences in romantic relationships and friendships. *Journal of Social and Personal Relationships, 19,* 463–481.

Stacey, J. (1996). *In the name of the father: Rethinking family values in a postmodern age.* Boston: Beacon.

Stafford, L. (2004). *Maintaining long-distance and cross-residential relationships.* Mahwah, NJ: Erlbaum.

Stafford, L., Dutton, M., & Haas, S. (2000). Measuring routine maintenance: Scale revision, sex versus gender roles, and the prediction of relational characteristics. *Communication Monographs, 67,* 306–323.

Stearns, C., & Stearns, P. (1986). *Anger: The struggle for emotional control in America's history.* Chicago: University of Chicago Press.

Steil, J. (2000). Contemporary marriage: Still an unequal partnership. In C. Hendrick & S. Hendrick (Eds.), *Close relationships: A sourcebook* (pp. 124–136). Thousand Oaks, CA: Sage.

Steiner-Pappalardo, N., & Gurung, R. (2002). The femininity effect: Relationship quality, sex, gender, attachment, and significant-other concepts. *Personal Relationships, 9,* 313–325.

Stephenson, S. J., & D'Angelo, G. (1973). *The effects of evaluative/empathic listening and self-esteem on defensive reactions in dyads.* Paper presented to the International Communication Association, Montreal, Quebec, Canada.

Sternberg, R. J. (1986). A triangular theory of love. *Psychological Review, 93,* 119–135.

Stewart, J. (1986). *Bridges, not walls* (4th ed.). New York: Random House.

Stewart, L. P., Stewart, A. D., Friedley, S. A., & Cooper, P. J. (1990). *Communication between the sexes: Sex differences and sex role stereotypes* (2nd ed.). Scottsdale, AZ: Gorsuch Scarisbrick.

Stone, A. (1996). *The war of desire and technology at the close of the mechanical age.* Cambridge: MIT Press.

Straus, T. (2000, September–October). Baby, I've got an e-crush on you. *Utne Reader,* p. 67.

Strege, J. (1997). *Tiger: A biography of Tiger Woods.* New York: Bantam Doubleday.

Sugarman, D., & Frankel, S. (1996). Patriarchal ideology and wife assault: A meta-analytic review. *Journal of Family Violence, 1,* 11–40.

Suitor, J. J. (1991). Marital quality and satisfaction with the division of household labor across the family life cycle. *Journal of Marriage and the Family, 53,* 221–230.

Surra, C. (1987). Mate selection as social transition. In D. Perlman & S. W. Duck (Eds.), *Intimate relationships: Development, dynamics and deterioration* (pp. 88–120). Newbury Park, CA: Sage.

Surra, C., Arizzi, P., & Asmussen, L. (1988). The association between reasons for commitment and the development and outcome of marital relationships. *Journal of Social and Personal Relationships, 5,* 47–64.

Survey. (2004, August 27). The almanac issue: Survey of public opinion on higher education. *Chronicle of Higher Education,* p. 35.

Swain, S. (1989). Covert intimacy: Closeness in men's friendships. In B. Risman & P. Schwartz (Eds.), *Gender and intimate relationships* (pp. 71–86). Belmont, CA: Wadsworth.

Swidler, A. (2001). *Talk of love.* Chicago: University of Chicago Press.

Sypher, B. (1984). Seeing ourselves as others see us. *Communication Research, 11,* 97–115.

Tannen, D. (1990). *You just don't understand: Women and men in conversation.* New York: William Morrow.

Tannen, D. (1995). *Talking nine to five.* New York: William Morrow.

Tavris, C. (1989). *Anger: The misunderstood emotion.* New York: Simon & Schuster.

Tavris, C. (1992). *The mismeasure of woman.* New York: Simon & Schuster.

Taylor, S. (2002). *The tending instinct: How nurturing is essential for who we are and how we live.* New York: Times Books.

Teachers' words may clash with cultures. (2000, February 23). *Raleigh News and Observer,* p. 4E.

Telework Advisory Group. (2005). Retrieved May 16, 2005, from http://www.telecommute.org.

Templin, N. (1994, October 17). Wanted: Six bedrooms, seven baths for empty nesters. *Wall Street Journal,* pp. B1, B7.

Thiabaut, J., & Kelley, H. H. (1959). *The social psychology of groups.* New York: Wiley.

Thomas, V. G. (1989). Body-image satisfaction among black women. *Journal of Social Psychology, 129,* 107–112.

Three million around the world contracted AIDS in last year. (1994, August 9). *Raleigh News and Observer,* p. 5A.

Ting-Toomey, S. (1988). Intercultural conflict styles: A face-negotiation theory. In Y. Kim & W. Gudykunst (Eds.), *Theories in intercultural communication* (pp. 213–235). Newbury Park, CA: Sage.

Ting-Toomey, S. (1991). Intimacy expressions in three cultures: France, Japan, and the United States. *International Journal of Intercultural Relations, 15,* 29–46.

Ting-Toomey, S., & Oetzel, J. (2001). *Managing intercultural conflict effectively.* Thousand Oaks, CA: Sage.

Ting-Toomey, S., & Oetzel, J. (2002). Cross-cultural face concerns and conflict styles. In W. Gudykunst & B. Mody (Eds.), *Handbook of international and intercultural communication* (2nd ed., pp. 143–163). Thousand Oaks, CA: Sage.

Tjaden, P., & Thoennes, N. (1998). *Prevalence, incidence, and consequences of violence against women: Findings from the National Violence Against Women Survey.* Atlanta, GA: Centers for Disease Control and Prevention, Center for Injury Prevention and Control.

Tolhuizen, J. H. (1989). Communication strategies for intensifying dating relationships: Identification, use, and structure. *Journal of Social and Personal Relationships, 6,* 413–434.

Totten, L. D. (2006). Who am I right now? Negotiating familial and professional roles. In J. T. Wood & S. W. Duck (Eds.), *Composing relationships: Communication in everyday life* (pp. 186–193). Belmont, CA: Wadsworth.

Trad, P. V. (1995). Adolescent girls and their mothers: Realigning the relationship. *American Journal of Family Therapy, 23,* 11–24.

Trainor, B. (1996, May 20). Commit suicide over a medal? An ex-general gives his view. *New York Times,* p. A8.

Treichler, P. A., & Kramarae, C. (1983). Women's talk in the ivory tower. *Communication Quarterly, 31,* 118–132.

Trotter, R. J. (1975, October 25). The truth, the whole truth, and nothing but . . . *Science News, 108,* 269.

Truman, D., Tokar, D., & Fischer, A. (1996). Dimensions of masculinity: Relations to date rape supportive attitudes and sexual aggression in dating situations. *Journal of Counseling and Development, 74,* 555–562.

Turner, L. H., & Shutter, R. (2004). African American and European American women's visions of workplace conflict: A metaphorical analysis. *Howard Journal of Communication, 15,* 169–183.

Tyre, P., & McGinn, D. (2003, May 12). She works, he doesn't. *Newsweek,* pp. 44–54.

Ueland, B. (1992, November/December). Tell me more: On the fine art of listening. *Utne Reader,* pp. 104–109.

Ullman, S., Karabatsos, G., & Koss, M. (1999). Alcohol and sexual assault in a national sample of college women. *Journal of Interpersonal Violence, 14,* 603–625.

Underwood, A., & Adler, J. (2005, April 25). When cultures clash. *Newsweek,* pp. 68–72.

Underwood, M. (2003). *Social aggression among girls.* New York: Guilford.

Urgo, J. (2000). *The age of distraction.* Jackson: Mississippi University Press.

U.S. Bureau of the Census. (1999). *Resident population estimates of the United States by sex, race, and Hispanic origin, April 1, 1990, to April 1, 1999.* Retrieved November 18, 2000, from http://www.census.gov/population/estimates/nation/intfile1-3

U.S. Bureau of the Census. (2004). Retrieved February 25, 2005, from http://www.census.gov/population/estimates/nation/intfile1-3

Vachss, A. (1994, August 28). You carry the cure in your own heart. *Parade*, pp. 4–6.

Van Gelder, L. (1991). The strange case of the electronic lover. In C. Dunlop & R. Kling (Eds.), *Computerisation and controversy: Value conflicts and social choices* (pp. 364–375). Boston: Academic Press.

Vangelisti, A. (1993). Couples' communication problems: The counselor's perspective. *Journal of Applied Communication Research, 22,* 106–126.

Vangelisti, A., & Crumley, L. (1998). Reactions to messages that hurt: The influence of relational context. *Communication Monographs, 65,* 173–196.

Van Styke, E. (1999). *Listening to conflict: Finding constructive solutions to workplace disputes.* New York: AMA Communications.

VanYperen, N. W., & Buunk, B. P. (1991). Equity theory and exchange and communal orientation from a crossnational perspective. *Journal of Social Psychology, 131,* 5–20.

Vedantam, S. (2002, September 1). "Family" illness might join list of diagnoses. *Raleigh News and Observer,* p. 16A.

Veroff, J. (1999). Marital commitment in the early years of marriage. In W. Jones and J. Adams (Eds.), *Handbook of interpersonal commitment and relationship stability* (pp. 149–162). New York: Plenum Press.

Vickers, S. (1999). *Native American identities: From stereotype to archetype in art and literature.* Albuquerque: University of New Mexico Press.

Villarosa, L. (1994, January). Dangerous eating. *Essence,* pp. 19–21, 87.

Vobejda, B., & Perlstein, L. (1998, June 7). Girls catching up with boys in ways good and bad, study finds. *Raleigh News and Observer,* 1A, 14A.

Vocate, D. (Ed.). (1994). *Intrapersonal communication: Different voices, different minds.* Hillsdale, NJ: Erlbaum.

Wagner, E. (2001, May 11). Listening: Hear today, probably gone tomorrow. *Business Journal,* p. 25.

Walker, M. B., & Trimboli, A. (1989). Communicating affect: The role of verbal and nonverbal content. *Journal of Language and Social Psychology, 8,* 229–248.

Walster, E., Traupmann, J., & Walster, G. W. (1978). Equity and extramarital sexuality. *Archives of Sexual Behavior, 7,* 127–141.

Walters, R. (1984). Forgiving: An essential element in effective living. *Studies in Formative Spirituality, 5,* 365–374.

Waltman, M. (2003). Strategems and heuristics in the recruitment of children into communities of hate: The fabric of our future nightmares. *Southern Journal of Communication, 69,* 22–36.

Waner, K. (1995). Business communication competencies needed by employees as perceived by business faculty and business professionals. *Business Communication Quarterly, 58,* 51–56.

Wann, D., & Schrader, M. (2000). Controllability and stability in the self-serving attributions of sports spectators. *Journal of Social Psychology, 140,* 160–176.

Watzlawick, P., Beavin, J., & Jackson, D. D. (1967). *Pragmatics of human communication.* New York: W. W. Norton.

Webb, L. M., Walker, K. L., Bollis, T. S., & Hebbani, A. G. (2004). Perceived parental communication, gender, and young adults' self-esteem. In O. M. Backlund & M. R. Williams (Eds.), *Readings in gender communication* (pp. 197–224). Belmont, CA: Thomson/Wadsworth.

Wegner, H., Jr. (2005). Disconfirming communication and self-verification in marriage: Associations among the demand/withdraw interaction pattern, feeling understood, and marital satisfaction. *Journal of Social and Personal Relationships, 22,* 19–31.

Weiner, N. (1967). *The human use of human beings.* New York: Avon.

Weinstock, H., Berman, S., & Cates, W., Jr. (2004). Sexually transmitted diseases among American youth: Incidence and prevalence estimates, 2000. *Perspectives on Sexual and Reproductive Health, 36,* 6–10.

Weinstock, J., & Bond, L. (2000). Conceptions of conflict in close friendships and ways of knowing among young college women: A developmental framework. *Journal of Social and Personal Relationships, 17,* 687–696.

Weiss, S. E. (1987). The changing logic of a former minor power. In H. Binnendijk (Ed.), *National negotiating styles* (pp. 44–74). Washington, DC: U.S. Department of State.

Wellman, B. (1985). Domestic work, paid work, and net work. In S. W. Duck & D. Perlman (Eds.), *Understanding personal relationships.* Beverly Hills, CA: Sage.

Werking, K. (1997). *We're just good friends: Women and men in nonromantic relationships.* New York: Guilford.

Werner, C., Altman, I., & Oxley, D. (1985). Temporal aspects of homes: A transactional perspective. In I. Altman & C. M. Werner (Eds.), *Home environments: 8. Human behavior and environment: Advances in theory and research* (pp. 1–32). Beverly Hills, CA: Sage.

Werner, C. M., Altman, I., Brown, B. B., & Ginat, J. (1993). Celebrations in personal relationships: A transactional/dialectical perspective. In S. W. Duck (Ed.), *Understanding relational processes: 3. Social context and relationships* (pp. 109–138). Newbury Park, CA: Sage.

Werner, C. M., & Haggard, I. M. (1985). Temporal qualities of interpersonal relationships. In G. R. Miller & M. L. Knapp (Eds.), *Handbook of interpersonal communication* (pp. 59–99). Beverly Hills, CA: Sage.

West, J. (1995). Understanding how the dynamics of ideology influence violence between intimates. In S. W. Duck & J. T. Wood (Eds.), *Understanding relationship processes: 5. Confronting relationship challenges* (pp. 129–149). Thousand Oaks, CA: Sage.

West, L., Anderson, J., & Duck, S. W. (1996). Crossing the barriers to friendship between men and women. In J. T. Wood (Ed.), *Gendered relationships*. Mountain View, CA: Mayfield.

West, R., & Turner, L. (2006). *Understanding interpersonal communication*. Belmont, CA: Thomson/Wadsworth.

Weston, K. (1991). *Families we choose: Lesbians, gays, kinship*. New York: Columbia University Press.

Whaley, K., & Rubenstein, T. (1994). How toddlers "do" friendship: A descriptive analysis of naturally occurring friendships in a group child care setting. *Journal of Social and Personal Relationships, 11*, 383–400.

Whan, K. (1997, August 10). UNC study observes link between health, loving support. *The Chapel Hill Herald*, p. 7.

What teens say about drinking. (1994, August 7). *Parade*, p. 9.

Wheatley, M. (2002). *Turning to one another*. San Francisco: Berrett-Koehler.

Whitbeck, L. B., & Hoyt, D. R. (1994). Social prestige and assortive mating: A comparison of students from 1956 and 1988. *Journal of Social and Personal Relationships, 11*, 137–145.

White, B. (1989). Gender differences in marital communication patterns. *Family Process, 28*, 89–106.

White, B. (1998). *The 100 best ways to stay together*. New York: Dell.

White, J., & Bondurant, B. (1996). Gendered violence in intimate relationships. In J. T. Wood (Ed.), *Gendered relationships*. Mountain View, CA: Mayfield.

Whorf, B. (1956). *Language, thought, and reality*. New York: MIT Press/Wiley.

Whybrow, P. (2005). *American mania: When more is not enough*. New York: W. W. Norton.

Wiemann, J. M., & Harrison, R. P. (Eds). (1983). *Nonverbal interaction*. Beverly Hills, CA: Sage.

Wilkie, J. R. (1991). The decline in men's labor force participation and income and the changing structure of family economic support. *Journal of Marriage and the Family, 53*, 111–122.

Williams, D. G. (1985). Gender, masculinity–femininity, and emotional intimacy in same-sex friendship. *Sex Roles, 12*, 587–600.

Williams, R., & Williams, V. (1998). *Anger kills*. New York: Harper-Perennial.

Willmott, P. (1987). *Friendship networks and social support*. London: Policy Studies Institute.

Winsor, J., Curtis, D., & Stephens, R. (1997). National preferences in business and communication education: An update. *Journal of the Association for Communication Administration, 3*, 170–179.

Winzeler, R. (1990). Amok: Historical, psychological, and cultural perspectives. In W. J. Karim (Ed.), *Emotions of culture: A Malay perspective* (pp. 97–122). Oxford, England: Oxford University Press.

Woo, E. (1995, December 18). Stereotypes may psych out students. *Raleigh News and Observer*, pp. 1A, 10A.

Wood, J. T. (1982). Communication and relational culture: Bases for the study of human relationships. *Communication Quarterly, 30*, 75–84.

Wood, J. T. (1986). Different voices in relationship crises: An extension of Gilligan's theory. *American Behavioral Scientist, 29*, 273–301.

Wood, J. T. (1992). Telling our stories: Narratives as a basis for theorizing sexual harassment. *Journal of Applied Communication Research, 4*, 349–363.

Wood, J. T. (1993). Engendered relations: Interaction, caring, power, and responsibility in intimacy. In S. W. Duck (Ed.), *Understanding relationship processes: 3. Social context and relationships* (pp. 26–54). Newbury Park, CA: Sage.

Wood, J. T. (1994a). Engendered identities: Shaping voice and mind through gender. In D. Vocate (Ed.), *Intrapersonal communication: Different voices, different minds* (pp. 145–167). Hillsdale, NJ: Erlbaum.

Wood, J. T. (1994b). Gender and relationship crises: Contrasting reasons, responses, and relational orientations. In J. Ringer (Ed.), *Queer words, queer images: The construction of homosexuality* (pp. 238–265). New York: New York University Press.

Wood, J. T. (1994c). Gender, communication, and culture. In L. Samovar & R. Porter (Eds.), *Intercultural communication: A reader* (7th ed., pp. 155–164). Belmont, CA: Wadsworth.

Wood, J. T. (1994d). *Who cares? Women, care, and culture*. Carbondale: University of Southern Illinois Press.

Wood, J. T. (1995a). Diversity in dialogue: Communication between friends. In J. Makau & R. Arnett (Eds.), *Ethics of communication in an age of diversity*. Urbana: University of Illinois Press.

Wood, J. T. (1995b). The part is not the whole: Studying diverse relationships. *Journal of Social and Personal Relationships, 12*, 563–567.

Wood, J. T. (Ed.). (1996). *Gendered relationships*. Mountain View, CA: Mayfield.

Wood, J. T. (1997). Clarifying the issues. *Personal Relationships, 4*, 221–228.

Wood, J. T. (1998). *But I thought you meant . . . : Misunderstandings in human communication*. Mountain View, CA: Mayfield.

Wood, J. T. (2000a). *Relational communication* (2nd ed.). Belmont, CA: Thomson/Wadsworth.

Wood, J. T. (2000b). That wasn't the real him: Women's dissociation of violence from the men who enact it. *Qualitative Research in Review, 1*. 1–7.

Wood, J. T. (2001). The normalization of violence in heterosexual romantic relationships: Women's narratives of love and violence. *Journal of Social and Personal Relationships, 18*, 239–261.

Wood, J. T. (2004). Monsters and victims: Male felons' accounts of intimate partner violence. *Journal of Social and Personal Relationships, 21,* 555–576.

Wood, J. T. (2005). *Gendered lives: Communication, gender, and culture* (7th ed.). Belmont, CA: Thomson/Wadsworth.

Wood, J. T. (2006). Chopping the carrots: Creating intimacy moment by moment. In J. T. Wood & S. Duck (Eds.), *Composing relationships: Communication in everyday life* (pp. 24–35). Belmont, CA: Thomson/Wadsworth.

Wood, J. T. (in press). Feminist, critical theories of the family. In D. Braithwaite & L. Baxter (Eds.), *Engaging theories in family communication: Multiple perspectives.* Thousand, Oaks, CA: Sage.

Wood, J. T., Dendy, L., Dordek, E., Germany, M., & Varallo, S. (1994). Dialectic of difference: A thematic analysis of intimates' meanings for differences. In K. Carter & M. Presnell (Eds.), *Interpretive approaches to interpersonal communication* (pp. 115–136). New York: State University of New York Press.

Wood, J. T., & Duck, S. W. (Eds.). (2006a). *Composing relationships: Communication in everyday life.* Belmont, CA: Thomson/Wadsworth.

Wood, J. T., & Duck, S. (2006b). Introduction: Composing relationships: Communication in everyday life. In J. T. Wood & S. Duck (Eds.), *Composing relationships: Communication in everyday life.* Belmont, CA: Thomson/Wadsworth.

Wood, J. T., & Inman, C. C. (1993). In a different mode: Masculine styles of communicating closeness. *Journal of Applied Communication Research, 21,* 279–295.

Woods, E., McDaniel, P., & Woods, T. (1998). *Training a tiger.* New York: HarperCollins.

Word for Word. (2005, March 6). *The New York Times,* p. WK 7.

Wren, C. S. (1990, October 16). A South Africa color bar falls quietly. *New York Times,* pp. Y1, Y10.

Wright, P. H., & Scanlon, M. B. (1991). Gender role orientations and friendship: Some attenuation but gender differences still abound. *Sex Roles, 24,* 551–566.

Wright, P. H., & Wright, K. (1995). Codependency: Personality syndrome or relationship process? In S. W. Duck & J. T. Wood (Eds.), *Understanding relationship processes: 5. Confronting relationship challenges* (pp. 109–128). Thousand Oaks, CA: Sage.

The wrong weight. (1997, November). *Carolina Woman,* p. 7.

WuDunn, S. (1991, April 17). Romance, a novel idea, rocks marriages in China. *New York Times,* pp. B1, B12.

Yager, J. (1999). *Friendshifts.* Stamford, CT: Hannacroix Creek.

Yamamoto, T. (1995). Different silence(s): The poetics and politics of location. In W. L. Ng, S. Chin, J. Moy, & G. Okihiro (Eds.), *Reviewing Asian America: Locating diversity* (pp. 132–145). Pullman: Washington State University Press.

Yerby, J., Buerkel-Rothfuss, N., & Bochner, A. (1990). *Understanding family communication.* Scottsdale, AZ: Gorsuch Scarisbrick.

Yum, J. (1987). Korean philosophy and communication. In D. Kincaid (Ed.), *Communication theory: Eastern and Western perspectives* (pp. 71–86). London: Academic Press.

Yum, J. (2000). The impact of Confucianism on interpersonal relationships and communication patterns in East Asia. In L. Samovar & R. Porter (Eds.), *Intercultural communication: A reader* (9th ed., pp. 63–73). Belmont, CA: Wadsworth.

Zachary, P. (2002, January 21). The new America. *In These Times,* pp. 22–23.

Zhang, Y. B., Harwood, J., & Hummert, M. L. (2005). Perceptions of conflict management styles in Chinese intergenerational dyads. *Communication Monographs, 72,* 71–91.

Zorn, T. (1995). Bosses and buddies: Constructing and performing simultaneously hierarchical and close friendship relationships. In J. T. Wood & S. W. Duck (Eds.), *Understanding relationship processes: 6. Off the beaten track: Understudied relationships* (pp. 122–147). Thousand Oaks, CA: Sage.

Index

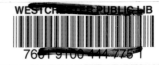
WHAT THE LEGO® COMMUNITY IS SAYING ABOUT
THE UNOFFICIAL LEGO® BUILDER'S GUIDE

"I owe a great deal to Allan and this book. His writing was excellent in illustrating techniques and made the art of LEGO interesting enough for me to devote an entire career to it."
—JASON POLAND, WINNER OF THE 2006 LEGOLAND MODEL BUILDER SEARCH

"Brilliant! Bedford guides you step-by-step through the wonderful, limitless LEGO system. . . . A must-read for every LEGO builder."
—TIM COURTNEY, LDRAW.ORG, CO-AUTHOR OF *VIRTUAL LEGO*

"An excellent resource for both the beginner and the expert LEGO builder. I recommend it highly."
—JOE MENO, EDITOR IN CHIEF OF *BRICKJOURNAL*, CO-AUTHOR OF *THE CULT OF LEGO*

"This is the book I wished I had as a kid and as an adult returning to the hobby. It's a great resource and is going to have a cherished place on my worktable for the foreseeable future."
—JACOB H. MCKEE, LEGO COMMUNITY DEVELOPMENT MANAGER FOR NORTH AMERICA, AUTHOR OF *GETTING STARTED WITH LEGO TRAINS*

"The benchmark on all aspects of the LEGO building hobby. A 'must-have' for those who are just starting to experiment with LEGO and experts looking for areas to expand."
—KIETH JOHNSON, AEROSPACE ENGINEER, UNITED SPACE ALLIANCE

"Makes for a great beginning for any future architects or LEGO hobbyists. The detailed model instructions . . . inspire you to go further and build anything you can think of."
—GARY ISTOK, LEGO BUILDER, COLLECTOR, AND HISTORIAN

"Explains in clear and concise language the things you will need to know to get started and develop your skills as a LEGO builder. This is a great springboard to unleashing the inner Master Model Builder that is in us all!"
—BILL VOLLBRECHT, FORMER MASTER BUILDER FOR LEGOLAND CALIFORNIA, OWNER OF WWW.BRICKCREATIONS.COM

"A clearly written and informative resource, an essential for any aspiring brickmeister whether adult or kid."
—JOHN BAICHTAL, *WIRED*'S GEEKDAD BLOGGER, CO-AUTHOR OF *THE CULT OF LEGO*

How many things are waiting to be created?